GATES

OR

a	b	a + b
0	0	0
0	1	1
1	0	1
1	1	1

AND

a	b	ab
0	0	0
0	1	0
1	0	0
1	1	1

NOT

a	a'
0	1
1	0

NAND

a	b	(a b)'
0	0	1
0	1	1
1	0	1
1	1	0

NOR

a	b	(a + b)'
0	0	1
0	1	0
1	0	0
1	1	0

Exclusive-OR

a	b	a ⊕ b
0	0	0
0	1	1
1	0	1
1	1	0

Exclusive-NOR

a	b	(a ⊕ b)'
0	0	1
0	1	0
1	0	0
1	1	1

Introduction to Logic and Computer Design

Introduction to Logic and Computer Design

Alan B. Marcovitz

Florida Atlantic University

 **Higher Education**

Boston   Burr Ridge, IL   Dubuque, IA   New York   San Francisco   St. Louis
Bangkok   Bogotá   Caracas   Kuala Lumpur   Lisbon   London   Madrid   Mexico City
Milan   Montreal   New Delhi   Santiago   Seoul   Singapore   Sydney   Taipei   Toronto

Higher Education

INTRODUCTION TO LOGIC AND COMPUTER DESIGN

1 2 3 4 5 6 7 8 9 0 DOC/DOC 0 9 8 7

ISBN 978–0–07–352949–3
MHID 0–07–352949–4

Executive Editor: *Michael S. Hackett*
Senior Developmental Editor: *Melinda D. Bilecki*
Executive Marketing Manager: *Michael Weitz*
Senior Project Manager: *Kay J. Brimeyer*
Lead Production Supervisor: *Sandy Ludovissy*
Media Project Manager: *Laurie Lenstra*
Associate Media Producer: *Christina Nelson*
Designer: *Rick D. Noel*
Cover/Interior Designer: *Rokusek Design*
Compositor: *Lachina Publishing Services*
Typeface: *10/12 Times Roman*
Printer: *R.R. Donnelley Crawfordsville, IN*

Library of Congress Cataloging-in-Publication Data

Marcovitz, Alan B.
  Introduction to logic and computer design / Alan B. Marcovitz. — 1st ed.
    p. cm.
  ISBN 978–0–07–352949–3 — ISBN 0–07–352949–4
   1. Logic design. 2. Logic circuits. 3. Electronic digital computers—Circuits. I. Title.

TK7888.4.M365 2008
621.39'5—dc22

                             2006048094

www.mhhe.com

BRIEF CONTENTS

CONTENTS

PREFACE

This book is intended as an introductory book for students in computer science, computer engineering and electrical engineering. Part One is suitable for a one semester course on *logic design*.* It has no prerequisites, although the maturity attained through an introduction to engineering course or a first programming course would be helpful. Part Two contains an introduction to the design of computers, utilizing the material from Part One. The whole book could be used for a two-semester course, or selected parts could be used in a one-semester course.

The book stresses fundamentals. It teaches through a large number of examples. The philosophy of the author is that the only way to learn design is to do a large number of design problems. Thus, in addition to the numerous examples in the body of the text, each chapter has a set of Solved Problems, that is, problems and their solutions, a Chapter Test (with answers in Appendix C), and a large set of Exercises (with answers to Selected Exercises in Appendix B).

Although computer-aided tools are widely used for the design of large systems, the student must first understand the basics. The basics provide more than enough material for a first course. The sections on Hardware Design Languages (HDLs) in Chapters 4 and 7 provide some material for a transition to a second course based on one of the computer-aided tool sets. For the computer design material, we introduce a simplified HDL that enables us to describe the hardware without spending excessive time on the details of some of the commercial tools such as Verilog or VHDL.

Chapter 1, after a brief introduction, gives an overview of number systems as it applies to the material of this book. (Those students who have studied this in an earlier course can skip this chapter.)

Chapter 2 discusses the steps in the design process for combinational systems and the development of truth tables. It then introduces switching algebra and the implementation of switching functions using common gates—AND, OR, NOT, NAND, NOR, Exclusive OR, and Exclusive NOR. We are only concerned with the logic behavior of the gates, not the electronic implementation.

---

*For a more complete introduction to logic design, including laboratory experiments, see Marcovitz, Alan B., *Introduction to Logic Design, Second Edition*, McGraw-Hill, 2005.

Chapter 3 presents the simplification of combinational systems using the Karnaugh map. It provides methods for solving problems (up to 5 variables) with both single and multiple outputs.

Chapter 4 is concerned with the design of larger combinational systems. It introduces a number of commercially available larger devices, including adders, comparators, decoders, encoders and priority encoders, and multiplexers. That is followed by a discussion of the use of logic arrays—ROMs, PLAs, and PALs for the implementation of medium scale combinational systems. Hardware Design Languages are introduced. Finally, two larger systems are designed.

Chapter 5 introduces sequential systems. It starts by examining the behavior of latches and flip flops. It then discusses techniques to analyze the behavior of sequential systems.

Chapter 6 introduces the design process for sequential systems. The special case of counters is studied next. Finally, the solution of word problems, developing the state table or state diagram from a verbal description of the problem is presented in detail.

Chapter 7 looks at larger sequential systems. It starts by examining the application of shift registers and counters. Then, PLDs (logic arrays with memory) are presented. Three techniques that are useful in the design of more complex systems, ASM diagrams, one-hot encoding, and HDLs for sequential systems, are discussed next. Finally, two examples of larger systems are presented.

Chapter 8 is concerned with computer organization. It discusses the basic structure of a computer and the various addressing modes and instruction types.

Chapter 9 looks at the logic required to move data in a large machine, and the structure of a controller. We introduce *Digital Design Language (DDL)*, a simple notation to describe the behavior of a digital system. We chose not to use one of the commercial systems because the amount of detail required to use it would detract from the fundamentals that we are teaching.

Chapter 10 deals with the details of the design of a sample computer, *MODEL*. We design the control sequence and examine the timing.

Chapter 11 describes some of the interaction of the CPU with the other components of a computer system, the primary and secondary memory and input/output controllers.

A feature of this text is the Solved Problems. Each chapter (other than 11, which is primarily descriptive) has a large number of problems, illustrating the techniques developed in the body of the text, followed by a detailed solution of each problem. Students are urged to solve each problem (without looking at the solution) and then compare their solution with the one shown.

Each chapter contains a large set of exercises. Answers to a selection of these are contained in Appendix B. Solutions will be made available to instructors through the Web.

Each Chapter then concludes with a Chapter Test; answers are given in Appendix C.

The material of Part One can be taught easily in a four-credit semester course. Five-variable maps could be eliminated without loss of continuity. (It is only needed for a few examples in Chapter 4.) The coverage of the larger examples of Sections 4.8 and 7.7 could be reduced. Indeed, most of Chapter 7 could be omitted.

The material of Part Two would work in a second-semester course, although some curricula cover computer organization in an earlier course. The material of Chapter 8 does not depend on Part One, but the remainder of the book does.

SUPPLEMENTS

In addition, the text is complemented by a wealth of supplemental resources presented through **McGraw-Hill's ARIS** (Assessment Review and Instruction System). ARIS makes homework meaningful-and manageable-for instructors and students.

Instructors can assign and grade text-specific homework within the industry's most robust and versatile homework management system.

Students can access multimedia learning tools and benefit from unlimited practice via algorithmic problems.

Go to aris.mhhe.com to learn more and register!

ACKNOWLEDGMENTS

I want to thank my wife, Allyn, for her encouragement and for enduring endless hours when I was closeted in my office working on the manuscript. Several of my colleagues at Florida Atlantic University have read parts of the manuscript and have taught from earlier drafts. Even more importantly, I want to thank my students who provided me with the impetus to write a more suitable text, who suffered through earlier drafts of the book, and who made many suggestions and corrections. The reviewers,

Michael Chelian, *California State University*, Long Beach

G.R. Dattatreya, *The University of Texas at Dallas*

Travis Doom, *Wright State University*

Clifford Fitzmorris, *The University of Oklahoma*

Donald Hung, *San Jose State University*

Cetin Kaya Koc, *Oregon State University*

Anselmo Lastra, *The University of North Carolina*

D.J. Lee, *Brigham Young University*

Hsien-Hsin Lee, *Georgia Institute of Technology*

Alex Martinez, *The Ohio State University*

Jacob Savir, *New Jersey Institute of Technology*

Eric Schwartz, *University of Florida*

provided many useful comments and suggestions. The book is much better because of their efforts. Finally, the staff at McGraw-Hill, particularly Michael Hackett, Melinda Bilecki, and Kay Brimeyer have been indispensable in producing the final product, as has my copy editor, Linda Davoli.

Introduction

This book concerns the design of *digital systems,* that is, systems in which all of the signals are represented by discrete values. Internally, digital systems usually are binary, that is, they operate with two-valued signals, which we will label 0 and 1. (Although multivalued systems have been built, two-valued systems are more reliable and thus almost all digital systems use two-valued signals.)

Computers and calculators are obvious examples of digital systems, but most electronic systems contain a large amount of digital logic. The music that we listen to on our CD players or iPods, the individual dots on a computer screen (and on the newer digital televisions), and most cell phone signals are coded into strings of binary digits, referred to as bits.

Part I of this book (Chapters 2 to 7) deals with design techniques for digital systems in general, a process often referred to as *logic design.* These techniques are limited to fairly small systems, although we will look at ways to break up larger systems into smaller subsystems. Part II of the book (Chapters 8 to 11) includes topics specific to the design of digital computers and similar large systems.

1.1 LOGIC DESIGN

A digital system, as shown in the Figure 1.1, may have an arbitrary number of inputs (*A, B,* . . .) and an arbitrary number of outputs (*W, X,* . . .). In addition to the data inputs shown, some circuits require a timing signal, called a clock (which is just another input signal that alternates between 0 and 1 at a regular rate). We will discuss the details of clock signals in Chapter 5.

A simple example of digital systems is described in Example 1.1.

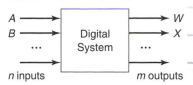

Figure 1.1 A digital system.

A system with three inputs, *A, B,* and *C,* and one output, *Z,* such that *Z*=1 if and only if* two of the inputs are 1.

EXAMPLE 1.1

---

*The term *if and only if* is often abbreviated "iff." It means that the output is 1 if the condition is met and is not 1 (which means it must be 0) if the condition is not met.

The inputs and outputs of a digital system represent real quantities. Sometimes, as in Example 1.1, these are naturally binary, that is, they take on one of two values. Other times, they may be multivalued. For example, an input may be a decimal digit or the output might be the letter grade for this course. Each must be represented by a set of binary digits. This process is referred to as coding the inputs and outputs into binary. (We will discuss the details of this later.)

The physical manifestation of these binary quantities may be one of two voltages, for example, 0 volts (V) or ground for logic 0 and 5 V for logic 1. It may also be a magnetic field in one direction or another (as on diskettes), a switch in the up or down position (for an input), or a light on or off (as an output). Except in the translation of verbal descriptions into more formal ones, the physical representation will be irrelevant in this text; we will be concerned with 0's and 1's.

We can describe the behavior of a digital system, such as that of Example 1.1, in tabular form. Since there are only eight possible input combinations, we can list all of them and what the output is for each. Such a table (referred to as a truth table) is shown in Table 1.1. We will leave the development of truth tables (including one similar to this) to the next chapter.

Four other examples are given in Examples 1.2 through 1.5.

Table 1.1 A truth table for Example 1.1.

A	B	C	Z
0	0	0	0
0	0	1	0
0	1	0	0
0	1	1	1
1	0	0	0
1	0	1	1
1	1	0	1
1	1	1	1

EXAMPLE 1.2

A system with eight inputs, representing two 4-bit binary numbers, and one 5-bit output, representing the sum. (Each input number can range from 0 to 15; the output can range from 0 to 30.)

EXAMPLE 1.3

A system with one input, A, plus a clock, and one output, Z, which is 1 iff the input was one at the last three consecutive clock times.

EXAMPLE 1.4

A digital clock that displays the time in hours and minutes. It needs to display four decimal digits plus an indicator for AM or PM. (The first digit display only needs to display a 1 or be blank.) This requires a timing signal to advance the clock every minute. It also requires a means of setting the time. Most digital clocks also have an alarm feature, which requires additional storage and circuitry.

EXAMPLE 1.5

A more complex example is a traffic controller. In the simplest case, there are just two streets, and the light is green on each street for a fixed period of time. It then goes to yellow for another fixed period and finally to red. There are no inputs to this system other than the clock. There are six outputs, one for each color in each direction. (Each output may control multiple bulbs.) Traffic controllers may have many more outputs, if, for example, there are left-turn signals. Also, there may be several inputs to indicate when there are vehicles waiting at a red signal or passing a green one.

The first two examples are *combinational*, that is, the output depends only on the present value of the input. In Example 1.1, if we know the value of A, B, and C right now, we can determine what Z is now.* Examples 1.3, 1.4, and 1.5 are *sequential*, that is, they require *memory*, since we need to know something about inputs at an earlier time (previous clock times).

We will concentrate on combinational systems in the first half of Part I and leave the discussion about sequential systems until later. As we will see, sequential systems are composed of two parts: memory and combinational logic. Thus, we need to be able to design combinational systems before we can begin designing sequential ones.

A word of caution about natural language in general, and English in particular, is in order. English is not a very precise language. The previous examples leave some room for interpretation. In Example 1.1, is the output to be 1 if all three of the inputs are 1, or only if exactly two inputs are 1? One could interpret the statement either way. When we wrote the truth table, we had to decide; we interpreted "two" as "two or more" and thus made the output 1 when all three inputs were 1. (In problems in this text, we will try to be as precise as possible, but even then, different people may read the problem statement in different ways.)

The bottom line is that we need a more precise description of logic systems. We will develop that for combinational systems in Chapter 2 and for sequential systems in Chapter 5.

1.2 A BRIEF REVIEW OF NUMBER SYSTEMS

This section gives an introduction to some topics in number systems, primarily those needed to understand the material in the remainder of the book. If this is familiar material from another course, skip to Chapter 2.

Integers are normally written using a positional number system, in which each digit represents the coefficient in a power series

$$N = a_{n-1}r^{n-1} + a_{n-2}r^{n-2} + \cdots + a_2r^2 + a_1r + a_0$$

where n is the number of digits, r is the radix or base, and the a_i are the coefficients, where each is an integer in the range

$$0 \le a_i < r$$

For decimal, $r = 10$, and the a's are in the range 0 to 9. For binary, $r = 2$, and the a's are all either 0 or 1. Another commonly used notation in computer documentation is hexadecimal, $r = 16$. In binary, the digits are usually referred to as *bits*.

---

*In a real system, there is a small amount of delay between the input and output, that is, if the input changes at some point in time, the output changes a little after that. The time frame is typically in the nanosecond (10^{-9} sec) range. We will ignore those delays almost all of the time, but we will return to that issue in Chapter 4.

The decimal number 7642 (sometimes written 7642_{10} to emphasize that it is radix 10, that is, decimal) thus stands for

$$7642_{10} = 7 \times 10^3 + 6 \times 10^2 + 4 \times 10 + 2$$

and the binary number

$$101111_2 = 1 \times 2^5 + 0 \times 2^4 + 1 \times 2^3 + 1 \times 2^2 + 1 \times 2 + 1$$
$$= 32 + 8 + 4 + 2 + 1 = 47_{10}$$

From this example,* it is clear how to convert from binary to decimal; just evaluate the power series. To do that easily, it is useful to know the powers of 2, rather than compute them each time they are needed. (It would save a great deal of time and effort if at least the first 10 powers of 2 were memorized; the first 20 are shown in the Table 1.2.)

We will often be using the first 16 positive binary integers, and sometimes the first 32, as shown in the Table 1.3. (As in decimal, leading 0's are often left out, but we have shown the 4-bit number including leading 0's for the first 16.) When the size of the storage place for a positive binary number is specified, then leading 0's are added so as to obtain the correct number of bits.

Table 1.2   Powers of 2.

n	2^n	n	2^n
1	2	11	2,048
2	4	12	4,096
3	8	13	8,192
4	16	14	16,384
5	32	15	32,768
6	64	16	65,536
7	128	17	131,072
8	256	18	262,144
9	512	19	524,288
10	1,024	20	1,048,576

Table 1.3   First 32 binary integers.

Decimal	Binary	4-bit	Decimal	Binary
0	0	0000	16	10000
1	1	0001	17	10001
2	10	0010	18	10010
3	11	0011	19	10011
4	100	0100	20	10100
5	101	0101	21	10101
6	110	0110	22	10110
7	111	0111	23	10111
8	1000	1000	24	11000
9	1001	1001	25	11001
10	1010	1010	26	11010
11	1011	1011	27	11011
12	1100	1100	28	11100
13	1101	1101	29	11101
14	1110	1110	30	11110
15	1111	1111	31	11111

Note that the number one less than 2^n consists of n 1's (for example, $2^4 - 1 = 1111 = 15$ and $2^5 - 1 = 11111 = 31$).

An n-bit number can represent the positive integers from 0 to $2^n - 1$. Thus, for example, 4-bit numbers have the range of 0 to 15, 8-bit numbers 0 to 255 and 16-bit numbers 0 to 65,535.

---

*Section 1.3, Solved Problems, contains additional examples of each of the types of problems discussed in this chapter. There is a section of Solved Problems in each of the chapters.

To convert from decimal to binary, we could evaluate the power series of the decimal number, by converting each digit to binary, that is

$$746 = 111 \times (1010)^{10} + 0100 \times 1010 + 0110$$

but that requires binary multiplication, which is rather time-consuming.

There are two straightforward algorithms using decimal arithmetic. First, we can subtract from the number the largest power of 2 less than that number and put a 1 in the corresponding position of the binary equivalent. We then repeat that with the remainder. A 0 is put in the position for those powers of 2 that are larger than the remainder.

EXAMPLE 1.6

For 746, $2^9 = 512$ is the largest power of 2 less than or equal to 746, and thus there is a 1 in the 2^9 (512) position.

$$746 = 1\,\_\,\_\,\_\,\_\,\_\,\_\,\_\,\_$$

We then compute $746 - 512 = 234$. The next smaller power of 2 is $2^8 = 256$, but that is larger than 234 and thus, there is a 0 in the 2^8 position.

$$746 = 1\,0\,\_\,\_\,\_\,\_\,\_\,\_\,\_$$

Next, we compute $234 - 128 = 106$, putting a 1 in the 2^7 position.

$$746 = 1\,0\,1\,\_\,\_\,\_\,\_\,\_\,\_$$

Continuing, we subtract 64 from 106, resulting in 42 and a 1 in the 2^6 position.

$$746 = 1\,0\,1\,1\,\_\,\_\,\_\,\_\,\_$$

Since 42 is larger than 32, we have a 1 in the 2^5 position, and compute $42 - 32 = 10$.

$$746 = 1\,0\,1\,1\,1\,\_\,\_\,\_\,\_$$

At this point, we can continue subtracting (8 next) or recognize that there is no $2^4 = 16$, and that the binary equivalent of the remainder, 10, is 1010, giving

$$746_{10} = 1 \times 2^9 + 0 \times 2^8 + 1 \times 2^7 + 1 \times 2^6 + 1 \times 2^5 + 0 \times 2^4 + 1 \times 2^3 + 0 \times 2^2 + 1 \times 2 + 0$$
$$= 1011101010_2$$

The other approach is to divide the decimal number by 2 repeatedly. The remainder each time gives a digit of the binary answer, starting at the least significant bit (a_0). The remainder is then discarded and the process is repeated.

EXAMPLE 1.7

Converting 746 from decimal to binary, we compute

$746/2 = 373$ with a remainder of 0	0
$373/2 = 186$ with a remainder of 1	10
$186/2 = 93$ with a remainder of 0	010

$$93/2 = 46 \text{ with a remainder of } 1 \qquad\qquad 1010$$
$$46/2 = 23 \text{ with a remainder of } 0 \qquad\qquad 01010$$
$$23/2 = 11 \text{ with a remainder of } 1 \qquad\qquad 101010$$
$$11/2 = 5 \text{ with a remainder of } 1 \qquad\qquad 1101010$$
$$5/2 = \text{ with a remainder of } 1 \qquad\qquad 11101010$$
$$2/2 = 1 \text{ with a remainder of } 0 \qquad\qquad 011101010$$
$$1/2 = 0 \text{ with a remainder of } 1 \qquad\qquad 1011101010$$

Do not forget the last division (1/2); it produces the most significant 1. We could continue dividing by 2 and get additional leading 0's. Thus, the answer is 1011101010 as before. In this method, we could also stop when we recognize the number that is left and convert it to binary. Thus, when we had 23, we could recognize that as 10111 (from Table 1.3) and place that in front of the bits we had produced, giving 10111 01010.

EXAMPLE 1.8	Convert 105 to binary

$$105/2 = 52, \text{ rem } 1 \qquad \text{produces} \qquad\qquad 1$$
$$52/2 = 26, \text{ rem } 0 \qquad\qquad\qquad\qquad 01$$
$$26/2 = 13, \text{ rem } 0 \qquad\qquad\qquad\qquad 001$$
$$\text{but } 13 = 1101 \qquad\qquad\qquad\qquad 1101\ 001$$

The method works because all of the terms in the power series except the last divide evenly by 2. Thus, since

$$746 = 1 \times 2^9 + 0 \times 2^8 + 1 \times 2^7 + 1 \times 2^6 + 1 \times 2^5 + 0 \times 2^4$$
$$+ 1 \times 2^3 + 0 \times 2^2 + 1 \times 2 + 0$$

$$746/2 = 373 \text{ and remainder of } 0$$
$$= 1 \times 2^8 + 0 \times 2^7 + 1 \times 2^6 + 1 \times 2^5 + 1 \times 2^4$$
$$+ 0 \times 2^3 + 1 \times 2^2 + 0 \times 2 + 1 + \text{rem } 0$$

The last bit became the remainder. If we repeat the process, we get

$$373/2 = 186 \text{ and remainder of } 1$$
$$= 1 \times 2^7 + 0 \times 2^6 + 1 \times 2^5 + 1 \times 2^4 + 1 \times 2^3 + 0 \times 2^2$$
$$+ 1 \times 2 + 0 + \text{rem } 1$$

That remainder is the second digit from the right. On the next division, the remainder will be 0, the third digit. This process continues until the most significant bit is found.

*[SP 1, 2; EX 1, 2]**

1.2.1   Hexadecimal

Hexadecimal, often referred to as *hex* ($r = 16$) is another base that is commonly used in computer documentation. It is just a shorthand notation for

---

*At the end of most sections, a list of solved problems and exercises that are appropriate to that section is given.

binary. In hexadecimal, binary digits are grouped in fours (starting at the least significant). For example, an 8-bit number,

$$N = (b_7 2^7 + b_6 2^6 + b_5 2^5 + b_4 2^4) + (b_3 2^3 + b_2 2^2 + b_1 2^1 + b_0)$$
$$= 2^4 (b_7 2^3 + b_6 2^2 + b_5 2^1 + b_4) + (b_3 2^3 + b_2 2^2 + b_1 2^1 + b_0)$$
$$= 16 h_1 + h_0$$

where the h_1 represent the hexadecimal digits and must fall in the range 0 to 15. Each term in parentheses is just interpreted in decimal. If the binary number does not have a multiple of four bits, leading 0's are added. The digits above 9 are represented by the first six letters of the alphabet (uppercase).

10	A
11	B
12	C
13	D
14	E
15	F

(from Examples 1.6 and 1.7)

EXAMPLE 1.9

$$1011101010_2 = 0010\ 1110\ 1010_2$$
$$= 2EA_{16}$$

To convert from hex to decimal, we evaluate the power series.

EXAMPLE 1.10

$$2EA_{16} = 2 \times 16^2 + 14 \times 16 + 10$$
$$= 512 + 224 + 10 = 746_{10}$$

Finally, to convert from decimal to hex, repeatedly divide by 16, producing the hex digits as the remainder.

EXAMPLE 1.11

$746/16 = 46$	rem 10	produces	A
$46/16 = 2$	rem 14		EA
$2/16 = 0$	rem 2		2EA

[SP 3, 4; EX 3, 4]

1.2.2 Binary Addition

A common operation required in computers and other digital systems is the addition of two numbers. In this section, we will describe the process for adding binary numbers.

Table 1.4   Binary addition.

$0 + 0 = 0$
$0 + 1 = 1$
$1 + 0 = 1$
$1 + 1 = 10$ (2, or a sum of 0 and a carry of 1 to the next bit)

To compute the sum of two binary numbers, say

```
0 1 1 0     6
0 1 1 1    +7
```

we add one digit at a time (as we do in decimal), producing a sum and a carry to the next bit. Just as we have an addition table for decimal, we need one for binary (but it is of course much shorter). (Table 1.4) A step-by-step addition is shown in Example 1.12.

EXAMPLE 1.12

First, the least significant bits (the rightmost bits) are added, producing a sum of 1 and a carry of 0, as shown in green.

```
        0
    0 1 1 0
    0 1 1 1
        1
```

Next, we must add the second digit from the right,

$$0 + 1 + 1 = 0 + (1 + 1) = 0 + 10 = 10$$
$$\text{(a sum of 0 and a carry of 1)}$$
$$\text{or } (0 + 1) + 1 = 1 + 1 = 10$$
$$\text{(the order of addition does not matter).}$$

That addition is highlighted in green.

```
      1 0
    0 1 1 0
    0 1 1 1
      0 1
```

The final two additions then become

```
    1 1              0 1
    0 1 1 0          0 1 1 0
    0 1 1 1          0 1 1 1
      1 0 1          1 1 0 1
```

Notice that in the third bit of addition, we had three 1's (the carry in plus the two digits). That produced a sum of 3 (11 in binary), that is, a sum bit of 1 and a carry of 1. The answer, of course, comes to 13 (in decimal). In this case, the last addition produced a carry out of 0, and thus the answer was 4-bits long. If the operands were larger (say, 13 + 5), the answer would require 5 bits as shown in the following addition, where the last carry is written as part of the sum. (This is, of course, no different from decimal addition, where the sum of two 4-digit numbers might produce a 4- or 5-digit result.)

```
    1 0 1
    1 1 0 1            1 3
    0 1 0 1             5
   ─────────         ─────
   1 0 0 1 0          1 8
```

In a computer with n-bit words, when an arithmetic operation produces a result that is out of range [for example, addition of n-bit positive integers produces an $(n + 1)$-bit result], it is called *overflow*. With the addition of 4-bit positive integers, overflow occurs when the sum is greater than or equal to 16 (that is, 2^4). In the previous example, there was overflow since the answer, 18, is greater than 15, the largest 4-bit positive integer.

After the addition of the least significant bits (which only has two operands), each remaining addition is a three-operand problem. We will denote the carry that is added in as c_{in} and the resulting carry from the addition c_{out}. The addition problem then becomes

$$
\begin{array}{r}
c_{in} \\
a \\
b \\
\hline
c_{out}\; s
\end{array}
$$

Table 1.5 shows a complete definition of the addition process.

A device that does this 1-bit computation is referred to as a *full adder*. To add 4-bit numbers, we might build four of these and connect them as shown in Figure 1.2. Notice that the carry input of the bit 1 adder has a 0 on it, since there is no carry into that bit. Sometimes a simpler circuit (called a *half adder*) is built for that bit. We will return to this problem in Chapter 2, when we are prepared to design the full adder.

Table 1.5 One-bit adder.

a	b	c_{in}	c_{out}	s
0	0	0	0	0
0	0	1	0	1
0	1	0	0	1
0	1	1	1	0
1	0	0	0	1
1	0	1	1	0
1	1	0	1	0
1	1	1	1	1

Figure 1.2 A 4-bit adder.

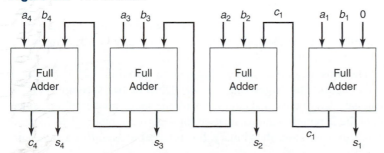

[SP 5; EX 5]

1.2.3   Signed Numbers

Up to this point, we have only considered positive integers, sometimes referred to as *unsigned numbers*. Computers must deal with *signed numbers*, that is, both positive and negative numbers. The human-friendly notation is referred to as *signed-magnitude* ($+5$ or -3 as decimal examples). This could be incorporated into a computer, using the first bit of a number as a sign indicator (normally 0 for positive and 1 for negative) and the remaining bits for the magnitude. Thus, in a 4-bit system, we would represent

$$+5 \rightarrow 0101 \quad -5 \rightarrow 1101 \quad -3 \rightarrow 1011$$

With 3 bits for magnitude, the range of numbers available would be from -7 to $+7$. (Of course, most computers use a larger number of bits to store numbers and thus have a much larger range.) Note that such a representation has both a positive (0000) and negative (1000) zero. Although that might cause confusion (or at least complicate the internal logic of the computer), the major problem with signed-magnitude is the complexity of arithmetic. Consider the following addition problems:

$$
\begin{array}{cccccc}
+5 & -5 & +5 & -5 & -3 & +3 \\
\underline{+3} & \underline{-3} & \underline{-3} & \underline{+3} & \underline{+5} & \underline{-5} \\
+8 & -8 & +2 & -2 & +2 & -2
\end{array}
$$

In the first two, where the signs of the two operands are the same, we just add the magnitudes and retain the sign. For these two, the computation is $5 + 3$. In each of the other examples, we must determine which is the larger magnitude. (It could be the first operand or the second.) Then, we must subtract the smaller from the larger, and finally, attach the sign of the larger magnitude. For these four, the computation is $5 - 3$. Although this could all be done, the complexity of the hardware involved (an adder, a subtractor, and a comparator) has led to another solution.

Signed binary numbers are nearly always stored in *two's complement* format. The leading bit is still the sign bit (0 for positive). Positive numbers (and zero) are just stored in normal binary. The largest number that can be stored is $2^{n-1} - 1$ (7 for $n = 4$). Thus, in a 4-bit system, $+5$ would be stored as 0101.

The negative number, $-a$, is stored as the binary equivalent of $2^n - a$ in an n-bit system. Thus, for example, -3 is stored as the binary for $16 - 3 = 13$, that is, 1101.

The most negative number that can be stored is -2^{n-1} (-8 in a 4-bit system). The largest number available in two's complement is about half that of unsigned numbers with the same number of bits, since half of the 2^n representations are used for negative numbers. This method extends to other bases than binary. It is referred to as *radix complement*.

Negative numbers, $-a$, in n digits are stored as $r^n - a$. In decimal for example, this is called ten's complement. In a 2-digit decimal system, -16 would be stored as $100 - 16 = 84$. (Numbers from 0 to 49 would be considered positive and those between 50 and 99 would be representations of negative numbers.)

An easier way to find the storage format for negative numbers in two's complement is the following three-step approach:

1. Find the binary equivalent of the magnitude.
2. Complement each bit (that is, change 0's to 1's and 1's to 0's)
3. Add 1.

		-5		-1		-0
1.	5:	0 1 0 1	1:	0 0 0 1	0:	0 0 0 0
2.		1 0 1 0		1 1 1 0		1 1 1 1
3.		1		1		1
	-5:	1 0 1 1	-1:	1 1 1 1		0 0 0 0
		(a)		(b)		(c)

EXAMPLE 1.13

Note that there is no negative zero; the process of complementing $+0$ produces an answer of 0000. In two's complement addition, the carry out of the most significant bit is ignored.

Table 1.6 lists the meaning of all 4-bit numbers both as positive (unsigned) numbers and as two's complement signed numbers.

To find the magnitude of a negative number stored in two's complement format (that is, one that begins with a 1), the second and third steps of the negation process are followed.

		-5:	1 0 1 1	-1:	1 1 1 1
2.	Bit-by-bit complement		0 1 0 0		0 0 0 0
3.	Add 1		1		1
		5:	0 1 0 1	1:	0 0 0 1

EXAMPLE 1.14

(We could subtract 1 and then complement, instead; that will give the same answer.)

The reason that two's complement is so popular is the simplicity of addition. To add any two numbers, no matter what the sign of each is, we just do binary addition on their representations. Three sample computations

Table 1.6 Signed and unsigned 4-bit numbers.

Binary	Positive	Signed (two's complement)
0000	0	0
0001	1	+ 1
0010	2	+ 2
0011	3	+ 3
0100	4	+ 4
0101	5	+ 5
0110	6	+ 6
0111	7	+ 7
1000	8	− 8
1001	9	− 7
1010	10	− 6
1011	11	− 5
1100	12	− 4
1101	13	− 3
1110	14	− 2
1111	15	− 1

are shown in Example 1.15. In each case, the carry out of the most significant bit is ignored.

EXAMPLE 1.15

−5	1 0 1 1	−5	1 0 1 1	−5	1 0 1 1
+7	0 1 1 1	+5	0 1 0 1	+3	0 0 1 1
+2	(1) 0 0 1 0	0	(1) 0 0 0 0	−2	(0) 1 1 1 0

In the first, the sum is 2. In the second, the sum is 0. In the third, the sum is −2, and, indeed, the representation of −2 is produced.

Overflow occurs when the sum is out of range. For 4-bit numbers, that range is $-8 \leq \text{sum} \leq +7$.

EXAMPLE 1.16

+5	0 1 0 1
+4	0 1 0 0
	(0) 1 0 0 1 (looks like −7)

The answer produced is clearly wrong because the correct answer (+9) is out of range.

Indeed, whenever we add two positive numbers (each beginning with a 0) and get a result that looks negative (begins with a 1), there is overflow. Similarly, adding two negative numbers and obtaining a sum more negative than -8 also produces overflow. (Also, we can detect overflow when the carry into the most significant bit [1 in this case] differs from the carry out.)

```
  −5       1 0 1 1
  −4       1 1 0 0
      (1)  0 1 1 1   (looks like +7)
```

This time, two negative numbers produced a sum that looks positive.

The addition of two numbers of the opposite sign never produces overflow, since the magnitude of the sum is somewhere between the magnitudes of the two operands. (Although overflow seems rather common when dealing with 4-bit examples, it is an unusual occurrence in most computer applications, where numbers are 16 or 32 bits or longer.) *[SP 6, 7, 8; EX 6, 7, 8, 9]*

1.2.4 Binary Subtraction

Subtraction (whether dealing with signed or unsigned numbers) is generally accomplished by first taking the two's complement of the second operand, and then adding. Thus, $a - b$ is computed as $a + (-b)$.

Consider the computation of $7 - 5$.

```
   5:  0 1 0 1       7:       0 1 1 1
       1 0 1 0      −5:     + 1 0 1 1
     +     1         2     (1) 0 0 1 0
  −5:  1 0 1 1
```

The 5 is first complemented. This same process is followed whether the computation involves signed or unsigned numbers. Then, the representation of -5 is added to 7, producing an answer of 2.

For signed numbers, the carry out of the high-order bit is ignored, and overflow occurs if the addition process operates on two numbers of the same sign and produces a result of the opposite sign. For unsigned numbers, the carry out of the high-order bit is the indicator of overflow, as in addition. However, in subtraction, a 0 indicates overflow. In Example 1.18, there was no overflow for either signed or unsigned numbers, since the answer, 2, is within range. The carry out of 1 indicates no overflow, for unsigned numbers. For signed numbers, the addition of a positive number to a negative one never produces overflow.

In most computer applications, the two additions (of the 1 in the complement computation and of the two operands) are done in one step.

The least significant bit of the adder (bit 1) has a zero carry input for addition. The 1 that was added in the process of complementing can be input to that carry input for subtraction. Thus, to compute $7 - 5$, we take the bit-by-bit complement of 5 (0101 becomes 1010) and add.

EXAMPLE 1.19

$7 - 5$

```
           1
        0 1 1 1
        1 0 1 0
     (1) 0 0 1 0
```

Of course, we could design a subtractor (in addition to the adder), but that is unnecessary additional hardware for most computers.

Note that this process works for unsigned numbers even if the operands are larger than could be represented in a two's complement system, as shown in Example 1.20, where the difference $14 - 10$ is computed.

EXAMPLE 1.20

```
          1
       1 1 1 0
      +0 1 0 1
    (1) 0 1 0 0 = 4
```

We see overflow for unsigned numbers in Example 1.21a and for signed numbers in Example 1.21b.

EXAMPLE 1.21

```
     5 - 7            7 - (-5)
        1                1
     0 1 0 1          0 1 1 1
     1 0 0 0          0 1 0 0
  (0) 1 1 1 0         1 1 0 0

     (a)              (b)
```

For unsigned numbers, overflow is indicated by the carry of 0. The result of (a) should be negative (-2), which cannot be represented in an unsigned system. For signed numbers, the result is correct. For signed numbers, overflow may occur if we subtract a negative number from a positive one or a positive number from a negative one, as shown in Example 1.21b. That is overflow because the addition process involved two positive numbers and the result looked negative. (Indeed, the answer should be 12, but that is greater than the largest 4-bit signed number, 7.)

[SP 9, 10; EX 10]

1.2.5 Fractions, Mixed Numbers and Floating Point Representation

Up to this point we have been dealing only with integers. We can easily extend the discussion to fractions and mixed numbers. A fraction (magnitude less than 1) is represented by the series

$$a_{-1}r^{-1} + a_{-2}r^{-2} + a_{-3}r^{-3} + \cdots$$

Thus, in binary,

$$.101 = 1/2 + 0/4 + 1/8 = .625$$

Conversion from decimal to binary is accomplished by multiplying the number by 2, using the integer part as the next digit (and then discarding the integer). For example

$$.625 \times 2 = 1.25 \qquad .1$$
$$.25 \times 2 = 0.50 \qquad .10$$
$$.50 \times 2 = 1.00 \qquad .101$$

Because the fractional part is now zero, we have an exact conversion. Trailing 0's can be added to make the number the correct size. Fractions do not always convert exactly. For example

$$.3 \times 2 = 0.6 \qquad .0$$
$$.6 \times 2 = 1.2 \qquad .01$$
$$.2 \times 2 = 0.4 \qquad .010$$
$$.4 \times 2 = 0.8 \qquad .0100$$
$$.8 \times 2 = 1.6 \qquad .01001$$
$$.6 \times 2 = 1.2 \qquad .010011$$

It now starts repeating; the fraction never goes to 0. Thus,

$$.3 = .010011001100110\ldots$$

For that reason, financial calculations are sometimes done using binary coded decimal (BCD), since fractions are coded exactly.

Mixed numbers contain an integer and a fraction, such as 24.375. The two parts are converted to decimal separately.

$$24 = 1\,1\,0\,0\,0$$
$$.375 = .011$$

Thus,

$$24.375 = 11000.011$$

Signed numbers are stored in two's complement (or possibly signed-magnitude).

If a computer stores mixed numbers, the binary point is predetermined. For 32-bit numbers, we might have 20 bits of integer (including the sign) and 12 bits of fraction. This only gives a range of ± 514 thousand and precision of just over 3 decimal digits to the right of the radix point.

A much larger range of numbers and more precision (particularly on small numbers) than is possible with a fixed-point system is often required. Thus, most computers provide for *floating-point* numbers, sometimes referred to as scientific notation. Numbers are represented by a fraction, called the *mantissa* and an exponent. They are usually normalized so that significant digits are a fraction with a leading nonzero digit (except when the number is zero). For example, in decimal, 24.375 is represented as

$$+.24375 \times 10^2$$

Only the mantissa, the sign, and the exponent need be stored. The exponent is also signed, because, for example, .0025 would be stored as

$$+.25000 \times 10^{-2}$$

Binary floating-point representation has been standardized by the Institute of Electrical and Electronic Engineers (IEEE). The standard notation (IEEE Standard 754) for 32-bit numbers uses a sign bit, an 8-bit exponent, and 23 bits for the significant digits. It uses signed-magnitude notation. The exponent is stored in Excess-127 ($+01111111$) notation (such that 0 is stored as 127, -5 as 122, and 127 as 254). Exponents in the range of -126 to $+127$ are allowed. It stores the significant digits in the range $1.000 \ldots$ to $1.111 \ldots _2$. Because the first significant digit is always a binary 1 (except when the number is 0), that leading 1 is not stored. For example, $.375 = .011 = 1.1 \times 2^{-2}$ would be stored with a sign bit of 0, an exponent of 125 (01111011_2) and the *significand* field of $1000 \ldots$ This field is called the significand because it is not quite the mantissa. The number 0 is the only one stored with an exponent field of 0. (It is stored as all 0's.) This allows a range of numbers (both positive and negative) from 1×2^{-127} to $2 \times 2^{+127}$ (or in decimal, approximately 10^{-38} to 10^{+38}).

EXAMPLE 1.22

The number $-27.875 = -11011.111 = 1.1011111 \times 2^4$ would be stored as

    1   10000011   10111110000000000000000

IEEE Standard 754 also allows for 64-bit numbers, with an 11-bit exponent (in Excess-1024 notation) and a 52-bit significand. (Other options that we will not discuss are also provided.)

Doing arithmetic on floating point numbers is more complex than for fixed-point numbers. To add two floating point numbers, the radix points must be lined up. To accomplish that, the exponent of the smaller number is increased and the mantissa is shifted right until the two exponents are equal.

			EXAMPLE 1.23
24.376	$.24376 \times 10^2$	$.24376 \times 10^2$	
$+\ \ .002$	$.20000 \times 10^{-2}$	$.00002 \times 10^2$	
24.378		$.24378 \times 10^2$	

Numbers (other than 0) are stored with a leading nonzero digit. The addition of two numbers could produce a mantissa greater than 1. In that case, after the addition, the mantissa is shifted to the right and the exponent increased.

			EXAMPLE 1.24
24.376	$.24376 \times 10^2$		
86.500	$.86500 \times 10^2$		
110.876	1.10876×10^2	$= .11088 \times 10^3$	

Sometimes, the addition of two numbers of opposite sign (or the subtraction of two numbers of the same sign) results in leading 0's. In that case, the result is adjusted by shifting the mantissa to the left to remove the 0's and decreasing the exponent.

		EXAMPLE 1.25
$+.24376 \times 10^2$		
$+\ \ -.23960 \times 10^2$		
$+.00416 \times 10^2$	$= +.41600 \times 10^0$	

[SP 11, 12, 13; EX 11, 12, 13]

1.2.6 Binary Coded Decimal (BCD)

Internally, most computers operate on binary numbers. However, when they interface with humans, the mode of communication is generally decimal. Thus, it is necessary to convert from decimal to binary on input and from binary to decimal on output. (It is straightforward to write software to do this conversion.) However, even this decimal input and output must be coded into binary, digit by digit. If we use the first 10 binary numbers to represent the 10 decimal digits (as in the first binary column in Table 1.7), then the number 739, for example, would be stored as

0111   0011   1001

Table 1.7 Binary-coded decimal codes.

Decimal digit	8421 code	5421 code	2421 code	Excess 3 code	2 of 5 code
0	0000	0000	0000	0011	11000
1	0001	0001	0001	0100	10100
2	0010	0010	0010	0101	10010
3	0011	0011	0011	0110	10001
4	0100	0100	0100	0111	01100
5	0101	1000	1011	1000	01010
6	0110	1001	1100	1001	01001
7	0111	1010	1101	1010	00110
8	1000	1011	1110	1011	00101
9	1001	1100	1111	1100	00011
unused	1010	0101	0101	0000	any of
	1011	0110	0110	0001	the 22
	1100	0111	0111	0010	patterns
	1101	1101	1000	1101	with 0, 1,
	1110	1110	1001	1110	3, 4, or 5
	1111	1111	1010	1111	1's

Each decimal digit is represented by 4 bits, and thus a 3-digit decimal number requires 12 bits (whereas, if it were converted to binary, it would require only 10 bits because numbers up to 1023 can be represented with 10 bits). In addition to the inefficiency of storage, arithmetic on BCD numbers is much more complex* than that on binary, and thus BCD is only used internally in small systems requiring limited computation.

We have already discussed the simplest code, using the first 10 binary numbers to represent the 10 digits. The remaining 4-bit binary numbers (1010, 1011, 1100, 1101, 1110, 1111) are unused. This code, and those in the next two columns of Table 1.7 are referred to as *weighted codes* because the value represented is computed by taking the sum of each digit times its weight. This first code is referred to as the 8421 code, since those are the weights of the bits. Each decimal digit is represented by

$$\mathbf{8} \times a_3 + \mathbf{4} \times a_2 + \mathbf{2} \times a_1 + \mathbf{1} \times a_0$$

It is also referred to as straight binary. Two other weighted codes (5421 and 2421) that are occasionally used are shown next.

Two other codes that are not weighted are shown in the Table 1.7. The first is *excess 3* (XS3) where the decimal digit is represented by the binary equivalent of 3 more than the digit. For example, 0 is stored as the binary 3 (0011) and 6 as the binary of $6 + 3 = 9$ (1001). The final column shows a 2 of 5 code, where each digit is represented by a 5-bit number, two of which are 1 (and the remaining three bits are 0). This provides some error detection capabilities, because, if an error is made in just one

---

*See Solved Problem 12 in Chapter 4 for an example of this.

of the bits (during storage or transmission), the result will contain either one or three 1's and can be detected as an error.

Note that in both the 5421 and 2421 codes, other combinations can be used to represent some of the digits (such as 0101 for 5). However, those shown in the table are the standard representations; the others are included in the unused category.

Each of the representations has advantages in various applications. For example, if signed (10's complement) numbers were stored, the first digit of that number would be in the range 5 to 9 for negative numbers. In the 5421, 2421, and excess 3 codes, that would correspond to the first bit of the number being 1. (We would only need to check 1 bit to determine if a number is negative.) In the 8421 code, however, more complex logic is required, because the first bit might be either 0 or 1 for negative numbers. In both 5421 and excess 3 codes, the 10's complement is computed by complementing each bit and adding 1 (as in two's complement). The process is more complex using the other codes. We will make use of some of these codes in later examples.

[SP 14, 15; EX 14, 15]

1.2.7 Other Codes

Other codes also appear in the digital world. Alphanumeric information is transmitted using the American Standard Code for Information Interchange (ASCII). Seven digits are used to represent the various characters on the standard keyboard as well as a number of control signals (such as carriage return). Table 1.8 lists the printable codes. (Codes beginning with 00 are for control signals.)

Table 1.8 ASCII code.

$a_3a_2a_1a_0$	$a_6a_5a_4$					
	010	011	100	101	110	111
0000	space	0	@	P	`	p
0001	!	1	A	Q	a	q
0010	"	2	B	R	b	r
0011	#	3	C	S	c	s
0100	$	4	D	T	d	t
0101	%	5	E	U	e	u
0110	&	6	F	V	f	v
0111	'	7	G	W	g	w
1000	(	8	H	X	h	x
1001	)	9	I	Y	i	y
1010	*	:	J	Z	j	z
1011	+	;	K	[	k	{
1100	,	<	L	\	l	|
1101		=	M	]	m	}
1110	.	>	N	^	n	~
1111	/	?	O	_	o	delete

This allows us to code anything that can be printed from the standard keyboard. For example, the word *Logic* would be coded

1001100	1101111	1100111	1101001	1100011
L	o	g	i	c

In a *Gray code*, consecutive numbers differ in only one bit. Table 1.9 shows a 4-bit Gray code sequence.

Table 1.9 Gray code.

Number	Gray code	Number	Gray code
0	0000	8	1100
1	0001	9	1101
2	0011	10	1111
3	0010	11	1110
4	0110	12	1010
5	0111	13	1011
6	0101	14	1001
7	0100	15	1000

A Gray code is particularly useful in coding the position of a continuous device. As the device moves from one section to the next, only 1 bit of the code changes. If there is some uncertainty as to the exact position, only 1 bit is in doubt. If a normal binary code were used, all 4 bits would change as it moved from 7 to 8.

The *Hamming code* (proposed by Richard Hamming in 1950) is a single-error-correcting code. Check bits are added to the information bits so that if at most 1 bit is changed in transmission or storage, the original value can be restored. The simplest organization is to number the bits starting at 1; those bits that are a power of 2 (1, 2, 4, 8) are check bits. The pattern of checking is shown below for 4 information bits and 3 check bits:

	a_1	a_2	a_3	a_4	a_5	a_6	a_7
Bit 1	X		X		X		X
Bit 2		X	X			X	X
Bit 4				X	X	X	X

The check bit is chosen so that the total number of 1's in the bits selected is even.* (This is referred to as a *parity* check.) Thus,

$$a_1 = a_3 \oplus a_5 \oplus a_7$$
$$a_2 = a_3 \oplus a_6 \oplus a_7$$
$$a_4 = a_5 \oplus a_6 \oplus a_7$$

---

*We could have made the total number of 1's odd, in which case the a's and e's would be the complement of the expressions shown.

The symbol $\oplus$ represents the Exclusive-OR, which is 1 if either operand is 1, but not both. When several variables are connected by Exclusive-ORs, the result is 1 if and only if an odd number of the operands are 1. (For a more detailed discussion, see Section 2.6.)

Table 1.10 shows the 16 coded words.

Table 1.10 Hamming code.

Data\Bit	a_1	a_2	a_3	a_4	a_5	a_6	a_7
0000	0	0	0	0	0	0	0
0001	1	1	0	1	0	0	1
0010	0	1	0	1	0	1	0
0011	1	0	0	0	0	1	1
0100	1	0	0	1	1	0	0
0101	0	1	0	0	1	0	1
0110	1	1	0	0	1	1	0
0111	0	0	0	1	1	1	1
1000	1	1	1	0	0	0	0
1001	0	0	1	1	0	0	1
1010	1	0	1	1	0	1	0
1011	0	1	1	0	0	1	1
1100	0	1	1	1	1	0	0
1101	1	0	1	0	1	0	1
1110	0	0	1	0	1	1	0
1111	1	1	1	1	1	1	1

When a word is received, the same bits are checked:

$$e_1 = a_1 \oplus a_3 \oplus a_5 \oplus a_7$$
$$e_2 = a_2 \oplus a_3 \oplus a_6 \oplus a_7$$
$$e_4 = a_4 \oplus a_5 \oplus a_6 \oplus a_7$$

If no errors were made, all three computations would produce 0. If one error was made, the checks produce the number of the bit in error,

$$4\,e_4 + 2\,e_2 + e_1$$

(Multiple errors will be misinterpreted.)

EXAMPLE 1.26

Received: 0010011

$e_1 = 0 \quad e_2 = 1 \quad e_4 = 0$

Bit 2 (a check bit) is in error. The correct word is 0110011, the data is 1011.
Received: 1101101

$e_1 = 1 \quad e_2 = 0 \quad e_4 = 1$

Bit 5 is in error. The correct word is 1101001, the data is 0001.

With n check bits (where $n \geq 2$), there can be $2^n - n - 1$ information bits.

Check bits	Data bits
2	1
3	4
4	11
5	26

[SP 16, 17; EX 16, 17]

1.3 SOLVED PROBLEMS

1. Convert the following positive binary integers to decimal.
  a. 110100101
  b. 00010111

  a. $110100101 = 1 + 4 + 32 + 128 + 256 = 421$
    Starting the evaluation from right (1's position) to left
    (2^8 position). (There are 0's in the 2, 8, 16, and 64 bits.)
  b. $00010111 = 1 + 2 + 4 + 16 = 23$
    Leading 0's do not change the result.

2. Convert the following decimal integers to binary. Assume all
  numbers are unsigned (positive) and represented by 12 bits.
  a. 47
  b. 98
  c. 5000

  a. 47

	$47 < 64$	Thus no 2^6 bit or greater
	$47 - 32 = 15$	gives a 2^5 bit
	$15 < 16$	no 2^4 bit
	$15 - 8 = 7$	2^3 bit
	$7 = 111$	thus last 3 bits are 111

  $47 = 000000101111$

  b. 98

$98/2 = 49$	remainder = 0	0
$49/2 = 24$	remainder = 1	10
$24/2 = 12$	remainder = 0	010
$12/2 = 6$	remainder = 0	0010
$6/2 = 3$	remainder = 0	00010
$3/2 = 1$	remainder = 1	100010
$1/2 = 0$	remainder = 1	1100010

We could keep dividing 0 by 2 and getting remainders of 0 until we had
12 bits or recognize that the leading bits must be 0.
$98 = 000001100010$
  As in part a., we could have stopped dividing when we recognized
the number, say that $12 = 1100$. We would take what we had already

found, the three least significant bits of 010 and put the binary for 12 ahead of that, getting the same answer, of course, 1100010 (with enough leading 0's to make up the appropriate number of bits).

    c. 5000: cannot represent in 12 bits because $5000 > 2^{12}$.

---

3. Convert the following to hexadecimal
    a. 11010110111_2
    b. 611_{10}

Leading 0's are added when necessary to make the number of bits a multiple of 4.

    a. 0110 1011 0111 = $6B7_{16}$
    b. $611/16 = 38$ rem   3   3
           $38/16 = 2$ rem   6   63
           $2/16 = 0$ rem   2   263

This equals 0010 0110 0011.

---

4. Convert the following hexadecimal integers to decimal
    a. 263
    b. 1C3

---

    a. $3 + 6 \times 16 + 2 \times 16^2 = 3 + 96 + 512 = 611$
    b. $3 + 12 \times 16 + 16^2 = 3 + 192 + 256 = 451$

---

5. Compute the sum of the following pairs of 6-bit unsigned integers. If the answer is to be stored in a 6-bit location, indicate which of the sums produces overflow. Also, show the decimal equivalent of each problem.
    a. $0\,0\,1\,0\,1\,1 + 0\,1\,1\,0\,1\,0$
    b. $1\,0\,1\,1\,1\,1 + 0\,0\,0\,0\,0\,1$
    c. $1\,0\,1\,0\,1\,0 + 0\,1\,0\,1\,0\,1$
    d. $1\,0\,1\,0\,1\,0 + 1\,0\,0\,0\,1\,1$

---

a.
```
                     0              1 0           0 1
  11          0 0 1 0 1 1     0 0 1 0 1 1     0 0 1 0 1 1
  26          0 1 1 0 1 0     0 1 1 0 1 0     0 1 1 0 1 0
  37                    1             0 1           1 0 1

            1 0              1 1             1
        0 0 1 0 1 1     0 0 1 0 1 1     0 0 1 0 1 1
        0 1 1 0 1 0     0 1 1 0 1 0     0 1 1 0 1 0
          0 1 0 1         0 0 1 0 1   0 1 0 0 1 0 1  = 37
```

Note that in this case the last carry result is 0 (it is shown as part of the sum) and thus the answer does fit in 6 bits (there is no overflow).

b.   0 1 1 1 1   (carries)
           1 0 1 1 1 1   47
           0 0 0 0 0 1 $\underline{1}$
           0 1 1 0 0 0 0   48

c.   0 0 0 0 0
           1 0 1 0 1 0   42
           0 1 0 1 0 1 $\underline{21}$
           0 1 1 1 1 1 1   63

d.   0 0 0 1 0
           1 0 1 0 1 0   42
           1 0 0 0 1 1 $\underline{35}$
           1 0 0 1 1 0 1   77   overflow (looks like 13)

Note that the answer is larger than 63, which is the largest 6-bit number.

6. The following decimal numbers are to be stored in a 6-bit two's complement format. Show how they are stored.
   a. $+ 14$
   b. $- 20$
   c. $+ 37$

   a. $+14 = 001110$ Positive numbers are just converted to binary.
   b. -20: $+20 = 010100$

   Complement every bit   1 0 1 0 1 1
   Add 1 $\underline{1}$
   -20 is stored as   1 0 1 1 0 0
   c. $+37$: Cannot be stored, the range of 6-bit numbers is $-32 \leq n \leq 31$. Converting 37 to binary would give 100101, but that represents a negative number.

7. The following 6-bit two's complement numbers were found in a computer. What decimal number do they represent?
   a. 001011
   b. 111010

   a. 001011: Because it begins with 0, it is positive $= 1 + 2 + 8 = 11$
   b. 111010: Because it begins with a 1, it is negative; take two's
      complement: 0 0 0 1 0 1
                           $\underline{1}$
                           0 0 0 1 1 0 $= 6$

   Thus 111010 represents -6

8. Each of the following pairs of signed (two's complement) numbers are stored in computer words (6 bits). Compute the sum as
it is stored in a 6-bit computer word. Show the decimal equivalents of each operand and the sum. Indicate if there is overflow.

   a. 1 1 1 1 1 1 + 0 0 1 0 1 1
   b. 0 0 1 0 0 1 + 1 0 0 1 0 0
   c. 0 0 1 0 0 1 + 0 1 0 0 1 1
   d. 0 0 1 0 1 0 + 0 1 1 0 0 0
   e. 1 1 1 0 1 0 + 1 1 0 0 0 1
   f. 1 0 1 0 0 1 + 1 1 0 0 0 1
   g. 1 1 0 1 0 1 + 0 0 1 0 1 1

a.   1 1 1 1 1 1 -1
           0 0 1 0 1 1 $+11$ The carry out is ignored and will not
    (1) 0 0 1 0 1 0 $+10$ be shown in the remaining examples.

b.   0 0 1 0 0 1 $+9$
           1 0 0 1 0 0 -28
           1 0 1 1 0 1 -19

c.   0 0 1 0 0 1 $+9$
           0 1 0 0 1 1 $+19$
           0 1 1 1 0 0 $+28$

d.   0 0 1 0 1 0 $+10$
           0 1 1 0 0 0 $+24$
           1 0 0 0 1 0   looks like -30; should be $+34$; overflow
                          sum of two positive numbers looks negative

e.   1 1 1 0 1 0 -6
           1 1 0 0 0 1 -15
           1 0 1 0 1 1 -21

f.   1 0 1 0 0 1 -23
           1 1 0 0 0 1 -15
           0 1 1 0 1 0   looks like $+26$; should be -38; overflow
                          sum of two negative numbers looks positive

g.   1 1 0 1 0 1 -11
           0 0 1 0 1 1 $+11$
           0 0 0 0 0 0 0

9. Subtract each of the following pairs of unsigned integers.
   a. 0 0 1 1 0 1 − 0 0 0 1 1 0
   b. 1 1 0 1 0 1 − 0 0 0 0 1 1
   c. 0 0 0 1 1 1 − 0 1 0 0 1 1

a. (This example is the same for either signed or unsigned numbers.)

$$
\begin{array}{ccc}
 & 1 & \\
0\,0\,1\,1\,0\,1 & 0\,0\,1\,1\,0\,1 & 13 \\
-0\,0\,0\,1\,1\,0 & 1\,1\,1\,0\,0\,1 & -6 \\
\hline
 & (1)\,0\,0\,0\,1\,1\,1 & 7 \\
\end{array}
$$

b.

$$
\begin{array}{ccc}
 & 1 & \\
1\,1\,0\,1\,0\,1 & 1\,1\,0\,1\,0\,1 & 53 \\
-0\,0\,0\,0\,1\,1 & 1\,1\,1\,1\,0\,0 & -3 \\
\hline
 & (1)\,1\,1\,0\,0\,1\,0 & 50 \\
\end{array}
$$

c.

$$
\begin{array}{ccc}
 & 1 & \\
0\,0\,0\,1\,1\,1 & 0\,0\,0\,1\,1\,1 & 7 \\
-0\,1\,0\,0\,1\,1 & 1\,0\,1\,1\,0\,0 & -19 \\
\hline
 & (0)\,1\,1\,0\,1\,0\,0 & \text{overflow, answer negative} \\
\end{array}
$$

10. Subtract each of the following pairs of signed integers.
 a. $1\,1\,0\,1\,0\,1 - 0\,0\,0\,0\,1\,1$
 b. $1\,1\,0\,1\,0\,1 - 0\,1\,1\,0\,0\,0$
 c. $0\,1\,0\,0\,0\,0 - 1\,0\,0\,1\,0\,0$

a.

$$
\begin{array}{ccc}
 & 1 & \\
1\,1\,0\,1\,0\,1 & 1\,1\,0\,1\,0\,1 & -11 \\
-0\,0\,0\,0\,1\,1 & 1\,1\,1\,1\,0\,0 & -(+3) \\
\hline
 & (1)\,1\,1\,0\,0\,1\,0 & -14 \\
\end{array}
$$

Note that this is the same binary number as in Solved Problem 9b.

b.

$$
\begin{array}{ccc}
 & 1 & \\
1\,1\,0\,1\,0\,1 & 1\,1\,0\,1\,0\,1 & -11 \\
-0\,1\,1\,0\,0\,0 & 1\,0\,0\,1\,1\,1 & -(+24) \\
\hline
 & (1)\,0\,1\,1\,1\,0\,1 & \text{overflow, answer looks positive} \\
\end{array}
$$

c.

$$
\begin{array}{ccc}
 & 1 & \\
0\,1\,0\,0\,0\,0 & 0\,1\,0\,0\,0\,0 & 16 \\
-1\,0\,0\,1\,0\,0 & 0\,1\,1\,0\,1\,1 & -(-28) \\
\hline
 & (0)\,1\,0\,1\,1\,0\,0 & \text{overflow, answer looks negative} \\
\end{array}
$$

11. In a fixed-point binary system, where signed numbers are stored in signed-magnitude, with a sign plus eight bits of integer and seven bits of fraction, how would each of the following decimal numbers be stored?
 a. 51.375
 b. −24.7

a. 51.375 $51/2 = 25$ rem 1   1
                $25/2 = 12$ rem 1   11
                    $12 = 1100$ 110011
            $.375 \times 2 = 0.75$ .0
            $.75 \times 2 = 1.50$ .01
            $.5 \times 2 = 1.0$ .011

$51.735 = 0$ 00110011   0110000

b. -24.7 $24 = 11000$
                $.7 \times 2 = 1.4$ .1
                $.4 \times 2 = 0.8$ .10
                $.8 \times 2 = 1.6$ .101
                $.6 \times 2 = 1.2$ .1011
                $.2 \times 2 = 0.4$ .10110
                $.4 \times 2 = 0.8$ .101100
                $.8 \times 2 = 1.6$ .1011001
                $.6 \times 2 = 1.2$ .10110011

This is rounded to 7 bits.

$-24.7 = 1$ 00011000 1011010

---

12. In IEEE Standard notation, how would each of the decimal numbers be stored?

a. 51.375

b. -0.1

---

a. $51.375 = 110011.011$ (from SP 11)
        $= 1.10011011 \times 2^5$

0   10000100   10011011000000000000000

b. $-0.1 = -.0001100110011 \ldots$
        $= 1.100110011 \ldots \times 2^{-4}$

1   1111011   10011001100110011001101

---

13. For each pair of decimal numbers, add them, leaving them in normalized decimal form (leading digit of the 5-digit mantissa nonzero).

a. $51.875 + 10461.$

b. $.00536 + .00871$

c. $24.611 - 24.632$

---

a. $.51876 \times 10^2$ $.00052 \times 10^5$
        $.10461 \times 10^5$ $.10461 \times 10^5$
        ───────────────── $.10513 \times 10^5 = 10513$

Note that numbers are rounded when digits fall off the end on a right shift.

    b. $.53600 \times 10^{-2}$

        $\dfrac{.87100 \times 10^{-2}}{1.40700 \times 10^{-2}}$ is stored as $.14070 \times 10^{-1} = .01407$

    c. $.24611 \times 10^{2}$

        $\dfrac{-.24632 \times 10^{2}}{-.00021 \times 10^{2}}$ is stored as $-.21000 \times 10^{-1} = -.02100$

14. We have a computer that can store 3 decimal digits. How are the following two numbers stored in each of the five codes?

    a. 491

    b. 27

  a. 8421   0100 1001 0001

      5421   0100 1100 0001

      2421   0100 1111 0001

      XS3   0111 1100 0100

      2 of 5   01100 00011 10100

    Note that the first four codes require 12-bit words; the 2 of 5 code requires 15-bit words.

  b. 8421   0000 0010 0111

      5421   0000 0010 1010

      2421   0000 0010 1101

      XS3   0011 0101 1010

      2 of 5   11000 10010 00110

15. We have the following numbers stored in a computer. What is the decimal value represented if the number is stored as

    i. BCD 8421   iv. BCD excess 3

    ii. BCD 5421   v. Binary unsigned

    iii. BCD 2421   vi. Binary signed

    a. 1000 0111

    b. 0011 0100

    c. 1100 1001

  a. 1000 0111

    i. BCD 8421   87

    ii. BCD 5421   — 0111 not used

    iii. BCD 2421   — 1000, 0111 not used

    iv. BCD excess 3   54

      v. Binary unsigned   135

     vi. Binary signed -121

b. 0011 0100

       i. BCD 8421   34

      ii. BCD 5421   34

     iii. BCD 2421   34

     iv. BCD excess 3   01

      v. Binary unsigned   52

     vi. Binary signed $+52$

c. 1100 1001

       i. BCD 8421   —   1100 not used

      ii. BCD 5421   96

     iii. BCD 2421   —   1001 not used

     iv. BCD excess 3   96

      v. Binary unsigned   201

     vi. Binary signed -55

16. a. Code the following into ASCII.

       i. HELLO

      ii. hello

  b. Translate the following into English.

       i. 1011001 1100101 1110011 0100001

      ii. 0110010 0101011 0110001 0111101 0110011

  a. i. 1001000 1000101 1001100 1001100 1001111

      ii. 1101000 1100101 1101100 1101100 1101111

  b. i. Yes!

      ii. 2+1=3

17. Using the version of the Hamming code shown

  a. Code the following data

       i. 1000

      ii. 0011

  b. If the following word was received, what word was sent (assuming no more than a single error)?

       i. 1111011

      ii. 1111010

  a. i. **111**0000

      ii. **1000**011

b. i. $e_1 = 1 \oplus 1 \oplus 0 \oplus 1 = 1$
$e_2 = 1 \oplus 1 \oplus 1 \oplus 1 = 0$
$e_4 = 1 \oplus 0 \oplus 1 \oplus 1 = 1$

bit 5 error, word sent 1111111, data sent 1111

ii. $e_1 = 1 \oplus 1 \oplus 0 \oplus 0 = 0$
$e_2 = 1 \oplus 1 \oplus 1 \oplus 0 = 1$
$e_4 = 1 \oplus 0 \oplus 1 \oplus 0 = 0$

bit 2 error, word sent 1011010, data sent 1010

1.4 EXERCISES*

1. Convert the following unsigned binary integers to decimal.
   *a. 11111   e. 10101010
   b. 1000000   f. 000011110000
   c. 1001101101   g. 110011001100
   *d. 101111   *h. 000000000000

2. Convert the following decimal integers to binary. Assume all
   numbers are unsigned (positive) and represented by 12 bits.
   *a. 73   c. 402   *e. 1000   *g. 4200
   b. 127   d. 512   f. 17   h. 1365

3. Convert the following to hexadecimal
   *a. 100101101011_2
   b. 10110100000101_2
   *c. 791_{10}
   d. 1600_{10}

4. Convert the following hexadecimal numbers to decimal
   a. 1000
   b. ABCD
   *c. 3FF

5. Compute the sum of the following pairs of 6-bit unsigned integers.
   If the answer is to be stored in a 6-bit location, indicate which of
   the sums produce overflow. Also, show the decimal equivalent of
   both operands and the result.
   *a. 000011 + 001100   *e. 001011 + 100111
   b. 010100 + 101101   f. 000101 + 000111
   c. 011100 + 011010   g. 101100 + 100100
   *d. 110011 + 001110

*Answers to Exercises marked with a star (*) are given in Appendix B.

6. The following decimal integers are to be stored in a 6-bit two's complement format. Show how they are stored.

    *a. +25   *c. +32   *e. −15   g. −1
    b.   0   d. +15   f. −45   h. −16

7. The following 6-bit two's complement integers were found in a computer. What decimal number do they represent?

    a. 000101 *c. 010101   e. 011111   g. 101010
    b. 111111 *d. 100100   f. 111001   *h. 100000

8. We have a computer that stores binary signed integers in two's complement form. All numbers are 8 bits long.

    a. What decimal number is represented by 01101011?

    b. What decimal number is represented by 10101110?

  *c. How is the number −113 stored?

  *d. How is the number +143 stored?

    e. How is the number +43 stored?

    f. How is the number −43 stored?

9. Each of the following pairs of signed (two's complement) integers are stored in computer words (6 bits). Compute the sum as it is stored in a 6-bit computer word. Show the decimal equivalents of each operand and the sum. Indicate if there is overflow.

    *a. 110101   c. 001100   e. 011010
          001111   110100   001100
    b. 111010   *d. 101010   *f. 111101
          000111   100110   110000

10. For each of the following pairs of integers, subtract the second from the first. Show the operands and the answers in decimal, assuming

   i. the numbers are unsigned

  ii. the numbers are signed (two's complement).

  Indicate overflow where appropriate.

    a. 010101   *c. 111010   e. 110010
          001100   000111   110111
  *b. 010001   *d. 100100   f. 111010
          011000   011000   101101

11. In a fixed-point binary system in which signed numbers are stored in signed-magnitude, with a sign plus 8 bits of integer and 7 bits of fraction, how would each of the following decimal numbers be stored?

  *a. 200.15625

    b. −48.5

    c.   121.95

  *d.   0.01

    e. -300.25

*12. In IEEE Standard 32-bit notation, how would each of the decimal numbers of Exercise 11 be stored?

13. For each pair of decimal numbers, add them, leaving them in normalized decimal form (leading digit of the 5-digit mantissa nonzero).

    a.   23.456 + 45.112

  *b.   2136431. + 47.

    c.   46.75 + 985.88

    d.   652.2 − 433.44

  *e.   513.95 − 514.03

14. We have a computer that can store 3 decimal digits. How are each of the following numbers stored in each of the five codes?

i.	8421	iv.	excess 3
ii.	5421	v.	2 of 5
iii.	2421		

  *a.   103   b.   999   c.   1   d.   0

15. We have the following numbers stored in a computer. What is the decimal value represented if the number is stored as

i.	BCD 8421	iv.	BCD excess 3
ii.	BCD 5421	v.	binary unsigned
iii.	BCD 2421	vi.	binary signed

a.	1111	1010	*d.	1001	0101
*b.	0001	1011	e.	1110	1101
c.	1000	0011	f.	0100	1000

16. a. Code the following into ASCII

i.	Problem 5	iii.	2 + 1 = 3
*ii.	"OK"	iv.	ABM

    b.   Translate the following into English

i.	1000001	1101100	1100001	1101110	
ii.	0100100	0110111	0101110	0111001	0110101
*iii.	0111001	0101111	0110011	0111101	0110011
iv.	1010100	1101000	1100101	0100000	1100101
	1101110	1100100			

17. Using the version of the Hamming code shown
   a. Code the following data

i. 0000	iii. 0101
*ii. 1011	iv. 1111

   b. If the following word was received, what word was sent (assuming no more than a single error)?

*i. 1011010	*iii. 0000110
ii. 0011010	iv. 1100110

1.5 CHAPTER 1 TEST (50 MINUTES)*

1. Convert the decimal number 347 to
   a. binary.
   b. hexadecimal.
   Show your work.

2. Add the two unsigned binary numbers; show both operands and the result in decimal as well as binary. (Be sure to show the carry as you add.) Indicate if there is overflow.

   0 1 0 1 1   1 0 1 0 1 1
   0 1 1 1 0   0 1 1 0 0 1

3. Show the decimal equivalent of each of the numbers if they are interpreted as (six answers).

                  1 0 0 1 0 1 0 1   0 1 1 1 0 0 1 1

   a. Unsigned binary
   b. Signed binary
   c. BCD (8421 code)

4. Add the three pairs of signed (two's complement) numbers. Be sure to show the carry as you add. Show both operands and the result of each addition in decimal as well as binary. Indicate if there is overflow.

   1 1 0 0   1 0 1 0   0 1 0 1
   1 1 0 1   0 1 1 1   0 0 1 1

5. Subtract the two pairs of numbers. Show the operands and the results in decimal and binary
   a. assuming they are unsigned.
   b. assuming they are signed.

   1 1 0 1 − 1 1 0 0   1 0 1 0 − 0 1 1 0

   Indicate if there is overflow.

---

*Tests assume students are allowed one sheet of $8\frac{1}{2} \times 11$ paper with any notes they wish on both sides. Solutions to Chapter Tests are given in Appendix C.

6. Convert each of the decimal numbers to IEEE Standard floating-point notation (sign, 8-bit excess 127 exponent, 23-bit significand).

   a.   −515.25

   b.   10.33

7. Convert the pair of decimal numbers to floating-point format with five significant digits. Then compute the sum, leaving them in standard form (fraction and exponent).

   24.368 + 981.42

Part I   Logic Design

Combinational Systems

In this chapter, we will develop the tools to specify combinational systems. Then, we will develop an algebraic approach for the description of these systems, their simplification, and their implementation. We will concentrate on rather small systems, which will enable us to better understand the process. We will look at larger problems in Chapter 4.

2.1 THE DESIGN PROCESS FOR COMBINATIONAL SYSTEMS

In this section, we will outline the process to be used to design combinational systems. (A similar process will be developed in Chapter 6 for sequential systems.) The design process typically starts with a problem statement, a verbal description of the intended system. The goal is to develop a block diagram of that system, utilizing available components and meeting the design objectives and constraints.

We will use the following five examples to illustrate the steps in the design process and, indeed, continue to follow some of them in subsequent chapters, as we develop the tools necessary to do that design.

Continuing Examples (CE)

CE1. A system with four inputs, *A, B, C,* and *D,* and one output, *Z,* such that $Z = 1$ iff three of the inputs are 1.

CE2. A single light (that can be on or off) that can be controlled by any one of three switches. One switch is the master on/off switch. If it is down, the lights are off. When the master switch is up, a change in the position of one of the other switches (from up to down or from down to up) will cause the light to change state.

CE3. A system to do 1 bit of binary addition. It has three inputs (the 2 bits to be added plus the carry from the next lower order bit) and produces two outputs: a sum bit and a carry to the next higher order position.

CE4. A display driver; a system that has as its input the code for a decimal digit and produces as its output the signals to drive a seven-segment display, such as those on most digital watches and numeric displays (more later).

CE5. A system with nine inputs, representing two 4-bit binary numbers and a carry input, and one 5-bit output, representing the sum. (Each input number can range from 0 to 15; the output can range from 0 to 31.)

> **Step 1:** Represent each of the inputs and outputs in binary.

Sometimes, as in CE1, 3, and 5, the problem statement is already given in terms of binary inputs and outputs. Other times, it is up to the designer. In CE2, we need to create a numeric equivalence for each of the inputs and outputs. We might code the light on as a 1 output and off as 0. (We could just as well have used the opposite definition, as long as we are coordinated with the light designer.) Similarly, we will define a switch in the up position as a 1 input and down as 0. For CE4, the input is a decimal digit. We must determine what BCD code is to be used. That might be provided for us by whoever is providing the input, or we may have the ability to specify it in such a way as to make our system simplest. We must also code the output; we need to know the details of the display and whether a 1 or a 0 lights each segment. (We will discuss those details in Section 2.1.1.) In general, the different input and output representations may result in a significant difference in the amount of logic required.

> **Step 2:** Formalize the design specification either in the form of a *truth table* or of an *algebraic expression*.

We will concentrate on the idea of a truth table here and leave the development of algebraic expressions for later in the chapter. The truth table format is the most common result of step 2 of the design process. We can do this in a digital system because each of the inputs only takes on one of two values (0 or 1). Thus, if we have n inputs, there are 2^n input combinations and thus the truth table has 2^n rows. These rows are normally written in binary order (if, for no other reason, than to make sure that we do not leave any out). The truth table has two sets of columns: n input columns, one for each input variable, and m output columns, one for each of the m outputs.

An example of a truth table with two inputs, A and B, and one output, Y, is shown as Table 2.1, where there are two input columns, one output column, and $2^2 = 4$ rows (not including the title row). We will look at truth tables for some of the continuing examples shortly, after presenting the other steps of the design process.

Table 2.1 A two-input truth table.

A	B	Y
0	0	0
0	1	1
1	0	1
1	1	1

> **Step 1.5:** If necessary, break the problem into smaller subproblems.

This step is listed here because sometimes it is possible to do this after having developed the truth table and sometimes, we must really break up the problem before we can even begin to do such a table.

It is not possible to apply most of the design techniques that we will develop to very large problems. Even CE5, the 4-bit adder, has nine inputs and would thus require a truth table of $2^9 = 512$ rows with nine input columns and five output columns. Although we can easily produce the entries for any line of that table, the table would spread over several pages and be very cumbersome. Furthermore, the minimization techniques of this chapter and Chapter 3 would be strained. The problem becomes completely unmanageable if we go to a realistic adder for a computer—say one that adds 32-bit numbers. There the table would be 2^{64} lines long, even without a carry input (approximately 1.84×10^{19}). (That means that if we were to write 1 million lines on each page and put 1 million pages in a book, we would still need over 18 million volumes to list the entire truth table. Or, if we had a computer that could process 1 billion lines of the truth table per second (requiring a supercomputer), it would still take over 584 years to process the whole table.)

Obviously, we have been able to solve such problems. In the case of the adder, we can imitate how we do it by hand, namely, add 1 bit at a time, producing 1 bit of the sum and the carry to the next bit. That is the problem proposed in CE3; it only requires an eight-line truth table. We can build 32 such systems and connect them together.

Also, it is often most economical to take advantage of subsystems that already have been implemented. For example, we can buy the 4-bit adder described in CE5 (on a single integrated circuit chip). We might want to use that as a component in our design. We will examine this part of the design process further in Chapter 4.

> **Step 3:** Simplify the description.

The truth table will lead directly to an implementation in some technologies (see, for example, the ROM in Chapter 4). More often, we must convert that to an algebraic form to implement it. But the algebraic form we get from the truth table tends to lead to rather complex systems. Thus, we will develop techniques for reducing the complexity of algebraic expressions in this chapter and the next.

> **Step 4:** Implement the system with the available components, subject to the design objectives and constraints.

A *gate* is a network with one output. Most of the implementations of this chapter and the next use gates as the components. The truth table used to illustrate step 2 (see Table 2.1) describes the behavior of one type of gate—a two-input OR gate. The final form of the solution may be a block diagram of the gate implementation, where the OR gate is usually depicted by the symbol of Figure 2.1. We may build the system in the laboratory using integrated circuit packages that contain a few such gates or we may simulate it on a computer. We will discuss each of these in more detail later.

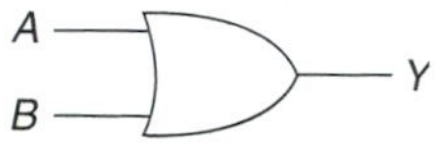

As mentioned earlier, more complex components, such as adders and decoders, may be available as building blocks, in addition to (or in place of) gates. (Of course, when we get to sequential systems, we will introduce storage devices and other larger building blocks.)

The design objective is often to build the least expensive circuit. That usually corresponds to the simplest algebraic expression, although not always. Since gates are usually obtained in packages (say 4 two-input OR gates in a package), the cost may be measured in terms of the number of packages. Thus, whether we need one of the four gates in a package, or all four, the cost would be the same. Sometimes, one of the objectives is speed, that is, to build as fast a circuit as possible. As we will see later, each time a signal passes through a gate, there is a small delay, slowing down the system. Thus, if speed is a factor, we may have a limit on the number of gates any one signal must pass through.

Figure 2.1   OR gate symbol.

2.1.1   Don't Care Conditions

Before we can develop the truth table for the display driver example (CE4), we must understand the concept of the *don't care*. In some systems, the value of the output is specified for only some of the input conditions. (Such functions are sometimes referred to as *incompletely specified functions*.) For the remaining input combinations, it does not matter what the output is, that is, we don't care. In a truth table, don't cares are indicated by an X. (Some of the literature uses d, ϕ, or φ.) Table 2.2 is such a truth table.

This table states that the f must be 0 when a and b are 0, that it must be 1 when $a = 0$ and $b = 1$ or when $a = 1$ and $b = 0$, and that it does not matter what f is when a and b are both 1. In other words, either f_1 or f_2 of Table 2.3 are acceptable.

When we design a system with don't cares, we may make the output either 0 or 1 for each don't care input combination. In the example of Table 2.3, that means that we can implement either f_1 or f_2. One of these might be much less costly to implement. If there are several don't cares, the number of acceptable solutions greatly increases, since each don't care can be either 0 or 1, independently. The techniques we develop in Chapter 3 handle don't cares very easily; they do not require solving separate problems.

Table 2.2   A truth table with a don't care.

a	b	f
0	0	0
0	1	1
1	0	1
1	1	X

Table 2.3   Acceptable truth tables.

a	b	f_1	f_2
0	0	0	0
0	1	1	1
1	0	1	1
1	1	0	1

In real systems, don't cares occur in several ways. First, there may be some input combinations that never occur. That is the case in CE4, where the input is the code for a decimal digit; there are only 10 possible input combinations. If a 4-bit code is used, then six of the input combinations never occur. When we build a system, we can design it such that the outputs would be either 0 or 1 for each of these don't care combinations, since that input never happens.

A second place where don't cares occur is in the design of one system to drive a second system. Consider the block diagram of Figure 2.2. We are designing System One to make System Two behave in a certain way. On some occasions, for certain values of *A, B,* and *C,* System Two will behave the same way whether *J* is 0 or 1. In that case, the output *J* of System One is a don't care for that input combination. We will see this behavior arise in Chapter 6, where System Two is a flip flop (a binary storage device).

Figure 2.2   Design example with don't cares.

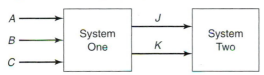

We will see a third kind of don't care in CE4; we may really not care what one output is.

2.1.2   The Development of Truth Tables

Given a word problem, the first step is to decide how to code the inputs. Then, the development of a truth table is usually rather straightforward. The number of inputs determines the number of rows, and the major problem generally revolves about the ambiguity of English (or any natural language).

For CE1, a 16-row truth table is required. There are four input columns and one output column. (In Table 2.4, three output columns are shown Z_1, Z_2, and Z_3 to account for the three interpretations of the problem statement.) There is little room for controversy on the behavior of the system for the first 15 rows of the table. If there are fewer than three 1's on the input lines, the output is 0. If three of the inputs are 1 and the other is 0, then the output is 1. The only question in completing the table is in relation to the last row. Does "three of the inputs are 1" mean *exactly* three or does it mean at *least* three? If the former is true, then the last line of the truth table is 0, as shown for Z_1. If the latter is true, then the last line of the table is 1, as shown in Z_2. Two other options, both shown as Z_3, are that we know that all four inputs will not be 1 simultaneously, and that we do not care what the output is if all four inputs are 1. In those cases, the last entry is don't care, X.

Table 2.4 Truth table for CE1.

A	B	C	D	Z_1	Z_2	Z_3
0	0	0	0	0	0	0
0	0	0	1	0	0	0
0	0	1	0	0	0	0
0	0	1	1	0	0	0
0	1	0	0	0	0	0
0	1	0	1	0	0	0
0	1	1	0	0	0	0
0	1	1	1	1	1	1
1	0	0	0	0	0	0
1	0	0	1	0	0	0
1	0	1	0	0	0	0
1	0	1	1	1	1	1
1	1	0	0	0	0	0
1	1	0	1	1	1	1
1	1	1	0	1	1	1
1	1	1	1	0	1	X

For CE2, even after coding the inputs and outputs, we do not have a unique solution to the problem. We will label the switches *a, b,* and *c* (where *a* is the master switch) and use a 1 to represent up (and a 0 for down). The light output is labeled *f* (where a 1 on *f* means that the light is on). When $a = 0$, the light is off (0), no matter what the value of *b* and *c*. The problem statement does not specify the output when $a = 1$; it only specifies what effect a change in the other inputs will have. We still have two possible solutions to this problem. If we assume that switches *b* and *c* in the down position cause the light to be off, then the fifth row of the table (100) will have an output of 0, as shown in Table 2.5a. When one of these switches is up (101, 110), then the light must be on. From either of these states, changing *b* or *c* will either return the system to the 100 input state or move it to state 111; for this, the output is 0.

We could have started with some other fixed value, such as switches *b* and *c* up means that the light is on or that switches *b* and *c* down means

Table 2.5 Truth tables for CE2.

a	b	c	f		a	b	c	f
0	0	0	0		0	0	0	0
0	0	1	0		0	0	1	0
0	1	0	0		0	1	0	0
0	1	1	0		0	1	1	0
1	0	0	0		1	0	0	1
1	0	1	1		1	0	1	0
1	1	0	1		1	1	0	0
1	1	1	0		1	1	1	1

(a)   (b)

that the light is on. Either of these would produce the truth table of Table 2.5b, which is equally acceptable.

We have already developed the truth table for CE3, the 1-bit binary full adder, in Section 1.2.2, Table 1.5 (although we did not refer to it as a truth table at that time).

Although we could easily construct a truth table for CE5, the 4-bit adder, we would need 512 rows. Furthermore, once we had done this, we would still find it nearly impossible to simplify the function by hand (that is, without the aid of a computer). We will defer further discussion of this problem to Chapter 4.

We will now examine the display driver of CE4. The first thing we must do is to choose a code for the decimal digit. That will (obviously) affect the table and, indeed, make a significant difference in the cost of the implementation. We will call the four binary inputs $W, X, Y,$ and Z and the seven outputs $a, b, c, d, e, f,$ and g. For the sake of this example, we will assume that decimal digits are stored in the 8421 code. (We will look at variations on this in Chapter 4.)

The next thing we need to know is whether the display requires a 0 or 1 on each segment input to light that segment. Both types of displays exist. In the solution presented in Table 2.6, we assume that a 1 is needed to light a segment.

The display has seven inputs, labeled $a, b, c, d, e, f, g,$ one for each of the segments. A block diagram of the system is shown in Figure 2.3, along with the layout of the display and how each digit is displayed. The solid lines represent segments to be lit and the dashed ones segments that are not lit for that digit. Note that there are alternative displays for the digits 6, 7, and 9. For 6, sometimes segment a is lit, and sometimes it is not. The design specification might state that it must be lit or that it must not be lit or that it doesn't matter; choose whatever is easier. The latter is the choice shown in Table 2.6. We will return to this problem in Chapter 4.

Figure 2.3 A seven-segment display.

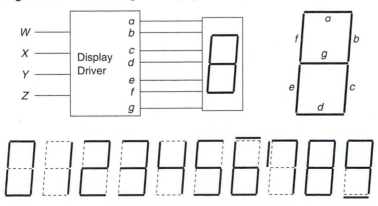

Table 2.6 A truth table for the seven-segment display driver.

Digit	W	X	Y	Z	a	b	c	d	e	f	g
0	0	0	0	0	1	1	1	1	1	1	0
1	0	0	0	1	0	1	1	0	0	0	0
2	0	0	1	0	1	1	0	1	1	0	1
3	0	0	1	1	1	1	1	1	0	0	1
4	0	1	0	0	0	1	1	0	0	1	1
5	0	1	0	1	1	0	1	1	0	1	1
6	0	1	1	0	X	0	1	1	1	1	1
7	0	1	1	1	1	1	1	0	0	X	0
8	1	0	0	0	1	1	1	1	1	1	1
9	1	0	0	1	1	1	1	X	0	1	1
–	1	0	1	0	X	X	X	X	X	X	X
–	1	0	1	1	X	X	X	X	X	X	X
–	1	1	0	0	X	X	X	X	X	X	X
–	1	1	0	1	X	X	X	X	X	X	X
–	1	1	1	0	X	X	X	X	X	X	X
–	1	1	1	1	X	X	X	X	X	X	X

EXAMPLE 2.1

We want to develop a truth table for a system with three inputs, a, b, and c, and four outputs, w, x, y, z. The output is a binary number equal to the largest integer that meets the input conditions:

$a = 0$: odd $a = 1$: even

$b = 0$: prime $b = 1$: not prime

$c = 0$: less than 8 $c = 1$: greater than or equal to 8

Some inputs may never occur; the output is never all 0's.
(A prime is a number that is only evenly divisible by itself and 1.) The following is a truth table for this system.

a	b	c	w	x	y	z
0	0	0	0	1	1	1
0	0	1	1	1	0	1
0	1	0	X	X	X	X
0	1	1	1	1	1	1
1	0	0	0	0	1	0
1	0	1	X	X	X	X
1	1	0	0	1	1	0
1	1	1	1	1	1	0

For the first four rows, we are looking for odd numbers. The odd primes are 1, 3, 5, 7, 11, and 13. Thus, the first row is the binary for 7 (the largest odd prime less than 8) and the second row is the binary for 13. The next two rows contain nonprimes. All odd numbers less than 8 are prime; therefore, the input is never 010 and the outputs are don't cares. Finally, 9 and 15 are odd nonprimes; 15 is larger. For the second half of the table, the only even prime is 2; thus, 101 never occurs. The largest even nonprimes are 6 and 14.

[SP 1, 2; EX 1,2]

2.2 SWITCHING ALGEBRA

In the last section, we went from a verbal description of a combinational system to a more formal and exact description—a truth table. Although the truth table is sufficient to implement a system using read-only memory (see Chapter 4), we need an algebraic description to analyze and design systems with other components. In this section, we will develop the properties of switching algebra.

We need the algebra for several reasons. Perhaps the most obvious is that if we are presented with a network of gates, we need to obtain a specification of the output in terms of the input. Since each gate is defined by an algebraic expression, we most often need to be able to manipulate that algebra. (We could try each possible input combination and follow the signals through each gate until we reached the output. That, however, is a very slow approach to creating a whole truth table for a system of gates.)

Second, in the design process, we often obtain an algebraic expression that corresponds to a much more complex network of gates than is necessary. Algebra allows us to simplify that expression, perhaps even minimize the amount of logic needed to implement it. When we move on to Chapter 3, we will see that there are other nonalgebraic ways of doing this minimization, methods that are more algorithmic. However, it is still important to understand the algebraic foundation behind them.

Third, algebra is often indispensable in the process of implementing networks of gates. The simplest algebraic expression, found by one of the techniques presented in this chapter or the next, does not always correspond to the network that satisfies the requirements of the problem. Thus, we may need the algebra to enable us to satisfy the constraints of the problem.

One approach to the development of switching algebra is to begin with a set of postulates or axioms that define the more general Boolean algebra. In Boolean algebra, each variable—inputs, outputs, and internal signals—may take on one of k values (where $k \geq 2$). Based on these postulates, we can define an algebra and eventually determine the meaning of the operators. We can then limit them to the special case of switching algebra, $k = 2$. Rather, we will define switching algebra in terms of its operators and a few basic properties.

2.2.1 Definition of Switching Algebra

Switching algebra is binary, that is, all variables and constants take on one of two values: 0 and 1. Quantities that are not naturally binary must then be coded into binary format. Physically, they may represent a light off or on, a switch up or down, a low voltage or a high one, or a magnetic field in one direction or the other. From the point of view of the algebra, the physical representation does not matter. When we implement a system, we will choose one of the physical manifestations to represent each value.

We will first define the three operators of switching algebra and then develop a number of properties of switching algebra:

OR (written as $+$)*
  $a + b$ (read a OR b) is 1 if and only if $a = 1$ **or** $b = 1$ or both
AND (written as $\cdot$ or simply two variables catenated)
  $a \cdot b = ab$ (read a AND b) is 1 if and only if $a = 1$ **and** $b = 1$.
NOT (written $'$)
  a' (read NOT a) is 1 if and only if $a = 0$.

The term *complement* is sometimes used instead of NOT. The operation is also referred to as inversion, and the device implementing it is called an inverter.

Because the notation for OR is the same as that for addition in ordinary algebra and that for AND is the same as multiplication, the terminology *sum* and *product* is commonly used. Thus, ab is often referred to as a product term and $a + b$ as a sum term. Many of the properties discussed in this chapter apply to ordinary algebra, as well as switching algebra, but, as we will see, there are some notable exceptions.

Truth tables for the three operators are shown in Table 2.7.

Table 2.7   Truth tables for OR, AND, and NOT.

a	b	$a + b$	a	b	ab	a	a'
0	0	0	0	0	0	0	1
0	1	1	0	1	0	1	0
1	0	1	1	0	0		
1	1	1	1	1	1		

We will now begin to develop a set of properties of switching algebra. (These are sometimes referred to as theorems.) A complete list of the properties that we will use may be found inside the front cover.[†] The first group of properties follow directly from the definitions (or the truth tables).

commutative **P1a.** $a + b = b + a$ **P1b.** $ab = ba$

Note that the values for both OR and AND are the same for the second and third lines of the truth table. This is known as the *commutative* property. It seems obvious because it holds for addition and multiplication, which

---

*OR is sometimes written $\vee$; AND is then written as $\wedge$. NOT x is sometimes written $\sim x$ or $\overline{x}$.

[†]This list is somewhat arbitrary. We are including those properties that we have found useful in manipulating algebraic expressions. Any pair of expressions that are equal to each other could be included on the list. Indeed, other books have a somewhat different list.

use the same notation. However, it needs to be stated explicitly, because it is not true for all operators in all algebras. (For example, $a - b \neq b - a$ in ordinary algebra. There is no subtraction operation in switching algebra.)

P2a. $a + (b + c) = (a + b) + c$ **P2b.** $a(bc) = (ab)c$ **associative**

This property, known as the *associative* law, states that the order in which one does the OR or AND operation doesn't matter, and thus we can write just $a + b + c$ and abc (without the parentheses). It also enables us to talk of the OR or AND of several things. We can thus extend the definition of OR to

$a + b + c + d + \cdots$ is 1 if any of the operands $(a, b, c, d, \ldots)$ is 1
and is 0 only if all are 0

and the definition of AND extends to

$abcd \ldots$ is 1 if all of the operands are 1 and is 0 if any is 0

The most basic circuit element is the gate. A *gate* is a circuit with one output that implements one of the basic functions, such as the OR and AND. (We will define additional gate types later.) Gates are available with two inputs, as well as three, four, and eight inputs. (They could be built with other numbers of inputs, but these are the standard commercially available sizes.) The symbols most commonly used (and which we will use throughout this text) are shown in Figure 2.4. (Note in Figure 2.4 the rounded input for the OR and the flat input for the AND; and the pointed output on the OR and the rounded output on the AND.)

Figure 2.4 Symbols for OR and AND gates.

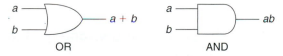

Property 2b states that the three circuits of Figure 2.5 all produce the same output.

Figure 2.5 AND gate implementation of Property 2b.

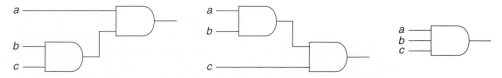

The third gate we will include is the NOT, which has the symbol shown in Figure 2.6. The triangle is just the symbol for an amplifier (from electronics). The circle (sometimes referred to as a bubble) on the output is

Figure 2.6   A NOT gate.

the symbol for inversion (NOT) and, as we will see later, is often shown attached to other gate inputs and outputs to indicate the NOT function.

Parentheses are used as in other mathematics; expressions inside the parentheses are evaluated first. When evaluating expressions without parentheses, the order of precedence is

NOT
AND
OR

Thus, for example,

$$ab' + c'd = [a(b')] + [(c')d]$$

Even without parentheses, the input b is complemented first and then ANDed with a. Input c is complemented and ANDed with d and then the two product terms are ORed. If the intent is to AND a and b and then complement them, it must be written $(ab)'$ rather than ab' and if the intent is to do the OR before the ANDs, it must be written $a(b' + c')d$.

In each of the properties, we use a single letter, such as $a, b, c, \ldots$ to represent any expression, not just a single variable. Thus, for example, Property 1a also states that

$$xy'z + w' = w' + xy'z$$

One other thing to note is that properties always appear in *dual* pairs. To obtain the dual of a property, interchange OR and AND, and the constants 0 and 1. The first interchange is obvious in P1 and P2; the other will be used in the next three properties. It can be shown that whenever two expressions are equal, the duals of those expressions are also equal. That could save some work later on, since we do not have to prove both halves of a pair of properties.

[SP 3; EX 3]

2.2.2   Basic Properties of Switching Algebra
We will next look at three pairs of properties associated with the constants 0 and 1.

identity	**P3a.**	$a + 0 = a$	**P3b.**	$a \cdot 1 = a$
null	**P4a.**	$a + 1 = 1$	**P4b.**	$a \cdot 0 = 0$
complement	**P5a.**	$a + a' = 1$	**P5b.**	$a \cdot a' = 0$

Properties 3a and 4b follow directly from the first and third lines of the truth tables; Properties 3b and 4a follow from the second and fourth lines. Property 5 follows from the definition of the NOT, namely, that either a or a' is always 1 and the other is always 0. Thus, P5a must be either $0 + 1$ or $1 + 0$, both of which are 1, and P5b must be either $0 \cdot 1$ or $1 \cdot 0$, both of which are 0. Once again, each of the properties comes in dual pairs.

Note that by combining the commutative property (P1a) with 3, 4, and 5, we also have

P3aa. $0 + a = a$ **P3bb.** $1 \cdot a = a$

P4aa. $1 + a = 1$ **P4bb.** $0 \cdot a = 0$

P5aa. $a' + a = 1$ **P5bb.** $a' \cdot a = 0$

Often, as we manipulate expressions, we will use one of these versions, rather than first interchanging the terms using the commutative law (P1).

Another property that follows directly from the first and last lines of the truth tables for OR and AND (see Table 2.7) is

P6a. $a + a = a$ **P6b.** $a \cdot a = a$ **idempotency**

By repeated application of Property 6a, we can see that

$$a + a + a + a = a$$

In the process of manipulating logic functions, it should be understood that each of these equalities is bidirectional. For example, $xyz + xyz$ can be replaced in an expression by xyz; but, also, it is sometimes useful to replace xyz by $xyz + xyz$.

The final property that we will obtain directly from the truth tables of the operators is the only one we will include on our list that is a self-dual.

P7. $(a')' = a$ **involution**

If $a = 0$, then $a' = 1$. However, when that is complemented again, that is, $(a')' = 1' = 0 = a$. Similarly, if $a = 1$, $a' = 0$ and $(a')' = 1$. Because there are no ANDs, ORs, 0's, or 1's, the dual is the same property.

The next pair of properties, referred to as the *distributive* law, are most useful in algebraic manipulation.

P8a. $a(b + c) = ab + ac$ **P8b.** $a + bc = (a + b)(a + c)$ **distributive**

P8a looks very familiar; we use it commonly with addition and multiplication. In right to left order, it is referred to as *factoring*. On the other hand, P8b is not a property of regular algebra. (Substitute 1, 2, 3 for a, b, c, and the computation is $1 + 6 = 7$ on the left and $4 \times 3 = 12$ on the right.) The simplest way to prove these properties of switching algebra is to produce a truth table for both sides of the equality and show that they are equal. That is shown for Property 8b in Table 2.8. The left three columns are the input columns. The left-hand side (LHS) of the equality is constructed by first forming a column for bc. That column has a 1 in each of the rows where both b and c are 1 and 0 elsewhere. Then LHS = $a + bc$ is computed using the column for a and that for bc. LHS is 1 when either of those columns contains a 1 or both are 1 and is 0 when they are both 0. Similarly, the right-hand side (RHS) is computed by first constructing a column for $a + b$, which contains a 1 when $a = 1$ or $b = 1$.

Table 2.8 Truth table to prove Property 8b.

a	b	c	bc	LHS	$a + b$	$a + c$	RHS
0	0	0	0	0	0	0	0
0	0	1	0	0	0	1	0
0	1	0	0	0	1	0	0
0	1	1	1	1	1	1	1
1	0	0	0	1	1	1	1
1	0	1	0	1	1	1	1
1	1	0	0	1	1	1	1
1	1	1	1	1	1	1	1

The column for $a + c$ is constructed in a similar fashion and finally RHS $= (a + b)(a + c)$ is 1 wherever both of the previous columns are 1.

The table could have been constructed by evaluating each of the expressions for each row (input combination). For the first row,

$$a + bc = 0 + (0 \cdot 0) = 0 + 0 = 0$$
$$(a + b)(a + c) = (0 + 0)(0 + 0) = 0 + 0 = 0$$

and for the sixth row (101)

$$a + bc = 1 + (0 \cdot 1) = 1 + 0 = 1$$
$$(a + b)(a + c) = (1 + 0)(1 + 1) = 1 \cdot 1 = 1$$

We would need to do this for all eight rows. If we need the whole table, the first method usually requires less work.

This method can also be used to determine whether functions are equal. To be equal, the functions must have the same value for all input combinations. If they differ in any row of the truth table, they are not equal.

EXAMPLE 2.2

Construct a truth table and show which of the three functions are equal. (Be sure to state whether they are equal.)

$$f = y'z' + x'y + x'yz'$$
$$g = xy' + x'z' + x'y$$
$$h = (x' + y')(x + y + z')$$

$x\,y\,z$	$y'z'$	$x'y$	$x'yz'$	f	xy'	$x'z'$	$x'y$	g	$x' + y'$	$x + y + z'$	h
0 0 0	1	0	0	1	0	1	0	1	1	1	1
0 0 1	0	0	0	0	0	0	0	0	1	0	0
0 1 0	0	1	1	1	0	1	1	1	1	1	1
0 1 1	0	1	0	1	0	0	1	1	1	1	1
1 0 0	1	0	0	1	1	0	0	1	1	1	1
1 0 1	0	0	0	0	1	0	0	1	1	1	1
1 1 0	0	0	0	0	0	0	0	0	0	1	0
1 1 1	0	0	0	0	0	0	0	0	0	1	0

The truth table was constructed for each of the three functions (using the same technique as we did in developing Table 2.8). For input combination 1 0 1, $f = 0$, but $g = h = 1$. Thus, f is not equal to either of the other functions. The columns for g and h are identical; thus, $g = h$.

[SP 4, 5; EX 4, 5]

2.2.3 Manipulation of Algebraic Functions

Before adding some properties that are useful in simplifying algebraic expressions, it is helpful to introduce some terminology that will make the discussion simpler.

A *literal* is the appearance of a variable or its complement. Examples are a and b'. In determining the complexity of an expression, one of the measures is the number of literals. **Each appearance** of a variable is counted. Thus, for example, the expression

$$ab' + bc'd + a'd + e'$$

contains eight literals.

A *product term* is one or more literals connected by AND operators. In the previous example, there are four product terms, ab', $bc'd$, $a'd$, and e'. Notice that a single literal is a product term.

A *standard product term*, also called a *minterm*, is a product term that includes each variable of the problem, either uncomplemented or complemented. Thus, for a function of four variables, w, x, y, and z, the terms $w'xyz'$ and $wxyz$ are standard product terms, but $wy'z$ is not.

A *sum of products* expression (often abbreviated SOP) is one or more product terms connected by OR operators. The previous expression meets this definition as do each of the following:

$w'xyz' + wx'y'z' + wx'yz + wxyz$	(4 product terms)
$x + w'y + wxy'z$	(3 product terms)
$x' + y + z$	(3 product terms)
wy'	(1 product term)
z	(1 product term)

It is usually possible to write several different SOP expressions for the same function.

A *canonical sum*, or *sum of standard product terms*, is just a sum of products expression where all of the terms are standard product terms. The first example is the only canonical sum (if there are four variables in all of the problems). Often, the starting point for algebraic manipulations is with canonical sums.

A *minimum sum of products* expression is one of those SOP expressions for a function that has the fewest number of product terms. If there is more than one expression with the fewest number of terms, then minimum is defined as one or more of those expressions with the fewest number of literals. As implied by this wording, there may be more than one minimum solution to a given problem. Each of the following expressions are equal (meaning that whatever values are chosen for x, y, and z, each expression produces the same value). Note that the first is a sum of standard product terms.

(1) $x'yz' + x'yz + xy'z' + xy'z + xyz$ 5 terms, 15 literals
(2) $x'y + xy' + xyz$ 3 terms, 7 literals
(3) $x'y + xy' + xz$ 3 terms, 6 literals
(4) $x'y + xy' + yz$ 3 terms, 6 literals

Expressions (3) and (4) are the minima. (It should be clear that those are minimum among the expressions shown; it is not so obvious that there is not yet another expression with fewer terms or literals.) (A word of caution: When looking for all of the minimum solutions, do **not** include any solution with more terms or more literals than the best already found.)

Actually, we have enough algebra at this point to be able to go from the first expression to the last two. First, we will reduce the first expression to the second:

$$x'yz' + x'yz + xy'z' + xy'z + xyz$$
$$= (x'yz' + x'yz) + (xy'z' + xy'z) + xyz \qquad \text{associative}$$
$$= x'y(z' + z) + xy'(z' + z) + xyz \qquad \text{distributive}$$
$$= x'y \cdot 1 + xy' \cdot 1 + xyz \qquad \text{complement}$$
$$= x'y + xy' + xyz \qquad \text{identity}$$

The first step takes advantage of P2a, which allows us to group terms in any way we wish. We then utilized P8a to factor $x'y$ out of the first two terms and xy' out of the third and fourth terms. Next we used P5aa to replace $z' + z$ by 1. In the final step, we used P3b to reduce the expression.

The last three steps can be combined into a single step. We can add a property

adjacency   **P9a.** $ab + ab' = a$ **P9b.** $(a + b)(a + b') = a$

where, in the first case, $a = x'y$ and $b = z'$. Thus, if there are two product terms in a sum that are identical, except that one of the variables is uncomplemented in one and complemented in the other, they can be combined, using P9a. (The proof of this property follows the same three steps we used before—P8a to factor out the a, P5a to replace $b + b'$ by 1, and finally P3b to produce the result.) The dual can be proved using the dual steps, P8b, P5b, and P3a.

The easiest way to get to expression (3), that is, to go to six literals, is to use P6a, and make two copies of $xy'z$, that is,

$$xy'z = xy'z + xy'z$$

The expression becomes

$$x'yz' + x'yz + xy'z' + xy'z + xyz + xy'z$$
$$= (x'yz' + x'yz) + (xy'z' + xy'z) + (xyz + xy'z)$$
$$= x'y(z' + z) + xy'(z' + z) + xz(y + y')$$
$$= x'y \cdot 1 + xy' \cdot 1 + xz \cdot 1$$
$$= x'y + xy' + xz$$

We added the second copy of $xy'z$ at the end and combined it with the last term (xyz). The manipulation then proceeded in the same way as before. The other expression can be obtained in a similar manner by using P6a on $x'yz$ and combining the second copy with xyz. Notice that we freely reordered the terms in the first sum of products expression when we utilized P6a to insert a second copy of one of the terms.

In general, we may be able to combine a term on the list with more than one other term. If that is the case, we can replicate a term as many times as are needed.

Another property that will allow us to reduce the system to six literals without the need to make extra copies of a term is

P10a. $a + a'b = a + b$ **P10b.** $a(a' + b) = ab$ **simplification**

We can demonstrate the validity of P10a by using P8b, P5a, and P3bb as follows:

$$a + a'b = (a + a')(a + b) \qquad \text{distributive}$$
$$= 1 \cdot (a + b) \qquad \text{complement}$$
$$= a + b \qquad \text{identity}$$

P10b can be demonstrated as follows:

$$a(a' + b) = aa' + ab = 0 + ab = ab$$

We can apply this property to the example by factoring x out of the last two terms:

$$x'y + xy' + xyz$$
$$= x'y + x(y' + yz) \qquad \text{distributive}$$
$$= x'y + x(y' + z) \qquad \text{simplification}$$
$$= x'y + xy' + xz \qquad \text{distributive}$$

We used P10a where $a = y'$ and $b = z$ in going from line 2 to 3. Instead, we could have factored y out of the first and last terms, producing

$$y(x' + xz) + xy'$$
$$= y(x' + z) + xy'$$
$$= x'y + yz + xy'$$

which is the other six literal equivalent.

Consider the following example, an expression in canonical form.

EXAMPLE 2.3

$a'b'c' + a'bc' + a'bc + ab'c'$

The first two terms can be combined using P9a, producing

$a'c' + a'bc + ab'c'$

Now, we can factor a' from the first two terms and use P10a to reduce this to

$a'c' + a'b + ab'c'$

and repeat the process with c' and the first and last terms, resulting in the expression

$a'c' + a'b + b'c'$

Although this expression is simpler than any of the previous ones, it is not minimum. With the properties we have developed so far, we have reached a dead end, and we have no way of knowing that this is not the minimum. Returning to the original expression, we can group the first term with the last and the middle two terms. Then, when we apply P9a, we get an expression with only two terms and four literals:

$$a'b'c' + a'bc' + a'bc + ab'c'$$
$$= b'c' + a'b$$

Later, we will see a property that allows us to go from the three-term expression to the one with only two terms.

Each terminology defined earlier has a dual that will also prove useful.

A *sum term* is one or more literals connected by OR operators. Examples are $a + b' + c$ and b' (just one literal).

A *standard sum term,* also called a *maxterm,* is a sum term that includes each variable of the problem, either uncomplemented or complemented. Thus, for a function of four variables, w, x, y, and z, the terms $w' + x + y + z'$ and $w + x + y + z$ are standard sum terms, but $w + y' + z$ is not.

A *product of sums* expression (POS) is one or more sum terms connected by AND operators. Examples of product of sums expressions:

$(w + x)(w + y)$	2 terms
$w(x + y)$	2 terms
w	1 term
$w + x$	1 term
$(w + x' + y' + z')(w' + x + y + z')$	2 terms

A *canonical product,* or *product of standard sum terms,* is just a POS expression in which all of the terms are standard sum terms. The last example above is the only canonical sum (if there are four variables in all of the problems). Often, the starting point for algebraic manipulations is with canonical sums.

Minimum is defined the same way for both POS and SOP, namely, the expressions with the fewest number of terms, and, among those with the same number of terms, those with the fewest number of literals. A given function (or expression) can be reduced to minimum sum of products form and to minimum product of sums form. They may both have the same number of terms and literals or either may have fewer than the other. (We will see examples later, when we have further developed our minimization techniques.)

An expression may be in sum of products form, product of sums form, both, or neither. Examples are

SOP: $x'y + xy' + xyz$

POS: $(x + y')(x' + y)(x' + z')$

both: $x' + y + z$ or xyz'

neither: $x(w' + yz)$ or $z' + wx'y + v(xz + w')$

We will now look at an example of the simplification of functions in maxterms form. (Later, we will look at methods of going from sum of products to product of sums and from product of sums to sum of products forms.)

$$g = (w' + x' + y + z')(w' + x' + y + z)(w + x' + y + z')$$

The first two terms can be combined, using P9b, where

$$a = w' + x' + y \quad \text{and} \quad b = z'$$

producing

$$g = (w' + x' + y)(w + x' + y + z')$$

That can most easily be reduced further by using P6b, to create a second copy of the first term, which can be combined with the last term, where

$$a = x' + y + z' \quad \text{and} \quad b = w$$

producing the final answer

$$g = (w' + x' + y)(x' + y + z')$$

We could also do the following manipulation (parallel to what we did with the SOP expression)

$$
\begin{aligned}
g &= (w' + x' + y)(w + x' + y + z') \\
&= x' + y + w'(w + z') && \textbf{[P8b]} \\
&= x' + y + w'z' && \textbf{[P10b]} \\
&= (x' + y + w')(x' + y + z') && \textbf{[P8b]}
\end{aligned}
$$

[SP 6, 7, 8, 9; EX 6, 7, 8, 9]

which, after reordering the literals in the first set of parentheses, is the same expression as before.

2.3   IMPLEMENTATION OF FUNCTIONS WITH AND, OR, AND NOT GATES

We will first look at the implementation of switching functions using networks of AND, OR, and NOT gates. (After all, the goal of our design is to produce the block diagram of a circuit to implement the given switching function.) When we defined minimum SOP expressions, we introduced, as an example, the function

$$f = x'yz' + x'yz + xy'z' + xy'z + xyz$$

A block diagram of a circuit to implement this is shown in Figure 2.7. Each of the product terms is formed by an AND gate. In this example, all of the AND gates have three inputs. The outputs of the AND gates are used as inputs to an OR (in this case a five-input OR). This implementation assumes that all of the inputs are available, both uncomplemented and complemented (that is, for example, both x and x' are available as inputs). This is usually the case if the input to the combinational logic circuit comes from a flip flop, a storage device in sequential systems. It is not usually true, however, if the input is a system input.

Figure 2.7   Block diagram of f in sum of standard products form.

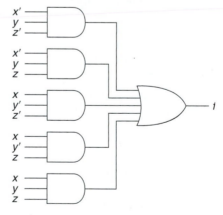

This is an example of a *two-level* circuit. The number of levels is the maximum number of gates through which a signal must pass from the input to the output. In this example, all signals go first through an AND gate and then through an OR. When inputs are available both uncomplemented and complemented, implementations of both SOP and POS expressions result in two-level circuits.

We saw that this same function can be manipulated to a minimum SOP expression, one version of which is

$$f = x'y + xy' + xz$$

This, of course, leads to a less complex circuit, namely, the one shown in Figure 2.8.

We have reduced the complexity of the circuit from six gates with 20 gate inputs (three to each of the five ANDs and five to the OR) to one with four gates and 9 gate inputs. The simplest definition of minimum for a gate network is minimum number of gates and, among those with the same number of gates, minimum number of gate inputs. For two-level circuits, this always corresponds to minimum sum of products or minimum product of sums functions.

If complemented inputs are not available, then an inverter (a NOT gate) is needed for each input that is required to be complemented (x and y in this example). The circuit of Figure 2.9 shows the NOT gates that must be added to the circuit of Figure 2.8 to implement f. Note that in this version we showed each input once, with that input line connected to whatever gates required it. That is surely what happens when we actually construct the circuit. However, for clarity, we will draw circuits more like the previous one (except, of course, we will only have one NOT gate for each input, with the output of that gate going to those gates that require it). (This is a three-level circuit because some of the paths pass through three gates: a NOT, an AND, and then an OR.)

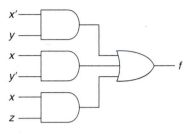

Figure 2.8 Minimum sum of product implementation of f.

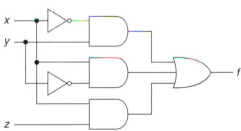

Figure 2.9 Circuit with only uncomplemented inputs.

A POS expression (assuming all inputs are available both uncomplemented and complemented) corresponds to a two-level OR–AND network. For this same example, the minimum POS (although that is not obvious based on the algebra we have developed to this point)

$$f = (x + y)(x' + y' + z)$$

is implemented with the circuit of Figure 2.10.

When we implement functions that are in neither SOP nor POS form, the resulting circuits are more than two levels. As an example, consider the following function:

$$h = z' + wx'y + v(xz + w')$$

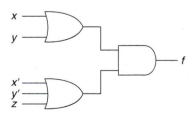

Figure 2.10 A product of sums implementation.

We begin inside the parentheses and build an AND gate with inputs x and z. The output of that goes to an OR gate, the other input of which is w'. That is ANDed with v, which is ORed with the input z' and the output of the AND gate, producing $wx'y$, which results in the circuit of Figure 2.11.

Figure 2.11   A multilevel circuit.

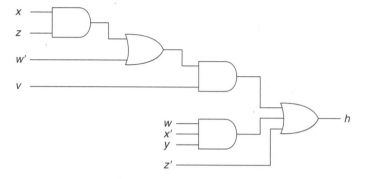

This is a four-level circuit because the signals x and z pass first through an AND gate, then an OR, then an AND, and finally through an OR—a total of four gates.

EXAMPLE 2.4

If we took the version of f used for Figure 2.8, and factored x from the last two terms, we obtain

$f = x'y + x(y' + z)$

That would result in the three-level circuit

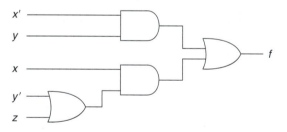

This (three-level) solution uses 4 two-input gates.

Gates are typically available in dual in-line pin packages (DIPs) of 14 connector pins. These packages are often referred to as *chips*. (Larger packages of 16, 18, 22, and more pins are used for more complex logic.) These packages contain *integrated circuits* (ICs). Integrated circuits are categorized as *small-scale integration* (SSI) when they contain just a few gates. Those are the ones that we will refer to in this chapter. Medium-scale (MSI) circuits contain as many as 100 gates; we will see examples of these later. The terminology *large-scale integration* (LSI), *very large-scale integration* (VLSI), and *giga-scale integration* (GSI) is used for even more complex packages, including complete computers.

Two of the connector pins are used to provide power to the chip. That leaves 12 pins for logic connections (on a 14-pin chip). Thus, we can fit 4 two-input gates on a chip. (Each gate has two input connections and one output connection. There are enough pins for four such gates.) Similarly, there are enough pins for 6 one-input gates (NOTs), 3 three-input gates, and 2 four-input gates (with two pins unused). In examples that refer to specific integrated circuits, we will discuss *transistor–transistor logic* (TTL) and, in particular, the 7400 series of chips.* For these chips, the power connections are 5 V and ground (0 V).

A list of the common AND, OR, and NOT integrated circuits that might be encountered in the laboratory is

7404   6 (hex) NOT gates

7408   4 (quadruple) two-input AND gates

7411   3 (triple) three-input AND gates

7421   2 four-input (dual) AND gates

7432   4 (quadruple) two-input OR gates

If a three-input OR (or AND) is needed, and only two-input ones are available, it can be constructed as follows:

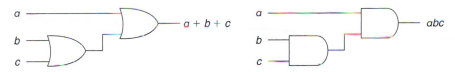

This idea can be extended to gates with larger numbers of inputs.[†]

Also, if we need a two-input gate and there is a leftover three-input one (because they come three to a package), we can connect the same signal to two of the inputs (since $aa = a$, and $a + a = a$).

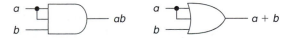

Also, we could connect a logic 1 ($+5$ V) to one of the inputs of an AND or a logic 0 (ground) to one of the inputs of an OR:

1
a $1 \cdot ab = ab$
b

0
a $0 + a + b = a + b$
b

---

*Even within the 7400 series, there are a number of variations, indicated by a letter or letters after the 74 (such as 74H10). We will not be concerned with that detail; it is left for a course on digital electronics.

[†]Caution: This approach does not work for NAND and NOR gates (which we will introduce in Section 2.6).

In the laboratory, logic 0 and logic 1 are represented by two voltages: often 0 and 5 V. Most commonly, the higher voltage is used to represent 1 and the lower voltage to represent 0. This is referred to as *positive logic*. The opposite choice is also possible, that is, use the higher voltage to represent 0. That is referred to as *negative logic*. When dealing with 1's and 0's, the concept does not really come up. However, the same electronic circuit has different logic meanings depending on which choice we make.

Consider the truth table of Table 2.9a, where the behavior of the gate is described just in terms of high (H) and low (L). The positive logic interpretation of Table 2.9b produces the truth table for an OR gate. The negative logic interpretation of Table 2.9c is that of an AND gate.

Table 2.9

a. High/Low				b. Positive logic				c. Negative logic		
a	*b*	*f*		*a*	*b*	*f*		*a*	*b*	*f*
L	L	L		0	0	0		1	1	1
L	H	H		0	1	1		1	0	0
H	L	H		1	0	1		0	1	0
H	H	H		1	1	1		0	0	0

Most implementations use positive logic; we will do that consistently throughout this book. Occasionally, negative logic, or even a mixture of the two, is used.

[SP 10, 11; EX 10, 11]

2.4   THE COMPLEMENT

Before we go further, we need to develop one more property. This property is the only one for which a person's name is commonly attached— *DeMorgan's theorem*.

DeMorgan   **P11a.** $(a + b)' = a'b'$ **P11b.** $(ab)' = a' + b'$

The simplest proof of this property utilizes the truth table of Table 2.10. In Table 2.10, we have produced a column for each of the expressions in the property. (The entries in the table should be obvious because they just

Table 2.10   Proof of DeMorgan's theorem.

a	*b*	$a + b$	$(a + b)'$	a'	b'	$a'b'$	ab	$(ab)'$	$a' + b'$
0	0	0	1	1	1	1	0	1	1
0	1	1	0	1	0	0	0	1	1
1	0	1	0	0	1	0	0	1	1
1	1	1	0	0	0	0	1	0	0
			11a			11a		11b	11b

involve the AND, OR, and NOT operations on other columns.) Note that the columns (labeled 11a) for $(a + b)'$ and $a'b'$ are the same and those (labeled 11b) for $(ab)'$ and $a' + b'$ are the same.

The property can be extended to more than two operands easily.

P11aa. $(a + b + c \ldots)' = a'b'c' \ldots$

$\qquad\qquad$ **P11bb.** $(abc \ldots)' = a' + b' + c' \ldots$

For P11aa, with three variables, the proof goes

$$(a + b + c)' = [(a + b) + c]' = (a + b)'c' = a'b'c'$$

CAUTION: The most common mistakes in algebraic manipulation involve the misuse of DeMorgan's theorem:

$$(ab)' \neq a'b'   \text{ rather }   (ab)' = a' + b'$$

The NOT (') cannot be distributed through the parentheses. Just look at the $(ab)'$ and $a'b'$ columns of the truth table and compare the expressions for $a = 0$ and $b = 1$ (or for $a = 1$ and $b = 0$):

$$(0 \cdot 1)' = 0' = 1   \quad 0' \cdot 1' = 1 \cdot 0 = 0$$

The dual of this is also false, that is,

$$(a + b)' \neq a' + b'$$

Once again, the two sides differ when a and b differ.

There will be times when we are given a function and need to find its complement, that is, given $f(w, x, y, z)$, we need $f'(w, x, y, z)$. The straightforward approach is to use DeMorgan's theorem repeatedly.

EXAMPLE 2.5

$f = wx'y + xy' + wxz$

then

$\quad f' = (wx'y + xy' + wxz)'$

$\quad\quad = (wx'y)'(xy')'(wxz)'$ $\qquad\qquad\qquad\qquad$ **[P11a]**

$\quad\quad = (w' + x + y')(x' + y)(w' + x' + z')$ $\qquad$ **[P11b]**

Note that if the function is in SOP form, the complement is in POS form (and the complement of a POS expression is a SOP one).

To find the complement of more general expressions, we can repeatedly apply DeMorgan's theorem or we can follow this set of rules:

1. Complement each variable (that is, a to a' or a' to a).
2. Replace 0 by 1 and 1 by 0.
3. Replace AND by OR and OR by AND, being sure to preserve the order of operations. That sometimes requires additional parentheses.

EXAMPLE 2.6

$f = ab'(c + d'e) + a'bc'$

$f' = (a' + b + c'(d + e))(a + b' + c)$

Note that in f, the last operation to be performed is an OR of the complex first term with the product term. To preserve the order, parentheses were needed in f'; making the AND the last operation. We could have used square brackets, [ ], in order to make the expression more readable, making it

$f' = [a' + b + c'(d + e')][a + b' + c]$

We would produce the same result, with much more work, by using P11a and P11b over and over again:

$f' = [ab'(c + d'e) + a'bc']'$

$= [ab'(c + d'e)]'[a'bc']'$

$= [a' + b + (c + d'e)'][a + b' + c]$

$= [a' + b + c'(d'e)'][a + b' + c]$

$= [a' + b + c'(d + e')][a + b' + c]$

[SP 12; EX 12]

2.5 FROM THE TRUTH TABLE TO ALGEBRAIC EXPRESSIONS

Table 2.11 A two-variable truth table.

a	b	f
0	0	0
0	1	1
1	0	1
1	1	1

Often, a design problem is stated in terms of the truth table that describes the output in terms of the inputs. Other times, verbal descriptions of systems can most easily be translated into the truth table. Thus, we need the ability to go from the truth table to an algebraic expression. To understand the process, consider the two-variable truth table of Table 2.11.

Because this is a two-variable problem, the truth table has $4(= 2^2)$ rows, that is, there are 4 possible combinations of inputs. (This is the truth table for the OR as we defined it at the beginning of this chapter, but that is irrelevant to this discussion.) What the table says is that

f is 1   if $a = 0$ AND $b = 1$ OR
            if $a = 1$ AND $b = 0$ OR
            if $a = 1$ AND $b = 1$

However, this is the same as saying

f is 1   if $a' = 1$ AND $b = 1$ OR
            if $a = 1$ AND $b' = 1$ OR
            if $a = 1$ AND $b = 1$

But $a' = 1$ AND $b = 1$ is the same as saying $a'b = 1$ and thus

f is 1   if $a'b = 1$ OR if $ab' = 1$ OR if $ab = 1$

That finally produces the expression

$$f = a'b + ab' + ab$$

Each row of the truth table corresponds to a product term. An SOP expression is formed by ORing those product terms corresponding to rows of the truth table for which the function is 1. Each product term has each variable included, with that variable complemented when the entry in the input column for that variable contains a 0 and uncomplemented when it contains a 1. Thus, for example, row 10 produces the term ab'. These product terms include all of the variables; they are minterms. Minterms are often referred to by number, by just converting the binary number in the input row of the truth table to decimal. Both of the following notations are common:

$$f(a, b) = m_1 + m_2 + m_3$$
$$f(a, b) = \Sigma m(1, 2, 3)$$

We show, in Table 2.12, the minterms and minterm numbers that are used for all functions of three variables.

For a specific function, those terms for which the function is 1 are used to form an SOP expression for f, and those terms for which the function is 0 used to form an SOP expression for f'. We can then complement f' to form a POS expression for f.

Table 2.12 Minterms.

ABC	Minterm	Number
0 0 0	$A'B'C'$	0
0 0 1	$A'B'C$	1
0 1 0	$A'BC'$	2
0 1 1	$A'BC$	3
1 0 0	$AB'C'$	4
1 0 1	$AB'C$	5
1 1 0	ABC'	6
1 1 1	ABC	7

EXAMPLE 2.7

ABC	f	f'
0 0 0	0	1
0 0 1	1	0
0 1 0	1	0
0 1 1	1	0
1 0 0	1	0
1 0 1	1	0
1 1 0	0	1
1 1 1	0	1

where the truth table shows both the function, f, and its complement, f'. We can write

$$f(A, B, C) = \Sigma m(1, 2, 3, 4, 5)$$
$$= A'B'C + A'BC' + A'BC + AB'C' + AB'C$$

Either from the truth table, or by recognizing that every minterm is included in either f or f', we can then write

$$f'(A, B, C) = \Sigma m(0, 6, 7)$$
$$= A'B'C' + ABC' + ABC$$

The two sum of minterm forms are SOP expressions. In most cases, including this one, the sum of minterms expression is not a minimum sum of products expression. We could reduce f from 5 terms with 15 literals to either of two functions with 3 terms and 6 literals as follows:

$$f = A'B'C + A'BC' + A'BC + AB'C' + AB'C$$
$$= A'B'C + A'B + AB' \qquad \textbf{[P9a, P9a]}$$
$$= A'C + A'B + AB'$$
$$= B'C + A'B + AB'$$

where the final expressions are obtained using P8a and P10a on the first term and either the second or the third. Similarly, we can reduce f' from 3 terms with 9 literals to 2 terms with 5 literals, using P9a:

$$f' = A'B'C' + AB$$

Using P11, we can then obtain the POS expression* for f, from the sum of minterms

$$f = (f')' = (A + B + C)(A' + B' + C)(A' + B' + C')$$

To find a minimum POS expression, we can either manipulate the previous POS expression (using P9b on the last two terms) to obtain

$$f = (A + B + C)(A' + B')$$

or we could simplify the SOP expression for f' and then use DeMorgan to convert it to a POS expression. Both approaches produce the same result.

In much of the material of Chapter 3, we will specify functions by just listing their minterms (by number). We must, of course, list the variables of the problem as part of that statement. Thus,

$$f(w, x, y, z) = \Sigma m(0, 1, 5, 9, 11, 15)$$

is the simplest way to specify the function

$$f = w'x'y'z' + w'x'y'z + w'xy'z + wx'y'z + wx'yz + wxyz$$

If the function includes don't cares, then those terms are included in a separate sum (Σ).

---

*It is possible to obtain POS expressions directly from the truth table without first finding the SOP expression. Each 0 of f produces a maxterm in the POS expression. We have omitted that approach here, because it tends to lead to confusion.

EXAMPLE 2.8

$f(a, b, c) = \Sigma m(1, 2, 5) + \Sigma d(0, 3)$

implies that minterms 1, 2, and 5 are included in the function and that 0 and 3 are don't cares, that is the truth table is as follows:

abc	f
0 0 0	X
0 0 1	1
0 1 0	1
0 1 1	X
1 0 0	0
1 0 1	1
1 1 0	0
1 1 1	0

Let us now return to the first three of our continuing examples and develop algebraic expressions for them.

EXAMPLE 2.9

Using Z_2 for CE1, we get

$Z_2 = A'BCD + AB'CD + ABC'D + ABCD' + ABCD$

directly from the truth table. The last term ($ABCD$) can be combined with each of the others (using P10a). Thus, if we make four copies of it (using P6a repeatedly) and then utilize P10a four times, we obtain

$Z_2 = BCD + ACD + ABD + ABC$

No further simplification is possible; this is the minimum sum of products expression. Notice that if we used Z_1, we would have

$Z_1 = A'BCD + AB'CD + ABC'D + ABCD'$

No simplification is possible. This expression also has four terms, but it has 16 literals, whereas the expression for Z_2 only has 12.

EXAMPLE 2.10

For CE2, we have either

$f = ab'c + abc'$ or $f = ab'c' + abc$

depending on which truth table we choose. Again, no simplification is possible.

For f', we have (for the first version)

$f' = a'b'c' + a'b'c + a'bc' + a'bc + ab'c' + abc$

$\quad = a'b' + a'b + ab'c' + abc$ **[P9a, P9b]**

$\quad = a' + ab'c' + abc = a' + b'c' + bc$ **[P9a, P10a]**

Thus, the product of maxterms is

$f = (a + b + c)(a + b + c')(a + b' + c)(a + b' + c')$
$\quad (a' + b + c)(a' + b' + c')$

and the minimum POS is

$f = a(b + c)(b' + c')$

EXAMPLE 2.11

For the full adder, CE3, (using c for the carry in, c_{in}, to simplify the algebraic expressions), we get from the truth table

$$c_{out} = a'bc + ab'c + abc' + abc$$
$$s = a'b'c + a'bc' + ab'c' + abc$$

The simplification of carry out is very much like that of Z_2 in Example 2.9, resulting in

$$c_{out} = bc + ac + ab$$

but s is already in minimum SOP form. We will return to the implementation of the full adder in Section 2.8.

We will next take a brief look at a more general approach to switching functions. How many different functions of n variables are there?

For two variables, there are 16 possible truth tables, resulting in 16 different functions. The truth table of Table 2.13 shows all of these functions. (Each output column of the table corresponds to one of the 16 possible 4-bit binary numbers.)

Table 2.13   All two-variable functions.

a	b	f_0	f_1	f_2	f_3	f_4	f_5	f_6	f_7	f_8	f_9	f_{10}	f_{11}	f_{12}	f_{13}	f_{14}	f_{15}
0	0	0	0	0	0	0	0	0	0	1	1	1	1	1	1	1	1
0	1	0	0	0	0	1	1	1	1	0	0	0	0	1	1	1	1
1	0	0	0	1	1	0	0	1	1	0	0	1	1	0	0	1	1
1	1	0	1	0	1	0	1	0	1	0	1	0	1	0	1	0	1

Some of the functions are trivial, such as f_0 and f_{15}, and some are really just functions of one of the variables, such as f_3. The set of functions, reduced to minimum SOP form, are

$$f_0 = 0 \qquad\qquad f_6 = a'b + ab' \qquad\qquad f_{12} = a'$$
$$f_1 = ab \qquad\qquad f_7 = a + b \qquad\qquad f_{13} = a' + b$$
$$f_2 = ab' \qquad\qquad f_8 = a'b' \qquad\qquad f_{14} = a' + b'$$
$$f_3 = a \qquad\qquad f_9 = a'b' + ab \qquad\qquad f_{15} = 1$$
$$f_4 = a'b \qquad\qquad f_{10} = b'$$
$$f_5 = b \qquad\qquad f_{11} = a + b'$$

Table 2.14   Number of functions of n variables.

Variables	Terms
1	4
2	16
3	256
4	65,536
5	4,294,967,296

[SP 13, 14; EX 13, 14, 15]

For n variables, the truth table has 2^n rows and thus, we can choose any 2^n-bit number for a column. Thus, there are 2^{2^n} different functions of n variables. That number grows very quickly, as can be seen from Table 2.14.

(Thus, we can find a nearly unlimited variety of problems of four or more variables for exercises or tests.)

2.6 NAND, NOR, AND EXCLUSIVE-OR GATES

In this section we will introduce three other commonly used types of gates, the NAND, the NOR, and the Exclusive-OR, and see how to implement circuits using them.

The NAND has the symbol shown in Figure 2.12. Like the AND and the OR, the NAND is commercially available in several sizes, typically two-, three-, four-, and eight-input varieties. When first introduced, it

Figure 2.12 NAND gates.

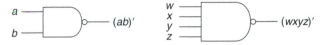

was referred to as an AND-NOT, which perfectly describes its function, but the shorter name, NAND, has become widely accepted. Note that DeMorgan's theorem states that

$$(ab)' = a' + b'$$

and thus an alternative symbol for the two-input NAND is shown in Figure 2.13. The symbols may be used interchangeably; they refer to the same component.

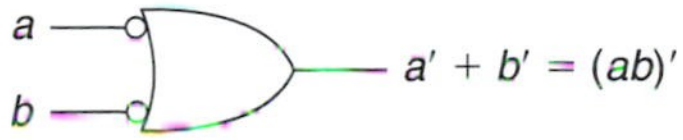

The NOR gate (OR-NOT) uses the symbols shown in Figure 2.14. Of course, $(a + b)' = a'b'$. NOR gates, too, are available with more inputs.

Figure 2.13 Alternative symbol for NAND.

$$a' + b' = (ab)'$$

Figure 2.14 Symbols for NOR gate.

Why use NAND and NOR gates, rather than AND, OR, and NOT gates? After all, the logic expressions are in terms of AND, OR, and NOT operators and thus the implementation with those gates is straightforward. Many electronic implementations naturally invert (complement) signals; thus, the NAND is more convenient to implement than the AND. The most important reason is that with either NAND or NOR, only one type of gate is required. On the other hand, both AND and OR gates are required; and, often, NOT gates are needed, as well. As can be seen from the circuits of Figure 2.15, NOT gates and two-input AND and OR gates can be replaced by just two-input NANDs. Thus, these operators are said to be *functionally complete*. (We could implement gates with more than two inputs using NANDs with more inputs. We could also implement AND, OR, and NOT gates using only NORs; that is left as an exercise.)

Using these gate equivalences, the function $f(= x'y + xy' + xz)$ that we first implemented with AND and OR gates in Figure 2.8 (Section 2.3) can now be implemented with NAND gates, as shown in Figure 2.16.

Figure 2.15   Functional completeness of NAND.

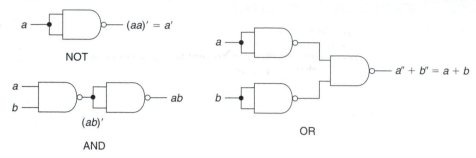

NOT

AND

OR

Figure 2.16   NAND gate implementation.

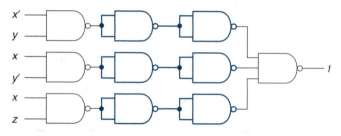

Figure 2.17   Better NAND gate implementation.

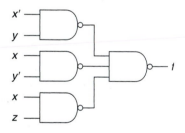

But note that we have two NOT gates in a row in each of the green paths. They serve no purpose logically (P7 states $(a')' = a$), and thus they can be removed from the circuit, yielding that of Figure 2.17. That is, all of the AND and OR gates of the original circuit became NANDs. Nothing else was changed.

This process can be greatly simplified when we have a circuit consisting of AND and OR gates such that

1. the output of the circuit comes from an OR,
2. the inputs to all OR gates come either from a system input or from the output of an AND, and
3. the inputs to all AND gates come either from a system input or from the output of an OR.

All gates are replaced by NAND gates, and any input coming directly into an OR is complemented.

We can obtain the same result by starting at the output gate and putting a bubble (a NOT) at both ends of each input line to that OR gate. If the circuit is not two-level, we repeat this process at the input of each of the OR gates. Thus, the AND/OR implementation of f becomes that of Figure 2.18, where all of the gates have become NAND gates (in one of the two notations we introduced earlier).

This approach works with any circuit that meets these conditions, with only one additional step. If an input comes directly into an OR gate,

there is no place for the second NOT; thus, that input must be complemented. For example, the circuit for h

$$h = z' + wx'y + v(xz + w')$$

is shown in Figure 2.19. Again, all of the AND and OR gates become
NANDs, but the two inputs that came directly into the OR gates were
complemented.

Figure 2.18 Double NOT gate approach.

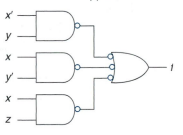

Figure 2.19 A multilevel NAND implementation.

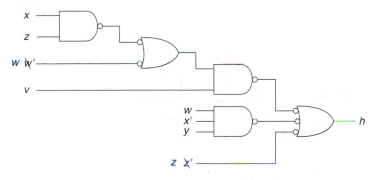

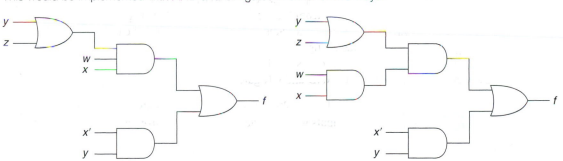

EXAMPLE 2.12

$$f = wx(y + z) + x'y$$

This would be implemented with AND and OR gates in either of two ways.

The first version can be directly converted to NAND gates, as follows.

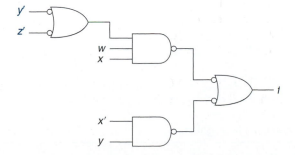

The second version cannot be converted to NAND gates without adding an extra NOT gate, because it violates the third rule—an AND gets an input from another AND. Thus, this circuit would become

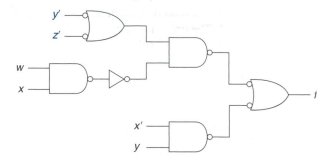

where the NOT is required to implement the AND that forms wx. Expressions such as this one are often obtained starting from SOP solutions. We will see some examples of this in Section 2.8.

The dual approach works for implementing circuits with NOR gates. When we have a circuit consisting of AND and OR gates such that

1. the output of the circuit comes from an AND,
2. the inputs to OR gates come either from a system input or from the output of an AND, and
3. the inputs to AND gates come either from a system input or from the output of an OR.

Then all gates can be converted to NOR gates, and, if an input comes directly into an AND gate, that input must be complemented.

EXAMPLE 2.13

$$g = (x + y')(x' + y)(x' + z')$$

is implemented

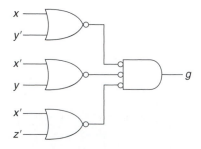

where all gates are NOR gates.

The Exclusive-OR gate implements the expression

$$a'b + ab'$$

which is sometimes written $a \oplus b$. The terminology comes from the definition that $a \oplus b$ is 1 if $a = 1$ (and $b = 0$) **or** if $b = 1$ (and $a = 0$), but not both $a = 1$ and $b = 1$. The operand we have been referring to as OR (+) is sometimes referred to as the Inclusive-OR to distinguish it from the Exclusive-OR. The logic symbol for the Exclusive-OR is similar to that for the OR except that it has a double line on the input, as shown in Figure 2.20a. Also commonly available is the Exclusive-NOR gate, as shown in Figure 2.20b. It is just an Exclusive-OR with a NOT on the output and produces the function

$$(a \oplus b)' = a'b' + ab.$$

This sometimes is referred to as a comparator, since the Exclusive-NOR is 1 if $a = b$, and is 0 if $a \neq b$.

A NAND gate implementation of the Exclusive-OR is shown in Figure 2.21a, where only uncomplemented inputs are assumed.

The two NOT gates (implemented as two-input NANDs) can be replaced by a single gate, as shown in Figure 2.21b, since

$$a(a' + b') + b(a' + b') = aa' + ab' + ba' + bb' = ab' + a'b$$

Figure 2.20 (a) An Exclusive-OR gate. (b) An Exclusive-NOR gate.

(a)

(b)

Figure 2.21 Exclusive-OR gates.

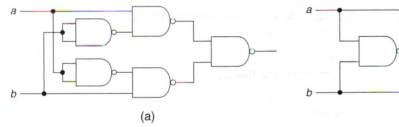

(a)   (b)

Some useful properties of the Exclusive-OR are

$$(a \oplus b)' = (a'b + ab')' = (a + b')(a' + b) = a'b' + ab$$
$$a' \oplus b = (a')'b + (a')b' = ab + a'b' = (a \oplus b)'$$
$$(a \oplus b') = (a \oplus b)'$$
$$a \oplus 0 = a = (a' \cdot 0 + a \cdot 1)$$
$$a \oplus 1 = a' = (a' \cdot 1 + a \cdot 0)$$

The Exclusive-OR has both the commutative and associative properties, that is,

$$a \oplus b = b \oplus a$$
$$(a \oplus b) \oplus c = a \oplus (b \oplus c)$$

A list of some of the more common NAND, NOR, and Exclusive-OR integrated circuit packages that we may encounter in the laboratory is as follows:

7400   4 (quadruple) two-input NAND gates
7410   3 (triple) three-input NAND gates
7420   2 (dual) four-input NAND gates
7430   1 eight-input NAND gate
7402   4 (quadruple) two-input NOR gates
7427   3 (triple) three-input NOR gates
7486   4 (quadruple) two-input Exclusive-OR gates

To build a circuit, we utilize packages. Even if we only need 1 three-input NAND gate, we must buy a package with three gates on it (a 7410). Recognize, however, that a three-input gate can be used as a two-input gate by connecting two of the inputs together or by connecting one of the inputs to a logic 1.

EXAMPLE 2.14

Consider the following circuit, constructed with ANDs and ORs; the input variables have been omitted because they are irrelevant to the discussion.

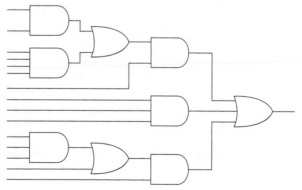

The number of gates and packages are shown in the left part of the following table

| | Gates | | Packs | | | | |
Inputs	AND	OR	AND	OR		NAND	Packs
2	3	2	1			5	1
3	2	1	1	1		3	1
4	1		1			1	1
Total	6	3	3	1		9	3

With AND and OR gates, four packages are needed: three ANDs and one OR package (because the 2 two-input OR gates can be constructed with the leftover three-input gates).

If all of the gates are converted to NANDs (and some of the inputs are complemented) the gate and package count is shown in the right part of the table. Only three packages are needed. The second four-input gate on the 7420 would be used as the fifth two-input gate (by tying three of the inputs together).

[SP 15, 16, 17; EX 16, 17, 18]

2.7 SIMPLIFICATION OF ALGEBRAIC EXPRESSIONS

We have already looked at the process of simplifying algebraic expressions, starting with a sum of minterms or a product of maxterms. The primary tools were

P9a. $ab + ab' = a$ **P9b.** $(a + b)(a + b') = a$

P10a. $a + a'b = a + b$ **P10b.** $a(a' + b) = ab$

although many of the other properties were used, particularly,

P6a. $a + a = a$ **P6b.** $a \cdot a = a$

P8a. $a(b + c) = ab + ac$ **P8b.** $a + bc = (a + b)(a + c)$

If the function is stated in other than one of the standard forms, two other properties are useful. First,

P12a. $a + ab = a$ **P12b.** $a(a + b) = a$ **absorption**

The proof of P12a uses P3b, P8a, P4aa, and P3b (again).

$$a + ab = a \cdot 1 + ab = a(1 + b) = a \cdot 1 = a$$

Remember that we only need to prove one half of the property, because the dual of a property is always true. However, we could have proven P12b using the duals of each of the theorems we used to prove P12a. Instead, we could distribute the a from the left side of P12b, producing

$$a \cdot a + ab = a + ab$$

However, that is just the left side of P12a, which we have already proved is equal to a.

P10a and P12a look very similar; yet we used two very different approaches to demonstrate their validity. In P10a, we did

$$a + a'b = (a + a')(a + b) = 1 \cdot (a + b) = a + b$$

$$\textbf{[P8b, P5a, P3bb]}$$

whereas for P12a, we used P3b, P8a, P4aa, and P3b. How did we know not to start the proof of P11a by using P8b to obtain

$$a + ab = (a + a)(a + b) = a(a + b)?$$

Those steps are all valid, but they do not get us anywhere toward showing that these expressions equal a. Similarly, if we started the proof of P10a by using P3b, that is,

$$a + a'b = a \cdot 1 + a'b$$

we also do not get anywhere toward a solution. How does the novice know where to begin? Unfortunately, the answer to that is either trial and error or experience. After solving a number of problems, we can often make the correct guess as to where to start on a new one. If that approach does not work, then we must try another one. This is not much of a problem in trying to demonstrate that two expressions are equal. We know that we can quit when we have worked one side to be the same as the other.

Before proceeding with a number of examples, some comments on the process are in order. There is no algorithm for algebraic simplification, that is, there is no ordered list of properties to apply. On the other hand, of the properties we have up to this point, 12, 9, and 10 are the ones most likely to reduce the number of terms or literals. Another difficulty is that we often do not know when we are finished, that is, what is the minimum. In most of the examples we have worked so far, the final expressions that we obtained appear to be as simple as we can go. However, we will see a number of examples where it is not obvious that there is not a more minimum expression. We will not be able to get around this until Chapter 3 when we develop other simplification methods. (Note that in the Solved Problems and the Exercises, the number of terms and literals in the minimum solution is given. Once that is reached, we know we are done; if we end up with more, we need to try another approach.)

We will now look at several examples of algebraic simplification.

EXAMPLE 2.15	
$xyz + x'y + x'y'$	
$= xyz + x'$	**[P9a]**
$= x' + yz$	**[P10a]**

where $a = x'$, $a' = x$, and $b = yz$

EXAMPLE 2.16	
$wx + wxy + w'yz + w'y'z + w'xyz'$	
$= (wx + wxy) + (w'yz + w'y'z) + w'xyz'$	
$= wx + w'z + w'xyz'$	**[P12a, P9a]**
$= wx + w'(z + xyz')$	
$= wx + w'(z + xy)$	**[P10a]**
$= wx + w'z + w'xy$	
$= w'z + x(w + w'y)$	
$= w'z + x(w + y)$	**[P10a]**
$= w'z + wx + xy$	

P10a could have been used first with wx and $w'xyz'$ (resulting in xyz'). That approach, however, would leave us with an expression

$w'z + wx + xyz'$

for which there are no algebraic clues as to how to proceed. The only way we can now reduce it is to add terms to the expression. Shortly, we will introduce another property that will enable us to go from this expression to the minimum one.

EXAMPLE 2.17

$$(x + y)(x + y + z') + y' = (x + y) + y' \qquad \text{[P12b]}$$
$$= x + (y + y') = x + 1 = 1 \qquad \text{[P5a, P4a]}$$

EXAMPLE 2.18

$$(a + b' + c)(a + c')(a' + b' + c)(a + c + d)$$
$$= (b' + c)(a + c')(a + d) \qquad \text{[P9b, P10b]}$$

where the second simplification really took several steps

$$(a + c')(a + c + d) = a + c'(c + d) = a + c'd = (a + c')(a + d)$$

One more tool is useful in the algebraic simplification of switching functions. The operator *consensus* (indicated by the symbol ¢) is defined as follows:

For any two product terms where exactly one variable appears un-complemented in one and complemented in the other, the consensus is defined as the product of the remaining literals. If no such variable exists or if more than one such variable exists, then the consensus is undefined. If we write one term as at_1 and the second as $a't_2$ (where t_1 and t_2 represent product terms), then, if the consensus is defined,

$$at_1 \text{ ¢ } a't_2 = t_1 t_2$$

EXAMPLE 2.19

$$ab'c \text{ ¢ } a'd = b'cd$$
$$ab'c \text{ ¢ } a'cd = b'cd$$
$$abc' \text{ ¢ } bcd' = abd'$$
$$b'c'd' \text{ ¢ } b'cd' = b'd'$$
$$abc' \text{ ¢ } bc'd = \text{undefined—no such variable}$$
$$a'bd \text{ ¢ } ab'cd = \text{undefined—two variables, } a \text{ and } b$$

We then have the following property that is useful in reducing functions.

P13a. $\quad at_1 + a't_2 + t_1 t_2 = at_1 + a't_2$

$\qquad$ **P13b.** $(a + t_1)(a' + t_2)(t_1 + t_2) = (a + t_1)(a' + t_2)$ $\qquad$ **consensus**

P13a states that the consensus term is redundant and can be removed from an SOP expression. (Of course, this property, like all of the others, can be used in the other direction to add a term. We will see an example of that shortly.)

CAUTION: It is the consensus term that can be removed ($t_1 t_2$), **not** the other two terms (**not** $at_1 + a't_2$). A similar kind of simplification can be obtained in POS expressions using the dual (P13b). We will not pursue that further.

First, we will derive this property from the others. Using P12a twice, the right-hand side becomes

$$at_1 + a't_2 = (at_1 + at_1 t_2) + (a't_2 + a't_1 t_2) \qquad \text{[P12a]}$$
$$= at_1 + a't_2 + (at_1 t_2 + a't_1 t_2)$$
$$= at_1 + a't_2 + t_1 t_2 \qquad \text{[P9a]}$$

It is also useful to look at the truth table for this theorem. From Table 2.15, we see that the consensus term, $t_1 t_2$, is 1 only when one of the other terms is already 1. Thus, if we OR that term with RHS, it does not change anything, that is, LHS is the same as RHS.

Table 2.15 Consensus.

a	t_1	t_2	at_1	$a't_2$	**RHS**	$t_1 t_2$	**LHS**
0	0	0	0	0	0	0	0
0	0	1	0	1	1	0	1
0	1	0	0	0	0	0	0
0	1	1	0	1	1	1	1
1	0	0	0	0	0	0	0
1	0	1	0	0	0	0	0
1	1	0	1	0	1	0	1
1	1	1	1	0	1	1	1

EXAMPLE 2.20

In Example 2.3 (Section 2.2.3), we reduced the function as

$$f = a'b'c' + a'bc' + a'bc + ab'c'$$

to

$$f_1 = a'c' + a'b + b'c'$$

by combining the first two terms using P9a, and then applying P10a twice. At that point, we were at a dead end. However, we found by starting over with a different grouping that we could reduce this to

$$f_2 = b'c' + a'b$$

Indeed, the term eliminated, $a'c'$, is the consensus of the other terms; we could use P13a to go from f_1 to f_2.

EXAMPLE 2.21

$$g = bc' + abd + acd$$

Because Properties 1 through 12 produce no simplification, we now try consensus. The only consensus term defined is

$$bc' \not\phi \, acd = abd$$

Property 13 now allows us to remove the consensus term. Thus,

$$g = bc' + acd$$

With the following function, there is no way to apply Properties 12, 9 and 10:

$$f = w'y' + w'xz + wxy + wyz'$$

Next, we try consensus. An approach that ensures that we try to find the consensus of all pairs of terms is to start with consensus of the second term with the first; then try the third with the second and the first; and so forth. Following this approach (or any other) for this example, the only consensus that exists is

$$w'xz \ \cent \ wxy = xyz$$

When a consensus term was part of the SOP expression, P13a allowed us to remove that term and thus simplify the expression. If the consensus term is not one of the terms in the SOP expression, the same property allows us to add it to the expression. Of course, we don't add another term automatically because that makes the expression less minimum. However, we should keep track of such a term, and, as a last resort, consider adding it to the function. Then, see if that term can be used to form other consensus terms and thus reduce the function. In this example, by adding xyz, f becomes

$$f = w'y' + w'xz + wxy + wyz' + xyz$$

Now, however,

$$xyz \ \cent \ wyz' = wxy \quad \text{and} \quad xyz \ \cent \ w'y' = w'xz$$

Thus, we can remove both wxy and $w'xz$, leaving

$$f = w'y' + wyz' + xyz \quad \text{(3 terms, 8 literals)}$$

We will now consider an example making use of consensus, as well as all of the other properties. The usual approach is to try to utilize properties 12, 9, and then 10. When we get as far as we can with these, we then turn to consensus.

EXAMPLE 2.22

$$A'BCD + A'BC'D + B'EF + CDE'G + A'DEF + A'B'EF$$
$$= A'BD + B'EF + CDE'G + A'DEF \qquad \text{[P12a, P9a]}$$

But $A'BD \ \cent \ B'EF = A'DEF$ and this reduces to
$$A'BD + B'EF + CDE'G$$

[SP 18; EX 19, 20, 21]

2.8 MANIPULATION OF ALGEBRAIC FUNCTIONS AND NAND GATE IMPLEMENTATIONS

In addition to the need to minimize algebraic expressions, there is sometimes the requirement to put an expression in a certain format, such as SOP, sum of minterms, POS, or product of maxterms. Secondly, to meet design constraints, we sometimes must manipulate the algebra. In this section we will look at some examples and introduce one more property.

If we have an SOP expression and need to expand it to sum of minterms, we have two options. First, we can create a truth table, and, from that, follow the approach of Section 2.5 to produce a sum of minterms.

Indeed, this approach will work for an expression in any format. The other approach is to use P9a to add variables to a term.

EXAMPLE 2.23

$f = bc + ac + ab$

$\quad = bca + bca' + ac + ab$

We can repeat the process on the other two terms, producing

$f = bca + bca' + acb + acb' + abc + abc'$

$\quad = abc + a'bc + abc + ab'c + abc + abc'$

$\quad = a'bc + ab'c + abc' + abc$

where P6a was used to remove the duplicate terms.

If two literals were missing from a term, that term would produce four minterms, using P9a repeatedly.

EXAMPLE 2.24

$g = x' + xyz = x'y + x'y' + xyz$

$\quad = x'yz + x'yz' + x'y'z + x'y'z' + xyz$

$g(x, y, z) = \Sigma m(3, 2, 1, 0, 7) = \Sigma m(0, 1, 2, 3, 7)$

since minterm numbers are usually written in numeric order.

To convert to product of maxterms, P9b can be used. For example,

---

EXAMPLE 2.25

$f = (A + B + C)(A' + B')$

$\quad = (A + B + C)(A' + B' + C)(A' + B' + C')$

One other property is useful in manipulating functions from one form to another.

P14a. $ab + a'c = (a + c)(a' + b)$

(The dual of this is also true; but it is the same property with the variables b and c interchanged.) This property can be demonstrated by first applying P8a to the right side three times:

$$(a + c)(a' + b) = (a + c)a' + (a + c)\,b = aa' + a'c + ab + bc$$

However, $aa' = 0$ and $bc = a'c \not\subset ab$ and thus, using P3aa and P13a, we get

$$aa' + a'c + ab + bc = a'c + ab$$

which is equal to the left side of the property.

This property is particularly useful in converting POS expressions to SOP and vice versa.

In Example 2.7, we found the sum of minterms and the minimum SOP expressions, as well as the product of maxterms and the minimum POS expression for

$$f(A, B, C) = \Sigma m \, (1, 2, 3, 4, 5)$$

In Example 2.26, we will start with the minimum POS, and use Property 14 to convert it to a SOP.

EXAMPLE 2.26

$f = (A + B + C)(A' + B') = AB' + A'(B + C) = AB' + A'B + A'C$

where the a of P14a is A, the b is $B + C$, and the c is B'. This, indeed, is one of the SOP solutions we found in Example 2.7 for this problem. Although the utilization of this property does not always produce a minimum SOP expression (as it does in this case), it does produce a simpler expression than we would get just using P8a.

$f = AA' + AB' + BA' + BB' + CA' + CB'$
$\quad = AB' + A'B + A'C + B'C$

The term $B'C$ can then be removed because it is the consensus of AB' and $A'C$.

To go from a POS expression (or a more general expression that is neither SOP nor POS) to an SOP expression, we use primarily the following three properties:

P8b. $a + bc = (a + b)(a + c)$

P14a. $ab + a'c = (a + c)(a' + b)$

P8a. $a(b + c) = ab + ac$

We try to apply them in that order, using the first two from right to left.

EXAMPLE 2.27

$(A + B' + C)(A + B + D)(A' + C' + D')$

$\quad = [A + (B' + C)(B + D)](A' + C' + D')$ **[P8b]**

$\quad = (A + B'D + BC)(A' + C' + D')$ **[P14a]**

$\quad = A(C' + D') + A'(B'D + BC)$ **[P14a]**

$\quad = AC' + AD' + A'B'D + A'BC$ **[P8a]**

The dual of these properties can be used to convert to POS as can be seen in Example 2.28.

EXAMPLE 2.28

$wxy' + xyz + w'x'z'$

$\quad = x(wy' + yz) + w'x'z'$ **[P8a]**

$\quad = x(y' + z)(y + w) + w'x'z'$ **[P14a]**

$\quad = (x + w'z')[x' + (y' + z)(y + w)]$ **[P14a]**

$\quad = (x + w')(x + z')(x' + y' + z)(x' + y + w)$ **[P8b]**

Another application of P14a and this type of algebraic manipulation comes when we wish to implement functions using only two-input NAND or NOR gates (or two- and three-input gates). (We will only consider examples of NAND gate implementations.) Consider the following problem.

The following expression is the only minimum SOP expression for the function f. Assume all inputs are available both uncomplemented and complemented. Find a NAND gate circuit that uses only two-input gates. No gate may be used as a NOT gate.*

$$f = ab'c' + a'c'd' + bd$$

(A two-level solution would require four gates, three of which would be three-input gates, and 11 gate inputs.)

To solve this problem, we must eliminate three-input gates. Thus, the starting point is to attempt to factor something from the three literal terms. In this example, there is a common c' in the first two terms and we can thus obtain

$$f = c'(ab' + a'd') + bd$$

This, indeed, solves the whole problem in one step because not only did we reduce the 2 three-input product terms to two inputs each, but we also got the final OR to a two-input one. Thus, the resulting circuit is shown in Figure 2.22, where we first implemented it with AND and OR gates and then, starting at the output, added double inverters in each path from the input of an OR back to the output of an AND. (In this example, no in-

Figure 2.22   A two-input NAND gate circuit.

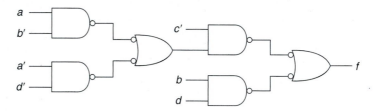

---

*We could always produce a circuit using two-input gates by replacing a three-input gate by 2 twos and a NOT. For example, a three-input NAND could be implemented as follows:

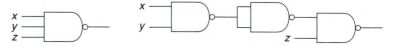

Larger gates could be replaced in a similar fashion. But this approach almost always leads to circuits with more gates than is necessary.

puts came directly into an OR.) This solution requires 6 gates and 12 inputs. It should be noted that either solution, this one or the two-level one mentioned earlier requires two integrated circuit packages. This requires two 7400s (4 two-input NANDs each) and would leave two of the gates unused. The two-level solution would require a 7410 (3 three-input gates) and a 7400 for the remaining two-input gate and would leave three of those gates unused. (If we had replaced each three-input gate by 2 two-input ones plus a NOT, the implementation would require 7 two-input gates plus three NOT gates.)

More complex examples of finding a two-input gate implementation often require the use of P14a as well as P8a. Consider the function in Example 2.29 (already in minimum sum of products form).

$$G = DE' + A'B'C' + CD'E + ABC'E$$

EXAMPLE 2.29

The four-literal product term is the first place we must attack. We could factor E from the last two terms. That would produce

$$G = DE' + A'B'C' + E(CD' + ABC')$$

But now, there is no way of eliminating the three-input gate corresponding to $A'B'C'$. Instead, we can factor C' from the second and the fourth terms, producing

$$G = C'(A'B' + ABE) + DE' + CD'E$$

We can apply P14a to the expression within the parentheses to get

$$G = C'(A' + BE)(A + B') + DE' + CD'E$$

or, using B instead of A,

$$G = C'(B' + AE)(B + A') + DE' + CD'E$$

In either case, we still have 2 three-input AND terms, that first product and the last one. (We cannot take the output of the OR gate that forms $B' + AE$ and the output of the OR gate that forms $B + A'$ and connect them to a two-input AND gate. We would then need to connect the output of that AND gate to the input of another AND gate with C' as its other input. This would violate the third rule for conversion to NAND gates—the inputs to AND gates may not come from the output of another AND gate.) We can reduce it to all two-input gates by applying P14a again, using the C' from the first complex term and the C from the last product term, producing (from the second version) the following expression:

$$G = (C' + D'E)[C + (B' + AE)(B + A')] + DE'$$

This requires 10 gates, as shown in the following NAND gate circuit.

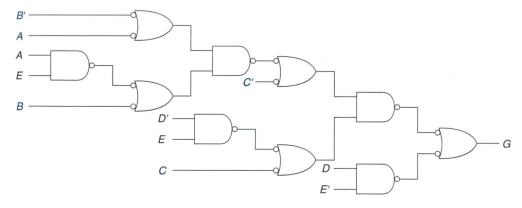

Again, we began by implementing the circuit with ANDs and ORs, starting at the inner most parentheses. Five of the inputs went directly to OR gates and were thus complemented (as shown in green in the circuit).

There is still another approach to manipulating this algebra.

$$G = C'(A' + BE)(A + B') + DE' + CD'E$$
$$= C'(A' + BE)(A + B') + (D + CE)(D' + E')$$
$$= (A' + BE)(AC' + B'C') + (D + CE)(D' + E')$$

In this case, we eliminated the three-input AND by distributing the C' (P8a) and used P14a on the last two product terms. We will leave the implementation of this as an exercise, but we can count 11 gates (one more than before) from the algebraic expression, as seen from the following count.

$$G = (A' + BE)(AC' + B'C') + (D + CE)(D' + E')$$
$$\quad\;\; 1\; 2\; 3\; 4 \quad 5 \quad 6 \qquad 7 \qquad 8\; 9\; 10 \quad 11$$

where each gate is numbered below the operator corresponding to that gate.

As an example of sharing a gate, consider the implementation of the following function with two-input NAND gates:

EXAMPLE 2.30

$$G = C'D' + ABC' + A'C + B'C$$
$$= C'(D' + AB) + C(A' + B')$$

The circuit for that expression is shown next.

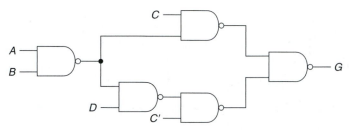

Note that only one NAND gate is needed for the product term AB and for the sum term $A' + B'$ (because inputs coming directly to an OR are complemented).

As a final example, we will return to the implementation of the full adder (CE3). The SOP expressions developed in Example 2.11 are repeated (where the carry input, c_{in}, is represented by just c).

EXAMPLE 2.31

$$s = a'b'c + a'bc' + ab'c' + abc$$

$$c_{out} = bc + ac + ab$$

A two-level implementation of these would require 1 four-input NAND gate (for s), 5 three-input NAND gates (four for s and one for c_{out}), and 3 two-input NANDs (for c_{out}), assuming all inputs are available both uncomplemented and complemented. But this assumption is surely not valid for c because that is just the output of combinational logic just like this (from the next less significant bit of the sum). Thus, we need at least one NOT gate (for c') and possibly three (one for each input). The implementation of this adder would thus require four integrated circuit packages (one 7420, two 7410s, and one 7400). (There would be one gate left over of each size, which could be used to create whatever NOTs are needed.)

Although s and c_{out} are in minimum SOP form, we can manipulate the algebra to reduce the gate requirements by first factoring c from two terms of s and from two terms of c_{out}, and factoring c' from the other two terms of s, yielding*

$$s = c(a'b' + ab) + c'(ab' + a'b)$$

$$c_{out} = c(a + b) + ab$$

This requires 11 two-input NAND gates, not including the three NOTs (because ab need only be implemented once for the two terms and $a + b$ is implemented using the same gate as $a'b'$).

Returning to the expression for sum, note that

$$s = c(a \oplus b)' + c'(a \oplus b) = c \oplus (a \oplus b)$$

Furthermore, we could write

$$c_{out} = c(a \oplus b) + ab$$

(That is a little algebraic trick that is not obvious from any of the properties. However, the difference between $a + b$ and $a \oplus b$ is that the former is 1 when both a and b are 1, but the latter is not. But the expression for c_{out} is 1 for $a = b = 1$ because of the ab term.)

---

*We could just as easily factor b and b' or a and a' from these expressions; the resulting circuits would have the same layout of gates.

Using these last two expressions, we could implement both the sum and carry using two Exclusive-ORs and 3 two-input NANDs as follows:

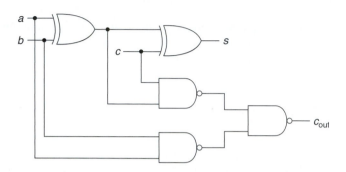

Packages with four Exclusive-OR gates are available (7486) and thus this circuit could be implemented with one of those packages and one 7400. Note that complemented inputs are not necessary for this implementation.

Finally, because we can implement each Exclusive-OR with 4 two-input NAND gates, without requiring complemented inputs, we obtain

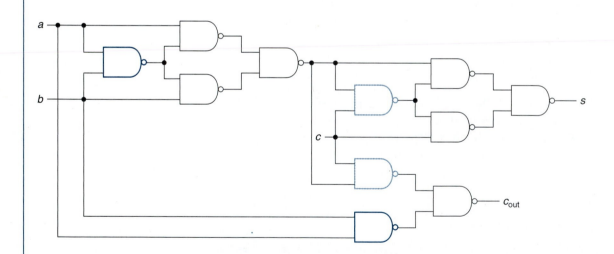

Note that the two green NAND gates have the same inputs and the two light green ones also have the same inputs. Only one copy of each is necessary, yielding the final circuit with only nine NAND gates.

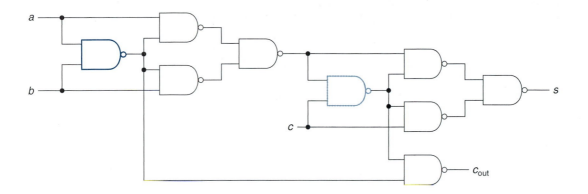

This implementation would require three 7400s if we were only building one bit of an adder. However, a 4-bit adder could be built with nine packages (36 two-input gates).

[SP 19, 20, 21, 22, 23; EX 22, 23, 24, 25, 26]

 2.9 SOLVED PROBLEMS

1. For each of the following problems, there are four inputs, A, B, C, and D. Show a truth table for the functions specified. (One truth table with four outputs is shown for the four examples.)

   a. The inputs represent a 4-bit unsigned binary number. The output, W, is 1 if and only if the number is a multiple of 2 or of 3 but not both.

   b. The inputs represent a 4-bit positive binary number. The output, X, is 0 if and only if the input is a prime (where 0 never occurs).

   c. The first two inputs (A, B) represent a 2-bit unsigned binary number (in the range 0 to 3). The last two (C, D) represent a second unsigned binary number (in the same range). The output, Y, is 1 if and only if the two numbers differ by two or more.

   d. The inputs represent a BCD number in Excess-3 code. Those combinations that do not represent one of the digits never occur. The output, Z, is 1 if and only if that number is a perfect square.

The truth table contains the answer to all four parts.

A	B	C	D	W	X	Y	Z
0	0	0	0	0	X	0	X
0	0	0	1	0	0	0	X
0	0	1	0	1	0	1	X
0	0	1	1	1	0	1	1
0	1	0	0	1	1	0	1
0	1	0	1	0	0	0	0
0	1	1	0	0	1	0	0
0	1	1	1	0	0	1	1
1	0	0	0	1	1	1	0
1	0	0	1	1	1	0	0
1	0	1	0	1	1	0	0
1	0	1	1	0	0	0	0
1	1	0	0	0	1	1	1
1	1	0	1	0	0	1	X
1	1	1	0	1	1	0	X
1	1	1	1	1	1	0	X

a. We don't care whether one considers 0 a multiple of 2 or 3 because it is either a multiple of neither or of both. In both cases, $W = 0$. For the next row, 1 is not a multiple of either 2 or 3; thus, $W = 0$. For the next three rows $W = 1$ because 2 and 4 are multiples of 2, but not 3, and 3 is a multiple of 3, but not 2. Both 5 and 7 are multiples of neither and 6 is a multiple of both; thus, for the next three rows, $W = 0$.

b. A prime number is one that is evenly divisible only by 1 or itself. Note that the problem specifies that the output is 0 for primes and is thus 1 for numbers that are not prime. The first nonprime is 4 (2×2). Indeed, all of the even numbers (other than 2) are nonprimes. Because 0 never occurs, the output for the first row is a don't care.

c. For the first four rows, the first number is 0. It is compared on successive rows with 0, 1, 2, and 3. Only 2 and 3 differ from 0 by 2 or more. In the next group of four rows, the first number is 1; it only differs from 3 by 2 or more. In the next four rows, 2 differs only from 0 by 2 or more. Finally, in the last 4 rows, 3 differs from 0 and 1 by 2 or more.

d. A perfect square is an integer obtained by multiplying some integer by itself. Thus, 0, 1, 4, and 9 are perfect squares. Note that the first three rows and the last three rows are all don't cares because those input combinations never occur.

2. The system is a speed warning device. It receives, on two lines, an indication of the speed limit on the highway. There are three possible values: 45, 55, or 65 mph. It receives from the automobile, on

two other lines, an indication of the speed of the vehicle. There are four possible values: under 45, between 46 and 55, between 56 and 65, and over 65 mph. It produces two outputs. The first, f, indicates whether the car is going above the speed limit. The second, g, indicates that the car is driving at a "dangerous speed"—defined as either over 65 mph or more than 10 mph above the speed limit. Show how each of the inputs and outputs are coded (in terms of binary values) and complete the truth table for this system.

The first step is to code the inputs, as shown in the following tables.

Speed limit	a	b	Speed	c	d
45	0	0	<45	0	0
55	0	1	46–55	0	1
65	1	0	56–65	1	0
unused	1	1	>65	1	1

The outputs will be 1 if the car is speeding or driving dangerously.

	a	b	c	d	f	g
	0	0	0	0	0	0
45	0	0	0	1	1	0
	0	0	1	0	1	1
	0	0	1	1	1	1
	0	1	0	0	0	0
55	0	1	0	1	0	0
	0	1	1	0	1	0
	0	1	1	1	1	1
	1	0	0	0	0	0
65	1	0	0	1	0	0
	1	0	1	0	0	0
	1	0	1	1	1	1
	1	1	0	0	X	X
	1	1	0	1	X	X
	1	1	1	0	X	X
	1	1	1	1	X	X

3. Show a block diagram of a circuit using AND and OR gates for each side of P8b: $a + bc = (a + b)(a + c)$

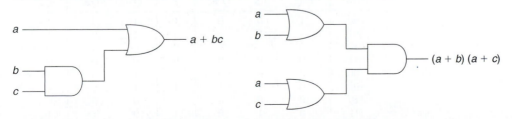

4. Show a truth table for the following functions:
   a. $F = XY' + YZ + X'Y'Z'$
   b. $G = X'Y + (X + Z')(Y + Z)$

(a)

XYZ	XY'	YZ	X'Y'Z'	F
000	0	0	1	1
001	0	0	0	0
010	0	0	0	0
011	0	1	0	1
100	1	0	0	1
101	1	0	0	1
110	0	0	0	0
111	0	1	0	1

(b)

XYZ	X'Y	X + Z'	Y + Z	()()	G
000	0	1	0	0	0
001	0	0	1	0	0
010	1	1	1	1	1
011	1	0	1	0	1
100	0	1	0	0	0
101	0	1	1	1	1
110	0	1	1	1	1
111	0	1	1	1	1

5. Determine, using truth tables, whether or not each of the groups of expressions are equal:

   a. $f = a'c' + a'b + ac$
   $g = bc + ac + a'c'$
   b. $f = P'Q' + PR + Q'R$
   $g = Q' + PQR$

(a)

abc	a'c'	a'b	ac	f	bc	ac	a'c'	g
000	1	0	0	1	0	0	1	1
001	0	0	0	0	0	0	0	0
010	1	1	0	1	0	0	1	1
011	0	1	0	1	1	0	0	1
100	0	0	0	0	0	0	0	0
101	0	0	1	1	0	1	0	1
110	0	0	0	0	0	0	0	0
111	0	0	1	1	1	1	0	1

The two functions are equal.

(b)

PQR	P'Q'	PR	Q'R	f	Q'	PQR	g
000	1	0	0	1	1	0	1
001	1	0	1	1	1	0	1
010	0	0	0	0	0	0	0
011	0	0	0	0	0	0	0
100	0	0	0	0	1	0	1	←
101	0	1	1	1	1	0	1
110	0	0	0	0	0	0	0
111	0	1	0	1	0	1	1

Note that for row 100 (marked with a green arrow), $f = 0$ and $g = 1$. Thus, the two functions are different.

6. For each of the following expressions, indicate which (if any) of the following apply (more than one may apply):

   i. Product term

   ii. Sum of products expression

   iii. Sum term

   iv. Product of sums expression

  a. ab'

  b. $a'b + ad$

  c. $(a + b)(c + a'd)$

  d. $a' + b'$

  e. $(a + b')(b + c)(a' + c + d)$

  a. i. product of two literals

      ii. sum of one product term

      iv. product of two sum terms

  b. ii. sum of two product terms

  c. none; second term is not a sum term

  d. ii. sum of two product terms

      iii. sum of two literals

      iv. product of one sum term

  e. iv. product of three sum terms

7. In the expressions of problem 6, how many literals are in each?

  a. 2   **b.** 4   **c.** 5   **d.** 2   **e.** 7

8. Using Properties 1 to 10, reduce the following expressions to a minimum SOP form. Show each step (number of terms and number of literals in minimum shown in parentheses).

  a. $xyz' + xyz$ (1 term, 2 literals)

  b. $x'y'z' + x'y'z + x'yz + xy'z + xyz$ (2 terms, 3 literals)

  c. $f = abc' + ab'c + a'bc + abc$ (3 terms, 6 literals)

  a. $xyz' + xyz = xy\,(z' + z) = xy \cdot 1 = xy$ **[P8a, P5aa, P3b]**

    or, in one step, using P9a, where $a = xy$ and $b = z'$

b. $x'y'z' + x'y'z + x'yz + xy'z + xyz$

Make two copies of $x'y'z$

$$
\begin{aligned}
&= (x'y'z' + x'y'z) + (x'y'z + x'yz) + (xy'z + xyz) && \text{[P6a]} \\
&= x'y'(z' + z) + x'z(y' + y) + xz(y' + y) && \text{[P8a]} \\
&= x'y' \cdot 1 + x'z \cdot 1 + xz \cdot 1 && \text{[P5aa]} \\
&= x'y' + x'z + xz && \text{[P3b]} \\
&= x'y' + (x' + x)z = x'y' + 1 \cdot z && \text{[P8a, P5aa]} \\
&= x'y' + z && \text{[P3bb]}
\end{aligned}
$$

or, without using P6a,

$$
\begin{aligned}
&= (x'y'z' + x'y'z) + x'yz + (xy'z + xyz) && \\
&= x'y' + x'yz + xz && \text{[P9a]} \\
&= x'(y' + yz) + xz && \text{[P8a]} \\
&= x'(y' + z) + xz && \text{[P10a]} \\
&= x'y' + x'z + xz && \text{[P8a]} \\
&= x'y' + z && \text{[P9a]}
\end{aligned}
$$

Note that we could follow a path that does not lead us to the correct answer, by combining the last two terms in the second line of this second sequence, yielding

$$
\begin{aligned}
&= x'y' + z(x'y + x) && \\
&= x'y' + z(y + x) && \text{[P10a]} \\
&= x'y' + yz + xz && \text{[P8a]}
\end{aligned}
$$

This is a dead end. It has more terms than the minimum (which was given) and we do not have the tools (in Properties 1 to 10) to reduce this further without backing up to the original expression (or, at least, the first reduction). We should then go back and start again.

c. There are two approaches to this problem. In the first, we note that abc can be combined with each of the other terms. Thus, we make three copies of it, using

$$
\begin{aligned}
abc &= abc + abc + abc && \text{[P6a]} \\
f &= (abc' + abc) + (ab'c + abc) + (a'bc + abc) && \\
&= ab + ac + bc && \text{[P9a]}
\end{aligned}
$$

In the second approach, we just use abc to combine with the term next to it, producing

$$
\begin{aligned}
f &= abc' + ab'c + a'bc + abc = abc' + ab'c + bc && \text{[P9a]} \\
&= abc' + c(b + b'a) = abc' + c(b + a) && \\
&= abc' + bc + ac && \text{[P10a]} \\
&= a(c + c'b) + bc = a(c + b) + bc && \\
&= ac + ab + bc && \text{[P10a]}
\end{aligned}
$$

or, in place of the last two lines,

$$= b(c + c'a) + ac = b(c + a) + ac$$
$$= bc + ab + ac \qquad \qquad \textbf{[P10a]}$$

In this approach, we used P10a twice to eliminate a literal from the second term and then the first. We could have done it in any order. Indeed, there were two ways to do the last step (as shown on the last two lines).

9. Using Properties 1 to 10, reduce the following expressions to a minimum POS form. Show each step (number of terms and number of literals in parentheses).

 a. $(a + b' + c)\,(a + b' + c')\,(a' + b + c)\,(a' + b' + c)$

    (2 terms, 4 literals)

 b. $(x' + y' + z')\,(x' + y + z')\,(x' + y + z)$ (2 terms, 4 literals)

 a. We group the first two and the last two terms, and use Property 9b

   $[(a + b' + c)(a + b' + c')][(a' + b + c)(a' + b' + c)] =$
   $[a + b'][a' + c]$

 b. We can make a second copy of the middle term and group it with each of the others

   $(x' + y' + z')(x' + y + z')(x' + y + z) = [(x' + y' + z')$
   $(x' + y + z')][(x' + y + z)(x' + y + z')] = [x' + z'][x' + y]$

 If we don't make the second copy, we get

 $[x' + z'](x' + y + z)$

 We can then use P8b to get

 $x' + z' (y + z) = x' + yz'$ **[P8a, P5bb, P3a]**
 $= (x' + y)(x' + z)$ **[P8b]**

10. Show a block diagram of a system using AND, OR, and NOT gates to implement the following function. Assume that variables are available only uncomplemented. Do not manipulate the algebra.
 $F = [A\,(B + C)' + BDE](A' + CE)$

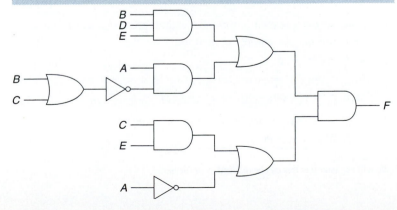

11. For each of the following circuits,
  i. find an algebraic expression
  ii. put it in SOP form.

a.

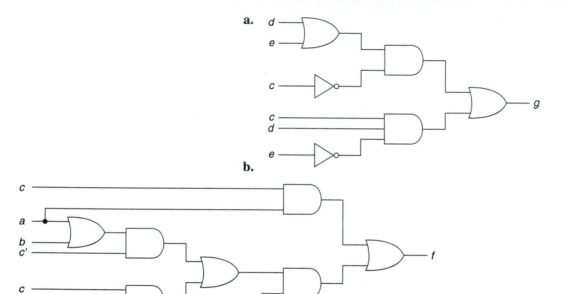

b.

a. i. $g = (d + e)c' + cde'$
  ii. $g = c'd + c'e + cde'$
b. i. $f = ac + ab'[cd + c'(a + b)]$
  ii. $f = ac + ab'cd + ab'c' + ab'c'b$
    $= ac + ab'cd + ab'c'$
    $= ac + ab'cd + ab'$*   **[P10a]**

12. Find the complement of the following expressions. Only single
  variables may be complemented in the answer.
  a. $f = x'yz' + xy'z' + xyz$
  b. $g = (w + x' + y)(w' + x + z)(w + x + y + z)$
  c. $h = (a + b'c)d' + (a' + c')(c + d)$

  a. $f' = (x + y' + z)(x' + y + z)(x' + y' + z')$
    SOP becomes POS.

---

* We will see later that this can be reduced even further.

b. $g' = w'xy' + wx'z' + w'x'y'z'$

POS becomes SOP.

c. $h' = [a'(b + c') + d][ac + c'd']$

or, step by step

$h' = [(a + b'c)d']'[(a' + c')(c + d)]'$

$\quad = [(a + b'c)' + d][(a' + c')' + (c + d)']$

$\quad = [a'(b'c)' + d][ac + c'd']$

$\quad = [a'(b + c') + d][ac + c'd']$

---

13. For the following truth table,

a b c	f
0 0 0	0
0 0 1	1
0 1 0	0
0 1 1	1
1 0 0	1
1 0 1	0
1 1 0	1
1 1 1	1

a. Show the minterms in numerical form.

b. Show an algebraic expression in sum of minterm form.

c. Show a minimum SOP expression (two solutions, three terms, six literals each).

d. Show the minterms of f' (complement of f) in numeric form.

e. Show an algebraic expression in product of maxterm form.

f. Show a minimum POS expression (two terms, five literals).

---

a. $f(a, b, c) + \Sigma m(1, 3, 4, 6, 7)$

b. $f = a'b'c + a'bc + ab'c' + abc' + abc$

c. $f = a'c + ac' + abc$

$\quad = a'c + ac' + ab$ (using P10a on last two terms)

$\quad = a'c + ac' + bc$ (using P10a on first and last term)

d. $f'(a, b, c) = \Sigma m(0, 2, 5)$

e. $f'(a, b, c) = \Sigma m(0, 2, 5)$

$\quad\quad\quad\quad = a'b'c' + a'bc' + ab'c$

$f = (a + b + c)(a + b' + c)(a' + b + c')$

f. Reordering the first two terms of f, we see that adjacency (P9b) is useful

$f = (a + c + b)(a + c + b')(a' + b + c')$

$\quad = (a + c)(a' + b + c')$

Or, we can minimize f' and then use DeMorgan's theorem:

$$f' = a'c' + ab'c$$
$$f = (a + c)(a' + b + c')$$

14. For the following function,

$$f(x, y, z) = \Sigma m(2, 3, 5, 6, 7)$$

   a. Show the truth table.
   b. Show an algebraic expression in sum of minterm form.
   c. Show a minimum SOP expression (two terms, three literals).
   d. Show the minterms of f' (complement of f) in numeric form.
   e. Show an algebraic expression in product of maxterm form.
   f. Show a minimum POS expression (two terms, five literals).

a.

$x\,y\,z$	f
0 0 0	0
0 0 1	0
0 1 0	1
0 1 1	1
1 0 0	0
1 0 1	1
1 1 0	1
1 1 1	1

b. $f = x'yz' + x'yz + xy'z + xyz' + xyz$

c. $f = x'y + xy'z + xy$
   $ = y + xy'z$
   $ = y + xz$

d. $f'(x, y, z) = \Sigma m(0, 1, 4)$

e. $f' = x'y'z' + x'y'z + xy'z'$
   $f = (x + y + z)(x + y + z')(x' + y + z)$

f. $f' = x'y'z' + x'y'z + xy'z' + x'y'z'$
   $ = x'y' + y'z'$
   $f = (x + y)(y + z)$

15. Show a block diagram corresponding to each of the expressions below using only NAND gates. Assume all inputs are available both uncomplemented and complemented. There is no need to manipulate the functions to simplify the algebra.

   a. $f = ab'd' + bde' + bc'd + a'ce$
   b. $g = b(c'd + c'e') + (a + ce)(a' + b'd')$

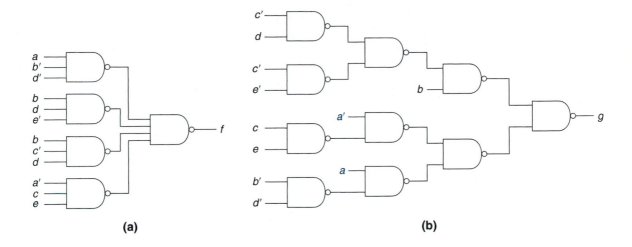

(a)   (b)

Note that in part (a), this is a two-level circuit. In part (b), the only inputs that go directly into an OR are *a* and *a'*; they are complemented.

16. Show a block diagram corresponding to each of the following expressions using only NOR gates. Assume all inputs are available both uncomplemented and complemented. There is no need to manipulate the functions to simplify the algebra.

   a. $f = (a + b')(a' + c + d)(b + d')$

   b. $g = [a'b' + a(c + d)](b + d')$

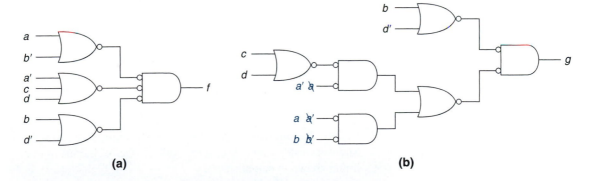

(a)   (b)

17. For each of the following circuits,

   i. Find an algebraic expression.

   ii. Put it in SOP form.

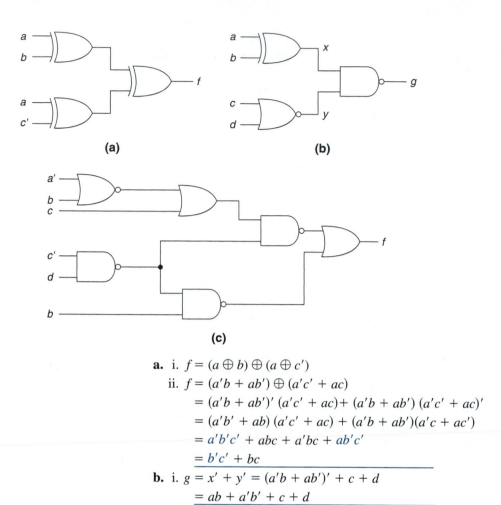

(a)

(b)

(c)

a. i. $f = (a \oplus b) \oplus (a \oplus c')$

　ii. $f = (a'b + ab') \oplus (a'c' + ac)$

　　　$= (a'b + ab')' (a'c' + ac) + (a'b + ab') (a'c' + ac)'$

　　　$= (a'b' + ab) (a'c' + ac) + (a'b + ab')(a'c + ac')$

　　　$= a'b'c' + abc + a'bc + ab'c'$

　　　$= b'c' + bc$

b. i. $g = x' + y' = (a'b + ab')' + c + d$

　　　$= ab + a'b' + c + d$

c. i. $f = \{[(a' + b)' + c](c'd)'\}' + [(b(c'd)']'$

　ii. $f = \{[(a' + b)' + c]' + (c'd)\} + [b' + c'd]$

　　　$= (a' + b)c' + c'd + b' + c'd$

　　　$= a'c' + bc' + c'd + b' = a'c' + c' + c'd + b'$

　　　$= c' + a'c' + c'd' + b' = c' + b'$

18. Reduce the following expressions to a minimum SOP form.
Show each step (number of terms and number of literals in minimum shown in parentheses).

a. $F = A + B + A'B'C'D$　　　　　　　　(3 terms, 4 literals)

b. $f = x'y'z + w'xz + wxyz' + wxz + w'xyz$

　　　　　　　　　　　　　　　　　(3 terms, 7 literals)

c. $H = AB + B'C + ACD + ABD' + ACD'$

　　　　　　　　　　　　　　　　　(2 terms, 4 literals)

d. $G = ABC' + A'C'D + AB'C' + BC'D + A'D$

$\qquad\qquad\qquad$ (2 terms, 4 literals)

e. $f = abc + b'cd + acd + abd'$

$\qquad\qquad\qquad$ (2 solutions, 3 terms, 9 literals)

a. $F = A + B + A'B'C'D$

$\qquad = (A + A'B'C'D) + B$

$\qquad = (A + B'C'D) + B$ $\qquad\qquad$ [P10a]

$\qquad = A + (B + B'C'D)$

$\qquad = A + B + C'D$ $\qquad\qquad\qquad$ [P10a]

We can also achieve the same result using a different approach.

$A + B + A'B'C'D = (A + B) + (A + B)'C'D$ $\qquad$ [P11a]

$\qquad\qquad = (A + B) + C'D$ $\qquad\qquad\qquad\quad$ [P10a]

b. $f = x'y'z + w'xz + wxyz' + wxz + w'xyz$

$\qquad = x'y'z + w'xz + wxyz' + wxz$ $\qquad\quad$ [P12a]

$\qquad = x'y'z + xz + wxyz'$ $\qquad\qquad\qquad\quad$ [P9a]

$\qquad = x'y'z + x(z + wyz')$

$\qquad = x'y'z + x(z + wy)$ $\qquad\qquad\qquad\quad$ [P10a]

$\qquad = x'y'z + xz + wxy$

$\qquad = z(x'y' + x) + wxy$

$\qquad = z(y' + x) + wxy$ $\qquad\qquad\qquad\qquad$ [P10a]

$\qquad = y'z + xz + wxy$

c. $H = AB + B'C + ACD + ABD' + ACD'$

$\qquad = AB + B'C + AC$ $\qquad\qquad\qquad$ [P12a, P9a]

$\qquad = AB + B'C$ $\qquad\qquad\qquad\qquad\quad$ [P13a]

d. $G = ABC' + A'C'D + AB'C' + BC'D + A'D$

$\qquad = ABC' + AB'C' + A'D + BC'D$ $\qquad$ [P12a]

$\qquad = AC' + A'D + BC'D$ $\qquad\qquad\qquad$ [P9a]

But,

$AC' \not\!\!{c} \; A'D = C'D$

$G = AC' + A'D + BC'D + C'D$ $\qquad\qquad$ [P13a]

$\qquad = AC' + A'D + C'D$ $\qquad\qquad\qquad$ [P12a]

$\qquad = AC' + A'D$ $\qquad\qquad\qquad\qquad$ [P13a]

Note that we used consensus to first add a term and then to remove that same term.

e. $f = abc + b'cd + acd + abd'$

Since

$abc \not\!\!{c} \; b'cd = acd$

the consensus term can be removed and thus

$$f = abc + b'cd + abd'$$

No further reduction is possible; the only consensus that exists among the terms in this reduced expression produces the term *acd*, the one that we just removed. None of the other properties can be used to reduce this function further.

However, if we go back to the original function, we note that another consensus does exist:

$$acd \ ¢ \ abd' = abc$$

and thus the term *abc* can be removed, producing

$$f = b'cd + acd + abd'$$

That is another equally good minimum solution (because no further minimization is possible). Even though we found two applications of consensus in this function, we cannot take advantage of both of them because no matter which one we use first, the term needed to form the second consensus has been removed.

19. Expand the following function to sum of minterms form

$$F(A, B, C) = A + B'C$$

We have a choice of two approaches. We could use P3b, P5aa (both from right to left) and P8a repeatedly to produce

$$A + B'C = A(B' + B) + (A' + A)B'C$$
$$= AB' + AB + A'B'C + AB'C$$
$$= AB'(C' + C) + AB(C' + C) + A'B'C + AB'C$$
$$= AB'C' + AB'C + ABC' + ABC + A'B'C + AB'C$$
$$= AB'C' + AB'C + ABC' + ABC + A'B'C$$

having removed the duplicated term ($AB'C$). Or we could use a truth table, such as

A B C	B'C	F
0 0 0	0	0
0 0 1	1	1
0 1 0	0	0
0 1 1	0	0
1 0 0	0	1
1 0 1	1	1
1 1 0	0	1
1 1 1	0	1

and thus,

$$F = A'B'C + AB'C' + AB'C + ABC' + ABC$$

which is the same as the previous expression reordered, or

$$F(A, B, C) = \Sigma m(1, 4, 5, 6, 7)$$

20. Convert each of the following expressions to SOP form:
    a. $(w + x' + z)(w' + y + z')(x + y + z)$
    b. $(a + b + c + d')(b + c + d)(b' + c')$

    a. $(w + x' + z)(w' + y + z')(x + y + z)$

$$\begin{aligned}
&= [z + (w + x')(x + y)](w' + y + z') &&\text{[P8b]} \\
&= (z + wx + x'y)(w' + y + z') &&\text{[P14a]} \\
&= z(w' + y) + z'(wx + x'y) &&\text{[P14a]} \\
&= w'z + yz + wxz' + x'yz' &&\text{[P8a]}
\end{aligned}$$

Note that this is not a minimum SOP expression, even though the original was a minimum POS expression. Using P10a, we could reduce this to

$$w'z + yz + wxz' + x'y$$

b. $(a + b + c + d')(b + c + d)(b' + c')$

$$\begin{aligned}
&= [b + c + (a + d')d](b' + c') &&\text{[P8b]} \\
&= (b + c + ad)(b' + c') &&\text{[P8b, P5b, P3a]} \\
&= bc' + b'(c + ad) &&\text{[P14a]} \\
&= bc' + b'c + ab'd &&\text{[P8a]}
\end{aligned}$$

or using c instead of b for P14a

$$\begin{aligned}
&= (b + c + ad)(b' + c') \\
&= b'c + c'(b + ad) \\
&= b'c + bc' + ac'd
\end{aligned}$$

These are two equally good solutions.

21. Convert the following expression to POS form:

    $a'c'd + a'cd' + bc$

    $a'c'd + a'cd' + bc$

$$\begin{aligned}
&= c(b + a'd') + c'a'd &&\text{[P8a]} \\
&= (c + a'd)(c' + b + a'd') &&\text{[P14a]} \\
&= (c + a')(c + d)(c' + b + a')(c' + b + d') &&\text{[P8b]}
\end{aligned}$$

Two comments are in order. This is not in minimum POS form. P12b allows us to manipulate the first and third terms so as to replace the third term by $(a' + b)$. We could have started the process by factoring a' from the first two terms, but that would require more work.

22. Implement each of the following expressions (which are already in minimum SOP form) using only two-input NAND gates. No gate may be used as a NOT. All inputs are available both uncomplemented and complemented. (The number of gates required is shown in parentheses.)
   a. $f = w'y' + xyz + wyz' + x'y'z$ (8 gates)
   b. $g = a'b'c'd' + abcd' + a'ce + ab'd + be$ (12 gates)

a. $f = y'(w' + x'z) + y(xz + wz')$

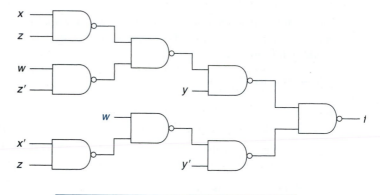

b. $g = a'b'c'd' + abcd' + a'ce + ab'd + be$

The first attempt at a solution yields one with 13 gates.

$$g = d'(a'b'c' + abc) + e(b + a'c) + ab'd$$
$$= (d' + ab')(d + a'b'c' + abc) + e(b + a'c)$$
$$= (d' + ab')(d + (a + b'c')(a' + bc)) + e(b + a'c)$$
$$\quad 1\ 2\ \ 3\ \ \ 4\qquad 5\ \ 6\ 7\ \ \ 8\ \ 9\ \ \ 10\ 11\ 12\ 13$$

Another approach is

$$g = a'(b'c'd' + ce) + a(bcd' + b'd) + be$$
$$= [a + b'c'd' + ce][a' + bcd' + b'd] + be$$
$$= [a + (c + b'd')(c' + e)][a' + (b + d)(b' + cd')] + be$$
$$\quad 1\quad\ \ 2\ \ \ 3\ 4\ \ \ 5\qquad 6\quad 7\ \ \ 3\ \ 8\quad 9\ 10\ \ \ 11\ 12$$

where gate three is used twice, as follows.

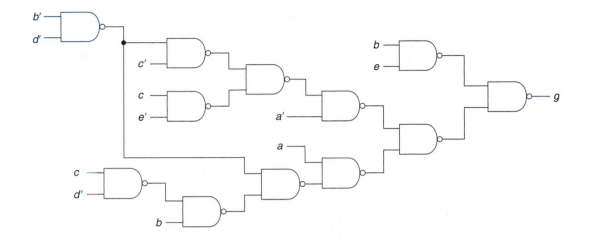

23. For the following function, show the block diagram for a NAND gate implementation that uses only four 7400 series NAND gate modules. No gate may be used as a NOT. Assume that all variables are available both uncomplemented and complemented. (Note that a two-level solution would require 2 six-input gates and a five-input gate (each of which would be implemented with a 7430 module containing 1 eight-input gate), plus a 7420 for the four-input gate and a 7410 for the 2 three-input gates and the 1 two-input gate.)

$$g = abcdef + d'e'f + a'b' + c'd'e' + a'def' + abcd'f'$$

$$g = abc(def + d'f') + d'e'(c' + f) + a'(b' + def')$$

This requires 1 four-input gate (for the first term), 4 three-input gates, and 5 two-input gates (one 7420, with the second gate used as a three-input one, one 7410, and two 7400s with three gates unused). If we required that no four-input gates be used, we could further manipulate the algebra as follows:

$$g = [a' + bc(def + d'f')][a + b' + def'] + d'e'(c' + f)$$

using P14a on the first and last terms, which would require 5 three-input gates and 6 two-input gates (still four modules).

We could also do a completely different factoring, yielding

$$g = de(abcf + a'f') + d'(abcf' + e'f + c'e') + a'b'$$
$$= [d' + e(abcf + a'f')][d + abcf' + e'f + c'e'] + a'b'$$
$$= [d' + e(a' + f)(f' + abc)]$$
$$\qquad \cdot [d + c'e' + (f + abc)(f' + e')] + a'b'$$

This requires 3 three-input gates and 10 two-input gates (also four modules), as shown below.

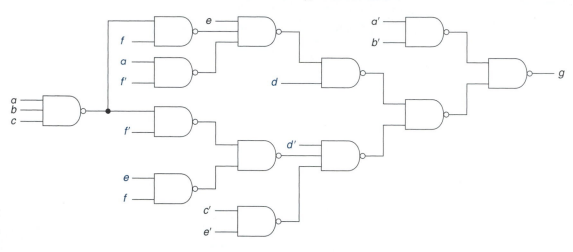

2.10 EXERCISES

1. Show a truth table for a 1-bit full subtractor that has a borrow input b_{in} and inputs x and y, and produces a difference, d, and a borrow output, b_{out}.

$$b^{in}$$
$$x$$
$$\underline{-y}$$
$$b_{out}\ d$$

2. Show truth tables for each of the following.

   *a. There are four inputs and three outputs. The inputs, w, x, y, z, are codes for the grade that may be received:

0000 A	0100 B−	1000 D+	1100 Incomplete
0001 A−	0101 C+	1001 D	1101 Satisfactory
0010 B+	0110 C	1010 D−	1110 Unsatisfactory
0011 B	0111 C−	1011 F	1111 Pass

   The outputs are

   1: a 1 if and only if the grade is C or better (only letter grades; C− is not C or better)

   2: a 1 if and only if the university will count it toward the 120 credits required for a degree (passing grade only)

   3: a 1 if and only if it will be counted in computing a grade point average (letter grades only).

b. This system has four inputs and three outputs. The first two inputs, *a* and *b*, represent a 2-bit binary number (range of 0 to 3). A second binary number (same range) is represented by the other two inputs, *c* and *d*. The output *f* is to be 1 if and only if the two numbers differ by exactly 2. Output *g* is to be 1 if and only if the numbers are equal. Output *h* is to be 1 if and only if the second number is larger than the first.

c. The system has four inputs. The first two, *a* and *b*, represent a number in the range 1 to 3 (0 is not used). The other two, *c* and *d*, represent a second number in the same range. The output, *y*, is to be 1 if and only if the first number is greater than the second or the second is 2 greater than the first.

*d. A system has one output, *F*, and four inputs, where the first two inputs (*A, B*) represent one 2-bit binary number (in the range 0 to 3) and the second two inputs (*C, D*) represent another binary number (same range). *F* is to be 1 if and only if the two numbers are equal or if they differ by exactly 1.

e. A system has one output, *F*, and four inputs, where the first two inputs (*A, B*) represent one 2-bit binary number (in the range 0 to 3) and the second two inputs (*C, D*) represent another binary number (same range). *F* is to be 1 if and only if the sum of the two numbers is odd.

f. The system has four inputs. The first two, *a* and *b*, represent a number in the range 0 to 2 (3 is not used). The other two, *c* and *d*, represent a second number in the same range. The output, *y*, is to be 1 if and only if the two numbers do not differ by more than 1.

g. The problem is to design a ball and strike counter for baseball. The inputs are how many balls (0, 1, 2, or 3) before this pitch, how many strikes (0, 1, 2) before this pitch, and what happens on this pitch. The outputs are how many balls after this pitch (0, 1, 2, 3, 4) or how many strikes after this pitch (0, 1, 2, 3).

In baseball, there are four outcomes of any pitch (from the point of view of this problem). It can be a strike, a foul ball, a ball, or anything else that will end this batter's turn (such as a hit or a fly out).

A foul ball is considered a strike, except when there are already two strikes, in which case the number of strikes remain 2. The output is to indicate the number of balls and strikes after this pitch (even if the pitch is the fourth ball or the third strike, in which case the batter's turn is over). If the batter's turn is over for any other reason, the output should indicate 0 balls and 0 strikes.

Show the code for the inputs (there are six inputs, two for what happened on that pitch, two for the number of balls, and two for the number of strikes) and for the outputs (there should be 5: 3 for balls and 2 for strikes). Then show the 64 line truth table.

*h. The months of the year are coded in four variables, *abcd*, such that January is 0000, February is 0001, . . . , and December is 1011. The remaining 4 combinations are never used. (Remember: 30 days has September, April, June, and November. All the rest have 31, except February. . . .) Show a truth table for a function, *g*, that is 1 if the month has 31 days and 0 if it does not.

i. The months of the year are coded as in 2h, except that February of a leap year is coded as 1100. Show a truth table with five outputs, *v, w, x, y, z* that indicates the number of days in the selected month.

j. Repeat 2i, except that the outputs are to be in BCD (8421 code). There are now six outputs, *u, v, w, x, y, z* (where the first decimal digit is coded 0, 0, *u, v* and the second digit is coded *w, x, y, z*).

k. The system has four inputs, *a, b, c,* and *d* and one output, *f*. The last three inputs (*b, c, d*) represent a binary number, *n*, in the range 0 to 7; however, the input 0 never occurs. The first input (*a*) specifies which of two computations is made.

$a = 0$: *f* is 1   iff *n* is a multiple of 2
$a = 1$: *f* is 1   iff *n* is a multiple of 3

l. The system has four inputs, *a, b, c,* and *d* and one output, *f*. The first two inputs (*a, b*) represent one binary number (in the range 0 to 3) and the last two (*c, d*) represent another number in the range 1 to 3 (0 never occurs). The output, *f*, is to be 1 iff the second number is at least two larger than the first.

3. Show a block diagram of a circuit using AND and OR gates for each side of each of the following equalities:

*a. P2a: $a + (b + c) = (a + b) + c$
b. P8a: $a(b + c) = ab + ac$

4. Show a truth table for the following functions:

*a. $F = X'Y + Y'Z' + XYZ$
b. $G = XY + (X' + Z)(Y + Z')$
c. $H = WX + XY' + WX'Z + XYZ' + W'XY'$

5. Determine, using truth tables, which expressions in each of the groups are equal:

a. $f = ac' + a'c + bc$
$g = (a + c)(a' + b + c')$

*b. $f = a'c' + bc + ab'$
    $g = b'c' + a'c' + ac$
    $h = b'c' + ac + a'b$

c. $f = ab + ac + a'bd$
    $g = bd + ab'c + abd'$

6. For each of the following expressions, indicate which (if any) of the following apply (more than one may apply):

   i.   Product term
   ii. SOP expression
   iii. Sum term
   iv. POS expression

   a. $abc'd + b'cd + ad'$
   *b. $a' + b + cd$
   c. $b'c'd'$
   *d. $(a + b)c'$
   e. $a' + b$
   *f. a'
   *g. $a(b + c) + a'(b' + d)$
   h. $(a + b' + d)(a' + b + c)$

*7. For the expressions of problem 4, how many literals are in each?

8. Using properties 1 to 10, reduce the following expressions to a minimum SOP form. Show each step (number of terms and number of literals in minimum shown in parentheses).

   *a. $x'z + xy'z + xyz$ (1 term, 1 literal)
   b. $x'y'z' + x'yz + xyz$ (2 terms, 5 literals)
   c. $x'y'z' + x'y'z + xy'z + xyz'$ (3 terms, 7 literals)
   *d. $a'b'c' + a'b'c + abc + ab'c$ (2 terms, 4 literals)
   e. $x'y'z' + x'yz' + x'yz + xyz$ (2 terms, 4 literals)
   *f. $x'y'z' + x'y'z + x'yz + xyz + xyz'$

                    (2 solutions, each with 3 terms, 6 literals)

   g. $x'y'z' + x'y'z + x'yz + xy'z + xyz + xyz'$

                    (3 terms, 5 literals)

   h. $a'b'c' + a'bc' + a'bc + ab'c + abc' + abc$

                    (3 terms, 5 literals)

9. Using Properties 1 to 10, reduce the following expressions to a minimum POS form. The number of terms and number of literals are shown in parentheses.

   a. $(a + b + c)(a + b' + c)(a + b' + c')(a' + b' + c')$

                    (2 terms, 4 literals)

    b. $(x + y + z)(x + y + z')(x + y' + z)(x + y' + z')$

                   (1 term, 1 literal)

    *c. $(a + b + c')(a + b' + c')(a' + b' + c')(a' + b' + c)$

         $(a' + b + c)$ (2 solutions, each with 3 terms, 6 literals)

10. Show a block diagram of a system using AND, OR, and NOT gates to implement the following functions. Assume that variables are available only uncomplemented. Do not manipulate the algebra.

    a. $P'Q' + PR + Q'R$

    b. $ab + c(a + b)$

    *c. $wx'(v + y'z) + (w'y + v')(x + yz)'$

11. For each of the following circuits,

     i.   find an algebraic expression

     ii.   put it in sum of product form.

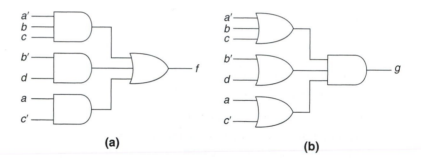

             (a)   **(b)**

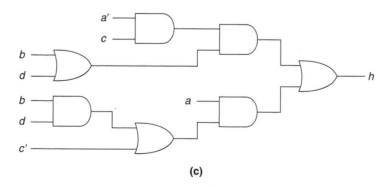

                             (c)

12. Find the complement of the following expressions. Only single variables may be complemented in the answer.

    *a. $f = abd' + b'c' + a'cd + a'bc'd$

    b. $g = (a + b' + c)(a' + b + c)(a + b' + c')$

    c. $h = (a + b)(b' + c) + d'(a'b + c)$

13. For each of the following functions:

$f(x, y, z) = \Sigma m(1, 3, 6)$
$g(x, y, z) = \Sigma m(0, 2, 4, 6)$

a. Show the truth table.

b. Show an algebraic expression in sum of minterms form.

c. Show a minimum SOP expression (a: 2 terms, 5 literals; b: 1 term, 1 literal).

d. Show the minterms of f' (complement of f) in numeric form.

e. Show an algebraic expression in product of maxterms form.

f. Show a minimum POS expression (f: 2 solutions, 3 terms, 6 literals; g: 1 term, 1 literal)

*14. For each of the following functions,

a b c	f	g
0 0 0	0	1
0 0 1	1	1
0 1 0	0	0
0 1 1	0	0
1 0 0	0	1
1 0 1	1	1
1 1 0	1	1
1 1 1	1	0

a. Show the minterms in numerical form.

b. Show an algebraic expression in sum of minterms form.

c. Show a minimum SOP expression (f: 2 terms, 4 literals; g: 2 terms, 3 literals).

d. Show the minterms of f' (complement of f) in numeric form.

e. Show an algebraic expression in product of maxterms form.

f. Show a minimum POS expression (f: 2 terms, 4 literals; g: 2 terms, 4 literals)

*15. Consider the following function with don't cares:

$G(X, Y, Z) = \Sigma m(5, 6) + \Sigma d(1, 2, 4)$

For each of the following expressions, indicate whether it could be used as a solution for G. (Note: it may not be a minimum solution.)

a. $XYZ' + XY'Z$ d. $Y'Z + XZ' + X'Z$

b. $Z' + XY'Z$ e. $XZ' + X'Z$

c. $X(Y' + Z')$ f. $YZ' + Y'Z$

16. Show that the NOR is functionally complete by implementing a NOT, a two-input AND, and a two-input OR using only two-input NORs.

17. For each of the following circuits,

  i. find an algebraic expression

 ii. put it in SOP form.

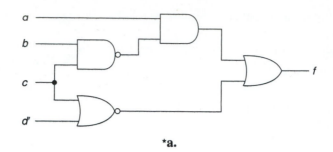

*a.

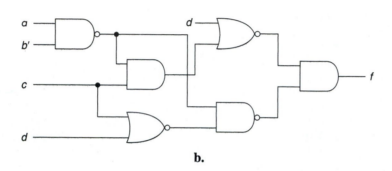

b.

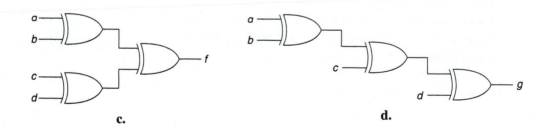

c.

d.

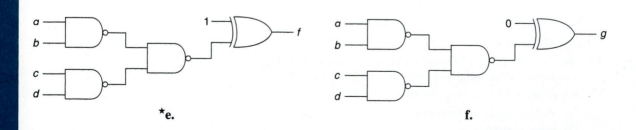

*e.

f.

18. Show a block diagram corresponding to each of the expressions below using only NAND gates. Assume all inputs are available both uncomplemented and complemented. Do not manipulate the functions to simplify the algebra.

   a. $f = wy' + wxz' + xy'z + w'x'z$

   b. $g = wx + (w' + y)(x + y')$

   c. $h = z(x'y + w'x') + w(y' + xz')$

   *d. $F = D[B'(A' + E') + AE(B + C)] + BD'(A'C' + AE')$

19. Reduce the following expressions to a minimum SOP form, using P1 through P12. Show each step (number of terms and number of literals in minimum shown in parentheses).

   a. $h = ab'c + bd + bcd' + ab'c' + abc'd$ (3 terms, 6 literals)

   b. $h = ab' + bc'd' + abc'd + bc$ (3 terms, 5 literals)

   *c. $f = ab + a'bd + bcd + abc' + a'bd' + a'c$
      (2 terms, 3 literals)

   d. $g = abc + abd + bc'd'$ (2 terms, 5 literals)

20. Reduce the following expressions to a minimum SOP form. Show each step and the property used (number of terms and number of literals in minimum shown in parentheses).

   a. $f = x'yz + w'x'z + x'y + wxy + w'y'z$ (3 terms, 7 literals)

   b. $G = A'B'C' + AB'D + BCD' + A'BD + CD + A'D$
      (4 terms, 9 literals)

   *c. $F = W'YZ' + Y'Z + WXZ + WXYZ' + XY'Z + W'Y'Z'$
      (3 terms, 7 literals)

   d. $g = wxz + xy'z + wz' + xyz + wxy'z + w'y'z'$
      (3 terms, 6 literals)

   *e. $G = B'C'D + BC + A'BD + ACD + A'D$
      (3 terms, 6 literals)

   f. $h = abc' + ab'd + bcd + a'bc$ (3 terms, 8 literals)

   *g. $g = a'bc' + bc'd + abd + abc + bcd' + a'bd'$
      (2 solutions, 3 terms, 9 literals)

21. i. For the following functions, use consensus to add as many new terms to the SOP expression given.

   ii. Then reduce each to a minimum SOP, showing each step and the property used.

   *a. $f = a'b'c' + a'bd + a'cd' + abc$ (3 terms, 8 literals)

   b. $g = wxy + w'y'z + xyz + w'yz'$ (3 terms, 8 literals)

22. Expand the following functions to sum of minterms form:

   a. $f(a, b, c) = ab' + b'c'$

   *b. $g(x, y, z) = x' + yz + y'z'$

   c. $h(a, b, c, d) = ab'c + bd + a'd'$

23. Convert each of the following expressions to SOP form:

   a. $(a + b + c + d')(b + c' + d)(a + c)$

   b. $(a' + b + c')(b + c' + d)(b' + d')$

   *c. $(w' + x)(y + z)(w' + y)(x + y' + z)$

24. Convert each of the following expressions to POS form:

   a. $AC + A'D'$

   b. $w'xy' + wxy + xz$

   *c. $bc'd + a'b'd + b'cd'$

25. Implement each of the following expressions (which are already in minimum SOP form) using only two-input NAND gates. No gate may be used as a NOT. All inputs are available both uncomplemented and complemented. (The number of gates required is shown in parentheses.)

   *a. $f = wy' + wxz' + y'z + w'x'z$　　　　　　(7 gates)

   b. $ab'd' + bde' + bc'd + a'ce$　　　　　　(10 gates)

   c. $H = A'B'E' + A'B'CD + B'D'E' + BDE' + BC'E + ACE'$

                                         (14 gates)

   *d. $F = A'B'D' + ABC' + B'CD'E + A'B'C + BC'D$　(11 gates)

   e. $G = B'D'E' + A'BC'D + ACE + AC'E' + B'CE$

                     (12 gates, one of which is shared)

26. Each of the following is already in minimum SOP form. All variables are available both uncomplemented and complemented. Find two solutions each of which uses no more than the number of integrated circuit packages of NAND gates (4 two-input or 3 three-input or 2 four-input gates per package) listed. One solution must use only two and three input gates; the other must use at least 1 four-input gate package.

   *a. $F = ABCDE + B'E' + CD'E' + BC'D'E + A'B'C$

         $+ A'BC'E$　　　　　　　　　　　(3 packages)

   b. $G = ABCDEF + A'B'D' + C'D'E + AB'CE' + A'BC'DF$

         $+ ABE'F'$　　　　　　　　　　　(4 packages)

2.11　CHAPTER 2 TEST (100 MINUTES, OR TWO 50-MINUTE TESTS)

1. The inputs of this system A and B represent one binary number in the range 0:3. The inputs C and D represent a second binary number (also in the range 0:3). There are three outputs, X, Y, and Z.

    Show a truth table such that Y and Z represent a number equal to the magnitude of the difference of the two inputs and X is 1 if and only if the first is larger. Two lines of the table are filled in.

A	B	C	D	X	Y	Z
0	0	0	0			
0	0	0	1			
0	0	1	0			
0	0	1	1			
0	1	0	0			
0	1	0	1			
0	1	1	0	0	0	1
0	1	1	1			
1	0	0	0			
1	0	0	1	1	0	1
1	0	1	0			
1	0	1	1			
1	1	0	0			
1	1	0	1			
1	1	1	0			
1	1	1	1			

2. Use a truth table to demonstrate whether or not the following functions are equal:

$f = a'b' + a'c' + ab$
$g = (b' + c')(a' + b)$

a b c	f	g
0 0 0		
0 0 1		
0 1 0		
0 1 1		
1 0 0		
1 0 1		
1 1 0		
1 1 1		

3. Reduce the following expression to a SOP expression with two terms and four literals. Show each step.

$a'b'c + a'bc + ab'c + ab'c'$

4. For each part, assume all variables are available both uncomplemented and complemented.

$f = ab'c + ad + bd$

a. Show a block diagram for a two-level implementation of f using AND and OR gates.

b. Show a block diagram for an implementation of f using only two-input AND and OR gates.

5. For the following truth table

x	y	z	f
0	0	0	1
0	0	1	0
0	1	0	1
0	1	1	1
1	0	0	0
1	0	1	1
1	1	0	0
1	1	1	1

   a.   Write a sum of minterms function in numeric form, for example,

$$\Sigma m(0, \ldots)$$

   b.   Write a sum of minterms function in algebraic form, for example,

$$x'yz + \cdots$$

   c.   Find one minimum SOP expression (3 terms, 6 literals).

   d.   Find a POS expression in product of maxterms form.

   e.   Find a minimum POS form (2 terms, 5 literals).

6. Assume all inputs are available both uncomplemented and complemented. Show an implementation of

$$g = wx + wz + w'x' + w'y'z'$$
$$= (w' + x + z)(w + x' + y')(w + x' + z')$$

   a.   using NAND gates of any size

   b.   using NOR gates of any size

   c.   using two-input NAND gates (none of which may be used as a NOT)

7. For each of the following functions find a minimum SOP expression (3 terms, 6 literals). Show each algebraic step.

   a. $f = b'd' + bc'd + b'cd' + bcd + ab'd$

5-POINT BONUS: Find a second minimum sum of products.

   b. $g = xy'z' + yz + xy'z + wxy + xz$

8. a. Expand the following to sum of minterms (sum of standard product terms). Eliminate any duplicates.

$$g = a' + ac + b'c$$

   b.   Manipulate the following to a SOP expression.

$$f = (x' + y)(w' + y + z')(y' + z)(w + y' + z')$$

9. Implement the following function using only two-input NAND gates. No gate may be used as a NOT gate. The function is in minimum SOP form. All inputs are available both uncomplemented and complemented.

$$f = ac + bcd + a'b'd' \hspace{3cm} \text{(7 gates)}$$

10. Implement the following function using only two-input NAND gates. No gate may be used as a NOT gate. The function is in minimum SOP form. All inputs are available both uncomplemented and complemented.

$$f = abc + ac'd'e' + a'd'e + ce + cd$$

(Full credit for 11 gates, 5-point bonus for 10 gates)

The Karnaugh Map

The algebraic methods developed in Chapter 2 allow us, in theory, to simplify any function. However, there are a number of problems with that approach. There is no formal method, such as first apply Property 10, then P14, etc. The approach is totally heuristic, depending heavily on experience. After manipulating a function, we often cannot be sure whether it is a minimum. We may not always find the minimum, even though it appears that there is nothing else to do. Furthermore, it gets rather difficult to do algebraic simplification with more than four or five variables. Finally, it is easy to make copying mistakes as we rewrite the equations.

In this chapter we will examine an approach that is easier to implement, the *Karnaugh map** (sometimes referred to as a K-map). This is a graphical approach to finding suitable product terms for use in sum of product expressions. (The product terms that are "suitable" for use in minimum SOP expressions are referred to as *prime implicants*. We will define that term shortly.) The map is useful for problems of up to six variables and is particularly straightforward for most problems of three or four variables. Although there is no guarantee of finding a minimum solution, the methods we will develop nearly always produce a minimum. We will adapt the approach (with no difficulty) to finding minimum POS expressions, to problems with don't cares, and to multiple output problems.

Other methods are presented in Marcovitz, Alan, *Introduction to Logic Design*, Second Edition, McGraw-Hill, 2005.

3.1 INTRODUCTION TO THE KARNAUGH MAP

In this section, we will look at the layout of two-, three-, and four-variable maps. The Karnaugh map consists of one square for each possible minterm in a function. Thus, a two-variable map has 4 squares, a three-variable map has 8 squares, and a four-variable map has 16 squares.

Three views of the two-variable map are shown in Map 3.1. In each, the upper right square, for example, corresponds to $A = 1$ and $B = 0$, minterm 2.

---

*This tool was introduced in 1953 by Maurice Karnaugh.

Map 3.1 Two-variable Karnaugh maps.

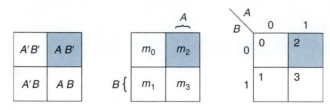

When we plot a function, we put a 1 in each square corresponding to a minterm that is included in the function, and put a 0 in or leave blank those squares not included in the function. For functions with don't cares, an X goes in the square for which the minterm is a don't care. Map 3.2 shows examples of these.

Map 3.2 Plotting functions.

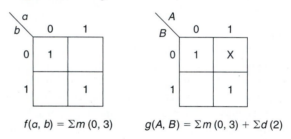

$$f(a, b) = \Sigma m\,(0, 3) \qquad g(A, B) = \Sigma m\,(0, 3) + \Sigma d\,(2)$$

Three-variable maps have eight squares, arranged in a rectangle as shown in Map 3.3.*

Map 3.3 Three-variable maps.

AB	$A'B'$	$A'B$	AB	AB'
C	00	01	11	10
$C'\ 0$	$A'\,B'\,C'$	$A'\,B\,C'$	$A\,B\,C'$	$A\,B'\,C'$
$C\ 1$	$A'\,B'\,C$	$A'\,B\,C$	$A\,B\,C$	$A\,B'\,C$

AB	00	01	11	10
C				
0	0	2	6	4
1	1	3	7	5

*Some people label the row(s) of the map with the first variable(s) and the columns with the others. The three-variable map then looks like

BC	00	01	11	10
A				
0	0	1	3	2
1	4	5	7	6

This version of the map produces the same results as the other.

Notice that the last two columns are not in numeric order. That is the key idea that makes the map work. By organizing the map that way, the minterms in adjacent squares can always be combined using the adjacency property,

P9a. $ab + ab' = a$

EXAMPLE 3.1

$m_0 + m_1$: $A'B'C' + A'B'C = A'B'$

$m_4 + m_6$: $AB'C' + ABC' = AC'$

$m_7 + m_5$: $ABC + AB'C = AC$

Also, the outside columns (and the outside rows when there are four rows) are adjacent. Thus,

$m_0 + m_4$: $A'B'C' + AB'C' = B'C'$

$m_1 + m_5$: $A'B'C + AB'C = B'C$

If we had ordered the columns in numeric order, as shown in Map 3.4 (where the algebraic version of the minterms is shown only for m_2 and m_4), we would not be able to combine adjacent squares:

Map 3.4   **Incorrect** arrangement of the map.

C \ AB	00	01	10	11
0	0	2 $A'BC'$	4 $AB'C'$	6
1	1	3	5	7

$m_2 + m_4 = A'BC' + AB'C' = C'(A'B + AB')$

However, we cannot manipulate that into a single term.

Product terms that correspond to the sum of two minterms appear as two adjacent 1's on the map. The terms of Example 3.1 are shown in Map 3.5.

It is sometimes more convenient to draw the map in a vertical orientation (that is, two columns and four rows) as shown in Map 3.6. Both versions of the map produce the same results.

In reading the map, it is useful to label the pairs of columns (in those arrangements where there are four columns) as shown in Map 3.7. Thus, 1's in squares 4 and 6 are in the A columns and the C' row (that is, not in the C row), producing the AC' term as shown earlier.

Map 3.5 Product terms corresponding to groups of two.

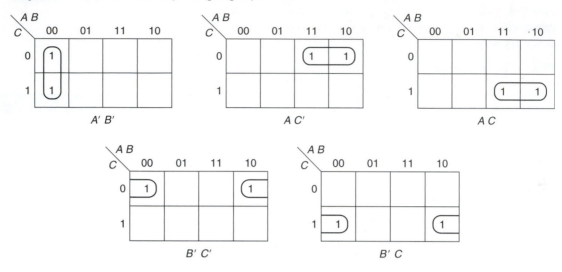

Map 3.6 Vertical orientation of three-variable map.

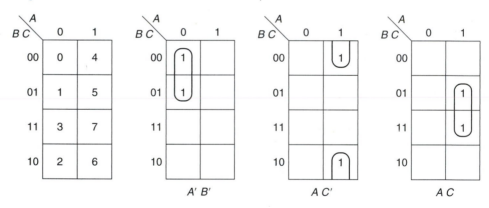

Map 3.7 Map with columns labeled.

The four-variable map consists of 16 squares in the 4 by 4 arrangement shown in Map 3.8.

As with the three-variable map, 1's in two adjacent squares (where the top and bottom rows as well as the left and right columns are considered to be adjacent) correspond to a single product term (combined using P9a). Example 3.2 shows three such terms.

Map 3.8 The four-variable map.

CD \ AB	00	01	11	10
00	0	4	12	8
01	1	5	13	9
11	3	7	15	11
10	2	6	14	10

CD \ AB	00	01	11	10
00	$A'B'C'D'$	$A'BC'D'$	$ABC'D'$	$AB'C'D'$
01	$A'B'C'D$	$A'BC'D$	$ABC'D$	$AB'C'D$
11	$A'B'CD$	$A'BCD$	$ABCD$	$AB'CD$
10	$A'B'CD'$	$A'BCD'$	$ABCD'$	$AB'CD'$

EXAMPLE 3.2

$m_{13} + m_9$: $ABC'D + AB'C'D = AC'D$

$m_3 + m_{11}$: $A'B'CD + AB'CD = B'CD$

$m_0 + m_2$: $A'B'C'D' + A'B'CD' = A'B'D'$

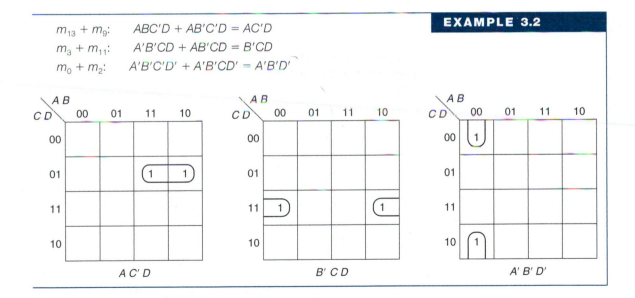

$A C' D$ $B' C D$ $A' B' D'$

Up to this point, all of the product terms that we have shown correspond to two minterms combined using P9a. These correspond to a product term with one literal missing, that is, with only two literals in a three-variable function and three literals in a four-variable function. Let us next look at the maps of Map 3.9 with a group of four 1's.

On the map to the left, we have circled two groups of two, one form-ing the term $A'C$ and the other forming the term AC. Obviously, P9a can be applied again to these two terms, producing

$$A'C + AC = C$$

Map 3.9 A group of four 1's.

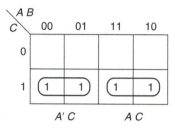 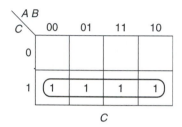

That is shown on the map to the right as a rectangle of four 1's. In gen-eral, rectangles of four 1's will correspond to a product term with two of the variables missing (that is, a single literal for three-variable problems and a two-literal term for four-variable problems).

We could have factored C from all of the terms producing

$$A'B'C + A'BC + ABC + AB'C = C(A'B' + A'B + AB + AB')$$

However, the sum inside the parentheses is just a sum of all of the minterms of A and B; that must be 1. Thus, we can get the result in just that one step. Indeed, we could have added a secondary property to P9, namely,

P9aa. $a'b' + a'b + ab + ab' = 1$

           P9bb. $(a' + b')(a' + b)(a + b)(a + b') = 0$

These can be proved by repeated application of P9, first to the first two terms, then to the last two terms, and finally to the resulting terms as shown

$$(a'b' + a'b) + (ab + ab') = (a') + (a) = 1$$
$$[(a' + b')(a' + b)][(a + b)(a + b')] = [a'][a] = 0$$

Some examples of such groups for four-variable problems are shown in Map 3.10.

The easiest way to identify the term from the map is by determining in which row(s) and column(s) all of the 1's are located. Thus, on the first map, the 1's in the group on the left are all in the 0 0 ($A'B'$) column and thus the term is $A'B'$. The other group has its 1's in the 11 and 10 columns; the common feature is the 1 in the A position (which corre-sponds to A). Furthermore, the 1's are in the 01 and 11 rows; there is a common 1 in the D position. Thus, the term is AD. In the middle map, the

Map 3.10 Examples of groups of four.

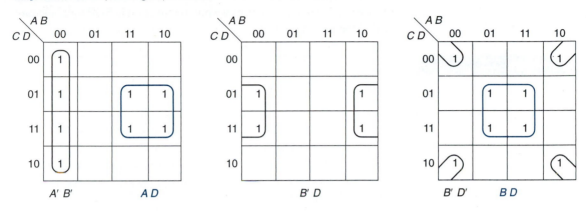

1's are in the 00 and 10 columns, producing B' and the 01 and 11 rows, resulting in D; the term is thus $B'D$. (Notice, by the way, that that term also appears on the first map, even though it was not circled.) On the last map, the four corners produce the term $B'D'$ (since all the 1's are in the 00 or 10 columns and the 00 or 10 rows). The middle group is BD. Any of these terms could also be obtained algebraically by first writing the minterms, then applying P10a to pairs of terms, and then applying it again to the two terms that resulted (as we did for the three-variable example). However, the whole idea of the map is to eliminate the need to do algebra.

Two adjacent groups of four can be combined in a similar way to form a group of eight squares (with three of the literals missing). Two such groups are shown in Map 3.11. The terms are A' for the map on the left and D' for the map on the right.

Map 3.11 Groups of eight.

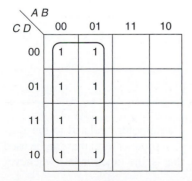
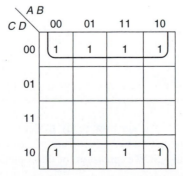

We can plot any function on the map. Either, we know the minterms, and use that form of the map, or we put the function in SOP form and plot each of the product terms.

EXAMPLE 3.3

Map

$$F = AB' + AC + A'BC'$$

The map for F follows, with each of the product terms circled. Each of the two-literal terms corresponds to two squares on the map (since one of the variables is missing). The AB' term is in the 10 column. The AC term is in the $C = 1$ row and in the 11 and 10 columns (with a common 1 in the A position). Finally, the minterm $A'BC'$ corresponds to one square, in the 01 ($A'B$) column and in the $C = 0$ row.

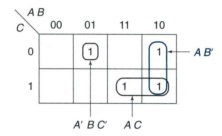

We could have obtained the same map by first expanding F to minterm form algebraically, that is,

$$F = AB'(C' + C) + AC(B' + B) + A'BC'$$
$$= AB'C' + AB'C + AB'C + ABC + A'BC'$$
$$= m_4 + m_5 + m_5 + m_7 + m_2$$
$$= m_2 + m_4 + m_5 + m_7$$

(removing duplicates and reordering)

We can then use the numeric map and produce the same result.

	AB			
C	00	01	11	10
0	0	2 \ 1	6	4 \ 1
1	1	3	7 \ 1	5 \ 1

We are now ready to define some terminology related to the Karnaugh map. An *implicant* of a function is a product term that can be used in a SOP expression for that function, that is, the function is 1 whenever the implicant is 1 (and maybe other times, as well). From the point of view of the map, an implicant is a rectangle of 1, 2, 4, 8, . . . (any power of 2) 1's. That rectangle may not include any 0's. All minterms are implicants.

Consider the function, F, of Map 3.12. The second map shows the first four groups of 2; the third map shows the other groups of 2 and the group of 4.

Map 3.12 A function to illustrate definitions.

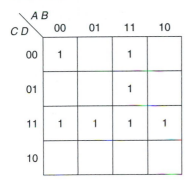 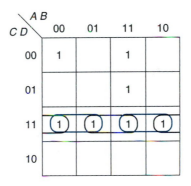 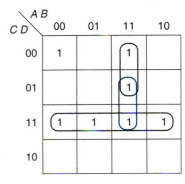

The implicants of F are

Minterms	Groups of 2	Groups of 4
$A'B'C'D'$	$A'CD$	CD
$A'B'CD$	BCD	
$A'BCD$	ACD	
$ABC'D'$	$B'CD$	
$ABC'D$	ABC'	
$ABCD$	ABD	
$AB'CD$		

Any SOP expression for F must be a sum of implicants. Indeed, we must choose enough implicants such that each of the 1's of F are included in at least one of these implicants. Such a SOP expression is sometimes referred to as a *cover* of F, and we sometimes say that an implicant *covers* certain minterms (for example, ACD covers m_{11} and m_{15}).

Implicants must be rectangular in shape and the number of 1's in the rectangle must be a power of 2. Thus, neither of the functions whose maps are shown in Example 3.4 are covered by a single implicant, but rather by the sum of two implicants each (in their simplest form).

EXAMPLE 3.4

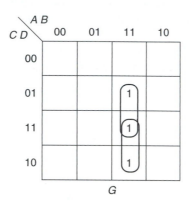

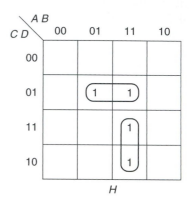

G consists of three minterms, *ABC'D, ABCD,* and *ABCD',* in the shape of a rectangle. It can be reduced no further than is shown on the map, namely, to *ABC + ABD,* since it is a group of three 1's, not two or four. Similarly, *H* has the same three minterms plus *A'BC'D*; it is a group of four, but not in the shape of a rectangle. The minimum expression is, as shown on the map, *BC'D + ABC.* (Note that *ABD* is also an implicant of *G,* but it includes 1's that are already included in the other terms.)

Map 3.13   Prime implicants.

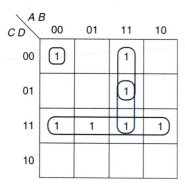

A *prime implicant* is an implicant that (from the point of view of the map) is not fully contained in any one other implicant. For example, it is a rectangle of two 1's that is not part of a single rectangle of four 1's. On Map 3.13, all of the prime implicants of *F* are circled. They are *A'B'C'D', ABC', ABD,* and *CD.* Note that the only minterm that is not part of a larger group is m_0 and that the other four implicants that are groups of two 1's are all part of the group of four.

From an algebraic point of view, a prime implicant is an implicant such that if any literal is removed from that term, it is no longer an implicant. From that viewpoint, *A'B'C'D'* is a prime implicant because *B'C'D', A'C'D', A'B'D',* and *A'B'C'* are not implicants (that is, if we remove any literal from that term, we get a term that is 1 for some input combinations for which the function is to be 0). However, *ACD* is not a prime implicant since when we remove *A,* leaving *CD,* we still have an implicant. (Surely, the graphical approach of determining which implicants are prime implicants is easier than the algebraic method of attempting to delete literals.)

The purpose of the map is to help us find minimum SOP expressions (where we defined minimum as being minimum number of product terms (implicants) and among those with the same number of implicants, the ones with the fewest number of literals. However, the only product terms that we need consider are prime implicants. Why? Say we found an implicant that was not a prime implicant. Then, it must be contained in some larger implicant, a prime implicant. But that larger implicant (say four 1's rather than two) has fewer literals. That alone makes a solution using the term that is not a prime implicant not a minimum. (For example, *CD* has two literals, whereas, *ACD* has three.) Furthermore, that larger implicant covers more 1's, which often will mean that we need fewer terms.

An *essential prime implicant* is a prime implicant that includes at least one 1 that is not included in any other prime implicant. (If we were to circle all of the prime implicants of a function, the essential prime implicants are those that circle at least one 1 that no other prime implicant circles.) In the example of Map 3.13, $A'B'C'D'$, ABC', and CD are essential prime implicants; ABD is not. The term *essential* is derived from the idea that we must use that prime implicant in any minimum SOP expression. A word of caution is in order. There will often be a prime implicant that is used in a minimum solution (even in all minimum solutions when more than one equally good solution exists) that is not "essential." That happens when each of the 1's covered by this prime implicant could be covered in other ways. We will see examples of that in Section 3.2.

[SP 1; EX 1]

3.2 MINIMUM SUM OF PRODUCT EXPRESSIONS USING THE KARNAUGH MAP

In this section, we will describe a method for finding minimum SOP expressions using the Karnaugh map. Although this method involves some heuristics, we can all but guarantee that it will lead to a minimum SOP expression (or more than one when multiple solutions exist) for three- and four-variable problems. (It also works for five- and six-variable maps, but our visualization in three dimensions is more limited. We will discuss five-variable maps in detail in Section 3.6.)

In the process of finding prime implicants, we will be considering each of the 1's on the map starting with the most *isolated* 1's. By isolated, we mean that there are few (or no) adjacent squares with a 1 in it. In an *n*-variable map, each square has *n* adjacent squares. Examples for three- and four-variable maps are shown in Map 3.14.

Map 3.14 Adjacencies on three- and four-variable maps.

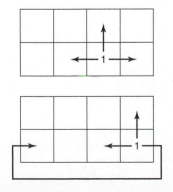

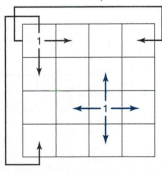

Map Method 1

1. Find all essential prime implicants. Circle them on the map and mark the minterm(s) that make them essential with a star ($\star$). Do this by examining each 1 on the map that has not already been circled. It is usually quickest to start with the most isolated 1's, that is, those that have the fewest adjacent squares with 1's in them.

2. Find *enough* other prime implicants to cover the function. Do this using two criteria:
   a. Choose a prime implicant that covers as many new 1's (that is, those not already covered by a chosen prime implicant).
   b. Avoid leaving isolated uncovered 1's.

It is often obvious what "enough" is. For example, if there are five uncovered 1's and no prime implicants cover more than two of them, then we need at least three more terms. Sometimes, three may not be sufficient, but it usually is.

We will now look at a number of examples to demonstrate this method. First, we will look at the example used to illustrate the definitions.

EXAMPLE 3.5

As noted, m_0 has no adjacent 1's; therefore, it ($A'B'C'D'$) is a prime implicant. Indeed, it is an essential prime implicant, since no other prime implicant covers this 1. (That is always the case when minterms are prime implicants.) The next place that we look is m_{12}, since it has only one adjacent 1. Those 1's are covered by prime implicant ABC'. Indeed, no other prime implicant covers m_{12}, and thus ABC' is essential. (Whenever we have a 1 with only one adjacent 1, that group of two is an essential prime implicant.) At this point, the map has become

and

$$F = A'B'C'D' + ABC' + \cdots$$

Each of the 1's that have not yet been covered are part of the group of four, CD. Each has two adjacent squares with 1's that are part of that group. That will always be the case for a group of four. (Some squares, such as m_{15} may have more than two adjacent 1's.) CD is essential because no other prime implicant covers m_3, m_7, or m_{11}. However, once that group is circled, we have covered the function:

resulting in

$$F = A'B'C'D + ABC' + CD$$

In this example, once we have found the essential prime implicants, we are done; all of the 1's have been covered by one (or more) of the essential prime implicants. We do not need step 2. There may be other prime implicants that were not used (such as ABD in this example).

We start looking at the most isolated 1, m_{11}. It is covered only by the group of two shown, wyz. The other essential prime implicant is $y'z'$ because of m_0, m_8, or m_{12}. None of these are covered by any other prime implicant; each makes that prime implicant essential. The second map shows these two terms circled.

EXAMPLE 3.6

That leaves two 1's uncovered. Each of these can be covered by two different prime implicants; but the only way to cover them both with one term is
shown on the first of the maps below.

Thus, the minimum sum of product solution is

$$f = y'z' + wyz + w'xz$$

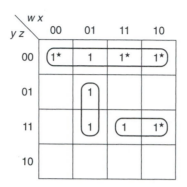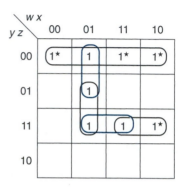

The other two prime implicants are $w'xy'$ and xyz, circled in green on the
last map. They are redundant, however, since they cover no new 1's. Even
though $w'xz$ must be used in a minimum solution, it does not meet the definition of an essential prime implicant; each of the 1's covered by it can be
covered by other prime implicants.

We will next look at the "dead end" example from Chapter 2
(Example 2.2).

EXAMPLE 3.7

$$f = a'b'c' + a'bc' + a'bc + ab'c'$$

In the first attempt at algebraic manipulation, we grouped the first two
minterms. But, as can be seen on the left map below, the two 1's that are left
could not be combined, and resulted in a three-term solution. Furthermore,
$a'c'$ is not an essential prime implicant. If, on the other hand, we used the
map, we could see that choosing the two essential prime implicants on the
right-hand map includes all of the minterms and produces the solution

$$f = a'b + b'c'$$

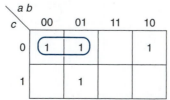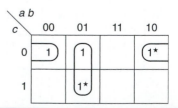

Sometimes, after selecting all of the essential prime implicants, there are two choices for covering the remaining 1's, but only one of these produces a minimum solution, as in Example 3.8.

EXAMPLE 3.8

$f(a, b, c, d) = \Sigma m(0, 2, 4, 6, 7, 8, 9, 11, 12, 14)$

The first map shows the function and the second shows all essential prime implicants circled. In each case, one of the 1's (as indicated with a star, *) can be covered by only that prime implicant. (That is obvious from the last map, where the remaining two prime implicants are circled.)

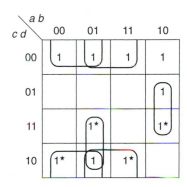 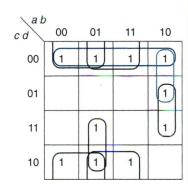

Only one 1 (m_8) is not covered by an essential prime implicant. It can be covered in two ways, by a group of four (in **green**) and a group of two (light green). Clearly, the group of four provides a solution with one less literal, namely,

$f = a'd' + bd' + a'bc + ab'd + c'd'$

When asking whether a 1 makes a group of four an essential prime implicant on a four-variable map, we need find only two adjacent 0's. If there are fewer than two adjacent 0's, this 1 must be either in a group of eight or part of two or more smaller groups. Note that in Example 3.8, m_2 and m_{14} have two adjacent 0's, and thus each makes a prime implicant essential. In contrast, m_0, m_4, m_8, and m_{12} each have only one adjacent 0 and are each covered by two or three prime implicants.

We will now consider some examples with multiple minimum solutions, starting with a three-variable function.

EXAMPLE 3.9

Let us now look back at the expressions used to illustrate the definition of minimum sum of products in Chapter 2:

$$x'yz' + x'yz + xy'z' + xy'z + xyz$$

A map of that function is·shown on the left. The two essential prime implicants are shown on the map on the right.

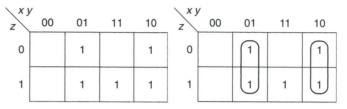

After finding the two essential prime implicants, m_7 is still uncovered. The following maps show the two solutions.

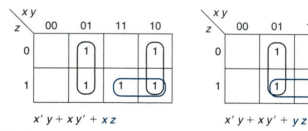

$$x'y + xy' + xz \qquad\qquad x'y + xy' + yz$$

EXAMPLE 3.10

$$g(w, x, y, z) = \Sigma m(2, 5, 6, 7, 9, 10, 11, 13, 15)$$

The function is mapped first, and the two essential prime implicants are shown on the second map, giving

$$g = xz + wz + \cdots$$

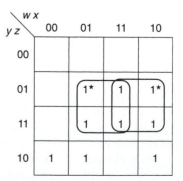

Although m_2 looks rather isolated, it can indeed be covered by $w'yz'$ (with m_6) or by $x'yz'$ (with m_{10}). After choosing the essential prime implicants, the remaining three 1's can each be covered by two different prime implicants. Since three 1's still need to be covered (after choosing the essential prime implicants), and since all the remaining prime implicants are groups of two and thus have three literals, we need at least two more of these prime implicants. Indeed, there are three ways to cover the remaining 1's with two more prime implicants. Using the first criteria, we choose one of the prime implicants that covers two new 1's, $w'yz'$, as shown on the left-hand map.

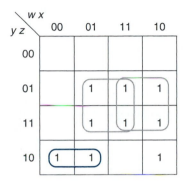
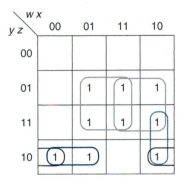
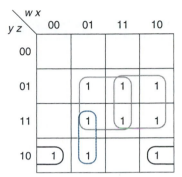

Then, only m_{10} remains and it can be covered either by $wx'y$ or by $x'yz'$, as shown on the center map. Similarly, we could have started with $x'yz'$, in which case we could use $w'xy$ to complete the cover, as on the right map. (We could also have chosen $w'yz'$, but that repeats one of the answers from before.) Thus, the three solutions are

$$g = xz + wz + w'yz' + wx'y$$
$$g = xz + wz + w'yz' + x'yz'$$
$$g = xz + wz + x'yz' + w'xy$$

All three minimum solutions require four terms and 10 literals.

At this point, it is worth stating the obvious. If there are multiple minimum solutions (as was true in this example), all such minimums have the same number of terms and the same number of literals. Any solution that has more terms or more literals is not minimum!

This example is one we call "don't be greedy."

EXAMPLE 3.11

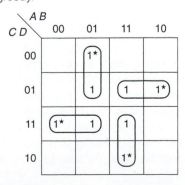

At first glance, one might want to take the only group of four (circled in light green). However, that term is not an essential prime implicant, as is obvious once we circle all of the essential prime implicants and find that the four 1's in the center are covered. Thus, the minimum solution is

$$G = A'BC' + A'CD + ABC + AC'D$$

EXAMPLE 3.12

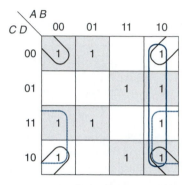

The four essential prime implicants are shown on the second map, leaving three 1's to be covered:

$$F = A'C'D' + AC'D + A'CD + ACD' + \cdots$$

These squares are shaded on the right-hand map. The three other prime implicants, all groups of four, are also shown on the right-hand map. Each of these covers two of the remaining three 1's (no two the same). Thus any two of $B'D'$, AB', and $B'C$ can be used to complete the minimum SOP expression. The resulting three equally good answers are

$$F = A'C'D' + AC'D + A'CD + ACD' + B'D' + AB'$$
$$F = A'C'D' + AC'D + A'CD + ACD' + B'D' + B'C$$
$$F = A'C'D' + AC'D + A'CD + ACD' + AB' + B'C$$

EXAMPLE 3.13

$$G(A, B, C, D) = \Sigma m(0, 1, 3, 7, 8, 11, 12, 13, 15)$$

This is a case with more 1's left uncovered after finding the essential prime implicant. The first map shows all the prime implicants circled. The only essential prime implicant is YZ; five 1's remain to be covered. Since all of the other prime implicants are groups of two, we need three more prime implicants. These 1's are organized in a chain, with each prime implicant linked to one on either side. If we are looking for just one solution, we should follow the guidelines of step 2, choosing two terms that each cover new 1's and then select a term to cover the remaining 1. One such example is

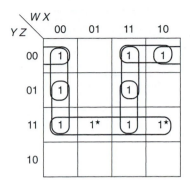 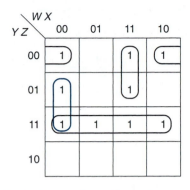 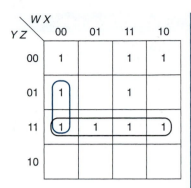

shown on the center map, starting with WXY' and $X'Y'Z'$. If we wish to find all of the minimum solutions, a methodical approach is to start at one end of the chain (as shown in the right-hand map). (We could have started at the other end, with m_{13}, and achieved the same results.) To cover m_1, we must either use $W'X'Z$, as shown in **green** above, or $W'X'Y'$ (as shown on the following maps). Once we have chosen $W'X'Z$, we have no more freedom since the terms shown on the previous center map are the only way to cover the remaining 1's in two additional terms. Thus, one solution is

$$F = YZ + W'X'Z + X'Y'Z' + WXY'$$

The next three maps show the solutions using $W'X'Y'$ to cover m_0.

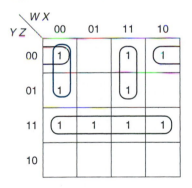 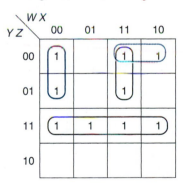 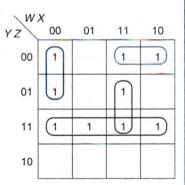

After choosing $W'X'Y'$, there are now three 1's to be covered. We can use the same last two terms as before (left) or use $WY'Z'$ to cover m_8 (right two maps). The other three solutions are thus

$$F = YZ + W'X'Y' + X'Y'Z' + WXY'$$
$$F = YZ + W'X'Y' + WY'Z' + WXY'$$
$$F = YZ + W'X'Y' + WY'Z' + WXZ$$

We will now look at two examples with no essential prime implicants. A classic example of such a function is shown in Example 3.14.

EXAMPLE 3.14

cd \ ab	00	01	11	10
00	1	1		
01		1	1	
11			1	1
10	1			1

cd \ ab	00	01	11	10
00	1	1		
01		1	1	
11			1	1
10	1			1

cd \ ab	00	01	11	10
00	1	1		
01			1	1
11			1	1
10	1			1

There are eight 1's; all prime implicants are groups of two. Thus, we need at least four terms in a minimum solution. There is no obvious place to start; thus, in the second map, we arbitrarily chose one of the terms, $a'c'd'$. Following the guidelines of step 2, we should then choose a second term that covers two new 1's, in such a way as not to leave an isolated uncovered 1. One such term is $bc'd$, as shown on the third map. Another possibility would be $b'cd'$ (the group in the last row). As we will see, that group will also be used. Repeating that procedure, we get the cover on the left map,

$$f = a'c'd' + bc'd + acd + b'cd'$$

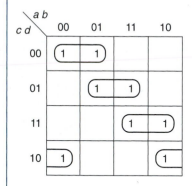

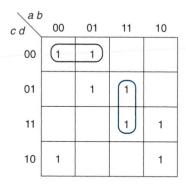

cd \ ab	00	01	11	10
00	1	1		
01		1		
11			1	1
10	1			1

Notice, that if, after starting with $a'c'd'$, we chose one of the prime implicants not included in this solution, such as abd, shown on the middle map, we leave an isolated uncovered 1 (which would require a third term) plus three more 1's (which would require two more terms). A solution using those two terms would require five terms (obviously not minimum since we found one with four).

The other solution to this problem starts with $a'b'd'$, the only other prime implicant to cover m_0. Using the same process, we obtain the map on the right and the only other minimum solution.

$$f = a'b'd' + a'bc' + abd + ab'c$$

EXAMPLE 3.15

$G(A, B, C, D) = \Sigma m(0, 1, 3, 4, 6, 7, 8, 9, 11, 12, 13, 14, 15)$

All of the prime implicants are groups of four. Since there are 13 1's, we need at least four terms. The left-hand map shows all of the prime implicants circled; there are nine. Any 1 that is circled only once would indicate an essential prime implicant. There are none, and thus, there are no essential prime implicants.

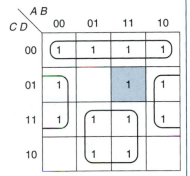

As a starting point, we choose one of the minterms covered by only two prime implicants, say m_0. On the second map, we used $C'D'$ to cover it. Next, we found two additional prime implicants that cover four new 1's each, as shown on the right-hand map. That leaves just m_{13} to be covered. As can be seen on the left-hand map that follows, three different prime implicants can be used. Now, we have three of the minimum solutions.

$$F = C'D' + B'D + BC + \{AB \quad \text{or} \quad AC' \quad \text{or} \quad AD\}$$

If, instead of using $C'D'$ to cover m_0, we use $B'C'$ (the only other prime implicant that covers m_0), as shown on the center map, we can find two other groups of four that each cover four new 1's and leave just m_{13} to be covered. Once again, we have three different ways to complete the cover (the same three terms as before).

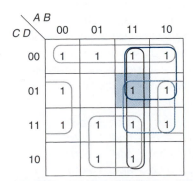
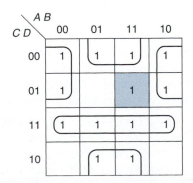
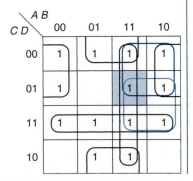

Thus, there are six equally good solutions

$$F = \begin{Bmatrix} C'D' + B'D + BC \\ B'C' + BD' + CD \end{Bmatrix} + \begin{Bmatrix} AB \\ AC' \\ AD \end{Bmatrix}$$

where one group of terms is chosen from the first bracket and an additional term from the second. We are sure that there are no better solutions, since each uses the minimum number of prime implicants, four. Although it may not be obvious without trying other combinations, there are no additional minimum solutions.

A number of other examples are included in Solved Problem 1. Example 3.16 is one of the most complex four-variable problems, requiring more terms than we might estimate at first.

EXAMPLE 3.16

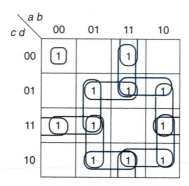

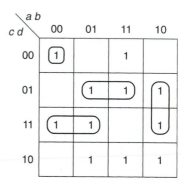

This function has one essential prime implicant (a minterm) and ten other 1's. All of the other prime implicants are groups of two. The center map shows all 13 prime implicants. Note that every 1 (other than m_0) can be covered by two or three different terms.

Since there are ten 1's to be covered by groups of two, we know that we need at least five terms, in addition to $a'b'c'd'$. The right-hand map shows the beginnings of an attempt to cover the function. Each term covers two new 1's without leaving any isolated uncovered 1. (The 1 at the top could be combined with m_{14}.) The four 1's that are left require three additional terms. After trying several other groupings, we can see that it is not possible to cover this function with fewer than seven terms. There are 32 different minimum solutions to this problem. A few of the solutions follow. The remainder are left as an exercise (Ex 2p).

$$f = a'b'c'd' + a'cd + bc'd + ab'd + abc' + a'bc + acd'$$
$$= a'b'c'd' + a'cd + bc'd + ab'd + abd' + bcd' + ab'c$$
$$= a'b'c'd' + b'cd + a'bd + ac'd + abd' + acd' + bcd'$$
$$= a'b'c'd' + b'cd + abc' + bcd' + a'bd + ab'c + ab'd$$

3.3 DON'T CARES

Finding minimum solutions for functions with don't cares does not significantly change the methods we developed in the previous section. We need to modify slightly the definitions of a prime implicant and clarify the definition of an essential prime implicant.

> A *prime implicant* is a rectangle of 1, 2, 4, 8, . . . 1's or X's not included in any one larger rectangle. Thus, from the point of view of finding prime implicants, X's (don't cares) are treated as 1's.

> An *essential prime implicant* is a prime implicant that covers at least one 1 not covered by any other prime implicant (as always). Don't cares (X's) do not make a prime implicant essential.

Now, we just apply the method of the previous section. When we are done, some of the X's may be included and some may not. But we *don't care* whether or not they are included in the function.

$F(A, B, C, D) = \Sigma m(1, 7, 10, 11, 13) + \Sigma d(5, 8, 15)$

EXAMPLE 3.17

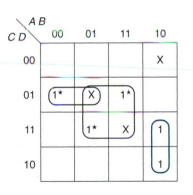

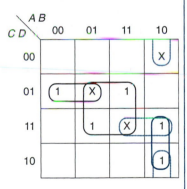

We first mapped the function, entering a 1 for those minterms included in the function and an X for the don't cares. We found two essential prime implicants, as shown on the center map. In each case, the 1's with a star cannot be covered by any other prime implicant. That left the two 1's circled in **green** to cover the rest of the function. That is not an essential prime implicant, since each of the 1's could be covered by another prime implicant (as shown in **light green** on the right-hand map). However, if we did not use $AB'C$, we would need two additional terms, instead of one. Thus, the only minimum solution is

$$F = BD + A'C'D + AB'C$$

and terms $AB'D'$ and ACD are prime implicants not used in the minimum solution. Note that if all of the don't cares were made 1's, we would need a fourth term to cover m_8, making

$$F = BD + A'C'D + AB'C + AB'D' \qquad \text{or}$$
$$F = BD + A'C'D + ACD + AB'D'$$

and that if all of the don't cares were 0's, the function would become

$$F = A'B'C'D + A'BCD + ABC'D + AB'C$$

In either case, the solution is much more complex than when we treated those terms as don't cares (and made two of them 1's and the other a 0).

EXAMPLE 3.18

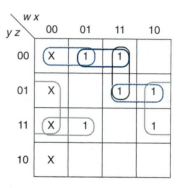

There are two essential prime implicants, as shown on the center map: $x'z$ and $w'yz$. The group of four don't cares, $w'x'$, is a prime implicant (since it is a rectangle of four 1's or X's) but it is not essential (since it does not cover any 1's not covered by some other prime implicant). Surely, a prime implicant made up of all don't cares would never be used, since that would add a term to the sum without covering any additional 1's. The three remaining 1's require two groups of two and thus there are three equally good solutions, each using four terms and 11 literals:

$$g_1 = x'z + w'yz + w'y'z' + wxy'$$
$$g_2 = x'z + w'yz + xy'z' + wxy'$$
$$g_3 = x'z + w'yz + xy'z' + wy'z$$

An important thing to note about Example 3.18 is that the three algebraic expressions are not all equal. The first treats the don't care for m_0 as a 1, whereas the other two (which are equal to each other) treat it as a 0. This will often happen with don't cares. They must treat the specified part of the function (the 1's and the 0's) the same, but the don't cares may take on different values in the various solutions. The maps of Map 3.15 show the three functions.

Map 3.15 The different solutions for Example 3.18.

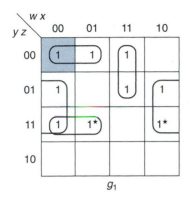 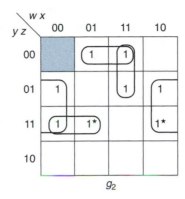 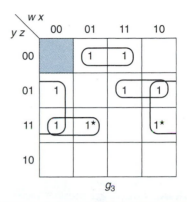

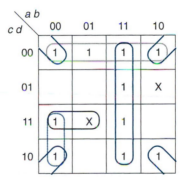

EXAMPLE 3.19

On the left-hand map, we have shown the only essential prime implicant, $c'd'$, and the other group of four that is used in all three solutions, ab. (This must be used since the only other prime implicant that would cover m_{15} is bcd, which requires one more literal and does not cover any 1's that are not covered by ab.) The three remaining 1's require two terms, one of which must be a group of two (to cover m_3) and the other must be one of the groups of four that cover m_{10}. On the second map, we have shown two of the solutions, those that utilize $b'd'$ as the group of four. On the right-hand map, we have shown the third solution, utilizing ad'. Thus, we have

$$g_1 = c'd' + ab + b'd' + a'cd$$
$$g_2 = c'd' + ab + b'd' + a'b'c$$
$$g_3 = c'd' + ab + ad' + a'b'c$$

Don't cares provide us with another approach to solving map problems for functions with or without don't cares.

Map Method 2

1. Find all essential prime implicants.
2. Replace all 1's covered by the essential prime implicants with X's. This highlights the 1's that remain to be covered.
3. Then choose enough of the other prime implicants (as in Method 1).

Step 2 works because the 1's covered by essential prime implicants may be used again (as part of a term covering some new 1's), but need not be. Thus, once we have chosen the essential prime implicants, these minterms are, indeed, don't cares.

EXAMPLE 3.20 $F(A, B, C, D) = \Sigma m(0, 3, 4, 5, 6, 7, 8, 10, 11, 14, 15)$

We first found the two essential prime implicants, $A'B$ and CD. On the center map, we converted all of the 1's covered to don't cares. Finally, we can cover the remaining 1's with AC and $B'C'D'$, producing

$$F = A'B + CD + AC + B'C'D'$$

Replacing covered minterms by don't cares accomplishes the same thing as the shading that we did in Example 3.12; it highlights the 1's that remain to be covered.

[SP 3; EX 4]

3.4 PRODUCT OF SUMS (POS)

Finding a minimum POS expression requires no new theory. The following approach is the simplest:

1. Map the complement of the function. (If there is already a map for the function, replace all 0's by 1's, all 1's by 0's and leave X's unchanged.)

2. Find the minimum SOP expression for the complement of the function (using the techniques of the previous two sections).

3. Use DeMorgan's theorem (P11) to complement that expression, producing a POS expression.

Another approach, which we will not pursue here, is to define the dual of prime implicants (referred to as prime implicates) and develop a new method.

EXAMPLE 3.21

$$f(a, b, c, d) = \Sigma m(0, 1, 4, 5, 10, 11, 14)$$

Since all minterms must be either minterms of f or of f', then, f' must be the sum of all of the other minterms, that is

$$f'(a, b, c, d) = \Sigma m(2, 3, 6, 7, 8, 9, 12, 13, 15)$$

Maps of both f and f' follow

cd \ ab	00	01	11	10
00	1	1		
01	1	1		
11				1
10			1	1

f

cd \ ab	00	01	11	10
00			1	1
01			1	1
11	1	1	1	
10	1	1		

f'

We did not need to map f, unless we wanted both the SOP expression and the POS expression. Once we mapped f, we did not need to write out all the minterms of f'; we could have just replaced the 1's by 0's and 0's by 1's. Also, instead of mapping f', we could look for rectangles of 0's on the map of f. This function is rather straightforward. The following are maps for the minimum SOP expressions for both f and f'.

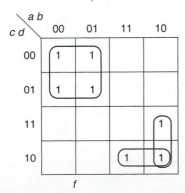

f

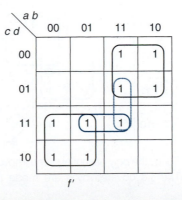

f'

There is one minimum solution for f and there are two equally good solutions for the sum of products for f':

$$f = a'c' + ab'c + acd' \qquad f' = ac' + a'c + abd$$
$$f' = ac' + a'c + bcd$$

We can then complement the solutions for f' to get the two minimum POS solutions for f:

$$f = (a' + c)(a + c')(a' + b' + d')$$
$$f = (a' + c)(a + c')(b' + c' + d')$$

The minimum SOP solution has three terms and eight literals; the minimum POS solutions have three terms and seven literals. (There is no set pattern; sometimes the SOP solution has fewer terms or literals, sometimes the POS does, and sometimes they have the same number of terms and literals.)

EXAMPLE 3.22

Find all of the minimum SOP and all minimum POS solutions for

$$g(w, x, y, z) = \Sigma m(1, 3, 4, 6, 11) + \Sigma d(0, 8, 10, 12, 13)$$

We first find the minimum SOP expression by mapping g. However, before complicating the map by circling prime implicants, we also map g' (below g). Note that the X's are the same on both maps.

For g, the only essential prime implicant, $w'xz'$, is shown on the center map. The 1's covered by it are made don't cares on the right map and the remaining useful prime implicants are circled. We have seen similar examples before, where we have three 1's to be covered in groups of two. There are three equally good solutions:

$$g = w'xz' + \begin{cases} w'x'y' + x'yz \\ w'x'z + x'yz \\ w'x'z + wx'y \end{cases}$$

For g', there are three essential prime implicants, as shown on the center map. Once all of the 1's covered by them have been made don't cares, there is only one 1 left; it can be covered in two ways as shown on the right map:

$$g' = x'z' + xz + wy' + \begin{cases} wx \\ wz' \end{cases}$$

$$g = (x + z)(x' + z')(w' + y) \begin{cases} (w' + x') \\ (w' + z) \end{cases}$$

Note that in this example, the SOP solutions each require only three terms (with nine literals), whereas the POS solutions each require four terms (with eight literals).

[SP 4; EX 5]

3.5 FIVE-VARIABLE MAPS*

A five-variable map consists of $2^5 = 32$ squares. Although there are several arrangements that have been used, we prefer to look at it as two layers of 16 squares each. The top layer (on the left in Map 3.16) contains the squares for the first 16 minterms (for which the first variable, A, is 0) and the bottom layer contains the remaining 16 squares, as pictured in Map 3.16:

Map 3.16 A five-variable map.

---

*For an introduction to six-variable maps, see Marcovitz, *Introduction to Logic Design*, 2nd ed., McGraw-Hill, 2005.

Each square in the bottom layer corresponds to the minterm numbered 16 more than the square above it. Product terms appear as rectangular solids of 1, 2, 4, 8, 16, . . . 1's or X's. Squares directly above and below each other are adjacent.

EXAMPLE 3.23

$m_2 + m_5 = A'B'C'DE' + AB'C'DE' = B'C'DE'$

$m_{11} + m_{27} = A'BC'DE + ABC'DE = BC'DE$

$m_5 + m_7 + m_{21} + m_{23} = B'CE$

These terms are circled on the following map.

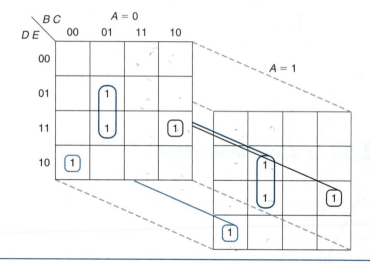

The techniques are the same as for four-variable maps; the only thing new is the need to visualize the rectangular solids. Rather than drawing the maps to look like three dimensions, we will draw them side by side. The function, F, is mapped in Map 3.17.

$$F(A, B, C, D, E) = \Sigma m(4, 5, 6, 7, 9, 11, 13, 15, 16, 18, 27, 28, 31)$$

As always, we first look for the essential prime implicants. A good starting point is to find 1's on one layer for which there is a 0 in the corresponding square on an adjoining layer. Prime implicants that cover that 1 are contained completely on that layer (and thus, we really only have a four-variable map problem). In this example, m_4 meets this criteria (since there is a 0 in square 20 below it). Thus, the only prime implicants covering m_4 must be on the first layer. Indeed, $A'B'C$ is an essential

Map 3.17 A five-variable problem.

A

<table>
<tr><td></td><td colspan="4" align="center">0</td></tr>
<tr><td>BC
DE</td><td>00</td><td>01</td><td>11</td><td>10</td></tr>
<tr><td>00</td><td></td><td>1</td><td></td><td></td></tr>
<tr><td>01</td><td></td><td>1</td><td>1</td><td>1</td></tr>
<tr><td>11</td><td></td><td>1</td><td>1</td><td>1</td></tr>
<tr><td>10</td><td></td><td>1</td><td></td><td></td></tr>
</table>

<table>
<tr><td></td><td colspan="4" align="center">1</td></tr>
<tr><td>BC
DE</td><td>00</td><td>01</td><td>11</td><td>10</td></tr>
<tr><td>00</td><td>1</td><td></td><td>1</td><td></td></tr>
<tr><td>01</td><td></td><td></td><td></td><td></td></tr>
<tr><td>11</td><td></td><td></td><td>1</td><td>1</td></tr>
<tr><td>10</td><td>1</td><td></td><td></td><td></td></tr>
</table>

prime implicant. (Note that the A' comes from the fact that this group is contained completely on the $A = 0$ layer of the map and the $B'C$ from the fact that this group is in the second column.) Actually, all four 1's in this term have no counterpart on the other layer and m_6 would also make this prime implicant essential. (The other two 1's in that term are part of another prime implicant, as well.) We also note that m_9, m_{16}, m_{18}, and m_{28} have 0's in the corresponding square on the other layer and make a prime implicant essential. Although m_{14} has a 0 beneath it (m_{30}), it does not make a prime implicant on the A' layer essential. Thus Map 3.18 shows each of the essential prime implicants that are contained on one layer circled.

So far, we have

$$F = A'B'C + A'BE + AB'C'E' + ABCD'E' + \cdots$$

Map 3.18 Essential prime implicants on one layer.

A

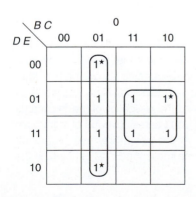

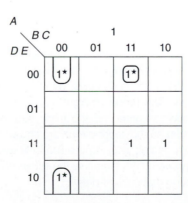

The two 1's remaining uncovered do have counterparts on the other layer. However, the only prime implicant that covers them is *BDE*, as shown on Map 3.19 in green. It, too, is an essential prime implicant. (Note that prime implicants that include 1's from both layers do not have the variable *A* in them. Such prime implicants must, of course, have the same number of 1's on each layer; otherwise, they would not be rectangular.)

Map 3.19   A prime implicant covering 1's on both layers.

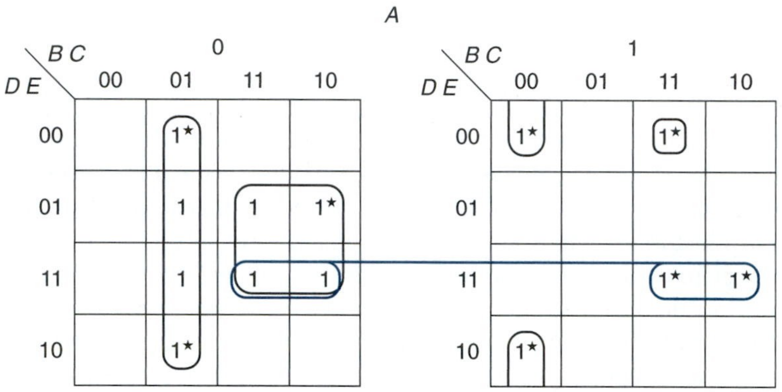

The complete solution is thus

$$F = A'B'C + A'BE + AB'C'E' + ABCD'E' + BDE$$

Groups of eight 1's are not uncommon in five-variable problems, as illustrated in Example 3.24.

EXAMPLE 3.24

$G(A, B, C, D, E) = \Sigma m(1, 3, 8, 9, 11, 12, 14, 17, 19, 20, 22, 24, 25, 27)$

The first map shows a plot of that function. On the second map, to the right, we have circled the two essential prime implicants that we found by considering 1's on one layer with 0's in the corresponding square on the other layer. The group of eight 1's, *C'E* (also an essential prime implicant), is shown in green on the third map (where the essential prime implicants found on the second map are shown as don't cares). Groups of eight have three literals missing (leaving only two). At this point, only two 1's are left uncovered; that requires the essential prime implicant, *BC'D'*, shown on the fourth map in light green.

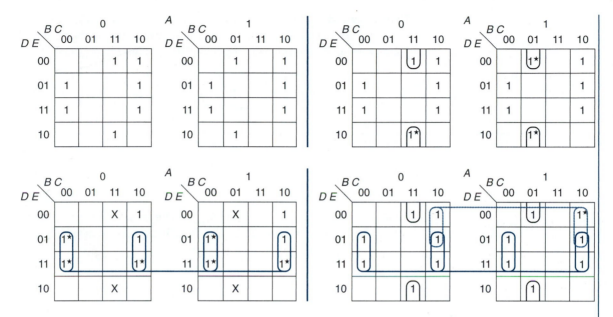

The solution is thus

$$G = A'BCE' + AB'CE' + C'E + BC'D'$$

Note that there is only one other prime implicant in this function, $A'BD'E'$; it covers no 1's not already covered.

The next problem is shown on the maps below. Once again, we start by looking for 1's that are on one layer, with a corresponding 0 on the other layer. Although there are several such 1's on the $A = 0$ layer, only m_{10} makes a prime implicant essential. Similarly, on the $A = 1$ layer, m_{30} is covered by an essential prime implicant. These terms, $A'C'E'$ and $ABCD$, are shown on the second map. The 1's covered are shown as don't cares on the next map.

EXAMPLE 3.25

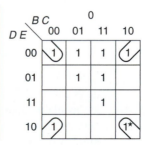

Three other essential prime implicants include 1's from both layers of the map; they are *CD'E*, *BCE*, and *B'C'DE'*, as shown on the left map below. These were found by looking for isolated 1's, such as m_{21}, m_{15}, and m_{18}.

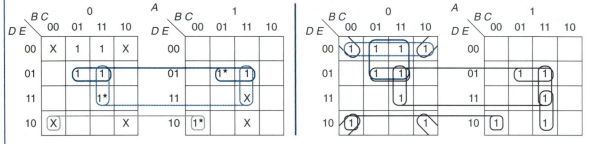

Finally, the remaining two 1's (m_4 and m_{12}) can be covered in two ways, as shown on the right map: *A'CD'* and *A'D'E'*. Thus, the two solutions are

$$F = A'C'E' + ABCD + CD'E + BCE + B'C'DE' + A'CD'$$
$$F = A'C'E' + ABCD + CD'E + BCE + B'C'DE' + A'D'E'$$

[SP 5; EX 6]

3.6 MULTIPLE-OUTPUT PROBLEMS

Many real problems involve designing a system with more than one output. If, for example, we had a problem with three inputs, *A*, *B*, and *C* and two outputs, *F* and *G*, we could treat this as two separate problems (as shown on the left in Figure 3.1). We would then map each of the functions, and find minimum solutions. However, if we treated this as a single system with three inputs and two outputs (as shown on the right), we may be able to economize by *sharing* gates.

Figure 3.1   Implementation of two functions.

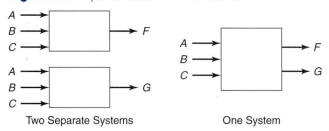

Two Separate Systems   One System

In this section, we will illustrate the process of obtaining two-level solutions using AND and OR gates (SOP solutions), assuming all variables are available both uncomplemented and complemented. We could convert each of these solutions into NAND gate circuits (using the same number of gates and gate inputs). We could also find POS solutions (by minimizing the complement of each of the functions and then using DeMorgan's theorem) and convert these to NOR gate circuits.

We will illustrate this by first considering three very simple examples.

EXAMPLE 3.26

$F(A, B, C) = \Sigma m(0, 2, 6, 7)$ $G(A, B, C) = \Sigma m(1, 3, 6, 7)$

If we map each of these and solve them separately,

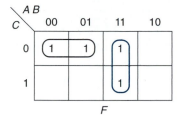 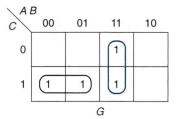

we obtain

$F = A'C' + AB$ $G = A'C + AB$

Looking at the maps, we see that the same term (AB) is circled on both. Thus, we can build the circuit on the left, rather than the two circuits on the right.

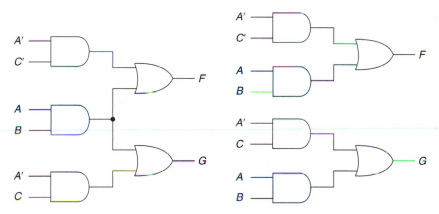

Obviously, the version on the left requires only five gates, whereas the one on the right uses six.

This example is the simplest. Each of the minimum SOP expressions contains the same term. It would take no special techniques to recognize this and achieve the savings.

Even when the two solutions do not have a common prime implicant, we can share as illustrated in the following example:

EXAMPLE 3.27

$F(A, B, C) = \Sigma m(0, 1, 6)$ $G(A, B, C) = \Sigma m(2, 3, 6)$

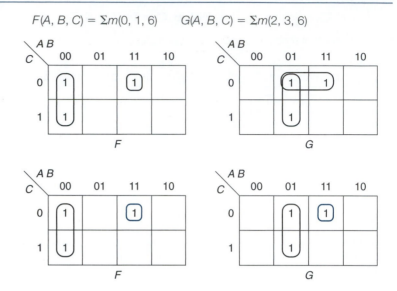

In the top maps, we considered each function separately and obtained

$$F = A'B' + ABC' \qquad G = A'B + BC'$$

This solution requires six gates (four ANDs and two ORs) with 13 inputs. However, as can be seen from the second pair of maps, we can share the term ABC' and obtain

$$F = A'B' + ABC' \qquad G = A'B + ABC'$$

(To emphasize the sharing, we have shown the shared term in green, and will do that in other examples that follow.) As can be seen from the following circuit, this only requires five gates with 11 inputs.

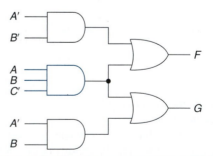

This example illustrates that a shared term in a minimum solution need not be a prime implicant. (In Example 3.27, ABC' is a prime implicant of F but not of G; in Example 3.28, we will use a term that is not a prime implicant of either function.)

EXAMPLE 3.28

$f(a, b, c) = \Sigma m(2, 3, 7) \qquad g(a, b, c) = \Sigma m(4, 5, 7)$

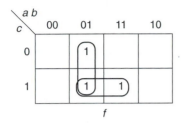

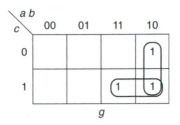

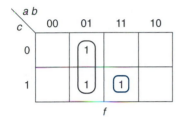

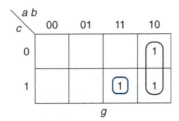

In the first pair of maps, we solved this as two problems. Using essential prime implicants of each function, we obtained

$f = a'b + bc \qquad g = ab' + ac$

However, as can be seen in the second set of maps, we can share the term *abc*, even though it is not a prime implicant of either function, and once again get a solution that requires only five gates:

$f = a'b + abc \qquad g = ab' + abc$

The method for solving this type of problem is to begin by looking at the 1's of each function that are 0's of the other function. They must be covered by prime implicants of that function. Only the shared terms need not be prime implicants. In this last example, we chose $a'b$ for f since m_2 makes that an essential prime implicant of f and we chose ab' for g since m_4 makes that an essential prime implicant of g. That left just one 1 uncovered in each function—the same 1—which we covered with *abc*. We will now look at some more complex examples.

EXAMPLE 3.29

$F(A, B, C, D) = \Sigma m(4, 5, 6, 8, 12, 13)$

$G(A, B, C, D) = \Sigma m(0, 2, 5, 6, 7, 13, 14, 15)$

The maps of these functions follow. In them, we have shown in green the 1's that are included in one function and not the other.

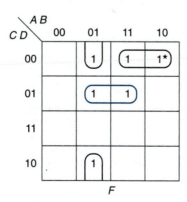

F

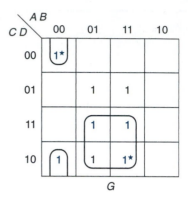

G

We then circled each of those prime implicants that was made essential by a green 1. The only green 1 that was not circled in F is m_4 because that can be covered by two prime implicants. Even though one of the terms would have fewer literals, we must wait. Next, we will use $A'BD'$ for F. Because m_6 was covered by an essential prime implicant of G, we are no longer looking for a term to share. Thus, m_6 will be covered in F by the prime implicant, $A'BD'$. As shown on the next pair of maps, that leaves m_4 and m_{12} to be covered in both functions, allowing us to share the term $BC'D$, as shown on the following maps circled in green.

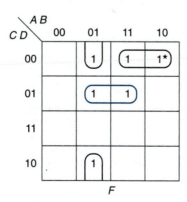

F

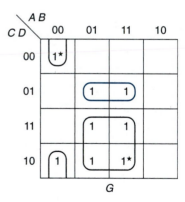

G

leaving

$$F = AC'D' + A'BD' + BC'D$$
$$G = A'B'D' + BC + BC'D$$

for a total of seven gates with 20 gate inputs. Notice that if we had minimized the functions individually, we would have used two separate terms for the third term in each expression, resulting in

$$F = AC'D' + A'BD' + BC'$$
$$G = A'B'D' + BC + BD$$

for a total of eight gates with 21 gate inputs. Clearly, the shared circuit costs less.

The shared version of the circuit, using NAND gates, follows.

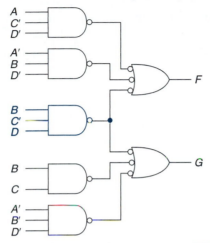

EXAMPLE 3.30

$F(A, B, C, D) = \Sigma m(0, 2, 3, 4, 6, 7, 10, 11)$
$G(A, B, C, D) = \Sigma m(0, 4, 8, 9, 10, 11, 12, 13)$

Once again the maps are shown with the unshared 1's in green and the prime implicants made essential by one of those 1's circled.

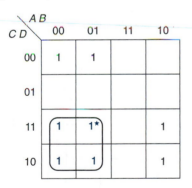

Each of the functions can be solved individually with two more groups of four, producing

$$F = A'C + A'D' + B'C \qquad G = AC' + C'D' + AB'$$

That would require eight gates with 18 gate inputs. However, sharing the groups of two as shown on the next set of maps reduces the number of gates to six and the number of gate inputs to 16. If these functions were implemented with NAND gates, the individual solutions would require a total of three packages, whereas the shared solution would require only two,

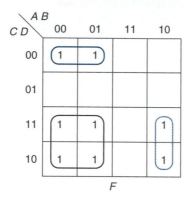 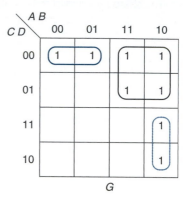

F   G

leaving the equations

$$F = A'C + A'C'D' + AB'C \quad G = AC' + A'C'D' + AB'C$$

The same techniques can be applied to problems with three or more outputs.

EXAMPLE 3.31

First, we show the solution obtained if we considered them as three separate problems.

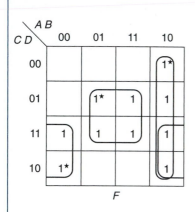 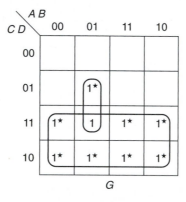 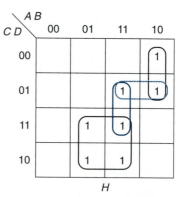

F   G   H

$$F = AB' + BD + B'C$$

$$G = C + A'BD$$

$$H = BC + AB'C' + (ABD \text{ or } AC'D)$$

This solution requires 10 gates and 25 gate inputs. There is no sharing. (Note that the term C in function G does not require an AND gate.)

The technique of first finding 1's that are only minterms of one of the functions does not get us started for this example, since each of the 1's is a minterm of at least two of the functions. The starting point, instead, is to choose C for function G. The product term with only one literal does not require an AND gate and uses only one input to the OR gate. Any other solution, say sharing $B'C$ with F and BC with H, requires at least two inputs to the OR gate. Once we have made that choice, however, we must then choose $B'C$ for F and BC for H, because of the 1's shown in green on the following maps. There is no longer any sharing possible for those 1's and they make those prime implicants essential in F and H.

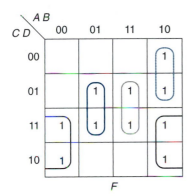

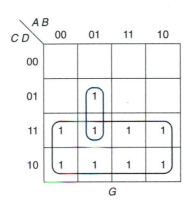

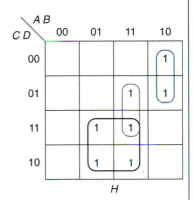

The term $AB'C'$ (circled in light green) was chosen next for H since it is an essential prime implicant of H and it can be shared (that is, all of the 1's in that term are also 1's of F, the only place where sharing is possible). $AB'C'$ is also used for F, since it covers two 1's and we would otherwise require an additional term, AB', to cover m_8. In a similar fashion, the term $A'BD$ is used for G (it is the only way to cover m_5) and can then be shared with F. Finally, we can finish covering F and H with ABD (a prime implicant of H, one of the choices for covering H when we treated that as a separate problem). It would be used also for F, rather than using another AND gate to create one of the prime implicants BD or AD. The solution then becomes

$$F = B'C + AB'C' + A'BD + ABD$$
$$G = C + A'BD$$
$$H = BC + AB'C' + ABD$$

which requires only eight gates and 22 gate inputs (a savings of two gates and three gate inputs).

EXAMPLE 3.32

$$F(A, B, C, D) = \Sigma m(0, 2, 6, 10, 11, 14, 15)$$
$$G(A, B, C, D) = \Sigma m(0, 3, 6, 7, 8, 9, 12, 13, 14, 15)$$
$$H(A, B, C, D) = \Sigma m(0, 3, 4, 5, 7, 10, 11, 12, 13, 14, 15)$$

The map below shows these functions; the only 1 that cannot be shared and makes a prime implicant essential is m_9 in G. That prime implicant, AC', is shown circled.

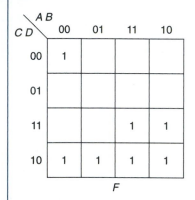

F

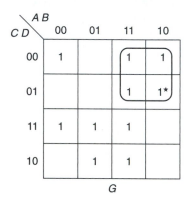

G

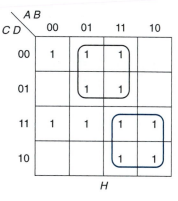

H

Next, we note that AC is an essential prime implicant of F (because of m_{11} and m_{15}) and of H (because of m_{10}). Furthermore, neither m_{10} nor m_{11} are 1's of G. Thus, that term is used for both F and H. Next, we chose BC' for H and BC for G; each covers four new 1's, some of which can no longer be shared (since the 1's that correspond to other functions have already been covered).

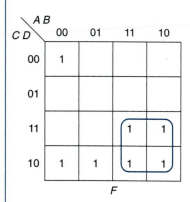

F

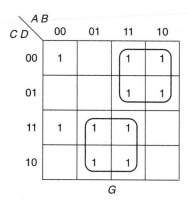

G

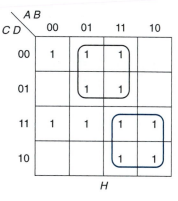

H

At this point, we can see that $A'B'C'D'$ can be used to cover m_0 in all three functions; otherwise, we would need three different three-literal terms. $A'CD$ can be used for G and H, and, finally, CD' is used for F, producing the following map and algebraic functions.

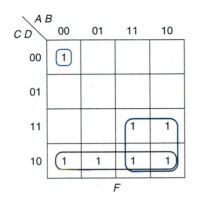

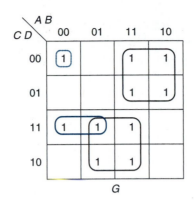

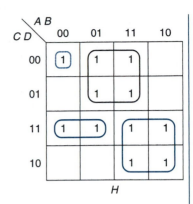

$$F = AC + A'B'C'D' + CD'$$
$$G = AC' + BC + A'B'C'D' + A'CD$$
$$H = AC + BC' + A'B'C'D' + A'CD$$

This solution requires 10 gates with 28 inputs, compared to 13 gates and 35 inputs if these were implemented separately.

EXAMPLE 3.33

Finally, we will consider an example of a system with don't cares:

$$F(A, B, C, D) = \Sigma m(2, 3, 4, 6, 9, 11, 12) + \Sigma d(0, 1, 14, 15)$$

$$G(A, B, C, D) = \Sigma m(2, 6, 10, 11, 12) + \Sigma d(0, 1, 14, 15)$$

A map of the functions follows, with the only prime implicant made essential by a 1 that is not shared circled, $B'D$.

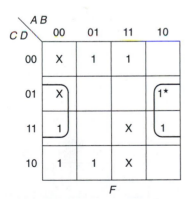

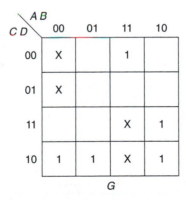

Since m_{11} has now been covered in F, we must use the essential prime implicant of G, AC, to cover m_{11} there. Also, as shown on the next maps, ABD' is used for G, since that is an essential prime implicant of G and the whole term can be shared. (We will share it in the best solution.)

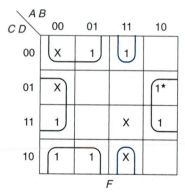

Since we need the term ABD' for G, one approach is to use it for F also. (That only costs a gate input to the OR gate.) If we do that, we could cover the rest of F with $A'D'$ and the rest of G with CD', yielding the map and equations that follow.

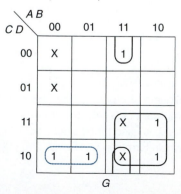

$$F = B'D + ABD' + A'D'$$
$$G = AC + ABD' + CD'$$

That solution uses seven gates and 17 inputs. Another solution using the same number of gates but one more input shares $A'CD'$. That completes G and then the cover of F is completed with BD'. The maps and equations are thus:

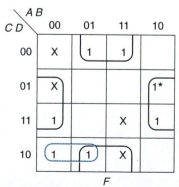

$$F = B'D + A'CD' + BD'$$
$$G = AC + ABD' + A'CD'$$

That, too, requires seven gates, but using a three-input AND gate instead of a two-input one, bringing the total number of inputs to 18.

[SP 6; EX 7]

3.7 SOLVED PROBLEMS

1. Plot the following functions on a Karnaugh map:
   a. $f(a, b, c) = \Sigma m(0, 1, 3, 6)$
   b. $g(w, x, y, z) = \Sigma m(3, 4, 7, 10, 11, 14) + \Sigma d(2, 13, 15)$
   c. $F = BD' + ABC + AD + A'B'C$

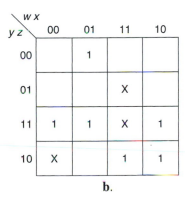

b.

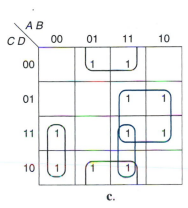

c.

a.

2. For each of the following, find all minimum SOP expressions. (If there is more than one solution, the number of solutions is given in parentheses.)
   a. $G(X, Y, Z) = \Sigma m(1, 2, 3, 4, 6, 7)$
   b. $f(w, x, y, z) = \Sigma m(2, 5, 7, 8, 10, 12, 13, 15)$
   c. $g(a, b, c, d) = \Sigma m(0, 6, 8, 9, 10, 11, 13, 14, 15)$

   (2 solutions)

   d. $f(a, b, c, d) = \Sigma m(0, 4, 5, 6, 7, 8, 9, 10, 11, 13, 14, 15)$

   (2 solutions)

   e. $f(a, b, c, d) = \Sigma m(0, 1, 2, 4, 6, 7, 8, 9, 10, 11, 12, 15)$
   f. $G(A, B, C, D) = \Sigma m(0, 1, 4, 5, 7, 8, 10, 13, 14, 15)$

   (3 solutions)

a. All of the prime implicants are essential, as shown on the map to the right.

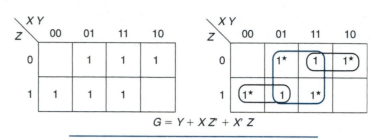

$$G = Y + X Z' + X' Z$$

b.

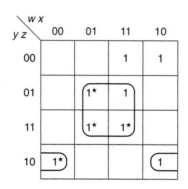

The essential prime implicants are shown on the second map, leaving two 1's to be covered. The third map shows that each can be covered by two different prime implicants, but the **green** group shown is the only one that covers both with one term. We would require both light green terms. The minimum is

$$f = xz + x'yz' + wy'z'$$

c.

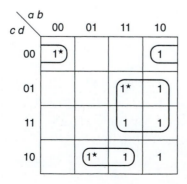
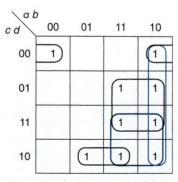

The three essential prime implicants are shown on the center map. The only 1 left to be covered can be covered by either of two groups of four, as shown circled in green on the third map, producing

$$g = b'c'd' + bcd' + ad + ab'$$

$$g = b'c'd' + bcd' + ad + ac$$

d.

cd \ ab	00	01	11	10
00	1	1		1
01		1	1	1
11		1	1	1
10		1	1	1

cd \ ab	00	01	11	10
00	1	1		1
01		1	1	1
11		1	1	1
10		1	1	1

cd \ ab	00	01	11	10
00	1	1		1
01		1	1	1
11		1	1	1
10		1	1	1

There are no essential prime implicants. We need one group of two to cover m_0; all other 1's can be covered by groups of four. Once we have chosen $a'c'd'$ to cover m_0 (center map), we would choose ab' to cover m_8. (Otherwise, we must use $b'c'd'$, a group of two to cover that 1. Not only is that more literals, it covers nothing else new; whereas ab' covered three additional uncovered 1's.) Once that has been done, the other two prime implicants become obvious, giving

$$f = a'c'd' + ab' + bc + bd$$

In a similar fashion (on the next map), once we choose $b'c'd'$ (the other prime implicant that covers m_0), $a'b$ is the appropriate choice to cover m_4:

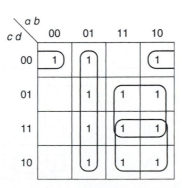

The only way to cover the remaining 1's in two terms is with ac and ad, as shown on the second map, leaving

$$f = b'c'd' + a'b + ac + ad$$

e. There are two essential prime implicants, as indicated on the first map, leaving six 1's to be covered. The essential prime implicants are shaded on the center map.

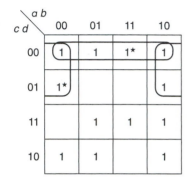
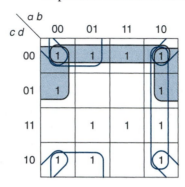
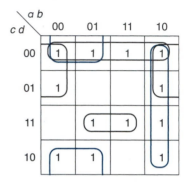

No prime implicant covers more than two of the remaining 1's; thus three more terms are needed. The three groups of four (two literal terms) are circled in **green** on the second map. We can cover four new 1's only using $a'd'$ and ab'. Note that m_7 and m_{15} are uncovered; they require a group of two, bcd. The only minimum solution, requiring five terms and 11 literals,

$$f = c'd' + b'c' + a'd' + ab' + bcd$$

is shown on the right map. There is another solution that uses five terms, but it requires 12 literals, namely,

$$f = c'd' + b'c' + b'd' + a'bc + acd$$

f. The first map shows all of the prime implicants circled; the 1's that have been covered only once are indicated with a star:

Essential prime implicants: $A'C'$, BD

Other prime implicants: $B'C'D'$, $AB'D'$, ACD', ABC

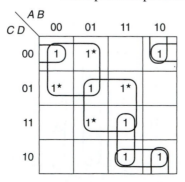
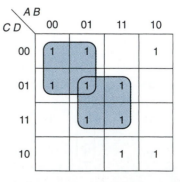

On the second map, the essential prime implicants have been shaded, highlighting the three 1' remaining to be covered. We need two terms to cover them, at least one of which must cover two of these remaining 1's. The three solutions are thus

$$F = A'C' + BD + ACD' + B'C'D'$$

$$F = A'C' + BD + AB'D' + ACD'$$

$$F = A'C' + BD + AB'D' + ABC$$

3. For each of the following, find all minimum SOP expressions. (If there is more than one solution, the number of solutions is given in parentheses.)

   a. $f(a, b, c, d) = \Sigma m(0, 2, 3, 7, 8, 9, 13, 15) + \Sigma d(1, 12)$

   b. $F(W, X, Y, Z) = \Sigma m(1, 3, 5, 6, 7, 13, 14) + \Sigma d(8, 10, 12)$

   (2 solutions)

   c. $f(a, b, c, d) = \Sigma m(3, 8, 10, 13, 15)$
   $$+ \Sigma d(0, 2, 5, 7, 11, 12, 14)$$

   (8 solutions)

   d. $f(a, b, c, d) = \Sigma m(0, 1, 4, 6, 10, 14)$
   $$+ \Sigma d(5, 7, 8, 9, 11, 12, 15)$$

   (13 solutions)

a.

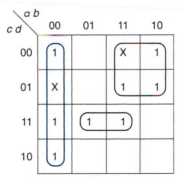

The left-hand map shows the one essential prime implicant, $a'b'$. The remaining 1's can be covered by two additional terms, as shown on the right-hand map. In this example, all don't cares are treated as 1's. The resulting solution is

$$f = a'b' + ac' + bcd$$

Although there are other prime implicants, such as $b'c'$, abd, and $a'cd$, three prime implicants would be needed in addition to $a'b'$ if any of them were chosen.

b.

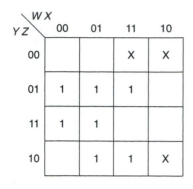

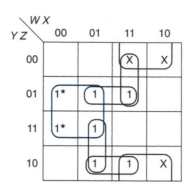

The center map shows all of the prime implicants circled. It is clear that only $W'Z$ is essential, after which three 1's remain uncovered. The prime implicant XYZ' is the only one that can cover two of these and thus appears in both minimum solutions. That leaves a choice of two terms to cover the remaining one—either WXY' (light green) or $XY'Z$ (gray). Note that they treat the don't care at m_{12} differently and thus, although the two solutions shown below satisfy the requirements of the problem, they are not equal:

$$F = W'Z + XYZ' + WXY'$$
$$F = W'Z + XYZ' + XY'Z$$

Also, the group of four (WZ') is not used; that would require a four-term solution.

c. There are no essential prime implicants in this problem. The left map shows the only two prime implicants that cover m_8; they also cover m_{10}. We must choose one of these. The next map shows the only prime implicants that cover m_{13}; both also cover m_{15}. We must choose one of these also. Finally, the last map shows the only two prime implicants that cover m_3.

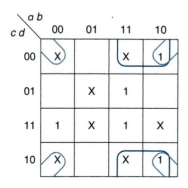

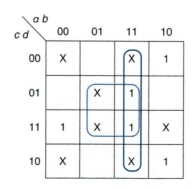

So, our final solution takes one from each group, giving us a total of eight solutions:

$$f = \begin{Bmatrix} ad' \\ b'd' \end{Bmatrix} + \begin{Bmatrix} ab \\ bd \end{Bmatrix} + \begin{Bmatrix} cd \\ b'c \end{Bmatrix}$$

or, written out

$$f = ad' + ab + cd$$
$$f = ad' + ab + b'c$$
$$f = ad' + bd + cd$$
$$f = ad' + bd + b'c$$
$$f = b'd' + ab + cd$$
$$f = b'd' + ab + b'c$$
$$f = b'd' + bd + cd$$
$$f = b'd' + bd + b'c$$

d. There are no essential prime implicants. The best place to start is with a 1 that can only be covered in two ways; in this problem there is only one, m_1. Any solution must contain either the term $a'c'$ (as shown on the first four maps) or the term $b'c'$ (as shown on the remaining two maps). There is no reason to use both, since $b'c'$ does not cover any 1's that are not already covered by $a'c'$. The first map shows $a'c'$. Note that there are three 1's left, requiring two more terms. At least one of these terms must cover two of the remaining 1's.

The second map shows two ways of covering m_6 and m_{14}, bc and bd'. In either case, only one 1 is left to be covered. The third map shows the previously covered 1's as don't cares and three ways of covering the last 1, m_{10}. Thus, we have as the first six solutions

$$f_1 = a'c' + bc + ab'$$
$$f_2 = a'c' + bc + ac$$
$$f_3 = a'c' + bc + ad'$$

$$f_4 = a'c' + bd' + ab'$$
$$f_5 = a'c' + bd' + ac$$
$$f_6 = a'c' + bd' + ad'$$

Next, we consider how we may cover both m_{10} and m_{14} with one term (in addition to those already found). That provides two more solutions shown on the left map that follows. (Other solutions that use these terms have already been listed.)

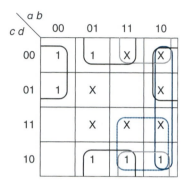

$$f_7 = a'c' + a'b + ad'$$
$$f_8 = a'c' + a'b + ac$$

We next consider the solutions that use $b'c'$. The middle map shows two of these, utilizing $a'b$. The right-hand map shows the final three, utilizing bd', instead; it has the same three last terms as in the first series. Thus, we have

$$f_9 = b'c' + a'b + ad'$$
$$f_{10} = b'c' + a'b + ac$$
$$f_{11} = b'c' + bd' + ab'$$
$$f_{12} = b'c' + bd' + ac$$
$$f_{13} = b'c' + bd' + ad'$$

---

4. For each of the following functions, find all of the minimum SOP expressions and all of the minimum POS expressions:

a. $f(w, x, y, z) = \Sigma m(2, 3, 5, 7, 10, 13, 14, 15)$

(1 SOP, 1 POS solution)

b. $f(a, b, c, d) = \Sigma m(3, 4, 9, 13, 14, 15) + \Sigma d(2, 5, 10, 12)$

(1 SOP, 2 POS solutions)

c. $f(a, b, c, d) = \Sigma m(4, 6, 11, 12, 13) + \Sigma d(3, 5, 7, 9, 10, 15)$

(2 SOP and 8 POS solutions)

a. The map of *f* follows.

yz \ wx	00	01	11	10
00				
01		1	1	
11	1	1	1	
10	1		1	1

yz \ wx	00	01	11	10
00				
01		1*	1*	
11	1	1	1	
10	1		1	1

Although there is only one essential prime implicant, there is only one way to complete the cover with two more terms, namely,

$$f = xz + w'x'y + wyz'$$

By replacing all the 1's with 0's and 0's with 1's, or by plotting all the minterms not in *f*, we get the map for *f*

yz \ wx	00	01	11	10
00	1	1	1	1
01	1			1
11				1
10		1		

yz \ wx	00	01	11	10
00	1	1	1*	1
01	1*			1
11				1*
10	1*			

There are four essential prime implicants, covering all of *f'*, giving

$$f' = x'y' + y'z' + w'xz' + wx'z$$

Using DeMorgan's theorem, we get

$$f = (x + y)\,(y + z)\,(w + x' + z)\,(w' + x + z')$$

In this case, the SOP solution requires fewer terms.

b. As indicated on the right-hand map that follows, all of the 1's are covered by essential prime implicants, producing the minimum SOP expression

Top-left map:

cd \ ab	00	01	11	10
00		1	X	
01		X	1	1
11	1		1	
10	X		1	X

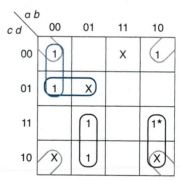

Top-right map:

cd \ ab	00	01	11	10
00	1*	X		
01	X	1	1*	
11	1*		1*	
10	X		1	X

$$f_1 = bc' + ab + a'b'c + ac'd$$

Now, replacing all of the 1's by 0's and 0's by 1's and leaving the X's unchanged, we get the map for f'

Left map:

cd \ ab	00	01	11	10
00	1		X	1
01	1	X		
11		1		1
10	X	1		X

Middle map:

cd \ ab	00	01	11	10
00	1		X	1
01	1	X		
11		1		1*
10	X	1		X

Right map:

cd \ ab	00	01	11	10
00	1		X	1
01	1	X		
11		1		1*
10	X	1		X

There is one essential prime implicant, $ab'c$. Although m_6 and m_7 can each be covered in two ways, only $a'bc$ covers them both (and neither of the other terms cover additional 1's). The middle map shows each of these terms circled, leaving three 1's to be covered. There is a group of four, covering two of the 1's (as shown on the right-hand map), $b'd'$. That leaves just m_1, which can be covered in two ways, as shown on the right-hand map in green and light green lines. Thus, the two minimum sum of product expressions for f' are

$$f_2' = ab'c + a'bc + b'd' + a'c'd$$
$$f_3' = ab'c + a'bc + b'd' + a'b'c'$$

producing the two minimum POS solutions

$$f_2 = (a' + b + c')(a + b' + c')(b + d)(a + c + d')$$
$$f_3 = (a' + b + c')(a + b' + c')(b + d)(a + b + c)$$

c. The map for f is shown next (on the left). There are two essential prime implicants, leaving only m_{11} to be covered.

There are two groups of four that can be used, as indicated on
the right map.

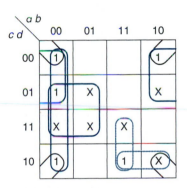

Thus the two SOP solutions are

$$f_1 = a'b + bc' + \boldsymbol{ad}$$
$$f_2 = a'b + bc' + cd$$

We then mapped f' and found no essential prime implicants.

We chose as a starting point m_8. It can be covered either by the
four corners, $b'd'$ (as shown on the middle map) or by $b'c'$, as
shown on the right-hand map. Whichever solution we choose,
we need a group of two to cover m_{14} (as shown in light green);
neither covers any other 1. After choosing one of these (and
$b'd'$), all that remains to be covered is m_1. The three green
lines show the covers. (Notice that one of those is $b'c'$.) If we
don't choose $b'd'$, then we must choose $b'c'$ to cover m_8 and
$a'b'$ to cover m_2 (since the only other prime implicant that
covers m_2 is $b'd'$ and we have already found all of the
solutions using that term). Thus, the eight solutions for f' are

$$f_3' = b'd' + abc + \boldsymbol{a'b'}$$
$$f_4' = b'd' + abc + \boldsymbol{a'd}$$
$$f_5' = b'd' + abc + \boldsymbol{b'c'}$$

$$f_6' = b'd' + acd' + a'b'$$
$$f_7' = b'd' + acd' + a'd$$
$$f_8' = b'd' + acd' + b'c'$$
$$f_9' = b'c' + abc + a'b'$$
$$f_{10}' = b'c' + acd' + a'b'$$

The POS solutions for f are thus

$$f_3 = (b + d)(a' + b' + c')(a + b)$$
$$f_4 = (b + d)(a' + b' + c')(a + d')$$
$$f_5 = (b + d)(a' + b' + c')(b + c)$$
$$f_6 = (b + d)(a' + c' + d)(a + b)$$
$$f_7 = (b + d)(a' + c' + d)(a + d')$$
$$f_8 = (b + d)(a' + c' + d)(b + c)$$
$$f_9 = (b + c)(a' + b' + c')(a + b)$$
$$f_{10} = (b + c)(a' + c' + d)(a + b)$$

5. Find the minimum SOP solution(s) for each of the following:

   a. $F(A, B, C, D, E) = \Sigma m(0, 5, 7, 9, 11, 13, 15, 18, 19, 22, 23, 25, 27, 28, 29, 31)$

   b. $F(A, B, C, D, E) = \Sigma m(0, 2, 4, 7, 8, 10, 15, 17, 20, 21, 23, 25, 26, 27, 29, 31)$

   c. $G(V, W, X, Y, Z) = \Sigma m(0, 1, 5, 6, 7, 8, 9, 14, 17, 20, 21, 22, 23, 25, 28, 29, 30)$ (3 solutions)

   d. $H(A, B, C, D, E) = \Sigma m(1, 3, 10, 14, 21, 26, 28, 30) + \Sigma d(5, 12, 17, 29)$

   a. We begin by looking at 1's for which the corresponding position on the other layer is 0. On the first map, all of the essential prime implicants that are totally contained on one layer of the map, $A'B'C'D'E'$, $A'CE$, $AB'D$, and $ABCD'$, are circled.

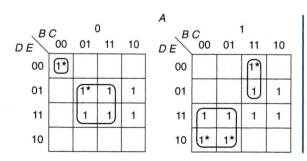

The 1's covered by these essential prime implicants are shown as don't cares on the second map. The remaining 1's are all part of the group of eight, *BE*, shown on the second map. Thus, the minimum solution is

$$F = A'B'C'D'E' + A'CE + AB'D + ABCD' + BE$$

b. On the left-hand map, the essential prime implicants are circled. Note that $A'C'E'$ is on the top layer, $AD'E$ is on the lower layer and CDE is split between the layers.

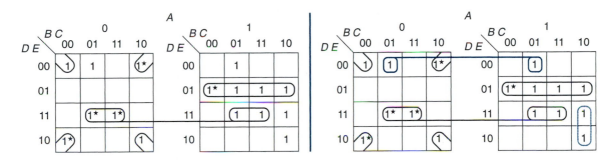

That leaves four 1's to be covered, using two groups of two as shown on the right map. The minimum is thus

$$F = A'C'E' + AD'E + CDE + B'CD'E' + ABC'D$$

c. On the first map, the two essential prime implicants, $V'X'Y'$ and XYZ', are circled. The term $W'XZ$ is circled on the second map; if it is not used, $W'XY$ would be needed to cover m_7 and m_{23}. But then, three more terms would be needed to cover the function.

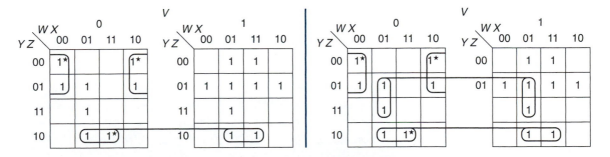

The following maps show the covered terms as don't cares and three ways of covering the remaining 1's. On the left map, the **green** term, $VY'Z$, is used with either of the other terms, VXY' or VXZ'. On the right map, VXY' and $X'Y'Z$ are used.

First group (WX / YZ) maps:

$V = 0$

YZ \ WX	00	01	11	10
00	X			X
01	X	X		X
11		X		
10		X	X	

$V = 1$

YZ \ WX	00	01	11	10
00	1	1		
01	1	X	1	1
11		X		
10		X	X	

$V = 0$

YZ \ WX	00	01	11	10
00	X			X
01	X	X		X
11		X		
10		X	X	

$V = 1$

YZ \ WX	00	01	11	10
00	1	1		
01	1	X	1	1
11		X		
10		X	X	

The three minimum solutions are thus

$$G = V'X'Y' + XYZ' + W'XZ + VY'Z + VXY'$$
$$G = V'X'Y' + XYZ' + W'XZ + VY'Z + VXZ'$$
$$G = V'X'Y' + XYZ' + W'XZ + VXY' + X'Y'Z$$

d. The two essential prime implicants, $A'B'C'E$ and BDE', are circled on the first map. Each of the remaining 1's can be covered in two ways, by a group of two contained completely on one layer or by the group of four shown.

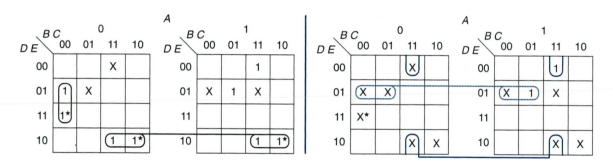

Thus, the minimum solution is

$$H = A'B'C'E + BDE' + BCE' + B'D'E$$

6. Find a minimum two-level circuit (corresponding to SOP expressions) using AND gates and one OR gate per function for each of the following sets of functions:

a. $f(a, b, c, d) = \Sigma m(0, 1, 2, 3, 5, 7, 8, 10, 11, 13)$

$g(a, b, c, d) = \Sigma m(0, 2, 5, 8, 10, 11, 13, 15)$

(7 gates, 19 inputs)

b. $f(a, b, c, d) = \Sigma m(1, 2, 4, 5, 6, 9, 11, 13, 15)$

$g(a, b, c, d) = \Sigma m(0, 2, 4, 8, 9, 11, 12, 13, 14, 15)$

(8 gates, 23 inputs)

c. $F(W, X, Y, Z) = \Sigma m(2, 3, 6, 7, 8, 9, 13)$
   $G(W, X, Y, Z) = \Sigma m(2, 3, 6, 7, 9, 10, 13, 14)$
   $H(W, X, Y, Z) = \Sigma m(0, 1, 4, 5, 9, 10, 13, 14)$
   (8 gates, 22 inputs)

d. $f(a, b, c, d) = \Sigma m(0, 2, 3, 8, 9, 10, 11, 12, 13, 15)$
   $g(a, b, c, d) = \Sigma m(3, 5, 7, 12, 13, 15)$
   $h(a, b, c, d) = \Sigma m(0, 2, 3, 4, 6, 8, 10, 14)$
   (10 gates, 28 inputs)

e. $f(a, b, c, d) = \Sigma m(0, 3, 5, 7) + \Sigma d(10, 11, 12, 13, 14, 15)$
   $g(a, b, c, d) = \Sigma m(0, 5, 6, 7, 8) + \Sigma d(10, 11, 12, 13, 14, 15)$
   (7 gates, 19 inputs)

a. The first pair of maps show the only prime implicant, $a'd$ in f, that covers a 1 not part of the other function.

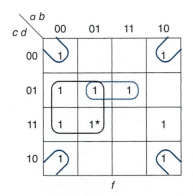

No other 1 (of either f or g) that is not shared makes a prime implicant essential (m_1 or m_3 in f or m_{15} in g). Two other terms, $b'd'$ and $bc'd$, are essential prime implicants of both f and g and have been thus chosen in the following maps.

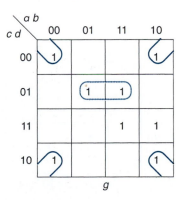

Although the term $ab'c$ could be shared, another term would be needed for g (either abd or acd). This would require seven gates and 20 gate inputs (one input too many). But, if acd is used for g, we could then complete covering both functions using $b'c$ for f as shown on the following maps.

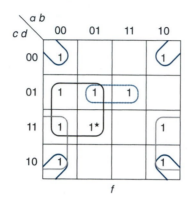 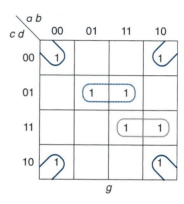

Thus,

$$f = a'd + b'd' + bc'd + b'c$$
$$g = b'd' + bc'd + acd$$

requiring seven gates and 19 inputs.

b. Scanning each function for 1's that are not part of the other function, we find m_1, m_5, and m_6 in f and m_0, m_8, m_{12}, and m_{14} in g. The only ones that make a prime implicant essential are $c'd$ for f and ab for g, as indicated on the maps below.

cd \ ab	00	01	11	10
00		1		
01	1*	1	1	1
11			1	1
10	1	1		

f

cd \ ab	00	01	11	10
00	1	1	1	1
01			1	1
11			1	1
10	1		1*	1

g

Next, we note that *ad* is an essential prime implicant of both functions, producing the following maps:

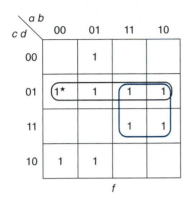

Unless we choose $c'd'$ to cover the remaining three 1's in the first row of *g*, we will need an extra term. Once we have done that, we see that the last 1 (m_2) of *g* can be covered by the minterm and shared with *f*. That leaves just two 1's of *f* that can be covered with the term $a'bd'$. The functions and the maps are shown next:

$$f = c'd + ad + a'b'cd' + a'bd'$$
$$g = ab + ad + c'd' + a'b'cd'$$

for a total of eight gates and 23 inputs.

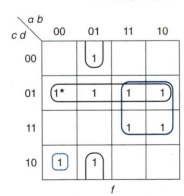

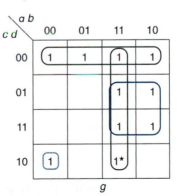

c. When minimizing three functions, we still look for 1's that are only included in one of the functions and that make a prime implicant essential. In this problem, the only ones that satisfy these conditions are m_8 in *F* and m_0 and m_4 in *H*, as shown on the following map.

F

Y Z \ W X	00	01	11	10
00				1*
01			1	1
11	1	1		
10	1	1		

G

Y Z \ W X	00	01	11	10
00				
01			1	1
11	1	1		
10	1	1	1	1

H

Y Z \ W X	00	01	11	10
00	1*	1*		
01	1	1	1	1
11				
10			1	1

Next, notice that $W'Y$ is an essential prime implicant of both F and G. Once that is chosen, the term $WY'Z$ covers the remaining 1 of F and two 1's in G and H. (That term would be used for both F and G in any case since it is an essential prime implicant of both and is shareable. It is used for H since the remaining 1's in the prime implicant $Y'Z$ are already covered.) Finally, WYZ', an essential prime implicant of H, finishes the cover of G and H. The maps and functions below show the final solution, utilizing eight gates and 22 inputs.

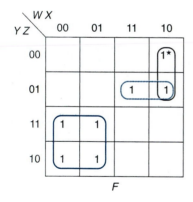

F

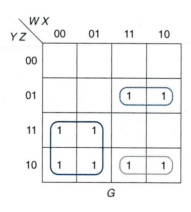

G

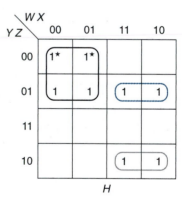

H

$$F = WX'Y' + W'Y + WY'Z$$
$$G = W'Y + WY'Z + WYZ'$$
$$H = W'Y' + WY'Z + WYZ'$$

d. On the following maps, the essential prime implicants that cover 1's not part of any other function are circled. In f, m_9 and m_{11} can each be covered with any of three prime implicants.

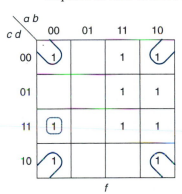

f

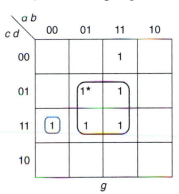

g

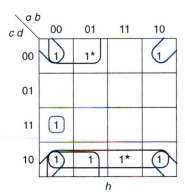

h

Next, we note that m_8 can only be covered by $b'd'$ in h and that $b'd'$ is also an essential prime implicant of f. That leaves only m_3 uncovered in h; by using the minterm for that, it can be shared with both f and g. (Otherwise, a new term would be required in each of those functions.) The resulting maps follow.

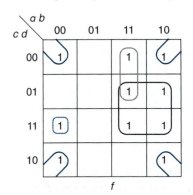

f

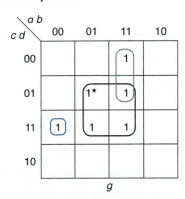

g

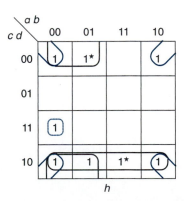

h

The only uncovered 1 in g is m_{12}. By using abc' for both that and for f, we can cover the three remaining 1's in f with ad, yielding the following maps and equations.

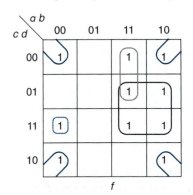

f

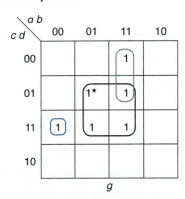

g

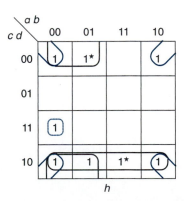

h

$$f = \mathbf{b'd'} + a'b'cd + abc' + ad$$
$$g = bd + a'b'cd + abc'$$
$$h = a'd' + cd' + \mathbf{b'd'} + a'b'cd$$

e. This example includes a number of don't cares, but that does not change the process significantly. There are two essential prime implicants, cd in f and bc in g, that cover 1's that cannot be shared. In addition, $a'b'c'd'$ must be used in f since it is the only prime implicant that covers m_0. (If a minterm is a prime implicant, we have no choice but to use it.) The maps below show these terms circled.

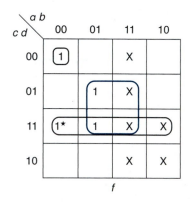

f

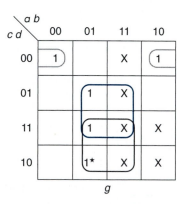

g

Next, we use bd to cover m_5 in both functions, and complete the cover of f. The obvious choice is to use $b'c'd'$ for the remaining 1's of g, producing the following maps and equations:

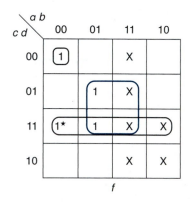

f

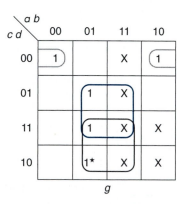

g

$$f = cd + a'b'c'd' + bd$$
$$g = bc + bd + b'c'd'$$

But, there is another solution, as shown in the following equations. By using $a'b'c'd'$ to cover m_0 in g (we already needed that term for f), we can cover the remaining 1 in g with a group of four, ad', producing the solution

$$f = cd + a'b'c'd' + bd$$
$$g = bc + bd + a'b'c'd' + ad'$$

as shown on the following maps. Both solutions require seven gates and 19 inputs.

f

g

3.8 EXERCISES

1. Plot the following functions on the Karnaugh map:
   a. $f(a, b, c) = \Sigma m(1, 2, 3, 4, 6)$
   *b. $g(w, x, y, z) = \Sigma m(1, 3, 5, 6, 7, 13, 14) + \Sigma d(8, 10, 12)$
   c. $F = WX'Y'Z + W'XYZ + W'X'Y'Z' + W'XY'Z + WXYZ$
   *d. $g = a'c + a'bd' + bc'd + ab'd + ab'cd'$
   e. $h = x + yz' + x'z$

2. For each of the following, find all minimum SOP expressions. (If there is more than one solution, the number of solutions is given in parentheses.)
   a. $f(a, b, c) = \Sigma m(1, 2, 3, 6, 7)$
   *b. $g(w, x, y) = \Sigma m(0, 1, 5, 6, 7)$ (2 solutions)
   c. $h(a, b, c) = \Sigma m(0, 1, 2, 5, 6, 7)$ (2 solutions)
   d. $f(a, b, c, d) = \Sigma m(1, 2, 3, 5, 6, 7, 8, 11, 13, 15)$
   *e. $G(W, X, Y, Z) = \Sigma m(0, 2, 5, 7, 8, 10, 12, 13)$
   f. $h(a, b, c, d) = \Sigma m(2, 4, 5, 6, 7, 8, 10, 12, 13, 15)$ (2 solutions)
   g. $g(a, b, c, d) = \Sigma m(0, 1, 2, 3, 4, 5, 6, 8, 9, 10, 12, 15)$ (2 solutions)

h. $g(w, x, y, z) = \Sigma m(2, 3, 6, 7, 8, 10, 11, 12, 13, 15)$

(2 solutions)

*i. $h(p, q, r, s) = \Sigma m(0, 2, 3, 4, 5, 8, 11, 12, 13, 14, 15)$

(3 solutions)

j. $F(W, X, Y, Z) = \Sigma m(0, 2, 3, 4, 5, 8, 10, 11, 12, 13, 14, 15)$

(4 solutions)

k. $f(w, x, y, z) = \Sigma m(0, 1, 2, 4, 5, 6, 9, 10, 11, 13, 14, 15)$

(2 solutions)

*l. $g(w, x, y, z) = \Sigma m(0, 3, 4, 5, 6, 7, 8, 9, 11, 13, 14, 15)$

*m. $H(W, X, Y, Z) = \Sigma m(0, 2, 3, 5, 7, 8, 10, 12, 13)$

(4 solutions)

*n. $f(a, b, c, d) = \Sigma m(0, 1, 2, 4, 5, 6, 7, 8, 9, 10, 11, 13, 14, 15)$

(6 solutions)

o. $g(w, x, y, z) = \Sigma m(0, 1, 2, 3, 5, 6, 7, 8, 9, 10, 13, 14, 15)$

(6 solutions)

p. $f(a, b, c, d) = \Sigma m(0, 3, 5, 6, 7, 9, 10, 11, 12, 13, 14)$

(32 solutions)

3. Map each of the following functions and find the minimum SOP expression:

   a. $F = AD + AB + A'CD' + B'CD + A'BC'D'$

  *b. $g = w'yz + xy'z + wy + wxy'z' + wz + xyz'$

4. For each of the following, find all minimum SOP expressions. (If there is more than one solution, the number of solutions is given in parentheses.) Label the solutions $f_1, f_2, \ldots$

   a. $f(w, x, y, z) = \Sigma m(1, 3, 6, 8, 11, 14) + \Sigma d(2, 4, 5, 13, 15)$

(3 solutions)

  *b. $f(a, b, c, d) = \Sigma m(0, 2, 3, 5, 7, 8, 9, 10, 11) + \Sigma d(4, 15)$

(3 solutions)

   c. $f(w, x, y, z) = \Sigma m(0, 2, 4, 5, 10, 12, 15) + \Sigma d(8, 14)$

(2 solutions)

   d. $f(a, b, c, d) = \Sigma m(5, 7, 9, 11, 13, 14) + \Sigma d(2, 6, 10, 12, 15)$

(4 solutions)

  *e. $f(a, b, c, d) = \Sigma m(0, 2, 4, 5, 6, 7, 8, 9, 10, 14) + \Sigma d(3, 13)$

(3 solutions)

   f. $f(w, x, y, z) = \Sigma m(1, 2, 5, 10, 12) + \Sigma d(0, 3, 4, 8, 13, 14, 15)$

(7 solutions)

5. For each of the following functions, find all of the minimum SOP expressions and all of the minimum POS expressions:

  *a. $f(A, B, C, D) = \Sigma m(1, 4, 5, 6, 7, 9, 11, 13, 15)$

   b. $f(W, X, Y, Z) = \Sigma m(2, 4, 5, 6, 7, 10, 11, 15)$

  *c. $f(a, b, c, d) = \Sigma m(0, 2, 4, 6, 7, 9, 11, 12, 13, 14, 15)$
                              (2 SOP and 1 POS solutions)

  d. $f(w, x, y, z) = \Sigma m(0, 4, 6, 9, 10, 11, 14) + \Sigma d(1, 3, 5, 7)$

  e. $f(a, b, c, d) = \Sigma m(0, 1, 2, 5, 7, 9) + \Sigma d(6, 8, 11, 13, 14, 15)$
                              (4 SOP and 2 POS solutions)

  f. $f(a, b, c, d) = \Sigma m(0, 1, 4, 6, 10, 14) + \Sigma d(5, 7, 8, 9, 11,$
          12, 15)   (13 SOP and 3 POS solutions)

  *g. $f(w, x, y, z) = \Sigma m(1, 3, 7, 11, 13, 14) + \Sigma d(0, 2, 5, 8, 10,$
          12, 15)   (6 SOP and 1 POS solutions)

6. For each of the following five variable functions, find all minimum SOP expressions. (If there is more than one solution, the number of solutions is given in parentheses.)

  a. $F(A, B, C, D, E) = \Sigma m(0, 1, 5, 7, 8, 9, 10, 11, 13, 15, 18, 20,$
          21, 23, 26, 28, 29, 31)$

  *b. $H(A, B, C, D, E) = \Sigma m(5, 8, 12, 13, 15, 17, 19, 21, 23, 24,$
          28, 31)$

  c. $F(V, W, X, Y, Z) = \Sigma m(2, 4, 5, 6, 10, 11, 12, 13, 14, 15, 16,$
          17, 18, 21, 24, 25, 29, 30, 31)$

  d. $G(V, W, X, Y, Z) = \Sigma m(0, 1, 4, 5, 8, 9, 10, 15, 16, 18, 19, 20,$
          24, 26, 28, 31)$

  *e. $H(V, W, X, Y, Z) = \Sigma m(0, 1, 2, 3, 5, 7, 10, 11, 14, 15, 16, 18,$
          24, 25, 28, 29, 31)$ (2 solutions)

  f. $F(A, B, C, D, E) = \Sigma m(0, 4, 6, 8, 12, 13, 14, 15, 16, 17, 18,$
          21, 24, 25, 26, 28, 29, 31)$ (6 solutions)

  *g. $G(V, W, X, Y, Z) = \Sigma m(0, 1, 5, 7, 8, 13, 24, 25, 29, 31)$
                     $+ \Sigma d(9, 15, 16, 17, 23, 26, 27, 30)$
                                (2 solutions)

  h. $H(A, B, C, D, E) = \Sigma m(0, 4, 12, 15, 27, 29, 30) + \Sigma d(1, 5,$
          9, 10, 14, 16, 20, 28, 31)$ (4 solutions)

  i. $F(A, B, C, D, E) = \Sigma m(8, 9, 11, 14, 28, 30) + d(0, 3, 4, 6, 7,$
          12, 13, 15, 20, 22, 27, 29, 31)$
                                (8 solutions)

7. Find a minimum two-level circuit (corresponding to SOP expressions) using AND and one OR gate per function for each of the following sets of functions.

  *a. $f(a, b, c, d) = \Sigma m(1, 3, 5, 8, 9, 10, 13, 14)$
     $g(a, b, c, d) = \Sigma m(4, 5, 6, 7, 10, 13, 14)$ (7 gates, 21 inputs)

  b. $f(a, b, c, d) = \Sigma m(5, 8, 9, 12, 13, 14)$
     $g(a, b, c, d) = \Sigma m(1, 3, 5, 8, 9, 10)$
                      (3 solutions, 8 gates, 25 inputs)

    c. $f(a, b, c, d) = \Sigma m(1, 3, 4, 5, 10, 11, 12, 14, 15)$
        $g(a, b, c, d) = \Sigma m(0, 1, 2, 8, 10, 11, 12, 15)$

(9 gates, 28 inputs)

    d. $F(W, X, Y, Z) = \Sigma m(0, 2, 3, 7, 8, 9, 13, 15)$
        $G(W, X, Y, Z) = \Sigma m(0, 2, 8, 9, 10, 12, 13, 14)$

(2 solutions, 8 gates, 23 inputs)

    e. $f(a, b, c, d) = \Sigma m(1, 3, 5, 7, 8, 9, 10)$
        $g(a, b, c, d) = \Sigma m(0, 2, 4, 5, 6, 8, 10, 11, 12)$
        $h(a, b, c, d) = \Sigma m(1, 2, 3, 5, 7, 10, 12, 13, 14, 15)$

(2 solutions, 12 gates, 33 inputs)

  *f. $f(a, b, c, d) = \Sigma m(0, 3, 4, 5, 7, 8, 12, 13, 15)$
        $g(a, b, c, d) = \Sigma m(1, 5, 7, 8, 9, 10, 11, 13, 14, 15)$
        $h(a, b, c, d) = \Sigma m(1, 2, 4, 5, 7, 10, 13, 14, 15)$

(2 solutions, 11 gates, 33 inputs)

    g. $f(a, b, c, d) = \Sigma m(0, 2, 3, 4, 6, 7, 9, 11, 13)$
        $g(a, b, c, d) = \Sigma m(2, 3, 5, 6, 7, 8, 9, 10, 13)$
        $h(a, b, c, d) = \Sigma m(0, 4, 8, 9, 10, 13, 15)$

(2 solutions for f and g, 10 gates, 32 inputs)

  *h. $f(a, c, b, d) = \Sigma m(0, 1, 2, 3, 4, 9) + \Sigma d(10, 11, 12, 13,$
                  $14, 15)$
        $g(a, c, b, d) = \Sigma m(1, 2, 6, 9) + \Sigma d(10, 11, 12, 13, 14, 15)$

(3 solutions for f, 6 gates, 15 inputs)

    i. $f(a, c, b, d) = \Sigma m(5, 6, 11) + \Sigma d(0, 1, 2, 4, 8)$
        $g(a, c, b, d) = \Sigma m(6, 9, 11, 12, 14) + \Sigma d(0, 1, 2, 4, 8)$

(2 solutions for g, 7 gates, 18 inputs)

3.9   CHAPTER 3 TEST (100 MINUTES, OR TWO 50-MINUTE TESTS)

1. Map each of the following functions (be sure to label the maps):

    a. $f(x, y, z) = \Sigma m(1, 2, 7) + \Sigma d(4, 5)$

	00	01	11	10
0				
1				

b. $g = a'c + ab'c'd + a'bd + abc'$

Circle each of the terms.

	00	01	11	10
00				
01				
11				
10				

2. Find the minimum SOP expression for each of the following functions (that is, circle the terms on the map and write the algebraic expressions).

a.

wx / yz

	00	01	11	10
00		1		1
01		1		
11		1	1	1
10		1		

b.

ab / cd

	00	01	11	10
00	1	1	1	
01	1	1	1	
11			1	1
10	1	1	1	

3. Find all four minimum SOP expressions for the following function. (Two copies of the map are given for your convenience.)

ab / cd

	00	01	11	10
00	1	1	1	
01	1		1	1
11	1		1	1
10		1	1	1

ab / cd

	00	01	11	10
00	1	1	1	
01	1		1	1
11	1		1	1
10		1	1	1

4. For the following function (three copies of the map are shown), find all four minimum solutions.

yz \ wx	00	01	11	10
00		1	1	X
01	X	X		X
11	X			1
10			1	1

yz \ wx	00	01	11	10
00		1	1	X
01	X	X		X
11	X			1
10			1	1

yz \ wx	00	01	11	10
00		1	1	X
01	X	X		X
11	X			1
10			1	1

5. For the following four-variable function, f, find both minimum SOP expressions and both minimum POS expressions.

cd \ ab	00	01	11	10
00			X	
01	X	1	X	1
11	1	1		X
10		X		

6. For the following function, f, find all four minimum SOP expressions and all four minimum POS expressions.

yz \ wx	00	01	11	10
00	X		1	
01	X	1	1	
11	X		X	1
10	X		X	

7. For the following five-variable problem, find both minimum SOP expressions.

A

$DE \backslash BC$	00	01	11	10
00	1		1	
01	1	1		
11	1			
10	1			

0

$DE \backslash BC$	00	01	11	10
00			1	
01		1	1	
11		1	1	1
10				1

1

8. For the following five-variable problem, find both minimum SOP expressions. (5 terms, 15 literals)

A

$DE \backslash BC$	00	01	11	10
00	1			1
01				1
11		1	1	1
10	1			1

0

$DE \backslash BC$	00	01	11	10
00	1	1	1	
01	1			1
11	1	1	1	1
10	1	1	1	

1

9. a. For the following two functions, find the minimum SOP expression for each (treating them as two separate problems).

$yz \backslash wx$	00	01	11	10
00		1	1	1
01				1
11				1
10			1	1

f

$yz \backslash wx$	00	01	11	10
00				
01	1	1		1
11	1	1		1
10		1		

g

b. For the same two functions, find a minimum SOP solution (corresponding to minimum number of gates, and among those with the same number of gates, minimum number of gate inputs). (7 gates, 19 inputs)

10. Consider the three functions, maps for which follow.

f yz\wx	00	01	11	10
00				1
01	1	1		
11	1	1	1	1
10	1	1		1

g yz\wx	00	01	11	10
00		1	1	1
01				
11			1	
10	1	1	1	

h yz\wx	00	01	11	10
00		1		1
01	1	1		
11	1	1	1	
10		1		

a. Find the minimum SOP expression (individually) for each of the three functions. Indicate which, if any, prime implicants can be shared.

b. Find a minimum two-level NAND gate solution. Full credit for a solution using 10 gates and 32 inputs. All variables are available both uncomplemented and complemented. Show the equations *and* a block diagram.

Designing Combinational Systems

4

Until now, we have concentrated on rather small systems—mostly systems with five or fewer inputs and three or fewer outputs. In this chapter, we want to expand our horizons. Large systems are usually designed by breaking them up into smaller subsystems. Indeed, these subsystems may need to be broken down still further.

In this chapter, we will first look at systems that consist of a number of identical blocks. (These are sometimes referred to as *iterative systems.*) Adders and other arithmetic functions are examples of this type of system.

Because signals in large systems pass through many layers of logic, the small delay encountered as a signal passes through a single gate adds up. We will use the design of a multibit adder to illustrate this.

Next, we will look at some common types of circuit—the binary decoder and encoder, and the multiplexer. Each of these have many applications in digital system design and are available commercially in a variety of forms.

Another class of circuits used in the design of medium- and large-size systems is *gate arrays*, sometimes referred to as *programmable logic devices (PLDs)*. As we will discuss in Chapter 7, some PLDs also contain memory. Gate arrays consist of a set of AND gates and a set of OR gates connected to form SOP expressions. The basic structure is standard; some of the connections can be specified by the user. Gate arrays are commonly available in three forms: *read only memory (ROM)*, *programmable logic array (PLA)*, and *programmable array logic (PAL)*.

We will also look at issues of testing and simulation of combinational circuits.

We will then look at the design of a decimal adder and a driver for a seven-segment display. We will use a variety of the techniques of this chapter and Chapter 3 in these designs. A large number of exercises (Ex 18–23) fall into this category.

4.1 ITERATIVE SYSTEMS

We will first look at adders as an example of a system that can be implemented with multiple copies of a smaller circuit. We will use the adder to illustrate the issue of delay in multiple-level circuits and then discuss other iterative circuits.

When we add two numbers by hand, we add the two least significant digits (plus possibly a carry-in) to produce one bit of the sum and a carry to the next bit. Such a one-bit adder (referred to as a full adder) is defined as CE3 and was designed with NAND gates in Example 2.31 (Section 2.8). If we wish to build an n-bit adder, we need only connect n of these. A 4-bit version is shown in Figure 4.1.

Figure 4.1   A 4-bit adder.

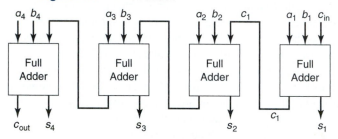

4.1.1   Delay in Combinational Logic Circuits

When the input to a gate changes, the output of that gate does not change instantaneously; but, there is a small delay, Δ. If the output of one gate is used as the input to another, the delays add. A block diagram of a simple circuit is shown in Figure 4.2a and the timing diagram associated with it in Figure 4.2b.

Figure 4.2   Illustration of gate delay.

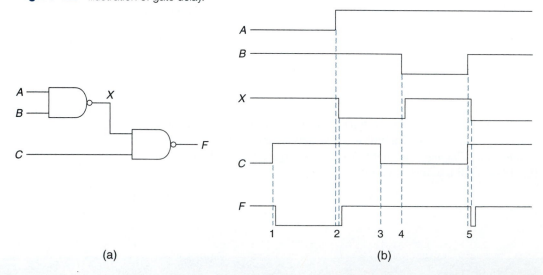

(a)   (b)

When a change in C causes F to change, F changes one delay time, Δ, later, as shown at time 1. If A or B changes, then point X changes one delay time later, and F changes one time after that, as indicated at time 2. At time 3, a change in C does not cause a change in F, and at time 4, a change in B causes a change in X, but not the output. Finally, at time 5, both B and C change simultaneously. The output F goes to 0 briefly when the change in C is recognized (Δ after the change in C), and then F returns to 1 when the change in B is propagated (2Δ after the change in B). This situation is known as a *hazard* or a *glitch*.

The output is stable after the longest delay path. We are not usually interested in the output until it is stable. In this case, that time is 2Δ. As a more complex example of delay, we will consider the *full adder,* the system of CE3. It adds two 1-bit numbers and a carry input from the next less significant digit and produces a sum bit and a carry out to the next more significant digit.

We will now look at the time it takes for the result of an addition to be available at the two outputs of the full adder. We will assume that all inputs are available at the same time. Figure 4.3 repeats the adder circuit of Example 2.31 (from Section 2.8), with the delay (from when inputs a and b change) indicated at various points in the circuit. Of course, if two inputs to a gate change at different times, the output may change as late as Δ after the last input change.

As shown, the delay from the time inputs a or b change to the time that the sum is available is 6Δ and to the time that the carry out is available is 5Δ. If a and b are established,* the delay from the carry-in to the

Figure 4.3 Delay through a 1-bit adder.

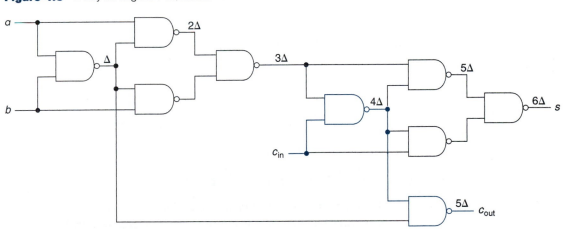

---

*All of the bits of the two multidigit numbers to be added are normally available at one time. Thus, after the least significant digit, all of the a's and b's are established before c_{in} arrives.

carry-out is only 2Δ, since c_{in} passes through only two gates on the way to c_{out}, as shown in the green path. This latter time is most critical, as we will see shortly. (Also, the delay from carry-in to sum is 3Δ.)

We can build an n-bit adder with n copies of the full adder; as shown in Figure 4.1. The total time required is calculated as the delay from the inputs to c_{out} (for the least significant bit) plus $n - 2$ times the delay from c_{in} to c_{out} (for the middle full adders), plus the longer of the delay from c_{in} to c_{out} or from c_{in} to s (for the most significant bit). For the multilevel adder, that equals $5\Delta + 2(n - 2)\Delta + 3\Delta = (2n + 4)\Delta$. For a 64-bit adder, the delay would be 132Δ.

4.1.2   Adders

As indicated in the previous section, one approach to building an n-bit adder is to connect together n 1-bit adders. This is referred to as a *carry-ripple adder*. The time for the output of the adder to become stable may be as large as $(2n + 4)\Delta$. It does not always take that long for all the outputs to be set, because, for any bit, if a_i and b_i are both 1, then a carry-out is always 1 (independent of the carry-in from lower order bits) and if a_i and b_i are both 0, then a carry-out is always 0.

To speed this up, several approaches have been attempted. One approach is to implement a multibit adder with an SOP expression. After all, an n-bit adder (with a carry-in to the least significant bit is just a $2n + 1$ variable problem. In theory, we can construct a truth table for that and get an SOP (or POS) expression.

The truth table for a 2-bit adder is shown in Table 4.1. This can be implemented by an SOP expression. The (five-variable) maps are shown in Map 4.1. The prime implicants are not circled because that would make the map unreadably cluttered.

The minimum SOP expressions are

$$c_{out} = a_2 b_2 + a_1 b_1 a_2 + a_1 b_1 b_2 + c_{in} b_1 b_2 + c_{in} b_1 a_2 + c_{in} a_1 b_2 + c_{in} a_1 a_2$$

$$s_2 = a_1 b_1 a_2' b_2' + a_1 b_1 a_2 b_2 + c_{in}' a_1' a_2' b_2 + c_{in}' a_1' a_2 b_2' + c_{in}' b_1' a_2' b_2 + c_{in}' b_1' a_2 b_2' + a_1' b_1' a_2 b_2' + a_1' b_1' a_2' b_2 + c_{in} b_1 a_2' b_2' + c_{in} b_1 a_2 b_2 + c_{in} a_1 a_2' b_2' + c_{in} a_1 a_2 b_2$$

$$s_1 = c_{in}' a_1' b_1 + c_{in}' a_1 b_1' + c_{in} a_1' b_1' + c_{in} a_1 b_1$$

The equations are very complex, requiring 23 terms with 80 literals. A two-level solution would require a 12-input gate for s_1. Clearly, we could repeat this process for a 3-bit or 4-bit adder, but the algebra gets very complex and the number of terms increases drastically. (We do not have seven- or nine-variable maps; other methods would work, although it

Table 4.1 Two-Bit Adder Truth Table

a_2	b_2	a_1	b_1	c_{in}	c_{out}	s_2	s_1
0	0	0	0	0	0	0	0
0	0	0	0	1	0	0	1
0	0	0	1	0	0	0	1
0	0	0	1	1	0	1	0
0	0	1	0	0	0	0	1
0	0	1	0	1	0	1	0
0	0	1	1	0	0	1	0
0	0	1	1	1	0	1	1
0	1	0	0	0	0	1	0
0	1	0	0	1	0	1	1
0	1	0	1	0	0	1	1
0	1	0	1	1	1	0	0
0	1	1	0	0	0	1	1
0	1	1	0	1	1	0	0
0	1	1	1	0	1	0	0
0	1	1	1	1	1	0	1
1	0	0	0	0	0	1	0
1	0	0	0	1	0	1	1
1	0	0	1	0	0	1	1
1	0	0	1	1	1	0	0
1	0	1	0	0	0	1	1
1	0	1	0	1	1	0	0
1	0	1	1	0	1	0	0
1	0	1	1	1	1	0	0
1	1	0	0	0	1	0	0
1	1	0	0	1	1	0	1
1	1	0	1	0	1	0	1
1	1	0	1	1	1	1	0
1	1	1	0	0	1	0	1
1	1	1	0	1	1	1	0
1	1	1	1	0	1	1	0
1	1	1	1	1	1	1	1

would be a lengthy process by hand.) We could also manipulate the algebra to produce multilevel solutions with fewer large gates, but that would increase the delay. Another problem that we would encounter in that implementation in the real world is that there is a limitation on the number of inputs (called *fan-in*) for a gate. Gates with 12 inputs may not be practical or may encounter delays of greater than Δ.

For the 2-bit adder, c_{out} can be implemented with two-level logic (with a maximum fan-in of seven). Thus, the delay from carry-in to carry-out of every two bits is only 2Δ (other than the first 2 and the last 2 bits) producing a total delay of

$$2\Delta + 2(n/2 - 2)\Delta + 3\Delta = (n + 1)\Delta$$

about half that of the previous solution.

Map 4.1   2-bit adder.

$a_2 = 0$

$c_{in}b_1$ \ b_2a_1	00	01	11	10
00				
01			1	
11			1	1
10			1	

$a_2 = 1$ c_{out}

$c_{in}b_1$ \ b_2a_1	00	01	11	10
00			1	1
01	·	1	1	1
11	1	1	1	1
10		1	1	1

$a_2 = 0$

$c_{in}b_1$ \ b_2a_1	00	01	11	10
00			1	1
01		1		1
11	1	1		
10		1		1

$a_2 = 1$ s_2

$c_{in}b_1$ \ b_2a_1	00	01	11	10
00	1	1		
01	1			1
11			1	1
10	1			1

$a_2 = 0$

$c_{in}b_1$ \ b_2a_1	00	01	11	10
00		1	1	
01	1			1
11		1	1	
10	1			1

$a_2 = 1$ s_1

$c_{in}b_1$ \ b_2a_1	00	01	11	10
00		1	1	
01	1			1
11		1	1	
10	1			1

There have been some compromises, where the carry is implemented with a two-level circuit and the sum is a less complex multilevel circuit. This only increases the delay by a few Δ (for the last sum), independent of n.

There are commercially available 4-bit adders: the 7483, 7483A, and 74283. Each is implemented differently, with a three-level circuit for the carry out. The 7483A and 74283 differ only in pin connections; each produces the sum with a four-level circuit, using a mixture of NAND, NOR, AND, NOT, and Exclusive-OR gates. Thus, the delay from carry-in to carry-out is 3Δ for each four bits, producing a total delay of $(3/4\,n + 1)\Delta$ (an extra delay for the last sum). The 7483 ripples the carry internally (although it has a three-level chip carry out); it uses an eight-level circuit for s_4.

When larger adders are needed, these 4-bit adders can be *cascaded*. For example, a 12-bit adder, using three of the adders of Figure 4.3, is shown in Figure 4.4, where each block represents a 4-bit adder.

Figure 4.4 Cascading 4-bit adders.

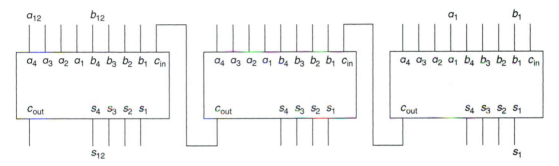

Still another approach is to build a *carry-look-ahead adder*. Each stage of the adder produces two outputs: a carry *generate* signal, g, and a carry *propagate* signal, p. The generate signal is 1 if that stage of the adder has a carry-out of 1, whether or not there was a carry-in. The propagate signal is 1 if that state produces a carry-out of 1 if the carry-in is 1. For a 1-bit adder,

$$g = ab \qquad p = a + b$$

We could build a three-level circuit for the carry-out of any stage. For example, the carry-out of the 4-bit adder we discussed earlier would be

$$c_{out} = g_4 + p_4 g_3 + p_4 p_3 g_2 + p_4 p_3 p_2 g_1 + p_4 p_3 p_2 p_1 c_{in}$$

The carry-out is 1 if the last bit generated a carry, or if it propagated a carry and the stage below it generated a carry, and so forth. This could be extended to any number of bits, limited only by the fan-in capabilities of the logic. (In the 4-bit example, we required a fan-in of five.)*

---

*For a more detailed discussion of carry-look-ahead adders, see Brown and Vranesic, *Fundamentals of Digital Logic with VHDL Design*, 2nd ed., McGraw-Hill, 2005.

4.1.3 Subtractors and Adder/Subtractors

To do subtraction, we could develop the truth table for a 1-bit full subtractor (See Solved Problem 3) and cascade as many of these as are needed, producing a borrow-ripple subtractor.

Most of the time, when a subtractor is needed, an adder is needed as well. In that case, we can take advantage of the approach to subtraction we developed in Section 1.2.4. There, we complemented each bit of the subtrahend and added 1.

To build such an adder/subtractor, we need a signal line that is 0 for addition and 1 for subtraction. We will call that a'/s (short for add'/subtract).* Remembering that

$$1 \oplus x = x' \quad \text{and} \quad 0 \oplus x = x$$

we can now build the circuit of Figure 4.5, using the 4-bit adder we have already designed. There needs to be an Exclusive-OR on each input. The carry-out from one stage is just connected to the carry-in of the next.

Figure 4.5 A 4-bit adder/subtractor.

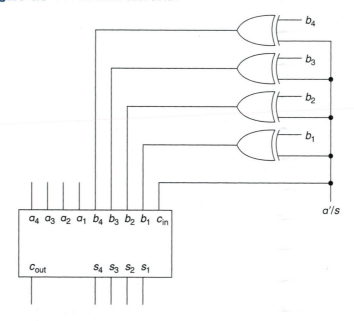

4.1.4 Comparators

A common arithmetic requirement is to compare two numbers, producing an indication if they are equal or if one is larger than the other. The

---

*This notation is quite common. The a' indicates that a 0 on this line calls for addition and the s implies that a 1 on this line calls for subtraction.

Exclusive-OR produces a 1 if the two inputs are unequal and a 0, otherwise. Multibit numbers are unequal if any of the input pairs are unequal. The circuit of Figure 4.6a shows a 4-bit comparator. The output of the NOR is 1 if the numbers are equal. In Figure 4.6b, we accomplished the same thing with Exclusive-NORs and an AND gate.

Figure 4.6 Two 4-bit comparators.

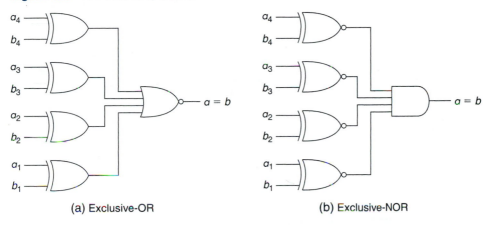

(a) Exclusive-OR (b) Exclusive-NOR

These comparators can be extended to any number of bits.

To build a 4-bit comparator that will indicate greater than and less than, as well as equal to (for unsigned numbers), we recognize that, starting at the most significant bit (a_4 and b_4),

$a > b$ if $a_4 > b_4$ or $(a_4 = b_4$ and $a_3 > b_3)$ or $(a_4 = b_4$ and $a_3 = b_3$ and $a_2 > b_2)$ or $(a_4 = b_4$ and $a_3 = b_3$ and $a_2 = b_2$ and $a_1 > b_1)$

$a < b$ if $a_4 < b_4$ or $(a_4 = b_4$ and $a_3 < b_3)$ or $(a_4 = b_4$ and $a_3 = b_3$ and $a_2 < b_2)$ or $(a_4 = b_4$ and $a_3 = b_3$ and $a_2 = b_2$ and $a_1 < b_1)$

$a = b$ if $a_4 = b_4$ and $a_3 = b_3$ and $a_2 = b_2$ and $a_1 = b_1$

This can, of course, be extended to any size, or 4-bit comparators can be cascaded, passing on the three signals, greater than, less than, and equal to. A typical bit of such a comparator is shown in Figure 4.7.

The 7485 is a 4-bit comparator, with cascading inputs and outputs. Like the adder, the cascading signals go from lower order module to higher order module (as opposed to the previous example). It thus computes the greater output as 1 if the a inputs to this module are greater than the b inputs or if they are equal and the cascading input is greater.

Figure 4.7 Typical bit of a comparator.

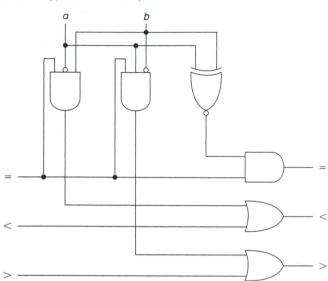

[SP 1, 2, 3, 4; EX 1, 2, 3, 4, 5, 6]

4.2 BINARY DECODERS

A *binary decoder* is a device that, when activated, selects one of several output lines, based on a coded input signal. Most commonly, the input is an *n*-bit binary number, and there are up to 2^n output lines.* (Some decoders have an enable signal that activates it; we will get to that shortly.)

The truth table for a two-input (four-output) decoder is shown in Table 4.2a. The inputs are treated as a binary number, and the output selected is made active. In this example, the output is *active high,* that is, the active output is 1 and the inactive ones are 0. (We will use the terms *active high* and *active low* (active value is 0) to refer both to inputs and outputs.) This decoder just consists of an AND gate for each output, plus NOT gates to invert the inputs. (We assume only *a* and *b* are available, not their complements.) The block diagram is given in Figure 4.8a. Output 0 is just $a'b'$; output 1 is $a'b$; output 2 is ab'; and output 3 is ab. Each output corresponds to one of the minterms for a two-variable function.

An active low output version of the decoder has one 0 corresponding to the input combination; the remaining outputs are 1. The circuit and the truth table describing it are shown in Figure 4.8b and Table 4.2b. The AND gates in the previous circuit are just replaced by NANDs.

Most decoders also have one or more enable inputs. When such an input is active, the decoder behaves as described. When it is inactive, all of the outputs of the decoder are inactive. In most systems with a single

---

*Although 4 inputs have 16 combinations, some decoders only have 10 outputs.

Figure 4.8a An active high decoder.

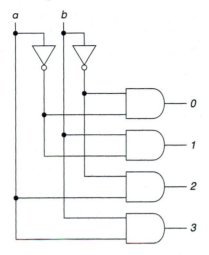

Table 4.2a An active high decoder.

a	b	0	1	2	3
0	0	1	0	0	0
0	1	0	1	0	0
1	0	0	0	1	0
1	1	0	0	0	1

Figure 4.8b An active low decoder.

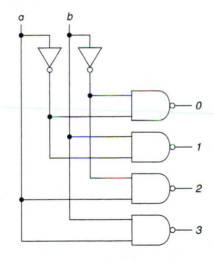

Table 4.2b An active low decoder.

a	b	0	1	2	3
0	0	0	1	1	1
0	1	1	0	1	1
1	0	1	1	0	1
1	1	1	1	1	0

enable input (not just decoders), that input is active low. The truth table, a block diagram, and the circuit for an active high output decoder with an active low enable input is shown in Figure 4.9. Note that the enable input is inverted and connected to each AND gate. When $EN' = 1$, a 0 is on the input to each AND gate and thus, all of the AND gate outputs are 0. When $EN' = 0$, the additional input (beyond those for the circuit without an enable) is 1, and, thus, the output selected by a and b is 1, as before. Active low signals are often indicated with a circle (bubble), as shown in the block diagram in Figure 4.9. In most commercial literature, such signals are labeled with an overbar ($\overline{EN}$), rather than as EN'.

Figure 4.9 Decoder with enable.

EN'	a	b	0	1	2	3
1	X	X	0	0	0	0
0	0	0	1	0	0	0
0	0	1	0	1	0	0
0	1	0	0	0	1	0
0	1	1	0	0	0	1

Notice that we have shortened the truth table (from eight rows to five) by the notation in the first row. That row says that if $EN' = 1$, we don't care what a and b are (X's); all outputs are 0. That notation will appear in many places where we discuss commercial circuits.

Larger decoders can be built; 3-input, 8-output as well as 4-input, 16-output decoders are commercially available. The limitation on size is based on the number of connections to the integrated circuit chip that is required. A 3-input decoder uses 11 logic connections (three inputs and eight outputs) in addition to two power connections and one or more enable inputs.

A truth table for the 74138 one of eight decoders is shown in Table 4.3 and the block diagram is shown in Figure 4.10. This chip has active low outputs and three enable inputs (thus requiring a 16-pin chip), one of which is active high ($EN1$) and the other two are active low. Only when all three ENABLES are active, that is, when

$$EN1 = 1, \quad EN2' = 0 \quad \text{and} \quad EN3' = 0$$

is the chip enabled. Otherwise, all outputs are inactive, that is, 1.

Notice that in this circuit (and this is true in many of the commercial integrated circuit packages) the inputs are labeled C, B, A (with C the high-order bit). In previous examples, we have made A the

Figure 4.10 The 74138 decoder.

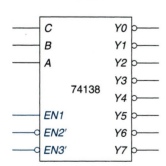

Table 4.3 The 74138 decoder.

Enables			Inputs			Outputs							
EN1	*EN2'*	*EN3'*	*C*	*B*	*A*	*Y0*	*Y1*	*Y2*	*Y3*	*Y4*	*Y5*	*Y6*	*Y7*
0	X	X	X	X	X	1	1	1	1	1	1	1	1
X	1	X	X	X	X	1	1	1	1	1	1	1	1
X	X	1	X	X	X	1	1	1	1	1	1	1	1
1	0	0	0	0	0	0	1	1	1	1	1	1	1
1	0	0	0	0	1	1	0	1	1	1	1	1	1
1	0	0	0	1	0	1	1	0	1	1	1	1	1
1	0	0	0	1	1	1	1	1	0	1	1	1	1
1	0	0	1	0	0	1	1	1	1	0	1	1	1
1	0	0	1	0	1	1	1	1	1	1	0	1	1
1	0	0	1	1	0	1	1	1	1	1	1	0	1
1	0	0	1	1	1	1	1	1	1	1	1	1	0

high-order bit. When using such a device, be sure which input has which meaning.

Two other commercially available decoder chips are the 74154, which is a four-input (plus two active low enables), 16-output decoder (implemented in a 24-pin package), and the 74155, which contains dual two-input, four-output decoders with common inputs and separate enables (such that it can be used as a three-input, eight-output decoder).

One application of decoders is to select one of many devices, each of which has a unique address. The address is the input to the decoder; one output is active, to select the one device that was addressed. Sometimes, there are more devices than can be selected with a single decoder. We will consider two such examples.

EXAMPLE 4.1

We have available 74138 decoders and wish to select one of 32 devices. We would need four such decoders. Typically, one of these would select one of the first eight addressed devices; another would select one of the next eight, and so forth. Thus, if the address were given by bits $a, b, c, d, e,$ then c, d, e would be the inputs (to C, B, A in order) for each of the four decoders, and a, b would be used to enable the appropriate one. Thus, the first decoder would be enabled when $a = b = 0$, the second when $a = 0$ and $b = 1$, the third when $a = 1$ and $b = 0$, and the fourth when $a = b = 1$. Since we have two active low enable inputs and one active high enable, only the fourth decoder would require a NOT gate for the enable input. The circuit is shown next.

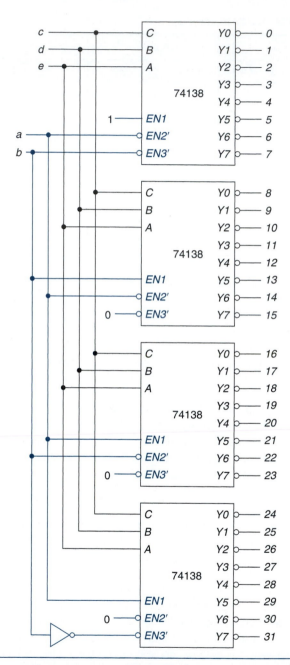

Sometimes, an extra decoder is used to enable other decoders. If, for example, we had a two-input, four-output active low decoder with an active low enable, and needed to select one of 16 devices, we could use one decoder to choose among four groups of devices, based on two of the inputs. Most commonly, the first two (highest order) inputs are used, so that the groupings are devices *0–3, 4–7, 8–11,* and *12–15.* Then, for each group, one decoder is used to choose among the four devices in that group. Such an arrangement is shown below.

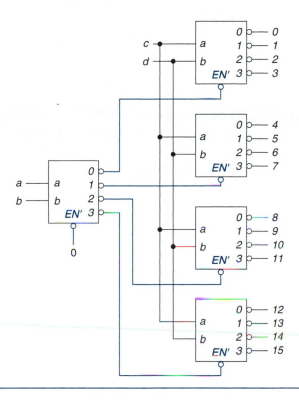

Another application of decoders is the implementation of logic functions. Each active high output of a decoder corresponds to a minterm of that function. Thus, all we need is an OR gate connected to the appropriate outputs. With an active low output decoder, the OR gate is replaced by a NAND (making a NAND-NAND circuit from an AND-OR). With more than one such function of the same set of inputs, we still only need one decoder, but one OR or NAND for each output function.

EXAMPLE 4.3

$f(a, b, c) = \Sigma m(0, 2, 3, 7)$

$g(a, b, c) = \Sigma m(1, 4, 6, 7)$

It could be implemented with either of the decoder circuits shown here.

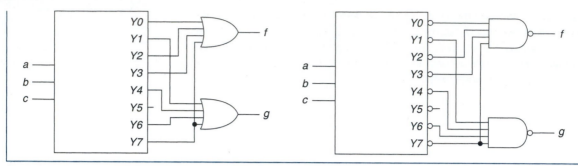

[SP 5, 6, 7, 11d; EX 7, 8, 9, 10]

4.3 ENCODERS AND PRIORITY ENCODERS

A *binary encoder* is the inverse of a binary decoder. It is useful when one of several devices may be signaling a computer (by putting a 1 on a wire from that device); the encoder then produces the device number. If we can assume that exactly one input (of A_0, A_1, A_2, A_3) is 1, then the truth table of Table 4.4 describes the behavior of the device.

If, indeed, only one of the inputs can be 1, then, this table is adequate and

$$Z_0 = A_2 + A_3$$
$$Z_1 = A_1 + A_3$$

This arrangement does not differentiate between device 0 and no device signaling. (If there is no device numbered 0, this is not a problem.) Otherwise, we could add another output, *N*, which indicates that no input is active.

$$N = A_0'A_1'A_2'A_3' = (A_0 + A_1 + A_2 + A_3)'$$

If more than one input can occur at the same time, then some priority must be established. The output would then indicate the number of the highest priority device with an active input. The priorities are normally arranged in descending (or ascending) order with the highest priority given to the largest (smallest) input number. The truth table for an eight-input priority encoder is shown in Table 4.5, where device 7 has the highest priority.

Table 4.4   A four-line encoder.

A_0	A_1	A_2	A_3	Z_0	Z_1
1	0	0	0	0	0
0	1	0	0	0	1
0	0	1	0	1	0
0	0	0	1	1	1

Table 4.5   A priority encoder.

A_0	A_1	A_2	A_3	A_4	A_5	A_6	A_7	Z_0	Z_1	Z_2	NR
0	0	0	0	0	0	0	0	X	X	X	1
X	X	X	X	X	X	X	1	1	1	1	0
X	X	X	X	X	X	1	0	1	1	0	0
X	X	X	X	X	1	0	0	1	0	1	0
X	X	X	X	1	0	0	0	1	0	0	0
X	X	X	1	0	0	0	0	0	1	1	0
X	X	1	0	0	0	0	0	0	1	0	0
X	1	0	0	0	0	0	0	0	0	1	0
1	0	0	0	0	0	0	0	0	0	0	0

The output *NR* indicates that there are no requests. In that case, we don't care what the other outputs are. If device 7 has an active signal (that is, a 1), then the output is the binary for 7, regardless of what the other inputs are (as shown on the second line of the table). Only when $A_7 = 0$ is any other input recognized. The equations describing this device are

$$NR = A_0'A_1'A_2'A_3'A_4'A_5'A_6'A_7'$$
$$Z_0 = A_4 + A_5 + A_6 + A_7$$
$$Z_1 = A_6 + A_7 + (A_2 + A_3)A_4'A_5'$$
$$Z_2 = A_7 + A_5A_6' + A_3A_4'A_6' + A_1A_2'A_4'A_6'$$

The 74147 is a commercial BCD encoder, taking nine active low input lines and encoding them into four active low outputs. The input lines are numbered $9'$ to $1'$ and the outputs are D', C', B', and A'. Note that all outputs of 1 (inactive) indicates that no inputs are active; there is no $0'$ input line. The truth table describing its behavior is shown in Table 4.6.

Table 4.6 The 74147 priority encoder.

$1'$	$2'$	$3'$	$4'$	$5'$	$6'$	$7'$	$8'$	$9'$	D'	C'	B'	A'
1	1	1	1	1	1	1	1	1	1	1	1	1
X	X	X	X	X	X	X	X	0	0	1	1	0
X	X	X	X	X	X	X	0	1	0	1	1	1
X	X	X	X	X	X	0	1	1	1	0	0	0
X	X	X	X	X	0	1	1	1	1	0	0	1
X	X	X	X	0	1	1	1	1	1	0	1	0
X	X	X	0	1	1	1	1	1	1	0	1	1
X	X	0	1	1	1	1	1	1	1	1	0	0
X	0	1	1	1	1	1	1	1	1	1	0	1
0	1	1	1	1	1	1	1	1	1	1	1	0

[SP 8; EX 11]

4.4 MULTIPLEXERS AND DEMULTIPLEXERS

A *multiplexer*, often referred as a *mux*, is basically a switch that passes one of its data inputs through to the output, as a function of a set of select inputs. Often, sets of multiplexers are used to choose among several multibit input numbers.

A two-way multiplexer and its logic symbol are shown in Figure 4.11.

Figure 4.11   Two-way multiplexer.

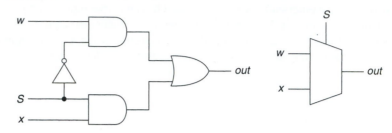

The output, *out,* equals *w* if $S = 0$, and equals *x* if $S = 1$.

A four-way multiplexer can be implemented with AND and OR gates, as shown in Figure 4.12a, or with three two-way multiplexers, as shown in Figure 4.12b. The logic symbol is shown in Figure 4.12c.

Figure 4.12   (a) A four-way multiplexer. (b) From two-way multiplexers. (c) Logic symbol.

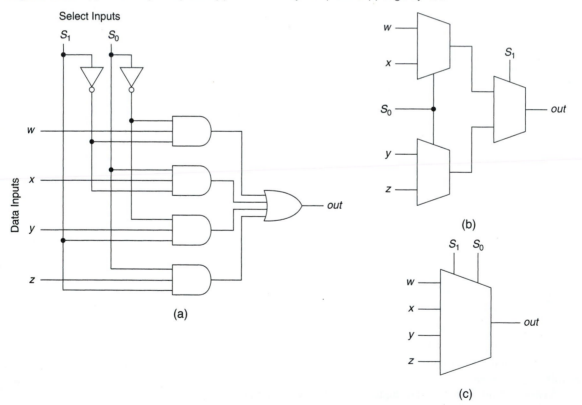

The output equals input *w* if the select inputs (S_1, S_0) are 00, *x* if they are 01, *y* if they are 10, and *z* if they are 11. The circuit is very similar to that of the decoder, with one AND gate for each select input combination. Some multiplexers also have enable inputs, such that *out* is 0 unless the enable is active.

If the inputs consist of a set of 16-bit numbers, and the control inputs choose which of these numbers is to be passed on, then we would need 16 multiplexers, one for each bit. We could build 16 of the circuits of Figure 4.12a, utilizing 64 three-input AND gates and 16 four-input OR gates. (Of course, all of the gates could be replaced by NAND gates.) The alternative is to use one decoder to drive all the multiplexers. The first 3 bits of such a circuit are shown in Figure 4.13.

There are still 16 four-input OR gates, but now the AND gates in the multiplexers require only two inputs. There are, of course, 4 two-input

Figure 4.13 A multibit multiplexer.

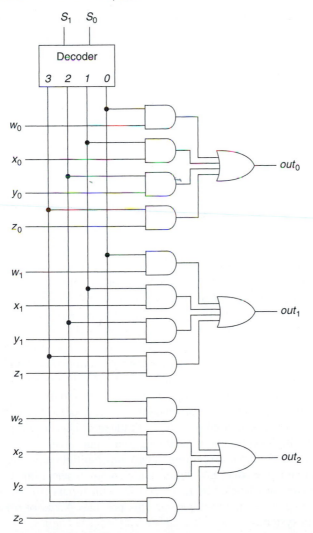

AND gates in the decoder. The total is then 68 two-input gates for a 16-bit multiplexer. If we were to implement this with 7400 series integrated circuits, this implementation would require 17 packages of two-input AND gates (four to a package), whereas the previous solution would require 22 packages of three-input AND gates (three to a package).

Multiplexers can be used to implement logic functions. The simplest approach is to use the select inputs to make a decoder and connect the constants 0 and 1 to the data inputs.

EXAMPLE 4.4

Implement the function

$$f(a, b) = \Sigma m(0, 1, 3)$$

A truth table and the circuit follow

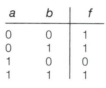

a	b	f
0	0	1
0	1	1
1	0	0
1	1	1

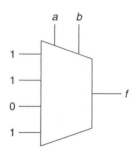

Other implementations to produce more complex functions are beyond the scope of this text.

We will briefly describe three of the commercially available multiplexer packages. The 74151 is a 1-bit eight-way multiplexer with one active low enable input, EN', and both an uncomplemented (active high) and a complemented (active low) output. The data inputs are labeled $A7$ through $A0$ (corresponding to the binary select) and the outputs are Y and Y'. The select inputs are labeled $S2$, $S1$, and $S0$, in that order.

The 74153 contains two (dual) four-way multiplexers, A and B, each with its own active low enable (ENA' and ENB'). The inputs to the first are labeled $A3$ to $A0$ and its output is YA; the inputs to the second are $B3$ to $B0$, with output YB. There are two select lines (labeled $S1$ and $S0$). The same select signal is used for both multiplexers. This would provide 2 bits of multiplexer for choosing among four input words.

The 74157 contains four (quad) two-way multiplexers, with a common active low enable, EN' and a single common select input (S). The multiplexers are labeled A, B, C, and D, with inputs $A0$ and $A1$ and output YA for the first multiplexer. This provides 4 bits of a two-way selection system.

A *demultiplexer (demux)* is the inverse of a mux. It routes a signal from one place to one of many. Figure 4.14 shows one bit of a four-way demux, where *a* and *b* select which way the signal, *in,* is directed. The circuit is the same as for a four-way decoder with the signal *in* replacing *EN*.

Figure 4.14 A four-way demux.

out₀

out₁

out₂

out₃

[SP 9,10; EX 12,13]

4.5 THREE-STATE GATES

Up to this point, we assumed that all logic levels were either 0 or 1. Indeed, we also encountered don't care values, but in any real circuit implementation, each don't care took on either the value 0 or 1. Furthermore, we never connected the output of one gate to the output of another gate, since if the two gates were producing opposite values, there would be a conflict. (In some technologies, it is possible to connect the output of two AND gates and achieve a "wired AND" or a "wired OR," but in others, there is a real possibility that one or more of the gates would be destroyed. Thus, we have not suggested this option in anything we have discussed so far.)

Some design techniques have been used that do allow us to connect outputs to each other. The more commonly used one today is referred to as *three-state* (or tristate) output gates. (We will not discuss other similar implementations, such as transmission gates and open-collector gates.)

In a three-state gate, there is an enable input, shown on the side of the gate. If that input is active (it could be active high or active low), the

Figure 4.15   A three-state buffer.

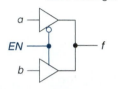

gate behaves as usual. If the control input is inactive, the output behaves as if it is not connected (as an open circuit). That output is typically represented by a Z. The truth table and the circuit representation of a three-state buffer (with an active high enable) is shown in Figure 4.15.

Three-state buffers with active low enables and/or outputs exist; in the latter case, it is a three-state NOT gate. Three-state outputs also exist on other more complex gates. In each case, they behave normally when the enable is active and produce an open circuit output when it is not. With three-state gates, we can build a multiplexer without the OR gate. For example, the circuit of Figure 4.16 is a two-way multiplexer. The enable is the control input, determining whether $f = a$ ($EN = 0$) or $f = b$ ($EN = 1$). The three-state gate is often used for signals that travel between systems. A *bus* is a set of lines over which data is transferred. Sometimes, that data may travel in either direction between devices located physically at a distance. The bus itself is really just a set of multiplexers, one for each bit in the set.

Figure 4.16   A multiplexer using three-state gates.

EXAMPLE 4.5

The following circuits show a bit of two implementations of the bus—one using AND and OR gates and the other using three-state gates.

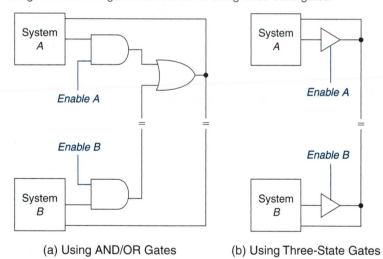

(a) Using AND/OR Gates   (b) Using Three-State Gates

The major difference is the two long wires per bit between the systems for the AND-OR multiplexer compared to only one for the three-state version.

When we discuss gate arrays, both in this chapter and in Chapter 7, we will see that many systems have three-state output buffers.

4.6 GATE ARRAYS*—ROMs, PLAs, AND PALs

Gate arrays are one approach to the rapid implementation of fairly complex systems. They come in several varieties, but all have much in common. The basic concept is illustrated in Figure 4.17 for a system with three inputs and three outputs where the dashed lines indicate possible connections. (This is much smaller than most real gate arrays.)

Figure 4.17 Structure of a gate array.

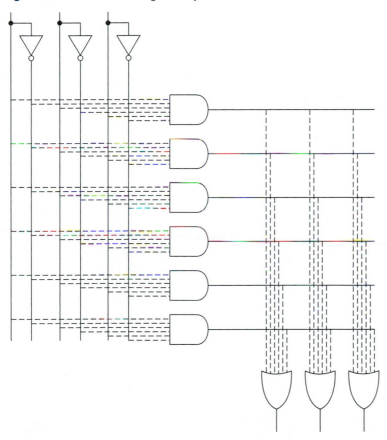

---

*A more general term is a *programmable logic device (PLD)*. That includes all of these, as well as devices that include gate arrays and memory. The term *field programmable gate array (FPGA)* is also commonly used for such devices.

.

What these devices implement are SOP expressions. (In this case, three functions of three variables can be implemented. However, since there are only six AND gates, a maximum of six different product terms can be used for the three functions.) The array only requires uncomplemented inputs; there is internal circuitry that produces the complement.

EXAMPLE 4.6a

The following circuit shows the implementation of

$$f = a'b' + abc$$
$$g = a'b'c' + ab + bc$$
$$h = a'b' + c$$

using such an array, where the solid lines show the actual connections.

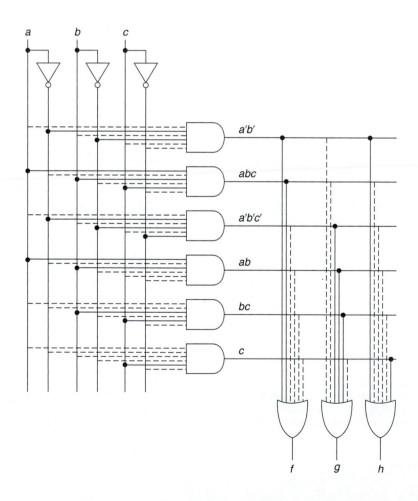

Two things should be noted in this diagram. First, the output of the AND gate that produces the *a′b′* is connected to the inputs of two of the OR gates. That is just sharing the term. Second, the term *c,* which does not require a gate in a NAND gate implementation (or in an AND/OR implementation), does require a term in a logic array. There is no other way to get *c* to the output.

This version of the diagram is rather cumbersome, particularly as the number of inputs and the number of gates increase. Thus, rather than showing all of the wires, only a single input line is usually shown for each gate, with X's or dots shown at the intersection where a connection is made. Thus, the previous circuit can be redrawn as in Example 4.6b.

EXAMPLE 4.6b

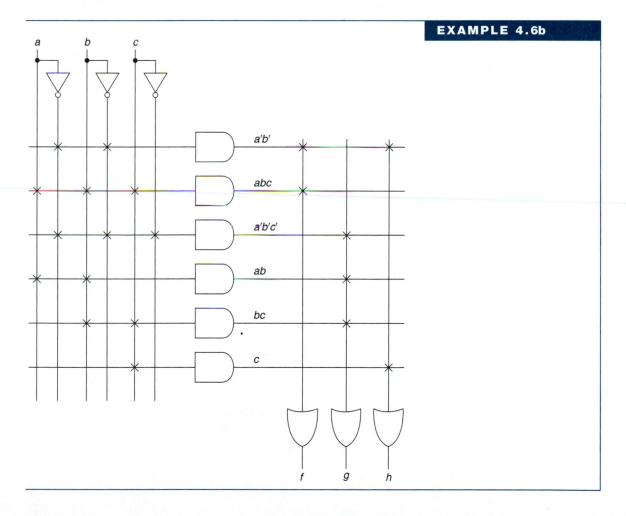

Sometimes, the AND and OR gates are not shown but are understood. (We will see examples of this shortly.)

There are three common types of combinational logic arrays. (We will discuss those with memory in Chapter 7.) The most general type (the one we have illustrated so far) is the *Programmable Logic Array (PLA)*. In the PLA, the user specifies all of the connections (in both the AND array and in the OR array). Thus, we can create any set of SOP expressions (and share common terms). The second type is the *Read-Only Memory (ROM)*. In a ROM, the AND array is fixed. It is just a decoder, consisting of 2^n AND gates for an n input ROM. The user can only specify the connections to the OR gate. Thus, he produces a sum of minterms solution. The third type is the *Programmable Array Logic (PAL)*, where the connections to the OR gates are specified; the user can determine the AND gate inputs. Each product term can be used only for one of the sums. We will discuss each of these in more detail in the sections that follow.

In each case, the base array is manufactured first, with the connections added later. One option is to have them added by the manufacturer on the user's specifications. There are also *field programmable* versions, where the user can enter the connections using a special programming device. The concept behind field programmable devices is to include a fuse in each connection line. If the user does not want the connection, he blows the fuse. (A blown fuse produces a 1 input to the AND gates and a 0 input to the OR gates. That fuse may be electronic, in which case it may be reset.) This sounds more complicated and time consuming than it is; the programming device does all of this automatically from inputs describing the desired array. This idea is carried one step further in the case of ROMs; there are *Erasable Programmable Read-Only Memories (EPROMs)*. (This does sound like an oxymoron, to have a writable read-only device, but they do exist.) One type of fuse can be reset by exposing the device to ultraviolet light for several minutes; another type can be reset electronically.

In addition to the logic shown above, many field programmable devices make the output available in either active high or active low form. (By active low, we really mean the complement of the output, that is, f' instead of f.) This just requires an Exclusive-OR gate on the output with the ability to program one of the inputs to 0 for f and to 1 for f'. The output logic for such a case is shown in Figure 4.18.

Figure 4.18 A programmable output circuit.

0 or 1

$f \oplus 0 = f$
$f \oplus 1 = f'$

f

Some programmable devices have a three-state buffer at the output, which may be enabled either by an enable input line or one of the logic AND gates. This allows the output to be easily connected to a bus.

Sometimes, the output is fed back as another input to the AND array. This allows for more than two-level logic (most commonly in PALs, as we will discuss later on). It also allows that output to be used as an input instead of an output, if a three-state output gate is added, as shown in Figure 4.19.

Figure 4.19 Three-state output.

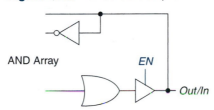

AND Array   EN

Out/In

Note that if the three-state gate is enabled, the connection from the OR array to the output and back as an input to the AND array is established. If the three-state gate is not enabled, the logic associated with that OR is disconnected, and this *Out/In* can be used as just another input to the AND array.

4.6.1 Designing with Read-Only Memories

To design a system using a ROM, you need only to have a list of minterms for each function. A ROM has one AND gate for each minterm; you connect the appropriate minterm gates to each output. This is really the same type of circuitry as the decoder implementation of a sum of product expression presented in Example 4.3.

EXAMPLE 4.7

$W(A, B, C, D) = \Sigma m(3, 7, 8, 9, 11, 15)$

$X(A, B, C, D) = \Sigma m(3, 4, 5, 7, 10, 14, 15)$

$Y(A, B, C, D) = \Sigma m(1, 5, 7, 11, 15)$

The rows of the ROM are numbered (in order) from 0 to 15 for the four-input ROM shown here. An X or a dot is then placed at the appropriate intersection. In the following circuit, the connections shown as X's are built into the ROM; the user supplied the ones shown as dots to implement the functions above.

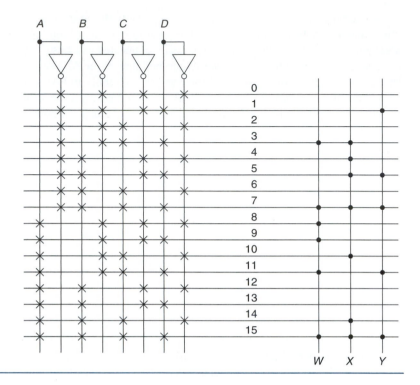

In spite of the terminology, that is, referring to this device as a memory, it is really a combinational logic device, as used in a circuit. The outputs are just a function of the present inputs. In Chapter 7, we will see programmable devices that do have memory in them. Typical commercial programmable ROMs have 8 to 12 inputs and 4 to 8 outputs.

4.6.2 Designing with Programmable Logic Arrays

To design a system using a PLA, you need only find SOP expressions for the functions to be implemented. The only limitation is the number of AND gates (product terms) that are available. Any SOP expression for each of the functions will do, from just a sum of minterms to one that minimizes each function individually to one that maximizes sharing (uses the techniques of Section 3.6).

| EXAMPLE 4.8 | Consider the same example we used to illustrate the ROM design: |

$$W(A, B, C, D) = \Sigma m(3, 7, 8, 9, 11, 15)$$
$$X(A, B, C, D) = \Sigma m(3, 4, 5, 7, 10, 14, 15)$$
$$Y(A, B, C, D) = \Sigma m(1, 5, 7, 11, 15)$$

The first set of maps shows the solution considering these as individual functions. *X* and *Y* have two solutions.

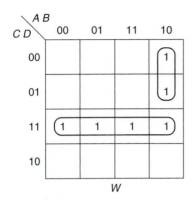

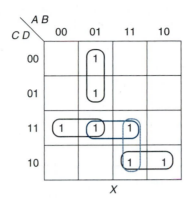

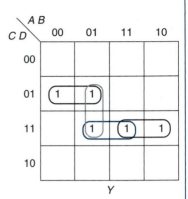

$$W = AB'C' + CD$$
$$Y = A'BC' + A'CD + ACD' + \{BCD \text{ or } ABC\}$$
$$Z = A'C'D + ACD + \{A'BD \text{ or } BCD\}$$

If we choose *BCD* for both *Y* and *Z*, this solution requires eight terms. Otherwise it requires nine terms.

We can use fewer terms, by treating this as a multiple-output problem, as shown in the following maps:

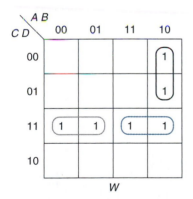

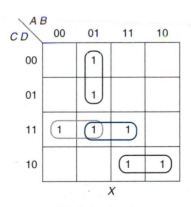

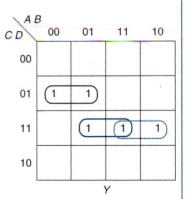

$$W = AB'C' + A'CD + ACD$$
$$X = A'BC' + ACD' + A'CD + BCD$$
$$Y = A'C'D + ACD + BCD$$

This solution only uses seven terms instead of eight or nine.

The following PLA shows both solutions. In the first set of output columns, we show the first solution. The first eight terms are used or the term *BCD* (green dots) can be replaced by *ABC* in *X* and *A'BD* in *Z* (as shown with X's), using a total of nine terms. In the second solution, the second term, *CD*, is not used; only seven product terms are needed. If the PLA to be used is as big as the one shown, it does not matter which solution is chosen.

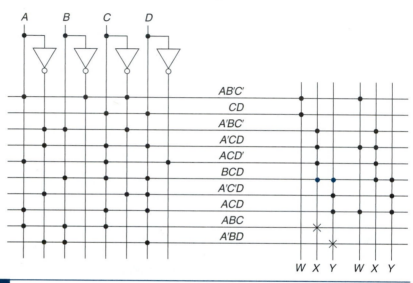

EXAMPLE 4.9

We will look at one other example, to illustrate what happens when there is a term with a single literal. In Example 3.31 (Section 3.6), we saw the following maps:

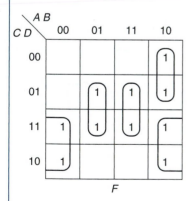

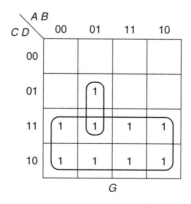

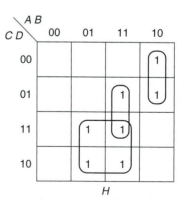

We chose the group of eight, *C* for *G*, because it did not require an AND gate and used only one input to the OR. In a PLA, however, even a single literal term requires a gate, and we are not counting gate inputs. We could reduce the number of terms needed by using $BC + B'C$ for G, since $B'C$ was required for F and BC was required for H. Thus, either set of output columns in the following PLA diagram would be a solution. Note that the term C is only used in the first implementation; the second requires one less term.

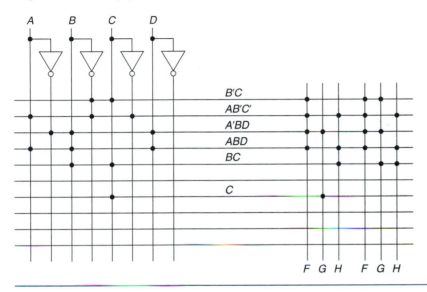

A typical commercially available PLA (PLS100) has 16 inputs, 48 product terms, and 8 outputs. Each output is programmable to be active high or low and has a three-state buffer, controlled by a common active low enable input. Note that this is less than one thousandth the number of product terms that would be required for a ROM with 16 inputs.

4.6.3 Designing with Programmable Array Logic

In a PAL, each output comes from an OR that has its own group of AND gates connected to it. The layout of a small PAL is shown in Figure 4.20.

For this PAL, there are six inputs and four outputs, with each OR gate having four input terms. When using a PAL, the output of each AND gate goes to only one OR. Thus, there is no sharing of terms and we would solve each function individually. However, most PALs provide for the possible feedback of some or all of the outputs to an input. Sometimes this is internal, that is, the output of some of the OR gates is available as another input to all of the AND gates. In other cases, an external connection is made (as implied in Example 4.11). This allows for more terms (more than

Figure 4.20   A PAL.

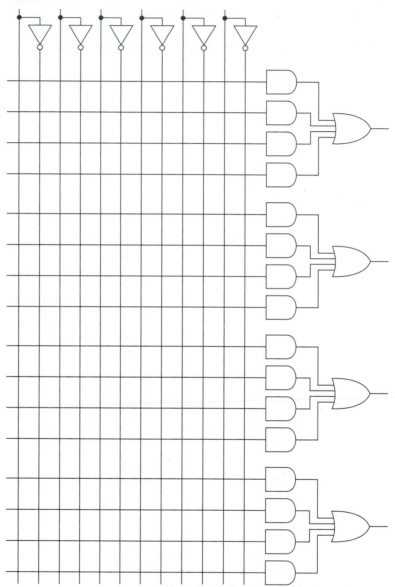

four in this example) in a sum of product expression, or for expressions that are not sum of product, or for sharing a group of terms. Many PALs have a three-state buffer on the output (before the feedback to the inputs), allowing that output to be used as an input as well.

EXAMPLE 4.10

We will first return to the example we used for ROMs and PLAs, namely,

$$W = AB'C' + CD$$
$$X = A'BC' + A'CD + ACD' + \{BCD \text{ or } ABC\}$$
$$Y = A'C'D + ACD' + \{A'BD \text{ or } BCD\}$$

There is no reason to consider sharing. Choosing the first of each of the optional terms, the implementation is

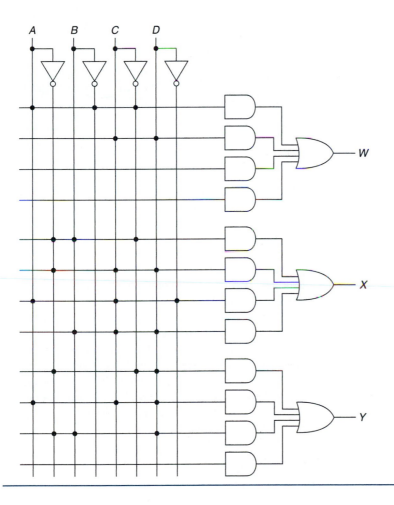

EXAMPLE 4.11

As an example of a system where feedback is useful, consider the functions shown in the following maps:

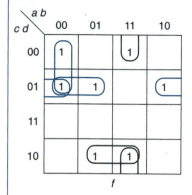

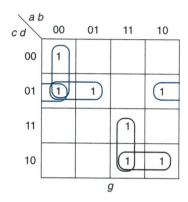

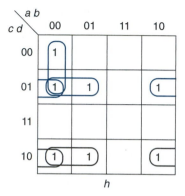

Note that the three green terms are essential prime implicants of each function; the other two are not. This results in the following equations:

$$f = a'b'c' + a'c'd + b'c'd + abd' + bcd'$$
$$g = a'b'c' + a'c'd + b'c'd + abc + acd'$$
$$h = a'b'c' + a'c'd + b'c'd + a'cd' + b'cd'$$

(This solution was obtained by considering each function individually. If we treated this as a multiple-output problem, we would use the term $ab'cd'$ in both g and h, rather than acd' in g and $b'cd'$ in h. That would reduce the number of different terms in the algebraic solution, but would not change the number of gates used in the PAL.) The PAL implementation is shown in the following circuit. The first three terms are implemented in the first OR gate, the output of which, t, is fed back to the input of one of the AND gates in each of the other three circuits. Note that the fourth AND gate of the t circuit has both a and a' connected at its input. Obviously, the output of that AND gate is 0. Some implementations require the user to connect unused AND gates in that way. (We did not do that for the other unused AND gates.)

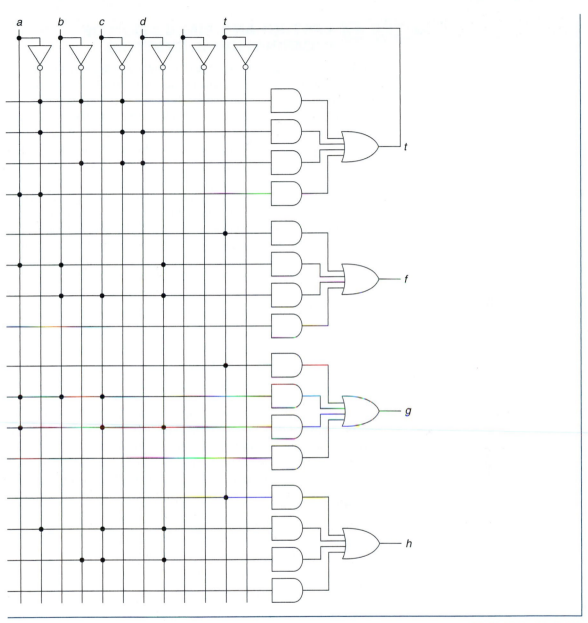

[SP 11; EX 14, 15, 16, 17]

4.7 TESTING AND SIMULATION OF COMBINATIONAL SYSTEMS

After designing a system, it is necessary to test it to make sure that it does what it was intended to do. For a small system, this means applying all possible input combinations and comparing the output with what was expected. As systems get a little larger, that process becomes very time-consuming. For example, if we are testing the behavior of a 4-bit adder (with carry input), there are 2^9 input combinations to test. We can be sure that it works by trying many fewer input sets, as long as we are careful to make sure that all parts of the circuit are tested (each sum circuit and each carry circuit).

When building a large system, it is often necessary to break it into several smaller systems and design and test each subsystem separately. If you are building a large number of a particular system, you would normally design an integrated circuit. Before committing to that design, you must test the design, either by building a circuit using small-scale components or simulating it.

4.7.1   An Introduction to Verilog

Most design of significant digital systems is done with computer-aided tools. They allow the user to specify either the behavior of the system or the structure of the system (or a mixture of the two) using a notation similar to a programming language. The two most widely used systems are *Verilog* and *VHDL*. They have many similarities, but differ in detail. In this section, we will show examples of Verilog code, both structural and behavioral, but a discussion adequate to allow the user to design using any HDL is beyond the scope of this book.*

We will first illustrate a structural Verilog description, using the full adder first discussed in Example 2.31 and shown here as Figure 4.21.

Figure 4.21   A full adder.

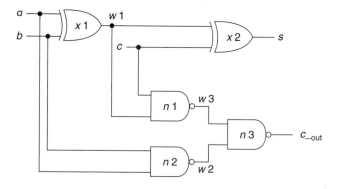

---

*For a detailed discussion of Verilog or VHDL, see Brown and Vranesic, *Fundamentals of Digital Logic with Verilog Design,* McGraw-Hill, 2003 or Brown and Vranesic, *Fundamentals of Digital Logic with VHDL Design,* 2nd ed. McGraw-Hill, 2005.

The corresponding Verilog code (description) is shown in Figure 4.22.

Figure 4.22 Verilog structural description of a full adder.

```
module full_adder (c_out, s, a, b, c);
     input a, b, c;
     wire a, b, c;
     output c_out, s;
     wire c_out, s;
     wire w1, w2, w3;
     xor x1 (w1, a, b);
     xor x2 (s, w1, c);
   nand n1 (w2, a, b);
     nand n2 (w3, w1, c);
     nand n3 (c_out, w3, w2);
   endmodule
```

The first line includes the key word `module` followed by the name of the module and the parameters, that is, the outputs and the inputs. Names may include character other than spaces; Verilog is case-sensitive, that is x1 means something different from X1. (The symbol _ is used to connect multiple word names.) Each module ends with the statement `endmodule`. Statements within Verilog are ended with a semicolon(;), other than `endmodule`. A list of inputs and outputs must be included, and each gate output must be declared a `wire`. Structural Verilog includes most standard gate types, such as `and, or, not, nand, nor, xor`. They are indicated by listing the key word (such as `xor`), a unique name for each copy of that device, their output wire name, and their inputs, as shown in Figure 4.22. The connections for the circuit are made exactly as in Figure 4.21. The order in which the logic statements are written does not matter. (That is not true in behavioral Verilog.)

A 4-bit adder can be built using the full adder as a building block, as shown in Figure 4.23. (We will use a full adder for the least significant bit, although a half adder would do.)

Figure 4.23 A 4-bit adder.

```
module  adder_4_bit (c, sum, a, b);
     input a, b;
     output c, sum;
     wire [3:0] a, b, sum;
     wire c0, c1, c2, c;
     full_adder f1 (c0, sum[0], a[0], b[0], 'b0);
     full_adder f2 (c1, sum[1], a[1], b[1], c0);
     full_adder f3 (c2, sum[2], a[2], b[2], c1);
     full_adder f4 (c, sum[3], a[3], b[3], c2);
endmodule
```

Some additional notation appears in this example. Multibit wires are labeled with brackets. The `wire [3:0] a, b, sum` declaration states that each of the inputs and the sum output are 4 bits (with the highest number on the left. When a module is used, such as `full_adder`, the order of the parameters is what matters, not the name. Thus, the first copy of the full adder adds the least significant bits, `a[0]` and `b[0]`, with a 0 in the carry position (denoted as `'b0`, where the `'b` indicates that the number following it is binary).

Verilog also provides for the description of the behavior of a system, without specifying the details of the structure. This is often the first step in the design of a complex system, made up of a number of modules. The behavioral description of each module can be completed and tested. That is often much more straightforward. Once that works, the individual modules can be designed and described structurally. The structural description can then replace the behavioral one, one module at a time. Behavioral Verilog uses notation very similar to the C programming language. Both the normal mathematics operators (such as $+$, $-$, $*$, and $/$) are available, as well as bitwise logical operators (not: $\sim$, and: $\&$, or: $|$, and exclusive or: $\wedge$). Two behavioral Verilog descriptions of the full adder are shown in Figure 4.24.

Figure 4.24 Behavioral Verilog for the full adder.

```
module full_adder (c_out, s, a, b, c);
    input a, b, c;
    wire a, b, c;
    output c_out, s;
    reg c_out, s;
    always
        begin
            s = a ^ b ^ c;
            c_out = (a & b) | (a & c_in) | (b & c_in);
        end
endmodule
```

(a) With logic equations.

```
module full_adder (c_out, s, a, b, c);
    input a, b, c;
    wire a, b, c;
    output c_out, s;
    reg c_out, s;
    always
        {c_out, s}  = a + b + c;
endmodule
```

(b) With algebraic equations.

Note that values set in behavioral models are referred to as `reg`, rather than `wire`.

4.8 LARGER EXAMPLES

In this section, we will look at the design of two systems that are somewhat larger than any we have considered so far. The design of much larger systems, such as a computer, is deferred to Part II of the text.

4.8.1 A One-Digit Decimal Adder

We want to design an adder to add two decimal digits (plus a carry in), where the digits are stored in 8421 code. This system would have nine inputs (two coded digits plus the carry in) and five outputs (the one digit and the carry out). Rather than trying to solve a nine-input problem, we can break it up into smaller parts, using the 4-bit binary adder that we already designed (or obtained on a single chip). We will assume that none of the unused inputs ever occur.

Decimal addition can be performed by first doing binary addition. Then, if the sum is greater than 9, a carry is generated and 6 is added to this digit. (That is to make up for the six combinations that are not used). For example,

		0		1	1
0011	3	0111	7	1000	8
0101	5	0101	5	1001	9
0 1000	8	0 1100	– –	1 0010	1 2
sum ≤ 9		0110	6	0110	6
no correction		1 0010	1 2	1 1000	1 8

We add the two numbers using a binary adder and detect whether the sum is greater than 10. If it is, we must add six (0110) to the result. A block diagram of the decimal adder, using two binary adders, is shown in Figure 4.25.

The carry detect circuit takes the output of the first adder (including the carry) and produces a 1 output if that number is greater than 9. That is the carry output from the decimal adder, as well as the correction indicator. When there is a carry out, 6 is added to the answer from the first adder; otherwise, 0 is added. A map for the carry detect circuit is shown as Map 4.2.

Figure 4.25 A decimal adder.

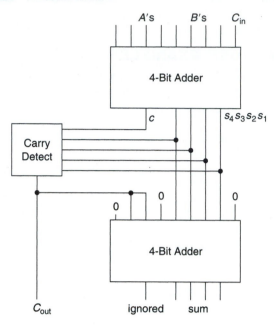

Map 4.2 Carry detect.

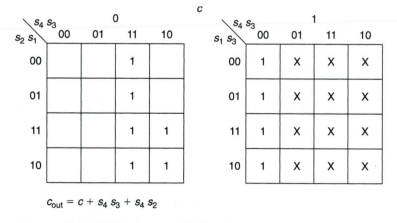

$$C_{out} = c + s_4\,s_3 + s_4\,s_2$$

4.8.2   A Driver for a Seven-Segment Display

In Chapter 2 (CE4), we introduced the seven-segment display commonly used for decimal digits. A block diagram of that display system is repeated as Figure 4.26.

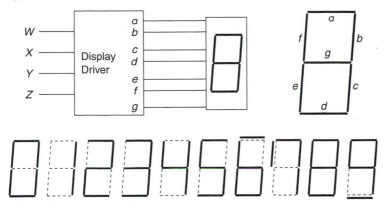

where the solid lines represent segments to be lit and the dashed ones segments that are not lit. For digits 6, 7, and 9, two alternative representations are shown (that is, one segment of each may or may not be lit).

This display driver is a problem with four inputs, W, X, Y, and Z and seven outputs, a, b, c, d, e, f, and g. If, indeed, the system is to display only a decimal digit, and the inputs are limited to only proper codes for those digits, then only 10 of the possible 16 input combinations can occur. The others can be treated as don't cares. In Section 2.1.2, we chose the 8421 code (straight binary) to represent the decimal digits and showed the truth table under the assumption that a 1 input to the display would cause that segment to be lit. Although this seems like a natural assumption, displays are available that require a 0 on a segment input to light that segment.

There are several approaches to this design. There are BCD-to-seven–segment converters available, such as the 7449, that could be used for this problem. (There are also chips that produce an active low output.)

We could solve each of these as individual functions (as in Section 3.3), or we could treat them as multiple-output problems, as in Section 3.6. We could also use a ROM, a PLA, or a PAL to complete the design. We will design the ROM and PLA solution for this problem.

Solving each as an individual function is very straightforward. There are several prime implicants that can be shared. The minimum is obtained by choosing one of the multiple solutions for g that takes advantage of sharing. A minimum solution, shown in Map 4.3, is

$a = W + Y + XZ + X'Z'$
$b = X' + YZ + Y'Z'$
$c = X + Y' + Z$
$d = X'Z' + YZ' + X'Y + XY'Z$
$e = X'Z' + YZ'$
$f = W + X + Y'Z'$
$g = W + X'Y + XY' + \{XZ' \text{ or } YZ'\}$

Map 4.3   Seven-segment display driver.

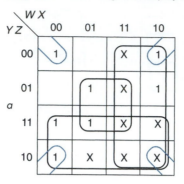

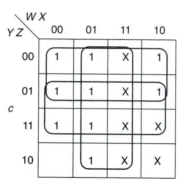

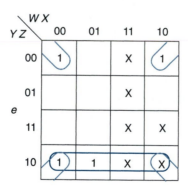

where the shared terms are shown in green, light green, and gray. There are eight unique terms requiring gates (since single literal terms do not require a gate). Thus, this would require a total of 15 gates, assuming all inputs are available both uncomplemented and complemented. (Otherwise, four additional NOT gates would be required.) If these were implemented with 7400 series NAND gates, then we would use

Type	Number	Number of modules	Chip number
2-in	8	2	7400
3-in	4	1	7410
4-in	3	2	7420

where only one 7410 is required since the extra four-input gate would be used as the fourth three-input gate. Treating this as a multiple-output problem, we could save one gate by using $XY'Z$ in function a in place of XZ.

A more interesting problem (in the sense that there is more of an advantage to treating the problem as a multiple-output one) results if we demand that all segments be unlit if the code is not one of those used for a decimal digit. The maps for this, with the minimum solutions circled, are shown in Map 4.4. All of the don't cares for minterms 10 to 15 have become 0's. (The don't cares for the alternative representations of 6, 7, and 9 remain.) The shared prime implicants are shown circled in green, light green, and gray. (There are multiple solutions to several of the functions; the one that provides the maximum sharing is shown.)

One way to display the answer is shown in Table 4.7, with a row for each product term and a column for each function. An X is placed in the column if that product term is used in the function.

Table 4.7 Seven-segment display driver (prime implicants only).

	a	b	c	d	e	f	g
$X'Y'Z'$	X			X	X		
$WX'Y'$	X					X	X
$W'Y$	X						
$W'XZ$	X						
$W'Y'Z'$		X				X	
$W'X'$		X					
$W'YZ$		X					
$X'Y'$		X	X				
$W'X$			X			X	
$W'Z$			X				
$W'YZ'$				X	X		X
$W'X'Y$				X			X
$W'XY'Z$				X			
$W'XY'$							X

Map 4.4   Seven-segment display driver (individual).

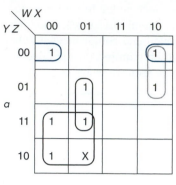
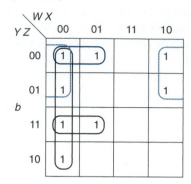
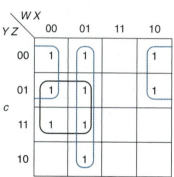

The algebraic expressions can be obtained by just ORing the terms included in each function. We can count the number of gates (one for each term, that is, each row and one for each output column). The number of gate inputs is also easy to compute, since we just add the number of literals in each term and the number of X's in each function (corresponding to OR gate inputs). For this example, the total is 21 gates and 62 gate inputs.

We next attempt to solve this by sharing terms wherever possible, even if the term is not a prime implicant. The first obvious spot is in a, where the prime implicant $W'XZ$ can be replaced by the term $W'XY'Z$, a term we already need for d. Map 4.5 shows a minimum solution, where terms that are shared are shown circled in green, light green, and gray. This results in the solution of Table 4.8.

Table 4.8 Seven-segment display driver (maximum sharing).

	a	b	c	d	e	f	g
$X'Y'Z'$	X			X	X		
$WX'Y'$	X					X	X
$W'XY'Z$	X			X			
$W'YZ$	X	X	X				
$W'X'Y$	X	X		X			X
$W'Y'Z'$		X				X	
$X'Y'$		X	X				
$W'X$			X			X	
$W'YZ'$				X	X		X
$W'XY'$							X

This solution requires only 10 terms and thus 17 gates, a savings of 4 gates, and 54 inputs, a savings of 8 gate inputs. The corresponding equations are thus

$a = X'Y'Z' + WX'Y' + W'XY'Z + W'YZ + W'X'Y$

$b = W'YZ + W'X'Y + W'Y'Z' + X'Y'$

$c = W'YZ + X'Y' + W'X$

$d = X'Y'Z' + W'XY'Z + W'X'Y + W'YZ'$

$e = X'Y'Z' + W'YZ'$

$f = WX'Y' + W'Y'Z' + W'X$

$g = WX'Y' + W'X'Y + W'YZ' + W'XY'$

If we are to implement each of these with 7400 series NAND gates, the system would require

Map 4.5   Seven-segment display driver (maximum sharing).

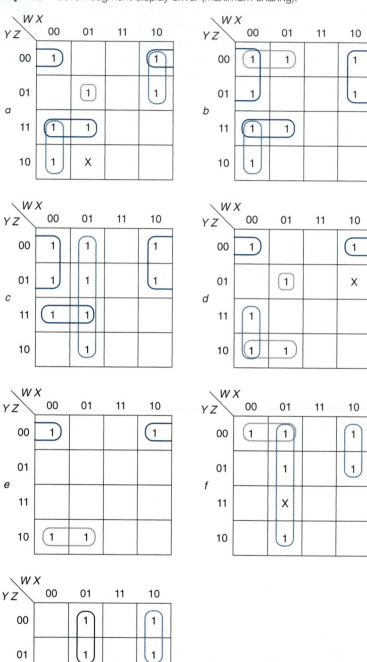

		Individually		Multiple output	
Type	**Chip number**	**Number**	**Number of modules**	**Number**	**Number of modules**
2-in	7400	6	2	3	1
3-in	7410	10	3	9	3
4-in	7420	5	3	4	2
8-in	7430	0		1	1
Total		21	8	17	7

Thus, we save four gates and one module by treating this as a multiple-output problem.

Notice that these two solutions are not equal. The first treats the don't care in d as 0 and the don't cares in a and f as 1's; the second treats the don't cares in a and d as 0's and only the one in f as a 1.

We could also implement this problem using the ROM shown in Figure 4.27. Note that we did not include any of the don't cares; we could have made any or all of them 1's. Notice that this solution is not equal to either of the other ones, since each of them treat at least one of the don't cares as 1.

Figure 4.27 ROM implementation of seven-segment display driver.

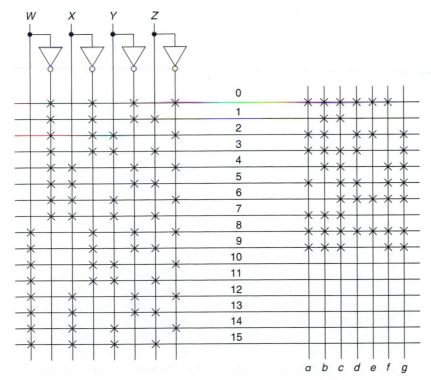

We could implement this system with the PLA of Figure 4.28 with four inputs, seven outputs, and 14 product terms. If all we had were 10 product terms, then we must use the minimum solution we found for the NAND implementation. If we have more terms, then a less minimum solution could be utilized.

Figure 4.28 PLA implementation of seven-segment display driver.

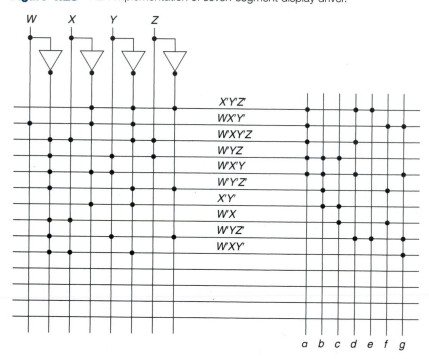

If we wished to implement this with a PAL, we would need seven OR gates (two of the circuits we discussed in the previous section). There are a number of variations to this problem, each of which creates a totally new problem. We could require 0's to light a segment, in which case the complement of each of these functions must be found. That would create a whole new set of maps. Once again, we could demand that the unused conditions be unlit, or we could allow them to be don't cares. We could specify the form for 6, 7, and/or 9, thus eliminating those don't cares. That would change the problem slightly. We could make this into a hexadecimal display, in which case the last six codes would represent A, B, C, D, E, and F. Finally, one of the other codes could have been used for the decimal digits, with each of the variations described earlier. Some of these are included in the Solved Problems and Exercises.

[SP 12, 13, 14; EX 18, 19, 20, 21, 22, 23]

4.9 SOLVED PROBLEMS

1. For the following circuit

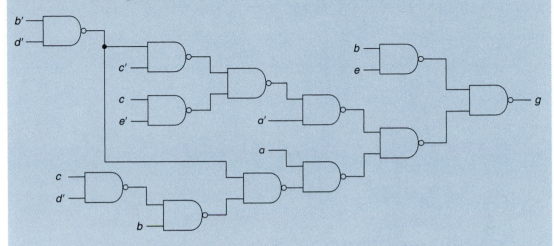

   a. Compute the maximum delay,

      i. Assuming that all inputs are available both uncomplemented and complemented.

      ii. Assuming only uncomplemented inputs are available and an additional gate must be added to complement each input.

   b. Compute the maximum delay from input a to the output, assuming that all inputs are available both uncomplemented and complemented.

   a. i. The signal from the gate whose inputs are b' and d' must pass through six gates.

      ii. Both b and d must be complemented and thus there is a seventh delay.

   b. Signal a passes through only three gates.

2. We want to build a NAND gate circuit to compute the parity of an **n**-bit number. The parity is defined as 1 if and only if there are an odd number of 1's in the number.* One way of doing this is to build the circuit 1 bit at a time (as in the adder), such that the circuit computes the parity after that bit as a function of the

*This is sometimes referred to as odd parity. However, the terminology is used in two different ways. Some use odd parity to mean an odd number of 1's in the word plus the parity bit (which is, of course, the opposite of what we defined). For our purposes, we will stick to the definition above.

parity up to that bit and the one input bit. A block diagram of
the first few bits of such a circuit is shown below.

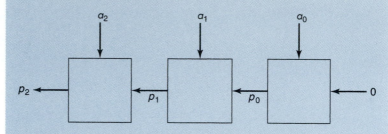

a. Show a NAND gate circuit to implement 1 bit and compute
the delay for **n** bits. Assume that inputs are available only
uncomplemented.

b. Reduce the delay by implementing 2 bits at a time.

a. Each block has a truth table

p_{i-1}	a_i	p_i
0	0	0
0	1	1
1	0	1
1	1	0

that is, the output parity indicates an odd number of 1's so far
if the input indicated there were an even number of 1's
($p_{i-1} = 0$) and this bit (a_i) is 1, or if the input indicated there
were an odd number of 1's ($p_{i-1} = 1$) and this bit (a_i) is 0. The
logic expression is

$$p_i = p'_{i-1}a_i + p_{i-1}a'_i$$

This requires a three-level NAND circuit; it is just an
Exclusive-OR, as shown here

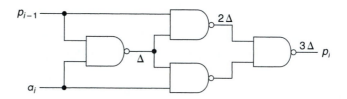

The delay from either input to the output is 3Δ. If we had an
n-bit number, the total delay would then be $3n\Delta$.

b. We can build a block that computes 2 bits of parity at a time. We will call the inputs a, b, and p_{in} and the output p_{out}. The truth table is thus

a	b	p_{in}	p_{out}
0	0	0	0
0	0	1	1
0	1	0	1
0	1	1	0
1	0	0	1
1	0	1	0
1	1	0	0
1	1	1	1

The equation for p_{out} is thus

$$p_{out} = a'b'p_{in} + a'bp'_{in} + ab'p'_{in} + abp_{in}$$

and the NAND circuit is

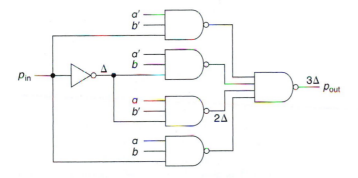

where the NOT gate required for p_{in} is shown (but not those for a and b). The total delay for the 2 bits is 3Δ and thus the **n**-bit delay is $1.5\,n\Delta$. We could reduce the delay by building a separate circuit for p'_{out} in each box. It would also require five NAND gates, since

$$p'_{out} = a'b'p'_{in} + a'bp_{in} + ab'p_{in} + abp'_{in}$$

However, now we do not need the NOT gate for the parity input and thus, these circuits are all two-level and the delay per two bits is 2Δ and the total delay for **n** bits is $n\Delta$.

3. Design a full subtractor, that is, a circuit which computes $a - b - c$, where c is the borrow from the next less significant digit and produces a difference, d, and a borrow from the next more significant bit, p.

The truth table for the full subtractor is as follows:

a	b	c	p	d
0	0	0	0	0
0	0	1	1	1
0	1	0	1	1
0	1	1	1	0
1	0	0	0	1
1	0	1	0	0
1	1	0	0	0
1	1	1	1	1

Note that the difference bit is the same as the sum bit for the adder. The borrow is 1 if there are more 1's in b and c than in a. Thus, the equations become

$$d = a'b'c + a'bc' + ab'c' + abc$$
$$p = bc + a'c + a'b$$

The eight-NAND gate circuit used for the adder could be used for d. However, the p circuit would be different from c_{out}.

$$p = bc + a'c + a'b = c(b + a') + a'b = c(a' \oplus b) + a'b$$
$$= c(a \oplus b)' + a'b$$

This would require two NAND gates and two NOT gates for the borrow (in addition to the eight NAND gates for the difference). The timing would be the same as for the adder, except that the first borrow out delay would now be 6Δ (an increase of 1).

If we wish to use the minimum number of gates, we would need to factor a from both functions, rather than c. An extra NAND and a NOT is needed (compared with the adder). One solution would be

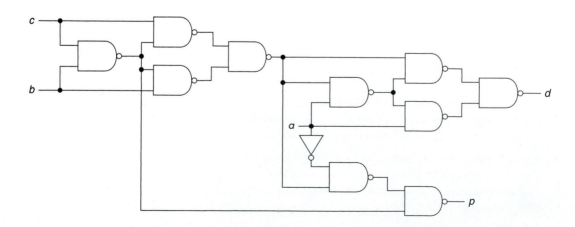

The disadvantage of this approach is that the delay from borrow in to borrow out is 5Δ.

4. We have two 4-bit comparators that produce greater than ($>$), equal ($=$), and less than ($<$) outputs. Show the external logic that can be used to cascade them.

The output indicates equal if both comparators show equal. It is greater than if the high-order one is greater than or if it is equal and the low-order one is greater than. Finally, it shows less than if the high-order one shows less than or if the high-order one is equal and the low-order one is less than. (This is how the internal logic of the 7485 works, although the details of the circuit are quite different.)

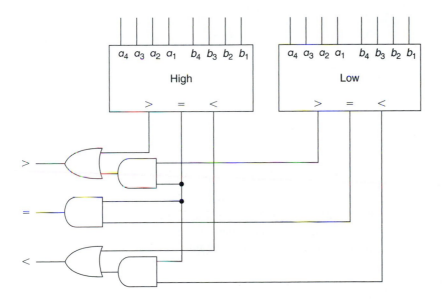

5. We have a decoder with three inputs, a, b, and c, and eight active low outputs, labeled 0 through 7. In addition, there is an active low enable input EN'. We wish to implement the following function using the decoder and as few NAND gates as possible. Show a block diagram.

$$f(a, b, c, e) = \Sigma m(1, 3, 7, 9, 15)$$

Note that all of the minterms are odd; thus, variable e is 1 for each of these. If we enable the decoder when $e = 1$, that is, connect e' to the enable input, and connect a, b, and c to the control inputs, the outputs of the decoder will correspond to minterms

1, 3, 5, 7, 9, 11, 13, and 15. Thus, the following circuit solves the problem:

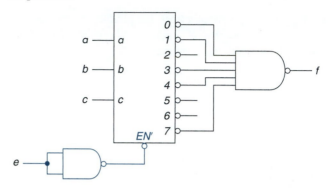

---

6. We wish to build a 32-way active high decoder, using only the four-way decoders shown here.

EN	a	b	0	1	2	3
0	X	X	0	0	0	0
1	0	0	1	0	0	0
1	0	1	0	1	0	0
1	1	0	0	0	1	0
1	1	1	0	0	0	1

The inputs are v, w, x, y, and z; the outputs are numbered 0 to 31.

We need eight of these decoders at the output. Each is enabled based on the first 3 bits of the input. Thus, we need an eight-way decoder for the enabling. That must be built in two levels, as shown in the following diagram.

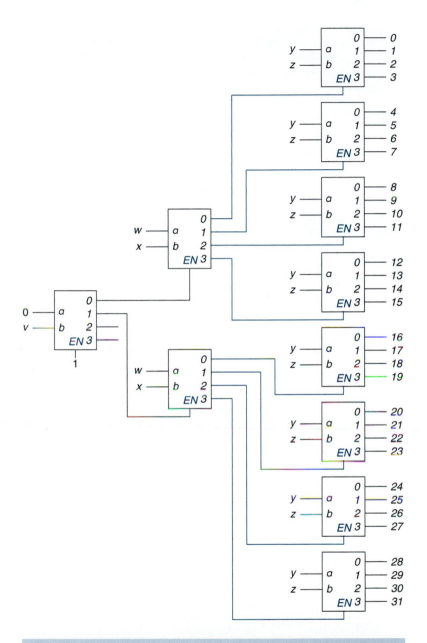

7. Professor Smith computes grades as follows: He uses only the first digit (that is, 9 for averages between 90 and 99). He never has an average of 100. He gives a P (pass) to anyone with an average of 60 or above and an F to anyone with an average below 60. That first digit is coded in 8421 code (that is, straight binary, 5 as 0101, for example); these are inputs *w*, *x*, *y*, and *z*.

Design a circuit using up to two of the decoders with active high outputs and an active low enable shown below, one NOT gate, and one OR gate to produce an output of 1 iff the student passes.

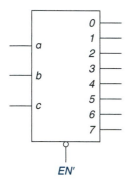

EN'	a	b	c	0	1	2	3	4	5	6	7
1	X	X	X	0	0	0	0	0	0	0	0
0	0	0	0	1	0	0	0	0	0	0	0
0	0	0	1	0	1	0	0	0	0	0	0
0	0	1	0	0	0	1	0	0	0	0	0
0	0	1	1	0	0	0	1	0	0	0	0
0	1	0	0	0	0	0	0	1	0	0	0
0	1	0	1	0	0	0	0	0	1	0	0
0	1	1	0	0	0	0	0	0	0	1	0
0	1	1	1	0	0	0	0	0	0	0	1

This problem has two solutions. The more straightforward one uses two decoders, where one is enabled when $w = 0$ and has outputs corresponding to minterms 0 to 7 and the other is enabled when $w = 1$ and has outputs corresponding to minterms 8 to 15 (although only 8 and 9 ever occur). The output is 1 for minterms 6, 7, 8, and 9.

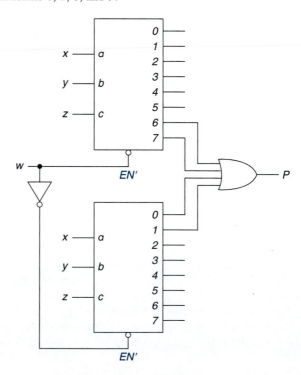

Another approach is to recognize that the only inputs that will lead to $P = 0$ are minterms 0, 1, 2, 3, 4, and 5. Thus, we can use just one decoder and the following circuit:

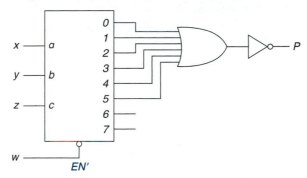

In this case, we OR together the first six outputs of the decoder, which produces a 1 for grades between 0 and 59 (and a 0 for passing grades).We then complement it to get the desired output.

8. Design a priority encoder with four active high inputs *0, 1, 2,* and *3* and three active high outputs, *A* and *B,* indicating the number of the highest priority device requesting service, and *N,* indicating no active requests. Input *0* is the highest priority (and *3* the lowest).

0	*1*	*2*	*3*	*A*	*B*	*N*
0	0	0	0	X	X	1
1	X	X	X	0	0	0
0	1	X	X	0	1	0
0	0	1	X	1	0	0
0	0	0	1	1	1	0

N is clearly just

$$N = 0'\ 1'\ 2'\ 3'$$

We can map *A* and *B* to obtain

2 3 \ 0 1	00	01	11	10
00	X			
01	1			
11	1			
10	1			

A

2 3 \ 0 1	00	01	11	10
00	X	1		
01	1	1		
11		1		
10		1		

B

$$A = 0'\ 1'$$
$$B = 0'\ 1 + 0'\ 2'$$

9. We have four 3-bit numbers: $w_2 - w_0, x_2 - x_0, y_2 - y_0$, and $z_2 - z_0$. We want to select one of these, based on the input s and t (where $st = 00$ selects w, $st = 01$ selects x and so forth). The answer is to appear on output lines $f_2 - f_0$. Use the 74153 multiplexer chip to do this.

The 74153 contains two 4-way multiplexers. Since we need three, we will use two such circuits as shown below. Note that one-half of the second 74153 is unused.

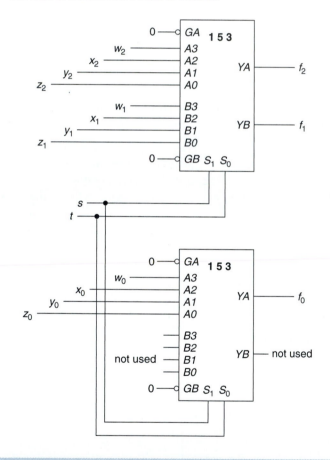

10. Create an eight-way multiplexer using some of the two-way multiplexers of Figure 4.11.

We build two four-way multiplexers as in Figure 4.12b and use a third layer of multiplexer to switch those two outputs. Assume S_2 is the high order select bit.

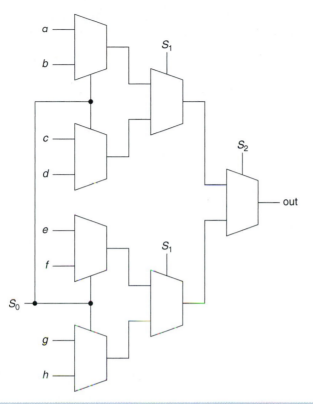

11. We have found a minimum SOP expression for each of two functions, F and G, minimizing them individually (no sharing):

$$F = WY' + XY'Z$$
$$G = WX'Y' + X'Z + W'Y'Z$$

a. Implement them with a PAL.

b. Implement them with a ROM.

c. Implement them with a PLA using no more than four terms.

d. For the same functions, we have available as many of the decoders described here as we need plus 2 eight-input OR gates. Show a block diagram for this implementation. All inputs are available both uncomplemented and complemented.

$EN1'$	$EN2$	A	B	0	1	2	3
X	0	X	X	0	0	0	0
1	X	X	X	0	0	0	0
0	1	0	0	1	0	0	0
0	1	0	1	0	1	0	0
0	1	1	0	0	0	1	0
0	1	1	1	0	0	0	1

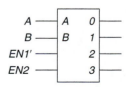

Note that this chip is enabled only when $EN1' = 0$ and $EN2 = 1$.

a. For the PAL, we need just implement the minimum SOP expressions.

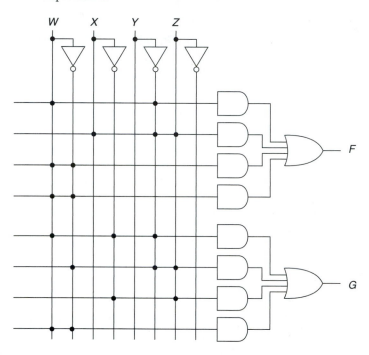

b. The first step is to find the minterm numbers. Since we will need to map the functions for part c, that is the easiest thing to do now. (We could, of course, expand the functions algebraically to sum of minterm form.)

YZ \ WX	00	01	11	10
00			1	1
01		1	1	1
11				
10				

F

YZ \ WX	00	01	11	10
00				1
01	1	1		1
11	1			1
10				

G

From this, we get

$$F(W, X, Y, Z) = \Sigma m\,(5, 8, 9, 12, 13)$$
$$G(W, X, Y, Z) = \Sigma m\,(1, 3, 5, 8, 9, 11)$$

This produces the following ROM diagram:

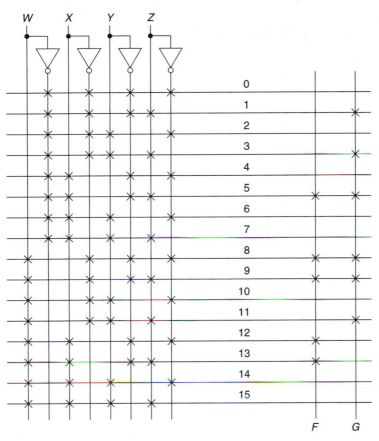

c. For the PLA, we need to find a SOP solution that uses only four different terms. The following maps show such a solution.

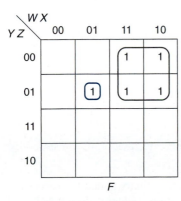

$F = WY' + W'XY'Z$
$G = X'Z + WX'Y' + W'XY'Z$

The following PLA implements this four-term solution.

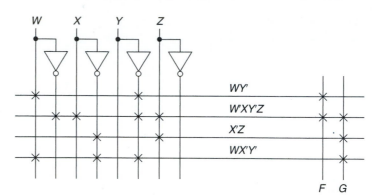

d. The straightforward approach is to use W and X to enable each of four decoders. However, looking at the maps, we see that the last row of each map contains no 1's. If we use Y and Z to enable the decoders, we only need three, enabled on 00, 01, and 11. The first decoder has active outputs for all of the minterms that end in 00, that is, 0, 4, 8, and 12. The circuit then becomes

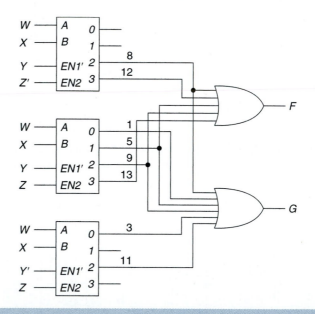

12. Design a 1-bit decimal adder, where decimal digits are stored in excess-three code.

When you add the two codes using a binary adder, the carry is always correct. The sum must be corrected by adding $+3$ if there is no carry or -3 if there is a carry.

```
    0011   0        1010    7
    0100   1        1001    6
 0  0111           1 0011
-3  1101          +3 0011
(1) 0100   1        0110    13
```

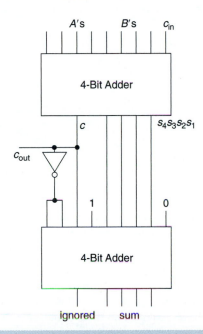

13. We have two different codes for the decimal digits that we sometimes use—the excess-3 code and the 2 of 5 code, shown here.

Digit	Excess-3 wxyz	2 of 5 abcde
0	0011	11000
1	0100	10100
2	0101	10010
3	0110	10001
4	0111	01100
5	1000	01010
6	1001	01001
7	1010	00110
8	1011	00101
9	1100	00011

All other combinations of input bits never occur. We wish to build a box that converts excess-3 code to 2 of 5 code. It thus has four inputs—w, x, y, and z—and has five outputs—a, b, c, d, and e. All inputs are available both complemented and uncomplemented.

a. Map each of the five functions and find all minimum SOP and POS solutions for each of the five functions individually.

b. Our building blocks consist of integrated circuit chips. We can buy any of the following chips:

7404:   6 inverters

7400:   4 two-input NAND gates   7402:   4 two-input NOR gates
7410:   3 three-input NAND gates   7427:   3 three-input NOR gates
7420:   2 four-input NAND gates   7425:   2 four-input NOR gates

All chips cost the same, 25¢ each.

Find one of the least expensive ($1.25) implementations of the five outputs. (The gates on any chip may be used as part of the implementation of more than one of the outputs.) Show the algebraic expression and the block diagram for the solution.

c. Find three solutions, one of which uses only 7400 and 7410 packages, one of which uses 7420s also (it must use at least one 4-input gate), and a solution that uses only NOR gates. Each of these must cost no more than $1.25. (Of course, one of these is the solution to part b.)

d. Implement this with a ROM.

e. Implement this with a PLA.

a. The maps of the five functions and their complements are shown next.

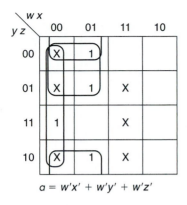

$$a = w'x' + w'y' + w'z'$$

$$a' = w + xyz$$
$$a = w'\,(x' + y' + z')$$

$$b = x'y' + w'yz$$

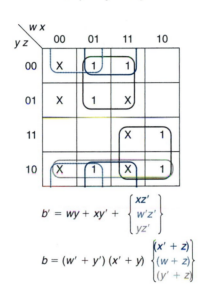

$$b' = wy + xy' + \begin{Bmatrix} xz' \\ w'z' \\ yz' \end{Bmatrix}$$

$$b = (w' + y')\,(x' + y) \begin{Bmatrix} (x' + z) \\ (w + z) \\ (y' + z) \end{Bmatrix}$$

$$b' = wy + xz' + w'y'$$
$$b = (w' + y')\,(x' + z)\,(w + y)$$

$$c = w'y'z' + xyz + wy$$

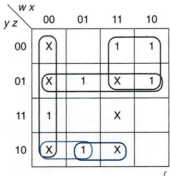

$$c' = w'x' + wy' + y'z + \begin{Bmatrix} xyz' \\ w'yz' \end{Bmatrix}$$

$$c = (w + x)\,(w' + y)\,(y + z') \begin{Bmatrix} (x' + y' + z) \\ (w + y' + z) \end{Bmatrix}$$

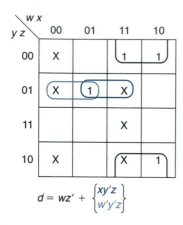

$$d = wz' + \begin{Bmatrix} xy'z \\ w'y'z \end{Bmatrix}$$

	wx=00	01	11	10
yz=00	X	1		
01	X		X	1
11	1	1	X	1
10	X	1	X	

$$d' = w'z' + \begin{Bmatrix} x'z \\ wz \end{Bmatrix} + \begin{Bmatrix} w'y \\ yz \end{Bmatrix}$$

$$d = (w + z) \begin{Bmatrix} (x + z') \\ (w' + z') \end{Bmatrix} \begin{Bmatrix} (w + y') \\ (y' + z') \end{Bmatrix}$$

	wx=00	01	11	10
yz=00	X	1		
01	X		X	1
11	1	1	X	1
10	X	1	X	

$$d' = w'z' + x'z + xy$$
$$d = (w + z)(x + z')(x' + y')$$

	wx=00	01	11	10
yz=00	X		1	
01	X		X	1
11			X	1
10	X	1	X	

$$e = wz + wx + \begin{Bmatrix} w'yz' \\ xyz' \end{Bmatrix}$$

	wx=00	01	11	10
yz=00	X	1		1
01	X	1	X	
11	1	1	X	
10	X		X	1

$$e' = x'z' + w'y' + w'z$$
$$e = (x + z)(w + y)(w + z')$$

Note that there are two SOP solutions for d and e, and that there are four POS solutions for b, two for c, and five for d.

b. If we were to use the solutions that we found in part a, there are no common product terms and thus no sharing is possible in the NAND gate implementation. We would need 10 two-input gates and 8 three-input gates, for a total of three 7400s and three 7410s (at a total cost of $1.50). For the NOR gate solution, we would use the product of sums. There is only one term that can be shared, $w + y$, in b and e. There would be a total of 1 four-input gate, 5 three-input gates, and 12 two-input gates, once again requiring six integrated circuit packages.

We must then attempt to do sharing. The following maps show that for the SOP solutions.

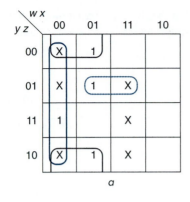

a

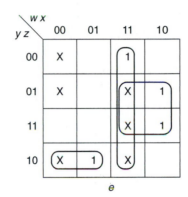

b

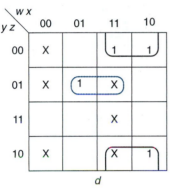

c

d

e

$$a = w'x' + xy'z + w'z'$$
$$b = x'y' + w'x' + xyz$$
$$c = w'y'z' + xyz + wy$$
$$d = wz' + xy'z$$
$$e = wz + wx + w'yz'$$

In this solution, three terms have been shared (as indicated by the colored circling and terms). There are some other choices ($w'y'z$ in place of $xy'z$ in *a* and *d*, and xyz' in place of $w'yz'$ in *e*) but they would not alter the gate count. This solution requires 8 two-input gates and 8 three-input gates and utilizes two 7400s and three 7410s (total cost $1.25).

c. The solution to part b could be used as one of the three solutions to part c and any of those shown here could have been used for part b. A solution that requires one less new product term is

$$a = w'x' + xy'z + w'y'z' + w'yz'$$

where the last two terms are required for (and shared with) *c* and *e*, respectively. This saves 1 two-input gate, but replaces a three-input gate with a four-input one (all in the implementation of *a*). This solution requires 1 four-input gate and 7 each of three-input and two-input gates. It utilizes one 7420, two 7430s (using the extra four-input gate for the 7th three-input one) and two 7400s (total cost $1.25).

There is also a solution using NOR gates, based on the POS solutions. The maps of the complements below produce one solution that almost works:

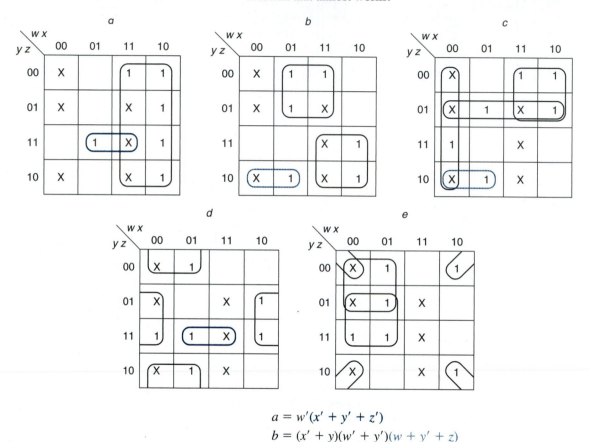

$$a = w'(x' + y' + z')$$
$$b = (x' + y)(w' + y')(w + y' + z)$$
$$c = (w + x)(w' + y)(y + z')(w + y' + z)$$
$$d = (w + z)(x + z')(x' + y' + z')$$
$$e = (x + z)(w + y)(w + z')$$

This solution requires 1 four-input gate, 5 three-input gates, and 11 two-input gates (utilizing six packages).

However, if we do not restrict ourselves to two-level solutions, we could eliminate the four-input gate, by rewriting c as

$$c = (w + x)(y + w'z')(w + y' + z)$$

Now, the gate count becomes 6 three-input gates and 10* two-input gates (utilizing five packages). (Similar manipulation could be done on *e,* replacing a three-input gate by a two-input one, but that would not change the package count.) A block diagram of the circuit is shown here.

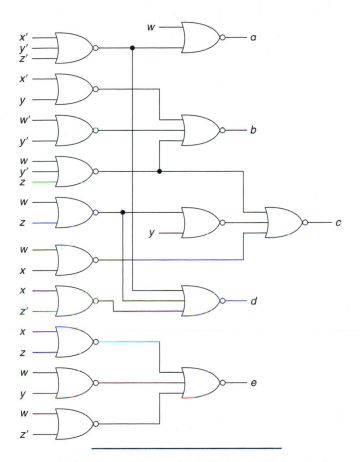

d, e. The implementation with a ROM and a PLA are rather straightforward. For the ROM, all we need is the minterms; the don't cares are ignored. For the PLA, any of the SOP solutions can be used, as long as we have enough terms. The two solutions follow.

---

*By doing this, we have saved a two-input gate, since the term $w'z'$ uses the same NOR gate as the term $w + z$.

d.

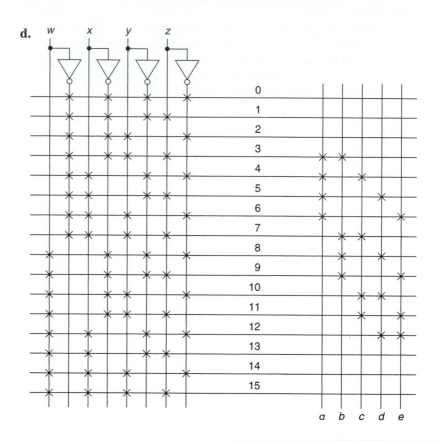

e.

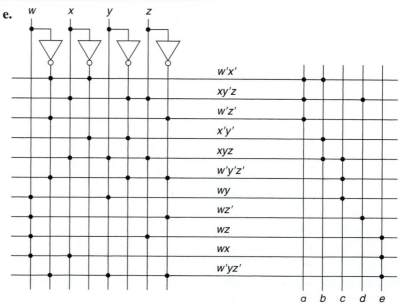

14. You are to design a driver for an eight-segment display as described below. It has four inputs, *a, b, c, d* and eight outputs, *X*1, . . . , *X*8.

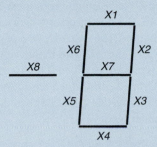

This is to display the decimal equivalent of a 4-bit binary number that is in one's complement format. In one's complement, the following values are coded:

0000	0	1000	−7
0001	1	1001	−6
0010	2	1010	−5
0011	3	1011	−4
0100	4	1100	−3
0101	5	1101	−2
0110	6	1110	−1
0111	7	1111	0

(Note that the minus sign (*X*8) is lit for −1 to −7, but not for either 0 or for 1 to 7.) Segment *X*1 may or may not be lit for the digit 6; segment *X*6 is not lit for digit 7. All inputs are available both complemented and uncomplemented.

a. Show the maps, equations, and a block diagram for a minimum two-level NAND gate solution that treats this as eight separate problems and uses only prime implicants of each of the functions. However, the gate implementation should share gates whenever possible. (Minimum is 36 gates, 107 inputs.)

b. Show the maps, equations, and a block diagram for a minimum two-level NAND gate solution—but this time gates are to be shared wherever possible. Restriction: There are no gates with more than eight inputs. Also, indicate how many modules you have used.

c. *X*4 requires at least eight terms and thus an eight-input NAND gate for a two-level solution. Find a minimum solution for *X*4 that uses only two-input gates. (This must, of course, be more than two levels.) Note: This part has nothing to do with part b. No gate may be used as a NOT.

d. Implement these functions using a PLA with as few terms as possible. Show a PLA diagram.

a. All but $X3$ and $X7$ have unique solutions. There are six solutions for $X3$, the first three of which can share two terms with other solutions. The maps for one of the best solutions, requiring 36 gates and 107 gate inputs, are shown on the next page. Shared terms are in green. The list of solutions is given here. The underlined subscripted terms are shared in this solution. Other terms that could be shared in a different solution are underlined:

$$X1 = b'd' + bd + \underline{ac'}_7 + a'c$$
$$X2 = a'b' + ab + \underline{c'd'}_6 + \underline{cd}$$
$$X3 = \underline{ab'}_5 + \underline{c'd'}_6 + a'd + bc$$
$$ = \underline{ab'} + bd' + \underline{cd} + a'c'$$
$$ = a'b + \underline{cd} + \underline{ad'} + b'c'$$
$$ = b'd + \underline{c'd'} + a'b + ac$$
$$ = a'c' + \underline{ad'} + b'd + bc$$
$$ = b'c' + ac + bd' + a'd$$
$$X4 = \underline{a'b'd'}_4 + b'cd' + a'b'c + \underline{a'cd'}_3 + abc' + \underline{abd}_2$$
$$ + bc'd + \underline{ac'd}_1$$
$$X5 = \underline{ac'd}_1 + \underline{abd}_2 + \underline{a'cd'}_3 + \underline{a'b'd'}_4$$
$$X6 = a'c'd' + a'bc' + \underline{a'bd'} + \underline{ab'd} + ab'c + acd$$
$$X7 = bc' + b'c + \{\underline{a'cd'}_3 \text{ or } \underline{a'bd'}\} + \{\underline{ac'd}_1 \text{ or } \underline{ab'd}\}$$
$$X8 = \underline{ab'}_5 + \underline{ac'}_7 + \underline{ad'}$$

The gate count for this solution is

$X1$:	2	2	2	2					4
$X2$:	2	2	2	2					4
$X3$:	2	(2)	2	2					4
$X4$:	3	3	3	3	3	3	3	3	8
$X5$:	(3)	(3)	(3)	(3)					4
$X6$:	3	3	3	3	3	3			6
$X7$:	2	2	(3)	(3)					4
$X8$:	(2)	(2)	2						3

2's:	14		7430s:	2	36 gates/107 inputs
3's:	15		7420s:	3	
4's:	5		7410s:	5	
6's:	1		7400s:	4	
8's:	1				

14 chips

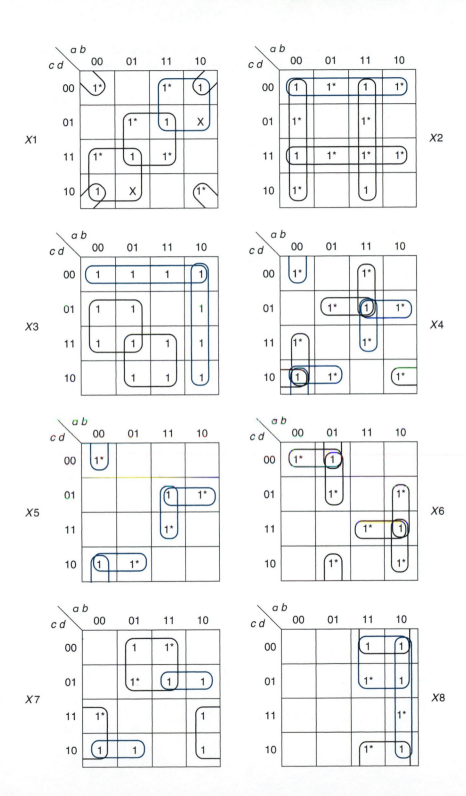

b. The best solution is shown in the following table and maps. It requires 24 gates with 95 inputs and only 13 chips.

	X1	X2	X3	X4	X5	X6	X7	X8	
$a'b'c'd'$	X			X	X	X			4
abc'	X	X		X			X	X	3
$a'b'c$	X	X		X			X		3
bd	X								2
$ab'd'$	X		X					X	3
$a'b'c'$		X	X						3
abd'		X	X					X	3
$c'd'$		X							2
cd		X	X						2
$a'bd'$			X			X	X		3
$a'bc'd$			X	X		X	X		4
$ab'd$			X			X	X	X	3
$ac'd$				X	X				3
$a'cd'$				X	X				3
$abcd$				X	X	X			4
$ab'cd'$				X		X	X		4
	5	6	7	8	4	6	6	4	

8-in	1		1
7-in	1		1
6-in	3		3
5-in	1		1
4-in	6		3
3-in	9		3
2-in	3		1
Total	24	13 chips	95 inputs

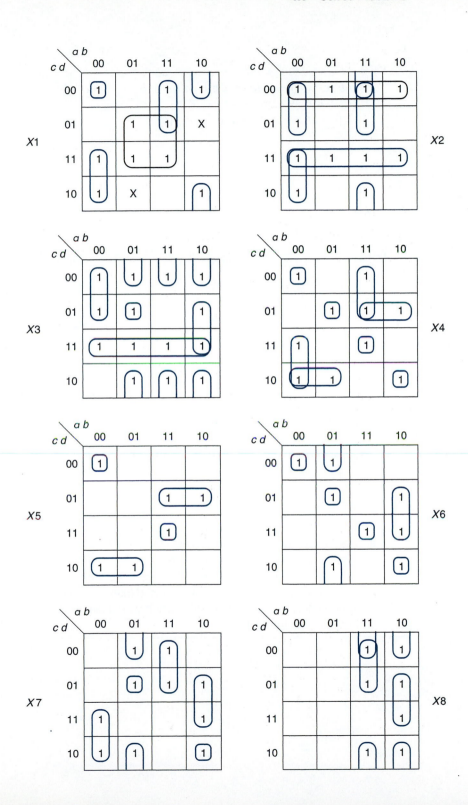

c.

$$X4 = a'b'd' + b'cd' + a'b'c + a'cd' + abc' + abd + bc'd + ac'd$$
$$= a'b'(c + d') + ab(c' + d) + cd'(a' + b') + c'd(a + b)$$
$$= [a' + b(c' + d)][a + b'(c + d')]$$
$$\quad + [c + d(a + b)][c' + d'(a' + b')]$$

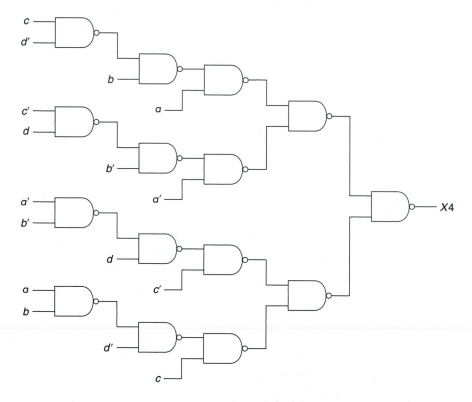

d. The solution to part b translates directly into a PLA with 16
product terms (where each row corresponds to a product
term). An equally good solution would be to design the PLA
as a ROM. It, too, would have 16 terms. (Note: the ROM
solution does not work for part b since it would require a
14-input gate for $X3$.)

4.10 EXERCISES

1. For the following circuit:

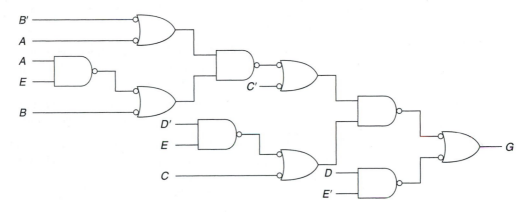

a. Compute the maximum delay,

   i. Assuming that all inputs are available both uncomplemented and complemented.

   ii. Assuming only uncomplemented inputs are available and an additional gate must be added to complement each input.

   b. Compute the maximum delay from input C to the output, assuming that all inputs are available both uncomplemented and complemented.

*2. We are building an adder to add the 32-bit constant

   10101010101010101010101010101010

   to an arbitrary 32-bit number. We will implement this with 16 identical adder modules, each of which will add 2 bits of the number to the constant (10) and a carry from the next lower pair of bits and produce 2 bits of the sum and the carry to the next bits. A block diagram of part of this is shown below:

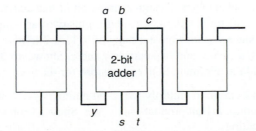

The problem each 2-bit adder solves is

$$
\begin{array}{cc}
 & c \\
a & b \\
1 & 0 \\
\hline
y \quad s & t
\end{array}
$$

a. Show a truth table for that 2-bit adder (it has three inputs, a, b, and c, and it has three outputs, y, s, and t), and find minimum SOP expressions for each output.

b. Compute the delay from the c input of each module to the y output of that module and the total delay for the 32 bits.

3. We want to build a circuit to compute the two's complement of an n-bit number. We will do this with n modules, each of which complements that bit and then adds the carry from the next lower bit. Thus, the first three bits of a block diagram of the circuit will look like

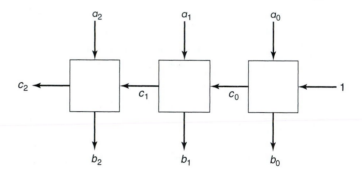

a. Show a block diagram for each of the boxes using NAND gates. (Design the first—on the right—box specially.)

b. Compute the delay for n bits.

c. Improve the speed by designing 2 bits at a time. Show a NAND gate circuit and compute the total delay.

4. We want to build an adder to simultaneously add three multi-digit binary numbers. Design a single bit of that adder. It has three inputs for that digit, x, y, and z, plus two carry inputs, u, and v (since you may have a carry of 0, 1, or 2). There are three outputs, a sum, s, and two carries, f and g. Show a truth table and find the minimum SOP expressions for the three outputs.

5. Design a circuit to multiply two 2-bit numbers—a, b and c, d and produce a 4-bit product—w, x, y, z. Show a truth table and the equations.

6. We need to determine whether a three-bit number, a_3, a_2, a_1, is equal to another number, b_3, b_2, b_1, or if it is greater than that number. (We do not need an output for less than.)

   a. Show how the 7485 would be connected to accomplish this.

   b. Implement this with AND and OR gates.

   c. Assuming that the 7485 costs $1, what must 7400 series AND and OR gate packages cost to make the AND/OR implementation less expensive?

*7. Consider the following circuit with an active high output decoder. Draw a truth table for X and Y in terms of a, b, and c.

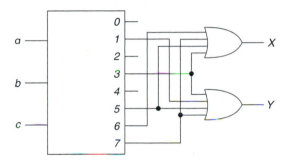

8. We wish to design a decoder, with three inputs, x, y, z, and eight active high outputs, labeled 0, 1, 2, 3, 4, 5, 6, 7. There is no enable input required. (For example, if $xyz = 011$, then output 3 would be 1 and all other outputs would be 0.)

   The **only** building block is a two-input, four-output decoder (with an active high enable), the truth table for which is shown here.

EN	A	B	0	1	2	3
0	X	X	0	0	0	0
1	0	0	1	0	0	0
1	0	1	0	1	0	0
1	1	0	0	0	1	0
1	1	1	0	0	0	1

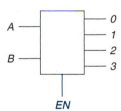

   Draw a block diagram of the system using as many of these building blocks as are needed.

*9. We want to implement a full adder; we'll call the inputs a, b, and c and the outputs s and c_{out}. As always, the adder is described by the following equations:

$$s(a, b, c) = \Sigma m(1, 2, 4, 7)$$
$$c_{out}(a, b, c) = \Sigma m(3, 5, 6, 7)$$

To implement this, all we have available are two decoders (as described here) and two OR gates. Inputs a and b are available both uncomplemented and complemented; c is available only uncomplemented. Show a block diagram for this system. Be sure to label all of the inputs to the decoders.

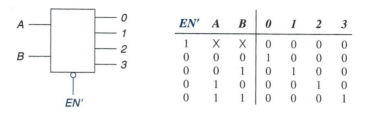

EN'	A	B	0	1	2	3
1	X	X	0	0	0	0
0	0	0	1	0	0	0
0	0	1	0	1	0	0
0	1	0	0	0	1	0
0	1	1	0	0	0	1

10. Show the block diagram for a decoder, the truth table for which is shown here. The available components are one-, two-, and three-input NAND gates. (A one-input NAND is an inverter.)

Inputs				Outputs		
E1	E2	a	b	1	2	3
0	X	X	X	1	1	1
X	0	X	X	1	1	1
1	1	0	0	1	1	1
1	1	0	1	0	1	1
1	1	1	0	1	0	1
1	1	1	1	1	1	0

11. Design, using AND, OR, and NOT gates, a priority encoder with seven active low inputs, $1', \ldots, 7'$ and three active high outputs, CBA that indicate which is the highest priority line active. Input $1'$ is highest priority; $7'$ is lowest. If none of the inputs are active, the output is 000. There is a fourth output line, M, which is 1 if there are multiple active inputs.

*12. Implement the function

$$f(x, y, z) = \Sigma m(0, 1, 3, 4, 7)$$

using two-way multiplexers.

13. In the following circuit, the decoder (DCD) has two inputs and four (active high) outputs (such that, for example, output 0 is 1 if and only if inputs A and B are both 0). The three multiplexers (MUX) each have two select inputs (shown on the top of the box), four data inputs (shown on the left) and an active high enable input (shown on the bottom). Inputs A, B, C, and D are select inputs; inputs N through Z are data inputs. Complete a

truth giving the value of F for each of the 16 possible select input combinations. (Comment: For some values, $F = 0$; for one value, $F = W$.)

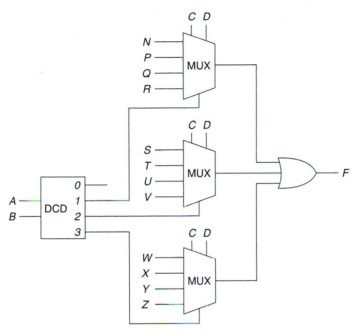

14. For the following sets of functions, design a system
    i. Using a ROM
    ii. Using a PLA with the number of product terms shown
    iii. Using a PAL

  a. $F(A, B, C) = \Sigma m(3, 4, 5, 7)$
       $G(A, B, C) = \Sigma m(1, 3, 5, 6, 7)$
       $H(A, B, C) = \Sigma m(1, 4, 5)$ (4 product terms)

  b. $W(A, B, C) = \Sigma m(0, 1, 4)$
       $X(A, B, C) = \Sigma m(0, 3, 4, 7)$
       $Y(A, B, C) = \Sigma m(1, 2, 6)$
       $Z(A, B, C) = \Sigma m(2, 3, 6, 7)$ (4 product terms)

  c. $f(a, b, c, d) = \Sigma m(3, 5, 6, 7, 8, 11, 13, 14, 15)$
       $g(a, b, c, d) = \Sigma m(0, 1, 5, 6, 8, 9, 11, 13, 14)$
                                (6 product terms)

  d. $F(A, B, C, D) = \Sigma m(1, 2, 6, 7, 8, 9, 12, 13)$
       $G(A, B, C, D) = \Sigma m(1, 8, 9, 10, 11, 13, 15)$
       $H(A, B, C, D) = \Sigma m(1, 6, 7, 8, 11, 12, 14, 15)$
                                  (8 product terms)

15. Consider the following three functions, f, g, and h of the four variables, a, b, c, and d, whose minimum solutions (treating each as a separate problem) are listed below. Throughout, all variables are available *only uncomplemented:*

$$f = b'c'd' + bd + a'cd$$
$$g = c'd' + bc' + bd' + a'b'cd$$
$$h = bd' + cd + ab'd$$

a. Implement them with a ROM.

b. Implement them on a PLA with six terms.

c. Implement them using only decoders of the type shown below (as many as needed) and three OR gates (each with as many inputs as you need). (No other gates are allowed.) Logic 0 and logic 1 are available.

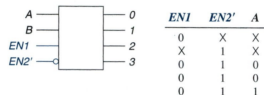

ENI	EN2'	A	B	0	1	2	3
0	X	X	X	0	0	0	0
X	1	X	X	0	0	0	0
0	1	0	0	1	0	0	0
0	1	0	1	0	1	0	0
0	1	1	0	0	0	1	0
0	1	1	1	0	0	0	1

*16. We have three functions, X, Y, Z of the four variables, A, B, C, D. Note: Each part can be solved without the other:

$$X(A, B, C, D) = \Sigma m(0, 2, 6, 7, 10, 13, 14, 15)$$
$$Y(A, B, C, D) = \Sigma m(2, 6, 7, 8, 10, 12, 13, 15)$$
$$Z(A, B, C, D) = \Sigma m(0, 6, 8, 10, 13, 14, 15)$$

a. Implement with a two-level NAND gate circuit. This can be done using only prime implicants of the individual functions with 13 gates. With sharing, it can be done with 10 gates. Assume that all variables are available both complemented and uncomplemented.

b. Implement these functions using a ROM.

c. Implement this with 2 three-input (plus active low enable) decoders as shown here, plus a minimum number of AND, OR, and NOT gates.

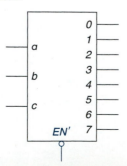

  d. Implement it with a PLA with eight terms. (You may not need to use all of them.)

  e. Implement them with the PAL shown in the text.

17. Implement the 2-bit adder of Section 4.1.2 using the PAL of Section 4.6.3. The problem is that one of the output functions requires 7 terms and another 12. This can be overcome by building the carry between the 2 bits and using that output as another input to compute s_1 and c_{out}.

18. In solved problem 13, we designed a converter from excess-3 to 2 of 5 code. In this exercise, we want to do the reverse, that is, design a converter from 2 of 5 code to excess-3. There will be four functions of five variables. We will assume that only legitimate digit codes are input; thus there will be 22 don't cares on each map. All inputs are available both uncomplemented and complemented.

  a. Map each of the four functions and find all minimum SOP and POS solutions for each of the four functions individually.

  b. Our building blocks consist of integrated circuit chips. We can buy any of the following chips:

7404: 6 inverters

7400: 4 two-input NAND gates   7402: 4 two-input NOR gates
7410: 3 three-input NAND gates   7427: 3 three-input NOR gates
7420: 2 four-input NAND gates   7425: 2 four-input NOR gates

  All chips cost the same, 25¢ each.

    Find one of the least expensive ($1.00) implementations of the four outputs. (The gates on any chip may be used as part of the implementation of more than one of the outputs.) Show the algebraic expression and the block diagram for the solution.

  c. Find two solutions, one of which uses only 7400 and 7410 packages, and a solution that uses only NOR gates. Each of these must cost no more than $1.00. (Of course, one of these is the solution to part b.)

  d. Implement this with a ROM.

  e. Implement this with a PLA.

  f. Implement this with the PAL described in the text.

*19. We have a special eight-segment display, as shown.

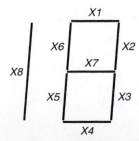

We want to display the numbers from 0 to 15, as shown on the next figure, where a dashed line means an unlit segment and a solid line a lit one. Note that for 6 and 9, one segment each may be lit or unlit, as you wish.

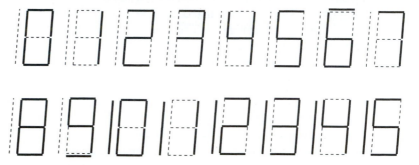

Design three versions of a system that accepts as an input a 4-bit number, A, B, C, D and produces the eight outputs, $X1$, $X2$, ..., $X8$ under each of the following constraints. (All inputs are available both complemented and uncomplemented.) For parts a and b, show the maps, the equations, and a block diagram.

a. Each output is minimized independently using a two-level NAND gate circuit, where minimum is minimum number of gates, and among those with the same number of gates, minimum number of gate inputs. (Each function must be a sum of prime implicants of that function. A gate can be shared among functions only if it implements a prime implicant of each function.) (Minimum solution: 31 gates, 93 inputs.)

b. Two-level NAND gates, using a minimum number of the following modules:

> Type 7400: 4 two-input NAND gates
> Type 7410: 3 three-input NAND gates
> Type 7420: 2 four-input NAND gates
> Type 7430: 1 eight-input NAND gate

(There is a solution that uses 11 modules.) (Note the solution to part a uses 13 modules.)

c. A PLA with the minimum number of terms.

20. We have a decimal digit stored in excess-3 code, that is

0	0011	5	1000
1	0100	6	1001
2	0101	7	1010
3	0110	8	1011
4	0111	9	1100

The bits of the code are labeled w, x, y, z (from left to right). We wish to display that digit on a seven-segment display. The layout is as in Figure 4.26. Note that there are two ways to display a 6, a 7, and a 9; choose whichever is most convenient. The display requires a 0 to light a segment and a 1 for it not to be lit.

Design the four-input, seven-output device that takes the code for the digit and produces the signals to drive the display. If any of the unused input combinations are applied to your device, the display is to be blank, that is all the outputs from the device are to be 1. Assume that the four inputs are available both uncomplemented and complemented.

We are looking for three different designs for this. For each, show the maps, the algebraic equations, and a block diagram. Please use color to make your solutions readable. For the first two parts, indicate how many of each type of package you need (7400, 7410, 7420, 7430). But minimum is defined as minimum number of gates, and among those with the same number of gates, minimum number of gate inputs.

a. First, find a minimum cost two-level NAND gate solution such that all terms are prime implicants of the individual functions. Only terms that are prime implicants of each function are to be shared. When there are multiple solutions, one answer will often lead to more sharing than others.

b. Second, reduce the number of gates by doing more sharing (including terms that are not prime implicants).

c. Third, implement this with a PLA, which has four inputs, seven outputs, and 12 product terms.

21. For the following three functions (of five variables)

$$f(a, b, c, d, e) = \Sigma m(0, 2, 5, 7, 8, 10, 13, 15, 16, 21, 23, 24, 29, 31)$$

$$g(a, b, c, d, e) = \Sigma m(2, 5, 7, 10, 13, 15, 16, 18, 20, 21, 22, 23, 25, 27)$$

$$h(a, b, c, d, e) = \Sigma m(2, 9, 10, 12, 13, 14, 16, 18, 20, 22, 28, 29, 30, 31)$$

a. Find all minimum SOP solutions for each. Show the maps and the algebraic equations for each.

b. Find a minimum solution, assuming a two-level NAND gate circuit. All variables are available both uncomplemented and complemented. Show the maps, the equations and a block diagram of the circuit. Also, indicate how many 7400 series packages you need (that is, 7400, 7410, 7420, 7430). (It can be done with no more than 12 gates.)

c. Show an implementation with a PLA with five inputs, three outputs, and 10 product terms.

22. Consider the following three functions:

$$f(a, b, c, d, e) = \Sigma m(2, 3, 4, 5, 8, 9, 12, 20, 21, 24, 25, 31)$$
$$g(a, b, c, d, e) = \Sigma m(2, 3, 4, 5, 6, 7, 10, 11, 12,$$
$$20, 21, 26, 27, 31)$$
$$h(a, b, c, d, e) = \Sigma m(0, 2, 3, 4, 5, 8, 10, 12, 16, 18,$$
$$19, 20, 21, 22, 23, 24, 28, 31)$$

All variables are available both uncomplemented and complemented.

a. Consider each as a separate problem and find all the minimum SOP expression(s). Both f and h have multiple solutions.

b. Assume that 7400, 7410, 7420, and 7430 packages are available at 25¢ each. Show the number of each size gate, how many of each package is required, and the total cost for a two-level solution. (Take advantage of sharing ONLY if the same term is a prime implicant of more than one function.)

c. For each function (again using the solutions of part a), find a solution that only uses 7400 and 7410 packages (25¢ each) (no four- or eight-input gates). Show the equations, indicating sharing, and a block diagram. Show the number of each size gate, how many of each package is required, and the total cost for a two-level solution.

d. Take maximum advantage of sharing to try to reduce the cost of a two-level solution. Use 7400, 7410, 7420, and 7430 packages (25¢ each). Show the maps, the equations, indicating sharing, and a block diagram. Show the number of each size gate, how many of each package is required, and the total cost for a two-level solution.

e. Implement this using a ROM and also using a PLA with five inputs, 12 product terms, and three outputs.

23. Design a system which has as its inputs a number from 1 to 10 and provides as its outputs (eight of them) the signals to drive the following display. The inputs are labeled W, X, Y, and Z and are normal binary. The input combinations 0000, 1011, 1100, 1101, 1110, and 1111 will never occur; they are to be treated as don't cares. The available building blocks are 7400, 7410, and 7420 integrated circuits. The design should use the minimum number of packages (which is five for all cases). The solution should include the maps for each of the functions and a block diagram of the circuit.

The display allows for the representation of Roman numerals (except that IIX is used to represent 8, whereas it is normally written as VIII).

There are a total of eight segments in the display, labeled A through H, as shown.

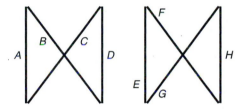

Version High: To light a segment, a 1 is placed on the appropriate display input (A, B, . . . , H).

Version Low: To light a segment, a 0 is placed on the appropriate display input (A, B, . . . , H). Note that for this version, each input is just the complement of the one for version high.

There are two ways to represent a 5 on this display.

Left: Light segments A and C (or E and G).

Right: Light segments B and D (or F and H).

The following illustration shows all digits as they should be coded for each of these, with a lit segment represented by a bold line and an unlit segment represented by a dashed line.

Left

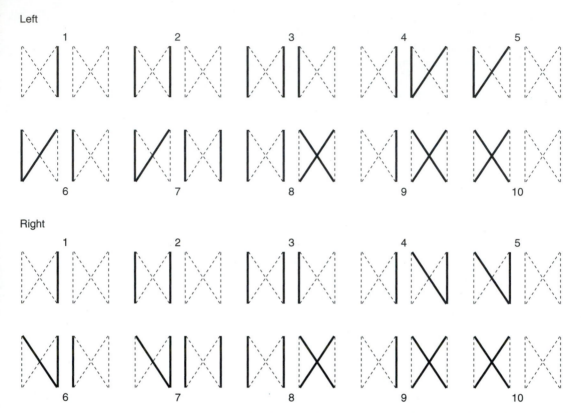

Right

This is really four separate problems, one for each version of the design.

4.11   CHAPTER 4 TEST (100 MINUTES)

1. Implement the following functions using only two of the decoders described below and two 8-input OR gates.

$$f(w, x, y, z) = \Sigma m(0, 4, 5, 6, 7, 12, 15)$$
$$g(w, x, y, z) = \Sigma m(1, 3, 12, 13, 14, 15)$$

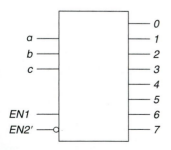

EN1	EN2'	a	b	c	0	1	2	3	4	5	6	7
0	X	X	X	X	0	0	0	0	0	0	0	0
X	1	X	X	X	0	0	0	0	0	0	0	0
1	0	0	0	0	1	0	0	0	0	0	0	0
1	0	0	0	1	0	1	0	0	0	0	0	0
1	0	0	1	0	0	0	1	0	0	0	0	0
1	0	0	0	1	0	0	0	1	0	0	0	0
1	0	1	0	0	0	0	0	0	1	0	0	0
1	0	1	0	1	0	0	0	0	0	1	0	0
1	0	1	1	0	0	0	0	0	0	0	1	0
1	0	1	0	1	0	0	0	0	0	0	0	1

2. We have two 74151 eight-way multiplexers, with an active low enable input (EN'), and both an active high and an active low output. Implement the function

$$W(A, B, C) = \Sigma m(1, 2, 3, 6, 7)$$

in two ways.

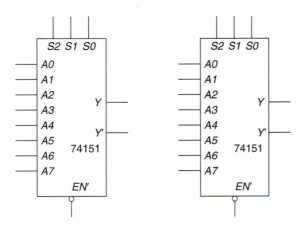

3. Consider the three functions, the maps of which are shown.

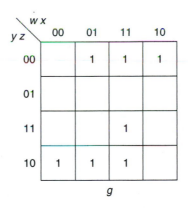

Implement them on the PLA shown here. Be sure to label the inputs and the outputs. Full credit if you use eight terms or fewer.

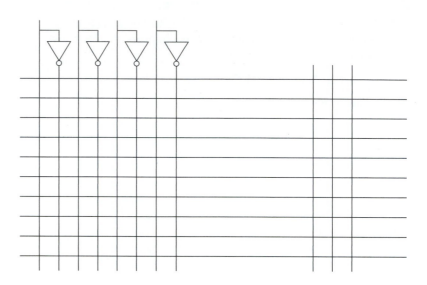

4. For the same set of functions, implement them with the ROM shown below. Be sure to label the inputs and the outputs.

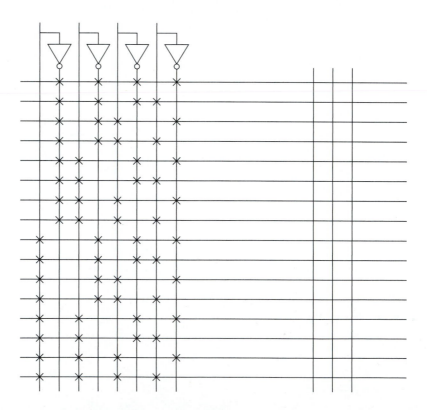

5. For the same set of functions, implement them with the following PAL. Be sure to label the inputs and the outputs.

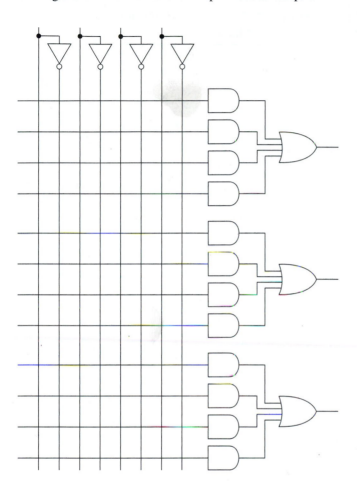

6. For the same set of functions, we have available as components three NAND gates (as many inputs as you need) and some active low output, active low enable decoders, as shown below (as many as you need).

EN	a	b	0	1	2	3
1	X	X	1	1	1	1
0	0	0	0	1	1	1
0	0	1	1	0	1	1
0	1	0	1	1	0	1
0	1	1	1	1	1	0

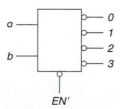

Show a diagram of a circuit to implement these functions with only these components.

5 points extra credit: Show a diagram that uses only 3 eight-input NAND gates and 4 of these decoders.

Analysis of Sequential Systems

U p to now everything has been combinational—that is, the output at any instant of time depends only on what the inputs are at that time. (This ignores the small delay between the time the input of a circuit changes and when the output changes.)

In the remainder of Part I, we will be concerned with systems that have memory, referred to as *sequential systems* or as *finite state machines*. Thus, the output will depend not only on the present input but also on the past history—what has happened earlier.

We will deal primarily with *clocked* systems (sometimes referred to as *synchronous*). A clock is just a signal that alternates (over time) between 0 and 1 at a regular rate.* Two versions of a clock signal are shown in Figure 5.1. In the first, the clock signal is 0 half of the time and 1 half of the time. In the second, it is 1 for a shorter part of the cycle. The same clock is normally connected to all flip flops.

The period of the signal (T on the diagram) is the length of one cycle. The frequency is the inverse ($1/T$). A frequency of 200 MHz (megahertz, million cycles per second) corresponds to a period of 5 nsec[†] (5 nanoseconds, 5 billionths of a second). The exact values are not important in most of the discussion that follows.

Figure 5.1 Clock signals.

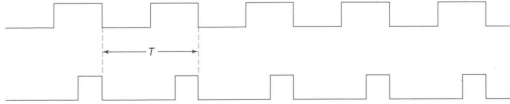

---

*Although the clock is usually a regular waveform as shown, the regularity of the clock is not crucial to the operation of most sequential systems.
[†]$1/(200 \times 10^6) = (1000/200) \times 10^{-9} = 5 \times 10^{-9} = 5$ nsec.

In most synchronous systems, change occurs on the transition of the clock signal. We will look at this in more detail as we introduce the several types of *flip flops,* clocked binary storage devices.

The block diagram of Figure 5.2 is a conceptual view of a synchronous sequential system. A sequential system consists of a set of memory devices and some combinational logic. This diagram depicts a system with n inputs (x's), in addition to the clock, k outputs (z's), and m binary storage devices (q's). Each memory device may need one or two input signals. Many systems have only one input and one output, although we will see examples with several of each, and some where there is no input, other than the clock.

Figure 5.2   Conceptual view of a sequential system.

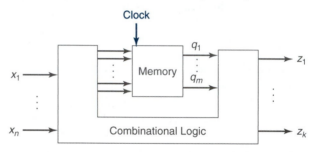

The outputs of the combinational logic are functions of the system inputs and the contents of memory; the combinational logic outputs are the system outputs and signals to update the memory.

In Section 5.2, we will introduce the simplest storage device, the *latch.* It is a static device constructed of gates. The output changes immediately whenever the input changes; there is no clock involved. Latches are used primarily for temporary (buffer) storage.

In Section 5.3, we will develop the most common binary storage device, the *flip flop,* a clocked device. A flip flop almost always has two outputs, q and q'; that is, both the bit stored and its complement. It may have one or two inputs (indeed, they used to make one with three); we will describe several types of flip flops.

In Section 5.1, we will introduce state table, state diagrams, and timing traces. In Section 5.4, we will discuss the analysis of sequential systems.

5.1   STATE TABLES AND DIAGRAMS

A simple example of a sequential system is the first of a set of continuing examples for sequential systems. (Others will be introduced in Chapter 6.)

CE6. A system with one input x and one output z such that $z = 1$ iff x has been 1 for at least three consecutive clock times.*

For this example, the system must store in its memory information about the last three inputs and produce an output based on that. What is stored in memory is the *state* of the system. Memory consists of a set of binary devices. They may just store the last few inputs, but it is often more economical to code the information in a different way. Sometimes, a finite number of recent inputs is not adequate.

A *timing trace* is a set of values for the input and the output (and sometimes the state or other variables of the system, as well) at consecutive clock times. It is often used to clarify the definition of system behavior or to describe the behavior of a given system. The inputs are an arbitrary set of values that might be applied to the system, chosen so as to demonstrate the behavior of the system. For CE6, the timing trace is shown in Trace 5.1.

Trace 5.1 Three consecutive 1's.

x	0	1	1	0	1	1	1	0	0	1	0	1	1	1	1	1	0	0
z	?	0	0	0	0	0	0	1	0	0	0	0	0	0	1	1	1	0	0	0	0

For CE6, the output depends only on the state of the system (not the present input) and, thus, occurs after the desired input pattern has occurred. Such a system is called a *Moore model*, named after E. F. Moore. The output for the first input is shown as unknown, because we have no history of what happened before. (If the system were initialized to indicate that no 1's had yet occurred, then that output would be 0.) After three consecutive inputs are 1, the system goes to a state where the output is 1, and remains there as long as the input remains 1.

Several designs are possible for this system. We will defer until Chapter 6 the techniques for designing a system from a verbal description. At this point, we will introduce two tools for describing sequential systems.

A *state table* shows, for each input combination and each state, what the output is and what the *next state* is, that is, what is to be stored in memory after the next clock.

A *state diagram* (or *state graph*) is a graphical representation of the behavior of the system, showing for each input combination and each state what the output is and what the *next state* is, that is, what is to be stored in memory after the next clock.

Table 5.1 shows an example of a state table, one that does describe CE6, although that is not obvious at this point.

---

*In Section 5.3, we will define exactly when during the clock that the input matters.

Table 5.1 A state table.

Present state	Next state x = 0	x = 1	Present output
A	A	B	0
B	A	C	0
C	A	D	0
D	A	D	1

We will refer to the present state as q and the next state as $q^\star$. (Some books use Q or $q+$ or $q(t + \Delta)$ to represent the next state.) The next state is what will be stored in memory after this clock transition. That will then become the present state at the next clock time. The next state is a function of the present state and the input, x. The output, in this example, depends on the present state, but not the present input. The output only changes when the state changes, at the time of a clock transition. The first row of the table signifies that if the system is in state A, that is, fact A is stored in memory and the input is a 0, then the next state is A (that is, A is to be stored in memory again); and if fact A is stored in memory and the input is a 1, then the next state is B. Whenever the system is in state A (or B or C), the output is 0.

    The state diagram that corresponds to this state table is shown in Figure 5.3. Each state is represented by a circle. Also included in the circle is the output for that state. Each line coming out of a circle represents a possible transition. The label on the line indicates the input that causes that transition. There must be one path from each state for each possible input combination. (In this example, there is only one input; thus, there are two paths.) Sometimes, the same next state is reached for both input combinations and a single line is shown either with two labels or with a don't care (X). This state diagram contains the identical information as the state table.

Figure 5.3 A state diagram.

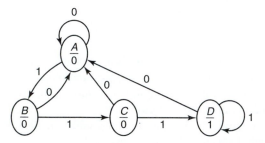

    If we were given the state table or diagram, we can construct the timing trace. In Trace 5.2, we repeat the previous trace but include the state.

Trace 5.2 Trace with state.

x	0	1	1	0	1	1	1	0	0	1	0	1	1	1	1	1	0	0			
q	?	A	B	C	A	B	C	D	A	A	B	A	B	C	D	D	D	A	A	?	
z	?	0	0	0	0	0	0	1	0	0	0	0	0	0	1	1	1	0	0	0	0

Whether we know the initial state or not, the state table and the state diagram both show that a 0 input takes the system to state A from all states. From state A, a 1 input takes the system to state B; from C, it goes to D; and from D, it remains in D.

In some systems, the output depends not only on the present state of the machine, but also on the present input. This type of system is referred to as a *Mealy model* (after G. B. Mealy). The state table has as many output columns as the next state portion (one for each possible input combination). An example (which we will return to in the next chapter) is shown in Table 5.2.

Table 5.2 State table for a Mealy model system.

	$q^\star$		z	
q	$x = 0$	$x = 1$	$x = 0$	$x = 1$
A	A	B	0	0
B	A	C	0	0
C	A	C	0	1

The Mealy model state diagram is different from the Moore model. The output is associated with the transition, rather than the state, as shown in Figure 5.4. Each path has a double label: the input causing the transition, followed by a slash and the output that occurs when the system is in that state and that is the input. Thus, from state A, the path to state B is labeled 1/0, meaning that that path is followed when $x = 1$, and the output produced is 0.

Figure 5.4 State diagram for the Mealy system of Table 5.2.

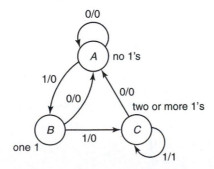

The timing trace (Trace 5.3) is constructed in much the same way as for a Moore model, except that the present output depends on the present input as well as the present state.

Trace 5.3 Timing trace.

x	0	1	1	0	1	1	1	0	0	1	0	1	0	1	1	1	1	1	0	0
q	?	A	B	C	A	B	C	C	A	A	B	A	B	A	B	C	C	C	C	A	A
Z	0	0	0	0	0	0	1	0	0	0	0	0	0	0	0	1	1	0	0	0	0

The analysis and design process for Moore and Mealy machines are very similar. We will return to that issues in Section 5.4 and again in Chapter 6.

[SP 1; EX 1]

5.2 LATCHES

A *latch* is a binary storage device, composed of two or more gates, with feedback—that is, for the simplest two-gate latch, the output of each gate is connected to the input of the other gate. Figure 5.5 shows such a latch, constructed with two NOR gates.

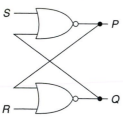

Figure 5.5 A NOR gate latch.

We can write the equations for this system:

$$P = (S + Q)'$$
$$Q = (R + P)'$$

The normal storage state is both inputs 0 (inactive). If S and R are 0, then both equations state that P is the opposite of Q, that is,

$$P = Q' \qquad Q = P'$$

The latch can store either a 0 ($Q = 0$ and $P = 1$) or a 1 ($Q = 1$ and $P = 0$). Thus, the P output is usually just labeled Q'. The letter S is used to indicate *set,* that is, store a 1 in the latch. If $S = 1$ and $R = 0$, then

$$P = (1 + Q)' = 1' = 0$$
$$Q = (0 + 0)' = 0' = 1$$

Thus, a 1 is stored in the latch (on line Q). Similarly, if the *reset* line, R, is made 1 and $S = 0$,

$$Q = (1 + P)' = 1' = 0$$
$$P = (0 + 0)' = 0' = 1$$

Finally, the latch is not operated with both S and R active, since, if $S = 1$ and $R = 1$,

$$P = (1 + Q)' = 1' = 0$$
$$Q = (1 + P)' = 1' = 0$$

Both outputs would be 0 (not the complement of each other). Further, if both S and R became inactive (went to 0) simultaneously, it is not clear to which state the latch would go (since either $Q = 0$ or $Q = 1$ would satisfy the logic equations). What happens would depend on such issues as whether they go to 0 at exactly the same time or one input goes to 0 ahead of the other, in which case the last 1 will dominate. Otherwise, such factors that are beyond the normal interest of the logic designer (such as the stray capacitance or the gain of the individual transistors) will determine the final state. To avoid this problem, we ensure that both inputs are not active simultaneously.

More complex latches can also be built. We will look at a gated latch, as shown in Figure 5.6. When the *Gate* signal is inactive (=0), *SG* and *RG* are both 0, and the latch remains unchanged. Only when *Gate* goes to 1, can a 0 or 1 be stored in the latch, exactly as in the simpler latch of Figure 5.5.

Figure 5.6   A gated latch.

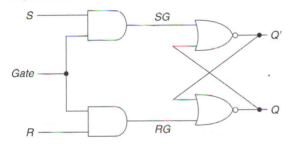

[SP 2; EX 2]

5.3 FLIP FLOPS

A *flip flop* is a clocked binary storage device, that is, a device that stores either a 0 or a 1. Under normal operation, that value will only change on the appropriate transition of the clock.* The state of the system (that is, what is in memory) changes on the transition of the clock. For some flip flops, that change takes place when the clock goes from 1 to 0; that is referred to as *trailing-edge triggered*. For others, that change takes place when the clock goes from 0 to 1; that is referred to as *leading-edge triggered*. What is stored after the transition depends on the flip flop data inputs and what was stored in the flip flop prior to the transition.

Flip flops have one or two outputs. One output is the state of the flip flop. If there are two, the other output is the complement of the state. Individual flip flops almost always have both outputs. However, when several flip flops are contained in one integrated circuit package, pin limitations may make only the uncomplemented output available.

---

*Many flip flops also have asynchronous clear and/or preset inputs that override the clock and put a 0 (clear) or a 1 (preset) in the flip flop immediately, in much the same way as in the simple *SR* latch. We will address that issue shortly.

We will concentrate on two types of flip flops, the *D* and the *JK*. The *D* flip flop is the most straightforward and is commonly found in programmable logic devices (Chapter 7). The *JK* flip flop almost always produces the simplest combinational logic. We will also introduce the *SR* and *T* flip flops, in between the discussion of the *D* and *JK*, since they naturally lead to the *JK*.

The simplest flip flop is the *D* flip flop. The name comes from **D**elay, since the output is just the input delayed until the next active clock transition. The next state of the *D* flip flop is the value of *D* before the clock transition. Block diagrams of *D* flip flops, both trailing-edge triggered and leading-edge triggered are shown in Figure 5.7. The triangle is used to indicate which input is the clock. A circle is usually shown on the clock input of a trailing-edge triggered flip flop. (We will do that consistently.) Caution is in order, however, since some publications do not differentiate in the diagram.

Figure 5.7 *D* flip flop diagrams.

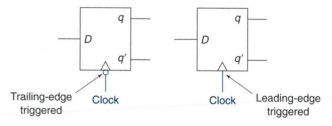

Trailing-edge triggered   Clock   Clock   Leading-edge triggered

We will use two forms of a truth table (Table 5.3) and a state diagram to describe the behavior of each type of flip flop. Although these are particularly simple for the *D* flip flop, we will show them here as well. In the first form of the truth table, the flip flop input(s) and the present state are in the input columns; in the second, only the flip flop input(s) are needed. The state diagram for a *D* flip flop is shown in Figure 5.8. It has two states (for all types of flip flops). The transition paths are labeled with the input that causes that transition, since the output of the flip flop is just the state. (The output is not shown in the circle since it is the same as the state.)

Figure 5.8 *D* flip flop state diagram.

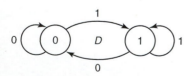

Table 5.3 The *D* flip flop behavioral tables.

D	q	$q^\star$
0	0	0
0	1	0
1	0	1
1	1	1

D	$q^\star$
0	0
1	1

The next state of a flip flop can be described algebraically as a function of its inputs and present state (by obtaining an equation directly from the first truth table). In the case of the D flip flop, the equation is

$$q^\star = D$$

The behavior of a trailing-edge triggered D flip flop is illustrated in the timing diagram of Figure 5.9a. Unless we know the initial value of q, that is, what was stored in the flip flop before we started to look, then q is unknown until after the first negative-going clock transition. That is indicated by the slashed section on the timing diagram. When the first trailing edge of the clock occurs, the state of the flip flop is established. Since D is 0 at that time, q goes to 0 (and, of course, q' goes to 1). Note that there is a slight delay in the output. The input, D, usually changes shortly after the transition, as shown for the first change, but may change at any time, as long as it has reached the correct value well before the next active transition. (Note that the second and third changes in D come later in the clock cycle.) As shown, the q' output is (as the name implies) the opposite of the q output. At the second trailing edge, D is 1; thus, q is 1 for the next clock period. At the third trailing edge, D is still 1, and q remains 1 for another clock period. Note that if the D input were to go back and forth between clock transitions, as shown in Figure 5.9b, the output would not be affected, since the value of D is only relevant near the time of a trailing edge. It would be the same as in Figure 5.9a.

Figure 5.9 *D* flip flop timing diagram.

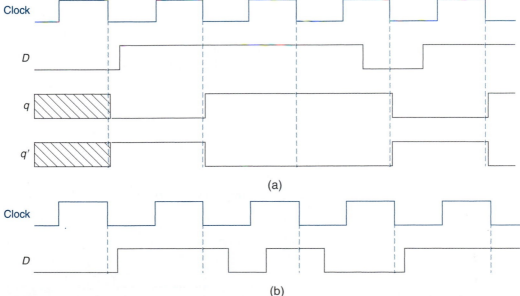

(a)

(b)

Next, we will look at the behavior of a leading-edge triggered version of that flip flop. The tables describing the flip flop need not be modified; the only difference is when the output changes relative to the clock. A timing diagram for a leading-edge triggered D flip flop, using the same input as before, is shown in Figure 5.10. The output (the state of the flip flop) changes shortly after the clock goes from 0 to 1 (based on the input just before that transition).

Figure 5.10   Leading-edge triggered D flip flop.

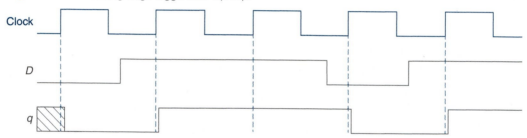

Since the behavior of the flip flop at a clock transition depends on the value of the flip flop inputs prior to that transition, we can connect the output of one flip flop to the input of another, as shown in Figure 5.11 (with trailing-edge triggered flip flops), and clock them simultaneously. At a clock transition when flip flop q changes, the old value of q is used to compute the behavior of r, as indicated in the timing diagram of Figure 5.12. The input to the first flip flop has not changed from the last example, and thus, q is the same as it was in Figure 5.9. (We have not shown q' on this diagram.) At the first trailing edge, the input to r (the output of the q flip flop) is unknown; thus, the output remains unknown after that clock. At the second trailing edge, the input to r is 0 and thus r goes to 0. That flip flop q changes from 0 to 1 as a result of this clock edge is not relevant; it is the value of the input *before* the clock edge that determines the behavior of r. The new value of q will be used to determine the behavior of r at the next clock transition. The output of flip flop r is a replica of that of q, delayed by one clock period.

Figure 5.11   Two flip flops.

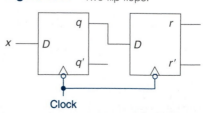

Figure 5.12 Timing for two flip flops.

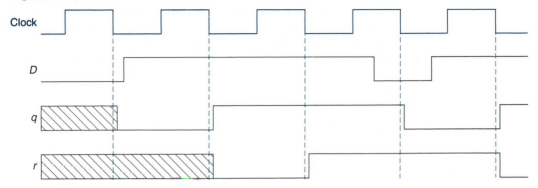

This type of behavior is common throughout sequential systems. Usually, all flip flops in the system are triggered by the same clock. Often, the inputs to flip flops are a function of the contents of the flip flops of the system, as was shown in the global view of a sequential system at the beginning of this chapter.

Before going on to look at other types of flip flops, we will examine the behavior of flip flops with static (asynchronous) clear* and preset inputs. Any type of flip flop may have one or both of these available. A D flip flop with active low (the most common arrangement) clear and preset inputs is shown in Figure 5.13. The version on the left uses over-bars for the complement (the most common notation in the integrated circuit literature); we will continue to use primes, as on the right, where the behavior of the flip flop is described by the truth table of Table 5.4. The clear and preset inputs act immediately (except for circuit delay) and override the clock, that is, they force the output to 0 and 1, respectively. Only when both of these static inputs are 1, does the flip flop behave as before, with the clock transition and the D input determining the behavior.

Figure 5.13 Flip flop with clear and preset inputs.

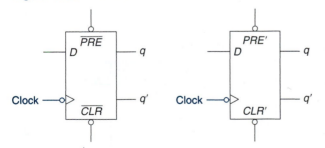

Table 5.4 D flip flop with clear and preset inputs behavioral table.

PRE'	CLR'	D	q	q*	
0	1	X	X	1	static
1	0	X	X	0	immediate
0	0	X	X	—	not allowed
1	1	0	0	0	
1	1	0	1	0	clocked
1	1	1	0	1	(as before)
1	1	1	1	1	

*Preset is sometimes referred to as *set,* in which case, clear may be referred to as *reset.*

A timing example is shown in Figure 5.14. The clear input becomes active near the beginning of the time shown, forcing q to 0. As long as that input remains 0, the clock and D are ignored; thus, nothing changes at the first trailing edge of the clock that is shown. Once the clear returns to 1, then the clock and D take over; but they have no effect until the next trailing edge of the clock. The output (q) does not change when CLR' (or PRE') returns to 1. The D input determines the behavior of the flip flop at the next four trailing edges. When the preset input goes to 0, the flip flop output goes to 1. When the preset input goes back to 1, the clock and D once again take over.

Figure 5.14   Timing for flip flop with clear and preset.

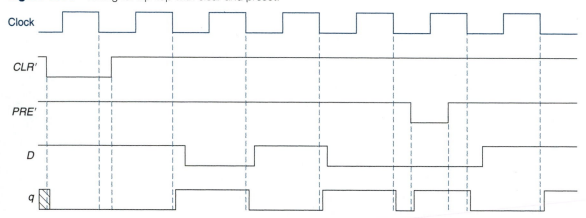

Next, we will look at the SR (**S**et-**R**eset) flip flop. It has two inputs, S and R, which have the same meaning as those for the SR latch. Its behavior is described by the truth tables of Table 5.5 and state diagram of Figure 5.15. The set (S) input causes a 1 to be stored in the flip flop at the next active clock edge; the reset (R) input causes a 0 to be stored. The S and R inputs are never made 1 at the same time. Although that would not damage the flip flop, as in the case of the latch, it is not certain what happens when S and R both go back to 0. Note that in the diagram, each

Figure 5.15   *SR* flip flop state diagram.

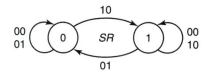

Table 5.5   *SR* flip flop behavioral tables.

S	R	q	q*
0	0	0	0
0	0	1	1
0	1	0	0
0	1	1	0
1	0	0	1
1	0	1	1
1	1	0	— not
1	1	1	— allowed

S	R	q*
0	0	q
0	1	0
1	0	1
1	1	— not allowed

label is 2 digits; the first is the value of S and the second the value of R. Two labels are on the path from 0 to 0 since either 00 or 01 will cause the flip flop to return to state 0. (There are also two input combinations that cause the flip flop to go from state 1 to 1.)

In Map 5.1, we map $q\star$ (from the first truth table). Notice that two of the squares are don't cares, since we will never make both S and R equal to 1 at the same time. This allows us to write an equation for the next state of the flip flop, $q\star$, in terms of the present state, q, and the inputs, S and R:

$$q\star = S + R'q$$

The equation says that after the clock, there will be a 1 in the flip flop if we set it ($S = 1$) or if there was already a 1 and we don't reset it ($R = 0$). A timing example (where there is only a clear input, not a preset one) is given in Figure 5.16. Note that we never made both S and R equal to 1 at the same time. Also, when both S and R are 0, q does not change.

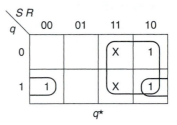

Map 5.1 *SR* flip flop behavioral map.

Figure 5.16 *SR* flip flop timing diagram.

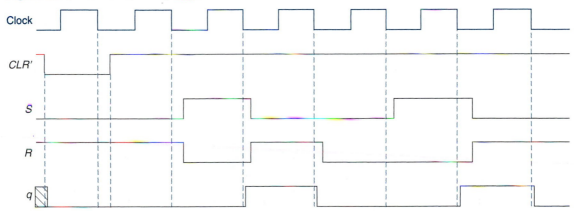

The third type of flip flop is the T (**T**oggle) flip flop. It has one input, T, such that if $T = 1$, the flip flop changes state (that is, is toggled), and if $T = 0$, the state remains the same. The truth tables describing the behavior of the T flip flop are given in Table 5.6 and the state diagram is shown in Figure 5.17.

Table 5.6 *T* flip flop behavioral tables.

T	q	$q\star$
0	0	0
0	1	1
1	0	1
1	1	0

T	$q\star$
0	q
1	q'

Figure 5.17 *T* flip flop state diagram.

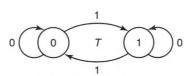

The behavioral equation is

$$q^\star = T \oplus q$$

and a timing example is shown in Figure 5.18.*

Figure 5.18 T flip flop timing diagram.

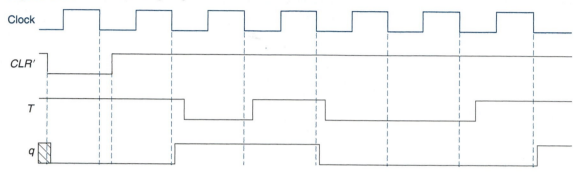

The last type of flip flop we will present is the JK (where the letters are not an acronym), which is a combination of the SR and T, in that it behaves like an SR flip flop, except that $J = K = 1$ causes the flip flop to change states (as in $T = 1$). The truth tables are given in Table 5.7 and the state diagram is shown in Figure 5.19.

Figure 5.19 JK flip flop state diagram.

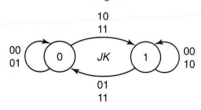

Table 5.7 JK flip flop behavioral tables.

J	K	q	$q^\star$
0	0	0	0
0	0	1	1
0	1	0	0
0	1	1	0
1	0	0	1
1	0	1	1
1	1	0	1
1	1	1	0

J	K	$q^\star$
0	0	q
0	1	0
1	0	1
1	1	q'

Map 5.2 JK flip flop behavioral map.

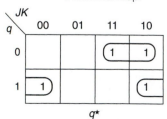

From the first truth table, we can derive Map 5.2 and the equation for $q^\star$:

$$q^\star = Jq' + K'q$$

---

*The T flip flop must have a static clear or preset, since the next state always depends on the previous one. For each of the other types of flip flops, there is at least one input combination that will force the flip flop to state 0.

A timing example for the *JK* flip flop is shown in Figure 5.20. Note that there are times when both *J* and *K* are 1 simultaneously; the flip flop just changes state at those times.

Figure 5.20 Timing diagram for *JK* flip flop.

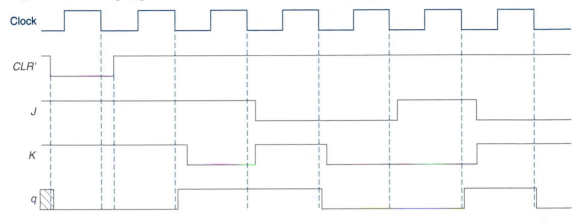

We now have the behavioral aspects of all of the flip flops and can begin to analyze more complex systems. Before we continue with that, we will look at some of the commercially available flip flop packages. *D* and *JK* flip flops are the most common. The Tables and State Diagrams describing all four types of flip flops, as well as the design tables we develop in the next chapter, are summarized on the inside back cover. We will now look at four commonly available packages.

The 7473 is a dual *JK* flip flop package. It contains two independent *JK* flip flops, each of which has an active low clear input, and both *q* and *q′* outputs. It is trailing-edge triggered (with separate clock inputs for each of the flip flops). (Each flip flop has four inputs—*J, K,* clear, and clock—and two outputs—*q* and *q′*; it fits in a 14-pin integrated circuit package.)

The 7474 is a dual *D* flip flop, also in a 14-pin package. Since there is only one data input per flip flop, there are two available pins; they are used for active low preset inputs. It is leading-edge triggered (with separate clock inputs for each of the flip flops).

There are packages of *D* flip flops with four or six flip flops. The 74174 is a hex (six) *D* flip flop package, with only a *q* output for each flip flop and a common leading-edge triggered clock. There is a common active low clear (sometimes referred to as a master reset). This is a 16-pin package.

Lastly, we have the 74175, a quad (four) *D* flip flop package. Each flip flop has both a *q* and *q′* output. There is a common leading-edge

[SP 3, 4; EX 3, 4, 5, 6]

triggered clock and a common active low clear. Once again, this is a 16-pin package.

5.4 ANALYSIS OF SEQUENTIAL SYSTEMS

In this section, we will examine some small state machines (consisting of flip flops and gates) and analyze their behavior, that is, produce timing diagrams, timing traces, state tables, and state diagrams. We will also look at the relationship between the state table and the timing.

The first example, the circuit of Figure 5.21, is a circuit with two trailing-edge triggered D flip flops. (We will call the flip flops q_1 and q_2; sometimes we will use names, such as A and B.)

Figure 5.21 A D flip flop Moore model circuit.

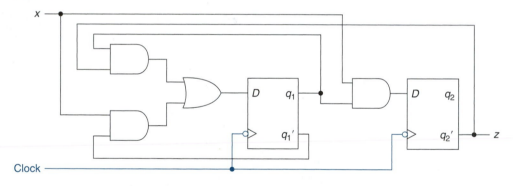

From the circuit, we find

$$D_1 = q_1 q_2' + x q_1'$$
$$D_2 = x q_1$$
$$z = q_2'$$

We will first construct the state table. Since this is a Moore model, the output depends only on the state and, thus, there is only one output column. The next state part is particularly easy for a D flip flop $q^* = D$. We first complete the output (z) column and the q_1^* part of the table as shown in Table 5.8a.

Finally, we add $q_2^*(D_2)$ to produce the complete state table of Table 5.8b.

Table 5.8a Partial state table.

| $q_1 q_2$ | $q_1^\star q_2^\star$ | | z |
	$x = 0$	$x = 1$	
0 0	0	1	1
0 1	0	1	0
1 0	1	1	1
1 1	0	0	0

Table 5.8b Complete state table.

| $q_1 q_2$ | $q_1^\star q_2^\star$ | | z |
	$x = 0$	$x = 1$	
0 0	0 0	1 0	1
0 1	0 0	1 0	0
1 0	1 0	1 1	1
1 1	0 0	0 1	0

Figure 5.22 A Moore state diagram.

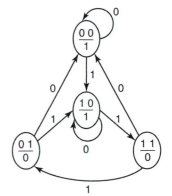

The corresponding state diagram is shown in Figure 5.22.

We will now look at a Moore model circuit with JK flip flops (see Figure 5.23).

Figure 5.23 A Moore model circuit.

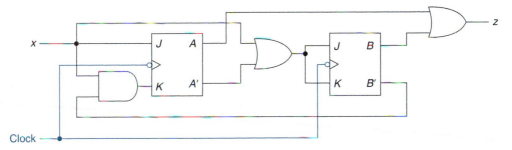

This is a Moore model, since the output z, which equals $A + B$, is only a function of the present state (that is, the contents of the flip flops) and not of the input x.

We will now write equations for the flip flop inputs and the output, and, from them, construct a state table:

$$J_A = x \qquad K_A = xB'$$
$$J_B = K_B = x + A'$$
$$z = A + B$$

The output column comes directly from the z equation. We can now fill in the next state section one entry at a time. For the first entry, since $x = A = B = 0$, $J_A = K_A = 0$ and $J_B = K_B = 1$. From the flip flop behavioral table of Table 5.7 (Section 5.2), we can see that A does not change state, but B toggles. Thus, the next state is 0 1. Next, for $x = A = 0$ and $B = 1$ (the second row of the first column), $J_A = K_A = 0$ and $J_B = K_B = 1$. Again, A does not change state, but once again B does. The resulting next state is 0 0. At this point, we have the state table of Table 5.9a.

Table 5.9a State table with first two entries.

A B	A⋆ B⋆ $x = 0$	$x = 1$	z
0 0	0 1		0
0 1	0 0		1
1 0			1
1 1			1

We can continue through the remaining entries or we can look at the equations for one flip flop at a time (as we did with the D flip flops). When $x = 0$ (no matter what A and B are), $J_A = K_A = 0$ and flip flop A does not change state. Thus, we can complete $A^\star$ for $x = 0$, as in Table 5.9b. When $x = 1$, $J_A = 1$ and $K_A = B'$. For the two rows where $B = 0$ (the first and third), J_A and K_A are both 1 and A toggles. For the two rows where $B = 1$ (the second and fourth), $J_A = 1$ and $K_A = 0$, putting a 1 in flip flop A. That results in the partial table (where $A^\star$ has been filled in) of Table 5.9b.

Table 5.9b State table with $A^\star$ entered.

A B	A⋆ B⋆ $x = 0$	$x = 1$	z
0 0	0	1	0
0 1	0	1	1
1 0	1	0	1
1 1	1	1	1

Now we can complete the $B^\star$ section of the table. When $A = 0$ (the first two rows of both columns), $J_B = K_B = 1$ and B changes state. When $A = 1$, $J_B = K_B = x$. For $x = 0$ (the first column, last two rows), B remains unchanged. Finally, for $A = 1$, $J_B = K_B = 1$ and B changes, producing the completed Table 5.9c.

Table 5.9c Completed state table.

A B	A⋆ B⋆ $x = 0$	$x = 1$	z
0 0	0 1	1 1	0
0 1	0 0	1 0	1
1 0	1 0	0 1	1
1 1	1 1	1 0	1

Another technique to construct the state table is to use the equations we developed in the last section for the next state, namely,

$$q^\star = Jq' + K'q$$

Using the values from this problem, we obtain

$$A^\star = J_A A' + K'_A A = xA' + (xB')'A = xA' + x'A + AB$$
$$B^\star = J_B B' + K'_B B = (x + A')B' + (x + A')'B$$
$$= xB' + A'B' + x'AB$$

We can now construct the state table as we did with D flip flops. These equations give exactly the same results as before.

For this example, we will produce a timing trace and a timing diagram, given the input x and the initial state.* The values of x and the initial values of A and B in Trace 5.4 are given.

Trace 5.4 Trace for Table 5.9.

x	0	0	1	0	1	1	0		
A	0 →	0	0	1	1	1	0	0	
B	0	1	0	1	1	0	1	0	1
	↓								
z	0	1	0	1	1	1	1	0	1

At the first clock edge, the values in the shaded box determine the present output (the box below), and the next state (the box to the right). The next state is obtained from the first row ($A\ B = 0\ 0$) and the first column ($x = 0$), the shaded square in Table 5.9c. The output is just the value of z in the first row. (Only the state is needed to determine the output.) For the next column of the timing trace, we start the process over again; this is effectively a new problem. The state is 0 1 (second row of the state table) and the input is 0, giving a next state of 0 0. This continues through successive inputs. The last input shown, a 0 when the system is in state 0 1, takes the system to state 0 0. We know that state and that output, even though we do not know the input any longer. Finally, for this example, we can determine the output and the value of B for one more clock time, since, from state 0 0, the next state is either 0 1 or 1 1, both of which have $B = 1$ and a 1 output. (We cannot go any further.)

In Figure 5.24, we will next look at a timing diagram for the same system with the same input sequence. We must look at the value of the variables (A, B, and x) just before the trailing edge. From that, we know the present state and the input, and can determine what the values for A and B must be during the next clock period. At any time that we know A and B, we can determine z.

We did not need to construct the state table to obtain either the timing diagram or the trace. We could, at each clock trailing edge, determine the

---

*The process is really a repetition of what we did in Timing Trace 5.3. The major differences are that there we had state names and here we have the values of the state variables (flip flops).

Figure 5.24   Timing diagram for Table 5.9.

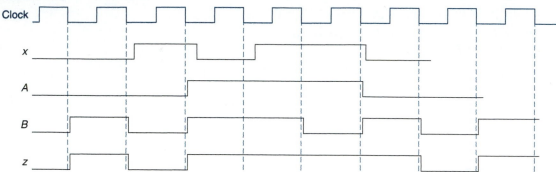

behavior of each flip flop. The output can then be constructed last, since it is just the OR of the two state variables (A and B). Thus, when the first clock edge arrives, $A = B = x = 0$ and, thus, $J_A = K_A = 0$, leaving A at 0. At the same time, $J_B = K_B = 1$ and thus B toggles, that is, goes to 1. We can now shift our attention to the next clock time and repeat the computations.

At this point, a word is in order about the initial value. For this example, we assumed that we knew what was stored in A and B when the first clock arrived. That may have been achieved using a static clear input, which was not shown to simplify this problem. In some cases, we can determine the behavior of the system after one or two clock periods even if we did not know the initial value. (That will be the case in the next example.) But, in this problem, we must initialize the system. (Try the other initial states and note that each follows a completely different sequence over the time period shown.) Finally, for this problem (a Moore model), the state diagram is given in Figure 5.25.

Figure 5.25   State diagram for Table 5.9.

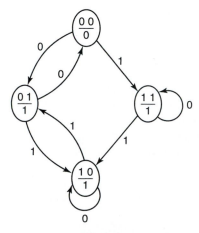

In some systems, the output depends on the present input, as well as the state. From a circuit point of view, that just means that z is a function of x, as well as the state variables. This type of circuit is a Mealy model. An example of such a system is shown in Figure 5.26.

Figure 5.26   A Mealy model.

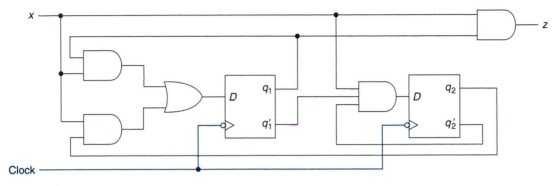

The flip flop input and the output equations are

$$D_1 = xq_1 + xq_2$$
$$D_2 = xq_1'q_2'$$
$$z = xq_1$$

Of course, with D flip flops, $q^\star = D$. Thus,

$$q_1^\star = xq_1 + xq_2$$
$$q_2^\star = xq_1'q_2'$$

From that, we obtain the state table of Table 5.10. Notice that we need two output columns, one for $x = 0$ and one for $x = 1$.

Table 5.10   State table for the Mealy system.

	$q^\star$		z	
q	$x = 0$	$x = 1$	$x = 0$	$x = 1$
0 0	0 0	0 1	0	0
0 1	0 0	1 0	0	0
1 0	0 0	1 0	0	1
1 1	0 0	1 0	0	1

Note that state 1 1 is never reached; this problem really only has three states (although when the system is first turned on, it could start in state 1 1). But after the first clock, it will leave that state and never return. That becomes obvious from the state diagram of Figure 5.27.

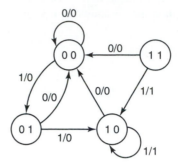

Figure 5.27   State diagram for a Mealy model.

Notice that there is no path into state 1 1. Also note that whenever there is a 0 input, we return to state 0 0. Thus, even if we do not initialize this system, it will behave properly after the first 0 input.

We will next look at the timing trace (see Trace 5.5, where the input is given and shown in light green) and then at the timing diagram for this system.

Trace 5.5   Mealy model timing.

x	0	1	1	0	1	1	1	1	0		
q_1	?	0 →	0	1	0	0	1	1	1	0	
q_2	?	0	1	0	0	1	0	0	0	0	
z	0	0	0	0	0	0	1	1	0	0	0

Even though we do not know the initial state (the ? for q_1 and q_2), the 0 input forces the system to state 0 0 at the next clock time and we can complete the trace. Note that the output is known for two clock periods after the input is not, since the system cannot reach state 1 0 (the only state for which there is a 1 output) any sooner than that. A word of caution: the present state and the present input determine the *present* output and the *next* state, as indicated.

The timing diagram for this example is shown in Figure 5.28. It illustrates a peculiarity of Mealy systems.* Note that there is a *false output* (sometimes referred to as a *glitch*), that is, the output goes to 1 for a short period even though that is not indicated in the timing trace nor in the state table.

The output comes from combinational logic; it is just xq_1. If the input x does not change simultaneously with the trailing edge of the

---

*In the timing diagram, the delay through the output AND gate is ignored since it is typically shorter than that of the flip flop.

Figure 5.28   Illustration of false output.

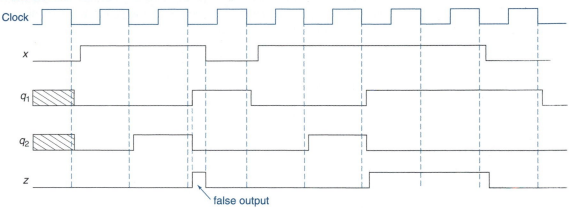

false output

clock (as is the case here), and it remains 1 after q_1 goes to 1, the output
will go to 1. But the output indicated by the state table or the timing trace
is based on the value of q_1 at the time of the next clock. The false output
is not usually important, since the output of a Mealy system is mainly of
interest at clock times (that is, just before the edge on which flip flops
might change state). Furthermore, it is often the case that system inputs
change simultaneously with the trailing edge of the clock.* The glitch
occurred only because x changed well after the flip flop change. As the
change in x gets closer (in time) to the changes in q (that is, the clock
edge), the glitch gets narrower and if x goes to 0 at the same time that q_1
goes to 1, the false output disappears.

Consider the following circuit with one JK and one D flip flop: **EXAMPLE 5.1a**

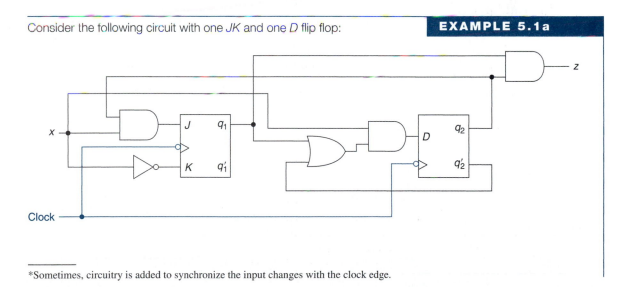

---
*Sometimes, circuitry is added to synchronize the input changes with the clock edge.

The output, $z = q_1 q_2$, does not depend on the input x; thus, this is a Moore model. (This system produces an output of 1 if the input is 1 for three or more consecutive clock periods (CE 6).)

The input equations for the system are

$$J_1 = xq_2 \qquad K_1 = x'$$
$$D_2 = x(q_1 + q_2')$$

Notice that when $x = 0$, J_1 is 0, K_1 is 1, and D_2 is 0; thus the system goes to state 0 0. When $x = 1$,

$$J_1 = q_2 \qquad K_1 = 0 \qquad D_2 = q_1 + q_2'$$

Flip flop q_1 goes to 1 when $q_2 = 1$ and is unchanged otherwise. (Of course, q_1 remains at 1 in state 1 0.) Flip flop q_2 goes to 1 when $q_1 = 1$ or $q_2 = 0$ and to 0 only if $q_1 = 0$ and $q_2 = 1$.

We could also use, for q_1, the equation

$$q^\star = Jq' + K'q$$

and obtain

$$q_1^\star = xq_2q_1' + xq_1 = x(q_2 + q_1)$$

From either approach, we get the following state table:

	$q_1^\star \, q_2^\star$		
$q_1 \, q_2$	$x = 0$	$x = 1$	z
0 0	0 0	0 1	0
0 1	0 0	1 0	0
1 0	0 0	1 1	0
1 1	0 0	1 1	1

This is the same state table as in Table 5.1 if we note that A has been coded as 0 0, B as 0 1, C as 1 0, and D as 1 1.

This system produces the following timing diagram:

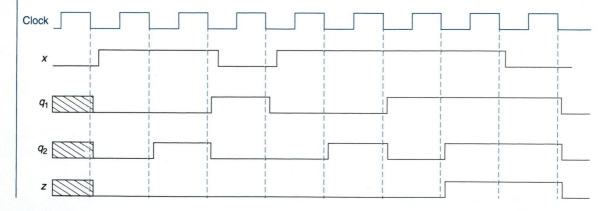

There is never a false output in a Moore model, since the output depends only on the state of the flip flops, and they all change simultaneously, on the trailing edge of the clock. The output is valid for a whole clock period, from just after one negative-going transition to just after the next.

EXAMPLE 5.1b

If the AND gate of Example 5.1a had a third input, x', then $z = x'q_1q_2$ and this would be a Mealy model. The next state portion of the state table and of the timing diagram would be unchanged. There would be two columns in the state table.

$q_1 q_2$	$q_1^* q_2^*$		z	
	$x = 0$	$x = 1$	$x = 0$	$x = 1$
0 0	0 0	0 1	0	0
0 1	0 0	1 0	0	0
1 0	0 0	1 1	0	0
1 1	0 0	1 1	1	0

The z in the timing diagram would remain 0 until after x goes to 0 (one clock time later than in Example 5.1a).

EXAMPLE 5.2

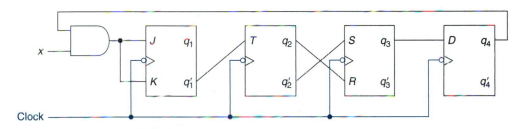

Complete the timing trace as far as possible. Assume that the system is initially in state 0 0 0 0. The given values are shown in green.

$$J_1 = K_1 = xq_4$$
$$T_2 = q_1'$$
$$S_2 = q_2' \quad R_2 = q_2$$
$$D_4 = q_3$$

Therefore,

q_1 changes state only when $xq_4 = 1$
q_2 changes state only when $q_1 = 0$
$q_3^* = q_2'$
$q_4^* = q_3$

$$x \quad 1\ 1\ 1\ 0\ 1\ 1$$
$$q_1 \quad 0\ 0\ 0\ 1\ 1\ 0\ 0\ 0\ 0$$
$$q_2 \quad 0\ 1\ 0\ 1\ 1\ 1\ 0\ 1\ 0\ 1$$
$$q_3 \quad 0\ 1\ 0\ 1\ 0\ 0\ 0\ 1\ 0\ 1\ 0$$
$$q_4 \quad 0\ 0\ 1\ 0\ 1\ 0\ 0\ 0\ 1\ 0\ 1\ 0$$

After the first clock, q_1 remains at 0, q_2 toggles, q_3 is loaded with 1 (q_2'), and q_4 goes to 0 (from q_3). After the last input is known for this circuit, we can determine the next value of q_1 as long as the present value of q_4 is 0 (since xq_4 will be 0). The next state of each of the other flip flops depends only on the present state of the one to its left. Thus, we can find a value for q_2 one clock time after q_1 is known, for q_3 one clock time after that, and for q_4 one additional clock time later.

[SP 4, 5, 6, 7, 8; EX 6, 7, 8, 9]

5.5 SOLVED PROBLEMS

1. For each of the following state tables, show a state diagram and complete the timing trace as far as possible (even after the input is no longer known).

   a.

q_1q_2	$q_1^\star q_2^\star$ $x=0$	$x=1$	z $x=0$	$x=1$
0 0	0 0	1 0	0	1
0 1	0 0	0 0	0	0
1 0	1 1	0 1	1	1
1 1	1 0	1 0	1	0

   $$x \quad 0\ 1\ 0\ 0\ 1\ 1\ 1\ 0$$
   $$q_1 \quad 0$$
   $$q_2 \quad 0$$
   $$z$$

   b.

q	$q^\star$ $x=0$	$x=1$	z
A	A	B	1
B	D	C	1
C	D	C	0
D	A	B	0

   $$x \quad 0\ 1\ 0\ 1\ 0\ 1\ 1\ 1\ 0\ 1\ 0\ 0\ 0\ 0$$
   $$q \quad A$$
   $$z$$

a.   **b.**

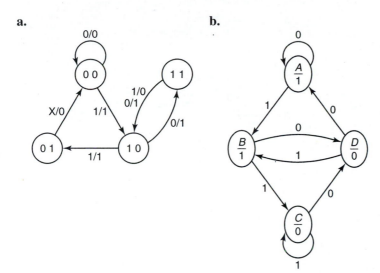

Note that in part a, state 0 1 goes to 0 0 always (input is don't care) and the output is always 0. State 1 1 always goes to 1 0, but the outputs are different for the two different inputs; thus two labels are shown on that path.

The timing traces are as follows:

a. x 0 1 0 0 1 1 1 0
$\quad q_1$ 0 0 1 1 1 0 0 1 1 1
$\quad q_2$ 0 0 0 1 0 1 0 0 1 0 1 0
$\quad z$ 0 1 1 1 1 0 1 1 ? 1

Since state 1 1 always goes to state 1 0 (independent of the input), we can determine the next state for the second clock after the input is no longer known. At the first clock after the last input, the output is unknown, but at the next one, we know that it must be 1, since the output is 1 from state 1 0, no matter what the input is. Note that we can determine q_2 for two additional clock times.

b. x 0 1 0 1 0 1 1 1 0 1 0 0 0 0
$\quad q$ A A B D B D B C C D B D A A A
$\quad z$ 1 1 1 0 1 0 1 0 0 0 1 0 1 1 1 1

Since state A goes to either A or B, and the output in each of those states is 1, we can determine the output for one extra clock time.

2. Analyze the following latch; give the appropriate inputs and outputs meaningful labels.

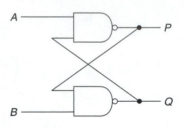

$$P = (AQ)' \qquad Q = (BP)'$$

If $A = B = 0$,

$$P = Q = 1$$

If $A = B = 1$,

$$P = Q' \qquad Q = P'$$

If $A = 0$ and $B = 1$,

$$P = 1 \qquad Q = 0$$

If $A = 1$ and $B = 0$,

$$Q = 1 \qquad P = 0$$

This is an active low input latch, where both inputs active ($A = B = 0$) is not allowed. The store state is $A = B = 1$ (inactive), where the outputs are the complement of each other. When A is active, P is made 1 (and $Q = 0$). When B is active, $Q = 1$ and $P = 0$. Thus, we could label the latch as follows:

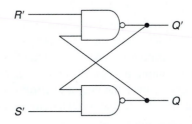

3. Consider the trailing-edge triggered flip flops shown.

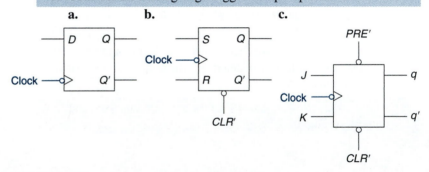

a. Show a timing diagram for *Q*.

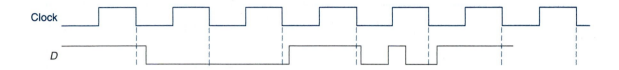

b. Show a timing diagram for *Q* if
  i. there is no *CLR′* input.
  ii. the *CLR′* input is as shown.

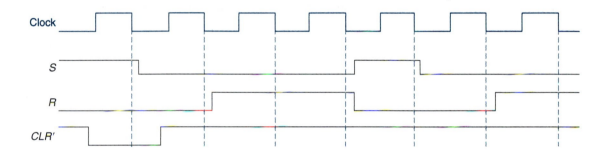

c. Show a timing diagram for *Q* if
  i. there is no *PRE′* input.
  ii. the *PRE′* input is as shown (in addition to the *CLR′* input).

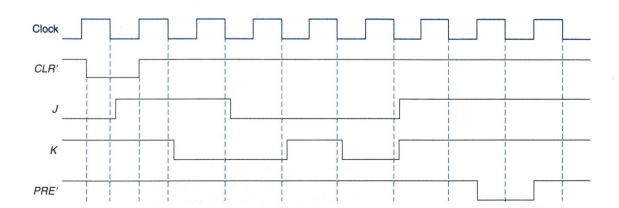

a.

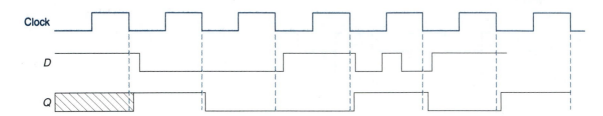

The state of the flip flop is not known until the first trailing edge. At that point, D determines what is to be stored. Thus, the first time, Q goes to 1; the second time, Q goes to 0; the third time, Q goes to (stays at) 0. When D changes between clock times, that does not affect the behavior; it is the value just before the trailing edge that matters.

b.

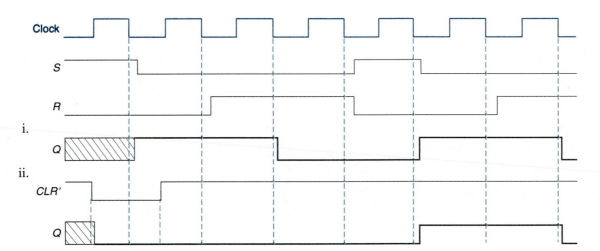

Without the clear, we do not know what Q is until after the first trailing edge. At that point, since $S = 1$, Q goes to 1. At the next clock, both S and R are 0; thus Q does not change. Since $R = 1$ for the next two clock times, Q goes to 0. Then $S = 1$, making $Q = 1$; both are 0 leaving Q at 1; and finally $R = 1$, returning Q to 0. With the clear, Q goes to 0 earlier and the first clock edge is ignored. Thus Q remains at 0 for the next three clock times. Then, this part behaves like the first part. (Once the Q from the second part is the same as that from the first, the behavior is identical.)

c.

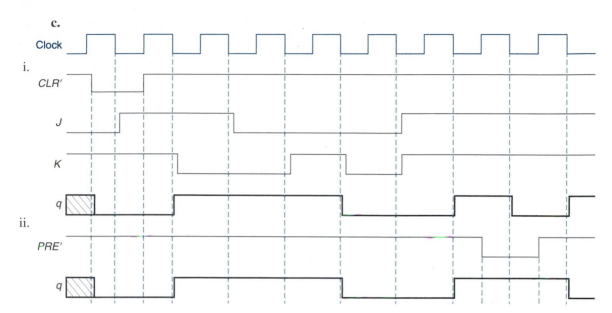

i.

ii.

The two parts are the same up to the time of the active preset input. In the second case, the preset overrides the clock and keeps the output at 1. Then, when the outputs start toggling (since J and K are 1), the two timing pictures are the opposite of each other.

4. We have a new flip flop with three inputs, S, R, and T (in addition to a trailing-edge triggered clock input). No more than one of these inputs may be 1 at any time. The S and R inputs behave exactly as they do in an SR flip flop (that is, S puts a 1 into the flip flop and R puts a 0 in the flip flop). The T input behaves as it does in a T flip flop (that is, it causes the flip flop to change state).

a. Show a state graph for this flip flop.

b. Write an equation for $Q^\star$ in terms of S, R, T, and Q.

a.   **b.**

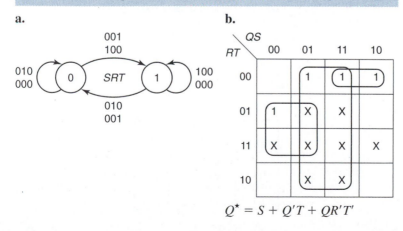

$$Q^\star = S + Q'T + QR'T'$$

5. For the following circuit,

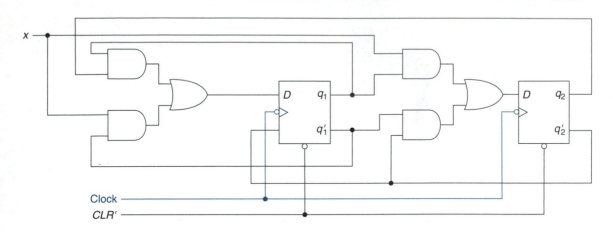

a. Ignore the *CLR'* input. Find a state diagram and a state table.

b. Assume that the flip flops are each initially in state 0 (and there is no *CLR'*), complete the timing trace for the states of the flip flops as far as possible.

  x   1   0   1   1   1   0

c. For the following inputs (both *x* and *CLR'*), complete the timing diagram for the state of each flip flop.

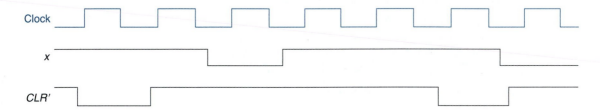

a. For this circuit,

$$D_1 = q_1 q_2 + x q_1' \qquad D_2 = x q_1 + q_1' q_2'$$

The state table is

$q_1 q_2$	$q_1^\star q_2^\star$ $x = 0$	$x = 1$
0 0	0 1	1 1
0 1	0 0	1 0
1 0	0 0	0 1
1 1	1 0	1 1

Since no outputs are shown, we will assume that the state is the only output. The state diagram becomes

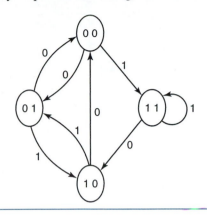

b. The timing trace for the given string is

x	1 0 1 1 1 0
q_1	0 1 1 0 1 0 0
q_2	0 1 0 1 0 1 0 1

c. The timing diagram is

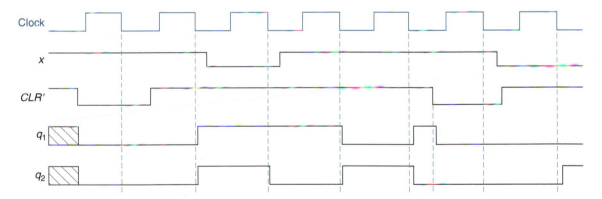

The flip flop contents are unknown until the *CLR'* signal goes to 0. The first transition of the clock has no effect. At the second negative-going transition of the clock, $x = 1$. Both flip flops go to 1. We can evaluate the flip flop inputs at the next three clock trailing edges and produce the balance of the timing, until *CLR'* goes to 0 again. At that time, q_1 and q_2 go to 0. The clock takes over again at the last transition.

6. For the following circuit, complete the timing diagram for the state of each flip flop and the output. All flip flops are trailing-edge triggered.

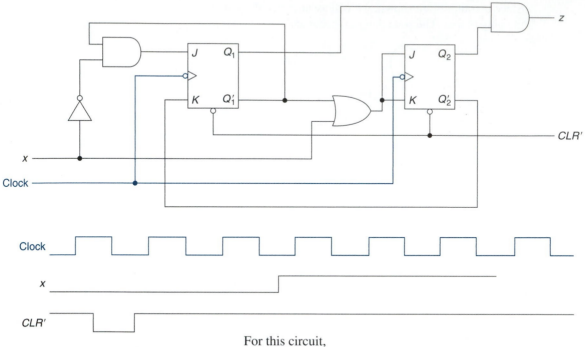

For this circuit,

$$J_1 = x'Q_1' \quad K_1 = Q_2' \quad J_2 = K_2 = x + Q_1' \quad z = Q_1Q_2$$

The output z is just a function of the state of the flip flops. It can be determined last (after completing the flip flop outputs). At the last clock transition, the input is not known and thus J_1 is unknown (since $Q_1' = 1$). Thus, we cannot determine the next value of Q_1. But, $J_2 = K_2 = 1$ (no matter what x is) and thus we can determine the value for Q_2.

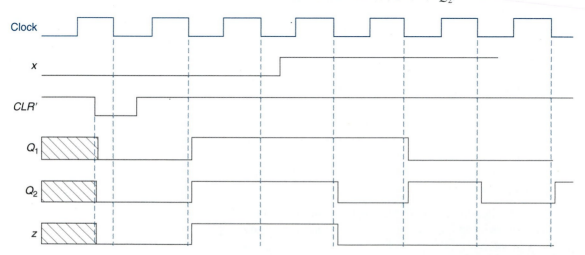

7. For each of the following circuits and input strings
- i. Construct a state table (calling the states 0 0, 0 1, 1 0, 1 1).
- ii. Show a timing trace for the values of the flip flops and the output for as far as possible. Assume all flip flops are initially in state 0.

a.

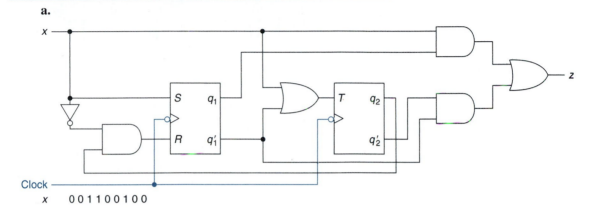

x 0 0 1 1 0 0 1 0 0

b.

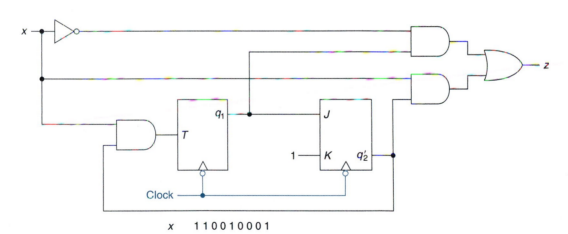

x 1 1 0 0 1 0 0 0 1

a. $S = x$ $R = x'q_2$ $T = q_1' + x$ $z = xq_1 + q_1'q_2'$

For $x = 0$, $S = 0$ and $R = q_2$. Thus, q_1 is unchanged when $q_2 = 0$ and cleared otherwise. For $x = 1$, q_1 is set. When $x = 1$

or $q_1 = 0$, q_2 toggles; otherwise it remains unchanged. That produces the following state table:

q_1q_2	$q_1^\star q_2^\star$ $x = 0$	$x = 1$	z $x = 0$	$x = 1$
0 0	0 1	1 1	1	1
0 1	0 0	1 0	0	0
1 0	1 0	1 1	0	1
1 1	0 1	1 0	0	1

x	0	0	1	1	0	0	1	0	0	
q_1	0	0	0	1	1	1	1	1	0	0
q_2	0	1	0	1	0	0	0	1	1	0	1
z	1	0	1	1	0	0	1	0	0	1

Note that at the first clock time when the input is unknown, we can determine the output even though we do not know the input, since $z = 1$ in state 0 0, for both $x = 0$ and $x = 1$. We know q_2 one additional clock time, since 0 0 goes to states 0 **1** or 1 **1**, both of which give $q_2 = 1$.

b. $T = xq_2'$ $J = q_1$ $K = 1$ $z = x'q_1 + xq_2'$
Note that q_1 toggles only when $x = 1$ and $q_2 = 0$; and that q_2 toggles when $q_1 = 1$, and goes to 0, otherwise.

q_1q_2	$q_1^\star q_2^\star$ $x = 0$	$x = 1$	z $x = 0$	$x = 1$
0 0	0 0	1 0	0	1
0 1	0 0	0 0	0	0
1 0	1 1	0 1	1	1
1 1	1 0	1 0	1	0

x	1	1	0	0	1	0	0	0	1	1	
q_1	0	1	0	0	0	1	1	1	1	1	0	0
q_2	0	0	1	0	0	0	1	0	1	0	1	0	0
z	1	1	0	0	1	1	1	1	0	1	0	

In this example, we can determine the state for two clocks after the input is no longer known, the value of q_2 for a third (since from state 0 0, we go either to 0 **0** or 1 **0**) and the output for one clock after the last known input.

8. For the following circuits, complete the timing trace as far as possible. The state of some flip flops can be determined as many as five or six clocks after the input is no longer known. Assume that all flip flops are initially 0.

a.

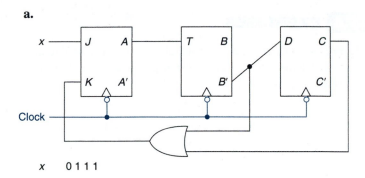

x   0 1 1 1

b.

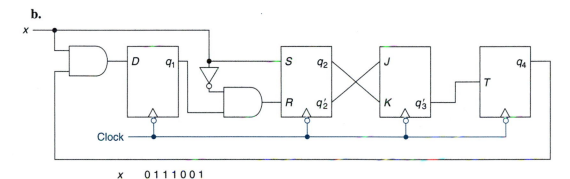

x   0 1 1 1 0 0 1

a. $J = x$ $K = B' + C$ $T = A$ $D = C^\star = B'$

```
x 0   1   1   1
A 0 0 1 0 1 1 0
B 0 0 0 1 1 0 1 1
C 0 1 1 1 0 0 1 0 0
```

Since flip flop B depends only on A, and C depends only on B, we know the value of C one clock time after B, and B one clock time after A. At the first clock time when x (and thus, J) is unknown, A contains a 1. If K is 0 (independent of J), flip flop A will still have a 1; if K is 1, it will go to 0. Thus, for this sequence, we are able to determine A for two clock times when x is unknown.

---

b. $D = xq_4$ $S = x$ $R = x' q_1$ $q_3^\star = q_2'$ $T = q_3'$

```
x     0   1   1   1   0   0   1
q₁ 0 0 1 1 1 0 0 0 0 0
q₂ 0 0 1 1 1 0 0 1 1 1 1
q₃ 0 1 1 0 0 0 1 1 0 0 0 0
q₄ 0 1 1 1 0 1 0 0 0 1 0 1 0
```

5.6 EXERCISES

1. For each of the following state tables, show a state diagram and complete the timing trace as far as possible (even after the input is no longer known).

a.

$q_1 q_2$	$q_1^\star q_2^\star$ $x = 0$	$x = 1$	z $x = 0$	$x = 1$
0 0	0 1	0 0	0	1
0 1	1 0	1 1	0	0
1 0	0 0	0 0	1	1
1 1	0 1	0 1	1	0

x	1 0 1 1 0 0 0 1
q_1	0
q_2	0
z	

*b.

q	$q^\star$ $x = 0$	$x = 1$	z
A	A	B	0
B	C	B	0
C	A	D	0
D	C	B	1

x	1 1 0 1 0 1 0 1 0 0 1 0 1 1
q	A
z	

c.

q	$q^\star$ $x = 0$	$x = 1$	z $x = 0$	$x = 1$
A	B	C	0	1
B	C	A	0	0
C	A	B	1	0

x	0 0 1 1 1 0 0 0 0 0 1 0
q	A
z	

d.

q	$q^\star$ $x = 0$	$x = 1$	z $x = 0$	$x = 1$
A	A	B	1	0
B	C	D	0	0
C	A	B	0	0
D	C	D	1	0

x 0 1 0 0 0 1 1 1 1 0 1

q A

z

2. Show the block diagram for a gated latch that behaves similarly to the one of Figure 5.6, but uses only NAND gates.

3. For the input shown below, show the flip flop outputs.

   a. Assume that the flip flop is a D flip flop without a clear or preset.

   b. Assume that the flip flop is a D flip flop with an active low clear.

   c. Assume that the flip flop is a D flip flop with active low clear and preset inputs.

   d. Assume that the flip flop is a T flip flop with the same input as part a, and that Q is initially 0.

   e. Assume that the flip flop is a T flip flop with an active low clear and the same inputs as part b.

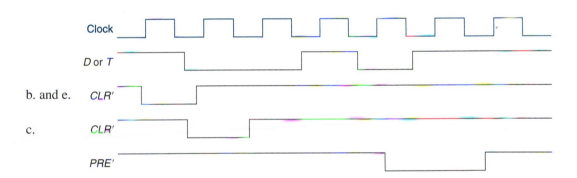

4. For the following JK flip flops, complete each of the timing diagrams. First, assume that CLR' and PRE' are inactive (1). Then, use the values shown.

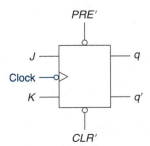

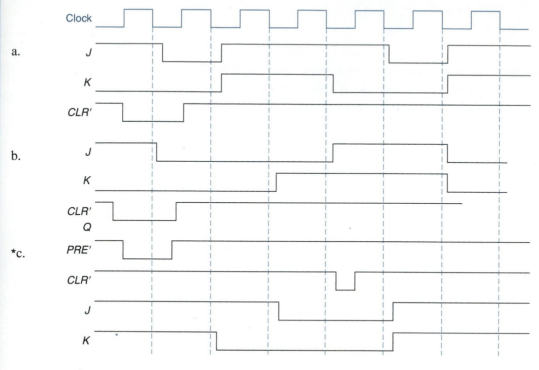

a.

b.

*c.

5. Consider the following flip flop circuit

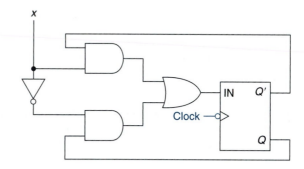

Complete the timing diagram below if that flip flop is

a. a *D* flip flop

b. a *T* flip flop

In both cases, the flip flop starts with a 0 in it.

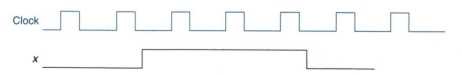

6. We have a new type of flip flop, with inputs A and B. If $A = 0$, then $Q^\star = B$; if $A = 1$, $Q^\star = B'$.

    a.   Show a state diagram for this flip flop.

    b.   Write an equation for $Q^\star$ in terms of A, B, and Q.

7. For each of the following circuits, complete the timing diagram for the state of each flip flop and the output, where shown. All flip flops are trailing-edge triggered. For those circuits in which there is no clear input, assume each flip flop starts at 0.

    a.

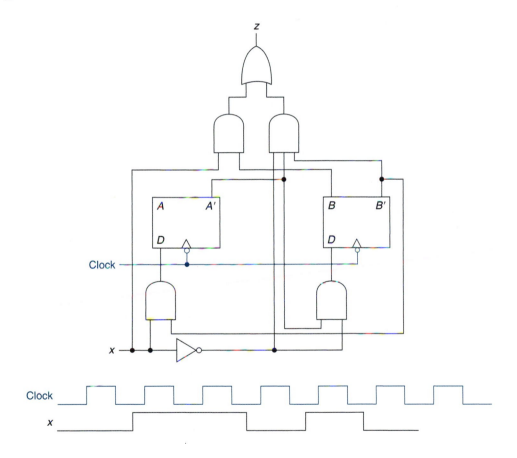

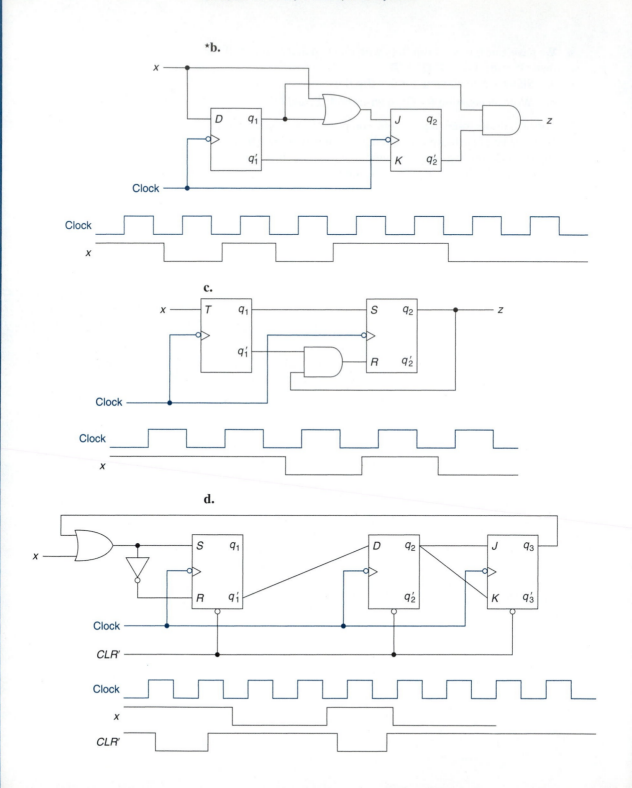

8. For each of the following circuits and input strings

   i. Construct a state table (calling the states 0 0, 0 1, 1 0, 1 1).

   ii. Show a timing trace for the values of the flip flops and the output for as far as possible. Assume that the initial value of each flip flop is 0.

*a.

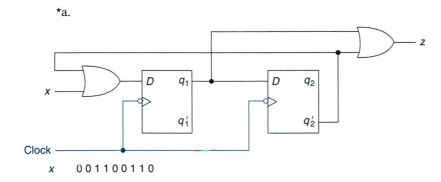

x   0 0 1 1 0 0 1 1 0

b.

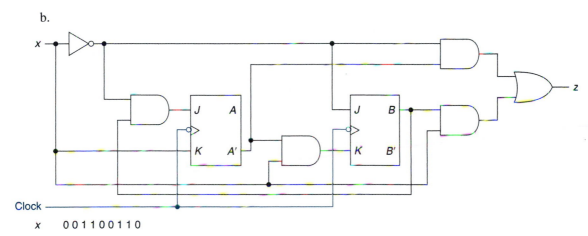

x   0 0 1 1 0 0 1 1 0

c.

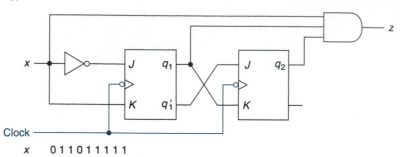

x 0 1 1 0 1 1 1 1 1

d.

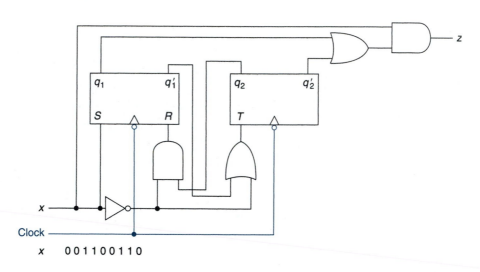

x 0 0 1 1 0 0 1 1 0

9. For the following circuits, complete the timing trace as far as possible. The state of some flip flops and the output can be determined for as many as three clocks after the input is no longer known. Assume that all flip flops are initially 0.

a.

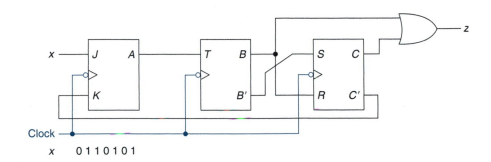

x   0 1 1 0 1 0 1

b.

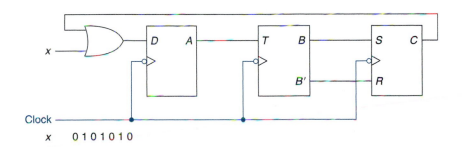

x   0 1 0 1 0 1 0

*c.

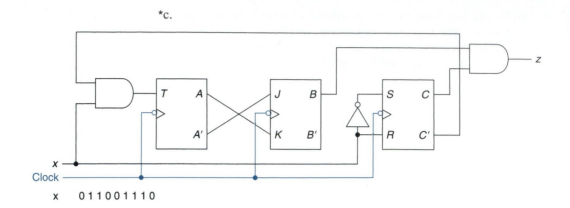

x   0 1 1 0 0 1 1 1 0

d.

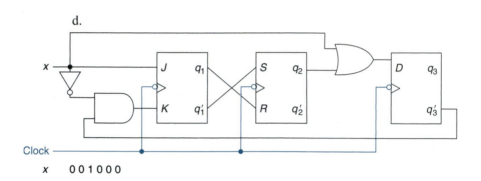

x   0 0 1 0 0 0

---

1. For the following state table, complete the timing trace as far as you can

	$q^\star$		z	
q	$x = 0$	$x = 1$	$x = 0$	$x = 1$
A	C	A	0	0
B	A	D	1	1
C	B	C	0	1
D	B	B	0	0

x 0 0 1 1 0 0 0 1 0 1

q A

z

2. For the following *JK* trailing-edge triggered flip flop with an active low clear, show the timing diagram for *Q*.
   a. Assuming no *CLR'* input.
   b. With the *CLR'* input shown.

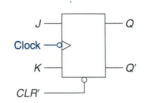

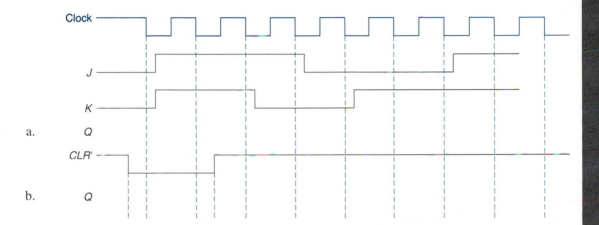

3. For the following circuit, construct the state table.

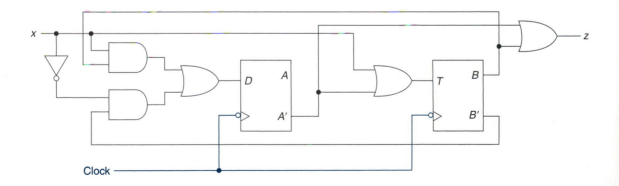

4. For the following circuit, complete the timing diagram.

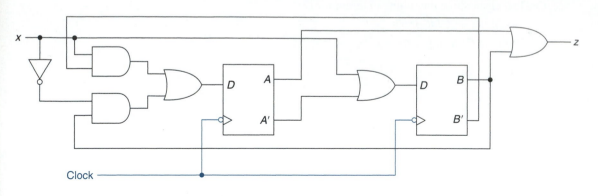

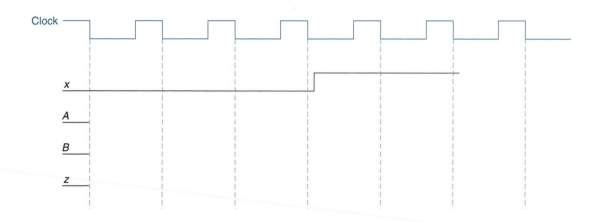

The Design of Sequential Systems

A s in the case of combinational systems, the design process typically starts with a problem statement, a verbal description of the intended behavior of the system. The goal is to develop a block diagram of the system utilizing the available components and meeting the design objectives and constraints.

We will first present five additional Continuing Examples, which we will use throughout the chapter to illustrate the design techniques.

Continuing Examples (CE)

CE7. A Mealy system with one input x and one output z such that $z = 1$ at a clock time iff x is currently 1 and was also 1 at the previous two clock times.*

CE8. A Moore system with one input x and one output z, the output of which is 1 iff three consecutive 0 inputs occurred more recently than three consecutive 1 inputs.

CE9. A Moore system with no inputs and three outputs, that represent a number from 0 to 7, such that the outputs cycle through the sequence 0 3 2 4 1 5 7 and repeat on consecutive clock inputs.

CE10. A Moore system with two inputs, x_1 and x_2, and three outputs, z_1, z_2, and z_3, that represent a number from 0 to 7, such that the output counts up if $x_1 = 0$ and down if $x_1 = 1$, and recycles if $x_2 = 0$ and saturates if $x_2 = 1$. Thus, the following output sequences might be seen

$x_1 = 0, x_2 = 0$:   0 1 2 3 4 5 6 7 0 1 2 3 4 5 6 7 . . .

$x_1 = 0, x_2 = 1$:   0 1 2 3 4 5 6 7 7 7 7 7 7 7 7 7 . . .

$x_1 = 1, x_2 = 0$:   7 6 5 4 3 2 1 0 7 6 5 4 3 2 1 0 . . .

$x_1 = 1, x_2 = 1$:   7 6 5 4 3 2 1 0 0 0 0 0 0 0 0 0 . . .

---

*This is very similar to CE6 (introduced in Chapter 5), except that the output goes to 1 simultaneously with the third consecutive 1 (whereas in CE6, the system went to a state with a 1 output when it received the third 1).

(Of course, x_1 and x_2 may change at some point so that the output would switch from one sequence to another.)

CE11. A bus controller that receives requests on separate lines, R_0 to R_3, from four devices desiring to use the bus. It has four outputs, G_0 to G_3, only one of which is 1, indicating which device is granted control of the bus for that clock period. (We will consider, in Section 6.4, the design for such a priority controller, where the low number device has the highest priority, if more than one device requests the bus at the same time. We look at both interrupting controllers (where a high-priority device can preempt the bus) and one where a device keeps control of the bus once it gets control until it no longer needs the bus.)

We will now look at the design process for systems similar to those we discussed in the previous chapter. In Chapters 7 and 9, we will look at other techniques that are more suitable for larger systems.

> **Step 1:** From a word description, determine what needs to be stored in memory, that is, what are the possible states.

Sometimes there may be different ways of storing the necessary information. For CE7, we could just store the last two values of the input. If we know that and we know the current input, then we know if all three have been 1. But we could also store how many consecutive 1's there have been—none, 1, or two or more. We can develop the state table either way; each will produce a properly working circuit. However, the cost might be quite different. Just consider what would have been the case if we wanted an output of 1 iff the input was now 1 and was also 1 for the last 27 consecutive clocks. The first approach would require us to store the last 27 inputs—in 27 flip flops. The second approach would require us to keep track of only 28 things, 0 consecutive 1's through 27 or more consecutive 1's. But 28 facts can be stored using only five binary storage devices, coding none as 00000, through 27 or more as 11011 (the binary equivalent of 27).

> **Step 2:** If necessary, code the inputs and outputs in binary.

This is the same problem as for combinational systems. Many problems are stated in such a way that this step is not necessary.

> **Step 3:** Derive a state table or state diagram to describe the behavior of the system.

In Moore systems, such as CE6 and CE8, the output depends only on the present state of the system. (The combinational logic that produces the output is just a function of the contents of the various flip flops.) (The output does, of course, depend on the input, since the state depends on the input, but the effect on the output is delayed until after the next clock.) In other examples, such as CE7, the output depends on the current input as well as the contents of memory.

Step 4: Use state reduction techniques to find a state table that produces the same input/output behavior, but has fewer states.

Fewer states may mean fewer storage devices. By reducing the number of flip flops, we also reduce the number of inputs to the combinational logic. Thus, for example, a system with one input and three flip flops requires four-variable combinational logic, whereas one with two flip flops would use only three-variable logic. This usually means a less expensive circuit. (This step could be omitted and a correctly working system designed.)

Step 5: Choose a state assignment, that is, code the states in binary.

Any coding will do, that is, will produce a correct solution. However, a good choice will lead to simpler combinational logic.

Step 6: Choose a flip flop type and derive the flip flop input maps or tables.

The state table and state assignment produce a table that tells what is to be stored in each flip flop as a function of what is in memory now and the system input. This part of the problem is to determine what input must be applied to each flip flop to get that transition to take place. In this chapter, we will look at the technique that is required for the various types of flip flops commonly used.

Step 7: Produce the logic equation and draw a block diagram (as in the case of combinational systems).

We will start with steps 6 and 7, assuming that we have a state table with the states already assigned binary values. Then, in Section 6.4, we will discuss the first three steps, developing a state table from a verbal description of the problem. For a discussion of state reduction and state assignment techniques, see Marcovitz, *Introduction to Logic Design,* 2nd ed., McGraw-Hill, 2005.

The state table of Table 5.1 and the state diagram of Figure 5.3 are repeated here as Figure 6.1.

Figure 6.1 Design example.

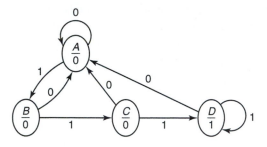

	$q^\star$		
q	$x = 0$	$x = 1$	z
A	A	B	0
B	A	C	0
C	A	D	0
D	A	D	1

Three state assignments are shown in Table 6.1

Table 6.1 State assignments.

q	q_1	q_2
A	0	0
B	0	1
C	1	0
D	1	1

(a)

q	q_1	q_2
A	0	0
B	1	1
C	1	0
D	0	1

(b)

q	q_1	q_2
A	0	0
B	0	1
C	1	1
D	1	0

(c)

These assignments were chosen arbitrarily. It is not clear which choice might lead to the least combinational logic.*

From either the state diagram or the state table, we construct the truth table of Table 6.2 for the next state. For this first example, we will use the state assignment of Table 6.1a.

Although the q column is not really needed, it is helpful in the development of the truth table, particularly if the states are assigned in some order other than numerical (such as in Table 6.1b and 6.1c). The first half of the design truth table corresponds to the first column of the state table ($x = 0$). The next state is 0 0 for the first four rows, since each of the

Table 6.2 Truth table for system design.

q	x	q_1	q_2	$q_1^\star$	$q_2^\star$
A	0	0	0	0	0
B	0	0	1	0	0
C	0	1	0	0	0
D	0	1	1	0	0
A	1	0	0	0	1
B	1	0	1	1	0
C	1	1	0	1	1
D	1	1	1	1	1

*It can be shown that all of the other possible state assignments result in the same amount of combinational logic as one of these. Each can be obtained either by a renumbering of the flip flops or the replacement of variables by their complement or both.

states go to state A on a 0 input. The second half of the table corresponds to $x = 1$.

For a Moore system, we construct a separate table for the output (Table 6.3), since it depends only on the two state variables. (As we will see shortly, the z column would be included as another column in the design truth table for a Mealy system.)

We can now map $q_1^{\star}$, $q_2^{\star}$, and z, as shown in Map 6.1. We prefer to draw the Karnaugh maps in the vertical orientation for such problems since the columns correspond to the input and the rows to the states.

Table 6.3 Output truth table.

q	q_1	q_2	z
A	0	0	0
B	0	1	0
C	1	0	0
D	1	1	1

Map 6.1 Next state and output maps.

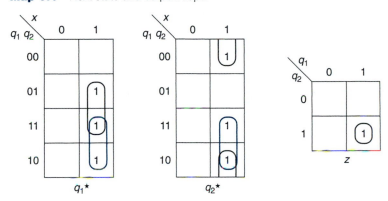

We thus have the equations

$$q_1^{\star} = xq_2 + xq_1$$
$$q_2^{\star} = xq_2' + xq_1$$
$$z = q_1q_2$$

(Although we took advantage of the obvious sharing available in this example, we will not emphasize sharing in the development of flip flop input equations.) Note that this SOP solution requires 4 two-input AND gates and 2 two-input OR gates (or 6 two-input NAND gates plus a NOT, since z comes from an AND, requiring a NAND followed by a NOT).*

---

*We assumed that q_1 and q_2 are available both uncomplemented and complemented, but x is only available uncomplemented (although the latter is irrelevant in this example).

EXAMPLE 6.1

If we use the state assignment of Table 6.1b, we get the following design truth table:

	x	q_1	q_2	$q_1^\star$	$q_2^\star$
A	0	0	0	0	0
D	0	0	1	0	0
C	0	1	0	0	0
B	0	1	1	0	0
A	1	0	0	1	1
D	1	0	1	0	1
C	1	1	0	0	1
B	1	1	1	1	0

q	q_1	q_2	z
A	0	0	0
D	0	1	1
C	1	0	0
B	1	1	0

The resulting maps for $q_1^\star$ and $q_2^\star$ are

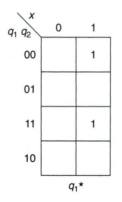

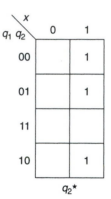

$$q_1^\star = xq_1'q_2' + xq_1q_2$$
$$q_2^\star = xq_1' + xq_2'$$
$$z = q_1'q_2$$

Note that this implementation requires an extra gate and three extra gate inputs.

[SP 1; EX 1]

The design using the state assignment of Table 6.1c is left as an exercise.

What we have done so far does not depend on the type of flip flop we will use to implement the system. We will use these results to complete the design in Section 6.1.

6.1 FLIP FLOP DESIGN TECHNIQUES

The truth table that we developed for the next state will be used in conjunction with the appropriate *flip flop design table* to obtain a truth table for the flip flop inputs. We will present this approach first and then look at a map approach that does not require the truth table and finally a *quick method* that saves a great deal of work but applies only to *JK* flip flops.

The flip flop design table is most readily obtained from the state diagram. Its general form is shown in Table 6.4. For each line of the truth table equivalent of the state table, and for each flip flop, we know its present value and the desired next state. This table allows us to then determine the inputs.

Although the *D* flip flop is trivial, we will use that to illustrate the process. The state diagram for the *D* flip flop is repeated as Figure 6.2. The diagram indicates that if the flip flop is in state 0 and the desired next state is also 0, the only path is $D = 0$. Similarly, to go from 0 to 1, *D* must be 1; from 1 to 0, *D* must be 0; and from 1 to 1, *D* must be 1. That produces the flip flop design table of Table 6.5 for the *D* flip flop.

For the *D* flip flop, we do not need separate columns in the truth table for D_1 and D_2, since they are identical to the $q_1^\star$ and $q_2^\star$ columns. We will use the truth table of Table 6.2 as an example throughout this section. Thus, for *D* flip flops,

$$D_1 = xq_2 + xq_1$$
$$D_2 = xq_2' + xq_1$$

A block diagram of the solution, using *D* flip flops and AND and OR gates, is shown in Figure 6.3.

Table 6.4 Flip flop design table.

q	$q^\star$	Input(s)
0	0	
0	1	
1	0	
1	1	

Figure 6.2 *D* flip flop state diagram.

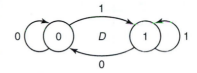

Table 6.5 *D* flip flop design table.

q	$q^\star$	D
0	0	0
0	1	1
1	0	0
1	1	1

Figure 6.3 Implementation using *D* flip flops.

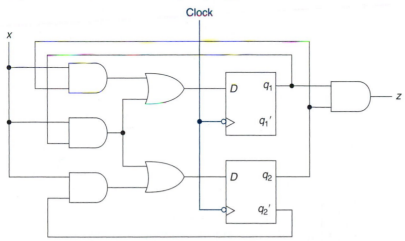

We will now repeat the process for the *JK* flip flop. The state diagram for the *JK* flip flop is repeated as Figure 6.4. To go from state 0 to state 0, we have two choices; we can make $J = 0$ and $K = 0$, or $J = 0$

Figure 6.4 JK flip flop state diagram.

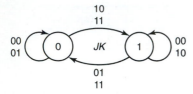

and $K = 1$. In other words, J must be 0 and it does not matter what K is, that is, K is a don't care. Similarly, to go from 1 to 1 K must be 0 and J is a don't care. To go from 0 to 1 J must be 1 and K is a don't care, and to go from 1 to 0 K must be 1 and J is a don't care. This results in the JK flip flop design table of Table 6.6. The truth table for the system design is thus shown in Table 6.7. Now, the truth table for the design requires four more columns for the four flip flop inputs. (The q column with state names has been omitted since the first five columns of this table are identical to the corresponding columns of Table 6.2.)

Table 6.6 JK flip flop design table.

q	$q^\star$	J	K
0	0	0	X
0	1	1	X
1	0	X	1
1	1	X	0

Table 6.7   Flip flop input table.

x	q_1	q_2	$q_1^\star$	$q_2^\star$	J_1	K_1	J_2	K_2
0	0	0	0	0	0	X	0	X
0	0	1	0	0	0	X	X	1
0	1	0	0	0	X	1	0	X
0	1	1	0	0	X	1	X	1
1	0	0	0	1	0	X	1	X
1	0	1	1	0	1	X	X	1
1	1	0	1	1	X	0	1	X
1	1	1	1	1	X	0	X	0

The shaded columns, q_1 and $q_1^\star$, produce the shaded flip flop input columns, using Table 6.6. The unshaded columns (for flip flop 2) produce the unshaded flip flop inputs. In each of the first two rows, q_1 goes from 0 to 0; thus, from the first row of the flip flop design table, $J_1 = 0$ and $K_1 = X$. In the first row, q_2 also goes from 0 to 0, producing $J_2 = 0$ and $K_2 = X$. In the second row, q_2 goes from 1 to 0; thus, from the third row of the flip flop design table, $J_2 = X$ and $K_2 = 1$. The rest of the table can be completed in a similar manner.

The resulting maps are shown in Map 6.2.

Map 6.2 JK input maps.

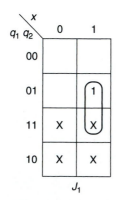

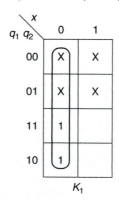

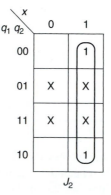

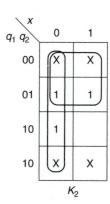

The flip flop input equations are

$$J_1 = xq_2 \qquad K_1 = x' \qquad z = q_1 q_2$$
$$J_2 = x \qquad K_2 = x' + q_1'$$

This requires just 2 two-input AND gates (including the output gate), 1 two-input OR gate, and a NOT for x', by far the least expensive solution. (For NAND gates, we would need 3 two-input gates and 2 NOTs.)

In Examples 6.2 and 6.3, we will repeat this process for the SR and T flip flops.

The state diagram for the SR flip flop is repeated here.

EXAMPLE 6.2

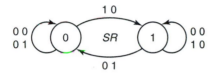

To go from state 0 to state 0 or from state 1 to state 1, we have the same two choices as for the JK. To go from 0 to 1, S must be 1 and R must be 0, and to go from 1 to 0, R must be 1 and S must be 0. The resulting SR flip flop design table is

q	q^*	S	R
0	0	0	X
0	1	1	0
1	0	0	1
1	1	X	0

Note that S and R will never both be made 1 (whatever values we choose for the don't cares). Following the same technique as for JK flip flops, we get

x	q_1	q_2	q_1^*	q_2^*	S_1	R_1	S_2	R_2
0	0	0	0	0	0	X	0	X
0	0	1	0	0	0	X	0	1
0	1	0	0	0	0	1	0	X
0	1	1	0	0	0	1	0	1
1	0	0	0	1	0	X	1	0
1	0	1	1	0	1	0	0	1
1	1	0	1	1	X	0	1	0
1	1	1	1	1	X	0	X	0

The maps for the flip flops inputs (the output z is still $q_1 q_2$) become

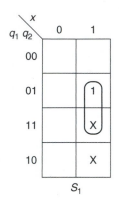 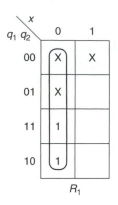 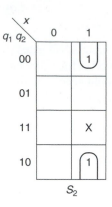 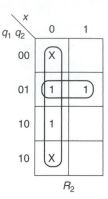

and the input equations are

$$S_1 = xq_2 \qquad R_1 = x' \qquad\qquad z = q_1 q_2$$
$$S_2 = xq_2' \qquad R_2 = x' + q_1' q_2$$

This requires 4 two-input AND gates (including the one for the output), 1 two-input OR gate, and 1 NOT gate for x'. (The NAND solution would require 3 additional NOT gates, for S_1, S_2, and for z.)

EXAMPLE 6.3

The state diagram for the T flip flop is

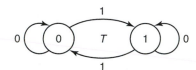

There is only one way to get from any state to any other state. The flip flop design table is thus

q	$q^\star$	T
0	0	0
0	1	1
1	0	1
1	1	0

and the truth table for the system design becomes

x	q_1	q_2	$q_1^\star$	$q_2^\star$	T_1	T_2
0	0	0	0	0	0	0
0	0	1	0	0	0	1
0	1	0	0	0	1	0
0	1	1	0	0	1	1
1	0	0	0	1	0	1
1	0	1	1	0	1	1
1	1	0	1	1	0	1
1	1	1	1	1	0	0

The maps for T and the equations follow.

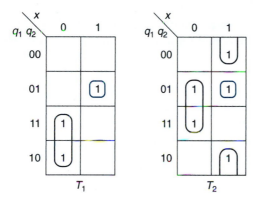

$$T_1 = x'q_1 + xq_1'q_2$$
$$T_2 = x'q_2 + xq_2' + xq_1'q_2$$
$$z = q_1q_2$$

This requires 4 two-input AND gates, 1 three-input AND gate, 1 two-input and 1 three-input OR gate, and a NOT for x. This is the most expensive solution for this example. (But, there are systems for which the T will result in a less expensive circuit than D or SR.)

The *JK* solution never requires more logic than either the *SR* or the *T*. Comparing the maps for the *SR* and the *JK* solutions, we see that both maps have 1's in exactly the same places. Further, all of the X's in the *SR* solution are also X's on the *JK* maps. The *JK* maps have additional don't cares. We could always choose to make those don't cares 0 and arrive at the *SR* solution. But, as we saw earlier, some of those X's were useful to make larger groupings and thus simplify the logic. From a different point of view, say we were to design a system for SR flip flops and build the combinational logic. If we then found that all we had available with which to build it was JK flip flops, we could use the logic and it would work. Similarly, if we designed for T flip flops, we could connect that logic to both J and K; the JK flip flop would behave like a T. (As in the case of the SR, there is often more logic required this way.) The relationship between the D and JK design is not quite so clear. However, if the logic for D is connected to J and the complement of that to K, the circuit will work. (Again, this might not be the best design for the JK flip flop; it certainly was not in this example.)

An important point to note is that the input equations for any flip flop are derived from the q and $q^\star$ columns for *that* flip flop. Thus, if two (or more) different types of flip flops were used, the same truth table would be developed as we have just done. Then the appropriate flip flop design table would be used for each flip flop. If, for example, a JK flip flop were used for q_1 and a D for q_2, then the logic equations would be

$$J_1 = xq_2 \qquad\qquad K_1 = x'$$
$$D_2 = xq_2' + xq_1$$
$$z = q_1q_2$$

These are the same equations that we obtained for J_1, K_1, and D_2 in this section.

Let us now go back and look at another approach to solving these problems without the use of the truth table. If the states are coded in binary, we can get maps for $q_1^\star$ and $q_2^\star$ directly from the state table as shown in Figure 6.5. (We are still using the state table of Figure 6.1 with the state assignment of Table 6.1a.)

Figure 6.5   State table to maps.

$q_1\,q_2$	$q_1^\star\,q_2^\star$ $x=0$	$q_1^\star\,q_2^\star$ $x=1$	z
00	0 0	0 1	0
01	0 0	1 0	0
10	0 0	1 1	0
11	0 0	1 1	1

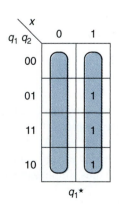

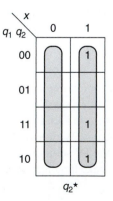

The columns of the state table shaded in light green produce the map for $q_1^\star$ and the gray columns on the truth table produce the map for $q_2^\star$. A word of caution is in order (although it does not come into play in this problem). The state table has the present state numbered in binary order; the map, of course has them numbered appropriately. The last two rows of the state table must be interchanged when they are copied onto the map. (Some people prefer to draw the state table in map order to avoid this problem, that is, 00, 01, 11, 10; that also works.)

For D flip flops, we are done, since the maps for $q_1^\star$ and $q_2^\star$ are also the maps for D_1 and D_2. Map 6.3a contains the maps for $q_1^\star$, J_1, and K_1 (from earlier in the section).

Map 6.3a First column of J_1 and K_1.

$q_1^\star$

q_1	q_2	x = 0	x = 1
0	0		
0	1		1
1	1		1
1	0		1

J_1

$q_1 q_2$	x = 0	x = 1
00		
01		1
11	X	X
10	X	X

K_1

$q_1 q_2$	x = 0	x = 1
00	X	X
01	X	X
11	1	
10	1	

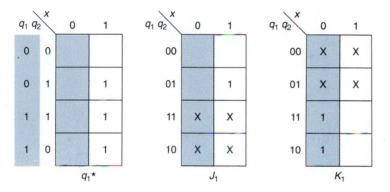

The shaded columns on the $q_1^\star$ map, together with the JK flip flop design table (Table 6.6) are used, row by row, to produce the shaded columns on the J_1 and K_1 maps. For example, the first two rows have q_1 going from 0 to 0, producing $J = 0$, $K = \text{X}$. The last two rows have q_1 going from 1 to 0, producing $J = \text{X}$, $K = 1$. To get the second column of the J_1 and K_1 maps, we use the second column of the $q_1^\star$ map but still the q_1 column (the first column) as shown shaded in Map 6.3b.

Map 6.3b Second column of J_1 and K_1.

$q_1^\star$

q_1	q_2	x = 0	x = 1
0	0		
0	1		1
1	1		1
1	0		1

J_1

$q_1 q_2$	x = 0	x = 1
00		
01		1
11	X	X
10	X	X

K_1

$q_1 q_2$	x = 0	x = 1
00	X	X
01	X	X
11	1	
10	1	

In the first row, 0 goes to 0, producing $JK = 0X$; in the second row, 0 goes to 1, producing $JK = 1X$; in the third and fourth rows, 1 goes to 1, producing $JK = X0$. The results are, of course, the same as before.

To find J and K for flip flop q_2, we map $q_2^\star$ and use the q_2 column, as shown in the shading for the first column of J_2 and K_2 in Map 6.3c. We then use the same column of q_2 with the other column of the $q_2^\star$ map to form the second columns of the J_2 and K_2 maps.

Map 6.3c   Computation of J_2 and K_2.

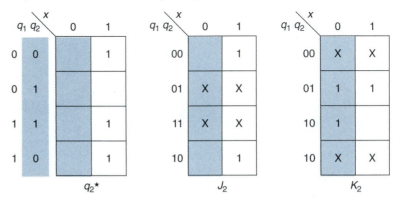

This same technique can be used with the other type of flip flops (using the appropriate flip flop design table). *Caution:* The q_1 input (the first input column) is used with both the first and second columns of $q_1^\star$ to obtain the inputs to the first flip flop. The q_2 input (the second input column) is used with both the first and second columns of $q_2^\star$ to obtain the inputs to the second flip flop.

The *quick* method for JK flip flop design (it does not apply to the other types of flip flop) takes advantage of a property of JK flip flops that we have not yet pointed out. Looking back at the JK flip flop input equations, we note that J_1 and K_1 do not depend on q_1 and J_2 and K_2 do not depend on q_2. That is not just a property of this particular problem, but there is always a minimum solution for which this is true (no matter how big the system). This can be seen by looking at the maps for J and K, repeated in Map 6.4. Note that half of each map contains don't cares (shown in green). (Indeed, sometimes, when all combinations of state variables are not used, there are even more don't cares. We will see an example of that later.) Each of the 1's on the map has a don't care in such a position that the 1 can be combined with the don't care to eliminate the variable involved. These are shown circled on the maps and the terms listed below. These terms are not necessarily prime implicants but those for J_1 and K_1 do not involve q_1 and those for J_2 and K_2 do not involve q_2.

Map 6.4 Pairing of 1's and don't cares in JK flip flop inputs.

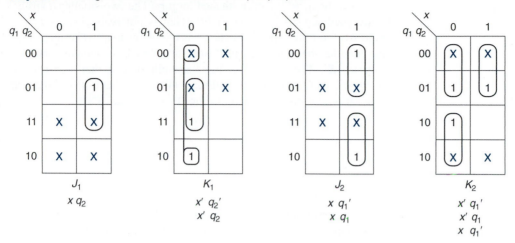

J_1
$x\, q_2$

K_1
$x'\, q_2'$
$x'\, q_2$

J_2
$x\, q_1'$
$x\, q_1$

K_2
$x'\, q_1'$
$x'\, q_1$
$x\, q_1'$

We can take advantage of this property by utilizing the equation we developed in Section 5.3,

$$q^\star = Jq' + K'q$$

Notice that when $q = 0$,

$$q^\star = J \cdot 1 + K' \cdot 0 = J$$

and when $q = 1$,

$$q^\star = J \cdot 0 + K' \cdot 1 = K'$$

Thus, the part of the map of $q^\star$ (for each variable) for which that variable is 0 is the map for J and the part for which that variable is 1 is the map for K'. On Map 6.5a, we show $q_1^\star$ with the $q_1 = 0$ section shaded in light

Map 6.5a Computing J_1 and K_1 using the quick method.

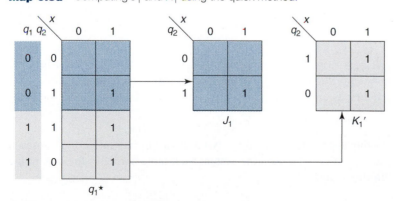

$q_1^\star$

J_1

K_1'

green and the $q_1 = 1$ section shaded in gray. The two smaller maps are then copied separately to the right. (That is not really necessary; we could work on the separate sections of the larger map.) The three variable map has been reduced to 2 two-variable maps, one for J and the other for K'. The variable q_1 has been eliminated; that was used to choose the section of the original map. (We could have drawn the map for K; it would just require replacing 0's by 1's and 1's by 0's.) From these maps, we see

$$J_1 = xq_2 \qquad K'_1 = x \qquad \text{or} \qquad K_1 = x'$$

These are, of course, the same answer we obtained using the other methods as in Map 6.2 and Maps 6.3a and b. Be careful in using the map for K'_1; the two rows are reversed, that is, the $q_2 = 1$ row is on the top. That does not affect this problem and just requires care in reading the map in other problems. (We could redraw the map and interchange the rows.)

We will repeat this process for the second flip flop on Map 6.5b, since the map geometry is somewhat different.

Map 6.5b   Computing J_2 and K_2 using the quick method.

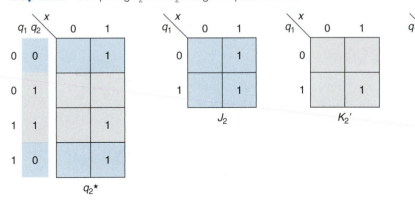

The $q_2 = 0$ portion of the map consists of the first and last rows; the $q_2 = 1$ portion is made up of the middle two rows. The maps for J_2, K'_2 and then K_2 are shown in Map 6.5b. As we found with the other methods,

$$J_2 = x \qquad K_2 = x' + q'_1$$

For this approach, it is really only necessary to plot maps of $q^\star$ for each variable. We do not need the system truth table nor maps for each of the flip flop inputs.

We will now look at a complete example. The state table and the state assignment are shown here.

q	$q^\star$ x = 0	x = 1	z x = 0	x = 1
A	B	C	1	1
B	A	B	1	0
C	B	A	1	0

q	q_1	q_2
A	1	1
B	1	0
C	0	1

From these, we create the following truth table, including a column with the state name.

	x	q_1	q_2	$q_1^\star$	$q_2^\star$	z
—	0	0	0	X	X	X
C	0	0	1	1	0	1
B	0	1	0	1	1	1
A	0	1	1	1	0	1
—	1	0	0	X	X	X
C	1	0	1	1	1	0
B	1	1	0	1	0	0
A	1	1	1	0	1	1

The resulting maps for the output and for D flip flop inputs follow.

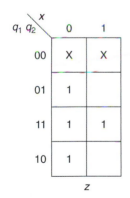

$q_1 q_2$ \ x	0	1
00	X	X
01	1	
11	1	1
10	1	

z

$q_1 q_2$ \ x	0	1
00	X	X
01	1	1
11	1	
10	1	1

$q_1^\star$

$q_1 q_2$ \ x	0	1
00	X	X
01		1
11		1
10	1	

$q_2^\star$

The resulting equations are

$$z = x' + q_1 q_2$$
$$D_1 = x' + q_1' + q_2'$$
$$D_2 = x q_2' + x' q_2$$

Notice that even the maps for D have don't cares, since one of the combinations of state variables is unused.

Columns for J and K are now added to the truth table, producing

	x	q_1	q_2	$q_1^\star$	$q_2^\star$	z	J_1	K_1	J_2	K_2
—	0	0	0	X	X	X	X	X	X	X
C	0	0	1	1	0	1	1	X	X	1
B	0	1	0	1	1	1	X	0	1	X
A	0	1	1	1	0	1	X	0	X	1
—	1	0	0	X	X	X	X	X	X	X
C	1	0	1	1	1	0	1	X	X	0
B	1	1	0	1	0	0	X	0	0	X
A	1	1	1	0	1	1	X	1	X	0

Even without mapping the functions, we can see that $J_1 = 1$. It is not unusual for one (or both) of the inputs to a JK flip flop to be 1. It is also noteworthy that more than half of the entries in the truth table are don't cares. The equations for the flip flop inputs follow. (The output is the same for all types of flip flops.)

$$J_1 = 1 \qquad K_1 = xq_2$$
$$J_2 = x' \qquad K_2 = x'$$

EXAMPLE 6.5

To conclude this section, we will look at one larger example. We wish to design the following system:

q	$q^\star$ $x = 0$	$x = 1$	z
S_1	S_2	S_1	0
S_2	S_3	S_1	0
S_3	S_4	S_1	0
S_4	S_4	S_5	1
S_5	S_4	S_6	1
S_6	S_4	S_1	1

The first issue is to make a state assignment. We will consider two different ones.

1.
q	A	B	C
S_1	0	0	0
S_2	0	0	1
S_3	0	1	0
S_4	0	1	1
S_5	1	0	0
S_6	1	0	1

2.
q	A	B	C
S_1	0	0	0
S_2	1	0	1
S_3	1	0	0
S_4	1	1	1
S_5	0	1	1
S_6	0	1	0

The first assignment just uses the first six binary numbers; the second uses an assignment meant to reduce the combinational logic (based on ideas beyond the scope of this book).

For the first assignment, we will consider the use of D and JK flip flops. It is easy to produce the maps for the three next states, $A^\star$, $B^\star$, and $C^\star$, without first drawing the truth table. The squares on each map correspond to the present state, as shown below (S_1 is 000; S_6 is 101; 110 and 111 are not used.) The left half of the map corresponds to $x = 0$, and the right half to $x = 1$.

BC \ xA	00	01	11	10
00	S_1	S_5	S_5	S_1
01	S_2	S_6	S_6	S_2
11	S_4	—	—	S_4
10	S_3	—	—	S_3

We can now complete the next state maps directly from the state table. Since S_1 goes to S_2 when $x = 0$, the upper left square for the maps become 0, 0, and 1. The complete maps are shown next. These are not only the maps of the next state, but also the D inputs. The output is only a function of the state variables (since this is a Moore model). We can now find the input equations and the output.

BC \ xA	00	01	11	10
00			1	
01				
11		X	X	1
10		X	X	

$A^\star$

BC \ xA	00	01	11	10
00		1		
01	1	1		
11	1	X	X	
10	1	X	X	

$B^\star$

BC \ xA	00	01	11	10
00	1	1	1	
01		1		
11	1	X	X	
10	1	X	X	

$C^\star$

$$D_A = xAC' + xBC$$
$$D_B = x'A + x'B + x'C$$
$$D_C = x'A + x'B + x'C' + AC'$$
$$z = A + BC$$

Using AND and OR gates, this requires 13 gates (including the NOT for x') with 30 inputs (including 1 four-input gate and 3 three-input gates).

To implement this with JK flip flops, we will go directly from the maps for Q^* of each flip flop to the maps for J and K.

A^*

BC \ xA	00	01	11	10
00			1	
01				
11		X	X	1
10		X	X	

J_A

BC \ xA	00	01	11	10
00		X	X	
01		X	X	
11		X	X	1
10		X	X	

K_A

BC \ xA	00	01	11	10
00	X	1		X
01	X	1	1	X
11	X	X	X	X
10	X	X	X	X

B^*

BC \ xA	00	01	11	10
00		1		
01	1	1		
11	1	X	X	
10	1	X	X	

J_B

BC \ xA	00	01	11	10
00		1		
01	1	1		
11	X	X	X	X
10	X	X	X	X

K_B

BC \ xA	00	01	11	10
00	X	X	X	X
01	X	X	X	X
11		X	X	1
10		X	X	1

C^*

BC \ xA	00	01	11	10
00	1	1	1	
01		1		
11	1	X	X	
10	1	X	X	

J_C

BC \ xA	00	01	11	10
00	1	1	1	
01	X	X	X	X
11	X	X	X	X
10	1	X	X	

K_C

BC \ xA	00	01	11	10
00	X	X	X	X
01	1		1	1
11		X	X	1
10	X	X	X	X

As we can see, the map for J_A has don't cares in the two columns for which A is 1 and the map for K_A has X's in the two columns for which A is O. Rows of don't cares are seen in the maps for $B^\star$ and $C^\star$.

$$J_A = xBC \qquad JB = x'A + x'C \qquad J_C = x' + A$$
$$K_A = x' + C \qquad K_B = x \qquad K_C = x + A'B'$$

Of course, the output does not depend on the flip flop type and thus

$$z = A + BC$$

This requires 11 gates (including the NOT for x') and 22 inputs (only 1 three-input gate).

Before considering the other state assignment, we will look at a related problem to this. Say we designed the system as shown and found that we had only one package of two D flip flops and one package of two JK flip flops. We already have done all the design work necessary; we can use the equation we found for D or those for JK for any of the flip flops. The following table shows the number of gates and gate inputs used in each of these arrangements (as well as those using only D or JK flip flops), including the output gates.

A	B	C	Gates	Inputs
D	D	JK	13	28
D	JK	D	13	29
JK	D	D	12	27
D	JK	JK	12	25
JK	D	JK	12	25
JK	JK	D	12	26
D	D	D	13	30
JK	JK	JK	11	22

As one might guess, the best solution uses two JK flip flops. Even the sharing provided by using D's for B and C requires more gate inputs. The D can be used equally well for A or B; other arrangements would require an extra gate and/or gate input(s).

Next, we will consider the solution using the second state assignment. For this, we will use the truth table approach. When dealing with state assignments that are not in numeric order, it is still best to list the truth table in binary order, but to list the state name next to the binary name. In that way, we can map the appropriate functions most directly.

The following truth table shows the next state and the *JK* inputs for each of the flip flops. Note that only the first eight rows are completed for the output column *z,* since *z* is not a function of the input *x.*

We can now find expressions for the output (with a three-variable map) and for the *D* inputs (using the A^*, B^*, and C^* columns) or for the *JK* inputs. First, the output map and equation are shown, since they apply to a solution using any type of flip flop (with this state assignment).

	x	A	B	C	z	A^*	B^*	C^*	J_A	K_A	J_B	K_B	J_C	K_C
S_1	0	0	0	0	0	1	0	1	1	X	0	X	1	X
—	0	0	0	1	X	X	X	X	X	X	X	X	X	X
S_6	0	0	1	0	1	1	1	1	1	X	X	0	1	X
S_5	0	0	1	1	1	1	1	1	1	X	X	0	X	0
S_3	0	1	0	0	0	1	1	1	X	0	1	X	1	X
S_2	0	1	0	1	0	1	0	0	X	0	0	X	X	1
—	0	1	1	0	X	X	X	X	X	X	X	X	X	X
S_4	0	1	1	1	1	1	1	1	X	0	X	0	X	0
S_1	1	0	0	0		0	0	0	0	X	0	X	0	X
—	1	0	0	1		X	X	X	X	X	X	X	X	X
S_6	1	0	1	0		0	0	0	0	X	X	1	0	X
S_5	1	0	1	1		0	1	0	0	X	X	0	X	1
S_3	1	1	0	0		0	0	0	X	1	0	X	0	X
S_2	1	1	0	1		0	0	0	X	1	0	X	X	1
—	1	1	1	0		X	X	X	X	X	X	X	X	X
S_4	1	1	1	1		0	1	1	X	1	X	0	X	0

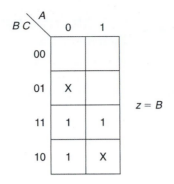

$z = B$

xA / BC map — A★

BC \ xA	00	01	11	10
00	1	1		
01	X	1		X
11	1	1		
10	1	X	X	

A★

xA / BC map — B★

BC \ xA	00	01	11	10
00		1		
01	X			X
11	1	1	1	1
10	1	X	X	

B★

xA / BC map — C★

BC \ xA	00	01	11	10
00	1	1		
01	X			X
11	1	1	1	
10	1	X	X	

C★

$$D_A = x'$$
$$D_B = x'B + BC + x'AC'$$
$$D_C = AB + x'C' + \{x'B \text{ or } x'A'\}$$

This requires a total of 9 gates with 20 inputs (including the NOT for x').

We could have solved the JK version using the quick method, but for this example, we have completed the truth table for J and K. We will leave the maps as an exercise for the reader; the equations are

$$J_A = x' \qquad K_A = x$$
$$J_B = x'AC' \qquad K_B = xC'$$
$$J_C = x' \qquad K_C = B' + xA'$$
$$z = B$$

This requires 5 gates with 10 inputs, significantly better than the D solution. Both the D and the JK solution for this assignment are considerably less expensive than the corresponding ones for the first state assignment.

[SP 2, 3; EX 2, 3, 4]

6.2 THE DESIGN OF SYNCHRONOUS COUNTERS

As additional examples of the design process for synchronous (clocked) sequential systems, we will look at the design of one class of circuit, referred to as *counters*. In the next section, we will look briefly at asynchronous counters, that is, those that do not require a clock input. In the next chapter, we will discuss some of the commercially available counters and the application of counters as part of a larger system.

Most counters are devices with no data input, that go through a fixed sequence of states on successive clocks. The output is often just the state of the system, that is, the contents of all of the flip flops. (In those cases, no output column is required in the state table.) We will also investigate counters with one or two control inputs that will, for example, determine whether the sequence is up (to the next larger number) or down.

Our first example is a 4-bit binary counter, that is one with four flip flops that cycles through the sequence

$$0, 1, 2, 3, 4, 5, 6, 7, 8, 9, 10, 11, 12, 13, 14, 15, 0, 1, \ldots$$

There are really no new techniques required for this design. The state table and the truth table are the same; they have 16 rows, 4 input columns, and 4 output columns, as shown in Table 6.8. Note that the flip flops are labeled *D, C, B,* and *A,* which is the common practice.

As can be seen, the next state for state 0 (0000) is 1 (0001), for 1 is 2, and so forth, until the next state for 15 (1111) is 0 (0000).

Table 6.8   A base-16 counter.

D	C	B	A	$D^\star$	$C^\star$	$B^\star$	$A^\star$
0	0	0	0	0	0	0	1
0	0	0	1	0	0	1	0
0	0	1	0	0	0	1	1
0	0	1	1	0	1	0	0
0	1	0	0	0	1	0	1
0	1	0	1	0	1	1	0
0	1	1	0	0	1	1	1
0	1	1	1	1	0	0	0
1	0	0	0	1	0	0	1
1	0	0	1	1	0	1	0
1	0	1	0	1	0	1	1
1	0	1	1	1	1	0	0
1	1	0	0	1	1	0	1
1	1	0	1	1	1	1	0
1	1	1	0	1	1	1	1
1	1	1	1	0	0	0	0

The maps for the four next state functions are shown in Map 6.6.

Map 6.6 *D* flip flop inputs for 16-state counter.

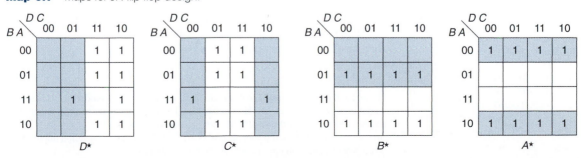

That produces

$$D_D = DC' + DB' + DA' + D'CBA$$

$$D_C = CB' + CA' + C'BA$$

$$D_B = B'A + BA'$$

$$D_A = A'$$

This solution would require 12 gates with 30 gate inputs. If we have Exclusive-OR gates available, we could simplify the expressions to

$$D_D = D(C' + B' + A') + D'CBA = D(CBA)' + D'(CBA)$$
$$= D \oplus CBA$$

$$D_C = C(B' + A') + C'BA = C(BA)' + C'(BA) = C \oplus BA$$

$$D_B = B'A + BA' = B \oplus A$$

$$D_A = A'$$

This would only require two AND gates and three Exclusive-OR gates.

Next, we will look at the *JK* design, using Map 6.7. (The *SR* design and the *T* design are left as exercises.) Using the quick method, the maps for *J* are the shaded parts of the next state maps (and those of *K'* are unshaded).

Map 6.7 Maps for *JK* flip flop design.

This produces the equations

$$J_D = K_D = CBA$$
$$J_C = K_C = BA$$
$$J_B = K_B = A$$
$$J_A = K_A = 1$$

We could extend the design to 5 flip flops, counting to 31 by adding flip flop E with inputs

$$J_E = K_E = DCBA$$

A circuit to implement this system using JK flip flops is shown in Figure 6.6.

Figure 6.6 A 4-bit counter.*

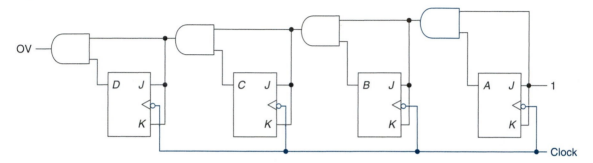

Table 6.9 An up/down counter.

x	C	B	A	C*	B*	A*
0	0	0	0	0	0	1
0	0	0	1	0	1	0
0	0	1	0	0	1	1
0	0	1	1	1	0	0
0	1	0	0	1	0	1
0	1	0	1	1	1	0
0	1	1	0	1	1	1
0	1	1	1	0	0	0
1	0	0	0	1	1	1
1	0	0	1	0	0	0
1	0	1	0	0	0	1
1	0	1	1	0	1	0
1	1	0	0	0	1	1
1	1	0	1	1	0	0
1	1	1	0	1	0	1
1	1	1	1	1	1	0

The green AND gate is not necessary if this is a stand-alone counter; the output of the A flip flop would be connected directly to J_B and K_B. The OV output is 1 when the counter is in state 15 (1111). OV could be connected to the JK inputs of another flip flop or, if we built two 4 flip flop circuits like the preceding one, we could connect the OV output of one to the input where a 1 is now connected to construct an 8-bit counter.

We will next look at an up/down counter, that is, one that can count in either direction, depending on a control input. We will label that control input x, such that the counter counts up when $x = 0$ and down when $x = 1$.[†] The state table for such a counter is shown as Table 6.9.

The maps for $C^\star$, $B^\star$, and $A^\star$ are shown in Map 6.8, with the $q = 0$ section shaded for the quick method with JK flip flops.

---

*Note that the combinational logic is multilevel. The term CBA is produced by using the output of the BA AND gate. In this way, we could extend the counter to any number of bits by adding as many flip flop/AND gate pairs as are needed.

[†]In commercial counters, this input is often labeled D/U', where the notation implies that down is active high and up is active low, just as we defined x.

Map 6.8 An up/down counter.

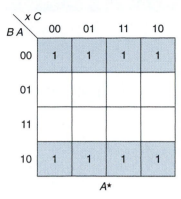

From these maps, we can see that

$$J_A = K_A = 1$$
$$J_B = K_B = x'A + xA'$$
$$J_C = K_C = x'BA + xB'A'$$

Just as in the case of the 4- and 5-bit up counters, this pattern continues, yielding (if we had two more flip flops)

$$J_D = K_D = x'CBA + xC'B'A'$$
$$J_E = K_E = x'DCBA + xD'C'B'A'$$

A block diagram for the 3-bit counter is shown in Figure 6.7.

Figure 6.7 An up/down counter.

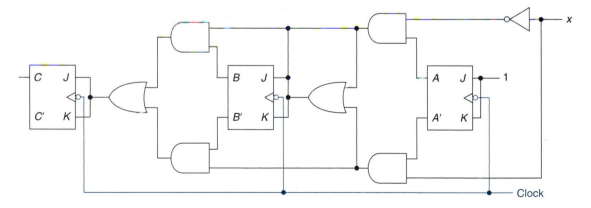

EXAMPLE 6.6

q_1	q_2	q_3	$q_1^\star$	$q_2^\star$	$q_3^\star$
0	0	0	0	1	1
0	0	1	1	0	1
0	1	0	1	0	0
0	1	1	0	1	0
1	0	0	0	0	1
1	0	1	1	1	1
1	1	0	X	X	X
1	1	1	0	0	0

We will next design a counter that goes through some sequence of states that are not in numeric order

0, 3, 2, 4, 1, 5, 7, and repeat

(This is CE9.) Note that the cycle is 7 states; it never goes through state 6. We can now draw the state table or go directly to the truth table, including a row for the unused state.

The table can be completed either by going through it row by row and seeing that state 0 goes to 3, state 1 goes to 5, and so forth, or by following the sequence, first filling in the next state for row 0 as 3, then a next state of 2 for state 3, and so forth. In the first approach, when we get to state 6, we find it not in the sequence and thus the next state is don't cares. In the second approach, when we get done with the cycle, we find that row 6 is empty and also put in don't cares. We surely write the truth table in numeric order.

The table is repeated below with columns for inputs to *SR* flip flops; we will use the quick method for *JK* flip flops.

q_1	q_2	q_3	$q_1^\star$	$q_2^\star$	$q_3^\star$	S_1	R_1	S_2	R_2	S_3	R_3
0	0	0	0	1	1	0	X	1	0	1	0
0	0	1	1	0	1	1	0	0	X	X	0
0	1	0	1	0	0	1	0	0	1	0	X
0	1	1	0	1	0	0	X	X	0	0	1
1	0	0	0	0	1	0	1	0	X	1	0
1	0	1	1	1	1	X	0	1	0	X	0
1	1	0	X	X	X	X	X	X	X	X	X
1	1	1	0	0	0	0	1	0	1	0	1

For *D* flip flops, we just use the $q_1^\star$, $q_2^\star$, and $q_3^\star$ columns, producing the following maps and equations.

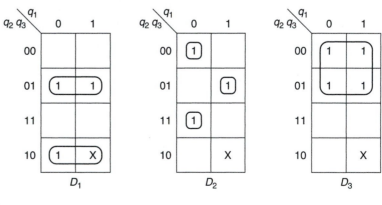

$$D_1 = q_2' q_3 + q_2 q_3'$$
$$D_2 = q_1' q_2' q_3' + q_1' q_2 q_3 + q_1 q_2' q_3$$
$$D_3 = q_2'$$

This solution requires 4 three-input gates and 3 two-input gates.

The maps and equations for the SR solution follow. Note that for state 6, where we don't care what the next state is, we then don't care what the inputs are. S and R are both don't cares for all three flip flops.

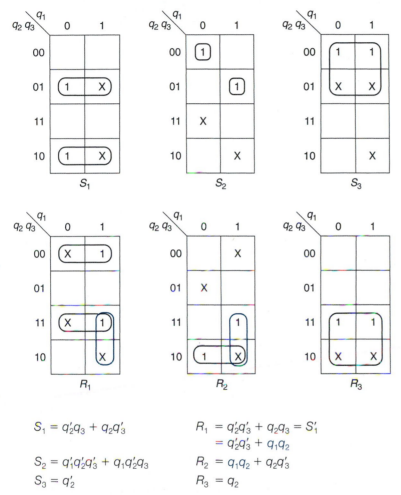

$$S_1 = q_2'q_3 + q_2q_3'$$

$$S_2 = q_1'q_2'q_3' + q_1q_2'q_3$$

$$S_3 = q_2'$$

$$R_1 = q_2'q_3' + q_2q_3 = S_1'$$
$$\quad = q_2'q_3' + q_1q_2$$

$$R_2 = q_1q_2 + q_2q_3'$$

$$R_3 = q_2$$

Even taking advantage of the sharing or using a NOT for R_1, this requires more logic than the D solution (10 or 11 gates).

Finally, we will solve this system using the quick method for JK flip flops as shown on the following maps and equations.

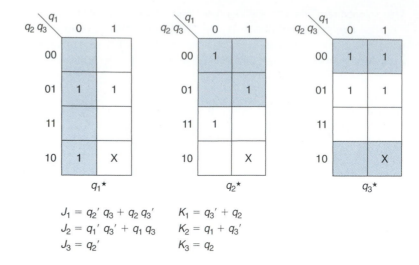

$$J_1 = q_2' \, q_3 + q_2 \, q_3' \qquad K_1 = q_3' + q_2$$
$$J_2 = q_1' \, q_3' + q_1 \, q_3 \qquad K_2 = q_1 + q_3'$$
$$J_3 = q_2' \qquad\qquad\quad K_3 = q_2$$

This solution requires 8 two-input gates, although the gate for K_1 could be replaced by a NOT gate and the gate for K_2 could be eliminated, since by choosing the don't cares as 1's in both places, we get

$$K_1 = J_1' \qquad \text{and} \qquad K_2 = J_2$$

If we do not have a static clear (or do not use it) and turn the system on, we do not know the initial state of each flip flop. If we care, we should clear the flip flops or use some combination of clears and presets to get the system into the proper initial state. Often, all we care about is that once this is turned on, it goes through the desired sequence after one or two clocks. That will always happen if it is initialized to one of the states in the sequence. But, if it is initialized to one of the unused states, it is not obvious what will happen. When we designed the systems of Example 6.6, we assumed that that state never happened and thus made the next state a don't care.

Once we complete the design, there are no longer any don't cares. The algebraic expressions (or the block diagrams) specify what happens for all possible combinations of variables including the unused state (state 6).

EXAMPLE 6.6 (Cont.)

We can determine what would happen by assuming we are in state 1 1 0. Thus, we would make $q_1 = 1$, $q_2 = 1$, and $q_3 = 0$ in the equations. For D flip flops, we would get

$$D_1 = q_2'q_3 + q_2q_3' = 00 + 11 = 1$$
$$D_2 = q_1'q_2'q_3' + q_1'q_2q_3 + q_1q_2'q_3 = 001 + 011 + 100 = 0$$
$$D_3 = q_2' = 0$$

In that case, the system would go to state 4 (1 0 0) on the first clock and continue through the sequence from there. (With the design shown, we would also go to state 4 with *SR* flip flops, and to state 0 with *JK* flip flops.)

If this were not satisfactory, we could go back and redesign the system by replacing the don't cares in row 110 of the truth table by the desired next state.

A state diagram, showing the behavior of the system designed with *D* or *SR* flip flops, including what happens if the system starts in the unused state, is shown next.

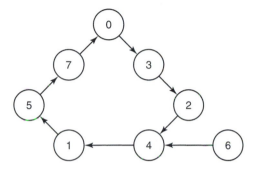

Note that there are no labels on the paths, since there is no input to the system, and the output is just equal to the state. (It is a Moore system.)

[SP 4, 5, 6, 7; EX 5, 6, 7, 8, 9, 10]

6.3 DESIGN OF ASYNCHRONOUS COUNTERS

Binary counters are sometimes designed without a clock input. They are constructed from the same clocked flip flops (typically *JK*) as synchronous counters, but each flip flop is triggered by the transition of the previous one. Consider the circuit of Figure 6.8 with two flip flops.

Figure 6.8 A 2-bit asynchronous counter.

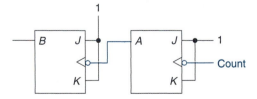

When the Count signal goes from 1 to 0, flip flop *A* is triggered. If it started out at 0, it goes to 1. The 0 to 1 transition on the output of *A*, and thus on the clock input of *B*, has no effect. When the next negative transition on Count occurs, *A* will go from 1 to 0, causing the clock input to

B to do the same. Since J and K are 1, flip flop B will change states. Since there is a delay from the clock edge to the output change, flip flop B is clocked somewhat later than A and thus its output changes later. This is emphasized in the timing diagram of Figure 6.9. We assume in this diagram that flip flops A and B both start at 0.

Figure 6.9   Timing delay in an asynchronous counter.

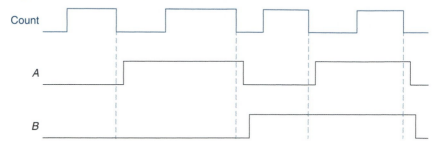

There are two things that are different about this timing diagram from the previous ones. Since the Count signal is not necessarily a clock, it might be rather irregular.* Second, the first flip flop (A) changes shortly after the negative edge of the clock (the dashed line), but the second flip flop (B) does not change until somewhat after A changes, and thus the delay from the clock is much greater. This becomes more significant as the changes ripple through several flip flops.

Note that the flip flops (BA) go through the sequence 00, 01, 10, 11, and repeat. Thus, this is a 2-bit counter. We can obtain a 4-bit counter by connecting four flip flops in the same fashion. A block diagram is shown in Figure 6.10.

Figure 6.10   A 4-bit asynchronous counter.

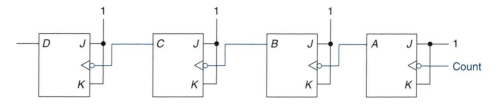

---

*The Clock input for synchronous counters is really a Count input also. Although the clock is usually regular, it need not be. The counter will change states on each negative transition.

The timing is shown in Figure 6.11, where there is one unit of delay through each flip flop and the clock period is 10 units.

Figure 6.11 Timing for the 4-bit counter.

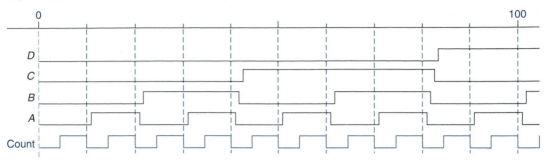

Notice that *A* changes one unit of time after the trailing edge of the clock, *B* one unit after a trailing edge of *A*, *C* after *B*, and *D* after *C*. Thus, the change in *D* occurs 4 units after the clock (almost at the next leading edge in this example).

Notice also that this counter does go through the sequence 0, 1, 2, 3, 4, 5, 6, 7, 8, 9, 10 (as far as the timing diagram goes) and would continue through 11, 12, 13, 14, 15, 0, . . .

The advantage of the asynchronous counter is the simplicity of the hardware. There is no combinational logic required. The disadvantage is speed. The state of the system is not established until all of the flip flops have completed their transition, which, in this case, is four flip flop delays. If the counter were larger or the clock faster, it might not reach its final state until after the next negative clock transition. In that case its value would not be available for other parts of the system at the next clock. Also, care must be taken when using outputs from this counter since it goes through unintended states. For example, a close inspection of the timing diagram as the counter moves from state 7 to state 8 shows that it is in state 6, state 4, and then state 0 before flip flop *D* goes to 1 and it reaches state 8. These short periods are not important if the outputs are used to light a display or as the inputs to a clocked flip flop, but they could produce spikes that would trigger a flip flop if used as a clock input.

EXAMPLE 6.7

Design an asynchronous base-12 counter using *JK* flip flops with active low clears and NAND gates.

The easiest way to do this is to take the 4-bit binary counter and reset it when it reaches 12. Thus, the following circuit computes (*DC*)' and uses that to reset the counter.

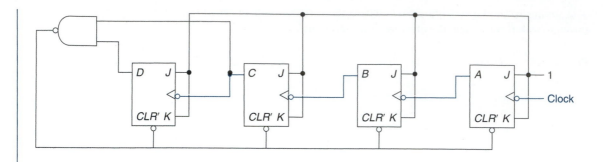

As can be seen from the timing diagram below, the counter cycles

0, 1, 2, 3, 4, 5, 6, 7, 8, 9, 10, 11, (12), 0

where it remains in state 12 for a short time. Note that there is a delay from the time that *A* changes to when *B* changes and so forth. The count is only valid after the last flip flop settles down.

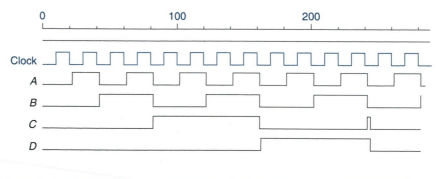

[SP 8; EX 11]

6.4   DERIVATION OF STATE TABLES AND STATE DIAGRAMS

In this section, we will start with verbal descriptions of sequential systems and develop state diagrams or tables. In some cases, we will carry the design further; but that is just a review of the material of earlier sections.

We will first look at Continuing Examples 6 and 7. Although the statement of CE6 does not include the term Moore, the wording of the problem implies a Moore system. That of CE7 is a Mealy model. We repeat CE6 here.

CE6. A system with one input *x* and one output *z* such that *z* = 1 iff *x* has been 1 for at least three consecutive clock times.

The timing trace of Trace 5.1 is repeated as Trace 6.1.

Trace 6.1 Three consecutive 1's.

| x | 0 | 1 | 1 | 0 | 1 | 1 | 1 | 0 | 0 | 1 | 0 | 1 | 1 | 1 | 1 | 1 | 0 | 0 |
| z | ? | 0 | 0 | 0 | 0 | 0 | 0 | 1 | 0 | 0 | 0 | 0 | 0 | 0 | 1 | 1 | 1 | 0 | 0 | 0 | 0 |

The first step in this problem (as it is in many word problems) is to determine what needs to be stored in memory. In this case, the question is: what do we need to know about previous inputs to determine whether the output should be 1 or not, and to update memory?

There are two approaches to step 1 for this problem. First, we could store the last three inputs. Knowing them we could determine the output. For memory, we would just discard the oldest input stored and save the last two plus the present one. The inputs are already coded in binary (step 2). If we store the oldest input in q_1, the next oldest in q_2, and the most recent one in q_3, we get the state table of Table 6.10.

The new value of q_3, $q_3^\star = x$; it will hold the most recent input. Similarly, $q_2^\star = q_3$ and $q_1^\star = q_2$. The output is only 1 when the system is in state 111.

For the second approach, we store in memory the number of consecutive 1's, as follows:*

A   none, that is, the last input was 0

B   one

C   two

D   three or more

That, too, is sufficient information, since the output is 1 if and only if there have been three or more.

The state diagram and the state table are the same as those in Figure 6.1 and are repeated here as Figure 6.12.

Table 6.10 Three flip flop state table.

| | | | $q_1^\star\ q_2^\star\ q_3^\star$ | | |
q_1	q_2	q_3	$x = 0$	$x = 1$	z
0	0	0	0 0 0	0 0 1	0
0	0	1	0 1 0	0 1 1	0
0	1	0	1 0 0	1 0 1	0
0	1	1	1 1 0	1 1 1	0
1	0	0	0 0 0	0 0 1	0
1	0	1	0 1 0	0 1 1	0
1	1	0	1 0 0	1 0 1	0
1	1	1	1 1 0	1 1 1	1

Figure 6.12 State diagram and state table.

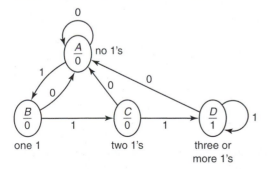

| | $q^\star$ | | |
q	$x = 0$	$x = 1$	z
A	*A*	*B*	0
B	*A*	*C*	0
C	*A*	*D*	0
D	*A*	*D*	1

_____

*We will just name the memory contents, that is, the state with letters *A, B, C, . . .* and deal with coding these into binary later.

This approach required only four states, whereas the first approach required eight. The first approach uses three flip flops, whereas the second uses only two. This is not much of a difference. Consider, however, what happens if the problem required a 1 output iff the input has been 1 for 25 or more consecutive clock times. For the first approach, we would need to save the last 25 inputs, using 25 flip flops. The state table would have 2^{25} rows. The second approach requires 26 states (no 1's through 25 or more 1's). They could be coded with just five flip flops.

The next step in the design process is to reduce the state table, if possible, to one with fewer states. That is beyond the scope of this book, but we can proceed to choose a state assignment and complete the design. (The first state table can be reduced to one with four states; the second cannot be reduced.)

For the first design, the state assignment has already been made. We labeled the flip flops q_1, q_2, and q_3. The flip flop inputs require no logic for D flip flops.

$$D_1 = q_2 \qquad D_2 = q_3 \qquad D_3 = x$$

For JK flip flops,

$$J_1 = q_2 \qquad J_2 = q_3 \qquad J_3 = x$$
$$K_1 = q_2' \qquad K_2 = q_3' \qquad K_3 = x'$$

A NOT gate is needed for x'. For either type of flip flop, one AND gate is needed for z:

$$z = q_1 q_2 q_3$$

For the second approach, we have already constructed the design truth table for one state assignment in Table 6.2 and found that

$$D_1 = q_1^\star = xq_2 + xq_1 \qquad \text{or} \qquad J_1 = xq_2 \qquad K_1 = x$$
$$D_2 = q_2^\star = xq_2' + xq_1 \qquad \text{or} \qquad J_2 = x \qquad K_2 = x' + q_1$$
$$z = q_1 q_2$$

The corresponding Mealy example is CE7.

CE7. A system with one input x and one output z such that $z = 1$ at a clock time iff x is currently 1 and was also 1 at the previous two clock times.

Another way of wording this same problem is

CE7#. A Mealy system with one input x and one output z such that $z = 1$ iff x has been 1 for three consecutive clock times.

The timing trace corresponding to this problem is shown in Trace 6.2.*

---

*The statement of CE7# has room for interpretation. Does "three consecutive clock times" mean *three or more* or *exactly three?* The timing trace clearly shows that the first interpretation is correct; otherwise, the output would be 0 at each clock time when there were five consecutive 1 inputs.

Trace 6.2 Timing trace for CE7.

x	0 1 1 0 1 1 1 0 0 1 0 1 1 1 1 1 0 0
z	0 0 0 0 0 0 1 0 0 0 0 0 0 1 1 1 0 0 0 0

There are two approaches for this problem, as well. We need only store the last two inputs (rather than three for the Moore model). This produces the state table of Table 6.11.

Table 6.11 State table for saving last two inputs.

q_1	q_2	$q_1^\star q_2^\star$ $x = 0$	$x = 1$	z $x = 0$	$x = 1$
0	0	0 0	0 1	0	0
0	1	1 0	1 1	0	0
1	0	0 0	0 1	0	0
1	1	1 0	1 1	0	1

For the second approach, we store in memory the number of consecutive 1's, as follows:

A none, that is, the last input was 0
B one
C two or more

That, too, is sufficient information since the output is 1 iff there were previously two or more 1's and the present input is a 1. If the present input is a 0, the next state is A; otherwise, we move from A to B and from B to C. The state diagram is shown in Figure 6.13.

Figure 6.13 State diagram for three consecutive 1's.

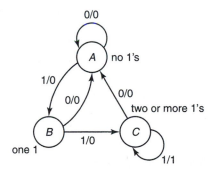

The description can also be written as a state table, as shown in Table 6.12.

Table 6.12 State table for three consecutive 1's.

q	$q^\star$ $x = 0$	$x = 1$	z $x = 0$	$x = 1$
A	A	B	0	0
B	A	C	0	0
C	A	C	0	1

To compare the behavior of the Mealy and Moore models, we will look at the timing diagram for each (using the four-state Moore model and the three-state Mealy model).

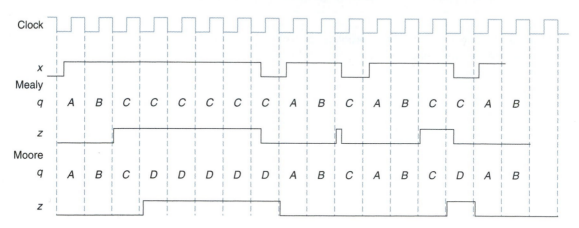

Basically, the Moore model output is the same as the Mealy, but delayed by one clock period. The Mealy model has a glitch when x is still 1 in state C. The Moore model does not have any false outputs, since z depends only on the flip flops, all of which change at the same time.

EXAMPLE 6.8

Design both a Moore and a Mealy system with one input x and one output z such that $z = 1$ iff x has been 1 for *exactly* three consecutive clock times.

A sample input/output trace for such a system is

x	0 1 1 1 1 1 1 1 0 1 1 0 1 1 1 0 1
z-Mealy	0 0 0 0 0 0 0 0 0 0 0 0 0 0 0 1 0 0 0*
z-Moore	0 0 0 0 0 0 0 0 0 0 0 0 0 0 0 0 1 0 0 0
	↑ ↑

We cannot tell whether there should be a 1 output when the third consecutive 1 input occurs. The past history and the present input are the same at the two places indicated with arrows. It is not until the next input arrives that we know that there have been exactly three 1's in a row. For the Mealy model, we now need five states,

      A   none, that is, the last input was 0
      B   one 1 in a row
      C   two 1's in a row
      D   three 1's in a row
      E   too many (more than 3) 1's in a row

---

*Notice that in this example, we can determine the output for two or three clocks after the input is no longer known, since even if both inputs were 1, the output would remain 0 at least until the clock time after the one shown.

The state diagram begins like that of the previous solution. However, when we get a third 1 input, we go to state D. From D, a 0 input produces a 1 output; a 1 input gets us to a new state, E. Sometimes, we think of state A as nowhere, that is, we are looking for the first 1 to get started on the successful path to a 1 output. In that case, state E is worse than nowhere, since we must first get a 0 before we can even begin to look for three 1's. The complete state diagram is shown next.

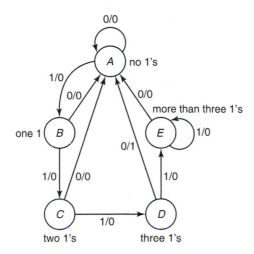

The implementation of this system requires three flip flops. The design is left as an exercise.

For the Moore model, we need a state D to indicate exactly three 1's. From there, it goes to E on another 1, indicating too many 1's. State F is reached on a 0 input; it is the state with a 1 output. The state table is shown below. (We could have constructed a state diagram for this version or a state table for the Mealy model.)

q	$q^\star$ $x = 0$	$x = 1$	z
A	A	B	0
B	A	C	0
C	A	D	0
D	F	E	0
E	A	E	0
F	A	B	1

EXAMPLE 6.9

Design a Mealy system whose output is 1 iff the input has been 1 for three consecutive clocks, but inputs are nonoverlapping. (That means that a 1 input can only be used toward one 1 output.)

A sample input/output trace for such a system is

```
x   0 1 1 1 1 1 1 1 0 1 1 0 1 1 1 0 1
z   0 0 0 1 0 0 1 0 0 0 0 0 0 0 1 0 0 0
```

As in CE7, only three states are needed. From state C, the system returns to state A whether the input is 0 or 1; the output is 1 if the input is 1 (third in a row) and 0 if the input is 0.

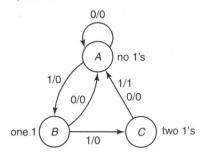

When the third 1 input occurs, we are, once again, nowhere; we need three more 1's to get a 1 output.

In each of the systems that we have considered so far, we have not worried about initializing the system. They all produce the correct output, once the first 0 input is received. If we are willing to ignore the output prior to that, we do not need to be concerned with initialization. If we need to know the output from the first input, then we must initialize the system to state A (or 0 0 0 in the first example). The next two examples do depend upon initializing the system to state A, that is, we need to know where the starting point is.

EXAMPLE 6.10

Design a Mealy system where the inputs are considered in blocks of three. The output is 1 iff the input is 1 for all three inputs in a block; obviously, that 1 output cannot occur until the third input is received.

A sample input/output trace for such a system is

```
x   0 1 1   1 1 1   1 0 1   1 1 0   1 1 1   0 1
z   0 0 0   0 0 1   0 0 0   0 0 0   0 0 1   0 0
```

where the blocks are indicated by extra space.

The initial state, A, is reached when the system is first turned on and before each new block (as the next state when the third input in a block is received). After receiving the first input in a block, the system goes to B if the input is 1 and C if it is 0; in either case, the output is 0. We could now have four states after the second input, D and E from B (on a 1 and a 0, respectively) and F and G from C (on a 1 and a 0, respectively).

A state table for this version, with seven states, is shown next.

q	q^*		z	
	$x = 0$	$x = 1$	$x = 0$	$x = 1$
A	C	B	0	0
B	E	D	0	0
C	G	F	0	0
D	A	A	0	1
E	A	A	0	0
F	A	A	0	0
G	A	A	0	0

But that creates two extra states. We only need D for the case where the first two inputs have been 1, and E for all of the other cases, as shown in the following state diagram.

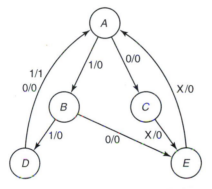

Note that the paths out of C and of E are denoted as X/0, meaning that we don't care what the input is; that path is followed and the output is 0.

Notice that the next state and output sections of the last three rows of the state table are identical. That indicates that it does not matter whether the system is in state E, F, or G; it behaves the same in all three cases. We could reduce the state table by combining these three rows into one. (Indeed, that is what the state diagram solution did.)

EXAMPLE 6.11

Design a Mealy system whose output is 1 for every third 1 input (not necessarily consecutive).

The initial state, A, is used for no 1's or a multiple of three 1's. When a 0 is received, the system stays where it is, rather than returning to the initial state, since a 0 does not interrupt the count of three 1's. A sample input/output trace for such a system is

```
x   0 1 1 1 1 1 1 1 0 1 1 0 1 0 1 0 0 1 0 1
z   0 0 0 1 0 0 1 0 0 0 1 0 0 0 0 0 1 0 0 0
```

The state diagram is thus

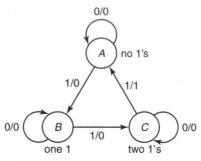

EXAMPLE 6.12

CE8. Design a Moore system whose output is 1 iff three consecutive 0 inputs occurred more recently than three consecutive 1 inputs.* A sample input/output trace for such a system is

x 1 1 1 0 0 1 0 1 1 1 0 0 1 0 0 0 0 1 1 1 1 0 1

z ? ? ? 0 0 0 0 0 0 0 0 0 0 0 0 0 0 1 1 1 1 0 0 0 0 0

We showed the first three outputs as unknown, assuming that we started looking at some time when the system was running or that we turned it on and did not know what state it came up in. The wording implies that when first turned on, the system should have a 0 output, since there have not recently been three consecutive 1's. (This is the same example that we did at the end of Section 6.1.)

We will call the initial state S_1. The first path to develop is to get the output to change from 0 to 1. That part of the state diagram is shown here.

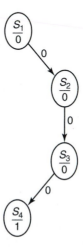

---

*We are assuming that three means three or more, not exactly three.

We had reached S_1 whenever the input was a 1 and the output was to be 0. To get the output to change to 1, we need three consecutive 0's, leading us to S_4. From there, three 1's will lead us back to S_1 as shown below on the left. On the right, we complete the state diagram, by showing that we return to S_1 when we are looking for 0's and get a 1 input and return to S_4 when we are looking for 1's and get a 0 input.

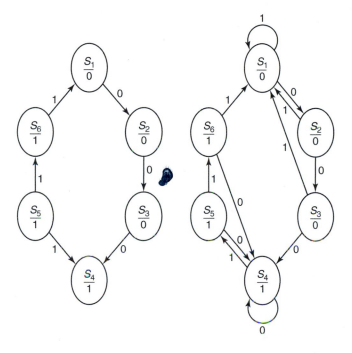

Design a Mealy system whose output is 1 iff there have been exactly two 1's followed by a 0 and then a 1.

EXAMPLE 6.13

a. Assume overlapping is allowed.
b. Assume overlapping is not allowed.

The following timing trace depicts the expected behavior for the overlapped case:

a.

x 0 0 1 1 0 1 1 0 1 1 0 1 1 1 0 1 1 0 1 1 0 1 1 0 1

z 0 0 0 0 0 1 0 0 1 0 0 1 0 0 0 0 0 0 1 0 0 1 0 0 0

The underlines indicate the 1101 pattern that is being searched for; the double underline is not an acceptable pattern since it does not begin with exactly two 1's. The behavior in the overlapping case is quite clear. When the final 1 input that produces a 1 output occurs, that 1 also counts as the first of two consecutive 1 inputs for the next 1 output. The two green underlines indicate overlapping patterns.

It is often easiest to begin the state diagram by following a success path, that is, one leading to the desired output, as follows.

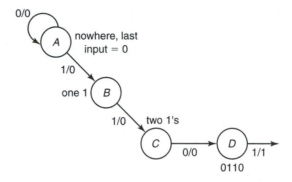

State *A* is the nowhere state, where we are looking for the first 1. On successive 1's, we move to *B* and *C;* a 0 takes us to *D* and then a 1 produces the 1 output. Since overlapping is allowed, that 1 is the first 1 toward a new sequence and we return to state *B* from *D*. We must also complete the failed paths. A 0 in any state other than *C* (where we are looking for a 0) returns us to state *A*. If, after getting two consecutive 1's, we get a third, we need another state, *E,* which indicates that we have too many 1's and are waiting for a 0 before we can go back to state *A* and start again. The complete state diagram for the overlapped solution is shown below.

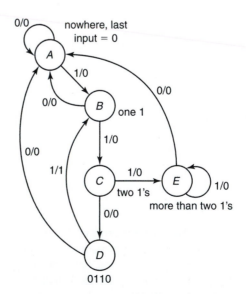

There are two interpretations to consider in the nonoverlapping case. The first is shown as *b-1*. In that case, when a 1 output occurs, there must be a 0 input before we can have exactly two 1's. Thus, after the first 1 output, we do not get started toward another 1 output until after a 0 input.

x   0 0 1 1 0 1 1 0 1 1 0 1 1 1 0 1 1 0 1 1 0 1

b-1   0 0 0 0 0 1 0 0 0 0 0 1 0 0 0 0 0 0 1 0 0 0 0 0

A second interpretation (perhaps a little far-fetched) is that once we have completed a pattern, we need exactly two more 1's followed by a 10; that is what accepts the double-underlined sequence.

x   0 0 1 1 0 1 1 0 1 1 0 1 1 1 0 1 1 0 1 1 0 1

b-2   0 0 0 0 0 1 0 0 0 0 0 1 0 0 0 1 0 0 0 0 0 1 0 0 0

The two solutions for the nonoverlapping versions are shown next. They begin exactly like the overlapping version, but behave differently when we get the input that produces a 1 output.

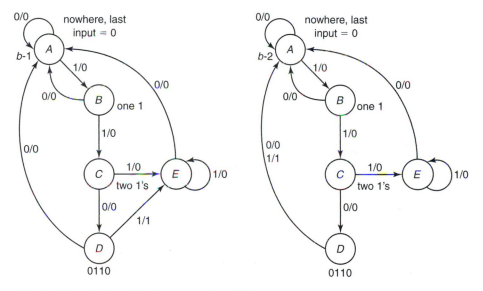

Finally, we will look at the design of the bus controller CE11.

CE11. Design a Moore model bus controller that receives requests on separate lines, R_0 to R_3, from four devices desiring to use the bus. It has four outputs, G_0 to G_3, only one of which is 1, indicating which device is granted control of the bus for that clock period. The low number device has the highest priority, if more than one device requests the bus at the same time. We look at both interrupting controllers (where a high priority device can preempt the bus) and one where a device keeps control of the bus once it gets it until it no longer needs it.

The bus controller has five states:

EXAMPLE 6.14

A: idle, no device is using the bus
B: device 0 is using the bus
C: device 1 is using the bus
D: device 2 is using the bus
E: device 3 is using the bus

We will first consider the case where once device *j* gets control of the bus ($G_j = 1$), it retains that control until it is no longer requesting it (until $R_j = 0$). Further, we will assume that it must return to the idle state for one clock period between allocations. This results in the following state diagram.

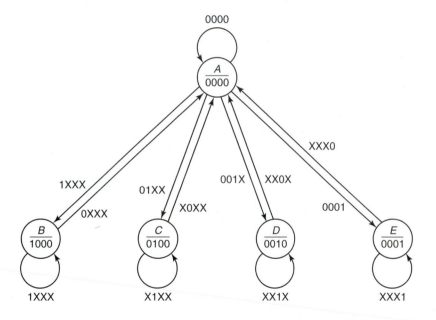

The system remains in the idle state if there are no requests. It goes to the highest priority state when there are one or more requests. Thus, it goes to state *B* if $R_0 = 1$, no matter what the other *R*'s are. Once it has granted the bus, it remains in that state if that device is still requesting the bus and returns to the idle state otherwise. If there is another request pending, it is idle for one clock period before granting the next highest priority request.

If the idle period is not necessary, the state diagram becomes much more complex. When any device no longer needs the bus, the controller will return to state *A* if no other device is requesting it; but it proceeds directly to granting the highest priority request. A state table for such a system is shown next.

q	q^*		$G_0G_1G_2G_3$
R_0	0 0 0 0 0 0 0 0 1 1 1 1 1 1 1 1		
R_1	0 0 0 0 1 1 1 1 0 0 0 0 1 1 1 1		
R_2	0 0 1 1 0 0 1 1 0 0 1 1 0 0 1 1		
R_3	0 1 0 1 0 1 0 1 0 1 0 1 0 1 0 1		
A	$A\ E\ D\ D\ C\ C\ C\ C\ B\ B\ B\ B\ B\ B\ B\ B$		0 0 0 0
B	$A\ E\ D\ D\ C\ C\ C\ C\ B\ B\ B\ B\ B\ B\ B\ B$		1 0 0 0
C	$A\ E\ D\ D\ C\ C\ C\ C\ B\ B\ B\ B\ C\ C\ C\ C$		0 1 0 0
D	$A\ E\ D\ D\ C\ C\ D\ D\ B\ B\ D\ D\ B\ B\ D\ D$		0 0 1 0
E	$A\ E\ D\ E\ C\ E\ C\ E\ B\ E\ B\ E\ B\ E\ B\ E$		0 0 0 1

Note that in this version, we can go from any state to any other state. There would be 20 paths on the state diagram. The following partial diagram shows just the paths to and from state C.

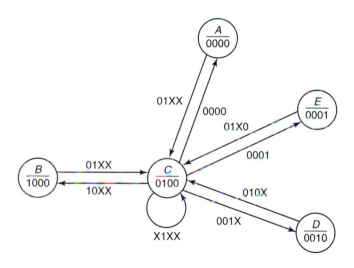

Finally, we will look at a preemptive controller, where a high-priority device will take control from a lower priority one, even if the lower priority one is still using the bus. For this case (whether we must return to state 0 or not), we remain in states C, D, and E only if that device is requesting the bus and no higher priority device is simultaneously requesting it. The state diagram for the system that must return to idle for one clock period is shown first and then the state table for the system that can go directly to the next state having use of the bus.

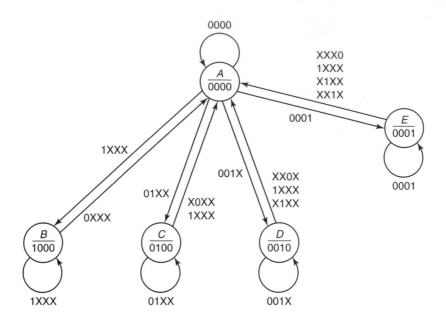

q	$q^\star$	$G_0\,G_1\,G_2\,G_3$
R_0	0 0 0 0 0 0 0 0 1 1 1 1 1 1 1 1	
R_1	0 0 0 0 1 1 1 1 0 0 0 0 1 1 1 1	
R_2	0 0 1 1 0 0 1 1 0 0 1 1 0 0 1 1	
R_3	0 1 0 1 0 1 0 1 0 1 0 1 0 1 0 1	
A	A E D D C C C C B B B B B B B B	0 0 0 0
B	A E D D C C C C B B B B B B B B	1 0 0 0
C	A E D D C C C C B B B B B B B B	0 1 0 0
D	A E D D C C C C B B B B B B B B	0 0 1 0
E	A E D D C C C C B B B B B B B B	0 0 0 1

Although the state diagram for this version would require the same 20 paths as was needed for the second version, the logic is much simpler. The condition for going to state B, from each state is 1XXX (R_1), to C is 01XX ($R_1'R_2$), to D is 001X ($R_1'R_2'R_3$), and to E is 0001 ($R_1'R_2'R_3'R_4$) (the same as the condition from state A in all of the versions).

[SP 9; EX 12, 13, 14, 15]

6.5 SOLVED PROBLEMS

1. For the following state table and state assignment, show equations for the next state and the output.

q	$q^\star$		z			q	q_1	q_2
	x = 0	x = 1	x = 0	x = 1				
A	C	A	1	0		A	0	1
B	B	A	0	1		B	1	1
C	B	C	1	0		C	0	0

We will first construct a truth table and map the functions.

q	x	q_1	q_2	z	$q_1^\star$	$q_2^\star$
C	0	0	0	1	1	1
A	0	0	1	1	0	0
—	0	1	0	X	X	X
B	0	1	1	0	1	1
C	1	0	0	0	0	0
A	1	0	1	0	0	1
—	1	1	0	X	X	X
B	1	1	1	1	0	1

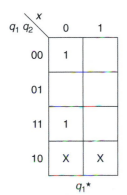

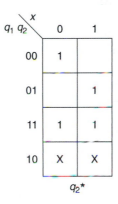

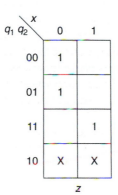

$$q_1^\star = x'q_2' + x'q_1$$
$$q_2^\star = q_1 + x'q_2' + xq_2$$
$$z = x'q_1' + xq_1$$

2. For each of the following state tables, design the system using

   i. *D* flip flops

   ii. *SR* flip flops

   iii. *T* flip flops

   iv. *JK* flip flops

Show the equations for each and a block diagram for the *JK* design (using AND, OR, and NOT gates).

a.

A B	A* B* x = 0	x = 1	z x = 0	x = 1
0 0	0 1	0 0	1	0
0 1	1 1	0 0	1	1
1 1	1 1	0 1	0	1

b.

A B	A* B* x = 0	x = 1	z
0 0	1 0	0 0	0
0 1	0 0	1 1	1
1 0	0 1	1 1	1
1 1	1 0	0 1	1

a. We can map $A^\star$, $B^\star$, and z directly from the state table, where the last row of the maps are don't cares, since state 10 is not used.

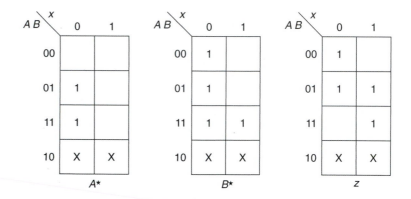

For all types of flip flops, z is the same, namely,

$$z = x'A' + xB$$

i. For the D flip flop,

$$D_A = A^\star = x'B \qquad\qquad D_B = B^\star = x' + A$$

ii. For the SR flip flop, we will use the truth table and the flip flop design table as follows:

x	A	B	A*	B*	S_A	R_A	S_B	R_B
0	0	0	0	1	0	X	1	0
0	0	1	1	1	1	0	X	0
0	1	0	X	X	X	X	X	X
0	1	1	1	1	X	0	X	0
1	0	0	0	0	0	X	0	X
1	0	1	0	0	0	X	0	1
1	1	0	X	X	X	X	X	X
1	1	1	0	1	0	1	X	0

The resulting maps are

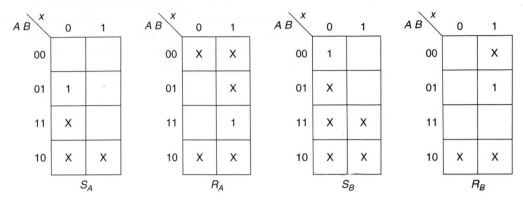

$$S_A = x'B \quad R_A = x \quad S_B = x' \quad R_B = xA'$$

We will develop the T maps directly from the next state maps. If the flip flop is to change, T is 1; otherwise, T is 0.

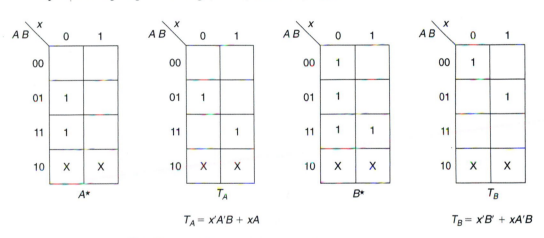

$$T_A = x'A'B + xA \qquad\qquad T_B = x'B' + xA'B$$

Finally, we will derive the JK inputs using the quick method. The following maps show the J sections shaded.

$$J_A = x'B \qquad K_A = x \qquad J_B = x' \qquad K_B = xA'$$

Note that these are the same equations as those for the *SR* flip flop and the same amount of logic as is required for the *D* flip flop. Only the *T* flip flop requires significantly more logic.

A block diagram of the system with *JK* flip flops follows.

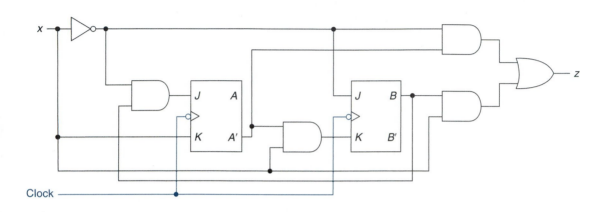

---

b. We can go to the truth table or we can first map $A^\star$ and $B^\star$ to find the *D* inputs. The output is only a two-variable problem. We do not need to map that to recognize that

$$z = A + B$$

The truth table follows (with columns for all types of flip flops).

x	A	B	$A^\star$	$B^\star$	S_A	R_A	S_B	R_B	T_A	T_B	J_A	K_A	J_B	K_B
0	0	0	1	0	1	0	0	X	1	0	1	X	0	X
0	0	1	0	0	0	X	0	1	0	1	0	X	X	1
0	1	0	0	1	0	1	1	0	1	1	X	1	1	X
0	1	1	1	0	X	0	0	1	0	1	X	0	X	1
1	0	0	0	0	0	X	0	X	0	0	0	X	0	X
1	0	1	1	1	1	0	X	0	1	0	1	X	X	0
1	1	0	1	1	X	0	1	0	0	1	X	0	1	X
1	1	1	0	1	0	1	X	0	1	0	X	1	X	0

Maps for each of the functions follow (where D_A is just $A^\star$).

D_A

A B \ x	0	1
00	1	
01		1
11	1	
10		1

D_B

A B \ x	0	1
00		
01		1
11		1
10	1	1

S_A

A B \ x	0	1
00	1	
01		1
11	X	
10		X

R_A

A B \ x	0	1
00		X
01	X	
11		1
10	1	

S_B

A B \ x	0	1
00		
01		X
11		X
10	1	1

R_B

A B \ x	0	1
00	X	X
01	1	
11	1	
10		

T_A

A B \ x	0	1
00	1	
01		1
11		1
10	1	

T_B

A B \ x	0	1
00		
01	1	
11	1	
10	1	1

J_A

A B \ x	0	1
00	1	
01		1
11	X	X
10	X	X

K_A

A B \ x	0	1
00	X	X
01	X	X
11		1
10	1	

J_B

A B \ x	0	1
00		
01	X	X
11	X	X
10	1	1

K_B

A B \ x	0	1
00	X	X
01	1	
11	1	
10	X	X

The corresponding equations are

$$z = A + B$$
$$D_A = x'A'B' + x'AB + xA'B + xAB'$$
$$D_B = xB + AB'$$
$$S_A = x'A'B' + xA'B \qquad R_A = x'AB' + xAB$$
$$S_B = AB' \qquad R_B = x'B$$
$$T_A = x'B' + xB \qquad T_B = x'B + AB'$$
$$J_A = K_A = x'B' + xB \qquad J_B = A \quad K_B = x'$$

Note that the logic required to implement the JK flip flop solution is the least, followed by the T and the SR, with the D requiring the most. A block diagram of the JK solution follows. To make the drawing clearer, we put flip flop B on the left.

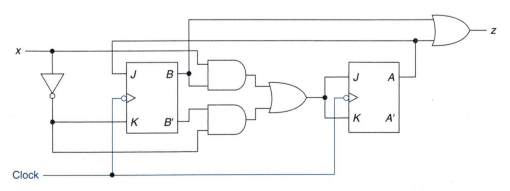

Comment: In either part of this problem, we could have specified that flip flop *A* was one type (say a *T*) and the other was a different type (say a *JK*). The solutions we have obtained are correct for each of the flip flops.

3. For the state table and each of the state assignments shown, design a system using *D* flip flops.

	$q^\star$		z	
q	$x = 0$	$x = 1$	$x = 0$	$x = 1$
A	*B*	*C*	1	0
B	*D*	*A*	0	0
C	*B*	*C*	1	1
D	*D*	*A*	1	0

a.

q	q_1	q_2
A	0	0
B	0	1
C	1	0
D	1	1

b.

q	q_1	q_2
A	0	0
B	0	1
C	1	1
D	1	0

c.

y	q_1	q_2
A	0	0
B	1	1
C	1	0
D	0	1

Each part of this is really a separate problem. (These are the only three assignments that produce significantly different hardware. Each of the other possible state assignments involve either interchanging variables or complementing variables or both.) Compare the amount of combinational logic for each state assignment.

a. Since the assignment is in normal binary order, it is easy to go directly to the maps.

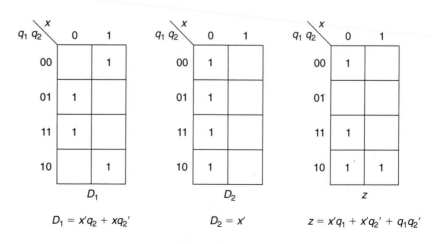

$$D_1 = x'q_2 + xq_2'$$

$$D_2 = x'$$

$$z = x'q_1 + x'q_2' + q_1q_2'$$

b. This assignment is in map order and once again we will go directly to the maps without first producing a truth table.

Top K-maps:

$q_1 q_2$ \ x	0	1
00		1
01	1	
11		1
10	1	

D_1

$q_1 q_2$ \ x	0	1
00	1	1
01		
11	1	1
10		

D_2

$q_1 q_2$ \ x	0	1
00	1	
01		
11	1	1
10	1	

z

$$D_1 = x'q_1'q_2 + x'q_1q_2' + xq_1'q_2' + xq_1q_2$$
$$D_2 = q_1'q_2' + q_1q_2 \qquad z = x'q_2' + q_1q_2$$

where the green terms are shared between D_2 and z.

c. For this part, we will first construct the truth table and then go to the maps.

q	x	q_1	q_2	z	$q_1^\star$	$q_2^\star$
A	0	0	0	1	1	1
D	0	0	1	1	0	1
C	0	1	0	1	1	1
B	0	1	1	0	0	1
A	1	0	0	0	1	0
D	1	0	1	0	0	0
C	1	1	0	1	1	0
B	1	1	1	0	0	0

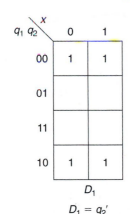

$q_1 q_2$ \ x	0	1
00	1	1
01		
11		
10	1	1

D_1

$q_1 q_2$ \ x	0	1
00	1	
01	1	
11	1	
10	1	

D_2

$q_1 q_2$ \ x	0	1
00	1	
01	1	
11		
10	1	1

z

$$D_1 = q_2' \qquad D_1 = x' \qquad z = x'q_1' + q_1q_2'$$

We really did not need to map D_1 and D_2; we should be able to see those from the truth table.

Comparing the three solutions we see a major difference, based on the three state assignments.

a. 8 gates   16 inputs
b. 11 gates   27 inputs
c. 4 gates   7 inputs

4. Design a decimal, or decade, counter, one that goes through the sequence

$$0, 1, 2, 3, 4, 5, 6, 7, 8, 9, 0, 1, \ldots .$$

The state (truth) table is similar to that for the binary counter, as seen here.

D	C	B	A	$D^\star$	$C^\star$	$B^\star$	$A^\star$
0	0	0	0	0	0	0	1
0	0	0	1	0	0	1	0
0	0	1	0	0	0	1	1
0	0	1	1	0	1	0	0
0	1	0	0	0	1	0	1
0	1	0	1	0	1	1	0
0	1	1	0	0	1	1	1
0	1	1	1	1	0	0	0
1	0	0	0	1	0	0	1
1	0	0	1	0	0	0	0
1	0	1	0	X	X	X	X
1	0	1	1	X	X	X	X
1	1	0	0	X	X	X	X
1	1	0	1	X	X	X	X
1	1	1	0	X	X	X	X
1	1	1	1	X	X	X	X

The next state for the 9 (1001) row is 0 (0000), and the remaining next states are don't cares, since states 10 through 15 are never reached. We have included rows in this table for the unused states because they are needed to produce don't cares on the maps. Some may write the state table without these rows and then convert it to this truth table (as we did in the previous section). The maps for the next state, with the J section shaded for finding J and K using the quick method are shown next.

$D^\star$

BA \ DC	00	01	11	10
00			X	1
01			X	
11		1	X	X
10			X	X

$C^\star$

BA \ DC	00	01	11	10
00		1	X	
01		1	X	
11	1		X	X
10		1	X	X

$B^\star$

BA \ DC	00	01	11	10
00			X	
01	1	1	X	
11			X	X
10	1	1	X	X

$A^\star$

BA \ DC	00	01	11	10
00	1	1	X	1
01			X	
11			X	X
10	1	1	X	X

From this we can see that

$$J_D = CBA \qquad K_D = A$$
$$J_C = K_C = BA$$
$$J_B = D'A \qquad K_B = A$$
$$J_A = K_A = 1$$

5. Design a synchronous counter that goes through the sequence

    1 3 5 7 4 2 0 6 and repeat

using D flip flops.

The truth table follows.

A	B	C	$A^\star$	$B^\star$	$C^\star$
0	0	0	1	1	0
0	0	1	0	1	1
0	1	0	0	0	0
0	1	1	1	0	1
1	0	0	0	1	0
1	0	1	1	1	1
1	1	0	0	0	1
1	1	1	1	0	0

The maps and equations for the D inputs are shown next.

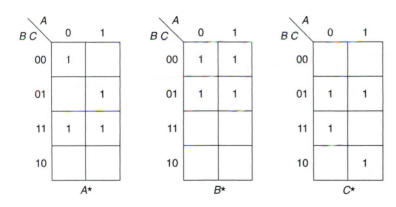

$$D_A = A'B'C' + AC + A'BC$$
$$D_B = B'$$
$$D_C = B'C + ABC' + A'BC$$

6. Design a synchronous counter that goes through the sequence

    2 6 1 7 5 and repeat

using

  i. *D* flip flops.

  ii. *JK* flip flops.

Show a state diagram, indicating what happens if it initially is in one of the unused states (0, 3, 4) for each of the designs.

The truth table is shown here. The next state for unused states is shown as don't cares.

A	*B*	*C*	$A^\star$	$B^\star$	$C^\star$
0	0	0	X	X	X
0	0	1	1	1	1
0	1	0	1	1	0
0	1	1	X	X	X
1	0	0	X	X	X
1	0	1	0	1	0
1	1	0	0	0	1
1	1	1	1	0	1

The maps and equations for the *D* inputs are shown next.

$BC \backslash A$	0	1
00	X	X
01	1	
11	X	1
10	1	

$A^\star$

$BC \backslash A$	0	1
00	X	X
01	1	1
11	X	
10	1	

$B^\star$

$BC \backslash A$	0	1
00	X	X
01	1	
11	X	1
10		1

$C^\star$

$$D_A = A' + BC$$
$$D_B = A' + B'$$
$$D_C = AB + \{A'B' \text{ or } A'C\}$$

There are two equally good solutions for D_C; as we will see shortly, the behavior of the system is different for those choices if it is initialized to one of the unused states.

Substituting the values for the three states not in the cycle:

    0 (0 0 0): $D_A = 1, D_B = 1, D_C = 1$ or $D_C = 0$

    3 (0 1 1): $D_A = 1, D_B = 1, D_C = 0$ or $D_C = 1$

    4 (1 0 0): $D_C = 0, D_B = 1, D_C = 0$

where the color indicates that the next state depends on the
choice for the second term of D_C.

The state diagrams for the two solutions follow.

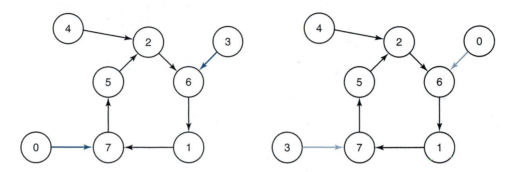

ii. The maps for the JK solution, with the J section shaded, and
the equations are shown here.

$$J_A = 1 \qquad K_A = B' + C'$$
$$J_B = 1 \qquad K_B = A$$
$$J_C = A \qquad K_C = AB'$$

Substituting the values for the three states not in the cycle:

$0\,(0\,0\,0)$: $J_A = K_A = 1, J_B = 1, K_B = 0,$
                  $J_C = K_C = 0 \Rightarrow 1\,1\,0$

$3\,(0\,1\,1)$: $J_A = 1, K_A = 0, J_B = 1, K_B = 0,$
                  $J_C = K_C = 0 \Rightarrow 1\,1\,1$

$4\,(1\,0\,0)$: $J_A = K_A = 1, J_B = K_B = 1,$
                  $J_C = K_C = 1 \Rightarrow 0\,1\,1$

This is still a different behavior for the unused states. Now, state
4 goes to 3 and then, on the next clock, it will get back into the
cycle. The state diagram follows.

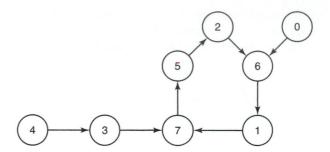

7. Design a 2-bit up/down, cycling/saturating counter. This counter has two flip flops, *A* and *B,* and thus only four states. It has two control inputs, *x* and *y*. If $x = 0$, it counts up and if $x = 1$, it counts down. If $y = 0$, it cycles, that is, goes 0, 1, 2, 3, 0, 1, . . . or 3, 2, 1, 0, 3, 2, . . . , and if $y = 1$, it saturates, that is, it goes 0, 1, 2, 3, 3, 3, . . . or 3, 2, 1, 0, 0, 0 . . . (This is a two-flip flop version of CE10.) The state table for this counter is

	$A^\star B^\star$			
A B	*xy* = 00	*xy* = 01	*xy* = 10	*xy* = 11
0 0	0 1	0 1	1 1	0 0
0 1	1 0	1 0	0 0	0 0
1 0	1 1	1 1	0 1	0 1
1 1	0 0	1 1	1 0	1 0

Since this is a problem with two inputs, there are four input combinations and thus four columns in the next state section. (If this were a Mealy system, there would also be four output columns.) This can easily be converted into a 16-row truth table or directly to maps. The latter is easiest if we are to implement this with either *D* or *JK* flip flops. In going to the maps, care must be taken since both the rows and columns are in binary order, not map order. The maps for D_A ($A^\star$) and D_B ($B^\star$) are shown.

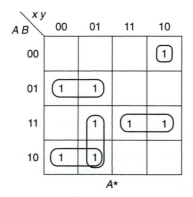

$A^\star$

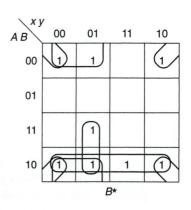

$B^\star$

The functions are rather complex.

$$D_A = x'A'B + x'AB' + x'yA + xAB + xy'A'B'$$
$$D_B = x'yA + AB' + x'B' + y'B'$$
$$\quad = x'yA + AB' + x'B' + xy'A'B'$$

Even if we were to implement this counter with JK flip flops, there is a great deal of combinational logic, as can be seen from the following maps and equations.

AB \ xy	00	01	11	10
00				1
01	1	1		
11		1	1	1
10	1	1		

$A\star$

AB \ xy	00	01	11	10
00	1	1		1
01				
11			1	
10	1	1	1	1

$B\star$

$$J_A = x'B + xy'B' \qquad K_A = xB' + x'y'B$$
$$J_B = x' + y' + A \qquad K_B = x + y' + A'$$

8. Construct a base 60 (0 to 59) asynchronous counter using JK flip flops.

We need six flip flops and must detect when the count reaches 60 and reset the counter. (That occurs when $FEDC = 1$.)

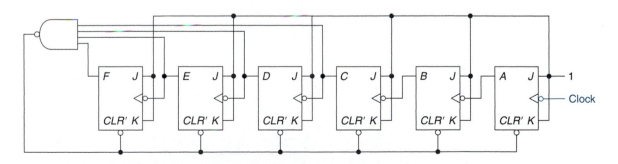

9. For each of the following problems show a state table or a state diagram. (A sample input/output trace is shown for each.)

a. A Mealy system that produces a 1 output iff there have been four or more consecutive 1 inputs or two or more consecutive 0 inputs.

x	0	1	1	0	0	1	0	0	1	1	1	1	1	0	0	0	1		
z	?	0	0	0	1	0	0	1	0	0	0	1	1	0	1	1	0	0	

b. A Mealy system whose output is 1 iff the last three inputs were 010
  i. assuming overlapping is allowed
  ii. assuming overlapping is not allowed.

x	1	1	0	1	0	1	0	1	0	0	1	0	0	1	0	0	1	1	0
$z\text{-}i$	0	0	0	0	1	0	1	0	1	0	0	1	0	0	1	0	0	0	0
$z\text{-}ii$	0	0	0	0	1	0	0	0	1	0	0	1	0	0	1	0	0	0	0

c. A Mealy system whose output is 1 iff the last four inputs were 1100 or the last output was a 1 and it is continuing on that pattern.

x	1	0	1	1	0	0	1	0	1	1	0	0	1	1	0	0	1	1	1	0	0	1	0
z	?	?	0	0	0	1	1	0	0	0	0	1	1	1	1	1	1	1	0	0	1	1	0	0	0	0

d. A Moore system whose output changes whenever it detects a sequence 110. (Assume that initially the output is 0.)

x	0	0	1	0	1	1	1	0	1	1	0	0	1	1	0	1	0	1				
z	0	0	0	0	0	0	0	0	1	1	1	0	0	0	0	1	1	1	1			

e. A Moore system whose output is 1 iff the input has been alternating for at least four clock periods.

x	0	0	1	0	1	1	0	1	0	1	0	1	0	0		
z	?	?	0	0	0	1	0	0	0	1	1	1	1	1	0	

a.

	$q^\star$		z	
q	$x = 0$	$x = 1$	$x = 0$	$x = 1$
A	A	B	1	0
B	A	C	0	0
C	A	D	0	0
D	A	D	0	1

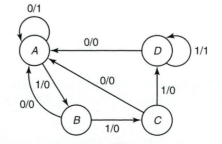

We start with a state for which the last input is 0. From there, we need four consecutive 1's to get a 1 output or another 0. Thus, on additional 0's, we loop back to state A. On a 1, we go to B; on a second 1, we go to C; and on a third 1, we go to D. In D, additional 1's produce a 1 output; 0's return the system to state A.

b. i.

q	$q^{\star}$		z	
	$x = 0$	$x = 1$	$x = 0$	$x = 1$
A	B	A	0	0
B	B	C	0	0
C	B	A	0	1

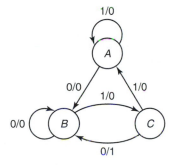

State A is the "nowhere" state, where we are looking for the first 0 in the pattern. A 0 gets us to B and then a 1 gets us to C. From there, a 0 input produces a 1 output. Since overlapping is allowed, that 0 input is the first 0 in a new string and thus, we return to state B.

In the case where overlapping is not allowed, we go from state C back to state A on a 0 input, since we are now nowhere, looking for a 010 pattern, as shown on the following state diagram.

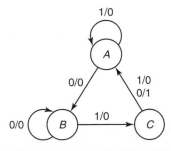

c. If we start with the "nowhere" state, that is, where the output is to be 0 and we are looking for the first 1, the success path consists of 1 1 0 0, at which point the output goes to 1. If that is followed by a 1, the output remains 1. It also remains 1 if there is another 1 input and then a 0 input (which gets the system back to state *D*). That produces the following start for the state diagram.

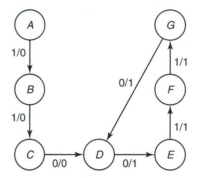

Now we can complete the failed paths. When we get a 0 while we are looking for 1's in states *A, B, E,* and *F,* we return to state *A*. We go next to state *C* on a 1 from either *C* or *G* (when there are more than two 1's in a row) and we go to *B* from *D* on a 1. Of course, all of these failed inputs produce a 0 output. The state diagram and then the state table are shown.

	$q^\star$		z	
q	$x = 0$	$x = 1$	$x = 0$	$x = 1$
A	*A*	*B*	0	0
B	*A*	*C*	0	0
C	*D*	*C*	0	0
D	*E*	*B*	1	0
E	*A*	*F*	0	1
F	*A*	*G*	0	1
G	*D*	*C*	1	0

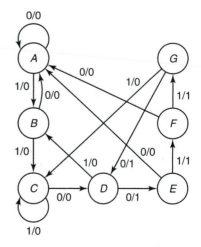

d. For a Moore system, the output is associated with the state. There are two "nowhere" states, A and D one for which the output is 0 and another, for which the output is 1. The state diagram and table follow:

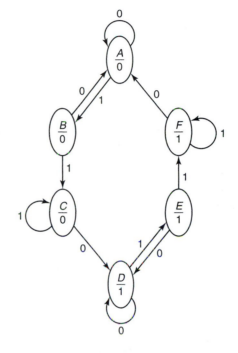

q	$q^\star$		z
	$x = 0$	$x = 1$	
A	A	B	0
B	A	C	0
C	D	C	0
D	D	E	1
E	D	F	1
F	A	F	1

When in the "nowhere" state and the input is 0, the system remains there. It progresses on the first 1 to B or E and on the second 1 to C or F. The system remains in C or F if 1's continue, and goes to the "nowhere" state with the opposite output on a 0 input.

e. We start with two "nowhere" states: A when the input has been 0 for two or more consecutive inputs, and B when it has been 1 for two or more consecutive inputs. From each of these there is a separate success path (from A to C to E to G or from B to D to F to H). States G and H have a 1 output. If the input continues to alternate, the system goes back and forth between these two states.

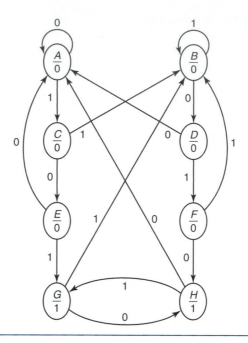

6.6 EXERCISES

1. Find equations for $q_1^\star$, $q_2^\star$, and Z for the state table of Figure 6.1, using the state assignment of Table 6.1c.

2. For each of the following state tables, design the system using
   i. D flip flops
   ii. SR flip flops
   iii. T flip flops
   iv. JK flip flops

   Show the equations for each and a block diagram for the JK design (using AND, OR, and NOT gates).

★a.

A B	$A^\star B^\star$		z	
	$x = 0$	$x = 1$	$x = 0$	$x = 1$
0 0	1 1	0 0	0	1
0 1	0 1	0 0	1	0
1 1	0 1	1 1	1	0

b.

A B	$A^\star B^\star$ $x = 0$	$A^\star B^\star$ $x = 1$	z $x = 0$	z $x = 1$
0 0	1 0	1 1	0	0
0 1	0 0	0 1	0	0
1 0	0 1	1 1	1	0
1 1	0 0	0 0	1	1

c.

A B	$A^\star B^\star$ $x = 0$	$A^\star B^\star$ $x = 1$	z
0 0	0 1	0 0	0
0 1	1 1	0 0	1
1 1	0 0	0 1	1

d.

A B	$A^\star B^\star$ $x = 0$	$A^\star B^\star$ $x = 1$	z
0 0	1 0	0 0	0
0 1	0 0	1 1	1
1 0	0 1	0 1	1
1 1	0 0	0 1	1

e.

A B	$A^\star B^\star$ $x = 0$	$A^\star B^\star$ $x = 1$	z
0 0	1 1	1 0	0
0 1	1 0	1 0	1
1 0	1 1	0 0	1
1 1	0 1	1 1	1

*f.

A B	$A^\star B^\star$ $x = 0$	$A^\star B^\star$ $x = 1$	z
0 0	1 0	0 1	1
0 1	1 1	0 0	1
1 0	0 0	1 1	0
1 1	0 1	0 0	0

g.

A B C	$A^\star B^\star C^\star$ $x = 0$	$x = 1$	z $x = 0$	$x = 1$
0 0 0	0 0 1	0 0 0	1	1
0 0 1	0 1 0	0 0 0	1	1
0 1 0	0 1 1	0 0 0	1	1
0 1 1	1 0 0	0 0 0	1	1
1 0 0	1 0 1	0 0 0	1	1
1 0 1	1 0 1	0 0 0	0	1

3. For each of the following state tables and state assignments, find the flip flop input equations and the system output equation for an implementation using

   i. D flip flops
   ii. JK flip flops

a.

q	$q^\star$ $x = 0$	$x = 1$	z
A	C	B	0
B	C	A	1
C	A	C	1

q	$q_1 q_2$
A	1 1
B	0 1
C	1 0

b.

q	$q^\star$ $x = 0$	$x = 1$	z $x = 0$	$x = 1$
A	C	B	1	1
B	A	A	1	0
C	C	A	1	0

q	$q_1 q_2$
A	0 0
B	1 1
C	0 1

⋆c.

q	$q^\star$ $x = 0$	$x = 1$	z
A	B	C	1
B	A	B	0
C	B	A	0

q	$q_1 q_2$
A	0 0
B	1 0
C	0 1

d.

q	$q^\star$ x = 0	x = 1	z x = 0	x = 1
A	B	B	0	0
B	D	A	1	0
C	D	B	0	0
D	C	D	1	0

q	$q_1 q_2$
A	0 0
B	1 1
C	1 0
D	0 1

e.

q	$q^\star$ x = 0	x = 1	z x = 0	x = 1
A	B	D	0	0
B	D	C	1	0
C	A	B	0	0
D	C	A	1	0

q	$q_1 q_2$
A	0 0
B	0 1
C	1 1
D	1 0

4. a. For the state table and each of the state assignments shown, design a system using D flip flops.

q	$q^\star$ x = 0	x = 1	z
A	B	D	0
B	C	A	1
C	B	B	1
D	D	C	1

i.

q	q_1	q_2
A	0	0
B	0	1
C	1	0
D	1	1

ii.

q	q_1	q_2
A	0	0
B	0	1
C	1	1
D	1	0

iii.

q	q_1	q_2
A	0	0
B	1	1
C	1	0
D	0	1

b, c. For each of the state tables and each of the state assignments shown, design a system using D flip flops.

*b.

q	$q^\star$ x = 0	x = 1	z x = 0	x = 1
A	B	C	1	0
B	A	B	0	1
C	B	B	0	0

c.

q	$q^\star$ $x = 0$	$x = 1$	z $x = 0$	$x = 1$
A	A	C	0	0
B	C	B	1	1
C	A	B	1	0

i.

q	q_1	q_2
A	0	0
B	0	1
C	1	0

ii.

q	q_1	q_2
A	0	0
B	0	1
C	1	1

iii.

q	q_1	q_2
A	0	0
B	1	1
C	1	0

5. Complete the design of the 4-bit binary counter (from Table 6.8 at the beginning of Section 6.2) with SR flip flops and with T flip flops.

6. If we build the decade counter of Solved Problem 4 using JK flip flops, show a state diagram, including what happens if it initially is in one of the unused states (10, 11, 12, 13, 14, 15).

7. Design, using
    i. D flip flops,
    ii. JK flip flops
   *a. a synchronous base-12 counter, one that goes through the sequence

      0, 1, 2, 3, 4, 5, 6, 7, 8, 9, 10, 11, . . .

   b. a synchronous binary down counter, one that goes through the sequence

      15, 14, 13, 12, 11, 10, 9, 8, 7, 6, 5, 4, 3, 2, 1, 0, . . .

8. Design synchronous counters that go through each of the following sequences
   a. 1 3 5 7 6 4 2 0 and repeat
  *b. 1 3 4 7 6 and repeat
   c. 6 5 4 1 2 3 and repeat
   d. 6 5 1 3 7 and repeat
   e. 7 4 3 6 1 2 and repeat

   using
   i. JK flip flops.
   ii. D flip flops.

Show a state diagram, indicating what happens if it initially is in one of the unused states for each of the designs.

9. Design a counter with two JK flip flops, A and B, and one input, x. If $x = 0$, it counts 1, 3, 0 and repeat; if $x = 1$, it counts 1, 2, 3 and repeat.

   a. Assume that x changes only when it is in state 1 or 3 (in which case there are two combinations which never occur—state 2 and $x = 0$, and state 0 and $x = 1$).

   b. After building the design of part a (with the two don't cares), what happens if somehow x is 0 in state 2 and what happens if somehow x is 1 in state 0?

*10. a. Design a counter with two JK flip flops (A and B) and an input (x) that counts 0 1 2 3 and repeat when $x = 0$ and counts 0 1 2 and repeat when $x = 1$. Design this assuming that x never is 1 when the count is 3. Show the minimum equations for each.

   b. What does happen when x goes to 1 when the count is 3?

11. Design an asynchronous base-10 counter, using T flip flops with a static active high clear.

12. Complete the design of CE6 using JK flip flops for the three different state assignments of Table 6.1.

13. Design the three-state version of CE7, using D flip flops and each of the following state assignments.

q	q_1	q_2
A	0	0
B	0	1
C	1	0

(a)

q	q_1	q_2
A	0	0
B	0	1
C	1	1

(b)

q	q_1	q_2
A	0	0
B	1	1
C	0	1

(c)

14. Design a system using JK flip flops that produces a 1 output iff there have been exactly three 1's in a row. (See Example 6.8.)

   a. Using the Mealy state diagram.

   b. Using the Moore state table.

15. For each of the following problems show a state table or a state diagram. (A sample input/output trace and the minimum number of states required is shown for each.)

a. A Moore system that produces a 1 output iff the input has been 0 for at least two consecutive clocks followed immediately by two or more consecutive 1's (five states).

x 0 1 0 0 1 0 0 1 1 0 0 0 1 0 1 0 0 0 1 1 1 1 0

z 0 0 0 0 0 0 0 0 0 1 0 0 0 0 0 0 0 0 0 1 1 1 0 0

*b. A Moore system, the output of which is 1 iff there have been two or more consecutive 1's or three or more consecutive 0's (five states).

x 0 0 0 0 1 0 1 1 0 0 1 1 1 0 0 0 1 0

z ? ? ? 1 1 0 0 0 1 0 0 0 1 1 0 0 1 0 0 0

c. A Mealy system that produces a 1 output iff the input has been 1 for three or more consecutive clock times or 0 for three or more consecutive clock times. When first turned on, it is in an initial state A. (There are four additional states.)

x 0 0 0 0 1 0 1 1 0 0 0 1 1 1 1 1 0 0 1

z 0 0 1 1 0 0 0 0 0 0 1 0 0 1 1 1 0 0 0 0

d. A Mealy system that produces a 1 output iff the input has been either 0 1 0 or 1 0 1. Overlapping is allowed. When first turned on, it is in an initial state A. (There are four additional states.)

x 0 0 1 0 0 1 0 1 0 0 1 1 0 1 1 0 1 0 0

z 0 0 0 1 0 0 1 1 1 0 0 0 0 1 0 0 1 1 0 0

e. A Mealy system that produces a 1 output iff the input is 0 for the first time after it has been 1 for at least two consecutive clocks or when it is 1 after having been 0 for at least two consecutive clocks. Overlapping is allowed. When first turned on, it is in an initial state A. (There are four additional states.)

x 0 1 0 0 0 1 1 1 1 1 0 0 1 1 0

z 0 0 0 0 0 1 0 0 0 0 1 0 1 0 1 0

*f. A Mealy system, the output of which is 1 iff the input had been at least two 0's followed by exactly two 1's followed by a 0. Overlapping is not allowed (five states).

x 1 1 1 0 0 0 1 1 0 0 1 1 0 0 1 1 1 0 0 0 0 1 1 0 0

z 0 0 0 0 0 0 0 0 1 0 0 0 0 0 0 0 0 0 0 0 0 0 1 0 0 0

g. A Mealy system, the output of which is 1 iff there have been exactly two consecutive 1's followed by at least two consecutive 0's (five states).

x 0 1 1 0 0 0 1 1 0 0 1 1 0 0 1 1 1 0 0 0 0 1 1 0 0

z ? 0 0 0 1 1 0 0 0 1 0 0 0 1 0 0 0 0 0 0 0 0 0 0 1

h. A Mealy system, the output of which is 1 iff there have been exactly two consecutive 0's or exactly two consecutive 1's.
   i. Overlapping is allowed (six states).
   ii. Overlapping is not allowed (six states).

x 0 1 1 1 0 1 1 0 0 1 1 0 1 0 1 0 0 1

z-i ? ? 0 0 0 0 0 1 0 1 0 1 0 0 0 0 0 1 0

z-ii ? ? 0 0 0 0 0 1 0 0 0 1 0 0 0 0 0 1 0 0

i. A Mealy system, the output of which is 1 iff there has been a pattern of 1 0 1 1.
   i. Overlapping is allowed (four states).
   ii. Overlapping is not allowed (four states).

x 0 0 1 0 1 1 0 1 1 0 1 1 1 0 0 1 0 1 0 1 1

z-i 0 0 0 0 0 1 0 0 1 0 0 1 0 0 0 0 0 0 1 0 0

z-ii 0 0 0 0 0 1 0 0 0 0 0 1 0 0 0 0 0 0 0 1 0 0 0

j. A Mealy system, the output of which is 0 iff there has been a pattern of 1 1 0 1. (The output is 1 most of the time.)
   i. Overlapping is allowed (four states).
   ii. Overlapping is not allowed (four states).

x 0 0 1 0 1 1 0 1 1 0 1 1 1 0 0 1 0 1 1 0 1 1

z-i 1 1 1 1 1 1 1 0 1 1 0 1 1 1 1 1 1 1 0 1 1

z-ii 1 1 1 1 1 1 1 0 1 1 1 1 1 1 1 1 1 1 1 0 1 1 1

*k. A Mealy system, the output of which is 1 iff the input has contained an even number of 0's (including no 0's) and a multiple of four 1's (including no 1's). When first turned on, the system is initialized to a state indicating no 0's and no 1's (but that state is reached again later) (eight states).

x 0 1 1 0 1 1 0 0 0 0 1 0 1 0 0 0 1 0 1 0

z 0 0 0 0 0 1 0 1 0 1 0 0 0 0 0 0 0 0 1 0

*l. A Moore system, the output of which is 1 iff the pattern 1 0 1 has occurred more recently than 1 1 1 (six states).

x 1 0 1 0 1 1 0 1 0 1 1 1 1 0 0 1 0 1 1 1

z ? ? ? 1 1 1 1 1 1 1 1 0 0 0 0 0 0 1 1 0 0

Determine from the sample whether overlapping is allowed.

m. A Mealy system, the output of which is 1 iff the input is exactly two 1's followed immediately by exactly one or two 0's. Full credit for solutions with six or fewer states.

x 1 0 0 1 1 0 0 1 1 0 1 1 1 0 0 1 1 0 0 0 0 0

z ? 0 0 0 0 0 0 1 0 0 1 0 0 0 0 0 0 0 0 0 0 0

n. A Mealy system, the output of which is 1 iff there has been a pattern of 1 1 0 0 0 (five states).

x 0 0 0 0 1 0 1 1 0 0 0 0 1 1 1 1 0 0 0 1

z ? ? ? 0 0 0 0 0 0 0 1 0 0 0 0 0 0 0 1 0 0 0 0

o. In this Mealy system, there are two inputs, a and b; they are to be treated as a binary number, that is 00 is 0, 01 is 1, 10 is 2, and 11 is 3. The output is to be 1 if the current number is greater than or equal to the previous one AND the previous one is greater than or equal to the one before that. It is to be 0 otherwise. There is an initial state for which there have been no previous numbers. Be sure to explain the meaning of each state (eight states in addition to the initial one.)

a 0 0 1 0 1 0 0 0 1 1 1 0 1 1

b 1 0 0 1 1 0 0 1 0 1 0 0 1 1

z 0 0 0 0 0 0 0 1 1 1 0 0 0 1

6.7 CHAPTER 6 TEST (75 MINUTES)

1. For the following state table, design a system using a D flip flop for A, a JK flip flop for B, and AND, OR, and NOT gates. Show the flip flop input equations and the output equation; you do **not** need to draw a block diagram.

	$A^\star B^\star$		z	
$A\ B$	$x = 0$	$x = 1$	$x = 0$	$x = 1$
0 0	1 1	0 1	0	1
0 1	0 0	1 0	0	0
1 0	1 0	0 1	1	1
1 1	0 1	1 0	1	0

2. For the following state table and state assignment, design a system using an SR flip flop for q_1 and a JK flip flop for q_2. Show

the flip flop input equations and the output equation; you do **not** need to draw a block diagram.

q	q^* $x = 0$	$x = 1$	z
A	A	B	1
B	B	C	1
C	A	C	0

q	q_1	q_2
A	0	0
B	1	0
C	1	1

3. For the following state table, design a system using D flip flops

q	q^* $x = 0$	$x = 1$	z
A	C	B	1
B	D	D	0
C	A	D	0
D	C	B	0

for each of the state assignments. Show equations for D_1, D_2, and z.

a.

q	q_1	q_2
A	0	0
B	0	1
C	1	0
D	1	1

b.

q	q_1	q_2
A	0	0
B	1	1
C	0	1
D	1	0

c. Show a block diagram for the solution to part b, using AND, OR, and NOT gates.

4. Design a counter that goes through the sequence

1   4   3   6   2   5   and repeat

using a D flip flop for A, a JK flip flop for B, and a T flip flop for C. *Five-point bonus:* Show a state diagram, including what happens if the system is initially in state 0 or 7.

5. a. Show the state table or state diagram for a Mealy system that produces a 1 output iff the input has been 1 0 1 0 for the last four clock times. Overlapping is allowed (four states).

  b. Show the state table or state diagram for a Mealy system that produces a 1 output iff the input has been 1 0 1 0 for the last four clock times. Overlapping is not allowed (four states).

Example:

x 1 1 0 1 0 1 1 1 0 1 0 1 0 1 0 0

z-a 0 0 0 0 1 0 0 0 0 0 1 0 1 0 1 0

z-b 0 0 0 0 1 0 0 0 0 0 1 0 0 0 1 0

6. Show the state table or state diagram for a Moore system that produces a 1 output iff the input has been 0 1 1 for the last three clock times (four states).

Example:

x 0 0 1 0 1 1 1 0 0 1 1 0 1 1

z ? 0 0 0 0 0 1 0 0 0 0 1 0 0 1

Solving Larger Sequential Problems

A s we get to larger problems, data is often stored in *registers,* rather than individual flip flops. A register is just a collection of flip flops, often with a common name (using subscripts to indicate the individual flip flops) and usually with a common clock. For example, in a computer, the two inputs to the adder (say 32 bits each) may come from two registers, each of which consists of 32 flip flops. It is nearly impossible to show a block diagram of such a system with all of the individual flip flops and gates.

In this chapter, we will look first at two classes of commercial medium-scale integrated circuits*: shift registers and counters. We will introduce programmable logic devices with memory to implement more complex problems such as CPLDs and FPGAs. We will then look briefly at a tool for dealing with these larger systems, ASM (Algorithmic State Machine) diagrams. We will then show some examples of Verilog descriptions of sequential systems. Lastly, we will then look at some larger design problems than we could manage in Chapter 6. We will concentrate on synchronous (clocked) systems.

7.1 SHIFT REGISTERS

A shift register, in its simplest form, is a set of flip flops, such that the data move one place to the right on each clock or shift input. A simple 4-bit shift register is shown in Figure 7.1, using *SR* flip flops. (Although shift registers are most commonly implemented with *SR* flip flops, *JK* flip flops could be used in place of the *SR*'s in the same circuit. *D* flip flops could also be used; the q output of one flip flop would be connected to the *D* input of the next.) At each clock, the input, *x,* is moved into q_1 and the contents of each of the flip flops is shifted one place to the right. A sample timing trace is shown in Trace 7.1, assuming that all flip flops are initially 0. The sample input is shown in green.

---

*When we look at the details of some of these circuits, we will simplify the logic somewhat by looking at just one bit and by eliminating some of the double NOT gates that are used for reducing load.

Figure 7.1 A simple shift register.

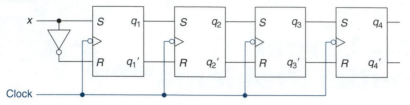

Trace 7.1 Shift register timing.

x	1	0	1	1	1	0	1	1	1	1	0	0	0			
q_1	0	1	0	1	1	1	0	1	1	1	1	0	0	0		
q_2	0	0	1	0	1	1	1	0	1	1	1	1	0	0	0	
q_3	0	0	0	1	0	1	1	1	0	1	1	1	1	0	0	0
q_4	0	0	0	0	1	0	1	1	1	0	1	1	1	1	0	0	0

In some commercial shift registers, a NOT gate is added at the clock input, as shown in Figure 7.2.

Figure 7.2 Leading-edge triggered shift register.

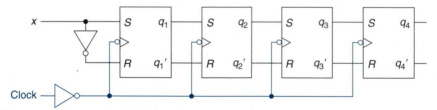

This accomplishes two things. The shift register is now leading-edge triggered (since the leading edge of the clock is the trailing edge of the flip flop clock input). Also, the clock input signal only goes to the NOT gate. Thus, this circuit presents a load of 1 to the clock, rather than a load of 4 (if the signal went to all four flip flops). When a trailing-edge triggered shift register is desired, a second NOT gate is added in series with the one shown. Sometimes, the x input is first inverted to present only a load of 1. Both of these changes are shown in the circuit of Figure 7.3.

Figure 7.3 Shift register with load reducing NOT gates.

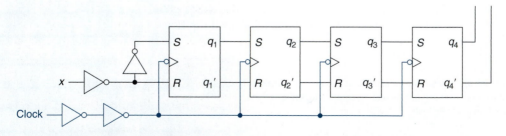

This version of the shift register is referred to as *serial-in, serial-out* in that only 1 bit (the left bit) may be loaded into the register at a time and, as shown, only 1 bit (the right bit) may be read. (Only the uncomplemented value, q_4, may be available or both the uncomplemented and complemented, q_4 and q_4', may be outputs.) The main limitation on the amount of logic that can fit on a single chip is the number of input and output connections. Thus, one could build a serial-in, serial-out shift register with a nearly unlimited number of bits on a chip, since there are only three or four logic connections.

One application of a large serial-in, serial-out shift register is a memory similar to a disk. If the output bit is connected back to the input as shown in Figure 7.4, when *Load* is 0, the data circulate around the n flip flops. It is available only when it is in q_n, once every n clock cycles. At that time it can be modified, by making *Load* = 1 and supplying the new value on x. If we needed a series of 8-bit numbers, we could build eight such shift registers, storing 1 bit in each. As we clocked all the shift registers we would obtain 1 byte (8 bits) at a time.

Figure 7.4   Shift register storage.

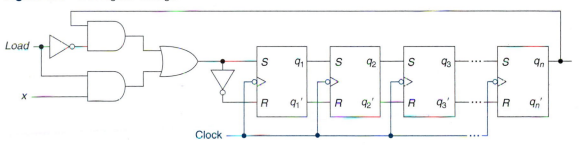

To initialize a 4-bit serial-in, serial-out shift register to all 0's, we would have to clock it four times, with 0 on input x each time. To avoid this, most shift registers have an active low (usually static) clear input. Many shift registers have a *parallel* output, that is, the contents of each of the flip flops is available. (Obviously, if we were building this with independent flip flops, this would just require connecting a wire to each flip flop output. If, however, the whole shift register were contained on a single integrated circuit, each output would require a pin.) There is an 8-bit serial-in, parallel-out shift register on one chip, using D flip flops (74164); it uses the 12 logic connections for 8 outputs, the clock, the clear, and 2 for serial input, as shown in Figure 7.5. (The x is replaced by A B, two inputs into a built-in AND gate.)

One application of a serial-in, parallel-out shift register is an input port from a modem. Data is transmitted serially over telephone lines. It is clocked into a shift register until a whole byte or word is received. Only then is there interaction with the computer's memory; the group of bits are read in parallel from the shift register and loaded into memory.

Figure 7.5 74164 serial-in parallel-out shift register.

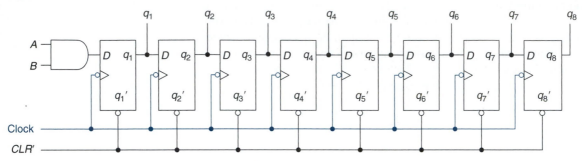

A *parallel-in* shift register allows the register to be loaded in one step. That, of course, requires an input line for each flip flop, as well as a control line to indicate load. Sometimes the loading is done statically (74165), as demonstrated for a typical bit (q_2) in Figure 7.6a. Sometimes it is done synchronously (74166), as shown in Figure 7.6b. Both of these are serial-out, that is, there is only one output connection, from the right flip flop. There is a serial input to the left bit for shift operations (going to the same place in the first flip flop logic that q_1 goes to in the typical bit below).

For the 74165, the clock input to the flip flops is inverted from the input to the chip and passed through only when *Load'* is high (don't load) and *Enable'* is low (enable shift). When *Load'* is high, both *CLR'* and *PRE'* are high, and the shift works. When *Load'* is low, the clock is disabled, IN_2' appears on *PRE'*, and IN_2 appears on *CLR'*, thus loading IN_2 into the flip flop.

For the 74166, there is an active low static clear, independent of the load. The clock is inverted when *Enable'* is 0; otherwise, the flip flops

Figure 7.6 Parallel-in shift registers.

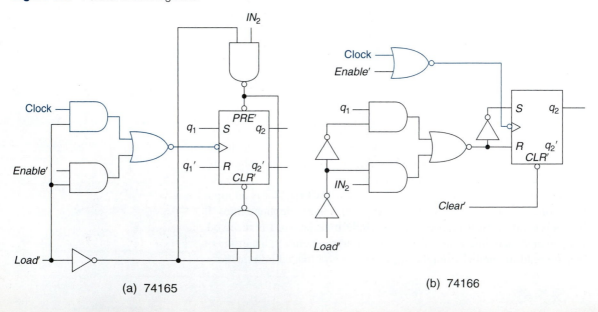

(a) 74165   (b) 74166

are not clocked and nothing changes. When enabled and *Load'* is 0, IN_2 is stored in q_2; when *Load'* is 1 (inactive), q_1 is shifted into q_2.

The parallel-in, serial-out shift register is used in the output process for serial data. A word is loaded (all at once) into the shift register from the computer. Then, bits are sent to the modem from the right end of the shift register one at a time.

Parallel-in, parallel-out shift registers are limited to 4 or 5 bits because of the number of connections required. The 7495 is very similar to the 74166 in control structure, except that it has a separate clock input for shifting and for loading.

In most computers, there are both left and right shift and rotate* instructions. To implement these, we might use a right/left shift register (such as the 74194, a synchronous parallel-in, parallel-out 4-bit shift register). For this, a three-way multiplexer is needed at each bit, since that bit can receive the bit to its left, the bit to its right or the input bit. A truth table describing the behavior of the shift register is shown in Table 7.1. Bits are numbered 1 to 4 from left to right.

Table 7.1   Right/left shift register.

	Clear'	S_0	S_1	$q_1^\star$	$q_2^\star$	$q_3^\star$	$q_4^\star$
Static clear	0	X	X	0	0	0	0
Hold	1	0	0	q_1	q_2	q_3	q_4
Shift left	1	0	1	q_2	q_3	q_4	LS
Shift right	1	1	0	RS	q_1	q_2	q_3
Load	1	1	1	IN_1	IN_2	IN_3	IN_4

The IN_i are the inputs for parallel load, *RS* is the serial input for a right shift, and *LS* is the serial input for a left shift. The hold combination is really the "don't shift, don't load" input. A typical bit (with the control circuitry) is shown in Figure 7.7.

Figure 7.7   Right/left shift register.

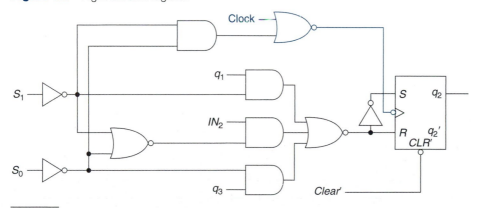

---

*A one place right rotate moves every bit one place to the right and moves the rightmost bit back into the left flip flop.

Note that when S_0 and S_1 are both 0, the clock input to the flip flop is 0; there is no edge and thus the flip flop holds. Otherwise, the clock is inverted and thus this is a leading-edge triggered shift register. (Note that for q_1, the left flip flop, RS comes into the top input of the multiplexer and for q_4, LS comes into the bottom input.)

These can be cascaded to form larger shift registers by connecting q_4 of the register on the left to the RS input of the one on the right and q_1 of the one on the right to the LS input of the left register.

As an example of an application of shift registers, consider the following problem.

EXAMPLE 7.1	We want to design a system with one output, z, which is 1 if the input, x, has been alternating for seven clock times (including the present). We have available an 8-bit serial-in, parallel-out shift register as shown:

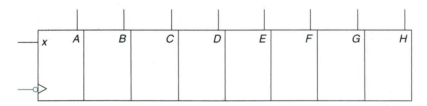

(The shift register probably also has a static clear input, but it is not needed for this problem.)

At any time, the register contains the value of x at the eight most recent clocks, with the most recent in A and the oldest in H. For this problem, we only need six of these. The following circuit computes the answer.

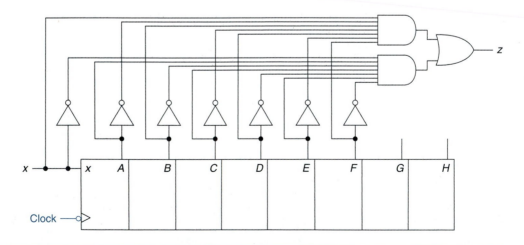

7.2 COUNTERS

In Chapter 6, we discussed the design of counters. In this section, we will look at some of the commercially available counters and applications of counters. A counter consists of a register and the associated logic.

Counters may be synchronous or asynchronous and may be base 10, 12, or 16 (that is, cycle through 10, 12, or 16 states on consecutive clock pulses). Most synchronous counters have parallel loads; they may be preset to a value, using the load signal and an input line for each bit. Many also have a clear (or *Master Reset*) signal to load the register with all 0's. These control signals are usually active low; they may be synchronous or asynchronous. Most asynchronous counters just have a static clear. In addition, some synchronous counters count both up and down. Most counters have a carry or overflow output, which indicates that the counter has reached its maximum and is returning to 0 (for up counters). That may be a logic 1 or it may be a clock pulse coincident with the pulse that causes the transition back to 0.

We will first look at the 74161 counter, which does synchronous counting and loading and has an asynchronous (active low) clear. It has two count enables: *ENT* and *ENP** (both of which must be 1 to enable counting). Labeling the bits D (high), C, B, and A, a block representation of the counter and the logic for a typical bit, bit C, is shown in Figure 7.8. Since the clock is inverted before going to the trailing-edge triggered flip flop, the counter is leading-edge triggered. The only difference between bits is the inputs to the green AND gate. That is the value for the J and K inputs to each bit when counting (ANDed with the enable). (Thus, D's input is ABC, C's input is AB, B's input is A, and A's input is 1.) When loading ($Load' = 0$), point x is 1, point y is 1, point z equals IN'_C, and point w equals IN_C. Thus, the flip flop is loaded with the value on IN_C. When $Load' = 1$, then point x equals 0, points w and z equal 1, and point y is just the output of the green AND gate. Thus, J and K are 1 when the green gate output is 1, that is, when this flip is to change during the count.

We could use two of these counters to count to 255 ($2^8 - 1$) or three to count to 4095 ($2^{12} - 1$). The block diagram of Figure 7.9 illustrates the 8-bit counter, where no parallel load inputs are shown.

If the counter is cleared initially, only the low-order counter (the one on the right) is enabled for the first 15 clocks. When that counter reaches 15 (1111), the overflow output (OV) becomes 1. That enables the second counter. On the next clock, the right counter goes to 0 (returning OV to 0) and the left counter increases by 1. (Thus, the count reaches 16.) Only the low-order counter increments on the next 15 clocks, as the count reaches 31. On the 32nd clock, the high-order counter is enabled again.

---

*Only *ENT* enables the overflow output.

Figure 7.8   The 74161 counter.

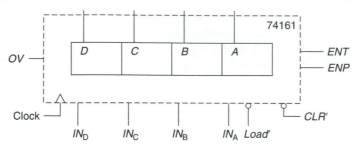

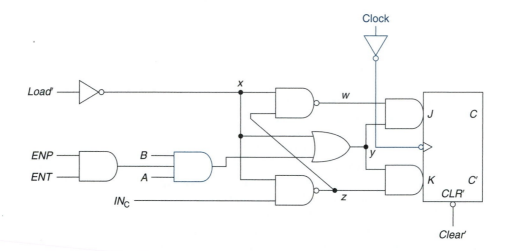

Figure 7.9   8-bit counter.

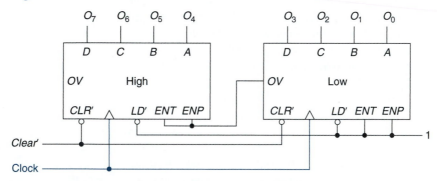

EXAMPLE 7.2

If we wanted to count through a number of states other than a power of 16, we would need to reset the counter when we reached the desired maximum. Since the 74161 counter has a static clear (similar to the asynchronous counter example in Example 6.7), we must count one beyond the desired maximum and use that to clear the counter. We will thus reach the extra state for a brief time (before the clear is effective), but that is well before the next clock time. For example, the counter of Figure 7.9 could be used to count through 120 states (0 to 119) by adding the NAND gate shown to clear it when it reaches 120 (01111000).

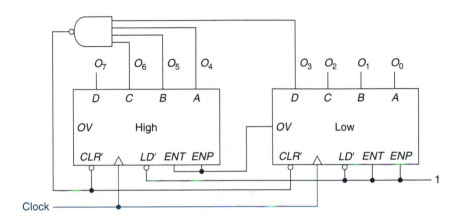

We do not need to AND O_2', O_1', O_0', or O_7', since we never reach a count over 120, and thus these are never 1 when O_6, O_5, O_4, and O_3 are all 1.

EXAMPLE 7.3

The 74163 is similar to the 74161, except that the clear is clocked. The internal structure of the circuit is modified so that an active clear input loads a 0 into each flip flop on the clock. To use it in a 120 state counter, we need to detect 119 and reset it on the next clock pulse, as shown. The advantage of this approach is that there is no period (not even a short one) where the counter reaches 120.

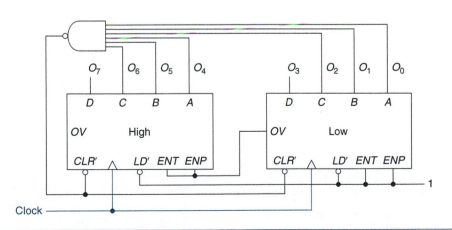

There are decade counters (counting 0 to 9) similar to the two binary counters we just described (74160 with a static clear and 74162 with a clocked clear).

There are both binary (74191 and 74193) and decade (74190 and 74192) up/down counters. The first of each type has a single clock input and a D/U' input (where a 1 indicates down and a 0 indicates up). The second has two separate clock inputs, one for counting down and the other for counting up; one of those must be a logic 1 for the other to work. All of these have static load inputs. Bit C of the 74191 binary counter is shown in Figure 7.10. When $Load'$ is 0, the preset input is low

Figure 7.10   Typical bit of the 74191 Down/Up' counter.

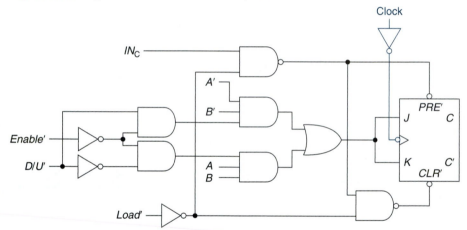

(active) if IN_C is 1 and the clear input is low (active) if IN_C is 0. (There is no clear input to the counter; that is accomplished by loading 0 into each bit.) If $Load'$ is 1, then both preset and clear are 1 (inactive) and the clock controls the counter. Note that J and K are BA when counting up and $B'A'$ when counting down.

A block diagram and a truth table for the 74191 counter are shown in Figure 7.11.

Figure 7.11   The 74191 Down/Up' counter.

LD'	EN'	D/U'	
0	X	X	Static load
1	1	X	Do nothing
1	0	0	Clocked count up
1	0	1	Clocked count down

The final group of counter we will discuss are asynchronous counters

7490	Base 10	(2 × 5)
7492	Base 12	(2 × 6)
7493	Base 16	(2 × 8)

Each of these is trailing-edge triggered and consists of a single flip flop and then a 3-bit counter (base 5, 6, and 8, respectively). The output from the single flip flop must be externally connected to the clock of the 3-bit counter to achieve the full count. Each has two static clear inputs, both of which must be 1 to clear all four flip flops. The decade counter also has a pair of static set inputs, which (when both are 1) sets the counter to 9 (1001); the set overrides the clear.

A simplified block diagram of the 7493 is shown in Figure 7.12.

Figure 7.12 7493 asynchronous binary counter.

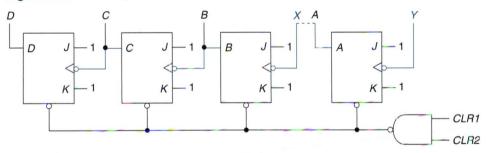

Note that to count to 8, the clock is connected to point X, and the outputs are from D, C, and B. To count to 16, the clock is connected to point Y, and points A and X must be connected (externally from the integrated circuit, as shown dashed).

EXAMPLE 7.4

We will now look at four solutions, each using a binary counter, to the following problem:

Design a system the output of which is a clock pulse for every ninth input clock pulse.

For this, the counter must go through nine states. The output is obtained by ANDing the clock with a circuit that detects any one of the nine states. One solution is to have the counter sequence

0 1 2 3 4 5 6 7 8 0 . . .

If we use a 74163, which has a clocked clear, the circuit is

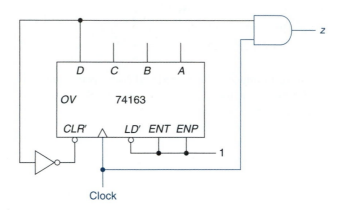

D is only 1 in state 8; thus it can be used to reset the counter to 0 and for the output.

If we use a 74161 with a static clear, then we must count to 9 before clearing it, as shown.

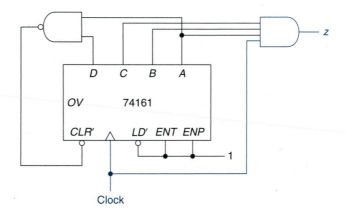

It will remain in state 9 for a short time (depending on the delays in the circuit). We cannot not use the same output circuit, because we would get a short output pulse at the beginning of state 9 (as well as the one in state 8), as shown in the following timing diagram.

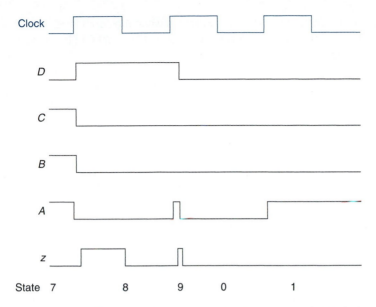

State   7   8   9   0   1

Another approach to this problem, using the first counter (74163), is to count

     8, 9, 10, 11, 12, 13, 14, 15, 0, 8 . . .

As before, this counter cycles through 9 states. When the count reaches 0, we load an 8 into the counter. Since the load is synchronous, this occurs on the next clock pulse. The output can be coincident with the time we are in state 0 (or any other state). This results in the following circuit, where the load inputs, IN_D, IN_C, IN_B, and IN_A, are shown down the right side of the block. The only state for which $D = 0$ is state 0; thus, the load is activated in that state and the output coincides with the clock pulse during that state.

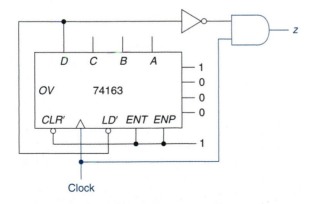

Finally, with the 74163, we could implement this to count the sequence

     7, 8, 9, 10, 11, 12, 13, 14, 15, 7, . . .

using the *OV* output. Since that indicates when the count is 15, we can invert it to create an active low load signal and connect 0111 to the parallel input lines, as shown.

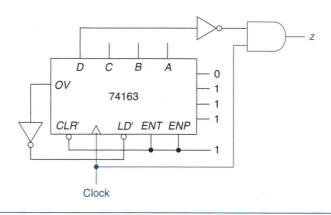

Clock

[SP 3, 4b; EX 3, 4a, 5, 6]

7.3 PROGRAMMABLE LOGIC DEVICES (PLDs)

Since a sequential system consists of memory and combinational logic, one approach to its implementation is to use a PAL (or other logic array described in Chapter 4) and some flip flops (for the memory). There are a variety of devices that combine a PAL and some *D* flip flops. One family of these devices is the 16R8,* 16R6, and 16R4. A simplified schematic of a portion of the 16R4 is shown in Figure 7.13. There are eight external inputs (two of which are shown). The *registered* outputs (all eight in the 16R8 and four in the 16R4) come from a flip flop, driven by a PAL (as shown for the first two outputs in Figure 7.13). Each PAL output circuit has eight AND gates (four of which are shown). There is a common clock and a common (active low) output enable, providing active low flip flop outputs (since the three-state gate inverts). Note that Q' is fed back to the AND array; but, it is then provided both uncomplemented and complemented, just as are the external AND array inputs. Thus, all the inputs to the combinational logic are available both uncomplemented and complemented.

The 16R8, by itself, is sufficient to implement only those sequential systems whose output is the state of the flip flops, such as counters.

---

*The 16 is the number of inputs to the AND array, the R indicates that at least some of the outputs are registered, that is, come from flip flops, and the 8 is the number of flip flops.

Figure 7.13 A PLD.

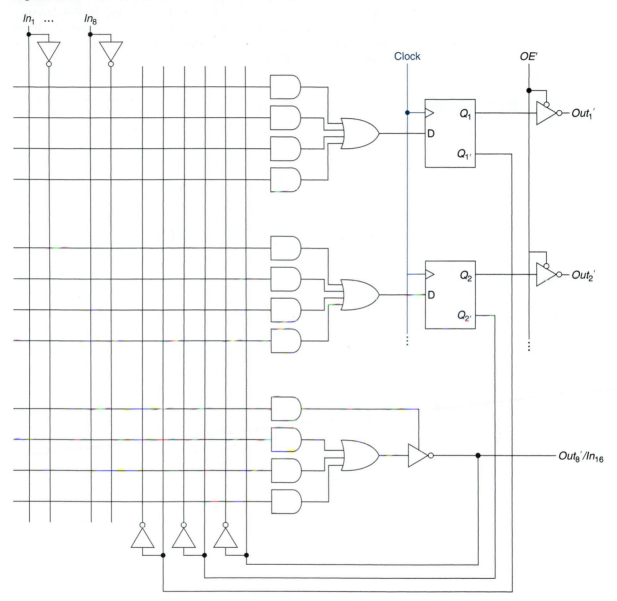

Those outputs that are not registered (as shown in the bottom of Figure 7.13) are enabled by one of the AND gates (and the PAL has only seven terms). Such an output can be used for a Mealy system. If it is not enabled, that pin can be used as an additional input (making as many as 12 inputs for the 16R4).

EXAMPLE 7.5

As an example, we will look at the design of the up/down counter from Solved Problem 7 of Chapter 6, where we have added two outputs, F and G, where F indicates that the counter is saturated and G indicates that the counter is recycling (that is, going from 3 back to 0 or from 0 back to 3). The state table is shown here.

	$A^{\star}B^{\star}$				$F\ G$			
$A\ B$	$xy = 00$	$xy = 01$	$xy = 10$	$xy = 11$	$xy = 00$	$xy = 01$	$xy = 10$	$xy = 11$
0 0	0 1	0 1	1 1	0 0	0 0	0 0	0 1	1 0
0 1	1 0	1 0	0 0	0 0	0 0	0 0	0 0	0 0
1 0	1 1	1 1	0 1	0 1	0 0	0 0	0 0	0 0
1 1	0 0	1 1	1 0	1 0	0 1	1 0	0 0	0 0

We developed the following equations for the D inputs in Solved Problem 7:

$$D_A = x'A'B + x'AB' + x'yA + xAB + xy'A'B'$$
$$D_B = x'yA + AB' + x'B' + y'B'$$

(There is no point in considering sharing, since the PAL does not permit it.) We can obtain the output equations from the state table (or we could construct maps):

$$F = x'yAB + xyA'B'$$
$$G = x'y'AB + xy'A'B'$$

A block diagram of that PAL, with only the gates that are used included, is shown next. Note that we did not show the output gates for the flip flops. We used five of the eight input lines (including one for a 1 to enable the two outputs). We used only two of the flip flops. This could be implemented with either a 16R6 or a 16R4.

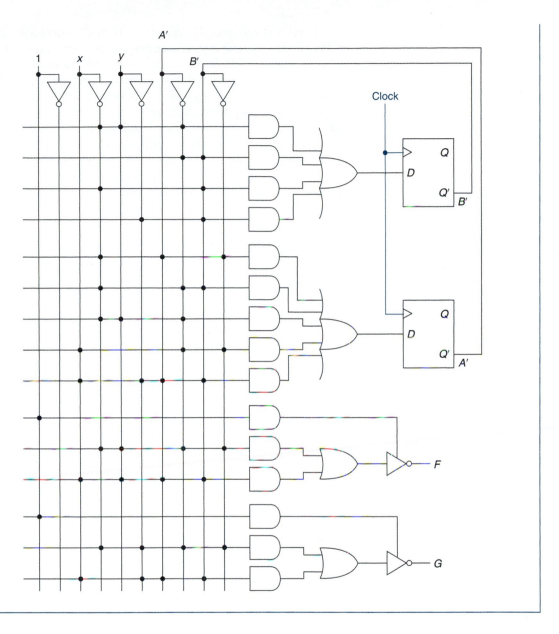

   The PLDs we have described are useful for relatively small circuits—
typically no more than a total of 32 inputs and outputs. Although it would
theoretically be possible to build them much larger, other approaches are
used.

A *complex programmable logic device* (CPLD*) incorporates an array of PLD-like blocks and a programmable interconnection network. Commercially available CPLDs have as many as a few hundred PLD blocks.

For larger circuits, *field programmable gate arrays* (FPGA) are used. Rather than containing PALs, FPGAs have as their basic building block a general purpose logic generator (typically three to five variables), with multiplexers and a flip flop. These blocks are connected by a programmable routing network, which also connects to Input/Output blocks. The logic generator is effectively a *lookup table* (LUT), often with a flip flop. A three-variable LUT is shown in Figure 7.14, with a flip flop that may be bypassed if control is 0. Each cell can be programmed to a 0 or a 1; thus, any three-variable function can be created.

Figure 7.14   A three-input lookup table.

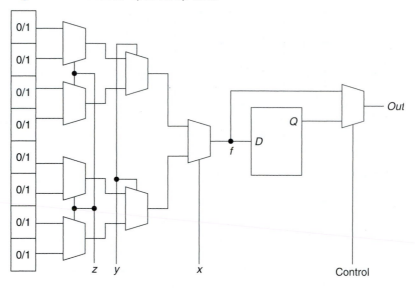

If, for example, the cells are programmed to 0, 0, 0, 1, 0, 0, 1, 1, then the function represented is $f = x'yz + xyz' + xyz = yz + xy$. To illustrate the interconnection network, Figure 7.15 shows an implementation of the function

$$f = x_1 x_2' + x_2 x_3$$

using two-input LUTs. The green input/output connectors, connections (X) and LUTs are active. All of the others are inactive. One LUT produces $f_1 = x_1 x_2'$, the second produces $f_2 = x_2 x_3$ and the third produces $f = f_1 + f_2$.

---

*For a more complete discussion of CPLDs and FPGAs, see Brown and Vranesic, *Fundamentals of Digital Logic with VHDL Design*, 2nd ed. McGraw-Hill, 2005.

Figure 7.15 A section of a programmed FPGA.

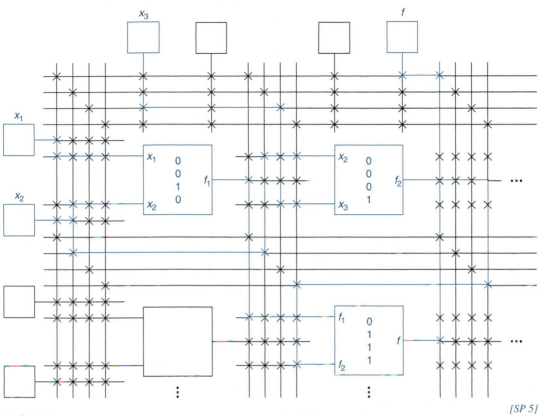

[SP 5]

7.4 DESIGN USING ASM DIAGRAMS

As we indicated in Chapter 5, the term state machine, also called finite state machine or *algorithmic state machine* (ASM) is the same as *sequential system*. A tool that is a cross between a state diagram and a flow chart is the ASM diagram (sometimes referred to as an ASM chart). We will first describe the basic elements and compare its structure to that of a state diagram. Then, we will apply this tool to a controller for a small system of registers (the place where this tool is most useful).

There are three types of blocks in an ASM diagram. The first is the state box. It is a rectangle, with one entry point and one exit point, as shown in Figure 7.16a.

The name of the state is shown above the box and the output(s) corresponding to that state is shown in the box. (This is a Moore type output, one that occurs whenever the system is in that state. We will see how to indicate a Mealy output shortly.) When an output is listed, it indicates that the output is 1; any output not listed is 0.

The second type of box is the decision box, as shown in Figure 7.16b, which allows a two-way branch based on a switching expression. It has one

Figure 7.16a State box.

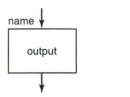

Figure 7.16b Decision box.

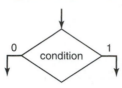

Figure 7.16c Mealy output box.

entry point and two exit points, one corresponding to the expression equal to 0, the other corresponding to a 1. If more than a two-way branch is needed, the exit of a decision box can go to the entry of another decision box.

The third type of box is the conditional output box (Figure 7.16c). It has one entry and one exit. It specifies the output that occurs when that state transition takes place. (It is the Mealy output.)

An ASM block consists of the state box and all the decision boxes and conditional output boxes connected to it. There is one entry to the block, but there may be one or more exits; each of these goes to the entry of a state box.

There is no symbol for a merge point; two or more exit paths may go to the same entry point, as will be seen in some examples that follow. A typical ASM block (associated with state A) is shown in Figure 7.17. The output, z, of this system is 1 when the system is in state A and the input, x, is 1. The system goes to state B when $x = 1$, and back to state A when $x = 0$.

Figure 7.17 An ASM block.

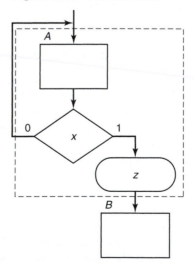

We will now look at the ASM diagram for the Moore system with an output of 1 iff the input has been 1 for at least three consecutive clocks (as first presented in Section 5.1). The state diagram is shown first in Figure 7.18 and then the corresponding ASM diagram.

Figure 7.18 Moore state diagram and ASM diagram.

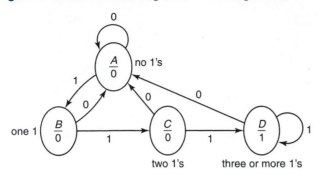

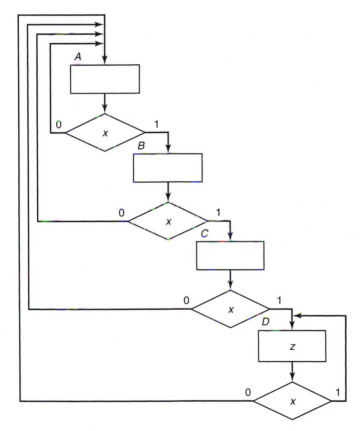

For the similar Mealy problem, with one input, x, and one output, z, such that $z = 1$ iff x has been 1 for three consecutive clock times, the state diagram (Figure 6.13) and the corresponding ASM diagram is shown in Figure 7.19. Note that the state assignment may be shown to the right of the state name, outside the state box.

Figure 7.19   Mealy state diagram and ASM diagram.

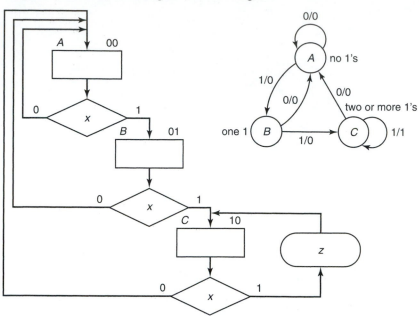

Finally, we will look at the design for a controller for a serial adder. The numbers are each stored in an 8-bit register (with shifting capability), and the answer is returned to one of those registers, as shown in the following diagram. We will assume that the two operands are already loaded into registers A and B.

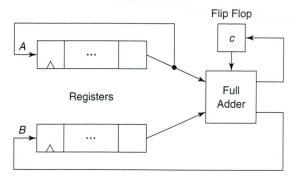

A signal of 1 on line s indicates that the system is to start the addition process. A 1 (for one clock period) on line d indicates that it is done. An ASM diagram for a controller for this system follows. The bits of the register are numbered 7 (left, most significant) to 0. Bits 0 of the numbers and the carry (c) are added and the result is loaded into the left bit (bit 7) of B as both registers are shifted to the right.

The main purpose of the controller is to send signals to the register and logic shown earlier. The notation ← indicates that the data on the right are clocked into the flip flop or register on the left. A detailed discussion of controller design is the subject of Chapter 9.

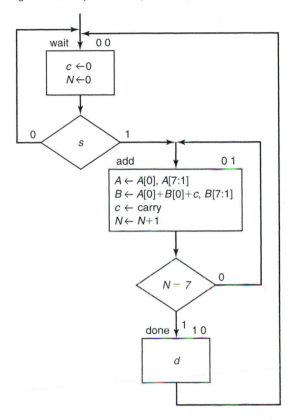

This controller can be implemented by a sequential machine with three states. It requires a 3-bit register, N, and an incrementer to count through the eight add/shift steps. This controller goes from state 00 to state 01 when $s = 1$ (and remains in state 00, otherwise). It goes from state 01 to 10 when register N contains three 1's (and returns to state 01, otherwise). It always goes from state 10 to 00 on the next clock. The design of the sequential circuit is left as an exercise.

[SP 6; EX 7, 8]

7.5 ONE-HOT ENCODING

Up until now, we have encoded states using the minimum number of flip flops. Another approach, particularly simple when designing from an ASM diagram, is to use one flip flop for each state. That flip flop is 1 (or *hot*) and all others are 0 when the system is in that state.

For the Moore system of Figure 7.18, we have four states and would thus have four flip flops. If we labeled them A, B, C, and D, we can see by inspection that

$$A^\star = x'(A + B + C + D) = x'$$

(since one of the state variables must be 1).

$$B^\star = xA$$

(since the condition box indicates that we go to state B when $x = 1$)

$$C^\star = xB$$
$$D^\star = x(C + D)$$

This produces very simple combinational logic for the next state (although the savings there is typically not adequate to make up for the cost of extra flip flops).

The output is 1 only when in state D; thus the output equation is

$$z = D$$

This approach is sometimes used in designing large controllers, where most states produce an output signal. As in the previous example, the output signal comes directly from a flip flop, rather than from combinational logic that decodes the state. We will return to this in Chapter 9.

7.6 VERILOG FOR SEQUENTIAL SYSTEMS*

In Section 4.7.1, we introduced Verilog constructs for combinational systems. Here, we will give examples of the use of Verilog for sequential systems.

We will now look at the structural model for a trailing-edge triggered D flip flop with an active low input, CLR' in Figure 7.20.

Figure 7.20 Structural model of a D flip flop.

```
module D_ff (q, ck, D, CLR);
    input ck, D, CLR;
    output q;
    reg q;
    always @ (negedge ck or negedge CLR)
        begin
            if (!CLR)
                q <= 0;
            else
                q <= D;
        end
endmodule
```

*For a detailed discussion of Verilog, see Brown and Vranesic, *Fundamentals of Digital Logic with Verilog Design,* McGraw-Hill, 2003, or for VHDL, see Brown and Vranesic, *Fundamentals of Digital Logic with VHDL Design,* 2nd ed. McGraw-Hill, 2005.

Note that q is referred to as a register (reg) rather than a wire, since it is storage. The symbol @ indicates the time when the following steps are executed. Only on the trailing edge (`negedge`) of the clock or the CLR input will anything happen. The symbol ! indicates *not,* and the arrowed equal (<=) is used to indicate time dependence. In the combinational models, an equal sign (=) was used since it did not matter in what order things happened.

We can use the flip flop we just described to build a 8-bit trailing-edge triggered shift register (shift right), as shown in Figure 7.21a.

Figure 7.21a Shift register using flip flop module.

```
module shift (Q, x, ck, CLR);
     input x, clock, CLR;
     output [7:0]Q;
     wire [7:0]Q;
     D_ff Stage 7 (Q[7], x, ck, CLR);
     D_ff Stage 6 (Q[6], Q[7], ck, CLR);
     D_ff Stage 5 (Q[5], Q[6], ck, CLR);
     D_ff Stage 4 (Q[4], Q[5], ck, CLR);
     D_ff Stage 3 (Q[3], Q[4], ck, CLR);
     D_ff Stage 2 (Q[2], Q[3], ck, CLR);
     D_ff Stage 1 (Q[1], Q[2], ck, CLR);
     D_ff Stage 0 (Q[0], Q[1], ck, CLR);
endmodule
```

Another approach is to define the shift register in a single module.

Figure 7.21b Single module shifter.

```
module shift (Q, x, ck, CLR);
     input x, clock, CLR;
     output [7:0]Q;
     wire [7:0]Q;
     reg [7:0]Q;
always (@ negedge ck)
     begin
          Q[0] <= Q[1];
          Q[1] <= Q[2];
          Q[2] <= Q[3];
          Q[3] <= Q[4];
          Q[4] <= Q[5];
          Q[5] <= Q[6];
          Q[6] <= Q[7];
          Q[7] <= x;
     end
endmodule
```

7.7 MORE COMPLEX EXAMPLES*

As the first example, consider the design of the following system:

> The system keeps track of how many consecutive 1 inputs occur on input line x and then, starting at the first time that the input x is 0, it outputs on line z that same number of 1's at consecutive clocks (z is 0 at all other times).

A sample timing trace of the input and output of such a system is shown in Trace 7.2.

Trace 7.2 Sample trace for input and output.

x	0 0 0 1 0 0 0 0 1 1 1 1 0 0 0 0 0 0 0 1 1 0 0 0
z	0 0 0 0 1 0 0 0 0 0 0 0 1 1 1 1 0 0 0 0 0 1 1 0

We will first assume that the available components are AND, OR, and NOT gates, a *JK* flip flop and a 74191 up/down counter with four outputs, labeled *D, C, B, A* (with *D* the high-order output). We will use the counter to count the number of consecutive 1's (counting up) and then count down to 0 as the 1's are output.

We will first look at the simplest solution and then examine the assumptions that must be made for this to be valid. We will then add circuitry so as to make the system work for a more general case. The circuit of Figure 7.22 is our first attempt at a solution. No clear was

Figure 7.22 A simple solution with a counter.

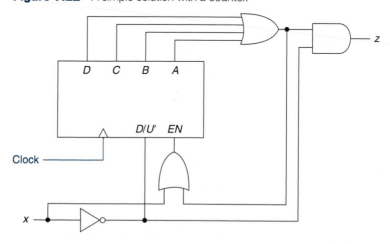

---

*Even larger examples are found in Chapters 9 and 10.

provided. Once the system produces its first set of 1 outputs, the counter will be left with 0 in it; so there is no need to clear it. When x is 1, the D/U' is set to 0 and the counter is enabled; thus, it counts up. When x returns to 0, it will count down, as long as it is enabled, that is, as long as there is a nonzero value in the counter. The output is 1 when x is 0 and there is a nonzero count. This solution works only if the count never exceeds 15, since on the 16th consecutive 1 input, the counter goes back to 0. If a larger number were required, we would need one or more additional counters so as to be able to count higher than 15. An alternative to that would be to limit the output to a maximum of 15 1's, even if the input included more than 15 consecutive 1's. In that case, we would disable the counter when we reached 15, if x remains 1. That would require the circuit of Figure 7.23.

Figure 7.23 Example with maximum of 16 outputs of 1.

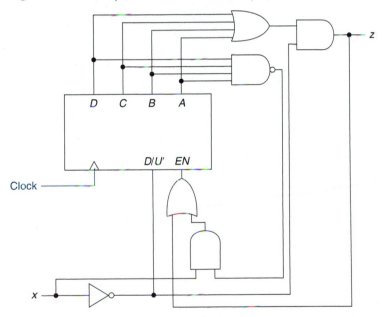

Now the counter is not enabled when the count is 15 (1111) and x is 1. Thus, if there are a large number of consecutive 1's, it will count to 15 and stop until x goes to 0; then it will count down, outputting fifteen 1's.

The other unstated assumption that we made was that x remains 0 until the 1 outputs are completed. That was the case in the sample trace. If that is not true, the counter will start counting up again as soon as x returns to 1. Assuming that we want to ignore the input until the 1 outputs are completed, we need a flip flop, Q, to keep track of when the system is counting down and we should ignore x. We must then consider the following possibilities.

$x = 0$ $Q = 0$ count $= 0$ $EN = 0$ $z = 0$ $D/U' = $ X*

$x = 0$ $Q = 0$ count $= 1^\dagger$ $EN = 1$ $z = 1$ $D/U' = 1$

$x = 0$ $Q = 0$ count > 1 $EN = 1$ $z = 1$ $D/U' = 1$ $Q \leftarrow 1$

$x = 1$ $Q = 0$ count $\neq 15$ $EN = 1$ $z = 0$ $D/U' = 0$

$x = 1$ $Q = 0$ count $= 15$ $EN = 0$ $z = 0$ $D/U' = $ X

$x = $ X‡ $Q = 1$ count > 1 $EN = 1$ $z = 1$ $D/U' = 1$

$x = $ X $Q = 1$ count $= 1$ $EN = 1$ $z = 1$ $D/U' = 1$ $Q \leftarrow 0$

Flip flop Q will be turned on when x is 0 and the count is not 0 or 1, and it will be turned off when it is 1 and the output gets down to 1. Thus,

$$J = x'(D + C + B) \qquad K = D'C'B'A$$

The output is 1 when Q is 1 or when x is 0 and Q is 0 but the count is not 0. Thus,

$$z = Q + x'Q'(D + C + B + A) = Q + x'(D + C + B + A)$$

The counter is enabled when $x = 1$ and the count is not at 15 (as in the last example, to allow for more than 15 consecutive 1 inputs) or when $z = 1$. Thus,

$$EN = x(ABCD)' + z$$

Finally,

$$D/U' = Q + x'(D + C + B + A)$$

the same as z, since at the only places where they differ, D/U' is a don't care (since the counter is not enabled).

We will now look at the same example, utilizing shift registers instead of a counter. We need some right/left shift registers (more than 1 if we are to allow more than four consecutive 1 outputs). If we set the limit at 12, we could use three 74194 shift registers. They would be connected as shown in Figure 7.24, where the parallel inputs are not shown, since they are not used.

---

*Since the counter is not enabled, it does not matter whether it is set to count up or down.
†If there is only one 1, that will cause the counter to increase to 1, but Q will not be set at the next clock time, since that is the last time the output is to be 1. The condition to set Q is just that the count is between 2 and 15, which yields, from the map, $D + C + B$.
‡When it is counting down (and the output is 1), the input is ignored; it does not matter.

Figure 7.24 Circuit using three right/left shift registers.

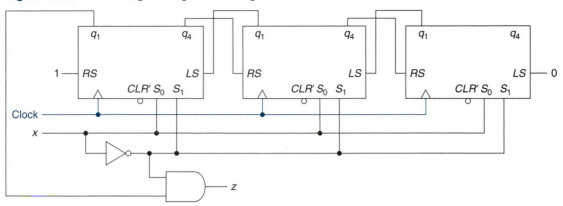

The three shift registers are connected to form one 12-bit shift register. When $x = 1$, $S_0 = 1$, and $S_1 = 0$, making the registers shift right. A 1 is shifted into the leftmost bit. When $x = 0$, the register shifts left, loading 0's from the right. After the input has been 0 for several clocks (or if the shift register is cleared), all bits will be 0. The output is 1 whenever there is a 1 in the left bit of the shift register and x is 0. Note that if there are more than 12 consecutive 1 inputs, the shift register will contain all 1's. When the input goes to 0, the output will be 1 for 12 clock times. Thus, this solution handles the situation where there are more 1 inputs than the register can hold (similar to the second counter design).

If the input could go to 1 again while the output is still 1, we need an extra flip flop, Q, here, as well. This flip flop is set ($J = 1$) when $x = 0$ and q_2 of the left shift register is 1 (indicating that there have been at least two 1's). It is cleared ($K = 1$) when q_2 is 0 (indicating that there are no more than one more 1 to be output). S_0 becomes xQ' and S_1 becomes $x' + Q$.

Design a counter that goes through the following sequence of 16 states

    1 2 4 7 11 0 6 13 5 14 8 3 15 12 10 9, and repeat

EXAMPLE 7.7

It does not matter where it starts. For the combinational logic, there are packages of NAND gates (7400, 7404, 7410, 7420, and 7430) available at 50¢ each. We will consider two alternative designs and compare them. The first uses four JK flip flops at a total cost of $2.00. The second uses a 4-bit synchronous counter (such as the 74161) and a combinational decoder block. This block takes the output of the counter that goes 0, 1, 2, 3, 4, . . . and translates the 0 to 1, the 1 to 2, the 2 to 4, and so forth.

First, we will design the counter using *JK* flip flops. The state table is shown.

D	C	B	A	D*	C*	B*	A*
0	0	0	0	0	1	1	0
0	0	0	1	0	0	1	0
0	0	1	0	0	1	0	0
0	0	1	1	1	1	1	1
0	1	0	0	0	1	1	1
0	1	0	1	1	1	1	0
0	1	1	0	1	1	0	1
0	1	1	1	1	0	1	1
1	0	0	0	0	0	1	1
1	0	0	1	0	0	0	1
1	0	1	0	1	0	0	1
1	0	1	1	0	0	0	0
1	1	0	0	1	0	1	0
1	1	0	1	0	1	0	1
1	1	1	0	1	0	0	0
1	1	1	1	1	1	0	0

We can map these functions and use the quick method to find the *JK* flip flop input equations, as follows.

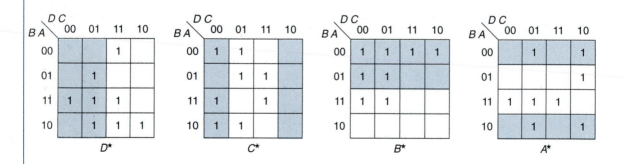

$$J_D = CA + CB + BA \qquad K_D = C'B' + C'A + B'A$$
$$J_C = D'A' + D'B \qquad K_C = DA' + D'BA$$
$$J_B = D' + A' \qquad K_B = D + A'$$
$$J_A = D'C + DC' \qquad K_C = D'B' + CB' + DC'B$$

This would require 18 two-input gates and 5 three-input gates or a total of 7 integrated circuit packages at 50¢ each. Thus, the total cost is $5.50.

For the other approach, we construct the following truth table for the decoder block:

D	C	B	A	W	X	Y	Z
0	0	0	0	0	0	0	1
0	0	0	1	0	0	1	0
0	0	1	0	0	1	0	0
0	0	1	1	0	1	1	1
0	1	0	0	1	0	1	1
0	1	0	1	0	0	0	0
0	1	1	0	0	1	1	0
0	1	1	1	1	1	0	1
1	0	0	0	0	1	0	1
1	0	0	1	1	1	1	0
1	0	1	0	1	0	0	0
1	0	1	1	0	0	1	1
1	1	0	0	1	1	1	1
1	1	0	1	1	1	0	0
1	1	1	0	1	0	1	0
1	1	1	1	1	0	0	1

The output maps follow.

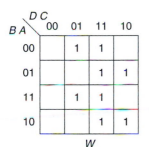

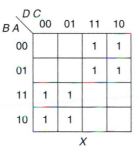

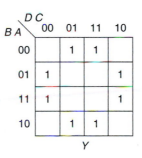

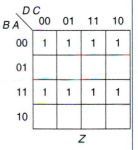

$W = CB'A' + DB'A + CBA + DBA'$

$X = DB' + D'B$

$Y = C'A + CA'$

$Z = B'A' + BA$

This requires 9 two-input gates, 4 three-input gates, and 1 four-input gate. In addition, we need four NOT gates (a 7404 package), since only the uncomplemented outputs from the counter (D, C, B, and A) are available. The total required is six packages. Thus, this approach costs $3.00 plus the cost of the counter and is less expensive if the counter costs less than $2.50.

It is interesting to note that if we built the counter using four JK flip flops, we would only need to create the functions BA and CBA. That would require just two NOT gates, since $(BA)'$ and $(CBA)'$ are used in W and Z. Thus, we end up with only six packages and a total cost of $5.00, which is less expensive than the first solution. This solution is best if the counter costs more than $2.00.

[SP 5, 6; EX 6, 9, 10, 11, 12, 13, 14, 15]

7.8 SOLVED PROBLEMS

1. Design a Mealy system using a 74164 shift register and whatever gates are needed to produce an output of 1 when the last six inputs have been 1, and 0 otherwise.

The shift register stores the previous eight inputs; we only need the five most recent ones. The circuit is shown below.

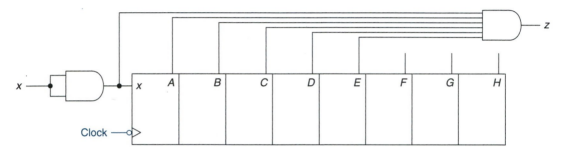

(We really only needed a 5-bit shift register, but it is easier and less expensive to use an 8-bit one than to build a 5-bit one with flip flops.)

2. Design a Moore circuit, using a 74164 shift register and AND, OR, and NOT gates to produce a 1 output for every 8th 1 input (not necessarily consecutive). We are not concerned about when the first output comes, as long as there is a 1 for every eight 1 inputs thereafter.

We will input a 1 to the shift register, clocking it only when the input is 1. When a 1 reaches the last flip flop, *H,* the shift register will be cleared. We can take the output from *G* (or from any of the first seven flip flops); it goes to 1 on the seventh 1 input and is cleared shortly after the eighth. A block diagram is as follows:

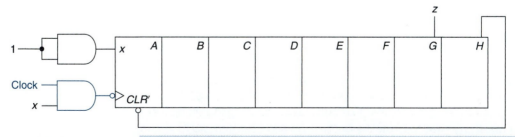

3. Design a Mealy system, using a 74161 counter and AND, OR, and NOT gates that produces a 1 output when the input has been 1 for at least 12 consecutive clock times.

The counter will be reset whenever the input is 0 and will be allowed to count when the input is 1 until the count reaches 11. At that point, if the input is 1, there will be a 1 output. A block diagram is shown below.

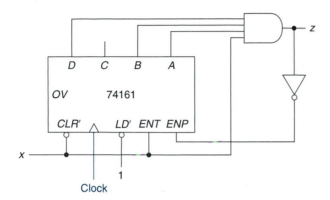

Note that the counter is enabled whenever $x = 1$ and the output is not already 1; that keeps it from counting beyond 11.

4. Design a system such that when the input, x, goes to 1 during one clock period, the output, z, will be the next eight consecutive clocks. At all other times z will be 0. Assume that x remains 0 throughout the period of nonzero output. Show the block diagram.

Example:

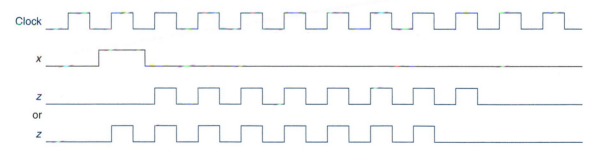

Use AND, OR, and NOT gates plus either

a. a trailing-edge triggered 8-bit serial-in, serial-out shift register with a static, active low clear, *CLR'*, or

b. a trailing-edge triggered 4-bit counter with a static, active low clear, *CLR'*.

Assume either that this has been running for a while or that we don't look at the output before the first time $x = 1$.

a. We will use x to clear the shift register and will clock a 1 into the leftmost bit at each clock time thereafter. The output will be taken from the right bit; when it is 0, there will be a clock pulse.

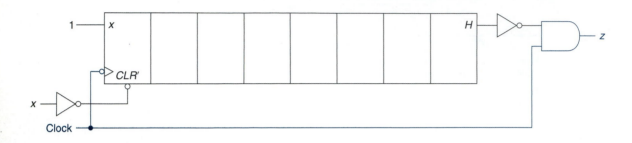

This circuit produces the second timing picture, since the first output occurs during the time x is 1. Note that this only uses the serial output; if H' is available, we do not need the output NOT gate.

---

b. For the counter design, we will use x to clear the counter and let it count as long as the count is less than 8 (that is, $D = 0$). Either of the following circuits could be used if the clear is static, and the timing is that of the second example. Only the circuit on the right can be used with a clocked clear; it produces the timing of the first example.

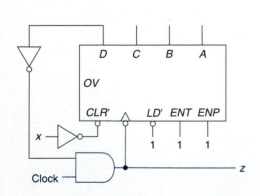

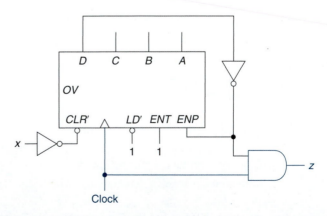

5. Design a system that counts up from 1 to 6 (and repeat) when input x is 0 and down from 6 to 1 when $x = 1$ and displays the results on a die. The die has seven lights (as shown in the diagram).

A 1 for each segment (a, b, c, d, e, f, g) indicates that it is lit; a 0 that it is not. The arrangement for the six numbers on a die are shown here, where the darkened circles are to be lit.

Design the counter, using three D flip flops to count from 1 (001) to 6 (110) and repeat. Then, design a decoder/driver that takes the outputs from the counter and produces the seven signals (a, b, c, d, e, f, g) to drive the display. Use a 16R4 PLD. (That works since there are really only four distinct outputs; a and g, b and f, and c and e are always the same.)

Labeling the flip flops F, G, and H, we get the following truth table for the system. There are only eight rows for the display inputs, since they do not depend on x.

x	F	G	H	D_F	D_G	D_H	$a = g$	$b = f$	$c = e$	d
0	0	0	0	X	X	X	X	X	X	X
0	0	0	1	0	1	0	0	0	0	1
0	0	1	0	0	1	1	1	0	0	0
0	0	1	1	1	0	0	1	0	0	1
0	1	0	0	1	0	1	1	0	1	0
0	1	0	1	1	1	0	1	0	1	1
0	1	1	0	0	0	1	1	1	1	0
0	1	1	1	X	X	X	X	X	X	X
1	0	0	0	X	X	X				
1	0	0	1	1	1	0				
1	0	1	0	0	0	1				
1	0	1	1	0	1	0				
1	1	0	0	0	1	1				
1	1	0	1	1	0	0				
1	1	1	0	1	0	1				
1	1	1	1	X	X	X				

The maps for the seven functions are shown below.

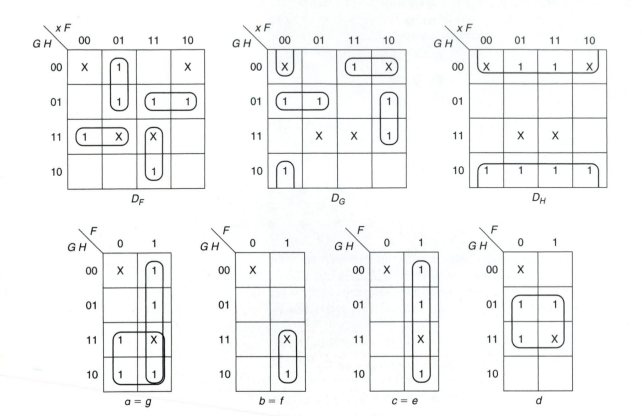

$$D_F = x'FG' + xG'H + xFG + x'GH$$
$$D_G = x'F'H' + x'G'H + xG'H' + xF'H$$
$$D_H = H'$$
$$a = g = F + G \qquad c = e = F$$
$$b = f = FG \qquad d = H$$

The PLD diagram is shown next. (Only those gates that are used are shown.)

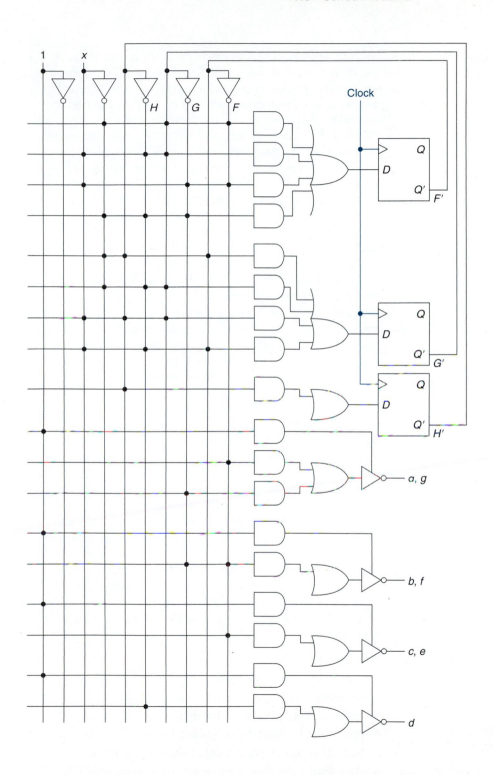

6. We are designing a rather rudimentary alarm system. The first part of the system includes a flip flop A that is 1 if the alarm is set (armed) and 0 if it is not, and a keypad (with 10 keys and 4 output lines). It produces an output of all 1's if no key is pushed or 0000 to 1001 if one of keys 0 to 9 are pushed. (You may assume that two keys are never pushed at the same time and that the keypad never produces one of the other five combinations.)

To set or clear the alarm, a 3-digit combination must be entered. Hidden away in the control box is a set of three 10-position switches (that contains the 3-digit alarm code). The switches each produce a 4-bit number, $R_{1:4}$, $S_{1:4}$, and $T_{1:4}$. As one pushes the buttons to enter the alarm code, the first digit will appear on the keypad output for several clock periods, followed by a hexadecimal F (indicating that no key is pushed) for several more clock periods, followed by the second digit, etc. We must design a system that watches the keypad and, if the right code is received, complements A. (Note: Like many alarms, the same code is used to arm the alarm, that is, put a 1 in A, as to disarm it.) Assume that there is at least one clock period when no key is pushed between digits. However, if another key is not depressed within 100 clocks, the system goes back to looking for the first digit.

The second part of the system is used to sound the alarm. There is an input signal, D, indicating that a door is open (1) or closed (0) and an output, N, indicating that the alarm is sounded (1) or not (0). (Of course, A is also an input to this part of the system.) When the alarm is first armed, the door must be closed within 1000 clock pulses or the alarm will sound. (Note that this gives the user the chance to set the alarm and go out without the alarm sounding.) Also, if the alarm has been armed for more than 1000 clock periods and the door is opened, the alarm will sound if it is not disarmed within 1000 clock periods.

Design both parts of this system. Available components include trailing-edge triggered *JK* flip flops, synchronous 4-bit binary or decimal counters, and whatever gates that are needed. Show a modular diagram that shows various parts, also a detailed block diagram or the equations for each part, and an ASM diagram for the first part.

One approach to the first part uses the following set of states:

1. Waiting for first input digit.
2. Have first input digit, waiting for key to be released.
3. Nothing pushed, but have first digit—waiting for second.
4. Have first two input digits, waiting for key to be released.
5. Nothing pushed, have two digits—waiting for third.
6. Have third input digit, waiting for key to be released.

An ASM diagram, ignoring the 100 clock timeout, is shown next.

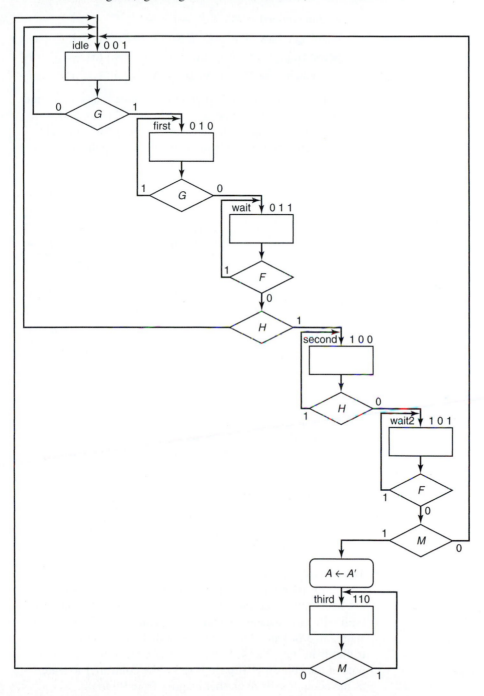

If we call the inputs from the keyboard $X_{1:4}$, then

Nothing pushed $= X_1X_2X_3X_4 = F$
First Digit $= (X_1 \oplus R_1)'(X_2 \oplus R_2)'(X_3 \oplus R_3)'(X_4 \oplus R_4)' = G$
Second digit $= (X_1 \oplus S_1)'(X_2 \oplus S_2)'(X_3 \oplus S_3)'(X_4 \oplus S_4)' = H$
Third digit $= (X_1 \oplus T_1)'(X_2 \oplus T_2)'(X_3 \oplus T_3)'(X_4 \oplus T_4)' = M$

This is a seven-variable problem: the three states q_1, q_2, and q_3, and the functions produced by the inputs, F, G, H, and M. We will code the states in binary (for example, 3 will be 011). We will then produce a table in binary, separating the three flip flop next state sections.

q_1	q_2	q_3	F	G	H	M	#	F	G	H	M	#	F	G	H	M	#
			$q_1^\star$					$q_2^\star$					$q_3^\star$				
0	0	0	X	X	X	X	X	X	X	X	X	X	X	X	X	X	X
0	0	1	0	0	0	0	0	0	1	0	0	0	1	0	1	1	1
0	1	0	0	0	X	X	X	1	1	X	X	X	1	0	X	X	X
0	1	1	0	0	1	0	0	1	0	0	0	0	1	1	0	1	1
1	0	0	1	X	1	X	X	0	X	0	X	X	1	X	0	X	X
1	0	1	1	0	0	1	0	0	0	0	1	0	1	1	1	0	1
1	1	0	0	X	X	1	X	0	X	X	1	X	1	X	X	0	X
1	1	1	X	X	X	X	X	X	X	X	X	X	X	X	X	X	X

where $\# = F'G'H'M'$. Note, only one of F, G, H, or M can be 1.

We found expressions for the next state by considering one column of the table at a time. Although this might not be minimum, it is close.

$$q_1^\star = Fq_1q_2' + H(q_2 + q_3') + Mq_1$$
$$q_2^\star = Fq_1'q_2 + G(q_1'q_2' + q_3') + Mq_1$$
$$q_3^\star = F + G(q_1 + q_2q_3) + H(q_1'q_2' + q_1q_3) + Mq_1'$$
$$+ F'G'H'M'$$

The control flip flop, A, is complemented when this controller goes from state 5 to 6, that is, on $q_1q_2'q_3M$. The one thing that has been omitted so far is the time out. A base 100 counter is built with two decade counters. It is cleared when going from state 2 to 3 or from 4 to 5 and is enabled whenever the controller is in state 2 or 4. It uses the static clear and preset inputs of the controller flip flops to set the controller to state 1 as the counter rolls over, that is, goes from 99 to 00.

Next we will design the alarm control. When A goes to 1, a three-digit decade counter will be cleared. When that reaches 1000, a second flip flop, B, will be set. When B is set and D goes to 1, we will start to count to 1000 again. If, by the time the counter gets to 1000, A does not go to 0, the alarm will sound; flip flop N will go to 1. Both B and N are cleared when A goes to 0. A diagram of the system follows.

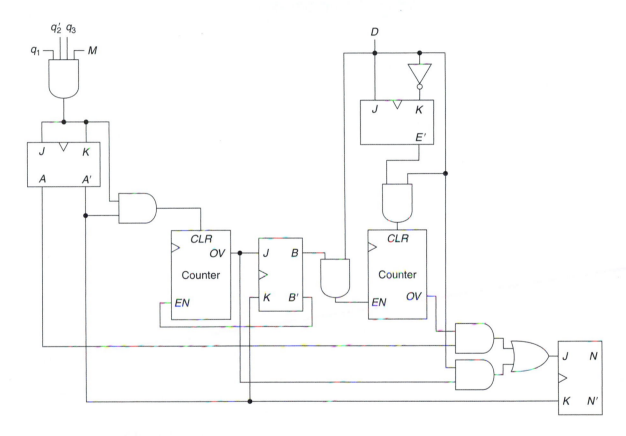

In this diagram, all of the clock inputs are connected to the system clock (but not shown to simplify the diagram). The two counters are base 1000 (that is, three decade counters cascaded); all inputs are assumed to be active high. When A goes to 1, the first counter is cleared. Flip flop B is 0, since it is cleared whenever A has been 0. It will be set when the counter reaches 1000. However, the alarm will be sounded if the door is still open (first counter overflows and door is open). The alarm flip flop (N) remains set until the code is entered to clear A. The E flip flop is used to produce a clear signal for the second counter when the door is first opened. That counter is enabled when the door is open and $B = 1$. The alarm will sound if it has not been disarmed (causing A and B to go to 0) within 1000 clocks.

7.9   EXERCISES

1. Using a 74164 shift register, design a Mealy system that produces an output of 1 when the last nine inputs were 0.

2. Using two 74164 shift registers, design a Moore system whose output is 1 when there have been exactly six 1's followed by exactly eight 0 inputs.

3. Design a system using a counter that produces a 1 output when the input has been 1 for eight or more consecutive clock times.

   a. Use a counter with a clocked active low clear and no enable input.

   b. Use a counter with a static active low clear and an active high enable.

*4. Design a system that has an output of 1 when the input has been 0 for exactly seven clock times. In addition to combinational logic blocks, one of the following is available:

   a. A 4-bit counter, with an active low clocked CLR'

   b. An 8-bit shift register

5. Design a sequential system that has a clock pulse input and produces a pulse that is coincident with every 25th clock pulse. (We do not care about initializing the system.)

   The only available components are

   1. AND gates (any number of inputs)

   2. Inverters (NOT gates)

   3. Two base 16 counters (as described below)

   The counter is trailing-edge triggered. It has four outputs: D (high order bit), C, B, and A. It has a clock input and an active low static $Clear'$ input. There is also an active low static $Load'$ input, along with data input lines, IN_D, IN_C, IN_B, and IN_A. (Assume that $Clear'$ and $Load'$ are never both 0 at the same time. When either is 0, it overrides the clock.)

   a. Design a system using these components that uses the $Clear'$ input, but not the $Load'$ input.

   b. Design a system using these components that uses the $Load'$ input, but not the $Clear'$ input.

6. Design a system using

 a. a 74190

 b. a 74192

 plus whatever other logic that is needed (including a flip flop) to go through the sequence

    0 1 2 3 4 5 6 7 8 9 8 7 6 5 4 3 2 1 (0 1) and repeat.

7. Implement the controller for the system of Example 7.6 using D flip flops and NAND gates.

*8. Show the ASM diagram for the controller of a system that has a 16-bit register, A, and a 4-bit register, N. When a signal of 1 appears on input line s, the register A is shifted right the number of places (0 to 15) as specified by N (with 0's put in the left bits). The register A can be shifted only one place at a time. The register N can be decremented (decreased by 1). When shifting is complete, a 1 is to appear on output line d for two clock periods.

*9. Design a system that consists of three components, a counter, a display driver, and a seven-segment display, as shown.

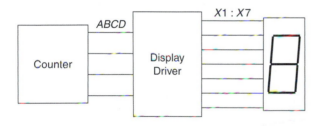

 a. Design the counter using four JK flip flops, A, B, C, and D, and a minimum number of NOR gates. The counter is binary-coded-decimal, using 2421 code (as described in Table 1.7) and is to go through the sequence:

    0 3 6 9 2 5 8 1 4 7 and repeat

 Thus, the counter sequences 0000, 0011, 1100, 1111, 0010, etc. After completing the design of this counter, draw a state graph. Make sure that it shows what happens if the counter is turned on and comes up in one of the unused states (for example, 0101).

 b. The outputs of the counter are inputs to the display driver. It is just a four-input, seven-output combinational circuit. If one of the unused codes turns up (for example, the counter is turned on and $ABCD = 0111$), the display should be blank (that is, all seven inputs should be 0). Find a near minimum sum of products implementation of *X1, X2, X3, X4, X5, X6,* and *X7.* (Use the versions of 6, 7, and 9 without the extra segment lit.) (There is a solution with 17 gates and 56 inputs.)

10. We already have a decimal counter that sequences

    0000 0001 0010 0011 0100 0101 0110 0111 1000 1001 and repeat.

    It has flip flops *W, X, Y,* and *Z.* We still want the display to cycle through 0, 3, 6, 9, 2, 5, 8, 1, 4, 7, and repeat (as in Exercise 9). Accomplish this by designing another box to go between the counter and the display driver of Exercise 9b. Note that this means, for example, that when the counter has $WXYZ = 0010$, the display is to be 6 and thus $ABCD = 1100$ (6 in 2421 code). Implement this box with a PLA with four inputs and four outputs.

11. Show a block diagram of a system whose output, *z,* is 1 if and only if at least two of the latest three inputs (including the - present one) are 0. There is no need to show a state table or state diagram. Any kind of flip flops and gates may be used.

*12. Design a sequential system (a counter) with one input line, *x,* and three flip flops, *A, B,* and *C.* When $x = 0$, the system sequences through the states (0, 1, 2, 3, 4), 0, . . . and when $x = 1$, the system sequences through the states (2, 3, 4, 5, 6, 7), 2, ... If, at any time, *x* is 0 when the system is in states 5, 6, or 7, or if *x* is 1 when the system is in states 0 or 1, it should go to state 3 on the next clock.

    a. The available components are

       7400, 7404, 7410, 7420, and 7430 (NAND
       gate packages)   25¢ each
       Dual *JK* trailing-edge triggered flip
       flop packages $1.00 each
       Dual *D* flip flop packages   cost to be determined

       Design the system two ways:
       i. First, using *JK* flip flops
       ii. Second, using *D* flip flops.
       Show the equations for both designs and a block diagram of one of them.

    b. Determine the price range for the *D* flip flop packages for which it would be more economical to use

       all *JK* flip flops
       one package of *JK* and one of *D*
       all *D* flip flops.

c. We would like to add an output that is 1 whenever the system is in state 3 and got there because it was out of sequence (when x is 0 and the system is in states 5, 6, or 7, or if x is 1 and the system is in states 0 or 1). This requires another flip flop.

d. Design the system of part c using a PLD. (Any of the ones we described will do.)

13. Design a clock display to show the time in hours, minutes, and seconds. Assume that we have a clock of exactly 1 KHz. (1000 clock pulses per second). It will use six seven-segment displays and operate either in military time (hours 00 to 23) or regular time (1 to 12, with AM and PM). An input line, x, differentiates between the two. A seventh display is used to show A or P in the latter case; it is blank otherwise. Assume that there is a BCD-to-seven-segment decoder driver available; one is needed for each display other than the AM/PM one.

a. Design this using asynchronous counters (utilizing the 7490 and 7492). The problem with these is that they can not be set arbitrarily.

b. Design this using synchronous counters with static load inputs. (They would require a large number of switches to set this to some arbitrary time, four for each digit.)

c. For either design, provide a set function for minutes and hours as follows:

> When input f is 0, the clock operates normally; when $f = 1$, we can adjust the time.
>
> When $f = 1$ and $g = 1$, the hour advances once every second.
>
> When $f = 1$ and $h = 1$, the minute advances once every second.
>
> Also, when $f = 1$, the seconds go to 00.

14. Design a counter that goes through the following sequence of 12 states

    10 4 5 1 2 8 11 3 9 12 13 0, and repeat.

It is not important where it starts. The available packages are NAND gates (7400, 7404, 7410, 7420, and 7430) at 50¢ each, plus the storage devices as described.

Consider three alternative designs and compare them. For each, show the equations and a block diagram. Label the four outputs in each design W (high-order bit), X, Y, Z.

a. The available storage devices are four JK flip flops at a total cost of $2.50.

b. The available storage devices are four *D* flip flops at a cost to be determined.

c. There is a 74161 4-bit synchronous counter and we must build a combinational decoder block. This block takes the output of the counter that goes 0, 1, 2, 3, 4, . . . and translates the 0 to 10, the 1 to 4, the 2 to 5, the 3 to 1, the 4 to 2, and so forth. It must also go back to state 0 from state 11.

    Comparing the three designs, how much must the *D* flip flops cost for design b to be less expensive than design a, and how much must the counter cost for design c to be less expensive than design a?

15. a. Repeat Solved Problem 5, so that we can count to 7, where a 7 lights all of the dots on the die display.

   b. Repeat Solved Problem 5, so that we can count from 0 (no lights lit) to 7, but the counter saturates (that is, it remains at 7 counting up or 0 counting down, rather than recycling).

7.10 CHAPTER 7 TEST (25 MINUTES)

Show two designs for a Mealy system that produces an output of 1 if and only if the input is 0 for exactly seven consecutive clock times. In addition to AND, OR, and NOT gates, we have available an 8-bit serial-in, parallel-out shift register, with an active low, clocked clear (that works whether or not the counter is enabled) for one and a 4-bit counter with an active low, static clear, and an active low enable for the other.

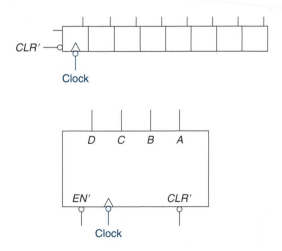

Part II   Computer Design

Computer Organization

8

U p to now, we have been studying general digital systems. The remainder of the book concentrates on the design of digital computers. In this chapter, we will look at a variety of organizations of computers. In Chapter 10, we will look more closely at the design of a sample computer that we call *MODEL*.

A block diagram of a computer is shown in Figure 8.1. The *Central Processing Unit (CPU)* contains all of the internal registers of the machine, the arithmetic and logic circuits (such as the adder), and the controller (which produces the timing signals to coordinate the activities of the machine). *BUS* is a set of wires, over which data, addresses, and control signals are transferred between the CPU and the rest of the machine. (In most computers, there are also one or more buses internal to the CPU.) We will examine the structure of buses in Chapter 9.

The *main memory* is a fast, random access* memory. There are usually *secondary memory* devices, such as disks, that are connected to BUS and include controllers (adaptors). The *Input/Output (I/O) controllers* interface between BUS and the outside world. We will discuss memory and I/O interfaces in detail in Chapter 11.

Figure 8.1   A computer.

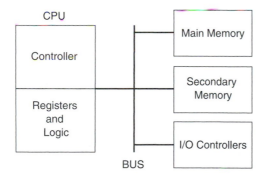

---

*By random access, we mean that the time to access (read or write) each word in memory is the same. In other devices, such as a disk, the access time depends on the location of the word relative to the read/write heads.

A memory *word* is the smallest addressable element. Word sizes are typically 16 to 64 bits, although both smaller and larger sizes have been used.* Modern computers have several million words of main memory, typically requiring addresses of 24 bits ($2^{24} \approx 16$ million) or more. Indeed, memories storing several gigabytes (billion bytes) are common.

Although main memory is fast, the CPU can often utilize information even faster than it can retrieve it from memory. The register and logic section of a computer has a number of internal registers, for storing information while an instruction is being processed. It may also include a small amount of user memory. Most machines have a set of user-addressable registers (often 16 to 64 of these) for the temporary storage of data. Access to these registers is usually faster than to main memory and does not utilize BUS, making BUS available for other activity. Also, a register address is shorter than a memory address, requiring only 5 bits for 32 (2^5) registers. Many machines also have a *cache* (not shown in Figure 8.1)—a small memory, with complex hardware, that stores recently used memory words (both instructions and data).

The workhorse of the register and logic section is the *Arithmetic and Logic Unit (ALU)*. It contains circuitry for adding and subtracting fixed-point numbers and bitwise logic operations such as AND and OR, and for shifting or rotating sets of bits. It may contain multiplication and division hardware or perform these operations by a sequence of additions or subtractions and shifts. It may also contain the logic for floating-point arithmetic, or that may be contained in a separate unit. The ALU gets all its operands from registers.

Computers execute a sequence of instructions, stored in memory. (Although some special purpose machines have separate memories for instructions and data, most computers have a single main memory.) Computers store instructions in sequence in the main memory. One register, usually referred to as the *program counter,* stores the address of the beginning of the next instruction. It is automatically updated as each instruction is executed.

Examples of computer instructions are

Add two numbers and store the result (ADD)

Increment (add one to) a number (INC)

Jump out of sequence if a flag bit[†] is zero (modify the program counter)

---

*Some computers address bytes (8 bits) and may provide instructions that work with data of various sizes.

[†]A flag bit is part of the register and logic section that stores information about machine operations. The contents of a flag bit is sometimes referred to as a condition code. For example, there may be a bit indicating whether the result of the last arithmetic operation was negative.

Each instruction must contain a code for the operation to be performed (the *op-code*), a specification of where to find the data, where to store the result, and, sometimes, the address of the next instruction.* In some computer architectures, each instruction fits in one memory word. In others, as we will see in the next section, some instructions require multiple words. Some structures pack more than one instruction into a word.

To execute a sequence of instructions, the computer performs the following step-by-step procedure (returning to step 1 after completing each instruction):

1. Send the address of the instruction (from the program counter) to memory to fetch the instruction. Save that word in an internal register of the CPU, sometimes called the *instruction register*. (When it is necessary to fetch more than one word to obtain the complete instruction, the program counter is incremented to get each additional word; see Section 8.1.1.)

2. Update the program counter so that it points to the (first word of the) next instruction. (That means incrementing it; possibly again if the present instruction required more than one word.)

3. Decode the instruction, that is, determine what operation is to be performed and what operands, if any, are needed. (In machines with variable-length instructions, this may be done as part of step 1.)

4. Obtain the operands. Some may be in registers and others in memory. In the latter case, the address may need to be computed and the data fetched from memory into a CPU register.

5. Execute the instruction, that is, do the computation (if any) required.

6. Store the result, if any, either in memory or in a register. (For jump instructions, the result may be the address of the next instruction, which is stored in the program counter.)

8.1 WORD STRUCTURE

In the design of a computer, two factors affect the number of bits in a word. One is the number of bits needed to specify an instruction. The other is the size of the data to be processed. The instruction word and the type of data to be processed often affect the word size in conflicting ways.

---

*In most modern computers, the first word of the next instruction is assumed to be stored in the location following the present instruction for all instructions other than branches. In some early computers, every instruction included the address of the next instruction.

Many internal registers of the CPU hold one word. Both internal and external busses typically can move one word at a time. Thus, a larger word makes the CPU hardware and the bus more expensive. On the other hand, it often speeds up the processing. (In some machines, it is possible to simultaneously access several words from memory, resulting in a larger bus, but not larger CPU registers.) The final design is generally a compromise between cost, speed, and efficiency.

8.1.1 Instruction Formats and Word Size

A typical two-operand instruction, such as ADD, must specify each of the operands as well as where the result is to be stored. One approach is to provide space for three addresses in the instructions, as shown in Figure 8.2a. Each address field in an instruction may specify a memory location, a register number, the actual data, or partial information with a key to computing the *effective address* (the memory address where the data is or the result is to be stored). Thus, the address field will often consist of two parts: the addressing mode and the address itself. In Section 8.3, we will consider a variety of addressing modes. If the three locations are all memory addresses, the instruction would be very long, 104 bits if the op-code was eight bits, the mode for each address required 4 bits, and memory addresses were 28 bits. This approach is not widely used for two reasons. First, it requires very long instructions. Second, two data words must be fetched from main memory, and the result must be stored in main memory. Since memory references are usually slower than the speed of the CPU, this slows the execution of the machine.

Several approaches have been taken to deal with this problem. One way to shorten the instruction would be to require that the result be stored in place of one of the operands. Thus, the first address would become Destination/Source1, as indicated in Figure 8.2b. (Thus, the sum

Figure 8.2 Instruction Formats.

a. Three-Address Instruction

OP	Destination	Source1	Source2

b. Two-Address Format

OP	Destination/Source1	Source2

c. One-Register/ One-Memory Address

OP	RN	Source2

would replace the first operand in an ADD instruction.) This does not address the speed issue, but does shorten the instruction by about 30%.

The main example that we will examine in Chapter 10, MODEL, shortens the instruction length further, by requiring that Destination/Source1 be a register, rather than a memory location. That reduces the first address field from 32–36 bits to only 6–8 bits, as seen in Figure 8.2c (where the RN field specifies a register number). This approach uses only one memory reference for data.

Some machines require that all computation be done on data stored in registers and that the result be returned to a register. Only *Read* and *Store* would reference memory. Although the format of ADD would be similar to that of Figure 8.2a, the address fields would all be short.

The formats of parts b and c of Figure 8.2 would also be used with two-address instructions, such as one to *Move* the contents of one location to another. (In a structure such as that of Figure 8.2c, these instructions are referred to as *Load* a register from memory and *Store* a register to memory.)

Many machines also have instructions that do not require any memory address, just one or more register references. They would require as little as 16 bits.

The most straightforward structure would have each instruction in a single word. But, that would require very long words for instructions with two or three addresses. Even for the single address structure of Figure 8.2c, the word would be 48 bits (8 + 8 + 32) or longer. However, not all instructions require that many bits, which would result in a great deal of wasted memory space.

A second approach is to provide enough space in one memory word for shorter instructions and require two or more words for longer ones. The format of the first word of a MODEL instruction is shown in Figure 8.2d. The Mode field determines whether or not a second word is needed.

Figure 8.2d   MODEL instruction format.

0	5 6	11 12	15 16	31
Op-Code	RN	Mode	Address	

A third approach is to have large words, for example, 64 bits. Each instruction uses as many 16-bit segments as are needed. Instructions may be contained in a single word or overlap words. Figure 8.3a shows an example, where instruction *A* uses two segments, instruction *B* uses one segment, instruction *C* uses three segments, and instruction *D* uses two segments.

Figure 8.3a Variable-length instructions.

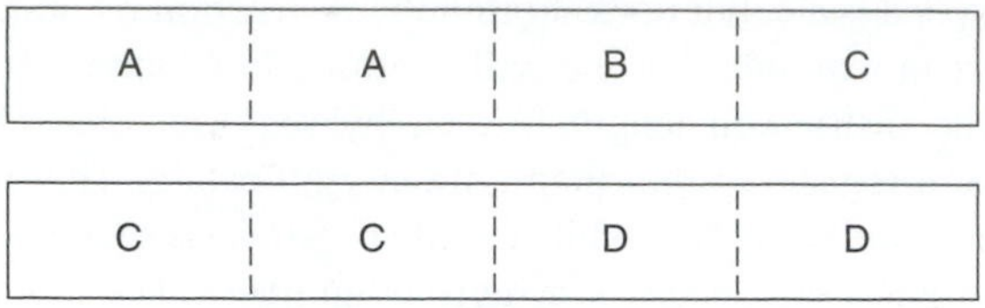

One problem with this arrangement is that instructions *B, C,* and *D* start in the middle of a word. If the machine can only address whole words, then all destinations of branches must be to instructions that start at the beginning of a word (such as *A*). If we wish to jump to instruction *D* (but not *B* or *C*), we would need to waste two segments and arrange instructions as shown in Figure 8.3b, where we insert no-op (no operation) in the last two segments of the second word.

Figure 8.3b Adding ability to jump to instruction *D*.

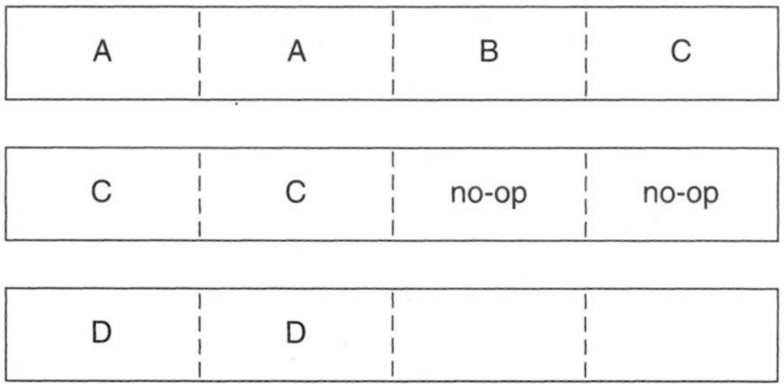

EXAMPLE 8.1

We have a computer with a maximum memory size of 1 Gwords (2^{30} words), 32 registers, and 200 instruction types (requiring an 8-bit op-code). In addition, 4 bits are required to specify the address type. For a machine in which instructions can reference one register and one memory address, an instruction would require

$$8 + 5 + 4 + 30 = 47 \text{ bits}$$

If we had a 24-bit word size, then instructions requiring an address would use 2 words. Instructions that used 1 (where the address type specified a 5-bit register number in place of a 30-bit address) could fit in one word.

[SP 1; EX 1]

8.1.2 Data and Word Sizes

The simplest structure would be to make the word large enough to hold the largest piece of data required.

> ASIDE: This is a completely separate consideration from the word size for an instruction. Indeed, the two needs often require a compromise.

The number of bits for data determines the precision of that data. For fixed-point data, 32 bits gives approximately 9.5 decimal digits of precision, and a range of integers of approximately ± 2 billion. If fractions are needed (such as dollars and cents*), then a smaller range is available.

Most computers provide floating-point numbers, as well as integers, providing about one third of the bits for the exponent and the remainder for the mantissa. (See Section 1.2.5.) Floating-point numbers usually require words of at least 32 bits.

Both greater precision and range can be achieved by using 2 (or more) words for data. Some machines provide both single- and double-precision instructions. Others provide for multiple-precision addition and subtraction by storing the carry from the most significant bit of the adder and providing instructions that use that carry as the input to the least significant bit for the next addition (or subtraction). (Obviously, this approach is slower, since it requires reading and decoding two instructions.)

As in the case of instructions, we often need different sizes of data (that is, sometimes more bits and other times fewer bits).

EXAMPLE 8.2

A machine with 24-bit words would have a range of

Unsigned integers	0 to $2^{24} - 1$	($\approx$ 16 million)
Signed integers	-2^{23} to $2^{23} - 1$	($\approx \pm 8$ million)

For floating point, it might use 8 bits for the exponent, giving a range $2^{\pm 128}$ or approximately $10^{\pm 38}$. There would be 16 bits for the mantissa (including sign), allowing about 4.5 decimal digits of precision.

8.2 REGISTER SET

Most machines have a set of general-purpose registers to hold both data and memory addresses. These registers are numbered; 32 (2^5) or 64 (2^6) are common sizes for that set. Some have separate sets of registers for floating-point data, and some machines have a much larger set of registers. Each register is the size of a memory word. There are two advantages to having data in registers. First, data can be accessed more quickly, typically in one CPU clock time. On the other hand, data in memory often requires a few clock periods (even several sometimes). Second, the number of bits to address a register is much smaller (5 or 6) compared with 20 to 32 to address a memory location. These registers are under the control of the programmer (user).

---

*Since cents (which are fractions) cannot be represented exactly in binary (See the discussion in Section 1.2.5.), BCD is sometimes used for financial data.

There are additional *user-accessible* registers, such as the stack pointer and the program counter.* In addition, there are internal registers used to store information during the execution of an instruction, such as the instruction register.

There is typically either a *status register* or a set of *flag bits*. Some of these bits indicate whether the result of the last instruction (that modified that bit) produced a zero or negative result, or produced overflow or a carry (from add or a borrow from subtract). Others may be used for input/output information.

The user-accessible registers (including the status register) are referred to as the *state* of the machine. They are the only registers that contain useful information between instructions.

EXAMPLE 8.3	**User Registers of Model**	**Internal Registers of Model**
	Register set (REG$^{0:63}$)	Instruction register (IR)
	Stack pointer (SP)	Effective address register (EA)
	Program counter (PC)	Working data (WORK)
	Flags (*z, n, c, v*)	

 **8.3 ADDRESSING MODES**

The addressing field is used either to obtain an *effective address (EA)*, the actual memory location to be used, or the data required for the instruction. It is obtained in various ways, based on the *addressing mode*. To illustrate the various addressing modes, we will use the Load (LOD) instruction, which moves data from the location specified by the Mode and Address to the register specified by the *RN* field, and the structure of MODEL (the machine to be designed in Chapter 10), the instruction format for which is shown in Figure 8.2d.

EXAMPLE 8.4	To illustrate the definitions, we will assume (where all addresses, register numbers, and data are in hexadecimal):
	$RN = 6$
	REG^{23} = 45361287
	ADDRESS = 0123
	second word (if needed) = 456789AB
	PC = 98765432

---

*The user controls the program counter through change-of-flow instructions, such as Jump.

M[00000123]* = 12345678
M[00001357] = 12312312
M[12345678] = CDEF0123
M[45361287] = 00112233
M[456789AB] = 91919191
M[91919191] = FFFFFFFF
M[98760123] = 44445555
M[98765556] = 00000000

The simplest mode is *direct addressing*. The address field contains a complete address. But the address must be large enough to specify a memory location (32 bits in the case of MODEL). For the format shown in Figure 8.2d, the address is contained in the second word of the instruction. The ADDRESS field in the first word is unused. If addresses were short enough, they could fit in the remainder of the first word (but that would imply a very small memory for a 32-bit word size); see Exercise 3. If addresses were longer than 32 bits, part of the address might be contained in the first word, or a third word of the instruction might be necessary (as in Example 8.6).

Direct

EXAMPLE 8.4a

EA = 456789AB $REG^6 \leftarrow 91919191^\dagger$

Page zero (sometimes called page zero direct) addressing views the memory as consisting of pages, where the first bits of the address specify the page number and the remaining bits specify the word on that page. Page zero is that page where the leading bits of the address are all 0. In MODEL, bits 16 to 31 of the first word specify the last 16 bits of a page zero address. This is often referred to as *zero-extending* the address. The advantage of page zero addressing is that it allows the user to specify a direct address with only one instruction word. Frequently referenced information is then located on page zero.

Page zero

EXAMPLE 8.4b

EA = 00000123 $REG^6 \leftarrow 12345678$

---

*The notation M[00000123] refers to memory location 00000123.
†The arrow ($\leftarrow$) implies that the location on the left is loaded with the value on the right, that is, REG^6 is loaded with 91919191.

A variation of page zero is *current page,* where the leading bits of the address are the same as the leading bits of the address of the current instruction (that is, the leading bits of the program counter). This allows referencing of words that are close to the current instruction.

EXAMPLE 8.4c   **Current page**

$$EA = 98760123 \qquad REG^6 \leftarrow 44445555$$

For *indirect addressing,* the address contained in the instruction is a pointer to the effective address. Indirect addressing can use either a full address or a page zero address for the pointer. The contents of that memory location is then used as the address. (In a few systems (not MODEL), 1 bit of that fetched address is used to indicate whether that is really the address or it is still indirect. This is referred to as multiple-level indirect addressing, and it may continue to an unlimited number of levels.) In machines where an address does not fit in a single word (Example 8.6), the indirect address may require two memory reads.

EXAMPLE 8.4d   **Full address indirect**

$$EA \leftarrow M[456789AB] = 91919191 \qquad REG^6 \leftarrow FFFFFFFF$$

EXAMPLE 8.4e   **Page zero indirect**

$$EA \leftarrow M[456789AB] = 91919191 \qquad REG^6 \leftarrow CDEF0123$$

Immediate addressing provides a constant. The data is contained in the instruction. This mode does not produce an effective address, only data. Immediate addressing is not used for instructions that store results or for branch instructions. Two forms of this are often available. Full immediate (usually just referred to as immediate) has the data in the second word. *Short immediate* extends the address field to produce a full word of data. It is usually *sign-extended,* that is, copies of the sign bit are added in the front.

EXAMPLE 8.4f   **Immediate**

$$REG^6 \leftarrow 456789AB$$

EXAMPLE 8.4g   **Short Immediate**

$$REG^6 \leftarrow 00000123$$

EXAMPLE 8.4h   **Short Immediate**

If, instead, Address = 9876, the leading bit is 1, and it is extended with leading (binary) 1's
$$REG^6 \leftarrow FFFF9876$$

Register addressing (or *register direct*) gets data from (or stores data to) one of the registers (64 in MODEL). Six bits of the address field are used to specify which register. In MODEL, it is the last 6 bits of Address. This form of addressing does not compute an effective address and can be used to obtain or store data (but not for an instruction address).

Register   **EXAMPLE 8.4i**

$REG^6 \leftarrow 45361287$

Register indirect or *address register* addressing gets the effective address from the register specified by 6 bits of the address field.

Register indirect   **EXAMPLE 8.4j**

$EA = 45361287 \qquad REG^6 \leftarrow 00112233$

Register indirect with auto-post-incrementing uses the contents of the register as the effective address for this instruction, but then increments (adds 1 to) that register. This is useful for manipulating arrays, that is, sets of data stored in consecutive memory locations. The register would be initialized to the address of the first element of the array. Each time it is referenced with this form of addressing, the pointer is advanced to the next vector element. Some machines provide auto-decrementing (subtract 1) instead of or in addition to auto-incrementing. Some machines pre-increment or -decrement, that is, they update the register before using it. (In machines that provide double-precision arithmetic operations, auto-incrementing would add 2 to the register.)

Register indirect with auto-post-incrementing   **EXAMPLE 8.4k**

$EA = 45361287 \qquad REG^6 \leftarrow 00112233$
$REG^{23} \leftarrow 45361288$

Relative addressing computes the effective address by adding the constant included in the address field to the address of the next instruction (contained in the program counter after it has been incremented during the fetch of this instruction). This is usually a 1-word instruction and the address field is sign-extended (which allows addresses before and after that of the next instruction). This addressing mode is used most commonly with branch instructions, but could be used for any address computation.

EXAMPLE 8.4l

Relative

EA = 98765432 + 1 + 00000123 = 98765556

REG^6 ← 00000000

Index register addressing uses a register as an offset from the address. The address part of the instruction is added to the contents of the index register to produce the effective address. The index register may be a special register, a specific one of the register set, or any of the registers. In the last case, a 6-bit field is needed to specify that register. This is another way of accessing a particular element of an array; the address of the first element is contained in the address field, and the offset or the element number or the *index* is stored in the index register (hence, the name. This could use 1 word, for data on Page zero, or 2 words, with the address in the second word.) This addressing mode is useful when referencing similar elements in two different arrays.

Base register addressing utilizes the same hardware as index register addressing. This terminology is used when the register contains the address, and the address section of the instruction contains an offset. Since offsets may be fairly small, the offset could be contained in the remaining bits of the address section, usually sign-extended.

EXAMPLE 8.4m

Index or base register

If the index or base register contained 1234, and page zero were used

EA = 00001234 + 00000123 = 00001357

REG^6 ← 12312312

Stack addressing utilizes a last-in/first-out data structure. The stack behaves like a pile of plates in a cafeteria. Items are *pushed* onto the stack, that is placed on top of the pile, everything else thereby being pushed down. Items can then be *popped* from the stack, that is, the top item is removed and all others pop up. Figure 8.4 shows a view of the stack, starting with an empty stack, followed by two pushes, a pop, and another push.

Figure 8.4 Stack operation.

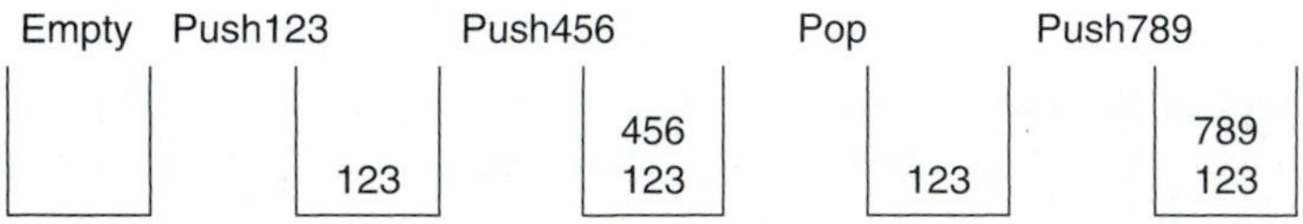

The stack is usually implemented by assigning a portion of main memory for it, with a register called the *stack pointer* used to indicate the

location of the top of the stack. We will discuss this in more detail in Chapter 10.

EXAMPLE 8.5

For each of the parts of Example 8.4, the number of memory references to fetch the instruction plus the number of references to compute the effective address plus the number to fetch the data is listed.

    a. $2 + 1 = 3$
    b. $1 + 1 = 2$
    c. $1 + 1 = 2$
    d. $2 + 1 + 1 = 4$
    e. $1 + 1 + 1 = 3$
    f. 2
    g. 1
    h. 1
    i. 1
    j. $1 + 1 = 2$
    k. $1 + 1 = 2$
    l. $1 + 1 = 2$
    m. $1 + 1 = 2$ for page zero
          $2 + 1 = 3$ for full address

For indirect (d and e), a memory reference is required to fetch the indirect addressing. For immediate and register addressing (f, g, h, and i), it is not necessary to fetch data from memory. In the next section, we will see how this computation must be modified for instructions other than Load.

EXAMPLE 8.6

Consider a machine with 20-bit words, 16 registers, and 2^{28} words of main memory. The instruction format of the first word of an instruction is

0	3	4	7	8	11	12	19

Op	Reg	Mode	Address

The last 8 bits of that word are the least significant bits of the 28-bit address. Each of the following are in hexadecimal. Those addressing modes that produce an address show the address; those that produce data show the data. For indirect and register indirect addressing, the word pointed to contains the last 8 bits of the address (in its right 8 bits). The first 20 bits are found in the next memory location or register. The register number is in the last 4 bits of Address.

    Address = 98

    PC = 1234567

    Second word (M[1234568]) = 34567

M[0000098] = 9ABCD
M[0000099] = 01234
REG^8 = 20304
REG^9 = 44444

Effective Address

Direct:	3456798
Page zero:	0000098
Current page:	1234598
Page zero indirect:	01234CD
Register indirect:	4444404

Register indirect, auto-post-incrementing:

4444404, $REG^8 \leftarrow$ 20305

Relative: 1234567 + 1 + 0000098 = 1234600

Data

Immediate:	34567
Short immediate:	FFF98
Register:	20304

[SP 2,3,4,5; EX 2,3,4,5]

8.4 INSTRUCTION SET

Instructions can be classified by the type of operation they perform, by the number of operands required, or the number of addresses required. We will use the first approach and look first at data movement instructions, then arithmetic instructions, logic and shift instructions, branch instructions, and input/output instructions.

Many of the instructions also affect one or more of the flag bits, based on the result of the operation. For example, a *zero* flag is set (to 1) if the result is 0 and cleared if the result is not. In the description of the MODEL instruction set in Chapter 10, the affected flags are specified.

8.4.1 Data Movement Instructions

The most basic operation in a computer is moving data from one location to another. The source of the data and the destination of the data each might be a register, a memory location, or the stack. The source might also be a constant (immediate addressing). *Caution:* Moving data, in computer terms, means making a copy of the data for the new location, leaving the original unchanged. (A few computers have a swap instruction, which interchanges data between two registers.)

Machines with a single memory address (like MODEL) usually have two separate instructions: *Load,* move data from the location specified by the address field* to the register specified by the register field, and *Store,* move data from the register to the location specified by the address field. Two-address machines have a single *Move* instruction. Immediate addressing is not permitted for store instructions (or other unary instructions, such as *Increment,* which read data and then store a result in the same location), since immediate addressing implies a constant.

Pop and *Push* load from the stack to a register and store the contents of a register on the stack.

Many machines also have special load and store instructions to move data from and to special registers (not part of the register set).

EXAMPLE 8.7a

Using the values of Example 8.6, with register 8 specified and Page zero addressing,

Load REG^8:	REG$^8 \leftarrow$ 9ABCD
Store REG^8:	M[0000098] $\leftarrow$ 20304

If the top of the stack contains FFFFF,

Pop REG^1:	REG$^1 \leftarrow$ FFFFF
Push REG^9:	Top of stack $\leftarrow$ 44444

8.4.2 Arithmetic Instructions

The simplest instructions are for the *Add* and *Subtract* for fixed-point numbers (usually integers). Since nearly all machines store signed numbers in two's complement format, the same instruction is used for both unsigned and signed numbers. In most machines, these instructions set flag bits to indicate if the result is zero or negative, and to store the carry from the most significant digit of the adder/subtractor. Machines that store the carry often provide separate add with carry and subtract with borrow instructions that allow for multiple-precision arithmetic. These add the carry or subtract the borrow from the last operation to the least significant bit of this one.

These instructions have two operands. In single-memory address machines, the first operand comes from a register and the result is stored back in that register; the second operand comes from the location specified in the address field. In two-address machines, both operands are specified by address fields and the result replaces the first operand.

A special case of addition is the *Increment* (*Decrement*) instruction, which adds the constant 1 (-1) to the location specified. It uses the

---

*That could be another register. In that case, *Load* and *Store* would perform the same data movement, but might affect the flags differently.

address field to specify both the operand and the location of the result.* Also, *Negate* (take the two's complement or subtract from 0) is usually available.

Some machines provide arithmetic operations on operands on the stack. For dyadic operations (two operands), the two operands are popped from the stack (in two steps), and the result is pushed back on the stack.

All but the smallest machines provide multiplication and division instructions. (Note that separate instructions are needed for unsigned and signed numbers.) Many machines also provide floating-point versions of the arithmetic instructions.

EXAMPLE 8.7b	Using the instruction format of Example 8.6 and values

$$\text{Reg} = 6$$
$$\text{REG}^6 = 43210$$
$$\text{REG}^8 = 20304$$
$$M[0000098] = 9ABCD$$
$$M[3456798] = 12121$$

Add, using Page zero addressing

43210
9ABCD
$DDDDD \rightarrow \text{REG}^6$

Subtract, using Page zero addressing

$\qquad$ 1
43210
65432   (bit-by-bit complement of M[0000098])
$A8643 \rightarrow \text{REG}^6$

Increment, using register addressing, (uses REG^8)

20304
00001
20305

Decrement, using direct addressing

$12121 - 1 = 12120$

---

*Some machines with short instruction words also provide an instruction to increment or decrement a register that requires only a register number (not a memory address field). The format for MODEL that was described in Figure 8.2 would allow register addressing using only one word.

8.4.3 Logic, Shift, and Rotate Instructions

Bitwise logic instructions (AND, OR, Exclusive-OR, and NOT) are available on most machines. As in arithmetic instructions, the address field specifies one operand, and the register field specifies the other operand and the location of the result. The AND instruction is sometimes used as a mask, to select one or more bits of a word. (The word is ANDed with a word containing 0's everywhere except for the bits to be chosen, producing a result with 0's everywhere except in that part of the selected portion where the mask had been 1's.) Examples throughout this subsection are shown in binary.

M[0000098] = 1001 1010 1011 1100 1101
REG^2 = 0000 1111 0000 0000 0000
REG^3 = 1111 1111 0000 1111 1111

AND REG^2, Page zero		**EXAMPLE 8.7c**
Mask:	0000 1111 0000 0000 0000	
Data:	1001 1010 1011 1100 1101	
Result:	0000 1010 0000 0000 0000 → REG^2	

Similarly, the OR can be used to fill portions of a data word with 1's.

OR REG^3, Page zero		**EXAMPLE 8.7d**
Mask:	1111 1111 0000 1111 1111	
Data:	1001 1010 1011 1100 1101	
Result:	1111 1111 1011 1111 1111 → REG^3	

A *Shift* moves the bits of the word in one direction (right or left), dropping the bits off the end. A *Rotate* takes the bits off one end and brings them around to the other end. Many machines provide for shifts and rotates of any number of places, by including a count field.

Two types of shifts are common: *logical* shifts and *arithmetic* shifts. The logical shift fills the vacated space with 0's. The arithmetic shift right preserves the leading bit (making copies) so as to keep the sign of the number the same. (The arithmetic shift left is the same as the logical shift left.)

Page Zero Addressing		**EXAMPLE 8.7e**
Data:	1001 1010 1011 1100 1101	
Left shift 5	0101 0111 1001 1010 0000 → M[0000098]	
Left rotate 5	0101 0111 1001 1011 0011 → M[0000098]	

Right logical shift 3	0001 0011 0101 0111 1001	→ M[0000098]
Right arithmetic shift 3	1111 0011 0101 0111 1001	→ M[0000098]
Right rotate 3	1011 0011 0101 0111 1001	→ M[0000098]

For integers, a shift to the right of one place is equivalent to dividing by 2, and a shift to the left of one place is equivalent to multiplying by 2. (An arithmetic shift is used for signed numbers, and a logical shift is used for unsigned numbers.) Results are rounded down to the next lower integer.

EXAMPLE 8.7f (Shift by one place, 8-bit data used)			
	Signed or Unsigned		
	Data:	0001 1010	(26)
	Shift left	0011 0100	(52)
	Shift right	0000 1101	(13)
	Signed		
	Data:	1100 0101	(−59)
	Shift left	1000 1010	(−118)
	Arithmetic shift right	1110 0010	(−30)
	Unsigned		
	Data:	1100 0101	(197)
	Shift left	1000 1010	(too large for 8 bits)
	Logic shift right	0110 0010	(98)

8.4.4   Branches

While executing most instructions, the program counter is incremented to point to (the first word of) the next instruction. *Branch* or *Jump* instructions are required when it is necessary to execute instructions out of order.

An *Unconditional Branch* loads the program counter with the effective address. The instruction following the unconditional branch is only reached by another instruction branching to it.

A *Conditional Branch* will cause a branch if some binary condition is satisfied; otherwise, it will continue to the next instruction. Typical conditions include whether one of the flag bits is zero or not. Also, many machines provide for branches after comparing two numbers (really, subtracting them), based on whether the first is greater than, greater than or equal to, less than, less than or equal to, equal to, or not equal to the second. (There are separate tests for signed numbers and unsigned numbers.)

Some machines have a *Skip*. This was popular in simpler machines where all instructions were one word long.

With the structure of Example 8.6,

$\quad$ PC = 1234567

$\quad$ Address = 98

$\quad$ Second word (M[1234568]) = 34567

$\quad$ Jump, Page zero $\quad$ PC ← 0000098

$\quad$ Branch on *carry,* direct

$\qquad$ If *carry* = 1 $\qquad$ PC ← 3456798

$\qquad$ If *carry* = 0 $\qquad$ PC ← 1234569

A *Subroutine* or *Procedure Call* is a branch (unconditional or conditional) that saves the address of the next instruction in order before branching. That address is most commonly pushed onto the stack and retrieved by a *Return* instruction. (The only requirement is that the subroutine leave the stack in the same state as it was before the call.) An example of the behavior is shown in Figure 8.5, where the subroutine call is at address 0511.* An example of the stack is shown before the call, while the procedure is executing and after the call. (The stack may not be empty before the call, but elements already on the stack will be unchanged by the process described.) The stack can be used by the

Figure 8.5 Calling and returning from a subroutine.

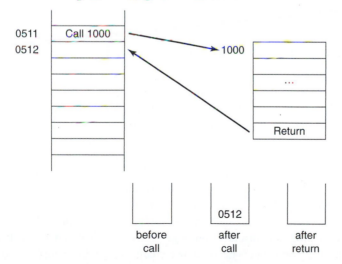

*For the purpose of this example, it is assumed that all instructions fit into one word. Word size is 16 bits and memory addresses are also 16 bits.

procedure as long as it first pushes items onto the stack and pops every-thing that it has pushed. Example 8.8 shows what happens if the first pro-cedure calls a second (nested subroutines).

Only addressing modes that produce an effective address are allowed with branches and calls. (You cannot get your next instruction from a constant or a register.)

EXAMPLE 8.8

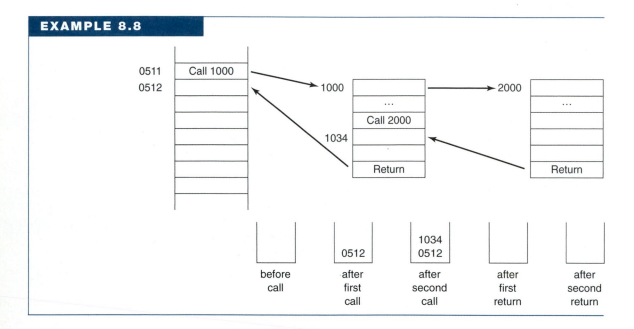

8.4.5 Input/Output and Interrupts

As indicated in Figure 8.1, input and output devices are connected to the main bus in a similar manner to memory. Since these devices operate at different speeds and often have different data configurations, an inter-face or controller is required between the device and BUS.

In some machines, special instructions are used for input and output. More commonly, the I/O controllers use some of the addresses that would otherwise be used by memory. That is referred to as *memory-mapped* I/O. In that case, the standard data movement instructions (described in Section 8.4.1) can be used.

An *interrupt* is a signal that something (usually not related to the piece of program currently running) needs immediate attention. It may come at any time, but is handled by the controller at the completion of the processing of an instruction. Although the source of the interrupt may be internal, it most commonly comes from external devices. The computer treats an interrupt like a subroutine call, except that the address to which control is branched is determined by hardware. If the interrupt processing program needs to use some of the user registers of the CPU, their contents must be stored and then replaced before returning to the program running. Sometimes, this is done automatically by the hardware; other times it is a software function. (See Chapter 11 for a discussion of this process.)

8.4.6 Instruction Timing

In many machines (those where the memory reference time is significantly slower than the clock), the time to fetch and execute most instructions is dominated by the time required to read from and write to memory. For those instructions for which an operand is fetched from memory or stored in memory (such as *Load*), one memory reference is required for data (see Example 8.5). Instructions using immediate or register addressing require no data memory references. Neither do branches. Some unary instructions, such as *Increment,* require two memory references: one to fetch the data and a second to store it. Instructions referencing the stack, such as *Call* and *Push,* require a memory reference for each stack reference.

The number memory references for each instruction of Example 8.7 is shown.

EXAMPLE 8.9

a. Load $1 + 1 = 2$

   Store $1 + 1 = 2$

   Pop $1 + 1 = 2$

   Push $1 + 1 = 2$

b. Add $1 + 1 = 2$

   Subtract $1 + 1 = 2$

   Increment   1

   Decrement $2 + 2 = 4$

c, d, and e $1 + 2 = 3$

g. Page zero   1

   Direct   2

[SP 5, 6; EX 6, 7, 8, 9]

8.5 SOLVED PROBLEMS

1. We have a machine that allows one and two address instructions (as well as some that require no address). The format of the first 24-bit segment of the instruction is

0	7 8	13 14	18 19	23
Op-Code		RN	Admode1	Admode2

Addresses are 24 bits; instructions that use one memory address require a second 24-bit segment and those that use two addresses require a second and third 24-bit segment. (For instructions with no address, 24 bits is sufficient.)

Consider the following instruction stream. (The three-segment instruction, *A,* is followed by a three-segment instruction, *B,* etc.):

Reference	A	B	C	D	E	F	G	H
Number of Segments	3	3	1	2	1	3	2	3

Memory word size is 96 bits. Show the layout of instructions when they are packed into each quarter-word if

a. any quarter can be addressed.

b. only the first quarter can be addressed and instructions *D* and *G* may be branched to.

a.

A	A	A	B
B	B	C	D
D	E	F	F
F	G	G	H
H	H		

b.

A	A	A	B
B	B	C	no-op
D	D	E	F
F	F	no-op	no-op
G	G	H	H
H			

2. Consider a machine with 16-bit words, 16 registers, and 2^{16} words of main memory. The format of the first word of the instruction is

Op-Code	RN	Mode

where the last 4 bits of the mode may be a register number, address, or data for some modes.

Assume the following values (before fetching the instruction):

PC = 0100

Reg No. = 1,   Bits 12:15 = 7

Second word = 1234

M[1234] = 5678

M[1336] = ABCD

M[5678] = FFFF

M[579B] = 2468

M[ABC4] = 1357

REG^0 = 4567

REG^7 = ABC4

If the instruction is *Load Register,* show the effective address and the changes to any register for each of the following address types.

a. Register

b. Register indirect

c. Register indirect with auto-post-incrementing

d. Short immediate (sign-extend bits 12:15)

e. Direct

f. Indirect

g. Relative

h. Immediate

i. Index (REG^0 is used as the index register)

a. no EA $REG^1 \leftarrow$ ABC4   PC $\leftarrow$ 0101

b. EA = ABC4 $REG^1 \leftarrow$ 1357   PC $\leftarrow$ 0101

c. EA = ABC4 $REG^1 \leftarrow$ 1357   PC $\leftarrow$ 0101
    $REG^7 \leftarrow$ ABC5

d. no EA $REG^1 \leftarrow$ 0007   PC $\leftarrow$ 0101

e. EA = 1234 $REG^1 \leftarrow$ 5678   PC $\leftarrow$ 0102

f. EA = 5678 $REG^1 \leftarrow$ FFFF   PC $\leftarrow$ 0102

g. EA = 0100 + 2 + 1234 = 1336   PC $\leftarrow$ 0102
    $REG^1 \leftarrow$ ABCD

h. no EA $REG^1 \leftarrow$ 1234   PC $\leftarrow$ 0102

i. EA = 4567 + 1234 = 579B   PC $\leftarrow$ 0102
    $REG^1 \leftarrow$ 2468

3. For the addressing modes of SP2, how many memory references are needed to fetch the instruction, compute the effective address, and execute the instruction?

   a. 1

   b. $1 + 1 = 2$

   c. $1 + 1 = 2$

   d. 1

   e. $2 + 1 = 3$

   f. $2 + 1 + 1 = 4$

   g. $2 + 1 = 3$

   h. 2

   i. $2 + 1 = 3$

4. We have a new addressing mode, indirect with auto-pre-decrementing. (Note this is memory indirect, not register indirect). In addition to all of the values in Solved Problem 3,

$$M[5677] = 2222$$

   If the instruction is *Load Register,* show the effective address and the changes to any register and memory location using this addressing mode. Also, find the number of memory references.

Memory location 1234 is read. That value is decremented and used as the effective address. It is also stored back into memory location 1234.

$EA = 5677$ $M[1234] \leftarrow 5677$ $REG^1 \leftarrow 2222$
$PC \leftarrow 0102$

Memory references $= 2 + 2 + 1 = 5$ ($M[1234]$ must be read from and written to during the address computation.)

5. Each of the following instructions is executed consecutively. Show the contents of the stack after each (assuming it was empty). The initial contents of the registers are

$REG^2 = 1357$
$REG^7 = ABC4$
$REG^8 = 4567$

   a. Push REG^2

   b. Push REG^7

   c. Pop REG^1

   d. Push REG^2

    e. Push REG^8

    f. Push REG^1

    g. Pop REG^3

    h. Pop REG^5

At c, $REG^1 \leftarrow ABC4$

At g, $REG^3 \leftarrow ABC4$

At h, $REG^5 \leftarrow 4567$

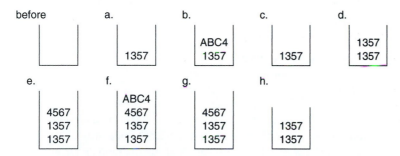

6. Using the structure of Solved Problem 2 and the following initial values,

PC = 0100

Bits 12:15 = 7

Second word = 1234

M[0007] = FF00

M[1234] = 5678

M[5678] = 1234

M[ABC4] = 1357

REG^7 = ABC4

REG^9 = 4567

carry bit = 1

stack:

| 1234 |
| 5678 |

Show the changes to all registers (including the PC) and memory locations. Indicate how many memory references are required. Each part is a separate problem.

a. Load* REG^2, Page zero

b. Load REG^2, Register

---

*The register specified next (REG^2 in this case) is what is specified by the RN field.

c. Store REG^9, Register indirect

d. Store REG^7, Register

e. Add REG^9, Direct

f. Add REG^9, Register

g. Add with carry REG^9, Page zero

h. Subtract REG^9, Register

i. Increment* register

j. Increment register indirect with auto-post-incrementing

k. Add stack

l. AND REG^9, Page zero

m. AND REG^9, Register

n. OR REG^7, Direct

p. NOT, Direct

For the shifts and rotates, assume that the RN field contains the number of places; it will be shown after the operation. The address field specifies the location of the operand and the result.

q. Left shift 3, Register

r. Logic right shift 4, Page zero

s. Arithmetic right shift 4, Page zero

t. Right rotate 5, indirect

u. Jump direct

v. Jump register indirect

w. Call indirect

x. Call immediate

y. Return

a. REG^2 ← FF00	PC ← 0101	Memory: 1 + 1 = 2
b. REG^2 ← ABC4	PC ← 0101	Memory: 1
c. M[ABC4] ← 4567	PC ← 0101	Memory: 1 + 1 = 2
d. REG^7 ← ABC4	PC ← 0101	Memory: 1
	no change in REG^7	
e. REG^9 ← 4567 + 5678 = 9BDF		PC ← 0102
		Memory: 2 + 1 = 3
f. REG^9 ← 4567 + ABC4 = F12B		PC ← 0101
		Memory: 1

---

*The RN field is ignored for instructions with one operand, such as Increment.

g. $REG^9 \leftarrow 4567 + FF00 + 1 = 4468$ $PC \leftarrow 0101$

                                            Memory: $1 + 1 = 2$

h. $REG^9 \leftarrow 4567 - ABC4 = 4567 + 543B + 1 = 99A3$

    $PC \leftarrow 0101$ Memory: 1

i. $REG^7 \leftarrow ABC5$ $PC \leftarrow 0101$ Memory: 1

j. $M[ABC4] \leftarrow 1358$ $REG^7 \leftarrow ABC5$ $PC \leftarrow 0101$

                                        Memory: $1 + 2 = 3$

k. $PC \leftarrow 0101$ Stack gets $1234 + 5678 = 68AC$

                                         Memory: $1 + 3 = 4$

```
|        |
|        |
| 68AC   |
```

l. $REG^9 \leftarrow$ 0100 0101 0110 0111 · 1111 1111 0000 0000

         $= 4500$ $PC \leftarrow 0101$ Memory: $1 + 1 = 2$

m. $REG^9 \leftarrow$ 0100 0101 0110 0111 · 1010 1011 1100 0100

         $= 0144$ $PC \leftarrow 0101$ Memory: 1

n. $REG^7 \leftarrow$ 1010 1011 1100 0100 + 0101 0110 0111 1000

         $= FFFC$ $PC \leftarrow 0102$ Memory: $2 + 1 = 3$

p. $M[1234] \leftarrow A987$ $PC \leftarrow 0102$ Memory: $2 + 2 = 4$

q. $REG^7 \leftarrow$ (1010 1011 1100 0100) shifted

         0101 1110 0010 0000 $= 5E20$ $PC \leftarrow 0101$

                                          Memory: 1

r. $M[0007] \leftarrow 0FF0$ $PC \leftarrow 0101$ Memory: $1 + 2 = 3$

s. $M[0007] \leftarrow FFF0$ $PC \leftarrow 0101$ Memory: $1 + 2 = 3$

t.   Rotate $M[5678] =$ 0001 0010 0011 0100

    $M[5678] =$ 1010 0000 1001 0001 $= A901$

    $PC \leftarrow 0102$ Memory: $2 + 1 + 2 = 5$

u. $PC \leftarrow 1234$ Memory: 2

v. $PC \leftarrow ABC4$ Memory: 1

w. $PC \leftarrow 5678$ Stack: Memory:

                                       $2 + 1 + 1 = 4$

```
|        |
| 0102   |
| 1234   |
| 5678   |
```

x.   not allowed

y. $PC \leftarrow 1234$ Stack: Memory: 2

```
|        |
|        |
| 5678   |
```

8.6 EXERCISES

1. Repeat Solved Problem 1 for a system with
   i. 48-bit words
   ii. 144-bit words

2. We have the instruction format of Figure 8.2d, with 64 registers and 2^{32} words of memory. The Address field contains data or part of an address. The last 6 bits are a register number for those addressing modes requiring a register.

   Assume the following (before fetching the instruction)

   PC = 11112222
   Reg. No. = 24,   Bits 16:31 = 9876
   Second word = 12304560
   M[00009876] = ABCDEF01
   M[10102323] = 22334455
   M[12304560] = 12345678
   M[12345678] = FFFFFFFF
   M[23416784] = 13572468
   REG^{36} = 10102323

   If the instruction is *Load Register,* show the effective address and the changes to any register for each of the following address types.
   a. Register
   b. Register indirect
   c. Register indirect with auto-post-incrementing
   d. Short immediate (sign-extend)
   e. Direct
   f. Indirect
   g. Relative
   h. Immediate

*3. We have a machine with 2^{20} 32-bit words of memory and 16 registers. All instructions fit in 1 word, with the following format:

0	3	4	7	8	11	12			31
Op-Code		RN		ADMODE		Address			

Assume the following (before fetching the instruction)

PC = 1234E
RN = 5,   Bits 12:31 = FEDC2
M[11111] = FFFFFFFF
M[45666] = 11223344
M[45678] = FFEEDCBA
M[FEDC2] = 12345666
REG^2: 12345678

If the instruction is *Load Register,* show the effective address and the changes to any register for each of the following address types. (The register number for parts a, b, and c is in bits 28:31.)

a. Register
b. Register indirect
c. Register indirect with auto-post-incrementing
d. Short immediate (sign-extend)
e. Direct
f. Indirect
g. Relative
h. Indirect with auto-post-incrementing

4. We have a machine with 2^{28} 20-bit words of memory and 16 registers, with the following format:

When a 28-bit address is required, the low order (right) 8 bits are contained in the first word and the first 20 bits are contained in the second word of the instruction. When an address is contained in a register or in memory, the word referenced contains the low order 8 bits (in its right 8 bits); the remainder of the address is contained in the next word.

Assume the following (before fetching the instruction)

PC = 1234567
Reg No. = 4,   Bits 12:19 = 12
Second word = 34567

M[0000012] = 12345
M[0000013] = ABCDE
M[1234567] = EDCBA
M[1234568] = 10102
M[1234578] = FFFFF
M[3456712] = 34567
M[3456713] = 12345
REG^0 = 02468
REG^2 = 45678
REG^3 = 12345

If the instruction is *Load Register,* show the effective address and the changes to any register for each of the following address types.

a.   Register

b.   Register indirect

c.   Register indirect with auto-post-incrementing

d.   Short immediate (sign-extend)

e.   Direct

f.   Indirect

g.   Immediate

h.   Indirect with auto-pre-incrementing

5.   For each part of

   a.   Exercise 2

  *b.   Exercise 3

   c.   Exercise 4

how many memory references are required to fetch the instruction, compute the effective address, and fetch data?

6.   Each of the following instructions is executed consecutively. Show the contents of the stack after each (assuming it was initially empty). Assume the initial contents of the registers are

REG^1 = 012
REG^3 = 345
REG^5 = 567
REG^6 = FF8

   a.   Push REG^1

   b.   Push REG^3

    c. Push REG^1

    d. Push REG^6

    e. Pop REG^9

    f. Pop REG^1

    g. Pop REG^3

    h. Push REG^1

    i. Pop REG^3

    j. Pop REG^6

*7. For the machine with the structure shown in Figure 8.2d (and Exercise 2) and the following initial values (*Note:* Register numbers are hexadecimal):

PC = 11112222

Bits 16:31 = 9876

Second word = 12304560

M[00009876] = ABCDEF01

M[10102323] = 22334455

M[12304560] = 12345678

M[12345678] = FFFFFFFF

REG^0 = 33333333

REG^{15} = 10203040

REG^{36} = 10102323

carry bit: = 1

Stack:
| 11223344 |
| 56789ABC |

Show the changes to all registers (including the PC) and memory locations. Each part is a separate problem. Also show the number of memory references.

    a.   Load REG^2, Page zero

    b.   Load REG^2, Register

    c.   Store REG^{15}, Register indirect

    d.   Store REG^0, Register

    e.   Add REG^{15}, Direct

    f.   Add REG^{15}, Register

    g.   Add with carry REG^{15}, Page zero

    h.   Subtract REG^{15}, Register

    i.   Increment indirect

j. Increment register indirect with auto-post-incrementing

k. Add Stack

l. AND REG^{15}, Page zero

m. AND REG^{15}, Register

n. OR REG^0, Direct

p. NOT, Direct

For the shifts and rotates, assume that the RN field contains the number of places; it will be shown after the operation. The address field specifies the location of the operand and the result.

q. Left shift 3, Register

r. Logic right shift 4, Page zero

s. Arithmetic right shift 4, Page zero

t. Right rotate 5, Indirect

u. Jump Direct

v. Jump Register indirect

w. Call Indirect

x. Return

8. For the machine of Exercise 3, and the following initial values,

PC = 12345

Bits 12:31 = FEDCB

M[45666] = 11223344

M[45678] = FFEEDCBA

M[FEDCB] = 12345666

REG^0 = 13579BDF

REG^B = 12345678

carry = 1

Stack is the same as in Exercise 7.

Show the changes to all registers (including the PC) and memory locations. Each part is a separate problem. Also show the number of memory references.

a. Load REG^2, Direct

b. Load REG^2, Register

c. Store REG^B, Register indirect

d. Store REG^0, Register

e. Add REG^B, Direct

f. Add REG^0, Register

g. Add with carry REG^B, Indirect

  h. Subtract REG^0, Register

  i. Increment Indirect

  j. Increment Register indirect with auto-post-incrementing

  k. Add Stack

  l. AND REG^0, Direct

  m. AND REG^0, Register

  n. OR REG^B, Direct

  p. NOT, Direct

For the shifts and rotates, assume that the RN field contains the number of places; it will be shown after the operation. The address field specifies the location of the operand and the result.

  q. Left shift 3, Register

  r. Logic Right shift 4, Register indirect

  s. Arithmetic Right shift 4, Stack

  t. Right rotate 5, Indirect

  u. Jump Direct

  v. Jump Register indirect

  w. Call Indirect

  x. Return

9. For the machine and initial values of Exercise 4, show the changes to all registers (including the PC) and memory locations. Also show the number of memory references. Each part is a separate problem.

  a. Load REG^2, Page zero

  b. Load REG^2, Register

  c. Store REG^3, Register indirect

  d. Store REG^0, Register

  e. Add REG^3, Direct

  f. Add REG^3, Register

  g. Add with carry REG^2, Page zero   (*carry* = 1)

  h. Subtract REG^3, Register

  i. Increment Indirect

  j. Increment Register indirect with auto-post-incrementing

  k. AND REG^2, Page zero

  l. AND REG^3, Short immediate

  m. NOT, Direct

  n. OR REG^3, Direct

For the shifts and rotates, assume that the RN field contains the number of places; it will be shown after the operation. The address field specifies the location of the operand and the result.

o. Left shift 3, Register

p. Logic right shift 4, Page zero

q. Arithmetic right shift 4, Page zero

r. Right Rotate 5, Indirect

s. Jump Direct

t. Jump Register indirect

8.7 CHAPTER 8 TEST (50 MINUTES)

1. (20) We have a machine where instructions require either 32 bits or 64 bits. The main memory has 96-bit words. Consider the following instruction stream:

Reference	A	B	C	D	E	F	G	H
Number of bits	32	64	64	32	64	32	64	64

Show the layout of instructions when they are packed into a third of a word if

a. any third can be addressed.

b. only the first third can be addressed and instructions *B* and *G* may be branched to.

2. (20) Each of the following instructions is executed consecutively. Show the contents of the stack after each (assuming it was initially empty). Assume the initial contents of the registers are

$REG^0 = 1234$

$REG^1 = 4567$

$REG^3 = 89AB$

a. Push REG^0

b. Push REG^0

c. Push REG^1

d. Pop REG^3

e. Pop REG^7

3. Consider a machine with 24-bit words, 64 registers, and 2^{32} words of main memory. The instruction format of the first word of an instruction is

0	5	6	11	12	15	16	23
Op-Code		RN		Mode		Address	

The last 8 bits of that word are the least significant bits of the 32-bit address. Each of the following is in hexadecimal. For indirect and register indirect addressing, the word pointed to contains the last 8 bits of the address (in its right 8 bits). The first 24 bits are found in the next (higher number) memory location or register. For modes that reference a register, the register number is in bits 18:23.

Address = 46

Second word = 123456

Address of this instruction: 00112222

M[00000046] = 6789AB

M[00000047] = 012345

M[00010203] = 765432

M[12345646] = FFFFFF

M[12345647] = 123456

M[123456FF] = 776655

M[44444403] = ABCDEF

REG^6 = 010203

REG^7 = 444444

a. (3 points per subpart) For each of the following addressing modes, show what gets stored in REG^1 for an instruction *Load Register* 1.

   i. Register

   ii. Page zero

   iii. Register indirect

   iv. Direct

   v. Short immediate

   vi. Immediate

b. (7 points per subpart) For each of the following instructions, show the value of all memory locations and registers (including the PC) that are changed. Also, show the number of memory references. Each part is a separate problem.

i.   Store* REG^7, Direct

ii. Add REG^7, Register

iii. Increment indirect

iv. OR REG^7, Register

v.   Left shift 1, Page zero

vi. Jump Direct

---

*The register specified next (REG^7 in this case) is what is specified by the RN field.

Computer Design Fundamentals

I n Section 4.7, we introduced two commercial hardware design languages: Verilog and VHDL. Although these languages, and the software associated with them, are useful for the testing and production of digital systems, we will not use them here. They entail a considerable investment in time to learn the details of their usage. They also, to some extent, hide the hardware that is used to implement as complex a device as a computer. In this and succeeding chapters, we will use a simplified language, *Design Description Language (DDL)*. Each step of that language represents an operation on data and is tied directly to the hardware to execute that operation. We will develop the language in this chapter and illustrate its use with a few small examples. In the next chapter, we will use DDL for the design of a computer.

Our main concern in Part II of this book is at the level of registers, including the movement of data between registers and the operations on data in those registers. But registers are just a collection of flip flops. For simplicity, we will use trailing-edge triggered D flip flops, as shown in Figure 9.1a. (These are the same D flip flops that we described in Chapter 5.) A sample clock signal and the corresponding values of Q and Q' are shown in Figure 9.1b. The value stored in the flip flop before the first clock, in this example, is assumed to be 0. We will assume that the D input does not change just before the trailing edge of the clock pulse. Indeed, that input, as well as most signals in our systems, will change at or shortly after the trailing edge of the clock. In a digital system, signals may pass through several layers of logic, in which case the delays will build up. We will assume that the clock speed and the delays are such that the transition always occurs before the next clock pulse.

A *register* is a set of flip flops with a common name. The bits of a register will be denoted by subscripts starting with the leftmost bit (the most significant bit for numeric data), which is numbered 0. Thus, the 32-bit register A consists of 32 flip flops labeled A_0, A_1, through A_{31}.

Figure 9.1 *D* flip flop and timing.

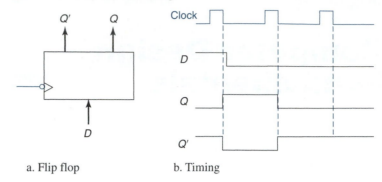

a. Flip flop   b. Timing

ASIDE: Computer literature is not consistent about the way in which the bits of a register are numbered. Many manufacturers use the notation just described, numbering from the left. On the other hand, most microprocessor literature numbers the rightmost bit 0 and thus the bits of *A* from left to right would be A_{31}, A_{30}, through A_0. There is no right way and no wrong way; you must learn to live with whatever method is used in the materials you are reading at the time.

It is possible to refer to individual bits of a register by their subscripted names (such as A_{14}) or to groups of consecutive bits by showing the first and last subscript separated by a colon (:). For example, the first 4 bits of register *C* may be specified as $C_{0:3}$ or by C_0, C_1, C_2, C_3.

The balance of the logic description that we will employ utilizes simple gates such as AND, OR, NOT, and Exclusive-OR and larger logic blocks, such as adders and decoders. We are not particularly concerned about the detailed implementation of the combinational logic blocks and will thus be satisfied with a concise verbal definition of each block. If that is not sufficient in a particular case, a block diagram or an algebraic description might be used, but we will not develop any mathematical notation to describe these combinational logic modules. We will also not be interested in whether the eventual implementation will use AND and OR gates or NAND gates. That decision and the modifications of the detailed logic to accommodate it are beyond the scope of these chapters. (Chapters 2 through 7 contain all the information necessary to implement these designs with any type of gates and flip flops.)

9.1 DATA MOVEMENT

A network providing for the transfer of the contents of the 4-bit register *A* to the 4-bit register *B* is shown in Figure 9.2. Note that the four flip flops of each register are run together and that a single clock input is shown for all the bits of register *B*. At this time, we will begin to introduce a little of the DDL notation so that by the time we get to a full

Figure 9.2 Transferring A to B.

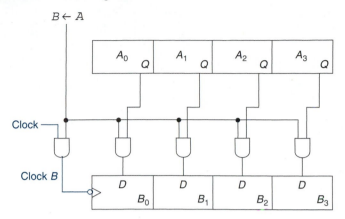

discussion of it later in the chapter, you will already be familiar with much of it.

The movement of A to B is denoted

$$B \leftarrow A$$

where the left-pointing arrow denotes "move to." The destination is to the left of the arrow and the source (that is, the information to be moved) is on the right. This notation will be used whenever we desire to clock data into a set of flip flops. The line labeled $B \leftarrow A$ is a line coming from the controller, commanding that this transfer take place. Actually, it serves two purposes. It enables the set of AND gates, thus opening the data path between A and B. It also, when ANDed with the clock, clocks whatever is on the D input (namely the bits of A) into register B.

Note that nothing is shown as an input to register A; the notation $B \leftarrow A$ implies only loading B, not changing A. (A is only loaded if there is also a signal $A \leftarrow$ "something.")

Figure 9.2 is really more complex than it needs to be for this very simple case. If, indeed, the only data path to B is the one from A, the AND gates are unnecessary. The output of flip flop A_i could be connected directly to the D input of flip flop B_i. Since register B is only clocked when it is desired to transfer something there, then there is no problem with A being there all the time.

But, the more common case is that different data may be clocked into register B at different times. If that is the case, then a multiplexer is required on each of the inputs to register B. Suppose we wish to be able to move one of three registers, A, C, and E, to B. Figure 9.3 shows the first 2 bits of such a system. There are three control signals, $B \leftarrow A$, $B \leftarrow C$, and $B \leftarrow E$, only one of which can be 1 at any time. These signals control the set of three-way multiplexors (the first of which is

Figure 9.3   Multiplexed inputs.

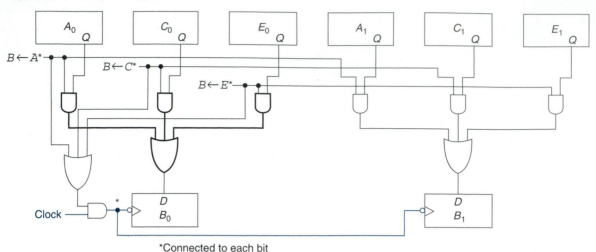

*Connected to each bit

bolded in Figure 9.3) that provide the D inputs to register B. There is a similar multiplexer for each bit of B with the same control signal (as indicated by the asterisk) going to each multiplexer. Also, the three control signals are ORed and then ANDed with the clock to provide the clock input to each of the bits of B. Obviously, this can be extended to more transfers to B with a larger multiplexer on each bit.

What we have described so far is a *point-to-point* data structure. For that approach, there is a set of multiplexers on the input to each of the registers. Thus, if there are n registers to be loaded, and each register is k bits, then there must be $n \times k$ multiplexers. The number of inputs to each varies, depending on the number of sources from which data may come. But there must be one input to each multiplexer for each source that may be transferred to that destination. One other point should be made here. A source might be some other register (as it was in this example), but it also might be a constant or the output of some logic module or shifting network. For example, some of the transfers to B might be

$B \leftarrow 6$ (hexadecimal constant)

$B \leftarrow A \cdot C$ (bit-by-bit AND)*

$B \leftarrow B'$ (bit-by-bit complement of B)

$B \leftarrow B_3, B_{0:2}$ (A right rotate)
$B \leftarrow \text{ADD}[C; E]$ (The sum of the numbers in C and E)

---

*In the remaining chapters, we will use the dot ($A \cdot C$) to indicate AND, rather than catenation, $A\ C$, so as to allow us to use names more than one character long, such as PC for program counter.

If all of these were required in addition to the ones for A, C, and E, there would be eight inputs to the multiplexer of Figure 9.3.

Show a typical bit of a system with three registers W, X, and Y that is organized with a point-to-point system allowing any register to be moved to any other register.

EXAMPLE 9.1

A *bus* requires a single multiplexer per bit, the output of which is referred to as the bus. The bits of the bus then go to the D inputs of each of the registers that are to receive data via the bus. Since only one multiplexor per bit is required instead of n, the amount of hardware is greatly reduced. On the other hand, that multiplexer can only pass one source at a time and thus a bus can only do one data transfer per clock. (In a point-to-point structure, each multiplexer can operate independently and thus more than one register can be clocked with different values.)

Figure 9.4 shows a typical bit of a bus where registers, A, C, and E as well as A' and $C \cdot E$ can be connected to the bus (and thus input to any register). The notation

$$BUS = A$$

means *connect* the output of register A to the bus. It is a signal that comes from the output of a flip flop in the controller and is thus 1 for a clock period.

Figure 9.4   A typical bit of a bus.

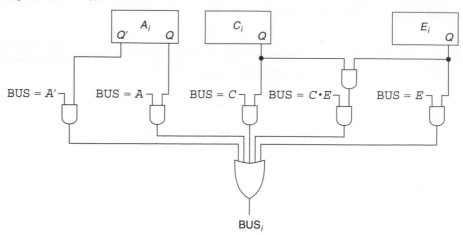

In most bus systems, all transfers use the bus, and thus no logic is required on the D input to the register; the bus is connected there. The clocking for the registers is the same as in a point-to-point structure, that is, register A is clocked whenever anything is to be transferred to that register.

Most of the time, detailed logic drawings of the bus structure are not needed. Rather, a busing diagram such as that of Figure 9.5 is provided to show what may be transferred by way of the bus. In this example, the five sources referred to in the last figure, A, A', C, $C \cdot E$, and E can be connected onto the bus. Any of them can be clocked into any of the three registers (A, C, or E). Note that in this example, there is no register B.

Figure 9.5   Busing diagram.

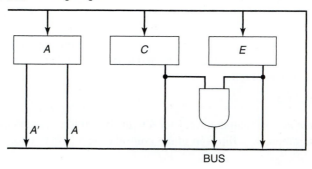

EXAMPLE 9.2

Implement the same set of transfers as in Example 9.1 using a bus.

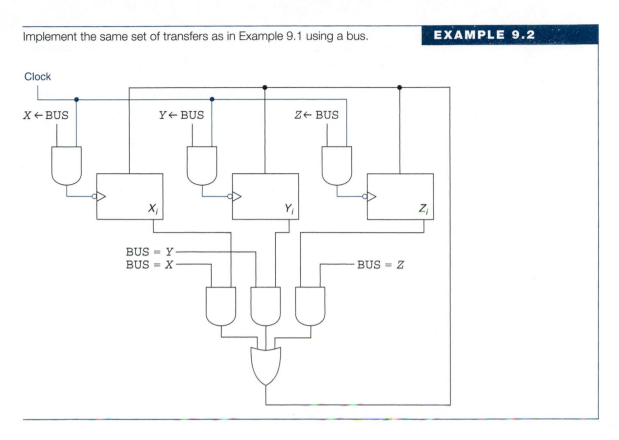

An important difference between a point-to-point system and a bus is that a bus may only transfer one piece of data at any clock time, whereas a point-to-point system can clock different data into different registers. In Example 9.1, it would be possible to move both $X \leftarrow Z$ and $Y \leftarrow X$ at the same time, since the two transfers involve different gates. In the bused system (Example 9.2), this would require two separate steps, since either Z or X could be connected to the bus, but not both at the same time.

[SP 1; EX 1, 2]

9.2 CONTROL SEQUENCE

A computer is a sequential system, that is, it executes its instructions by following a sequence of steps. The user describes what he or she wants the computer to do by providing it with a sequence of instructions, called a program. If that program is written in a higher level language (such as C++), it must first be translated into the machine language of the computer on which it will be run. Each instruction in the higher-level language typically translates into several instructions in machine language. But even machine language is not the appropriate detail for the hardware.

The control sequence specifies each step that is to be performed. Some of the steps are register transfers, moving information from one register to another. Others are branches, selecting which step in the sequence is to be executed next as a function of which instruction is being executed or as a function of the data in some register or flip flop.

We will specify the control sequence for the digital systems in this book using DDL. Once some preliminary design decisions have been made, such as the data interconnection structure and the type of controller, that description will be adequate to completely describe the hardware of the system and the design of the controller.

At this point, we will look at the structure of a simple controller. We will defer until Chapter 10 a more complete discussion of the design of a computer controller. Figure 9.6a shows the block diagram of a four-state one-hot controller, and Figure 9.6b shows the timing signals associated with that controller.

On the trailing edge of each clock pulse, all of the flip flops in the controller are triggered and the state may change. (In this example, the state does change on each clock pulse.) As can be seen from the timing diagram, on the trailing edge of the first clock shown, a 1 is clocked into flip flop 1 and a 0 into each of the others. At the next clock pulse, Q_1 is 1 and therefore D_2 is also 1. Thus, that clock will cause a 1 to be stored in flip flop 2. The D input to each of the other flip flops is 0 at that time. (Since Q_2 is 0, the output of both AND gates connected to Q_2 and thus D_3 and D_4 are both 0. Since Q_3 and Q_4 are both 0, their OR is also 0 and thus D_1 is 0.) Thus, the second clock will put a 1 in flip flop 2 and 0 in each of the other flip flops. At the next clock time, Q_2 is 1 and thus either D_3 or D_4 is one, depending on the value of x. In the

Figure 9.6a A simple controller.

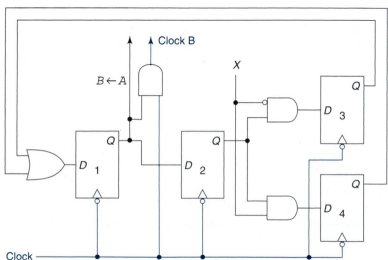

Figure 9.6b   Timing for a simple controller.

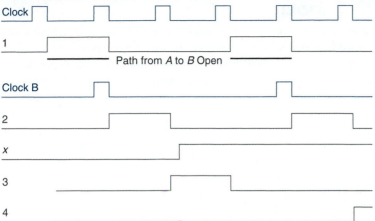

example, x is 0 at this time and thus the 1 from flip flop 2 is steered to flip flop 3. (The next time the system is in state 2, that is, flip flop 2 has a 1 in it, x is 1 and the transition is to state 4, as shown at the right of Figure 9.6b.)

Two output signals are shown from this controller. The one labeled $B \leftarrow A$ is connected directly to the output of a controller flip flop. It is 1 for one clock period (that is, from the trailing edge of one clock pulse to the trailing edge of the next.) It is used to establish a data path. As we can see in Figure 9.2, it enables the gates that transfer data to the D inputs of a register. The other signal, labelled Clock B, is a pulse, coincident with the clock. It is used to trigger the destination register. Thus, the path is established for one clock period, at the end of which the information is clocked into the destination register.

> ASIDE: The AND gate that produces the signal Clock B is sometimes thought of (and drawn) as part of the controller and sometimes thought of as part of the register transfer system. Indeed, that gate is shown in Figures 9.2 and 9.6. The distinction is not important; that pulse must be produced once. Also, there would likely be signals from the output of flip flops 2 and 3 to control other data transfers.

This sequence would be described in DDL

```
1. B ← A.
2. next: 4 (x), 3 (x').
3. "other transfer"
   next: 1.
4. "other transfer"
   next: 1.
```

where "other transfer" are not specified.

9.3 DESIGN DESCRIPTION LANGUAGE (DDL)

The purpose of a design description language is to compactly describe the hardware that is being designed. In some ways, it looks like a programming language, in that what is being described is the movement of data among registers in an appropriate sequence. Thus, the main operations are the transfer of data to registers and the determination of the next step to be executed. But, unlike a programming language, each step is tied directly to the hardware.

To introduce DDL, we will consider an example of a system description in that language. The illustration will explain many of the commonly used features of the language. The hardware implications of this system description will be explored next. We will then describe the whole language in detail.

```
SYSTEM NAME: MAGNITUDE
    INPUT LINES: start, X[0:7].
    OUTPUT LINES: request, ready, REG[0:7].
    FLIP FLOPS: WK[0:7], REG[0:7].
    INITIALIZE: 1.
    1. next: 2 (start), 1 (start').
    2. request = 1.
    3. WK ← X.
    4. next: 5 (WK₀), 7 (else).
    5. WK ← WK'.
    6. WK ← INC[WK].
    7. REG ← WK.
    8. ready = 1;
       next: 1.
END DESCRIPTION
```

A system description consists of two main parts: some definitions and the control sequence specification. In this example, the first five lines define the name of the system, its inputs, its outputs, the internal storage (that is, the flip flops that make up the registers and individual bits of the logic and register section of the system), and the step at which the system will begin when it is first turned on.

The definition lines contain lists (separated by commas). Scalars (single lines or flip flops) are denoted by lowercase boldface letters. Vectors (registers or sets of input or output lines) are denoted by uppercase letters. One of the purposes of the definition part is to specify what the inputs, outputs, and storage are. All flip flops other than those in the controller must be included on the FLIP FLOP definition line. The other is to specify the number of bits of each. The range of bits in each vector is contained in brackets following the name.

Figure 9.7 shows a block diagram of MAGNITUDE at the level of detail specified by the definition lines. It shows the inputs, the outputs, and the two 8-bit registers, but it does not show the data paths, the internal logic, or the controller.

Figure 9.7 Block diagram of MAGNITUDE.

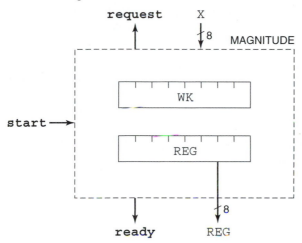

The definition line

```
INITIALIZE: 1.
```

states that when the system is turned on, it is in state 1. Sometimes the contents of registers are initialized as well.

The eight steps in the control sequence are then listed. The first step contains the key word `next`. It states that what is to follow is a specification of which step in the control sequence is to be executed following this one. If there is no such specification (as in steps 2, 3, 5, 6, and 7), the controller just goes to the next step numerically. The "next" specification is required whenever that is not to be the case. In step 8, control always returns to step 1. In step 1, it specifies that step 2 is executed next if **start** is 1 and that step 1 is executed again if **start′** is 1 (that is, if **start** is 0). A third form of the `next` is found in step 4, where it specifies going to step 5 if WK_0 is 1 and to step 7 otherwise. The key word `else` specifies what happens if none of the other conditions are met.

Step 2 indicates that the constant 1 is connected to line **request** whenever that step is executed. The equal sign means connect a value to the line(s) specified to the left. Once the control proceeds beyond that step, the connection is no longer made. In contrast, the left-facing arrow in step 3 indicates that whatever is on line X is stored in register WK. The arrow indicates that the register on the left is to be clocked.

Both steps 5 and 6 indicate computations. In 5, the complement (bit-by-bit) of register WK is computed and transferred into WK. Step 6 takes the output of some combinational logic module INC, the input of which is the output of register WK, and clocks it into WK. This description is not complete unless the behavior or INC is defined. For our purposes, the following definition will do:

> INC takes the 8-bit binary input and adds 1 to it, putting that sum on the eight output lines. The carry out of the addition is ignored. (Thus, INC[FF_{16}] produces 00.)

A timing diagram for this controller is shown in Figure 9.8, assuming that WK_0 is 0 for this execution of the sequence. When we first start to look at this system, **start** is 0 and the system is at step 1. As long as **start** remains 0, the branch at step 1 returns control to step 1. When **start** goes to 1 after clock pulse 2, control proceeds to step 2 on the trailing edge of the next clock pulse. At each clock, control proceeds to the next step, to 3 and then to 4. At 4, since WK_0 is 0, the else branch is executed and control goes on to step 7. From there, it continues to step 8 and then back to step 1 to wait for a new **start**. If **start** is still 1 or is 1 again, it will continue on to step 2. At step 4, it will continue on to steps 5 and 6 before going to 7 if the number in WK is negative (that is, if WK_0 is 1), computing the two's complement of that number. But, in this case, flip flops 5 and 6 remain at 0.

Figure 9.8   Timing for MAGNITUDE.

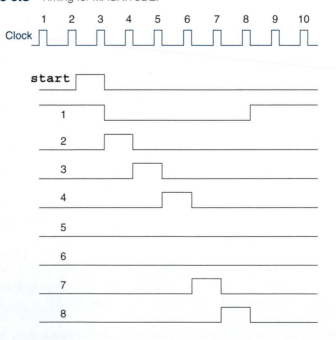

Figure 9.9 shows a block diagram of a hard-wired controller for that system. Each step of the sequence corresponds to a flip flop in the controller. In many steps, the next step to be executed is just the next step numerically. In that case, the Q output of the controller flip flop is just connected to the D input of the next flip flop. That is the case for steps 2, 3, 5, and 7. The `next` statement at step 8 just implies that its output wire goes to the input of flip flop 1 instead of 9. An OR gate is needed when more than one step may go to the same next step, such as in front of flip flop 1, where the input may come from the output of step 1 or from flip flop 8. The conditional `nexts` correspond to a set of AND gates that steer the output to the appropriate place. For Example, the `next` at step 1 is a two-way branch and thus there are two AND gates. The output of flip flop 1 goes to the input of each of them. The input **start** goes to one, the output of which goes to step 2, as specified by that step. The complement of that input, **start'**, goes to the other AND gate and its output goes to flip flop 1.

Figure 9.9 Hard-wired controller for MAGNITUDE.

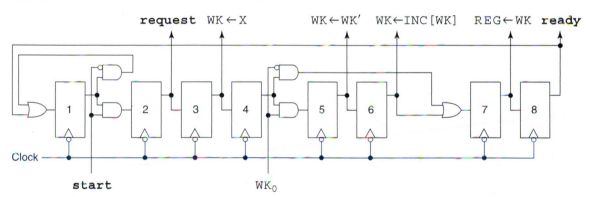

The data transfer steps imply signals from the controller to the register and logic section of the system, as shown in Figure 9.10. The signal

$$WK \leftarrow X$$

controls the transfer of the input vector X into the register WK. The signals **request** and **ready** are output lines from this system to the system with which it is interacting (getting operands and returning results).

Each of the registers is 8 bits long. Rather than attempting to show all the bits of these registers, Figure 9.10 shows a typical bit of the register and logic section of MAGNITUDE. There is a three-way multiplexor on the inputs to each bit of WK, since three different quantities may be transferred to that register. The numbers in circles refer to the states of the controller; those lines come directly from the output of the flip flop of the same number. Register WK is clocked whenever the controller wants to load WK, that is, whenever it is in state 3, 5, or 6. The clock input to WK_i, goes to each bit of WK; there is no need to replicate the AND and OR gates that produces that signal. The INC circuit has eight inputs and eight outputs; the i-th one is connected to this bit. REG is clocked from state 7. No gating is required on its D input since only WK is ever transferred there.

Figure 9.10   Typical bit of MAGNITUDE.

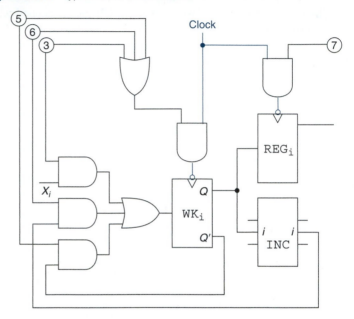

EXAMPLE 9.3

Design the controller and a typical bit of the system named SHIFTER.

When the system receives a 1 on line **compute**, it inputs a 20-bit number which is available on input lines IN. Based on input lines **a** and **b**, it does one of the following:

a b

0 0 no computation

0 1 shifts the input 1 place to the right

1 0 shifts the input 2 places to the right

1 1 shifts the input 3 places to the right

(Assume that **a** and **b** only change while the system is waiting for a 1 on **compute**.) The system then makes the answer available on output lines OUT and puts a 1 on line **done** for 1 clock period. After completing that, it goes back to wait for a new **compute** signal.

One version of a control sequence for this system is

```
SYSTEM NAME: SHIFTER
      INPUT LINES: compute, a, b, IN[0:19].
      OUTPUT LINES: OUT[0:19], done.
```

```
FLIP FLOPS: T[0:19], OUT[0:19].
1. next: 1 (compute'), 2(compute).
2. T ← IN.
3. next / a, b: 7, 6, 5, 4.
4. T ← 0, T₀:₁₈.
5. T ← 0, T₀:₁₈.
6. T ← 0, T₀:₁₈.
7. OUT ← T.
8. done = 1;
   next: 1.
END DESCRIPTION
```

The only new notation in this controller is at step 3. The `next` is followed by a binary string (in this case 2 bits) and then a list of steps. There is one entry on the list for each possible combination of the binary number (four in this case). It goes to the first when that number is 0, the second when it is 1, and so forth. Steps 5, 6, and 7 can each be reached in two ways, as can step 1. The diagram of the controller is shown on the next page.

A typical bit of the register and logic section is shown here. (The output from T_4 is shown since it is needed as an input to T_5.)

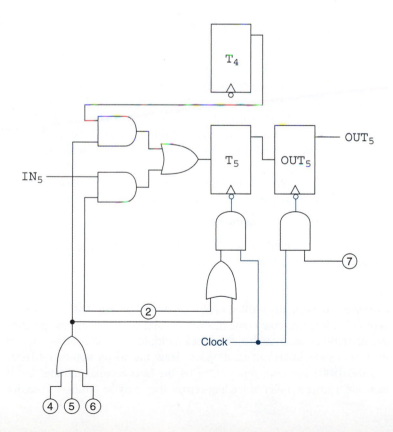

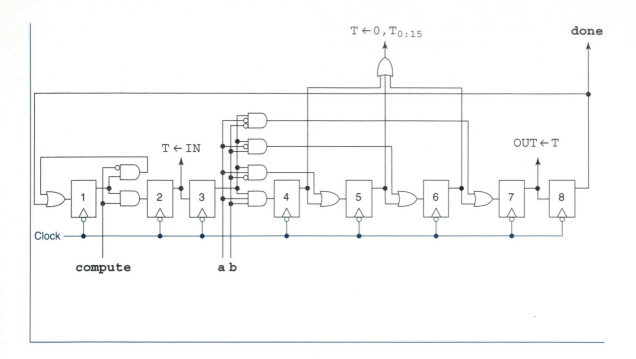

9.3.1 Specification of DDL

Now that we have seen many of the features of DDL, we are ready to define it more completely.

The objects to be operated on are scalars (single values), vectors (one-dimensional arrays, a set of values with the same name, distinguished by subscripts), two-dimensional arrays (with subscripts and superscripts), and constants. The scalars may reference flip flops or be the name of a wire (such as an input or an output). Similarly, the vectors may reference registers or sets of wires.

A scalar is represented by one or more boldface lowercase letters or letters and numbers, starting with a letter, such as:

a   **w2**   **compute**

A vector is represented by one or more boldface uppercase letters or letters and numbers starting with a letter, such as:

A   MEM   REG

Constants are normally written in hexadecimal. The length of the constant is usually clear from the context, since the size of all vectors is specified in a definition line. If the length is not a multiple of 4, the leading bit(s) of the first hexadecimal digit are dropped. Thus, the binary numbers 101001 and 00101001 are both represented by the hexadecimal number 29. If there are a large number of leading zeroes, they may be omitted. Thus, for example, the 16-bit number 0009 may be written more simply as 9. When there may be confusion as to the length of the number, or if you wish to emphasize that length, its length (in bits) may be included as a superscript. Thus 9^{16} implies a 16-bit number, hexadecimal 0009.

Individual bits of a vector are denoted by subscripts, with the left (the numerically most significant) bit numbered 0. Thus, the 4-bit register A consists of flip flops A_0, A_1, A_2, and A_3. You can refer to consecutive bits by showing the first and last bit separated by a colon. Thus, $A_{1:3}$ refers to A_1, A_2, and A_3.

Arrays are also represented by one or more uppercase alphanumeric characters, beginning with a letter. The rows of an array are referenced with superscripts. Thus the first row of array M is referred to as M^0.

Combinational logic is denoted in two ways. Simple bit-by-bit operations involving straightforward logic can be represented using the standard logic operators: AND $(\cdot)$,* OR $(+)$,[†] Exclusive-OR $(\oplus)$, and NOT $(')$. Thus, if A and B are 4-bit vectors, then $A \cdot B$ produces the 4-bit vector,

$$A_0 \cdot B_0, \quad A_1 \cdot B_1, \quad A_2 \cdot B_2, \quad A_3 \cdot B_3$$

The notation is also used where one operand is a scalar. In that case, the scalar operates on each element of the vector. Thus $\mathbf{x} + B$ produces

$$\mathbf{x} + B_0, \quad \mathbf{x} + B_1, \quad \mathbf{x} + B_2, \quad \mathbf{x} + B_3$$

If the logic is more complicated, a logic block must be defined. It is named following the same rules as for vectors, with its inputs enclosed in brackets and (if there is more than one) separated by semicolons. Thus, there might be blocks

```
INC[A]
ADD[A; B; 0].
```

Each such block must be defined by a block diagram, logic equations, or a verbal description. We will define a few such blocks in what follows, using the verbal description. When implementing a simulator for DDL, a more formal approach will be required.

ADD[A; B; **c**]: Adds two n-bit inputs, A and B, and a carry input (**c**) and produces a $(n + 1)$-bit result (the sum and the carry out).

Once this logic block is defined, you can use it with other inputs and thus

```
ADD[W; T; 0]
```

---

*Because we are using multicharacter names for some flip flops and lines, we will always use $A \cdot B$ in DDL, since AB might be the name of a register.

[†]The symbol $+$ indicates OR, not addition. Addition requires more logic than a single gate per bit.

would describe another copy of the same adder, but with 16-bit inputs W and T and a carry input of 0.

A system description consists of two parts: some definitions and the control sequence specification. We will first define the steps of a sequence and then go on to a description of the whole system.

The control sequence is a list of numbered steps, where each step can specify one or more of the following:

the movement of data

the connection of data

the flow of control in the sequence.

Each step is numbered (decimal numbers followed by a period) and the step is terminated with a period. Steps begin on a new line, usually indented, such that the numbers line up. Each step may include any number of data transfers and connections, separated by semicolons, followed by a branch in control, if necessary. We will be more exact in the definition after we have defined each of the things that can be included in a step.

The transfer of information to a register is denoted by a left-facing arrow ($\leftarrow$). Thus, the statement

    A ← B

means transfer the value of B to register A. B may be another register or a set of lines. However, it must be the same number of bits as A. Thus, if A is 4 bits long, then B must also be 4 bits. The source, B, is unchanged by this transfer. On the other hand, if B is a register, a second transfer loading B could be included in that step. Other valid transfers would include

A ← 7	(loading the binary value 0111 into A)
A ← A′	(loading the bit-by-bit complement of A into A)
A ← A · B	(loading the output of the AND logic, that is, four AND gates into A)

The left side of a transfer statement must always refer to a set of flip flops; it could be a single register or flip flop or it could be a string of registers such as A, B, **c**. That would specify 9 bits, first the 4 bits of A, then the 4 bits of B, and finally the 1 bit of **c**.

If C is a 3-bit register, then neither C ← A nor A ← C is legal, since they are not well defined. In either case, it is not clear which three bits of A are involved. One could write, for example, $A_{1:3} \leftarrow$ C (in which case C would be moved to the right 3 bits of A and A_0 would be unchanged) or $A_{0:2} \leftarrow$ C (in which case C would be moved to the left 3 bits of A and A_3 would be unchanged) or A ← 0, C (in which case a 0 would go to A_0 and C would go the right 3 bits of A) or A ← C, 0 (in which case C goes to the left 3 bits of A and 0 goes to A_3).

The value on a set of lines (be they a bus, an output vector, or just some internal lines) can be defined using a connection statement. It takes the same form as a transfer except that the arrow is replaced by an equal (=). Thus the statement

```
OUT = A
```

means connect A to the lines OUT. As before, both sides of the equal must have the same number of bits. The connection statement defines a *transitory situation*, that is, the connection is made *only during the time the statement is in effect*. It does not store the value. Thus, OUT must be the name of lines, not the name of a register. When a line is not connected, it is 0.

Sometimes, transfers or connections are to be made only if a certain condition is met. That is denoted by listing the condition first, followed by a colon, followed by the transfer. For example,

```
x: B ← A
```

denotes if the condition, **x** is 1, transfer A to B. Since nothing else is indicated, it implies that no transfer would take place if **x** is 0. You could specify two or more conditional transfer in one step; for example,

```
x': D ← C;
x: B ← A
```

It is often convenient to structure a set of registers as an array, where the first register is the first row of the array. Thus, the array of 16 registers, REG, includes REG^0, REG^1, through REG^{15}. When referencing that array, an address is usually provided. (In this case, that would be a 4-bit binary number, since 4 bits provide 2^4 combinations.) The register of the array REG referenced by register A is denoted by

```
REG / A.
```

This notation implies decoding hardware and a multiplexor or switch. Thus, if register A contained (hexadecimal) 6, then

```
D ← REG / A
```

would load REG^6 into D.

After the execution of the transfers and connections in a step, control continues with the next step (in ascending numerical order) unless otherwise specified. Such specification is provided by a line

```
next: 7.
```

to specify that the next step executed is always step 7 (that is, the word next followed by a colon and the step number). The construct for a conditional branch is next followed by a colon followed by a list. Each item in the list is a step number with a condition in parentheses. For example,

```
6. next: 14 (a), 7 (a').
```

says go to step 7 if **a** is 1 and to 14 if **a'** is 1 (or, equivalently, **a** is 0). The conditions must be mutually exclusive and one of them must be 1 at all times. Thus, there is a branch to one and only one place. The list can include any number of branches. The last condition can be shown as else, which is 1 if none of the other conditions are 1. Thus, the branches

```
6. next: 14 (a), 7 (a').
6. next: 14 (a), 7 (else).
6. next: 7 (a'), 14 (else).
```

all do exactly the same thing. The conditions are evaluated simultaneously, not sequentially. This step corresponds to a pair of AND gates in the hard-wired implementation of this, as shown in Figure 9.11a. Thus, if you want to branch to step 14 if **a** is 1, to step 20 if **b** is 1 (but not **a**), and to step 7 if both are 0, you must write

```
6. next: 14 (a), 20 (a' · b), 7 (else).
```

as shown in Figure 9.11b, or as two steps,

```
6. next: 14 (a), 6a (else).
6a. next: 20 (b), 7 (else).
```

It is not proper to write

```
6. next: 14 (a), 20(b) 7 (else).
```

Unless you know that **a** and **b** will never be one at the same time.

One additional branch step is provided, to allow a multiway branch on the basis of a vector:

```
next / A: {list of step numbers}.
```

If A is an n-bit vector, then the list includes 2^n step numbers, one for each combination of A.

Figure 9.11   Implementation of conditional branches.

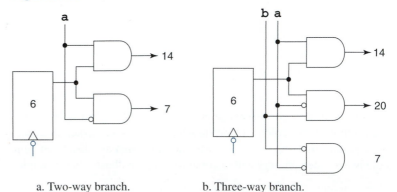

a. Two-way branch.   b. Three-way branch.

We will now be a little more exact about the definition of a step. Following the step number (and a period), there may be any number (including none) of transfers and connections, separated by semicolons (;). These may be followed by at most one branch (next). If so, it is separated from the transfers and connections by a semicolon. The step is ended with a period. It is possible to have a step containing no transfers or connections (such as in steps 1 and 3 in Example 9.3) or no branch (such as in step 2). Indeed, it is also possible to have one with neither— just the step number followed by a period. In that case, nothing happens during the clock period when the system is at that step. This is sometimes required to satisfy the timing constraints of the problem.

If a step has multiple transfers, they all take place at the same time. The order in which they are written is not important. For example,

    D ← A; A ← C

behaves the same as

    A ← C; D ← A.

Both move what was in A before the clock to D and what was in C before the clock to A. Also, if a conditional branch is included in that step, it depends on the values in registers before the transfers specified in that step. (See Examples 9.4 and 9.5.)

The definition section of a system description begins with a line

    SYSTEM NAME:

where the key words are followed by a name for this system. Next, the inputs, outputs, buses, and flip flops of the logic and register section of the system must be defined. Each follows the same format: key word(s), followed by a colon, followed by a list. The list includes all items in the category. In the case of vectors, the range of that vector is included in brackets. For arrays, the range of each dimension is included in brackets, separated by commas (rows first). The key words are:

    INPUT LINE
    OUTPUT LINE
    INTERNAL BUS
    INTERSYSTEM BUS
    FLIP FLOP

They are made plural when appropriate. We have seen many of these in the last example. INTERNAL BUS is used to define a bus connecting various components within this system. INTERSYSTEM BUS is used to define a bus connecting this system to another. An example of a definition line is

    FLIP FLOPS: **x,** A[0:7], REG[0:15, 0:31].

defining a single flip flop, **x**, an 8-bit register, A, and an array REG, consisting of 16 rows of 32 bits each.

There are three other types of definition lines:

```
CONNECTION
INITIALIZE
NAME
```

The line

```
CONNECTION: Z = A.
```

is used to specify that the lines Z (usually an output) are always connected to A (usually a register).

The line

```
INITIALIZE: 1, A = 00.
```

specifies that when the system is turned on, the hardware puts it in state 1 (that is, at step 1 in the sequence) and stores 00 in register A. The initialization only works when the system is first turned on, not each time it returns to step 1.

The line

```
NAME: SP = REG³ᶠ
```

allows us to use either name for the same set of flip flops or lines. Only one of them needs to be defined in the FLIP FLOP or LINE definitions.

The system description is concluded with the line

```
END DESCRIPTION.
```

Although step numbers are often continuous, it is permissible to skip numbers. This is particularly convenient when developing a complex sequence in which a branch to two subsequences occurs. Under one condition, you may want to go to the next step. Under the other condition, you want to go to a different sequence. But until you have written that first sequence, you do not know how many steps are required and therefore do not know the step number. You may choose a sufficiently large number (say, 50); nonexistent step numbers are ignored. Also, after writing a lengthy sequence, you might find a mistake and need to insert one or more steps. You may number the steps between 11 and 12 as 11a, 11b, etc. (That would probably not be possible if you were running a computer simulation of the system.)

EXAMPLE 9.4

The behavior of each of the following DDL steps is examined.

```
5. B ← AD; AD ← INC[AD].
5. AD ← INC[AD]; B ← AD.
```

In both cases, the contents of register AD are transferred to register B, and 1 is added to the contents of AD. (Both B and AD are clocked at the same time; the old value of AD is moved to B.) To move the incremented value of AD to B, you would either have to write it as two steps.

```
5.  AD ← INC[AD].
5a. B ← AD.
```

or move the output of the incrementer to B

```
5.  B ← INC[AD]; AD ← INC[AD].
```

In all of these, the next step would be step 6, since there is no branch.

```
10.  COUNT ← DEC[COUNT];
     next: 20 ((OR[COUNT])'), 11 (else).
```

DEC is a logic block that decrements (subtracts 1 from) a number. OR represents an OR gate that has as its inputs all the bits of COUNT. OR[COUNT] is 1 if any bit of COUNT is 1; (OR[COUNT])' is 1 if COUNT contains all 0's.

This is a typical loop control step. The branch is executed at the same time as COUNT is loaded. Thus, it is the old value of COUNT that is used. In this case, 1 is subtracted from COUNT; if it had a 0 in it *before* decrementing, the next step to be executed is 20. Otherwise, it goes on to step 11.

9.3.2 A Timing Refinement

In each of the controllers we have seen so far, each step takes one clock time. (See Figures 9.6b or 9.8.) If a system is being implemented with a hard-wired controller, a timing refinement can be made that will improve the speed and reduce the complexity of the controller. Sometimes it is possible to execute two or more consecutive steps at the same time. A good example is steps 2 and 3 of the controller in Example 9.3, the control sequence for which is repeated here.

```
1.  next: 1 (compute'), 2(compute).
2.  T ← IN.
3.  next / a, b: 7, 6, 5, 4.
4.  T ← 0, T_{0:18}.
5.  T ← 0, T_{0:18}.
6.  T ← 0, T_{0:18}.
7.  OUT ← T.
8.  done = 1;
    next: 1.
```

The branch conditions do not depend on the value being loaded into T at the previous step. One way of doing this is just to rewrite these steps as one, namely

```
2. T ← IN;
   next / a, b: 7, 6, 5, 4.
```

In this example, there is no need to renumber the other steps; there just is no step 3. (No problem is created by leaving out step numbers in a DDL sequence as long as control never branches to a nonexistent step.) Note that this solution eliminates flip flop 3 in the sequencer; the output from flip flop 2 goes directly to the inputs to the set of 4 AND gates. It also reduces the execution time by one clock pulse, since step 3 is no longer there to be executed.

Another way is to indicate that a step is *undelayed*, that is, may be executed at the same time as the previous one (and therefore its flip flop is removed from the controller), is to enclose the step number in parentheses. Thus,

```
2.    T ← IN.
(3.) next / a, b: 7, 6, 5, 4.
```

behaves precisely the same way as the earlier one-step implementation. We can use a timing trace as well as a timing diagram. Each step other than the undelayed one is written on a separate line. For undelayed step 3, the timing trace is written with the 3 on the same line as the 2 (following a comma).

```
1
:
1
2, 3
5
6
7
8
```

The timing is measured by counting lines (and thus 2, 3 counts as only one clock). There is little reason to use this notation in a simple case like this one; we might just as well have combined steps. But there are places where there is no other convenient way to introduce this speed improvement into the notation.

In order to be able to utilize this technique, two conditions must be satisfied. First, the undelayed step must not depend on the results of the step or steps being done at the same time. For example, step 4 could not be executed at the same time as 3 (and 2) since 4 uses the contents of register T (it is on the right side of a transfer statement), which is being loaded at that same time (by step 2). A second condition that must be observed is that two steps cannot be done at the same time if they utilize the same resource. In a bused system, it is not possible to do two data transfers simultaneously by way of the same bus. We will see more of this in the next chapter when we look at the implementation of MODEL. Finally, whenever you are considering taking advantage of this, you must look at all previous steps. If this step can be reached from more than one place, you must examine both predecessors since either may be executed simultaneously with this step. (And, if either of those steps is undelayed, you must continue back to other steps that would be executed simultaneously with these.)

EXAMPLE 9.6

Sometimes, it is convenient to write branches as separate steps, rather than as one complex step. For example,

```
6.    next: 12 (ready), 7 (else).
(7.)  next: 10 (AND[COUNT]), 8 (else).
```

Since the braches at steps 6 and 7 are unrelated, we might choose to write it this way, rather than combining it into one step

```
6.   next: 12 (ready), 10 (ready' · AND[COUNT]),
     8 (else).
```

The former is much more readable; the amount of logic is very similar, as shown here.

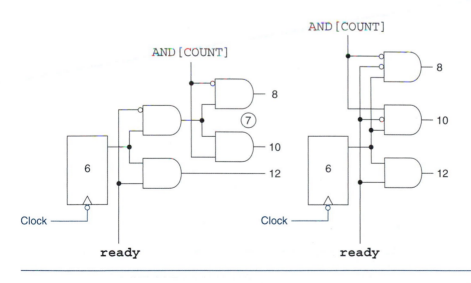

[SP 2, 3, 4; EX 3, 4, 5, 6, 7, 8]

9.4 DESIGNING A CONTROLLER

In this section, we will look at the design process, starting from the verbal description.

> On a **start** signal, the system reads in four 24-bit numbers and computes their sum. (Ignore overflow.) When the system desires an input number, it makes line **inready** 1 for one clock period. A new number will be available on the 24-bit input lines X at the next clock. The answer is placed on the 24-bit output lines Z and then line **done** is made 1 for one clock period.

First, let us make sure that we understand the implications of the wording. English can be rather vague. In a real-world design situation, it is often necessary to go back to the person who wrote the specifications for clarification. Or, once you propose a solution to the problem, the specifier may tell you that that is not quite what he or she had in mind, and you must modify the design.

What is meant by "On a **start** signal" is when the line **start** goes to 1. We will assume that **start** remains 1 for only 1 clock period, although it really will not make any difference in our design, as long as **start** has returned to 0 by the time the process is complete and the system returns to look for a new **start**. The timing for **inready** is clear. That signal is 1 for one clock period. The new number is not on lines X until after the next clock. If **inready** remains 1 for two or more clock periods, new values will appear on X as indicated in Figure 9.12. The only issue is how long does a number remain on X. Figure 9.12 shows it there until after the next time **inready** is 1. It could be that it is available for only one clock period. As it will turn out in our design, either is acceptable, since we use X as soon as it is available. You might read the problem to imply that all four input numbers must first be copied into the system and then added. That was not the intent in this case; they will be obtained one at a time and added into a partial sum. On the other hand, a solution that did store the four numbers before doing

Figure 9.12 Timing for **inready**.

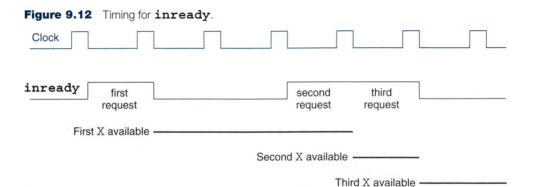

the computation would also be acceptable (but more expensive). Finally, it is clear that the answer must be available on lines Z before **done** is made 1. What is not clear is how long they should remain there. The simplest solution will connect the output there until the next **start**, after which the lines Z will have no useful information on them until the next **done**. (We will look at some alternatives to that later.)

We will design the system with a single internal 24-bit register, SUM, and thus the block diagram of Figure 9.13 will serve to describe the system.

Figure 9.13   Block Diagram of ADDER SYSTEM.

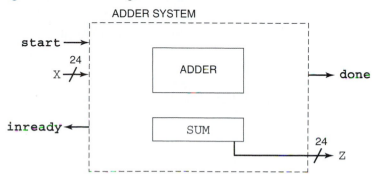

The definition lines can be readily seen from that diagram.

```
SYSTEM NAME: ADDER SYSTEM
        INPUT LINES: start, X[0:23].
        OUTPUT LINES: inready, done, Z[0:23].
        FLIP FLOPS: SUM[0:23].
        CONNECTION: Z = SUM.
```

where the connection line is required since the output Z always remains connected to the register SUM.

A straightforward approach to the control sequence is as follows:

```
1. next: 1 (start'), 2 (start).
2. SUM ← 000000.
3. inready = 1.
4. SUM ← ADD[SUM; X].
5. inready = 1.
6. SUM ← ADD[SUM; X].
7. inready = 1.
8. SUM ← ADD[SUM; X].
9. inready = 1.
10.SUM ← ADD[SUM; X].
11.done = 1;
   next: 1.
```

This system assumes that the module ADD has been defined as a binary adder, adding two 24-bit numbers and producing a 24-bit result (and the carry out of the last stage is ignored).

Notice that the pairs of steps (3, 4), (5, 6), (7, 8), and (9, 10) are identical. Thus, we have four pairs of identical steps to add four numbers. This approach can be extended to any size set of numbers; it requires, in addition to steps 1, 2 and 11, $2n$ steps to add a set of n numbers. It is true that one step could have been saved. Step 2 is unnecessary if step 4 is replaced by

```
4.  SUM ← X.
```

That is often not done so as to maximize the repetitive steps for use in a loop. We will look at the loop implementation in more detail shortly.

Given the input timing, there is no reason why this system could not ask for the next number while doing the addition. A new X does not appear until after the clock when **inready** is 1. Also, steps 2 and 3 could be done simultaneously. We could make steps, 3, 5, 7, and 9 undelayed or rewrite the controller

```
1.  next: 1 (start'), 2 (start).
2.  SUM ← 000000; inready = 1.
3.  SUM ← ADD[SUM; X]; inready = 1.
4.  SUM ← ADD[SUM; X]; inready = 1.
5.  SUM ← ADD[SUM; X]; inready = 1.
6.  SUM ← ADD[SUM; X].
7.  done = 1;
    next: 1.
```

A timing trace for these two approaches is shown in Figure 9.14a and b. It is obvious that the second is four clocks faster than the first. One further timing improvement is possible. Step 2 could be executed during the last clock period the system is in step 1. If this is to be implemented with a hard-wired controller, we could make step 2 undelayed (denoting that with parentheses). If not, step 1 could be rewritten

```
1.  start: SUM ← 000000; inready = 1;
    next: 1 (start'), 3 (start).
```

Figure 9.14   Timing traces for ADDER SYSTEM.

(a) 1   ...   1   2   3   4   5   6   7   8   9   10   11

(b) 1   ...   1   2   3   4   5   6   7

(c) 1   ...   1   2   3   4   3   4   3   4   3   4   5

(d) 1   ...   1,2,3   4,3   4,3   4,3   4   5

In that case, SUM would be clocked and **inready** set to 1 on the last clock time the system was in state 1, namely, when **start** had gone to 1. Either of them would save one clock.

Steps 3, 4, and 5 are identical. If we were adding n numbers, we would need $n - 1$ copies of that step in addition to steps 1, 2, 6, and 7.

For large n, it is more economical to replace these common steps by a loop. Even for the four numbers of this example, the loop approach has advantages. An additional register, COUNT[0:1], is used to control the loop. It is initialized to 0 and incremented each time through the loop. The loop is terminated after n times. We will first produce an ASM diagram, as in Figure 9.15, where the logic block INC computes the number 1 larger than the input. If the input is all 1's (hexadecimal 3 in this example), the output is 0.

The first time, the system reaches step 4, COUNT = 1, having been incremented at step 3. The second time, COUNT = 2, and the third time, COUNT = 3. In each of these cases, OR[COUNT] is 1, and the branch at step 4 is back to step 3. On the fourth pass, COUNT = 0, since the 2-bit counter recycles to 0 when it reaches its maximum (3). Control then falls through to step 5. The timing for this is shown in Figure 9.14c.

Thus, our first control sequence would become

1. next: 1 (**start'**), 2 (**start**).
2. SUM ← 000000; COUNT ← 0.
3. **inready** = 1; COUNT ← INC[COUNT].
4. SUM ← ADD[SUM; X];
   next: 3 (OR[COUNT]), 5 (else).
5. **done** = 1;
   next: 1.

Note that the loop version takes the same amount of time as the original version. This could be made to run faster by making step 3 undelayed. In each of these examples, we could save one more clock time by making step 2 undelayed.

If n were larger than 4, the changes that would be required are that COUNT would need to be larger, INC would represent a larger incrementer, and the test in step 4 may have to be modified. For example, if n were 32, COUNT would be 5 bits. Step 4 would look the same, although OR[COUNT] would imply a five-input OR gate instead of a two-input one. That would be the case whenever the size of the set of inputs is a power of 2. If, on the other hand, there were 20 numbers, then the branch in step 4 would become

next: 5 ($COUNT_0 \cdot COUNT_2$), 3 (else)

that is, the loop is terminated when COUNT reaches 20 (10100).*

---

*There is no need to test the other bits of COUNT since the first time that $COUNT_0$ and $COUNT_2$ are both 1 is when COUNT reaches 20.

Figure 9.15   ASM diagram for adder system.

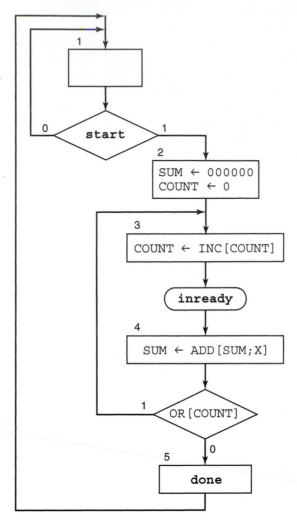

In this example, the counter was incremented at one clock time and tested at the next. Sometimes, both of these occur at the same time. In that case, COUNT is tested *before* it is incremented, and thus the test must be for $n - 1$. Remember that COUNT is loaded on the trailing edge of the clock pulse, whereas the 1 is clocked into either flip flop 3 or 5 based on the conditions existing at the beginning of that clock pulse. Our four number adder becomes

1.   next: 1 (**start'**), 2 (**start**).
2.   SUM ← 000000; COUNT ← 0.
3.   **inready** = 1.

4.   SUM ← ADD[SUM; X]; COUNT ← INC[COUNT];
     next: 5 (AND[COUNT]), 3 (else).
5.   **done** = 1;
     next: 1.

Control returns to step 3 until COUNT reaches all 1's. The timing for this version is the same as for the last one (See Figure 9.14c.).

Finally, we can get this to operate faster by making steps 2 and 3 undelayed (as we did in the nonloop version). That timing is shown in Figure 9.14d.

1.   next: 1 (**start'**), 2 (**start**).
(2.) SUM ← 000000; COUNT ← 0.
(3.) **inready** = 1.
4   SUM ← ADD[SUM; X]; COUNT ← INC[COUNT];
     next: 5 (AND[COUNT]), 3 (else).
5.   **done** = 1;
     next: 1.

A block diagram of the controller is shown in Figure 9.16, where the flip flops that have been eliminated (corresponding to undelayed steps) are shown dashed.

Figure 9.16 Controller with undelayed steps.

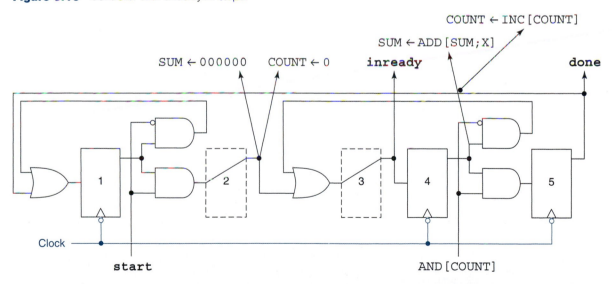

We want to design a device, SUMMER, that computes the sum of a set of numbers. The numbers are stored in consecutive locations in a memory. To read from that memory, put a 1 on line **read** and the memory address on

EXAMPLE 9.7

ADIN for one clock period. By the end of that clock period, the contents of that memory location are available on DATA and can be clocked into a register.

When this device receives a 1 on input line **start** (for one clock period), the 16-bit address of the first number is on intersystem bus DD (during the same clock period). At the next clock period, the address of the last number of the set is also on intersystem bus DD for one clock period. This device then computes the sum of these numbers and, when it is done, puts a 1 on output line **sum** for one clock period and puts the sum of the numbers on bus DD during the following clock period. It then returns to wait for a new **start**. Assume that there is no overflow.

```
SYSTEM NAME: SUMMER.

        FLIP FLOPS: SUM[0:15], FST[0:15],
        LST[0:15], TEMP[0:15].
        INPUT LINE: start.
        OUTPUT LINES: sum, read, ADIN[0:15].
        INTERSYSTEM BUSSES: DATA[0:15], DD[0:15].
        1.  FST ← DD; SUM ← 0000;
            next: 1 (start'), 2 (else).
        2.  LST ← DD.
        3.  ADIN = FST; read = 1; TEMP ← DATA.
        4.  SUM ← ADD[SUM; TEMP].
        5.  next: 6(OR[FST ⊕ LST]), 10 (else).
        6.  FST ← ADD[FST; 0001];
            next: 3.
        10. sum = 1.
        11. DD = SUM;
            next: 1.
END DESCRIPTION
```

Note that SUM is set to 0 and DD is loaded into FST over and over again as the system waits for **start** to go to 1. This is not a problem since DD is not used until after **start** is 1. The data read from memory is stored in a temporary register, TEMP. If memory were fast enough so that data was available in time to do the addition at the same clock, we could combine steps 3 and 4 to

```
3. ADIN = F; read = 1;
   SUM ← ADD[SUM; DATA].
```

The Exclusive-OR produces a 16-bit word that contains 1's where the bits of `FST` and `LST` differ, and 0's elsewhere. When they are equal, the 16-bit OR gate produces 0 and step 5 jumps to step 10 in order to output the answer.

[SP 5, 6, 7, 8;
EX 9, 10, 11, 12, 13, 14]

9.5 SOLVED PROBLEMS

1. I am constructing a system with four 16-bit registers: *A, B, C,* and *D*. I am considering two approaches to the design.

   a. Design 1 involves a bus, connecting all registers. The controller will then produce such signals as BUS = A, BUS = B, . . . and A ← BUS, . . . Show a block diagram of a typical bit of such a design. How many AND gates are required to implement the multiplexers for this system?

   b. Design 2 is a point-to-point scheme. Each register has two-way multiplexers on its inputs and can thus receive data directly from two of the three other registers, namely,

   > *A* from *B* and *D*
   > *B* from *A* and *C*
   > *C* from *B* and *D*
   > *D* from *A* and *C*

   The controller now sends such signals as *A* ← *B*, . . . Show a block diagram of a typical bit of such a design. How many AND gates are required to implement the multiplexers for this system?

   c. If design 1 is used, what transfers are available that are not available in design 2.

   d. I wish to accomplish the following three transfers simultaneously

   > *C* ← *A*; *A* ← *C*; *B* ← *D*

   If I had a complete point-to-point connection (that is, the ability to do all possible transfers), I would do these all in one step. But neither of the designs permits that; I must do them in two or more steps. Show the sequence of transfers for each of the designs. Be sure that after the sequence, register *D* contains the value it started with.

   a. This requires four AND gates per bit for the multiplexers or a total of 64 AND gates for the multiplexers. There are four more AND gates for the clock. (The output of the clock AND gates go to each bit of that register.) This allows only one transfer at a time. Bit 2 of the system is shown.

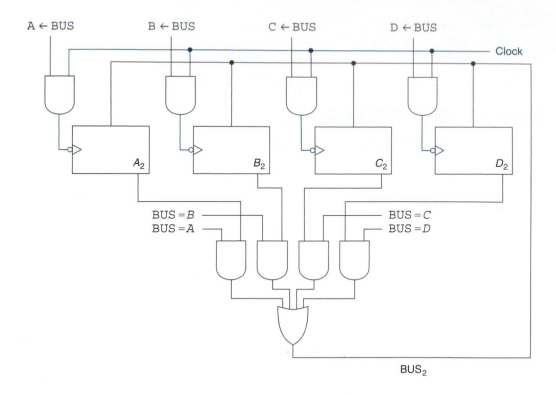

b. This requires eight AND gates per bit for the multiplexers, a total of 128 AND gates for the multiplexers. There are four more AND gates for the clock. This solution also uses many more OR gates (four per bit rather than one, plus four more for the clocks).

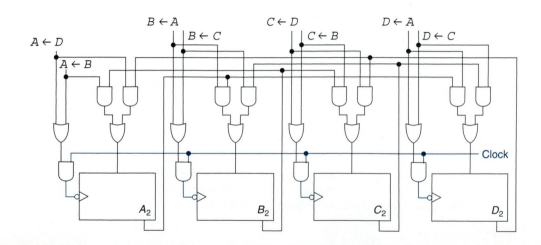

c. $A \leftarrow C, B \leftarrow D, C \leftarrow A, D \leftarrow B$

d. Assuming we want to preserve the contents of register D, we must move it somewhere temporarily and restore it at the end. The contents of the four register is shown after each step.

		BUS				*Point-to-Point*		
	A	*B*	*C*	*D*	*A*	*B*	*C*	*D*
$B \leftarrow D$					$A \leftarrow D; B \leftarrow A$			
	A	*D*	*C*	*D*	*D*	*A*	*C*	*D*
$D \leftarrow C$					$B \leftarrow A; C \leftarrow B; D \leftarrow C$			
	A	*D*	*C*	*C*	*D*	*D*	*A*	*C*
$C \leftarrow A$					$A \leftarrow D; D \leftarrow A$			
	A	*D*	*A*	*C*	*C*	*D*	*A*	*D*
$A \leftarrow D$								
	C	*D*	*A*	*C*				
$D \leftarrow B$								
	C	*D*	*A*	*D*				

2. Design a faster version of SHIFTER (Example 9.3), where there is hardware to shift one, two, or three places in one clock time.

The sequence is very similar. Steps 4 and 5 shift three and two places, and then go directly to step 7. Thus steps 2 through 8 take four clock times compared with up to seven clock times in Example 9.3. (Note that OUT is only loaded with the correct answers in either approach.) Indeed, steps 4 to 7 could be undelayed, reducing the time to three clock times.

```
SYSTEM NAME: SHIFTER
        INPUT LINES: compute, a, b, IN[0:19].
        OUTPUT LINES: OUT[0:19], done.
        FLIP FLOPS: T[0:19], OUT[0:19].
        1. next: 1 (compute'), 2 (compute).
        2. T ← IN.
        3. next / a, b: 7, 6, 5, 4.
        4. OUT ← 0³, T₀:₁₆;
           next: 8.
        5. OUT ← 0², T₀:₁₇;
           next: 8.
        6. OUT ← 0, T₀:₁₈;
           next: 8.
        7. OUT ← T.
```

8. **done** = 1;

next: 1.

END DESCRIPTION

This solution requires a four-way multiplexor for each bit, as shown here.

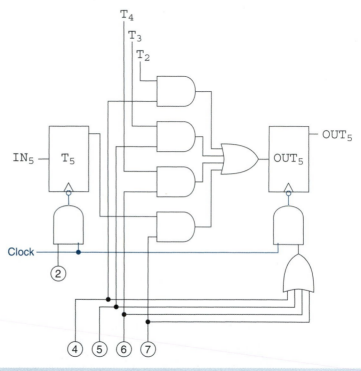

3. For the following system, show a block diagram of the register and logic section. Show all of the flip flops, the output line **d**, the clock inputs, and the signal lines coming from the controller

```
SYSTEM NAME: MOVER
      INPUT LINES: A[0:1].
      OUTPUT LINE: d.
      FLIP FLOPS: B[0:1], C[0:1].
      1.  B ← A; C ← A.
      2.  C ← B'; B ← A.
      3.  B ← C · B.
      4.  d = OR [B ⊕ C];
          next: 1.
END DESCRIPTION
```

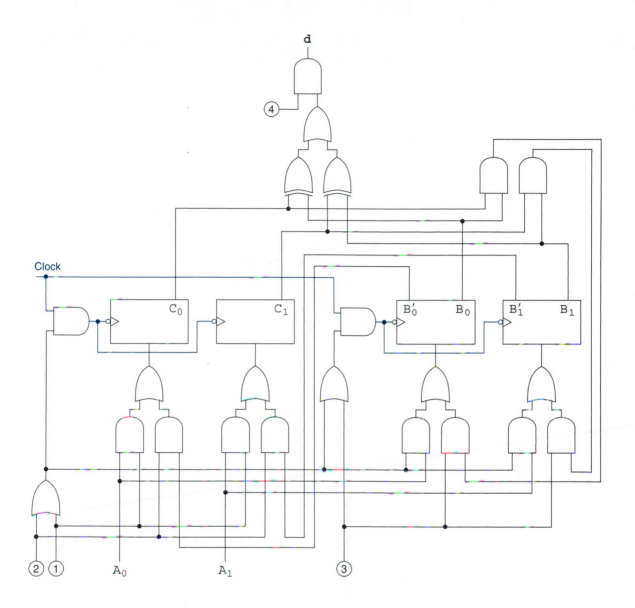

Each flip flop needs a two-way multiplexor. Since A is moved to B at both steps 1 and 2, we need only one AND for that transfer. The AND gate on the output is required to ensure that **d** is 1 only during the clock period the system is at step 4.

4. Consider the following DDL

```
SYSTEM NAME: TESTER
     INPUT LINE: .
    OUTPUT LINE: .
```

```
FLIP FLOPS: .
1. start = 1.
2.  .
3. A ← IN.
4. A ← A_{1:14}, 0^1.
5. A ← A_{1:14}, 0^1.
(6.) next: 1 (ok), 7 (else).
7. next: 6.
END DESCRIPTION
```

a. Complete the definition lines.

b. Draw a block diagram of the sequencer.

c. Complete the following timing diagram. Assume that you reach state 1 at the first clock.

a. INPUT LINE: IN[0:14], **ok.**

    OUTPUT LINE: **start.**

    FLIP FLOPS: A[0:14].

We know that A and IN must be 15 bits since the transfers at steps 4 and 5 move 15 bits into A.

b.

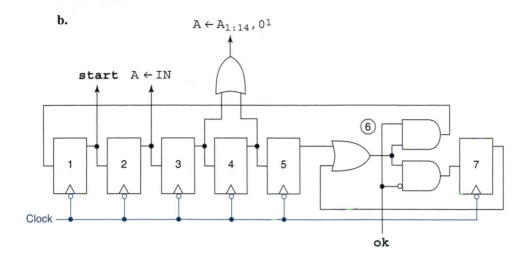

$$A \leftarrow A_{1:14}, 0^1$$

start $A \leftarrow IN$

Clock

ok

c.

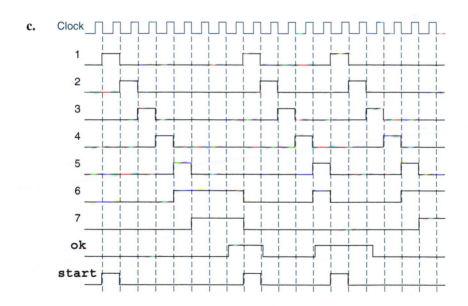

Clock

1

2

3

4

5

6

7

ok

start

5. Write a complete DDL description of a hard-wired controller for the following system, ONE.

When the input line **stop** goes to 0, the output line **out** starts alternating between 1 and 0. It continues until **stop** returns to 1. (It repeats the process when **stop** goes to 0 again.)

```
SYSTEM NAME: ONE
     INPUT LINES: stop
     OUTPUT LINES: out
     1.   next: 1 (stop), 2 (else).
     (2.) out = 1.
     3.   next: 1
END DESCRIPTION
```

Line **out** is 1 at the same time **stop** is 0. As long as **stop** remains 0, this system's timing trace is

1, 2
3
1, 2
3
1, 2
3

when **stop** goes to 1, it remains in state 1.

6. Write a complete DDL description of a system, COUNT. It has an input line **start** and a 15-bit input set, $X[0:14]$. When **start** goes to 1 for one clock period, a new 15-bit number will appear on X at the next clock time. The system computes how many 0's there are in that number. It then outputs that count on lines ZERO$[0:3]$. Output line **done** is made 1 for two clock periods when the answer is available.

There are three possible timing situations for the output.

a. ZERO has the answer only when **done** is 1 and is 0^4 at all other times.

b. ZERO has the answer only when **done** is 1 but may contain anything at all other times.

c. ZERO has the answer starting when **done** is 1 until **start** is 1 again and is 0^4 at all other times.

a. The first solution for part (a) uses a counter, C, to keep track of how many bits. C is initialized to 0 and allows us to go around the loop 15 times. (Note that on the 15th time, C contains 14, 1110, and the test is based on AND[INC[C]].) The left bit of A is tested as it is shifted to the left. (In this case, it really doesn't matter what is loaded into the right bit of A.) In both solutions for timing (a) the output is connected to ZERO only when **done** is 1.

```
SYSTEM NAME: COUNT
      INPUT LINES: start, X[0:14].
      FLIP FLOPS: A[0:14], N[0:3], C[0:3].
      OUTPUT LINES: ZERO[0:3], done.
      1. next: 2 (start), 1 (else).
      2. A ← X; N ← 0⁴; C ← 0⁴.
      3. A₀': N ← INC[N].
         A ← A₁:₁₄, 1;
         C ← INC[C];
         next: 4 (AND[INC[C]]), 3 (else).
      4. done = 1; ZERO = N.
      5. done = 1; ZERO = N;
         next: 1.
END DESCRIPTION
```

The second solution takes advantage of the fact that if we shift in 1's, we can quit counting when A contains all 1's. We do not need to count the number of bits in the word (C can be eliminated).

```
SYSTEM NAME: COUNT
      INPUT LINES: start, X[0:14].
      FLIP FLOPS: A[0:14], N[0:3].
      OUTPUT LINES: ZERO[0:3], done.
      1. next: 2 (start), 1 (else).
      2. A ← X; N ← 0⁴.
      3. A₀': N ← INC[N].
         A ← A₁:₁₄, 1;
         next: 4(AND[A₁:₁₄]), 3(else).
      4. done = 1; ZERO = N.
      5. done = 1; ZERO = N;
         next: 1.
END DESCRIPTION
```

b. In this solution, the computation is done in register ZERO, which is always connected to the output. It has the answer until the next time it reaches step 2. At other times, it has an intermediate result.

```
SYSTEM NAME: COUNT
      INPUT LINES: start, X[0:14].
```

FLIP FLOPS: A[0:14], ZERO[0:3].

OUTPUT LINES: ZERO[0:30], **done**.

1. next: 2 (**start**), 1 (else).

2. A ← X; ZERO ← 0^4.

3. A_0': ZERO ← INC[ZERO].

   A ← $A_{1:14}$, 1;

   next: 4 (AND[$A_{1:14}$]), 3 (else).

4. **done** = 1.

5. **done** = 1;

   next: 1.

END DESCRIPTION

c. In this version, ZERO is loaded with the answer as **done** is made 1, and then is cleared when **start** goes to 1.

SYSTEM NAME: COUNT

   INPUT LINES: **start**, X[0:14].

   FLIP FLOPS: A[0:14], N[0:3], ZERO[0:3].

   OUTPUT LINES: ZERO[0:30], **done**.

1. **start:** ZERO ← 0^4;

   next: 2 (**start**), 1 (else).

2. A ← X; N ← 0^4.

3. A_0': N ← INC[N].

   A ← $A_{1:14}$, 1;

   next: 4 (AND[$A_{1:14}$]), 3 (else).

4. ZERO ← N.

5. **done** = 1

6. **done** = 1;

   next: 1.

END DESCRIPTION

7. Write the complete DDL description of a system, PATTERN, with one input line, **in**, and one output line, **out**. At some time, line **in** goes to 1 for one or more clock periods. When it returns to 0, line **out** goes to 1 for two clock periods and then 0 for one clock period, repeating this so that **out** is 110 the same number of clock times that **in** was 1. If **in** is 1 for more than 15 clock times, the pattern continues for 15 times. Input **in** is ignored while **out** is going through its cycle. When it is finished, the system goes back and looks at **in** again. Note: **out**

can go to 1 at the first clock that **in** is 0 or the next one. Also, the system may return to watch **in** immediately after the last 1 output or one clock time later.

```
SYSTEM NAME: PATTERN
      INPUT LINE: in.
      OUTPUT LINE: out.
      FLIP FLOPS: C[0:3].
      1. next: 2 (in), 1 (else).
      2. C ← 1⁴;
         next: 3 (in), 4 (else).
      3. (AND[C])': C ← INC[C];
         next: 3 (in), 4 (else).
      4. out = 1.
      5. out = 1.
      6. C ← DEC[C];
         next: 4 (OR[DEC[C]]), 1 (else).

   END DESCRIPTION
```

Note that C is loaded with the hexadecimal constant 1 (0001 in binary) at step 2.

8. Design a system to multiply two unsigned 16-bit numbers and output the 32-bit result. When there is a 1 on input line **multiply** for one clock period, a 16-bit number is available on bus DATA. A second number is available when **multiply** goes to 1 again. When the product is computed, the least significant 16 bits are placed on DATA and line **ready** is made 1. They remain until there is a 1 on line **thanks**. That process is then repeated for the most significant 16 bits.

```
SYSTEM NAME: MULTIPLIER
      INPUT LINES: multiply, thanks.
      OUTPUT LINE: ready.
      INTERSYSTEM BUS: DATA[0:15].
      FLIP FLOPS: OP1[0:15], OP2[0:15],
      PRODUCT[0:15], COUNT[0:3],t.
      1.   next: 1 (multiply'), 2 (else).
      (2.) OP1 ← DATA.
      3.   next: 3 (multiply'), 4 (else).
      (4.) OP2 ← DATA.
```

(5.)   PRODUCT $\leftarrow$ 0000; COUNT $\leftarrow$ 0, **t** $\leftarrow$ 0.

6.   next: 8 (OP2$_{15}'$), 16 (else).

(7.)   **t**, PRODUCT $\leftarrow$ ADD[OP1; PRODUCT; **t**].

8.   **t**, PRODUCT, OP2 $\leftarrow$ 0, **t**, PRODUCT, OP2$_{0:14}$.

(9.)   C $\leftarrow$ INC[C];

next: 6 (OR[C]), 10 (else).

10.   **ready** = 1; DATA = OP1;

next: 10 (**thanks**), 11 (else).

11.   **ready** = 1; DATA = PRODUCT;

next: 11 (**thanks**), 1 (else).

END OF DESCRIPTION

The adder adds two 16-bit numbers plus a carry input and produces a 17-bit answer, clocked into **t** and PRODUCT. OP1 stores the multiplicand, and OP2 initially stores the multiplier. The product is computed in the 32-bit location, consisting of PRODUCT and OP2. The bits of the multiplier are examined. If the bit is 1, the multiplicand is added into the partial product. That is then shifted right (corresponding to our shifting the multiplicand left when we do multiplication by hand). This controller takes 32 clock times from the time the operands are received until the result is ready (steps 6 through 9).

9.6 EXERCISES

1. We have four 32-bit registers: *R, S, T,* and *U*. We need the following transfers:

R $\leftarrow$ S   R $\leftarrow$ T   R $\leftarrow$ T$'$

S $\leftarrow$ R   S $\leftarrow$ U   S $\leftarrow$ S$'$

T $\leftarrow$ R

U $\leftarrow$ S   U $\leftarrow$ T   U $\leftarrow$ T$'$ U $\leftarrow$ S$'$

a. Show a typical bit of a point-to-point system to perform only these transfers. How many AND gates are required for the multiplexers?

b. Show a typical bit of a bus system to perform these transfers. How many AND gates are required for the multiplexers? What additional transfers are also available?

2. We have three 8-bit registers: *A, B,* and *C.* We need the
following transfers:

$$A \leftarrow B \qquad A \leftarrow A' \qquad A \leftarrow C$$

$$B \leftarrow A' \qquad B \leftarrow 0, B_{0:6} \qquad$$

$$C \leftarrow A \qquad C \leftarrow B \qquad C \leftarrow A'$$

Show bits 0 and 1 of the three registers and all of the data
transfer logic

a. for a point-to-point system.

b. for a bused system.

3. For the following system

```
SYSTEM NAME: ONE
        INPUT LINES: start, X[0:2].
        OUTPUT LINES: done, S[0:2].
        FLIP FLOPS: R[0:2], S[0:2].
        1.   next: 2 (start), 1 (else).
        2.   start': R ← X;
             next: 2 (start), 3 (else).
        3.   next: 4 (start), 3 (else).
        (4.) S ← X.
        5.   S ← R + S.
        6.   done = 1;
             next: 1.
    END DESCRIPTION
```

a. Show a block diagram of the sequencer (the logic
corresponding to steps 1 to 6).

b. Show a block diagram of the register and logic section,
including all of the flip flops.

c. Complete the following timing diagram. Show the output of
each of the flip flops of the controller, as well as **done**. Show
when there must be an input on lines X. (Note that initially, the
system is in state 1.)

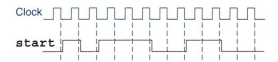

*4. I wrote a solution to the following problem:

> When **start** goes to 1, the system begins inputting a string of bits on line **in**. (There is an input whenever **start** = 1.) It continues inputting bits until it has 8 or until **start** goes to 0. After **start** goes to 0, it outputs the string on line **out** in reverse order, and a 1 on line **done**. (Note that up to 8 bits are output, but only after **start** goes to 0.)

```
SYSTEM NAME: REVERSE
      FLIP FLOPS: C[0:2], A[0:7].
      INPUT LINES: start, in.
      OUTPUT LINES: out, done.
      1.   C ← 0³;
             next: 2 (start), 1 (else).
      (2.) AND[C]': A ← in, A₀:₆.
      3.   AND[C]': C ← INC[C];
             next: 2 (start), 4 (else).
      4.   out = A₀;
           A ← A₁:₇, 0;
           C ← DEC[C];
           next: 5 (OR[DEC[C]]), 4(else).
      5.   done = 1;
           next: 1.

END DESCRIPTION
```

a. Counting the first clock period when **start** is 1 through the clock period when **done** is 1, how many clock periods does this take as a function of how many clock times, N, that **start** is 1. (Note that the answer needs to be given in two parts: when N is less than 8 and when N is greater than or equal to 8.) Show your work!!

b. Draw a block diagram for the sequencer.

c. Draw a block diagram of the register and logic section. You may have three-input, three-output blocks INC and DEC. Show the three flip flops of C and the logic associated with $A_{6:7}$.

d. This does not really work the way I said it should. What is wrong? Fix the problem statement so that it says what the DDL does.

5. For the following DDL

```
SYSTEM NAME: PROBLEM ONE
        FLIP FLOPS:
        INPUT LINES:
        OUTPUT LINES:
        1.   next: 2 (go), 1 (else).
        (2.)A ← B;
             next: 4 (x), 3 (else).
        3.   A ← A'.
        4.   A ← 0¹, A₀:₂;
        5.   y = OR[A];
             next: 5 (go), 1 (else).
```

END DESCRIPTION

a. Complete the definition lines.

b. Show a block diagram of the sequencer (the flip flops and logic corresponding to steps 1 to 5).

c. Show a block diagram of the register and logic section (including all of the flip flops).

d. Complete the following timing diagram.

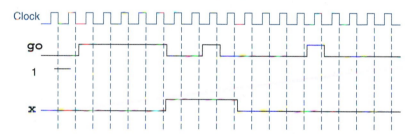

6. For the following system, show a block diagram of the register and logic section. You need only show a typical bit, but you must show the clock inputs and the signal lines coming from the controller.

```
SYSTEM NAME: MOVER
        INPUT LINES: A[0:3].
        OUTPUT LINES: D[0:3].
        FLIP FLOPS: B[0:3], C[0:3].
        1.  B ← A.
        2.  C ← B'; B ← A.
```

```
       3.  B  ←  C  ⊕  B.
       4.  D  =  B;
           next: 1.

   END DESCRIPTION
```

7. Consider the following DDL:

```
   SYSTEM NAME: TESTER
          INPUT LINE: go.
          OUTPUT LINE: out.
       1.  next: 2 (start), 1 (else).
       2.  out = 1.
       3.  out = 1.
       4.  .
       5.  out = 1;
           next: 2 (start), 6 (else).
       6.  .
       7.  next: 1.

   END DESCRIPTION
```

Draw a block diagram of the sequencer.

8. Consider the following DDL sequence:

```
   SYSTEM NAME: TEST1
          INPUT LINES:
          OUTPUT LINES:
          FLIP FLOPS:
       1.  start = 1.
       2.  A ← X;
           next: 3 (d), 4 (else).
       3.  A ← 0, A_{0:2};
           next: 5.
       4.  A ← A_{1:3}, 0.
       5.  Z = A;
           next: 1.

   END DESCRIPTION
```

a. Complete the definition lines.

b. Show a block diagram of the sequencer (the logic corresponding to steps 1 to 5).

c. Show a block diagram of the register and logic section (including all of the flip flops).

9. You are to design a small system called FINDME that meets the following specifications:

> The system watches an input signal, **start**. When it goes to 1 for one clock period, a 4-bit number is available on input lines, X[0:3] (during the same clock period that **start** is 1). The line **start** is then ignored until after output line **done** goes to 1 and back to 0. This system must now ask for more data. To do that, it puts a 1 on output line **sendme** for one clock period. Each time it does that, a new number is available on X during the second clock period after **sendme** is 1. This system repeatedly inputs numbers in that way until either a number is equal to the one received when **start** was 1 or until it has tested 14 numbers. When either of those has happened, it puts a 1 on output line **done** for two clock periods and places how many numbers have been tested on output lines Y[0:3] if there has been a match or all 1's on Y, otherwise. Y should be all 0's when **done** is not 1. It then returns to watch **start** again.

a. Write a complete DDL description of this system, assuming a hard-wired controller. Make it run as fast as possible.

b. Show a block diagram of the hard-wired controller.

c. Show a block diagram of the register and logic section, including all of the flip flops. The only logic block available other than AND, OR, NOT, and Exclusive-OR gates is a 4-bit incrementer, INC.

d. Show a timing diagram that corresponds to your DDL for the case when the third test is satisfied. The diagram must show the clock, lines **start**, **sendme**, and **done**, and indicate when there is a number on X and on Y.

e. I changed my mind about how to handle a long string of no matches. The output line **done** should not be 1 until there is a match. If there have been 15 or more tests, the output on Y will be all 1's when **done** = 1.

10. Write a complete DDL description for a system, THREE, that behaves as follows:

> When the input line **start** is 1 for one or more clock periods, the system gets a 4-bit input number from lines IN

at the first clock period after **start** is 1. The input is available at the next clock period. At each of the next four clock times, it outputs one bit of the number (from left to right) on line **out** and a 1 on line **done** at each period. It then returns to watch for a new **start**.

The only logic that is available (in addition to flip flops, AND, OR, and NOT gates) is one or two 4-bit incrementers, INC.

*11. Write a complete DDL description of a system, COUNT, with one input, **go**. When **go** becomes 1, the system counts how many consecutive clock times that **go** is 1. (If that count is greater than or equal to 15, the count is to be 15). After **go** is 0 for exactly two clock periods, the count is to be placed on output lines OUT[0:3] and a 1 on output line **done** for one clock period. The system then returns to watch for a 1 on **go**. (Assume that when **go** becomes 0, it remains that way for several clock periods.)

12. Write a complete DDL description for a system, PROBLEM TWO. When the input **start** goes to 1 for one clock period, there is an 11-bit input available on lines IN (during the time that **start** is 1). The first 8 bits of IN are treated as a word of data and the last 3 bits are a count. The system is to shift the data to the left (putting 0's in the right bit) the number of places specified by the count (0 to 7). When the shifting is completed and the answer is available on lines OUT, output line **stop** is made 1 for two clock periods. OUT must contain the answer from the time **stop** goes to 1 until the next time that **start** goes to 1. (It does not matter what is on OUT at other times.) In addition to flip flops, AND, OR, and NOT gates, you may use an incrementer, a decrementer, and/or a one-place shifter.

*13. You are to design a small system called HPONE that meets the following specifications:

The system watches input line **start**. It goes to 1 for one or more clock periods. During the first clock period after **start** returns to 0, an input is available on lines X[0:19] for one clock period. That input contains control information in the first 4 bits followed by 2 bytes of data (8 bits each).

The system is to output 2 bytes on the 8-bit data output lines, Z[0:7]. The first two control bits specify the first output on those lines; the next 2 bits specify the second output. For each control field, the first bit specifies which byte is involved: a 0 indicates the first byte (what was on $X_{4:11}$), a 1 the second byte (what was on $X_{12:19}$). The second bit of the

control field indicates whether the byte is output (bit $=$ 0) or
the bit-by-bit complement of the byte is output (bit $=$ 1).

Examples: X = 0011 01010101 11001100
           Z = 01010101 followed by 00110011

           X = 1010 00000000 01011010
           Z = 01011010 followed by 01011010

To output a byte, this system first puts a 1 on line **ready**,
holding it there until input line **ok** goes to 1. The output is
connected to Z only during the time that **ok** is 1. After the
first byte output, the system must wait two clock periods
before sending a new signal on **ready**. After the second
byte output, it returns to wait for a new **start**.

a. Write a complete DDL description of this system, assuming a
   hard-wired controller. Make it run as fast as possible.

b. Show timing diagrams that correspond to your DDL for the
   case where **ok** goes to 1 two clock periods after **ready**. Be
   sure to indicate when the input must be available and when
   the output is available.

9.7 CHAPTER TEST (90 MINUTES)

For the following DDL,

```
SYSTEM NAME: PROBLEM ONE
      FLIP FLOPS:
      INPUT LINES:
      OUTPUT LINES:
   1.  next: 2 (go), 1 (else).
   2.  next: 3 (go), 1 (else).
  (3.)A ← B;
      next: 5 (x), 4 (else).
   4.  A ← A'.
   5.  A ← 1¹, A₀:₂;
   6.  y = AND[A];
      next: 6 (go), 1 (else).
END DESCRIPTION
```

a. Complete the definition lines.

b. Show a block diagram of the sequencer (the flip flops and
   logic corresponding to steps 1 to 6).

c. Show a block diagram of the register and logic section (including all of the flip flops).

d. Complete the timing diagram, indicating when **x** and B must be available and when **y** is made available.

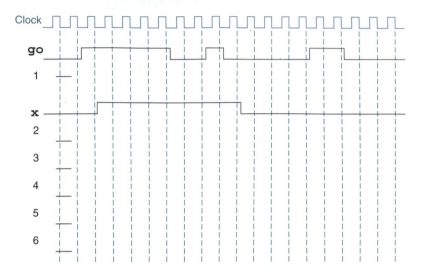

2. Write a complete DDL description for a hard-wired controller for a small system called TWO that meets the following specifications:

At the first clock period after input line **go** has been 1 for three or more clock periods (and then returns to 0), an input is available on lines IN[0:4]. That specifies the number of additional inputs that are to be summed (from 1 to 32, where 00000 indicates 32). Then, starting at the second clock time after receiving the count on IN, data is available every other clock period on input lines DATAIN[0:10]. This system is to compute the sum (treating the numbers as unsigned) and connect that to output lines DATAOUT[0:15]. Output line **ready** is to be 1 at that time as well. DATAOUT should be available for two clock periods and be 0^{16} at all other times.

You have available a 4-bit decrementer and a 16-bit adder.

The Design of a Central Processing Unit

In this chapter, we will discuss the design of the controller for parts of a computer, called MODEL. MODEL has a word size of 32 bits. Instructions may require one or two words, depending on the addressing mode.

The format for the first word of a MODEL instruction is shown in Figure 10.1, where RN specifies the register number and AM specifies the address mode.

Figure 10.1 Instruction format for MODEL.

0   5 6   11 12   15 16   31
Op-Code	RN	AM	Address

10.1 DESCRIPTION OF MODEL

In this section, we will specify the addressing modes and the instructions for which we will show the control sequence and discuss the timing. MODEL would surely have a wider variety of instructions and more addressing modes. However, those that we specify will be adequate to demonstrate the process of design.

10.1.1 Memory and Register Set

MODEL has a memory space of 2^{32} words,* each 32 bits wide. To access memory, the address is placed on lines AD[0:31] for one clock period. For read, a 1 is placed on line **read** at that same time, and the contents

---

*This implies a 32-bit address and a maximum memory of 2^{32} words. Not all of the memory needs to be there for the system to work properly.

of that memory location will be available on bus `DATA[0:31]` during that clock period. Thus, a typical memory fetch step might be

`AD = PC; read = 1; IR ← DATA.`

To store in memory, the word is connected to `DATA` (at the same time as the address is on `AD`) and a `1` is put on line **write**, for example

`AD = EA; DATA = WORK; write = 1.`

We will examine the modifications needed to handle a slower memory in Section 10.4.

`DATA` is an `INTERSYSTEM BUS`. `ADIN`, **read**, and **write** could be thought of as `OUTPUT LINES` from `MODEL` or as an `INTERSYSTEM BUS`. We will treat them as the latter; they are part of `BUS`, as shown in Figure 8.1.

The register set of `MODEL` includes the following registers:

`PC[0:31]`	The program counter
`IR[0:31]`[§]	The instruction register—a place to store the first word of an instruction while it is being decoded and executed
`REG[0:63; 0:31]`[*]	A set of 64 general-purpose registers
`WORK[0:31]`[§]	A register to hold data temporarily
`EA[0:31]`[§]	Register in which the effective address is computed
z	Zero flag bit—set to 1 when the result of some instructions is zero[†] (0 otherwise)
n	Negative flag bit—set to 1 when the result of some instructions is negative (stores the leading bit)
c	Carry (and borrow) bit—stores the carry out of the most significant bit of the adder
v	Two's complement overflow bit—set to 1 if the result of an operation is out of range, assuming operands are in two's complement notation (0 otherwise)

Registers indicated with a § contain no useful information between instructions. If we expand the instruction set, we may need to add some registers.

---

[*]REG^{3F} will be used as the stack pointer; we will use the notation SP in the DDL, but will define it as REG^{3F} with a NAME definition line.

[†]When we describe the instructions in Section 10.1.2, we will specify which instructions modify which flag bits.

The stack in MODEL is stored in memory. The register SP points to the next empty place on the stack. Elements are stored in descending order on the stack. Thus, if the stack pointer contains 7FFFFFFF and something is pushed onto the stack, it is stored in location 7FFFFFFF and the stack pointer is then decremented to 7FFFFFFE. Figure 10.2 shows the behavior of the stack with two items being pushed onto the stack and then one popped from the stack. Note that the SP is decremented on pushes and incremented on pops. When something is popped, it is not erased; it is copied to the Central Processing Unit (CPU) and the pointer is incremented. After the pop, the contents of 7FFFFFFE are still there but will never be used by a stack instruction. A push would write over it; a pop would first increment SP and take the contents of 7FFFFFFF.

Figure 10.2 Operation of the stack pointer.

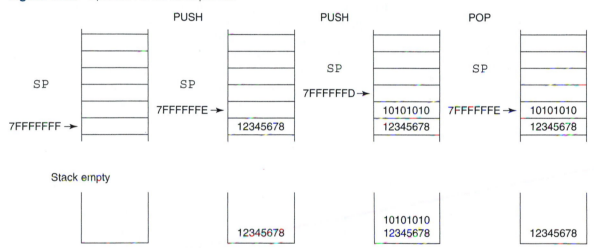

Internally, data is transferred by way of a 32-bit internal bus, CPUBUS. In addition, the arithmetic and logic unit has two 32-bit input buses: INA and INB. In describing the behavior of the machine, these buses are not referenced most of the time. A statement

$$REG/IR_{6:11} \leftarrow WORK.$$

implies that WORK is connected to CPUBUS and the data on that bus is clocked into the register, that is,

$$CPUBUS = WORK; \quad REG/IR_{6:11} \leftarrow CPUBUS.$$

EXAMPLE 10.1

$$WORK \leftarrow ADD_{1:32}[FFFFFFFF; WORK; 0]$$

implies the constant FFFFFFFF is connected to one 32-bit input of the adder, WORK is connected to the other 32-bit input, 0 is connected to the

c_{in} input, the right 32 bits of the adder output is connected to CPUBUS, and the bus is clocked into WORK. In this example, the carry output of the adder is not stored anywhere,

$$INA = FFFFFFFF; \; INB = WORK; \; c_{in} = 0;$$
$$BUS = ADD_{1:32}[INA; \; INB; \; c_{in}]; \; WORK \leftarrow CPUBUS$$

If we wanted to store that in the **c** flip flop, we would have written

$$c, \; WORK \leftarrow ADD[FFFFFFFF; \; WORK; \; 0]$$

Since there is no other way to move data, it is not necessary to be more specific.

Figure 10.3 shows a simplified block diagram of the bus structure. The constants, partial register connections, and shifted WORK are not shown, (For example, WORK $\leftarrow$ FFFF, $IR_{16:31}$ implies the constant FFFF is connected to the left half of CPUBUS and only the right half of IR is connected to the right half of CPUBUS.)

In addition to the three internal busses, there are two intersystem busses: DATA and AD. (The bus signals **read** and **write** are not shown.) Note that INA, INB, AD, **read** and **write** are really only multiplexors, with data only going in one direction. (However, in a larger

Figure 10.3   MODEL bus diagram.

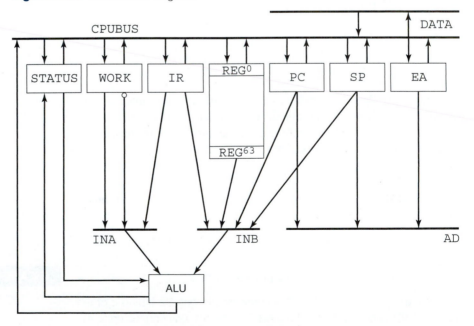

system where memory is used by more than one subsystem, AD, **read**, and **write** may be buses.)

10.1.2 Addressing Modes

We will define seven addressing modes (of the 16 possibilities with 4 bits), treating the remaining nine as no-ops (no operation). Some of the Examples, Solved Problems, and Exercises will suggest others. In each of the following examples, we will show what happens for a load register instruction (LOD), where RN is assumed to be 5 (05). The first four modes require a one-word instruction; the others require a second word. The AM field is shown in binary, rather than hexadecimal, to simplify the discussion later.

Register (AM = 0000)   The data comes from or is stored in the one of the 64 registers specified by $IR_{26:31}$.* This mode is not valid for branch instructions, since they require a memory address.

>   *Example*: LOD REG^5, REG^E [$IR_{26:31}$ = OE]
>   The data in Register 14 is loaded into Register 5.

Register indirect (AM = 0010)   The register specified by $IR_{26:31}$ contains the address in main memory of the data or where the result is to be stored or the jump is to go.

>   *Example*: LOD REG^5, (REG^E)   [$IR_{26:31}$ = OE]
>   where REG^E: 12345678
>   The data in memory location 12345678 is loaded into Register 5.

Page zero (AM = 0110)   Bits $IR_{16:31}$ are zero-extended to produce the effective address.

>   *Example*: LOD REG^5, z1234   [$IR_{16:31}$ = 1234]
>   The data in memory location 00001234 is loaded into Register 5.

Relative (AM = 0111)   Bits $IR_{16:31}$ are sign-extended and added to the program counter (after the program counter has been incremented to point to the next instruction) to produce the effective address.

>   *Example*: LOD REG^5, @1234   [$IR_{16:31}$ = 1234]
>   If this instruction is at address 01120111, the effective address is
>
> $$00001234 + 01120111 + 1 = 01121346.$$
>
>   The data in memory location 01121346 is loaded into Register 5.

---

*In those modes where the address field specifies a register, $IR_{16:25}$ (the rest of the address field) are ignored.

Example: LOD REG^5, @8000   [IR$_{16:31}$ = 8000]
If this instruction is at address 01120111, the effective address is

FFFF8000 + 01120111 + 1 = 01118112.

The data in memory location 01118112 is loaded into Register 5.

Direct (AM = 1000)   [IR$_{16:31}$ are ignored]   A second word of the
instruction is required. That word contains the effective address.

Example: LOD REG^5, 12345678
The contents of memory location 12345678 is loaded into Register 5.

Indirect (AM = 1001)   [IR$_{16:31}$ are ignored]   A second word of
the instruction is required. It contains the address in memory where the
effective address of data is found.

Example: LOD REG^5, (12345678)

M[12345678] = 56789ABC

The contents of 12345678 are fetched. Then the contents of memory
location 56789ABC are loaded into Register 5.

Immediate (AM = 1100)   [IR$_{16:31}$ are ignored]   A second word of
the instruction is required. It contains the data. This type is not valid for
any instruction that requires an address (for storing a result or branching).

Example: LOD REG^5, #12345678
The number 12345678 is loaded into Register 5. (The constant 12345678 is
contained in the second word of the instruction.)

EXAMPLE 10.2

We have an instruction to ADD the number specified by the addressing to
REG^4, where

This instruction is at location 12341234
The second word of the instruction (if any) is 20000000
Bits 16 to 31 of this instruction word are AB07
REG^4 = 00000102
REG^7 = 00123344
M[0000AB07] = 11111111
M[00123344] = FFFFFFFE
M[1233BD3C] = 44332211
M[20000000] = 00123344

We will examine which registers (not including the flag bits) are changed for
each addressing type.

Register   REG^4 ← 00123446   (00000102 + 00123344)
                  PC ← 12341235

Register indirect	REG^4 ← 00000100	(00000102 + FFFFFFFE)
	PC ← 12341235	
Page zero	REG^4 ← 11111213	(00000102 + 11111111)
	PC ← 12341235	
Relative	Address = 12341234 + 1 + FFFFAB07 =	
	1233BD3C	
	REG^4 ← 44332313	(00000102 + 44332211)
	PC ← 12341235	
Direct	REG^4 ← 00123446	(00000102 + 00123344)
	PC ← 12341236	
Indirect	REG^4 ← 00000100	(00000102 + FFFFFFFE)
	PC ← 12341236	
Immediate	REG^4 ← 20000102	(00000102 + 20000000)
	PC ← 12341236	

[SP 1, 2; EX 1]

10.1.3 Instruction Set of MODEL

In this section, we will define a subset of the instructions, enough to illustrate the design of the controller. For each, we will specify a three-letter mnemonic and the flag bits that are affected. We will not assign an op-code; rather, we will implement the controller, assuming that an appropriate decoder is included. However, those instructions that do not use the address portion (for example, Return from subroutine) begin with a 1; others begin with a 0. For each of the examples, we will assume that we used direct addressing and that

The effective address is 12345678
M[12345678] = 10101234
REG^3 = FFFFFFF8
SP = 7FFFFFF6
M[7FFFFFF7] = 98765432

Data Movement[*]

LOD z n Load register with data specified by the address field[†]

    Example: LOD REG^3, 12345678

       REG^3 ← 10101234 z ← 0 n ← 0

STO   Store register in location specified by the address field (either memory or a register)

---

[*]We will use REG^{3F} for the stack pointer and thus will not need special instructions to load or store SP.

[†]Either the contents of the memory location specified by EA, or the data for immediate or register addressing.

Example: STO REG^3, 12345678

    M[12345678] ← FFFFFFF8

PSH   Push register onto the stack

Example: PSH REG^3

    M[7FFFFFF6] ← FFFFFFF8   SP ← 7FFFFFF5

PSH and POP use only a register; the address field is ignored.

POP *z n*   Pop top of stack to register

Example: POP REG^3

    SP ← 7FFFFFF7 REG^3 ← 98765432 z ← 0 n ← 1

Arithmetic Instructions

ADD *z n c v*   Add number specified by the address field to the register

Example: ADD REG^3, 12345678

    FFFFFFF8

    <u>10101234</u>

   (1) 1010122C

    REG^3 ← 1010122C z ← 0 n ← 0 c ← 1 v ← 0

ADC *z n c v*   Add with carry; add number specified by the address field to the register and the *c* flag

Example: ADC REG^3, 12345678   (*c* was 1)

    REG^3 ← 1010122D z ← 0 n ← 0 c ← 1 v ← 0

Example: ADC REG^3, 12345678   (*c* was 0)

    REG^3 ← 1010122C z ← 0 n ← 0 c ← 1 v ← 0

SUB *z n c v*   Subtract number specified by the address field from the register

Example: SUB REG^3, 12345678

             1

    FFFFFF F8

    <u>EFEFEDCB</u>

   (1) EFEFEDC4

    REG^3 ← EFEFEDC4 z ← 0 n ← 1 c ← 1 v ← 0

CMP *z n c v*   Compare; behaves the same as subtract, but does not store the difference back to the register. (It is used to compare the same number with several words from memory without having to reload the register.)

Example: CMP REG^3, 12345678

$z \leftarrow 0$ $n \leftarrow 1$ $c \leftarrow 1$ $v \leftarrow 0$

INC z n Increments number specified by the address; ignores RN

Example: INC 12345678

M[12345678] $\leftarrow$ 10101235 $z \leftarrow 0$ $n \leftarrow 0$

Logic, Shift, and Rotate Instructions

NOT z Bit-by-bit complement; ignores RN

Example: NOT 12345678

M[12345678] $\leftarrow$ EFEFEDCB $z \leftarrow 0$

AND z n Bit-by-bit AND of register with number specified by the address

Example: AND REG^3, 12345678

	1111	1111	1111	1111	1111	1111	1111	1000
AND	0001	0000	0001	0000	0001	0010	0011	0100
	0001	0000	0001	0000	0001	0010	0011	0000

REG^3 $\leftarrow$ 1010230 $z \leftarrow 0$ $n \leftarrow 0$

ASR z Arithmetic shift right of number specified by the address; number of places specified by the right 5 bits of RN (IR$_{7:11}$)*

Example: ASR 3, 12345678

M[12345678] $\leftarrow$ 02020246 $z \leftarrow 0$

ROR   Rotate right number specified by the address; number of places specified by the right 5 bits of RN

Example: ROR 3, 12345678

M[12345678] $\leftarrow$ 82020246

Branch Instructions

JMP[†]   Jump to the address if the condition specified by the right 4 bits of RN (IR$_{8:11}$) is met; otherwise, continue to the next step. Branch conditions are specified in Table 10.1.

CLL   Call subroutine, save return address on the stack. Branch conditions are specified in Table 10.1.

RTS   Return from subroutine (unconditional). Pop address from stack.

---

*The right 5 bits of the RN field is treated as a number between 0 and 31, not as a register reference.

[†]For conditional Jumps and Calls, the condition is specified by a hexadecimal digit, such as JM2 for Jump if n is 1 or CL7 for Call if $v = 0$.

Table 10.1   Branch conditions.

$RN_{8:11}$	Condition	$RN_{8:11}$	Condition
0000	z	1000	not used
0001	z'	1001	not used
0010	n	1010	not used
0011	n'	1011	not used
0100	c	1100	not used
0101	c'	1101	not used
0110	v	1110	not used
0111	v'	1111	always

EXAMPLE 10.3

We will look at instructions referencing register 4 (REG^4), using Page zero addressing, where

Bits 16 to 31 of this instruction word are AB07
PC = 12341234
REG^4 = 00000102
REG^{3F} (SP) = 7FFFFFF5
M[0000AB07] = 81111111
M[7FFFFFF6] = 00000000

We will examine which registers and memory locations are changed for each instruction type. Unless indicated otherwise, the PC is incremented to 12341235.

LOD	$REG^4 \leftarrow 81111111$ $z \leftarrow 0$ $n \leftarrow 1$
STO	M[0000AB07] $\leftarrow$ 00000102
PSH	M[7FFFFFF5] $\leftarrow$ 00000102 REG^{3F}(SP) $\leftarrow$ 7FFFFFF4
POP	REG^{3F} (SP) $\leftarrow$ 7FFFFFF6 $REG^4 \leftarrow$ 00000000
	$z \leftarrow 1$ $n \leftarrow 0$
ADD	$REG^4 \leftarrow 81111213$ $z \leftarrow 0$ $n \leftarrow 1$ $c \leftarrow 0$ $v \leftarrow 0$
ADC	For $c = 0$, same as ADD; for $c = 1$
	$REG^4 \leftarrow 81111214$ $z \leftarrow 0$ $n \leftarrow 1$ $c \leftarrow 0$ $v \leftarrow 0$
SUB	$REG^4 \leftarrow 7EEEEFF1$ $z \leftarrow 0$ $n \leftarrow 0$ $c \leftarrow 0$ $v \leftarrow 0$
CMP	$z \leftarrow 0$ $n \leftarrow 0$ $c \leftarrow 0$ $v \leftarrow 0$
INC	M[0000AB07] $\leftarrow$ 81111112 $z \leftarrow 0$ $n \leftarrow 1$
NOT	M[0000AB07] $\leftarrow$ 7EEEEEEE $z \leftarrow 0$
AND	$REG^4 \leftarrow 00000100$ $z \leftarrow 0$ $n \leftarrow 0$
ASR	M[0000AB07] $\leftarrow$ F8111111 $z \leftarrow 0$ (4 places)
ROR	M[0000AB07] $\leftarrow$ 18111111
JMP	PC $\leftarrow$ 0000AB07
CLL	PC $\leftarrow$ 0000AB07 M[7FFFFFF5] $\leftarrow$ 12341235
	REG^{3F} (SP) $\leftarrow$ 7FFFFFF4
RTS	REG^{3F} (SP) $\leftarrow$ 7FFFFFF6 PC $\leftarrow$ 00000000

[SP 3, 4; EX 2, 3]

10.2 CONTROL SEQUENCE FOR MODEL*

In this section, we will develop a straightforward control sequence to implement that part of MODEL described in the previous two sections. In the next sections, we will look at its implementation with a hard-wired controller and a microprogrammed controller.

The first word of an instruction is read into the Instruction Register (IR) in the first step of the control sequence. Next, at step 2, the program counter is incremented to point to the next word (either the second word of this instruction or, if this is a one-word instruction, the first word of the next instruction). Throughout the design of the sequencer, we will use INC to represent an incrementer and DEC to represent a decrementer. In practice, there may be such a device as part of the ALU, or these may be implemented using the adder, putting a 1 or -1 on one of the inputs. Also, at step 2, we branch to step 60, the instruction decode step for those instructions where no address is required, or continue to step 3 for address computation.

```
1. AD = PC; read = 1; IR ← DATA.
2. PC ← INC[PC];
   next: 60 (IR₀), 3 (else).
```

The addressing mode of all one-word instructions begins with a 0, and that for two-word instructions begins with a 1. At step 3, we separate these.

```
3. next: 12 (IR₁₂), 4 (else).
4. next/IR₁₃:₁₅: 5, 1, 6, 1, 1, 1, 10, 11.
```

Unused codes are treated as no-ops, branching back to step 1 to fetch a new instruction. When addressing is completed, the address (if there is one) is stored in EA; control then goes to step 18 to fetch data. Those addressing modes that produce data, but no address (immediate and register), store that data in WORK and branch to step 20.

For register and register indirect addressing, bits 26 to 31 specify the register. Thus, at step 5, that register is moved to WORK (for register addressing), and control goes next to step 20. At steps 6 (for register indirect), that register is moved to EA, with control going to step 18.

Register

```
5. WORK ← REG/IR₂₆:₃₁;
   next: 20.
```

Register indirect

```
6. EA ← REG/IR₂₆:₃₁;
   next: 18.
```

---

*A complete listing of the control sequence for a hard-wired controller implementation of MODEL is found in Appendix A. To follow the design from this section, ignore the parentheses around step numbers in the appendix.

For Page zero addressing, the address field ($IR_{16:31}$) is zero-extended (that is, leading 0's are added to make the number 32 bits). For relative addressing, the sign-extended address field is added to the program counter (which had already been incremented to point to the next instruction at step 2). Both produce an address and thus branch to step 18.

Page zero

```
10. EA ← 0000, IR₁₆:₃₁;
    next: 18.
```

Relative

```
11. IR₁₆: EA ← ADD₁:₃₂[FFFF, IR₁₆:₃₁; PC; 0];
    IR₁₆′: EA ← ADD₁:₃₂[0000, IR₁₆:₃₁; PC; 0];
    next: 18.
```

The remaining three address modes all require a second word. At steps 13 and 14, the second word of the instruction is read into EA, and the program counter is incremented. For direct addressing, the second word is the effective address and is sent to EA. For indirect addressing, the second word is the address where the effective address will be found. Thus, after the second word is read at step 13, that memory location is read (step 15) and its contents are sent to EA.

Read second word, Direct

```
13. AD = PC; read = 1; EA ← DATA.
14. PC ← INC[PC];
    next/IR₁₃:₁₅: 18, 15, 1, 1, 16, 1, 1, 1.
```

Indirect

```
15. AD = EA; read = 1; EA ← DATA;
    next: 18.
```

For immediate addressing, the second word is the data and is sent to WORK, and control branches to step 20 (since a read is not needed for data).

Immediate

```
16. WORK ← EA;
    next: 20.
```

At step 18, we read the data from the effective address register, EA, into WORK. We could have a branch to skip this step for those instructions that do not require data (such as store, jump, and call).

Data read

```
18. AD = EA; read = 1; WORK ← DATA;
    next: 20.
```

We want to add two new addressing modes; register indirect with auto-post-incrementing, and short immediate. Assume that step 4 branches to steps 7 and 9 for these. Register indirect with auto-post-incrementing produces the same address as register indirect, but also increments the register after using it. For short immediate, the address field is sign-extended.

Register indirect with auto-post-incrementing

7. EA ← REG/IR$_{26:31}$.
8. REG/IR$_{26:31}$ ← INC[REG/IR$_{26:31}$];
   next: 18.

Short immediate

9. IR$_{16}$: WORK ← FFFF, IR$_{16:31}$;
   IR$_{16}$′: WORK ← 0000, IR$_{16:31}$;
   next: 20.

The details of the instruction decode step (or steps) are not shown, since we did not specify the coding of the op-code and we are implementing the controller for only a few instructions. We will show the implementation of the individual instructions, using step numbers beginning at 25.

Load register requires only one step, after which it returns to step 1 to fetch a new instruction. On *Store*, the result goes to the register specified by IR$_{26:31}$ for register addressing (IR$_{12}$′ · IR$_{13}$′ · IR$_{14}$′ · IR$_{15}$′) and to memory for all other types. Store does not permit immediate addressing; it is treated as a no-op.

LOD

25. REG/IR$_{6:11}$ ← WORK; z ← (OR[CPUBUS])′;
    n ← CPUBUS$_0$;
    next: 1.

STO

26. WORK ← REG/IR$_{6:11}$.
27. next: 28 (IR$_{12}$′ · IR$_{13}$′ · IR$_{14}$′ · IR$_{15}$′),
    1 (IR$_{12}$ · IR$_{13}$ · IR$_{14}$′ · IR$_{15}$′), 29 (else).
28. REG/IR$_{26:31}$ ← WORK;
    next: 1.
29. ADIN = EA; DATA = WORK; **write** = 1;
    next: 1.

Push and *Pop* are implemented after a decoding branch from step 60. *Push* writes to the location pointed to by the stack pointer and then decrements the pointer. *Pop* first increments the stack pointer and then reads.

PSH

65. ADIN = SP; DATA = REG/$IR_{6:11}$; **write** = 1.
66. SP ← DEC[SP];

    next: 1.

POP

67. SP ← INC[SP].
68. ADIN = SP; **read** = 1; REG/$IR_{6:11}$ ← DATA;

    z ← (OR[CPUBUS])'; n ← $CPUBUS_0$;

    next: 1.

The addition and subtraction instructions are each only one step. The adder has a 33-bit output, the left bit being the carry. Two's complement overflow is detected when two numbers have the same sign (INA_0 = INB_0) and the result has the opposite sign ($CPUBUS_0$). The expressions for each of the flag bits is the same for almost all instructions.

ADD

30. c, REG/$IR_{6:11}$ ← ADD[REG/$IR_{6:11}$; WORK; 0];

    z ← (OR[CPUBUS])'; n ← $CPUBUS_0$;

    v ← INA_0 · INB_0 · $CPUBUS_0'$ +
        INA_0' · INB_0'· $CPUBUS_0$;

    next: 1.

ADC

31. c, REG/$IR_{6:11}$ ← ADD[REG/$IR_{6:11}$; WORK; c];

    z ← (OR[CPUBUS])'; n ← $CPUBUS_0$;

    v ← INA_0 · INB_0 · $CPUBUS_0'$ +
        INA_0' · INB_0'· $CPUBUS_0$;

    next: 1.

SUB

32. c, REG/$IR_{6:11}$ ← ADD[REG/$IR_{6:11}$; WORK'; 1];

    z ← (OR[CPUBUS])'; n ← $CPUBUS_0$;

    v ← INA_0 · INB_0 · $CPUBUS_0'$ +
        INA_0' · INB_0'· $CPUBUS_0$;

    next: 1.

CMP

34. $c \leftarrow ADD_0[REG/IR_{6:11}; WORK'; 1];$
    $CPUBUS = ADD_{1:32}[REG/IR_{6:11}; WORK'; 1];$
    $z \leftarrow (OR[CPUBUS])'; n \leftarrow CPUBUS_0;$
    $v \leftarrow INA_0 \cdot INB_0 \cdot CPUBUS_0' +$
        $INA_0' \cdot INB_0' \cdot CPUBUS_0;$
    next: 1.

The next two instructions operate on numbers in WORK and ignore the RN field. The results are stored back in either a register or memory, using the steps already implemented for STO.

INC

36. $WORK \leftarrow ADD_{1:32}[00000001; WORK; 0];$
    $z \leftarrow (OR[CPUBUS])'; n \leftarrow CPUBUS_0;$
    next: 27.

NOT

40. $WORK \leftarrow WORK'; z \leftarrow (OR[CPUBUS])';$
    next: 27.

AND uses operands from a register and WORK, storing the result back in that register.

AND

42. $REG/IR_{6:11} \leftarrow REG/IR_{6:11} \cdot WORK;$
    $z \leftarrow (OR[CPUBUS])'; n \leftarrow CPUBUS_0;$
    next: 1.

The instruction decode step reaches step 43 for all of the shifts and rotates. We assume that the op-code for ASR ends in 00, and ROR ends in 10. We shift one place at a time; step 43 transfers to the step for the store instruction when $IR_{7:11}$ counts down to 0. $IR_{7:11} = 00000$ is treated as zero, making these instructions no-ops.

43. $IR_{7:11} \leftarrow DEC[IR_{7:11}];$
    next: 44 $(OR[IR_{7:11}])$, 27 (else).
44. next: 45 (IR_4), 47 (else).

ASR

45. $WORK \leftarrow WORK_0, WORK_{0:30};$
    $z \leftarrow (OR[CPUBUS])';$
    next: 43.

ROR

```
47. WORK ← WORK₃₁, WORK₀:₃₀;
        next: 43.
```

If faster shifting were required, we could build a *barrel shifter*, which would allow a shift of any number of places in one step. The hardware for that is more complex, since each bit of WORK could be loaded with any other bit or with 0. In contrast, the implementation we have shown only requires that each bit be loaded with the bit on either side (or 0 for the first and last bits).

The conditional jump and call instructions depend on the variable **br**, where

$$\mathbf{br} = \mathrm{OR}[\mathrm{DCD}(\mathrm{IR}_{8:11}) \cdot (\mathbf{z}, \mathbf{z'}, \mathbf{n}, \mathbf{n'}, \mathbf{c}, \mathbf{c'}, \mathbf{v}, \mathbf{v'}, 0, 0, 0, 0, 0, 0, 0, 1)]$$

DCD is a decoder with four inputs and 16 outputs, one of which is 1. That is ANDed with the 16-bit vector with each of the conditions, as specified in Table 10.1. Thus, **br** is 1 if the specified branch condition is satisfied and 0, otherwise. (Unused codes are treated as never branch. They could be treated as an unconditional branch by changing all of the 0's to 1's.)

On jump, the program counter is loaded with the effective address if the condition is met; otherwise, it returns to step 1. On a successful call, the contents of the program counter are first pushed onto the stack and then the effective address is moved to the PC.

JMP

```
50. br: PC ← EA;
        next: 1.
```

CLL

```
51. next: 1 (br), 52 (else)
52. ADIN = SP; DATA = PC; write = 1.
53. SP ← DEC[SP].
54. PC ← EA;
        next: 1.
```

Finally, the return from subroutine (unconditional) pops the address from the stack and loads that into the program counter.

RTS

```
70. SP ← INC[SP].
71. ADIN = SP; read = 1; PC ← DATA;
        next: 1.
```

EXAMPLE 10.5

Add a new instruction to decrement the register pointed to by the RN field and jump to the address if the result is 0. (This is a loop control instruction.)

The simplest way is to do the addressing and jump to step 55 from step 20.

```
55. WORK ← REG/IR₆:₁₁.
56. REG/IR₆:₁₁ ← ADD₁:₃₂[FFFFFFFF; WORK; 0];
    next: 1 (OR[CPUBUS]), 57 (else).
57. PC ← EA;
    next: 1.
```

Since step 57 is identical to step 54, the branch at step 56 could go to 54, eliminating step 57. It was necessary to move the register to WORK (step 55) because the bus structure up until this point put both the register and the constant on INA. If the bus structure were modified, we could combine steps 55 and 56.

EXAMPLE 10.6

Add a new instruction, *Stack add*. It adds the top two entries on the stack and pushes the answer back onto the stack. The operands are destroyed. No flags are involved.

This requires an additional register, WORK2, to store the second number. (That register would be needed by more complex instructions, such as *Multiply*.) We pop the two operands, add them, and then push the result onto the stack.

```
80. SP ← INC[SP].
81. ADIN = SP; read = 1; WORK ← DATA.
82. SP ← INC[SP].
83. ADIN = SP; read = 1; WORK2 ← DATA.
84. WORK ← ADD₁:₃₂[WORK2; WORK; 0].
85. ADIN = SP; DATA = WORK; write = 1.
86. SP ← DEC[SP];
    next: 1.
```

EXAMPLE 10.7

Modify **br** so as to provide conditional branches for comparing two signed and unsigned numbers.

Two numbers can be compared by subtracting them and then using a conditional jump. The comparisons are between the number in the register (REG/IR₆:₁₁), *a*, compared with the number specified by the address, *b*. There are separate tests for signed and unsigned numbers based on the flag bits.

For signed numbers, when $a < b$, the result is negative unless there is overflow. Thus, the condition is $\mathbf{n} \oplus \mathbf{v}$. For less than or equal, we have $\mathbf{z} + (\mathbf{n} \oplus \mathbf{v})$. The opposite of less than is greater than or equal, $(\mathbf{n} \oplus \mathbf{v})'$, and greater than is the complement of less than or equal, $\mathbf{z} + (\mathbf{n} \oplus \mathbf{v})$. For unsigned numbers, $a < b$ is indicated by $\mathbf{c}'$, less than or equal by $\mathbf{c}' + \mathbf{z}$, greater than by $(\mathbf{c}' + \mathbf{z})'$, and greater than or equal by $\mathbf{c}$.

If the following codes are added to the list in Table 10.1,

$$
\left.
\begin{array}{ll}
1000 & < \\
1001 & \leq \\
1010 & \geq \\
1011 & >
\end{array}
\right\} \text{After SUB for signed numbers}
$$

$$
\left.
\begin{array}{ll}
1100 & \leq \\
1101 & >
\end{array}
\right\} \text{After SUB for unsigned numbers}
$$

then the definition of *br* becomes

$$
\begin{aligned}
\mathbf{br} = \; & \mathrm{OR}[\mathrm{DCD}(\mathrm{IR}_{8:11}) \cdot (\mathbf{z}, \mathbf{z}', \mathbf{n}, \mathbf{n}', \mathbf{c}, \mathbf{c}', \mathbf{v}, \\
& \mathbf{v}', \mathbf{n} \oplus \mathbf{v}, \mathbf{z} + (\mathbf{n} \oplus \mathbf{v}), (\mathbf{n} \oplus \mathbf{v})', \\
& (\mathbf{z} + (\mathbf{n} \oplus \mathbf{v}))', \mathbf{c}' + \mathbf{z}, \mathbf{c} \cdot \mathbf{z}', 0, 1)]
\end{aligned}
$$

EXAMPLE 10.8

Include a new instruction to add a set of numbers stored in consecutive memory locations. The address field specifies the location of the first number. The register specified by RN contains the size of the set (how many numbers to be added) and is replaced by the sum. The flag bit $\mathbf{c}$ is set to one iff any of the additions produced unsigned overflow.

Step 20 branches to step 90. We need three registers, in addition to EA, in this process: one to hold the count, one to hold the sum as we are adding, and one to hold each new number as it is read. One approach is to store the sum in the register and the count in WORK. The additional register, WORK2, would be connected to INB. (Note that this is a different connection from Example 10.6.)

```
90. WORK ← REG/IR₆:₁₁;
    next: 91 (OR[CPUBUS]), 1 (else).
91. REG/IR₆:₁₁ ← 00000000; c ← 0.
92. AD = EA; read = 1; WORK2 ← DATA.
93. REG/IR₆:₁₁ ← ADD₁:₃₂[REG/IR₆:₁₁; WORK2; 0];
    c ← c + ADD₀[REG/IR₆:₁₁; WORK2; 0].
94. WORK ← DEC[WORK];
    next: 95 (OR[CPUBUS]), 1 (else).
95. EA ← INC[EA];
    next: 92.
```

On the first step, if the count is 0, the register already has the sum of 0 and the instruction is complete. When the count goes to 0, the process is complete. Since the sum is already in the register, we can go back to step 1 to fetch a new instruction. Note that EA must be connected to INA to implement step 95. (That connection was not previously required.)

[SP 5, 6, 7, 8; EX 4, 5, 6, 7, 8, 9]

10.3 IMPLEMENTATION OF MODEL CONTROL SEQUENCE WITH A HARDWIRED CONTROLLER

The simplest implementation is to use a one-hot controller (where each step corresponds to one flip flop). One flip flop of the controller has a 1 in it, and all others have a 0 (similar to the controller of Figure 9.9).

Such a controller for the instruction fetch and addressing portion of the control sequence is shown in Figure 10.4. So as to make the figure readable, the clock input line to each flip flop has been omitted, as have the output signal lines from each of the flip flops (There are no outputs from steps 3 and 4, which are only branches). Note at steps 11, there is a pair of AND gates for the conditional data transfers.

Figure 10.4 Controller for instruction fetch and addressing.

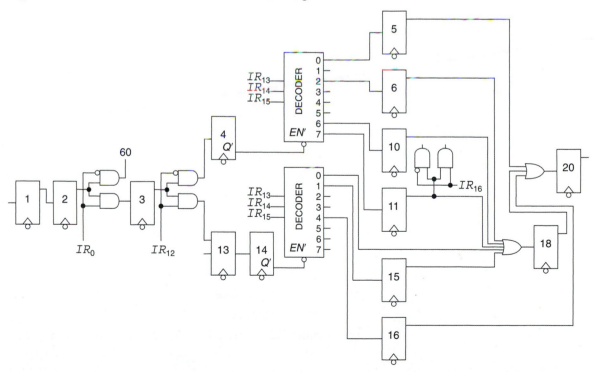

The eight-way decoder for the 1-word instructions is enabled by the Q' output of flip flop 4. One of the outputs of that decoder is active when the controller is in step 4, putting a 1 into one of flip flops 5, 6, 10, or 11 at the next clock. (The unused addressing code outputs (1, 3, 4, and 5) are not shown connected, but would all go to an OR gate at the input of flip flop 1.) A second eight-way decoder for the 2-word instructions is enabled by the Q' output of flip flop 14.

From the controller block diagram, it is easy to see that register addressing takes five clocks to reach step 20 (steps 1, 2, 3, 4, and 5). (For the purpose of timing discussions, we will include the time in step 20 in the execution portion.) Register indirect (step 6), Page zero (step 10), and Relative (step 11) each require five clocks (steps 1, 2, 3, 4, and one of 6, 10, or 11) to reach step 18 and a sixth to reach step 20. Direct addressing takes six clocks (steps 1, 2, 3, 13, 14, and 18). Indirect uses a seventh clock period (step 15). Immediate takes six clocks. (It uses step 16, but does not need step 18.)

The speed of the system can be greatly increased by taking advantage of undelayed steps. Since IR was not changed at steps 3 and 4, step 3 can be undelayed. Next, we note that either step 4 or all of the steps reached directly from step 4 can be made undelayed. That would mean that steps 5, 6, 10, and 11 would be executed at the same time as the branch at step 4, which does not change any registers nor utilize the internal bus. Steps 1 to 18 become

1. AD = PC; **read** = 1; IR ← DATA.

2. PC ← INC[PC];

    next: 60 (IR_0), 3 (else).

(3.) next: 12 (IR_{12}), 4 (else).

4.   next/$IR_{13:15}$: 5, 1, 6, 1, 1, 1, 10, 11.

(5.) WORK ← REG/$IR_{26:31}$;

    next: 20.

(6.) EA ← REG/$IR_{26:31}$;

    next: 18.

(10.) EA ← 0000, $IR_{16:31}$;

    next: 18.

(11.) IR_{16}: EA ← $ADD_{1:32}$[FFFF, $IR_{16:31}$; PC; 0];

    IR_{16}': EA ← $ADD_{1:32}$[0000, $IR_{16:31}$; PC; 0];

    next: 18.

13.   AD = PC; **read** = 1; EA ← DATA.

14.   PC ← INC[PC];

    next/$IR_{13:15}$: 18, 15, 1, 1, 16, 1, 1, 1.

15.   AD = EA; **read** = 1; EA ← DATA;

       next: 18.

16.   WORK ← EA;

       next: 20.

18.   AD = EA; **read** = 1; WORK ← DATA;

       next: 20.

This reduces the execution time for all 1-word addressing modes by two clocks and the 2-word modes by one clock. That eliminates five (of the 13) flip flops associated with steps 1 to 18. The controller is shown in Figure 10.5.

One other small timing improvement could be made by checking at step 18 whether it was necessary to fetch data. In particular, *Jump*, *Call*, and *Store* do not require data. If the op-codes for those instructions (and only those instructions) have a 1 in bit 2, then we could rewrite

(18.) next: 20 (IR_2), 19 (else).

19.   AD = EA; **read** = 1; WORK ← DATA.

That would save one clock time for these instructions.

Figure 10.5 Controller for instruction fetch and addressing.

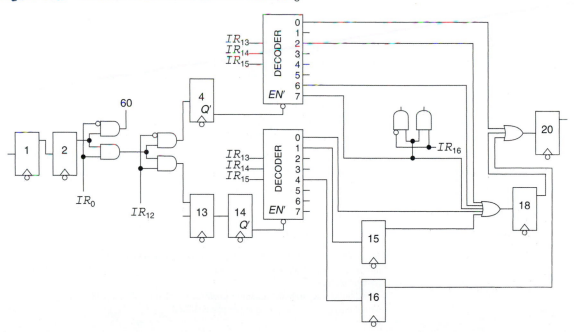

We could make step 20 undelayed. But then the first step of the execution part of any of the instructions would be delayed, because they all involve using the bus (which was also used in each of the steps leading to step 20). If step 20 is delayed, we can save a number of flip flops in the controller by making the first step of each memory reference instruction (24, 26, 30, . . .) undelayed.* Most instructions would take only one clock time for execution (that at step 20). Exceptions include those that require a store (STO, NEG, INC, DEC, and NOT), which have a second clock at either step 28 or 29, and CLL, which requires two extra clock times to push the program counter onto the stack. The shifts and rotates also require two clocks for each place plus one extra as it leaves the loop at step 43.† The DDL for MODEL is shown in Appendix A.

The timing of the instructions is summarized in Table 10.2. The dashes indicate that this addressing mode is not allowed for those instructions.

Table 10.2   Timing of Instructions.

Instruction		(REG),PG-0			
	REG	**REL**	**DIR**	**IND**	**IMM**
LOD,ADD,ADC,					
SUB,CMP,AND	4	5	6	5	5
STO,INC,NOT	5	6	7	6	—
JMP	—	5	6	5	—
CLL	—	7	8	7	—
ASR,ROR	$5 + 2n$	$6 + 2n$	$7 + 2n$	$6 + 2n$	—
PSH,POP,RTS		3 (no addressing)			

---

*This approach results in the machine being slower by one clock for failed conditional jumps and calls. We could rewrite step 50 as

```
(50.)     next: 50a (br), 1 (else).

50a.      PC ← EA;

          next: 1.
```

Thus, if step 20 were undelayed, step 50 could still be undelayed, and failed conditional jumps (and calls if we also modified step 51 in the same way) would take no clock times for execution.

†If we build a separate decrementer to count, we could make step 43 undelayed and would only need one clock time per place shifted.

EXAMPLE 10.9

We will look at the timing for the new addressing mode and instructions described in Examples 10.4, 10.5, 10.6, and 10.8.

10.4: Steps 7 and 9 can be undelayed. For the controller of Figure 10.5, Register Indirect with Auto-post-increment would take one more clock time than register indirect. Short immediate would take the same time as Register addressing.

10.5: Steps 55 can be undelayed. From step 20, this will take two clock times if it does not jump (Steps 20 and 56) or three clock times if it does jump (Steps 20, 56, and 57).

10.6: Only step 80 can be undelayed. This will take eight clock times (including steps 1 and 2).

10.8: Step 90 can be undelayed, requiring one clock time if there are zero numbers to add. Step 91 is executed once, and steps 92, 93, and 94 are each executed n times and step 95 is executed $n - 1$ times, for a total of $4n + 1$ (in addition to the time for steps 1 to 18).

EXAMPLE 10.10

In order to speed the machine, one thought was to add an incrementer for PC that does not use the bus. (Thus, instead of PC receiving all its inputs from CPUBUS, there would be a multiplexer on the input to PC.)

Steps 4 and 14 could then be made undelayed (or 4, 15, and 16), since the only reason that they are delayed is that the incrementing of PC used the bus. Step 2 cannot be made undelayed, because the branch uses the data being loaded into IR at step 1.

This would reduce the execution time of all instructions by one clock.

[SP 9, 10, 11; Ex 10, 11, 12, 13]

10.4 MODEL WITH A SLOWER MEMORY

If the main memory always took a fixed number of clock times, we could modify the read and write steps accordingly. Say that we could connect the address to ADIN and put a 1 on **read** at one clock time, and the contents of that location would be on DATA two clock times later. Then, steps 1, 2, 3, and 4 might be rewritten

```
1.      AD = PC; read = 1.
2.      PC ← INC[PC].
3.      IR ← DATA.
4.      next: 60 (IR₀), 4a (else).
(4a.)   next: 12 (IR₁₂), 6 (else)
(4b.)   next/IR₁₃:₁₅: 5, 1, 6, 1, 1, 1, 10, 11.
```

This only adds one clock time, since now PC can be incremented during the read process.

Steps 13 and 14 would now become

```
13.  AD = PC; read = 1.
14.  PC ← INC[PC].
14a. EA ← DATA;
     next/IR₁₃:₁₅: 18, 15, 1, 1, 16, 1, 1, 1.
```

again, adding one clock time.

The write at step 29 would become

```
29.  ADIN = EA; DATA = WORK; write = 1.
29a. .
29b. next: 1.
```

The other steps involving memory (for *Call*, *Return*, *Push*, and *Pop*) would also have to be rewritten.

If memory required that the address and **read** be kept 1 for all three clock times, that would not change the timing. Steps 1 to 3 would become

```
1.   AD = PC; read = 1.
2.   AD = PC; read = 1; PC ← INC[PC].
3.   AD = PC; read = 1; IR ← DATA.
```

If write also required the signals to remain, then step 29 would become

```
29.  ADIN = EA; DATA = WORK; write = 1.
29a. ADIN = EA; DATA = WORK; write = 1.
29b. ADIN = EA; DATA = WORK; write = 1;
     next: 1.
```

If the amount of time for a read and write of memory were variable (possibly depending on memory being used by another component), there would need to be a signal from memory, such as **memready**. If we must hold the inputs to memory until there is an answer, then step 1 is replaced by

```
1.   AD = PC; read = 1;
     next: 2 (memready), 1 (else).
(2.) IR ← DATA.
```

PC cannot be loaded until the next clock time. If the memory inputs were only required during the first clock period, we could replace steps 1 and 2 by

```
1.     AD = PC; read = 1;
(2.)   next: 4 (memready), 3 (else).
3.     next: 2.
(4.)   IR ← DATA.
```

For these two cases, the write at step 29 would become

```
29.    ADIN = EA; DATA = WORK; write = 1;
       next: 1 (memready), 29 (else).
```

or

```
29.    ADIN = EA; DATA = WORK; write = 1.
(29a.) next: 1 (memready), 29b (else).
29b.   next: 29a.
```

10.5 A MICROPROGRAMMED CONTROLLER

In this section, we will examine the ideas behind the design of micro-programmed controllers. Such a controller replaces the sequential circuit of a hard-wired controller by a small amount of control logic and a special memory in which a representation of the control sequence (the DDL) is stored. The steps of that sequence (the microinstructions) are fetched and executed by the control logic.

> ASIDE: A computer with a microprogrammed controller has two distinct memories: the main memory of the computer in which instruction and data are stored, and the special memory, often referred to as the control store, where the representation of the control sequence is stored. These memories are independent and are typically different sizes. The control store is often a Read-Only Memory (ROM), since the control sequence that is stored in it rarely, if ever, changes.

The block diagram of Figure 10.6 shows the basic structure of a microprogrammed controller and its connections to the rest of the machine. Those connections are identical for both the hard-wired and microprogrammed controller. It is only the structure of the inside of the controller box that has changed.

The MAR contains the location in the control store of the current microinstruction (the one that is being executed during this clock period). The output of the ROM is a set of lines containing that microinstruction. As each instruction is executed, the *next address logic* produces the address of the next microinstruction (DDL step). Often, that logic just performs incrementation. For data transfers and connections, the *decode logic* produces the appropriate control signals for the rest of the machine.

The sequencer is a very small hard-wired controller that controls the fetching and sequencing of the microinstructions from the control store.

Figure 10.6   A microprogrammed controller.

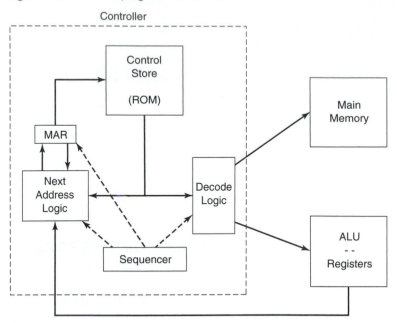

It contains only one (or at most two or three) flip flops. The decode logic, which produces the signals to the rest of the machine, depends only on what data transfers and connections are required. The next address logic is based on the branch conditions in the DDL steps. Both logic blocks are fairly simple. Neither depends on the details of the control sequence. That sequence is stored (in coded form) in the ROM. One advantage of microprogramming is that the controller logic is simpler than for the hard-wired version. The largest part of the controller is the control store. But that can be implemented using a rather inexpensive off-the-shelf ROM. The hard-wired controller for a large computer consists of an irregular collection of flip flops and gates, which must be fabricated from scratch for each new controller.

Another advantage of microprogramming becomes apparent when the designer wishes to make a modification in the control sequence. This may occur because of an error in the original version or because a new or modified instruction is being introduced. We must then rewrite a portion of the DDL sequence. If this has been implemented in a hard-wired controller, then the logic must be changed and a new sequencer fabricated. If the sequencer was implemented on a VLSI chip, the old chip is now useless and a new one must be produced. On the other hand, in a microprogrammed controller, the modifications are usually easier. If, as is usually the case, the data movements and branch conditions required for this change were already implemented (either because they were needed for some other instruction or because the hardware designer provided extra features for possible later expansion), then no hardware modifications need be made. All that must be done is that a new sequence must be loaded into the control store. ROM programmers allow that to be done quickly and inexpensively.

The major disadvantage of microprogramming is speed. A microprogrammed machine is usually slower than a hard-wired one. This is partly a result of the limitations of how much can be stored in a single word in the control store. Whereas a DDL step can contain an unlimited number of data transfers and connections, as well as a multiway branch and conditional data transfers, it is not practical to allow for all of these possibilities in the coding of microinstructions. Thus, some DDL steps will result in two or more steps in a microprogrammed implementation. A second factor is that each step must be obtained from memory; that takes a clock time. Those steps that are undelayed in a hard-wired implementation do require a clock time in a microprogrammed machine.

10.6 SOLVED PROBLEMS

1. We have two new address types in MODEL
   a. Page zero indirect
   b. Indexed, where $IR_{26:31}$ specify which register is used as an index register. The contents of the second word is added to the index register.

   Specify what happens on an instruction that loads REG^5 using the following values:

   This instruction is at location 10000000

   The second word of the instruction (if any) is 12345678

   Bits 16 to 31 of this instruction word are 9ABC

   REG^4 = FFEE0000

   REG^{3C} = 22446688

   M[00009ABC] = 12345678

   M[12345678] = FDECBA98

   M[3478BD00] = 11223344

   a. $REG^5 \leftarrow$ FDECBA98   PC $\leftarrow$ 10000001

      The Page zero address (00009ABC) contains the address of the data to be loaded.
   b. Address = 22446688 + 12345678 = 3478BD00

      $REG^5 \leftarrow$ 11223344   PC $\leftarrow$ 10000002

      The index register is specified by the last 6 bits of the first instruction word ($11\ 1100_2 = 3C_{16}$)

2. We have an instruction to store REG^4 at the location specified by the address field. Assume the values of Solved Problem 1. What registers and memory locations are changed for each of the address types?

   a. Register
   b. Register indirect
   c. Page zero
   d. Relative
   e. Direct
   f. Indirect
   g. Immediate

   a. Register $REG^{3C} \leftarrow FFEE0000$ $PC \leftarrow 10000001$
   b. Register indirect $M[22446688] \leftarrow FFEE0000$
       $PC \leftarrow 10000001$
   c. Page zero $M[00009ABC] \leftarrow FFEE0000$ $PC \leftarrow 10000001$
   d. Relative EA = 10000000 + 1 + FFFF9ABC = 0FFF9ABD
       $M[0FFF9ABD] \leftarrow FFEE0000$ $PC \leftarrow 10000001$
   e. Direct $M[12345678] \leftarrow FFEE0000$ $PC \leftarrow 10000002$
   f. Indirect $M[FDECBA98] \leftarrow FFEE0000$ $PC \leftarrow 10000002$
   g. Immediate $PC \leftarrow 10000001$ (This is treated as a no-op since Immediate is not allowed for stores.)

3. For each of the following instructions, what registers, flag bits, and memory locations are changed for each of the address types? Assume the following initial values for each instruction:

   This instruction is at location 10000000
   $z = 0$ $n = 1$ $c = 1$ $v = 0$
   $REG^5 = 12345678$
   $REG^{12} = 22446688$
   $REG^{3F} = 88888888$
   $M[00009ABC] = EDCBA988$
   $M[12345678] = 2468ACE0$
   $M[20001000] = 7E110000$
   $M[7E110000] = 345678FF$
   $M[88888887] = 00112233$
   $M[88888888] = 11223344$
   $M[88888889] = 22334455$

   a. STO REG^{12}, (REG^5)
   b. PSH REG^5

c. POP REG^5

d. ADD REG^5, 20001000

e. ADC REG^5, 20001000

f. ADD REG^5, z9ABC

g. SUB REG^5, REG^{3F}

h. CMP REG^{12}, 88888888

i. INC 00009ABC

j. NOT REG^{12}

k. AND REG^5, (20001000)

l. ASR 3, REG^{3F}

m. ASR 5, 20001000

n. ROR 8, (REG^5)

o. JMP (REG^5)

p. JM4 (REG^5)

q. JM5 12341234

r. CLL (REG^5)

s. RTS

a. Register indirect, EA = 12345678

M[12345678] ← 22446688   PC ← 10000001

b. M[88888888] ← 12345678   REG^{3F} ← 88888887

PC ← 10000001

c. REG^{3F} ← 88888889   REG^5 ← 22334455 z ← 0 n ← 0

PC ← 10000001

d. 12345678

7E110000

90455678

REG^5 ← 90455678 z ← 0 n ← 1 c ← 0 v ← 1

PC ← 10000002

Note that there is signed number overflow since both operands are positive but the result looks negative.

e. REG^5 ← 90455679 z ← 0 n ← 1 c ← 0 v ← 1

PC ← 10000002

f.   1 2 3 4 5 6 7 8

EDCBA988

(1) 0 0 0 0 0 0 0 0

REG^5 ← 00000000 z ← 1 n ← 0 c ← 1 v ← 0

PC ← 10000001

g. $\qquad$ 1

12345678

<u>77777777</u>

89ABCDF0

$REG^5 \leftarrow 89ABCDF0 \quad z \leftarrow 0 \quad n \leftarrow 1 \quad c \leftarrow 0 \quad v \leftarrow 1$

$PC \leftarrow 10000001$

h. $\qquad$ 1

22446688

<u>EEDDCCBB</u>   (Bit-by-bit complement of 11223344)

(1)11223344

$z \leftarrow 0 \quad n \leftarrow 0 \quad c \leftarrow 1 \quad v \leftarrow 0 \quad PC \leftarrow 10000002$

REG^{12} is not changed.

i. $M[00009ABC] \leftarrow EDCBA989 \quad PC \leftarrow 10000002 \quad z \leftarrow 0$
$n \leftarrow 1$

Note that this uses direct addressing and requires a 2-word instruction. We could achieve the same result using Page zero addressing as in part (f).

j. $REG^{12} \leftarrow DDBB9977 \quad z \leftarrow 0 \qquad PC \leftarrow 10000001$

k. 12345678   AND   345678FF

$\quad REG^5 \leftarrow 10145078 \quad z \leftarrow 0 \quad n \leftarrow 0 \qquad PC \leftarrow 10000002$

l. $REG^{3F} \leftarrow 11111111 \quad z \leftarrow 0 \qquad PC \leftarrow 10000001$

m. $M[20001000] \leftarrow 03F08800 \quad z \leftarrow 0 \qquad PC \leftarrow 10000002$

n. $M[12345678] \leftarrow E02468AC \quad z \leftarrow 0 \qquad PC \leftarrow 10000001$

o. $PC \leftarrow 12345678$

p. $PC \leftarrow 12345678$ (since $c = 1$)

q. $PC \leftarrow 10000002$ (since $c = 0$)

It does not jump but likely reads the second word.

r. $PC \leftarrow 12345678 \qquad M[88888888] \leftarrow 10000001$
$\quad REG^{3F} \leftarrow 88888887$

s. $REG^{3F} \leftarrow 88888889 \qquad PC \leftarrow 22334455$

4. For each part, a set of consecutive instructions are executed. Use the initial values of Solved Problem 3. Indicate what changes are made at the end of each set.

a. ADD REG^{12}, z9ABC
ADC REG^5, 7E110000

b. PSH REG^5
PSH REG^{12}
POP REG^1

c. CLL 2000000

RTS

a. First instruction

22446688

EDCBA988

$(1)\ 10101010 \rightarrow REG^{12}\quad z \leftarrow 0\quad n \leftarrow 0\quad c \leftarrow 1\quad v \leftarrow 0$

Second instruction

$\qquad\quad 1$

12345678

345678FF

468ACF78

$REG^{12} \leftarrow 10101010\quad REG^5 \leftarrow 468ACF78\quad PC \leftarrow 10000003$

$z \leftarrow 0\quad n \leftarrow 0\quad c \leftarrow 0\quad v \leftarrow 0$

b. First instruction

$M[88888888] \leftarrow 12345678\qquad REG^{3F} \leftarrow 88888887$

Second instruction

$M[88888887] \leftarrow 22446688\qquad REG^{3F} \leftarrow 88888886$

Third instruction

$REG^{3F} \leftarrow 88888887\qquad REG^1 \leftarrow 22446688\quad z \leftarrow 0\quad n \leftarrow 0$

Note that M[88888887] still has 22446688.

c. First instruction

$PC \leftarrow 20000000\qquad M[88888888] \leftarrow 10000002$

$REG^{3F} \leftarrow 88888887$

Second instruction

$PC \leftarrow 10000002\qquad REG^{3F} \leftarrow 88888888$

Note that M[88888888] still has 10000002.

5. In Solved Problem 1, we discussed two additional address types. Show the changes in the DDL needed to implement these if Page zero indirect is coded 0101 and Indexed is coded 1010.

4. next/$IR_{13:15}$: 5, 1, 6, 1, 1, 7, 10, 11.

Page zero indirect

7. EA $\leftarrow$ 0000, $IR_{16:31}$.

8. AD = EA; **read** = 1; EA $\leftarrow$ DATA;

next: 18.

Indexed

14. PC ← INC[PC];

next/IR$_{13:15}$: 18, 15, 17, 1, 16, 1, 1, 1.

17. EA ← ADD$_{1:32}$[REG/IR$_{26:31}$; EA; 0].

This assumes that the EA register is connected to INA, which was not the case in Figure 10.3. Otherwise, we would need to move EA to WORK first.

17. WORK ← EA

17a. EA ← ADD$_{1:32}$[REG/IR$_{26:31}$; WORK; 0];

next: 18.

6. Another possible addressing mode is indirect with auto-pre-decrementing. Assume the branch at step 14 goes to step 17.

17. WORK ← DEC[EA].

17a. AD = EA; DATA = WORK; **write** = 1.

17b. EA ← WORK;

next: 18.

Note that we must preserve the second word of the instruction to store the decremented address there. Thus, the effective address is not loaded into EA until the last step.

7. We wish to add a new addressing type—multilevel indirect addressing. When an indirect address is fetched, the first bit is an indicator of whether that is the effective address or is still indirect. In this mode, all indirect addresses begin with the same bit as the address in the instruction. The branch at step 14 will branch to step 90 for this address type.

90. AD = EA; **read** = 1; EA$_{1:31}$ ← DATA$_{1:31}$;

next: 90 (DATA$_0$), 18 (else).

Step 90 will be executed repeatedly until the first bit of the address being read is 0. This could result in an endless loop. To prevent that, some machines count how many times it loops, and terminate this after a fixed number of levels of indirection.

90. WORK ← 00000000.

91. AD = EA; **read** = 1; EA$_{1:31}$ ← DATA$_{1:31}$;

next: 92 (DATA$_0$), 18 (else).

```
92.   WORK ← INC[WORK];
      next: 1 (AND[CPUBUS₂₈:₃₁]), 91 (else).
```

On the 15th pass through the loop, WORK contains $0000000E$, and the right 4 bits of the incrementer output are all 1's, terminating the instruction (treating it as a no-op).

8. Design an instruction to multiply two unsigned numbers and store the result (or the 32 less significant bits) in the register from which the first operand comes. We will need to add two registers to implement this. The instruction sets the **c** flag if the answer does not fit into 1 word, and the **z** flag.

We initialize by setting a new 5-bit register, COUNT, to 0, putting one operand (the multiplier) in WORK, and putting the other (the multiplicand) in the new 32-bit register, WORK2. The partial product is stored in the register from which one operand came, which is also initialized to 0.

```
100.  WORK2 ← REG/IR₆:₁₁.
101.  REG/IR₆:₁₁ ← 00000000; COUNT ← 00;
      c ← 0.
102.  WORK ← 0, WORK₀:₃₀;
      next: 104 (WORK₃₁'), 103 (else).
103.  REG/IR₆:₁₁ ← ADD₁:₃₂[REG/IR₆:₁₁; WORK2;
      0];
      z ← (OR[CPUBUS])';
      c ← c + ADD₀[REG/IR₆:₁₁; WORK2; 0].
104.  COUNT ← INC[COUNT];
      next: 105 (OR[CPUBUS]), 1 (else).
105.  WORK2 ← WORK2₁:₃₁, 0;
      next: 102.
```

If the right bit of the multiplier is 1, we add the multiplicand to the partial product, shifting the multiplier one place to the right. (Each time we come back to step 103, we will look at another bit of the multiplier.) COUNT keeps track of the number of bits (32). After adding, the multiplicand is shifted to the left (as we do in multiplication by hand). If there is a carry out of the adder at any stage, the c bit is set and remains set. Note that if there is overflow, we only get the lower 32 bits of the answer.

9. We wish to design a new instruction to perform double-precision addition. The first operand and the result come from a register pair, specified by the first 5 bits of the RN field. The low-order half of the number is stored in the odd register (register number ending in 1), and the high-order half is in the even register. The

other operand comes from two consecutive memory locations, where the low-order part comes from the location specified by EA and the high-order part comes from the previous location. (Register and Immediate addressing is not allowed.) Step 20 branches to step 100 for this instruction.

$$(100.) \quad \mathbf{c}, \text{REG}/(\text{IR}_{6:10}, 1) \leftarrow$$
$$\text{ADD}[\text{REG}/(\text{IR}_{6:10}, 1); \text{WORK}; 0];$$
$$\mathbf{z} \leftarrow (\text{OR}[\text{CPUBUS}])'.$$

101. $\text{EA} \leftarrow \text{DEC}[\text{EA}].$

102. $\text{AD} = \text{EA}; \mathbf{read} = 1; \text{WORK} \leftarrow \text{DATA}.$

103. $\mathbf{c}, \text{REG}/(\text{IR}_{6:10}, 0) \leftarrow$
$$\text{ADD}[\text{REG}/(\text{IR}_{6:10}, 0); \text{WORK}; \mathbf{c}];$$
$$\mathbf{z} \leftarrow \mathbf{z} \cdot (\text{OR}[\text{CPUBUS}])'; \mathbf{n} \leftarrow \text{CPUBUS}_0;$$
$$\mathbf{v} \leftarrow \text{INA}_0 \cdot \text{INB}_0 \cdot \text{CPUBUS}_0' +$$
$$\text{INA}_0' \cdot \text{INB}_0' \cdot \text{CPUBUS}_0;$$

next: 1.

The carry from the first addition is used to make the second one an add with carry. The $\mathbf{z}$ flag is set only if both halves of the answer is 0. The $\mathbf{n}$ and $\mathbf{v}$ flags are determined by the most significant bit.

10. Using the controller design from Appendix A, show a block diagram of the hard-wired controller to implement the STO instruction.

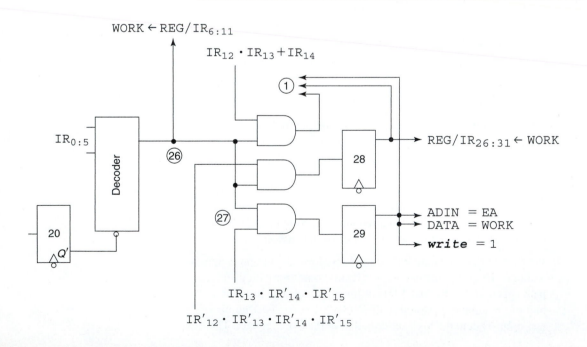

The flip flop and the decoder of step 20 are shown first. Steps 26 and 27 are undelayed, and thus there is no flip flop there. On completion of this instruction, the controller returns to step 1.

11. Compare the speed of double-precision addition, assuming direct addressing, for an ADD instruction followed by ADC with the double-precision instruction designed in Solved Problem 9.

ADD: 6   ADC: 6   Total: 12   (from Table 10.2)

In the new instruction, step 100 is undelayed, and thus it would take 9 clocks (1, 2, 13, 14, 18, 20, 101, 102, 103). If we had a special incrementer for EA (that does not use the bus), step 101 could also be undelayed, reducing the time to 8.

12. Design a small computer with the following instruction format:

```
0    23  45  67                                         31
┌─────┬────┬────┬──────────────────────────────────────┐
│ OP  │ RN │ AT │               Address                │
└─────┴────┴────┴──────────────────────────────────────┘
```

where memory has 2^{25} words, 32 bits each. All instructions fit in a single word. There are four 32-bit registers (similar to the 64 in MODEL). The bus structure and the memory signaling is the same as in MODEL. There are no flag bits.

The are four addressing types

00   Direct

01   Immediate (sign-extended)

10   Relative to this instruction

11   Indirect (up to three levels)

   Bit 0 of the address word indicates direct (0) or indirect (1). After three levels, bit 0 is ignored.

The operations are

000   Load

001   Increment (RN ignored)

010   Add

011   Subtract

100   Jump unconditional (RN ignored)

101   Jump conditional—only allows relative addressing

   Based on number in register with condition specified by AT

      00 $= 0$

      01 > 0

      10 $\neq 0$

$$11 \quad < 0$$

110   Store

111   not used in this problem

Write a complete DDL description of a hard-wired controller for this machine. Do not worry about unused or illegal combinations. Annotate your DDL. Make it run as fast as possible by making steps undelayed.

The first step here is

1. ADIN = PC; **read** = 1; IR $\leftarrow$ DATA.

There is one adder for all addition, subtraction, and incrementing, as in MODEL. It has two 32-bit inputs and a carry-in. There is only a 32-bit output (no need for the carry-out).

Show a table indicating the execution time for each instruction and each addressing type.

```
SYSTEM NAME: NEW COMPUTER
    FLIP FLOPS: PC[0:24], IR[0:31], W[0:31],
    R[0:3; 0:31].
    COMMUNICATION BUSES: DATA[0:31],
    ADIN[0:24].
    INTERNAL BUSES: CPUBUS[0:31], INA[0:31],
    INB[0:31].
    OUTPUT LINES: read, write.
    1.        ADIN = PC; read = 1; IR ← DATA.
    2.        next: 5 (IR₀ · IR₁' · IR₂), 3 (else).
    (3.)      next/IR₅:₆: 10, 4, 5, 6.
```

Immediate

```
    (4.)      IR₇': W ← 00, IR₇:₃₁;
              IR₇: W ← 7F, IR₇:₃₁;
              next: 12.
```

Relative

```
    (5.)      IR₇:₃₁ ← ADD₇:₃₁[IR; 0⁷, PC; 0];
              next: 10.
```

Indirect

(6.) $\text{ADIN} = \text{IR}_{7:31}$; **read** $= 1$;

        $\text{IR}_{7:31} \leftarrow \text{DATA}_{7:31}$;

        next: 7 (CPUBUS_0), 10 (else).

7. $\text{ADIN} = \text{IR}_{7:31}$; **read** $= 1$;

        $\text{IR}_{7:31} \leftarrow \text{DATA}_{7:31}$;

        next: 8 (CPUBUS_0), 10 (else).

8. $\text{ADIN} = \text{IR}_{7:31}$; **read** $= 1$;

        $\text{IR}_{7:31} \leftarrow \text{DATA}_{7:31}$;

        next: 10.

Data fetch?

(10.) next: 12 (IR_0), 11 (else).

11. $\text{ADIN} = \text{IR}_{7:31}$; **read** $= 1$;

        $\text{W} \leftarrow \text{DATA}$.

Decode

12. $\text{PC} \leftarrow \text{ADD}[1^{32}; 0^7, \text{PC}; 0]$;

        next/$\text{IR}_{0:2}$: 15, 16, 18, 19, 20, 21, 26, 1.

Load

15. $\text{R}/\text{IR}_{3:4} \leftarrow \text{W}$;

        next: 1.

Increment

16. $\text{W} \leftarrow \text{ADD}[1^{32}; \text{W}; 0]$

17. $\text{ADIN} = \text{IR}_{7:31}$; $\text{DATA} = \text{W}$; **write** $= 1$;

        next: 1.

Add

18. $\text{R}/\text{IR}_{3:4} \leftarrow \text{ADD}[\text{R}/\text{IR}_{3:4}; \text{W}; 0]$;

        next: 1.

Subtract

> 19. $R/IR_{3:4} \leftarrow ADD[R/IR_{3:4}; W'; 1];$
>
>   next: 1.

Jump

> 20. $PC \leftarrow IR_{7:31};$
>
>   next: 1.

Jump conditional

> 21. $CPUBUS = R/IR_{3:4};$
>
> $next/IR_{5:6}:$ 22, 23, 24, 25.
>
> (22.) next: 1 (OR[CPUBUS]), 20 (else).
>
> (23.) next: 20 ($CPUBUS_0'$ · OR[CPUBUS]),
>
>   1 (else).
>
> (24.) next: 20 (OR[CPUBUS]), 1 (else).
>
> (25.) next: 20 ($CPUBUS_0$), 1 (else).

Store

> 26. $ADIN = IR_{7:31};$ $DATA = R/IR_{3:4};$
>
>   write = 1;
>
>   next: 1.

> END DESCRIPTION

Note that we did not increment the Program Counter until after the addressing, since relative addressing is based on the address of the current instruction (not the next, as in MODEL).

The following graph shows the sequence of steps. The first step of the execution phase cannot be undelayed, since the decode step uses the bus while incrementing the PC.

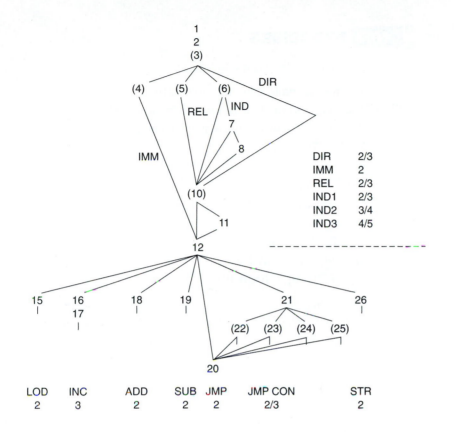

	LOD ADD SUB	INC	STO JMP UNC JMP FAIL	JMP SUC
DIR	5	6	4	—
IMMED	4	—	—	—
REL	5	6	4	5
IND 1	5	6	4	—
IND 2	6	7	5	—
IND 3	7	8	6	—

10.7 EXERCISES

1. For the following values (in MODEL):

   This instruction is at location 76543210

   The second word of the instruction (if any) is 22223333

   Bits 16 to 31 of this instruction word are 4547

   $REG^1 = 79864322$

   $REG^2 = 12341234$

   $REG^7 = FFFFFF00$

   $M[00000001] = 22222222$

   $M[00004547] = 23423423$

   $M[22223333] = 00000001$

   $M[76547758] = 11223300$

   $M[FFFFFF00] = 10101010$

   Show what registers are changed for each of the addressing types and each of these instructions (including the PC, but not the flag bits):

   i. Load REG^1

   *ii. Add to REG^2

   a. Register
   b. Register Indirect
   c. Page zero
   d. Relative
   e. Direct
   f. Indirect
   g. Immediate

2. For each of the following instructions, what registers, flag bits, and memory locations are changed for each of the address types? Assume the following initial values for each instruction:

   $PC = 11111111$

   $z = 1 \quad n = 1 \quad c = 1 \quad v = 1$

   $REG^1 = 12345678$

   $REG^2 = FFFFFFFF$

   $REG^3 = 87654321$

   $REG^{3F} = FFFFFFF0$

   $M[00001234] = 00000010$

   $M[10000000] = 91110000$

M[12345678] = 2468ACE0

M[2468ACE0] = 3456789A

M[FFFFFFEF] = 00112233

M[FFFFFFF0] = 11223344

M[FFFFFFF1] = 22334455

a. i.   STO REG^2, (REG^3)

   ii.   STO REG^1, 10000000

   iii. STO REG^3, z1000

   iv.   STO REG^2, REG^3

   v.   LOD REG^2, REG^3

b. i.   PSH REG^1

   ii.   POP REG^1

c. i.   ADD REG^1, REG^2

   ii.   ADD REG^2, REG^1

   iii. ADD REG^1, #34565432

   iv.   ADD REG^1, 10000000

   v.   ADD REG^3, 10000000

d. i.   ADC REG^2, (REG^{3F})

   ii.   ADC REG^2, z1234

   iii. ADC REG^2, #FFFFFFFF

e. i.   SUB REG^2, 00001234

   ii.   SUB REG^1, REG^2

f. i.   CMP REG^3, 2468ACE0

   ii.   CMP REG^3, #87654321

   iii. CMP REG^3, REG^2

g. i.   INC 10000000

   ii.   INC REG^2

   iii. INC (REG^1)

h. i.   NOT REG^1

   ii.   NOT (12345678)

i. i.   AND REG^1, z1234

   ii.   AND REG^3, #000000F0

   iii. AND REG^1, (FFFFFFF1)

j. i.   ASR 3, REG^{3F}

   ii.   ASR 5, 10000000

   iii. ASR 5, (REG^1)

k. i.   ROR 8, (REG^1)

   ii.   ROR 31, REG^3

l. i.   JMP (REG^3)
    ii. JMP z4567
    iii. JM6 z4567
    iv. JM7 z4567

m. i.   CLL (REG^1)
    ii. CL4 22223333

n. RTS

3. For each part, a set of consecutive instructions are executed. Use the initial values of Exercise 2. Indicate what changes are made at the end of each set.

   a. ADD REG^1, REG^7
       ADC REG^2, #00004567

   *b. PSH REG^1
       PSH REG^2
       POP REG^3
       PSH REG^1
       POP REG^4
       POP REG^5
       POP REG^6

   c. CLL 1000000
       PSH REG^2
       POP REG^6
       RTS

4. Modify the DDL of MODEL to add two new addressing types: modes 1010 and 1011:

   a. Indirect, then indexed by the register specified by $IR_{26:31}$
   b. Indexed by the register specified by $IR_{26:31}$, then indirect

5. Design a different version of multiple indirect from the one in Solved Problem 7. The address will be Page zero and all indirect addresses will also be Page zero.

6. Solved Problem 8 only provides a 32-bit product. Modify the design so that it will produce a 64-bit product, storing the answer in a register pair. (See Solved Problem 9.) Only the **z** bit should be changed.

7. a. Revise the solution to Solved Problem 9 to allow the second operand to come from a register pair.
   b. Also, allow the second operand to be immediate. In the case of immediate, the instruction becomes three words long, with the low-order half stored in the second word.

8. *a. We wish to provide several double-precision instructions. They work on data from a register pair and from another register pair, memory, or immediate (as described in Exercise 7b). Revise steps 1 to 18 to, for double-precision, fetch the data specified by the address field into WORK for the least significant part and into WORK2 for the most significant half. Assume that only such instructions have a 1 in bit 2 (IR_2) of the op-code. (It is still to work as before for single-precision, $IR_2 = 0$.)

   b. Redo Solved Problem 9 to accommodate this change.

9. Show the DDL for an instruction to count the number of 1's in the word specified by the address field, storing the answer in the register specified by RN.

10. Using the controller design from Appendix A, show a block diagram of the hard-wired controller to implement the shifts and rotates (starting at step 43), assuming the decoder at step 20 reaches step 43.

11. Consider the multiplication instruction of Solved Problem 8.
   a. How long does the execution take, as a function of the number of 1's in the multiplier, n?
   b. If registers could be cleared without using the bus and COUNT could be incremented without using the bus, what steps could be undelayed? How much improvement in speed would result?
   c. Add a branch that quits the loop once the multiplier reaches 0.
   d. Compare the speed of the three approaches for a multiplier of 0000 0000 0001 1010 0001 0011 0001 1000

*12. You are designing parts of a computer with a memory of 2^{25} 20-bit words. Instructions require 1, 2, or 3 words depending on the address modes. There is a bus structure similar to that of MODEL. Memory signals are the same as in MODEL, **but** reads and writes take two clocks. The first two steps of the DDL are

```
1. ADIN = PC; read = 1 ;
     PC ← ADD25[1²⁵; PC].

2. IR ← DATA.
```

Note: There are two adders: a 25-bit adder (with no carry-in or carry-out) for addresses (as used in step 1), and a 20-bit adder with carry-in and carry-out for all arithmetic. There are thirty-two 20-bit registers.

The first word of the instruction has the following format:

0	3 4	11 12	19
OP	AD1	AD2	

Some instructions (OP beginning with 0) have two addresses; others have only 1 (using only AD1 for address computation).

The following address types are available. Those beginning with a 0 are complete in the AD field; those beginning with a 1 require an extra word. If both addresses require a second word, the word associated with AD2 comes first.

000xxxxx Register Addressing

001xxxxx Register indirect (Page zero)

010xxxxx Register indirect with auto-pre-decrementing
  where xxxxx represents a register number

100xxxxx Direct, where xxxxx are the first 5 bits of the address

101xxxxx Indirect, where xxxxx are the first 5 bits of the address and the indirect address

110xxxxx AD1: Relative (second word sign-extended)
  AD2: Immediate (three words)

111xxxxx unused

The following are the instructions included in the problem (with flags affected shown):

0000	Add	z, s
0001	Add double-precision*	z, s
0010	Subtract	z, s
0011	Subtract double-precision*	z, s
0100	Compare	z, s
0101	AND	$z, , s$
0110	Move (from AD2 to AD1)	$z, , s$
0111	Move block of 16 words, not for register or immediate addressing	
1000	Increment	z, s

---

*For double-precision, the low-order half is at an even address or register number, and the high-order half is at an odd address or register number. We will assume that the programmer always enters an even address.

1001	Decrement	z, s
1010	Jump to subroutine (unconditional); return address stored in register specified by right 5 bits of AD2	
1011	Jump—condition specified by right 3 bits of AD2	

	0XX	unconditional
	1 0 0	z
	1 0 1	z'
	1 1 0	s
	1 1 1	s'

a. Write the DDL description of the machine. You may assume that only legal instructions occur. Make steps undelayed where possible to make it run reasonably fast. **Annotate your DDL!**

b. Produce a set of timing tables for all the instructions and all address types.

13. Design a computer with 128 Mwords of memory that operates on data of 32 and 64 bits. Memory is word-addressable, that is, addresses are 27 bits. The memory bus is 64 bits, and thus 2 consecutive words are accessed at once. These are always aligned so that the first 26 bits of the address of all instructions and 64-bit data is the same. All data comes from memory, and all results go to memory. Thus, there are no user registers comparable to REG in MODEL. There is a bus structure similar to that of MODEL.

   All instructions require 64 bits. Thus, the PC need only be 26 bits (since all instruction addresses end in 0). The instruction format is as follows (where the details of the first 10 bits are specified below):

0	9 10	36 37	63
INST	Address1	Address2	

	0	4 5 6	7 8	9
INST	OP	SZ	AT1	AT2

The result always goes to the location specified by Address1. For those instructions requiring one operand, its location is specified by Address2; for those requiring two operands, the first comes from the location specified by Address1, and the second from the location specified by Address2. The size of the data is specified by the SZ field as follows:

0	32 bits	word (W)
1	64 bits	double word (DW)

You may assume that all double-word addresses end in 0. Or, if you prefer, you may ignore the last bit.

The following address types are allowed:

00	Direct
01	Indirect*
10	Indirect with auto-post-incrementing*,†
11	Relative (to the first word of the next instruction) for Address1 Immediate for Address2 (sign-extended)

Only the following instructions are to be implemented:

00010	ADD‡
00011	SUB(tract)‡
00100	AND
00101	OR
10000	MOV(e)
1010x	Convert from the size specified by SZ to the other size. If the conversion is to a smaller size, then overflow may occur and the appropriate flags should be set. When making numbers longer, sign-extend them.
11 xyz	JMP

Jump is available both conditionally and unconditionally. Address1 is the address of the next instruction. Bits xyz contain the condition code, as follows:

000	Number specified by Address2 is 0.
001	Number specified by Address2 is nonzero.
010	Number specified by Address2 is negative.

---

*Indirect addresses occupy the right 27 bits of a word.

†*Caution*: You add 1 for W and 2 for DW.

‡There are two overflow flags: one to indicate signed overflow (v), and one to indicate unsigned overflow (c). They can be tested by the jump instruction.

011	Number specified by Address2 is greater than or equal to 0.
100	Signed overflow (v)
101	Unsigned overflow (c)
110	Unconditional
111	CLL* (subroutine, unconditional)

All others unused

The CPU has a 64-bit adder that is used for all arithmetic operations including incrementing. Word operations use the right 32 bits. Address computation is also done using the right bits of that adder. When words (32-bit data) are read from or written to memory, they may appear on either the first 32 bits of DATA or the last 32 bits of DATA. You must account for that. There are two write signals. Both must be made 1 to write 64-bit words. It has memory connections ADIN[0:26], DATA[0:63], **read, write0** (for even addresses) and **write1**.

Example—to read word data, the address of which is in EA

```
ADIN = EA₀:₂₅; read = 1;
EA₂₆': WORK ← 00000000, DATA₀:₃₁;
EA₂₆: WORK ← 00000000, DATA₃₂:₆₃.
```

a. Write a complete DDL description of a hard-wired controller for this machine (including undelayed steps). You may assume that unused codes and illegal combinations do not happen. You may add whatever internal registers you need (such as WORK in MODEL). You are to make this machine run reasonably fast (that is, take advantage of undelayed steps wherever possible), without writing very complex code. **You must annotate your solution**—at least to show where the steps for each op-code and each addressing type begin.

b. Compute the timing for each instruction and addressing type. (The timing should be the same for both sizes of data; but if it isn't, you must include that in your computation.) **You must show a diagram or a listing for the steps executed for each.** Display your results in a readable manner. You need not show a table as we did for MODEL; it would require three dimensions. Rather, you can show the timing as composed of the sum of

---

*The return address is stored in the last word of memory (that is, addresses 7FFFFFF). No provision is made to nest subroutines. You do not have to check.

three or four parts (for example, instruction fetch plus address 1 plus address 2 plus execution), with a table for each part. Just make sure that it is clear how you compute the timing for any instruction.

10.8 CHAPTER TEST (75 MINUTES)

1. (25) For the following values in MODEL:

PC = 12000122
Bits 16:31 of this instruction word are 9402
REG^3 = 98765432
M[00000000] = FF000011
M[12121212] = 00000000

Show the changes to registers, flag bits, and memory locations for each of the following instructions. Also specify the number of memory references to fetch and execute each instruction.

a. LOD REG^2, 12121212
b. STO REG^3, z4567
c. ADD REG^3, #80112233
d. AND REG^3, (12121212)
e. JMP @9000

2. (25) I wish to create a new instruction for MODEL. It only works for those addressing types that produce a memory address in EA, but you need not modify the addressing section to check for that. You will need an extra register, TEMP (if you don't want to change any other registers or memory locations).

   This instruction, SWP, compares the unsigned number in the memory location pointed to by EA with the unsigned number in the location following that. If the second number is greater, it swaps the two numbers; otherwise, it does nothing. Write the DDL to implement this instruction beginning at step 60.

Examples: SWP   00001234

Before:	00001234: 7	After:	00001234: 8
	00001235: 8		00001235: 7
Before:	00001234: 8	After:	00001234: 8
	00001235: 7		00001235: 7

3. (50) You are involved in the design of a small specialized computer, SMALL. It has a memory of 2^{16} 16-bit words. Instructions may only be executed from the first 2^{10} words; thus the PC need only be 10 bits and the Address part of the instruction is large enough to hold a complete address for the jump instructions. The machine has two registers, REG^0 and REG^1. There are no flag bits. The adder adds two 16-bit numbers and produces a 16-bit result. The bus structure is similar to MODEL. The instruction format is as follows:

The AT field specifies the addressing type, as follows:

0	1	2	3	4	5	6	15

OP	R	AT	Address

00	Page zero (that is, 6 leading 0's)
01	Unused
10	Page zero indirect
11	Immediate (only allowed for first four OP codes, zero-extended)

The OP field specifies one of eight instructions, six of which are defined as follows:

000	Load register from memory (or immediate)
001	AND number from memory (or immediate) to register
010	Add number from memory (or immediate) to register
011	unused
100	Store number from register into memory
101	unused
110	Jump (to Address), condition specified by AT*

00	always
01	$REG = 0$
10	$REG > 0$
11	$REG < 0$

---

* Only Page zero addressing is allowed for the two jump instructions.

111   DJZ*: Decrement register (specified by R) and jump (to Address) if register had been (before decrementing) 0 (AT is ignored)

The R bit specifies which register.

Write the DDL code for this machine. Assume that the unused codes and improper combinations (such as store immediate) never occur.

---

* Only Page zero addressing is allowed for the two jump instructions.

Beyond the Central Processing Unit

The term *memory* includes a wide range of devices. The smallest memory in a computer is a flip flop, capable of storing one bit. A *register* is just a set of flip flops with the same name, where the bits are numbered. (In this book, we have numbered the bits starting at 0 on the left end; however, some people, particularly integrated circuit manufacturers, number with the rightmost bit as 0.) Most computers have a set of numbered registers, addressed by a few bits. (For example, MODEL has a set of 64 registers and requires a 6-bit address.) In addition, there are several other registers, independently named.

Each computer has several levels of storage, starting with the smallest, fastest, and most expensive down to the largest, slowest, and least expensive. We have already mentioned the first group, the registers of the CPU. They are accessible in one clock time, on the order of 1 nsec (billionth of a second) or less.* We will discuss each of these in detail in the other sections of this chapter.

The main memory of a computer is referred to as a *RAM* (*Random Access Memory*); it is really just a large set of registers. The name implies that the time to access any one word is the same as that to access any other word. The *access time* for a RAM is how long it takes to read or write a word.[†] Generally, the access time for main memory is a few clock periods, compared with one clock period for registers. Main memory is electronic; it may consist of static (SRAM) circuits or dynamic (DRAM) circuits. The former are somewhat faster, but require more circuitry per bit. The latter only requires one transistor and capacitor per bit, but must be refreshed regularly to keep the capacitor from losing its charge.

In the ideal world, there would be a huge amount of very fast memory. Since that is impractical, a solution has been developed that utilizes a *cache*, a small fast memory that automatically saves the most recently

---

*All of the times, sizes, and costs are changing rapidly. By the time you read this, memories will likely be faster, larger, and less expensive.

[†]In some technologies, the time to read may be different from the time to write.

used words (both program and data), under the assumption that the same words are likely to be used again soon. If a word is found in the cache, its access time is usually the same as for registers (one CPU clock cycle), always much faster than from main memory.

Even though main memories now can hold a gigabyte (GB; 1 billion bytes) or more, modern software (and graphics and pictures) consume that space rapidly. Also, the main memory (even using static RAMs) is volatile; that is, its contents are lost if power is shut off. For both of these reasons, computers have another level of storage, *secondary memory*. The most common form of secondary memory is the magnetic disk. Even laptop computers have *hard drives*, built-in disks that hold 100 GB or more. Magnetic disks are both readable and writable and do not require power to maintain their contents. They are available in portable form (some referred to as floppy disks and others as zip drives). Another device, used mainly to transfer data from one computer to another, is *flash* memory, a small electronic storage device that can hold as much as a few gigabytes of data. Two other forms of secondary storage are the optical disks, the *CD-ROM* (compact disk—read-only memory) and the DVD (Digital Versatile Disk). Originally developed for the storage of audio and video, these have become a popular form of storage for the transfer of large amounts of data or software. Many computers have drives that can write to a CD-ROM and to a DVD. A block diagram of the multilevel memory system is shown in Figure 11.1.

The CPU communicates with main and secondary memory and input/output devices by way of the BUS (as shown in Figure 11.1). Main memory is typically 5 to 10 times slower than the CPU, and the remaining devices are much slower than that. Although it would seem natural that the CPU would always be the *bus master*, the unit in charge of what device has control of the bus, that would keep the CPU busy for long periods to move a block of data. Because of that, the transfer of blocks of data between main memory and other devices is not controlled by the

Figure 11.1 The memory hierarchy.

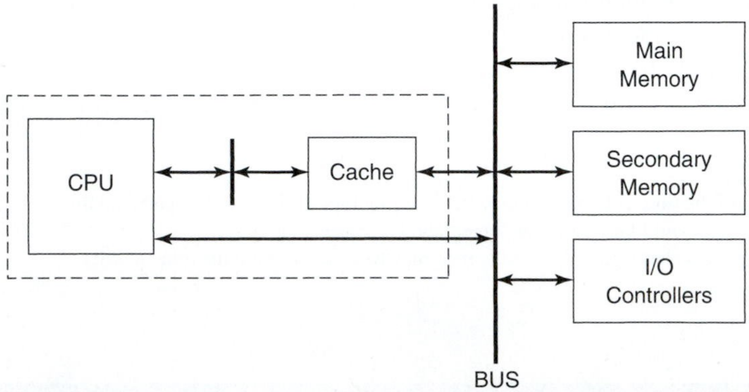

CPU. Other device controllers can become the bus master. This requires an approach to arbitrating who has control of the bus.

Data is transferred between secondary storage and main memory in blocks, typically 4 kilobytes (kB, $2^{12} = 4096$). The primary reason for this is that the time to find a group of bytes, referred to as the *latency*, is quite long, depending on how far the disk must rotate until it reaches the read/write heads and how far the heads must move in or out. This is typically in the range of a few milliseconds. Once the heads are positioned over the data, the transfer rates can be in the 100 megabytes per second (MB/sec) range (that is, 10 nsec/byte).

Input/output (I/O) devices are connected to controllers that are connected to the main system bus (in the same way as secondary memory). Although some machines had separate I/O instructions and a separate address space for I/O devices, most modern computers use the same address space for I/O and memory. Thus, all memory reference instructions can reference I/O device controllers and secondary memory controllers. I/O devices are connected through a controller that takes care of the difference in data rate and format. When large amounts of data are being transferred, I/O devices can control that transfer without interrupting the CPU. That is referred to as *Direct Memory Access (DMA)*.

11.1 RANDOM ACCESS MEMORY

The bus connected to main memory consists of three separate subbuses. The first is a set of address lines, selecting the word in memory. The second is the data bus, used for both input and output. Finally, there is the read/write' line, which indicates the direction in which data is flowing.

There are a variety of internal structures for memories. Logically, a single-bit storage cell behaves like the circuit shown in Figure 11.2a.

Figure 11.2a One-bit storage cell.

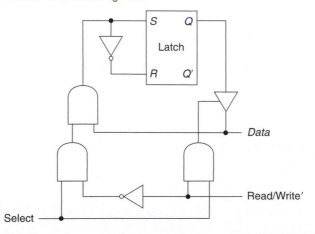

The select line comes from a decoder that activates all of the cells in one word. The line, *Data*, represents 1 bit of the data bus and is connected to all of the cells for that bit position of a word. The three-state output gate is enabled when that word is selected and there is a read operation. In some designs, there are two select lines, both of which must be activated to read from or write to that cell. Both select lines would be connected to the two AND gates in Figure 11.2a. A block diagram notation for that cell (with a single select line) is shown in Figure 11.2b.

Figure 11.2b   Block diagram notation for storage cell.

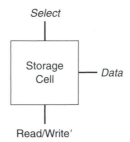

Figure 11.3 shows an array of such cells for a tiny memory: four words with 6 bits in each. Since there are only four words, a 2-bit address is decoded to produce the select line. The 6-bit data bus is connected to each word. The selected word is connected to the data bus on a read operation; otherwise, memory does not connect anything to *Data*.

Although this approach would theoretically work for any size memory, the size of the decoder becomes impractical for large memory chips. For a chip holding one million words, we would need a 20-input, 2^{20} output decoder (regardless of the number of bits per word). Aside from the huge size of this device, it implies 20-input AND gates to implement that decoder. Those are not practical; fan-in (the maximum number of inputs to a gate) is usually limited to 8–10. To solve this problem, a two- (or sometimes three-) dimensional array of cells is constructed.

For a two-dimensional array, half of the bits of the address are decoded in one decoder and the other half in a second decoder.* The first decoder enables a row of bits; the second enables a column. This is referred to as *coincident selection*. Each cell has two select inputs that are ANDed together. Figure 11.4 shows a very small example, a 1-bit, 16-word memory (using a cell with two enable lines). The cells are numbered 0 to 15.

---

*Other arrangements are possible, but we will limit our discussion to this one.

Figure 11.3 A four-word, 6-bit memory.

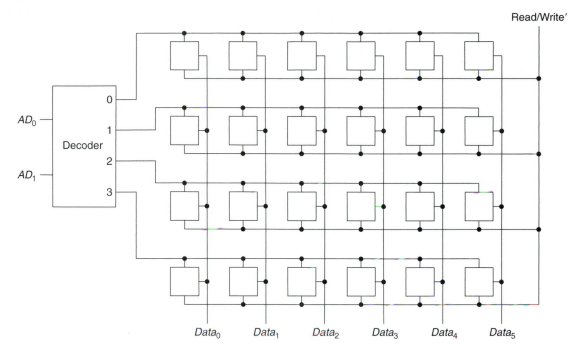

A large memory is generally built using a number of chips. If we require a memory of a billion 64-bit words ($2^{30} \times 2^6$ bits), we cannot find a single chip that large.* Such a chip would require a package with nearly 100 connectors (30 address pins, 64 data pins, plus read/write', one or more select inputs, and power). Although the size of memory chips is generally stated in bytes, they may be organized with a word size of 1, 2, 4, 8, or more bytes. The advantage of a small word size is that the number of connectors is smaller. The disadvantage is that you need several chips for a word.

The most common design today in computers is to mount a set of memory chips on a 168-pin *DIMM* (*Dual In-Line Memory Module*), a board that plugs into the main computer board. The term *dual* implies that there are connectors on both sides of the board. An older design used SIMMs (Single In-Line Memory Modules). There are typically eight chips on the board, each of which provides 8 bits of a word.

A memory chip storing 256 MB organized as 8-bit words would require 28 address lines, 8 data lines, and one or more enable lines. For this example, we will assume one active high enable. We could build a

---

*Of course, that may have changed by the time you read this book because memory sizes have been growing in size every year. However, users will still want even larger memories and the same issues discussed here will still be relevant.

Figure 11.4   Two-dimensional array.

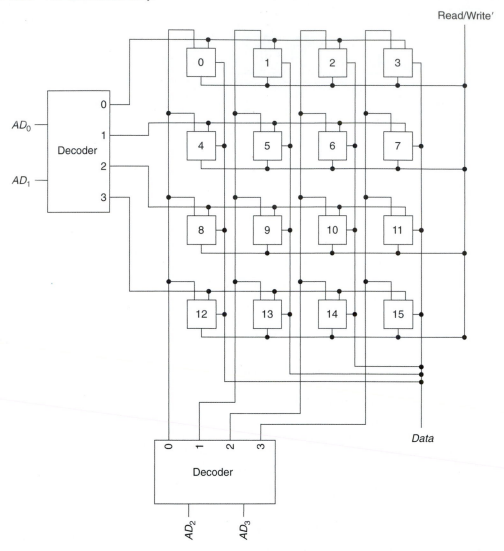

memory of 512 Mwords, 32 bits each, using eight of these chips, as shown in Figure 11.5. The top row contains the first 256 Mwords (spread over the four chips); it is activated by $Addr_0'$. (In this diagram, we are assuming that the computer produces a 29-bit address, allowing a total memory of 512 Mwords.) If the computer were to produce 32-bit addresses to allow a maximum 4-Gword memory, then these chips would contain only the first 512 Mwords. (It is not necessary to fill all of the DIMM slots. A 16-way decoder would choose one of 16 rows of four

Figure 11.5 A 512-Mword, 32-bit memory.

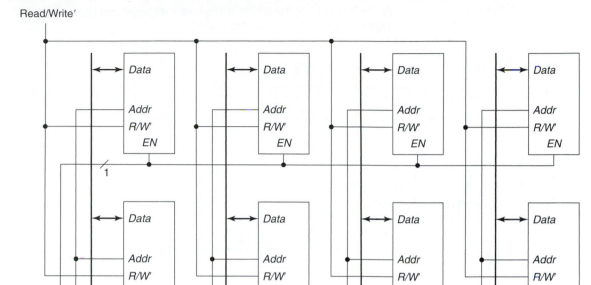

chips. $Addr_{0:3}$ would go to the decoder (and $Addr_{4:31}$ to each chip's address inputs). The first two outputs of the decoder enable these two rows of chips.*

Compare building a 1-MB memory using 1-Mbit chips organized as 1 Mbit $\times$ 1 as opposed to those organized 128 Kbit $\times$ 8. Each requires eight chips. The 1 Mbit $\times$ 1 chips require 20 address lines, one data line, and no decoding of the enable. The 128 Kbit $\times$ 8 chips have 17 address lines, eight data lines, and require a three-to-eight decoder.

In the first diagram, each chip has 1 bit of every word. The data lines are grouped to form an 8-bit set. All of the chips are always enabled. (If they were part of a larger memory, they would all be enabled by the same signal.)

EXAMPLE 11.1

---

*If this memory is implemented with 512-MB DIMMs, the decoder may be one of eight, with bit 3 of the address used to differentiate between the rows.

In the second diagram, a decoder selects one of the eight chips based on the first 3 bits of the address. The data lines are all tied together (assuming three-state data lines on the chips).

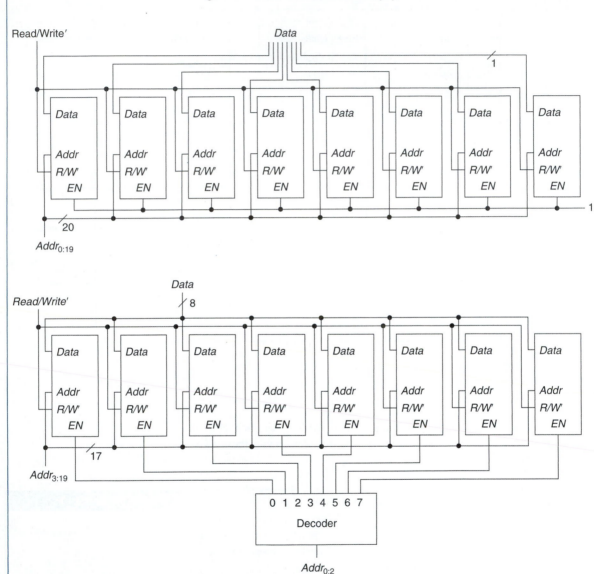

11.2 CACHE MEMORY

A *cache* is a fast memory that temporarily stores words from main memory. Accessing main memory usually takes a few clock cycles, whereas a cache is usually accessible in one cycle. Words are moved to the cache when the word is first referenced. Often, a block of words containing the referenced word is all moved into the cache. This use of the cache is based on two assumptions. First, if a word is accessed, it is likely to be accessed again in the near future, sometimes referred to as *temporal locality*. Second, if a word is referenced, other words with addresses close to it are likely to be referenced, referred to as *spacial locality*. Since computer programs store instructions and store arrays of data in consecutive locations, they exhibit spacial locality. The most heavily used instructions are usually in a loop, meaning that they are used over and over again, exhibiting temporal locality. We will look first at the simplest idea, and then expand it to a more practical approach.

For the first example, we will use a main memory of 2^{32} words and a cache of 256 words. Each word of the cache has four components: an address, the word from memory, a *valid* bit, and a *changed* (or *dirty*) bit. Each word in the cache can store any memory word whose last 8 bits equal the address of that cache word. For example, cache word 01 (hexadecimal) can store words from memory locations 00000001, 00000101, 00000201, . . . , FFFFFF01. This is referred to as a *direct-mapped* cache and is shown in Figure 11.6. The *valid* bit indicates that something is stored in that word of the cache. (When the computer is first turned on, all of the valid bits are set to 0.)

When the CPU produces an address, the last 8 bits select a word from the address section of the cache and, if the valid bit is set, compare that word with the first 24 bits of the address. If they match, the word referenced is in the cache and is immediately accessed. (That is referred to as a *hit*.) If the valid bit is not set or if they do not match (a *miss*), main memory must be accessed for a read and that word is brought into the cache and the CPU.* On a write, the word can be written into the cache. The *hit ratio*, the fraction of memory references that can be found in the cache, is a measure of how effectice the cache is.

One approach to improving the hit ratio for a cache is to bring into the cache a block of words (often referred to as a *line*) whenever any word in that block is referenced. Figure 11.7 shows a direct-mapped cache with 64 lines of four words each (same total size as the previous example). Words in any block have the same first 30 address bits. The assumption made is that if a word is referenced, the other words in its vicinity are also going to be referenced. This approach works particularly well if the data path from memory is wide enough to hold four words, that is, four words can be read from or written to memory at one time. This approach can be applied to the other types of cache that we will describe later on.

---

*Shortly, we will look at the issue of what to do about the word being replaced in the cache.

Figure 11.6 A direct-mapped cache.

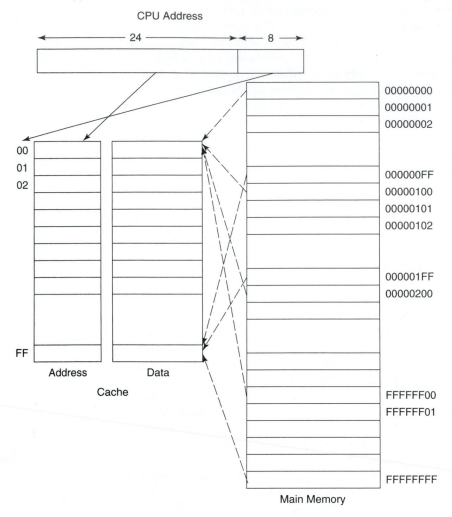

This approach works reasonably well if there is a set of consecutive words (less than the number of spaces in the cache) that are addressed repeatedly. One potential problem is that the instructions and the data may have the same least significant bits, which could cause a large number of misses. There are several solutions to that problem. The simplest is to build two separate caches: one for instructions and one for data. A second solution is to build a *fully associative cache*. Instead of reserving a word in the cache for all of those words that end in the same 8 bits, any memory word can be stored in any cache location. But now, the address portion of the cache must store a complete address. Rather than using the last 8 bits of the address to select a row of the cache, the CPU address

Figure 11.7 Direct-mapped cache with a four-word line.

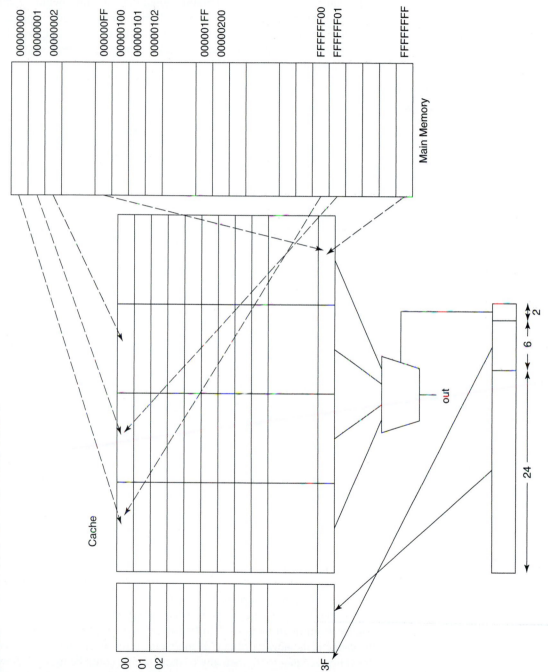

must be compared with the address portion of each cache address word. This requires a very complex combinational logic circuit, including 256 32-bit comparators. (It must be done with combinational logic; comparing addresses sequentially would make the cache too slow.) Figure 11.8 shows this form of cache, including a valid bit, with six words from main memory valid.

Figure 11.8   A fully associative cache.

v	Address	Data
1	00000001	word b
1	00000002	word c
1	00000102	word d
0		
1	FFFFFF01	word f
1	00000000	word a
0		
0		
1	FFFFFF00	word e
0		

Cache

word a	00000000
word b	00000001
word c	00000002
	000000FF
	00000100
	00000101
word d	00000102
	000001FF
	00000200
word e	FFFFFF00
word f	FFFFFF01
	FFFFFFFF

Main Memory

When an address comes from the CPU, it is compared with each address in the cache. If there is a match and the valid bit is 1, then the corresponding data word is returned to the CPU. If not, the word is fetched from main memory. This raises some new problems. Where in the cache is the new word put? If there are some unused locations (with the valid bit equal to 0), then any of those words could be used. If, however, the cache is full (which will normally happen after a short time), then something must be removed to make room. The *replacement policy* determines which word is removed. We could pick a word at random or cycle through the cache, using a first-in, first-out policy. Either of these will give fairly good behavior. Somewhat better would be to remove the word least recently used (LRU). This usually improves the hit ratio, but requires additional hardware to keep track of when a word was last used. When this policy is used, a counter is added to each word. The counter is set to 0 when a word is first brought into the cache and is incremented each time another word is used (saturating when it reaches all 1's). One of the words with the largest value in the counter is then removed. Usually, the counter is only a few bits; any word whose counter is all 1's is replaced. This is referred to as pseudo-LRU.

Since fully associative caches are so much more expensive than direct-mapped caches, a compromise has been developed. We can build a cache that is direct-mapped, but, instead of having only one place to store a word, we could have two or four (or any power of 2). Figure 11.9

Figure 11.9 A two-way associative cache.

000000	word a	00	FFFFFF	word e	
000000	word b	01	FFFFFF	word f	
000000	word c	02	000001	word d	
FFFFFE	word g	FF	000000	word h	

Cache

word a	00000000
word b	00000001
word c	00000002
word h	000000FF
	00000100
	00000101
word d	00000102
	000001FF
word j	00000200
word g	FFFFFEFF
word e	FFFFFF00
word f	FFFFFF01
	FFFFFFFF

Main Memory

shows such a cache with 512 words. (For simplicity, we have omitted the valid bits.) The last 8 bits of the address determine which row of the cache is used. In the example shown, words *a* to *h* fit into one or the other sides. When word *j* is referenced, either word *a* or word *e* must be removed. The least recently used algorithm could easily be implemented for this arrangement by assigning a single bit to each row, that gets set to 0 whenever the left word is used and to 1 whenever the right word is used. Note that if the simpler direct-mapped cache were used, there would be conflicts for words *d, e, f,* and *h,* even before the problem with word *j.*

One issue remains. What happens when the CPU writes to memory? Two approaches have been used. The first is referred to as *write through.* Any write is written both to the cache and to main memory. Thus, when a word is replaced in the cache, it can just be written over. The disadvantage of this is that it requires extra memory references when that word is being written to many times, such as when it is being used as a counter. The other approach is to include a *changed bit* (sometimes referred to as a *dirty bit*), which is set to 1 whenever there is a write to that word of the cache. When the word is replaced, it is written back to memory if the changed bit is set (or just written over, otherwise). This approach creates a problem if main memory might be accessed by some other processor or I/O device while this program is running; it might then use stale information (that is, data that has been changed in the cache.)

EXAMPLE 11.2

Consider a 16-word cache organized as

a.   direct-mapped
b.   direct-mapped with two-word lines
c.   fully associative
d.   two-way associative

For the following address sequence (in hexadecimal), show the contents of the cache at the end of the sequence.

121   206   122   123   206   124   125   126   121   206   122
123   206   129   12A   207

The contents of the direct-mapped cache show the address of the word stored in the cache at various stages of execution. The first seven references load words into the cache. Word 6 in the cache is needed both for word 206 and 126. When the next reference is to 126, that replaces 206. Later 126 is replaced by 206 and no further replacement is required.

For the direct-mapped cache with two-word lines, both 120 and 121 are loaded into the cache when 121 is loaded. That happens again when loading 122 (and 123) and several other places. There is still a conflict between 126 and 206. The status of the cache at the end of the execution is shown.

The fully associative cache has room for all 10 words used and is not shown.

The two-way associative cache has room for two words that have the same three last digits. (Words ending in 0 and 8 go on the same line.) All of the words for this memory reference stream would fit, as shown. If, however, there were a reference to 131, 201, or 209, line 1 of the cache would be full, and either 121 or 129 would have to be removed. (If an LRU replacement policy were used, 121 would be replaced.)

	after 7		after 8		end
0		0		0	
1	121	1	121	1	121
2	122	2	122	2	122
3	123	3	123	3	123
4	124	4	124	4	124
5	125	5	125	5	125
6	206	6	126	6	206
7		7		7	207
8		8		8	
9		9		9	129
A		A		A	12A
B		B		B	12B
C		C		C	
D		D		D	
E		E		E	
F		F		F	

Direct-mapped

	0	1
0	120	121
2	122	123
4	124	125
6	206	207
8	128	129
A	12A	12B
C		
E		

Two-word lines

0		
1	121	129
2	122	12A
3	123	
4	124	
5	125	
6	206	126
7	207	

Two-way associative

11.3 SECONDARY MEMORY

The primary type of secondary memory today is the magnetic disk. It stores information in a magnetic field on very small spots on one or more circular platters (typically on both sides). The layout of one side of a platter is illustrated in Figure 11.10. The disk rotates at a constant speed, typically 7200 rpm (120 revolutions per second, or one revolution per 8.33 ms.). Information is stored in tracks and is read or written when the bit passes the read/write head. There may be 1024 or more tracks on a platter. Each track is divided into sectors, holding a fixed number of bytes, most commonly 512. Figure 11.10 shows eight sectors (shaded) for all tracks. A modern disk would have at least 64. (Some disks have more sectors on outer tracks and fewer on inner tracks.) Read/write heads are located on a radius and must be moved in or out to align with the track being referenced.

Figure 11.10   A magnetic disk.

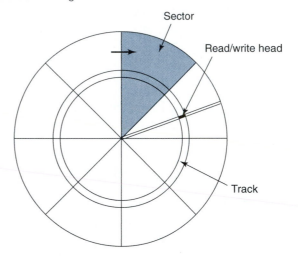

Unlike RAMs, the time it takes to get information from a disk depends on the location of the information relative to the read/write head. There are three factors involved. First, the *seek time* is how long it takes for the head to move to the correct track. That is quoted as an average, since we do not know how far the heads must move for any given access. An average seek time of 10 msec is typical. Then, we must wait for the platter to rotate so that the beginning of the desired sector is under the read/write head. The average is half a rotation. For the previous example (7200 rpm), that is 4.17 msec. Finally, the information is read as the sector goes by the head. If there are 64 sectors, that would be 8.33 msec/64 = 130 μsec/sector or 0.25 μsec/byte. That is a rate of approximately 3.9 MB/sec.*

More recently, optical storage devices are used, primarily for very large amounts of data and for portable memory. CD-ROMs (Compact Disk Read-Only-Memories)[†] and DVDs (Digital Video Memory or Digital Versatile Memory) are being used for computer data, as well as music and movies.

11.4 VIRTUAL MEMORY

When we discussed the cache, we saw that only a portion of the user's memory requirements fit into the cache at any one time. Similarly, we may only be able to accommodate a portion of a user's memory requirements in main memory at one time. This is particularly true in a large computer with multiple users. The most common approach to solving this problem is referred to as *virtual memory*. In a virtual memory system, the user may have a very large address space, larger than the physical main memory and much larger than his share of main memory (when it is being shared by multiple users). The concept of virtual memory is to make it appear as if all of the user's memory space is available to him and to relieve him of the responsibility of maneuvering words back and forth between main and secondary memory (much as he was relieved of that responsibility with the cache).

The address space is organized in blocks, referred to as *pages*, often 1024 (2^{10}) words each. Each page of a user's memory space is assigned to a block of main memory (referred to as a *page frame*) when it is active. The operating system maintains a *page table* that translates between the user's page number (that is, the leading bits of the user address) and the physical page frame in main memory. Actually, there are two tables. The first contains, for every user page, the location of that page in secondary memory and its location in main memory (if any). That table is contained on a page in main memory when that program is running. If that were the only table, it would take at least two memory references to access any word, one to read the table, and one to reference the word. In most systems, a second table is kept in hardware (possibly a special cache) of the active pages of a program, sometimes referred to as a *Translation*

---

*That is referred to as the *sustained rate*, the speed at which it would transfer several consecutive sectors. The *burst rate*, how fast data is being transferred during the time the sector is being transferred, is about 5% faster, since each sector has several bytes of error checking and synchronization information in addition to the 512 bytes of data.
[†]Although they are called read-only, CD-ROMs can be written to. Those labeled CD-R can be written to once, and those labeled CD-RW can be written to many times.

Lookaside Buffer (TLB). That table is shown in Figure 11.11. Each entry has a valid bit and a changed bit, just as in a cache.

When the CPU produces an address, it checks the hardware table. If it is found there, the reference is done quickly. If it is not in the hardware table, the memory table is checked. If the page is in memory, the hardware table is updated and the reference is completed in two memory cycles. If the required page is not in main memory, then it must be fetched from secondary memory, requiring several milliseconds. In a multiuser system, control is generally given to another program while the page is being fetched.

Figure 11.11   Virtual address translation.

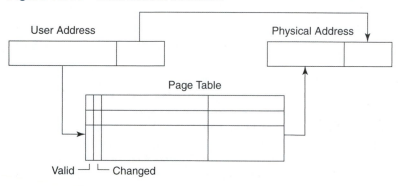

Valid ⌐└ Changed

EXAMPLE 11.3

A program consists of eight pages, of which four are in main memory. A typical Page Table is shown below.

Main Memory

	v	Frame		Frame Number		
0	1	7		0	Page 3
1	1	1		1	Page 1
2	1	3		2	
3	1	0		3	Page 2
4	0	-		4	
5	0	-		5	
6	0	-		6	
7	0	-		7	Page 0
	Page Table			8	
				9	

11.5 INTERRUPTS

An *interrupt* is a signal from outside the CPU controller requesting service by the CPU.* (You can see that the terminology is from the CPU point of view.) When the CPU receives such a signal, it normally interrupts what it is doing and executes a section of code (program) called the interrupt handler. (That is just a set of regular instructions stored in memory like any other program. The user can write his own interrupt handler although it is often part of the system's programs.) When the interrupt handler is finished, control must return to the program that was running when the interrupt handler was activated. That program must then be able to continue at the point where it was interrupted. Since that program had no way of knowing when (or if) an interrupt would occur, it could make no special preparations for the interrupt. The hardware and interrupt handler software must be so designed to ensure that the original program can continue running undisturbed.

Each device that is capable of producing a request has an output line that it activates when it wishes to be served. (Whether active is a logic 1 or logic 0 is a hardware detail that varies from machine to machine; we will assume that a 1 is a request.) Each device controller's interrupt request line may be connected to its own CPU input or all of these request lines may be tied together (ORed), producing a 1 on the CPU's interrupt request line when any of them is 1. The request must be held active until the CPU responds by issuing an appropriate I/O instruction to that device, at which time the device controller will clear the request line.

As an interrupt structure is developed, a number of issues arise in this scenario. First, there is typically no relationship between the interrupt itself and the program that is running when the interrupt is serviced. It is possible that the interrupt is related to that program, but usually it has nothing to do with what is happening at the moment of the interrupt. If the latter is the case, then we must take care that when we return to the original program, it can truly pick up where it left off. Sometimes the contents of all user-accessible registers (and flags) is referred to as the *state* of the machine. When an interrupt is to be processed, we must save enough of the state so that when we return to the original program, the entire state can be restored.

Second, typically several sources are capable of requesting service. Each needs its own special kind of service, its own interrupt handler. We must provide a way of determining which source caused the interrupt. Also, we must handle the possibility that two or more sources are requesting service simultaneously, and we must choose among them,

---

*Some computers refer to software interrupts or traps, but they are normally just subroutine calls to special error-handling subroutines generated by such problems as overflow or illegal instructions. We will not discuss them here.

delaying the others until the first has been handled. One approach to this is to have each device's interrupt request come into a priority encoder (see Section 4.3.). Another approach to priority control is referred to as a *daisy chain*. The request lines are all ORed. The grant line is connected as shown in Figure 11.12. The CPU issues a single *intgrant* signal, which goes to the highest priority device. Within each device, there is an AND gate, the inputs of which are the *intgrant* input and the complement of that device's request, *intreq'*. The output of that AND gate goes to the input of the next device's *intgrant*. Thus, once a device that requested an interrupt receives its *intgrant*, all lower priority devices get a 0 on their *intgrant* input.

Figure 11.12   Daisy chain.

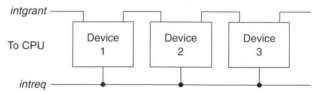

Finally, there are times when what is going on in the CPU is so important that we do not want to allow an interrupt. We must provide a way to turn off interrupts, that is, allow the machine to ignore, for the time being, all or some of the interrupt requests (under user control).

In order to process an interrupt without disturbing the program currently running (other than delay its completion), we recognize a service request only between instructions, that is, at the point where we are about to fetch a new instruction. If we call the signal that generates an interrupt within the CPU **interrupt***, then step 1 of the MODEL DDL must be replaced by

```
1.    next: 300 (interrupt), 1a (else).
1a.   AD = PC; read = 1; IR ← DATA;
      PC ← INC[PC].
```

In a hardwired controller, step 1 would be undelayed and thus, if **interrupt** were 0, step 1a would be executed without any time lost checking for the service request. The steps to begin processing this request start at 300. First, the program counter is pushed onto the stack, as in a subroutine call.

---

*The name **interrupt** was chosen to imply that this signal is 1 when service has been requested and the CPU is ready to respond to that request. It is 0 whenever there is no outstanding request or when interrupts are disabled.

```
300.    ADIN = SP; DATA = PC; write = 1.
301.    SP ← DEC[SP].
```

Eventually the program counter will be loaded with the address of the first instruction of the interrupt handler program. We must emphasize here that the structure to respond to a service request consists of two distinct parts: hardware and software. The hardware includes the generation of the signal **interrupt** and the additional control steps (1, 300, . . .) that we are inserting into the MODEL DDL. There will also be some new instructions to be implemented, as we will see shortly. The software is the interrupt handler programs (one for each source of service requests).

If we are to truly return to the original program in the same state as when the interrupt was processed, then the interrupt handler must leave all user registers ($REG^{0:63}$, PC, z, n, c, v) exactly as they were. We have already satisfied that requirement for PC since we pushed it onto the stack. SP will also be preserved, assuming that the interrupt handler pops from the stack everything that it pushes onto it. (If it does not, we have an even greater problem since the return will not load PC properly.) With respect to the registers, there are two alternatives: a hardware approach and a software one. For the former, the sequence at step 300 would also push each of the registers and the flag bits onto the stack (requiring 65 writes and 65 decrements). There would have to be a special return from interrupt handler instruction (RIH) that retrieved the registers, the flags, and the PC from the stack. The software approach places the burden on the programmer of the interrupt handler. None of the registers is automatically saved on the stack. It is up to the programmer to save those registers that he plans to use and to restore them before returning. Thus, at the beginning of the interrupt handler program, there would be a series of store or push instructions and, just before the return, these registers would be reloaded from memory.* Comparing the two approaches, the hardware version will be much faster if most of the registers are needed by the interrupt handler. It takes only two clock periods per register, whereas the software approach requires the execution of at least one instruction (several clock periods) for each register. On the other hand, if only one or two registers is needed, then the hardware approach wastes a great deal of time and space by storing and retrieving the contents of many registers unnecessarily. There is a middle ground, as well. The hardware could save the flags and a few registers, say the first four. The interrupt handler program would be able to use those without having to save them. If it needed additional registers, it would need to use the software approach for the others.

---

*There would need to be two new instructions: one to save the flags onto the stack and another to restore them from the stack (since any meaningful interrupt handler program would surely write to some or all of the flag bits).

One more issue must be examined before we are ready to describe a simple, but complete interrupt structure. There are times when interrupt processing must be suspended. The oversimplified approach described earlier will not work because as soon as the first instruction of the interrupt handler is about to be fetched—before the interrupting device has been signalled to turn off the service request—it will find that **interrupt** is 1 at step 3 and return to 300, never getting anything accomplished. Thus, the set of steps starting at 300 must disable interrupts before jumping to the interrupt handler. The programmer then needs the ability to enable them or disable them at will.

Figure 11.13a shows a snapshot of the computer at the time an interrupt occurs, when the controller is at step 20, having fetched the operand (into WORK) of the add instruction (from locations 00000102 and 00000103)*. The execution of that instruction is completed and then control proceeds to step 1 and then 300. By that time, REG^1 and the flags have been loaded by step 30 (the addition step in the control sequence), as shown in Figure 11.13b. Following the execution of the interrupt handler, REG^1, the flags, and PC must be restored, as well as any other registers that were used by the interrupt handler. (WORK, however, need not be, since it contains no information that is used by the next instruction.)

Figure 11.13   A snapshot of MODEL at the time of an interrupt.

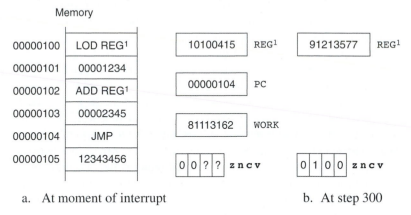

a.   At moment of interrupt   b.   At step 300

EXAMPLE 11.4

We will design the hardware to save the flags and the first two registers on the stack and then branch to memory location FFFFFFF0, where there are instructions to direct the program to the proper interrupt handler program. We will add a flag, **ie**, to indicate that interrupts are enabled. (Note that **interrupt** is only 1 if interrupts are enabled, that is, **ie** = 1.) Finally, we will write the steps for the RIH instruction, beginning at step 320.

---

*There would be at least one more flag to indicate whether interrupts were enabled.

```
302.   ADIN = SP;
       DATA = 0000000, z, n, c, v, ie;
       write = 1.
303.   SP ← DEC[SP].
304.   ADIN = SP; DATA = REG⁰; write = 1.
305.   SP ← DEC[SP].
306.   ADIN = SP; DATA = REG¹; write = 1.
307.   SP ← DEC[SP].
308.   PC ← FFFFFFF0; ie ← 0;
       next: 1.
```

The return from interrupt instruction leaves the interrupt enable where it was and restores all the registers.

```
320.   SP ← INC[SP].
321.   ADIN = SP; read = 1; REG¹ ← DATA.
322.   SP ← INC[SP].
323.   ADIN = SP; read = 1; REG⁰ ← DATA.
324.   SP ← INC[SP].
321.   ADIN = SP; read = 1;
       z, n, c, v, ie ← DATA₂₇:₃₁.
326.   SP ← INC[SP].
321.   ADIN = SP; read = 1; PC ← DATA;
       next: 1.
```

11.6 DIRECT MEMORY ACCESS

If the CPU were to control the transfer of blocks of data between main memory and secondary memory or an I/O device, it would not allow the CPU to do anything else for a long period of time. (For example, if the CPU clock rate is 2 GHz and the time to access and transfer a 512-word block to or from a disk is 7.8 msec, then 15.6 million clock cycles would be utilized to transfer a block of 512 64-bit words.) To get around this problem, an approach called *Direct Memory Access (DMA)* is commonly used.

In DMA, the CPU issues a few output commands to the device to begin the operation. For a disk transfer, that would include the address on the disk, the address in main memory, and the size of the block to transfer. The DMA controller manages the transfer of the data, getting control of the bus when it needs it (and delaying the CPU because the CPU cannot access the bus and main memory while the DMA controller has it).

Generally, the CPU has the lowest priority for use of the bus, since mechanical devices like a disk cannot wait for data; it must have it as the disk passes the write head.

There must be some way of deciding who is the bus master when more than one device requests the bus. One approach is to build a bus controller, as described in Section 6.4. Another approach is to use the daisy chain, as described in the Section 11.4.

When a DMA device is ready to transfer data, it issues a bus request. When it receives a grant, it puts an address on the address bus (and data on the bus for a write) and a read/write' signal. Unless this is a very high speed device (capable of data transfers at or near the main memory rate), it releases the bus. Unless there is another device waiting for the bus, the CPU can then proceed, having lost a few clock cycles. The DMA device then prepares for the next transfer (by incrementing address registers and decrementing the count if it is a secondary memory transfer) or, if it is finished, sends an interrupt to the CPU to indicate that the transfer is complete.

Summary of MODEL Controller Design

SYSTEM NAME: MODEL CONTROLLER

> FLIP FLOPS: PC [0:31], IR[0:31], WORK[0:31], REG[0:63, 0:31], EA[0:31], **z, n, c, v**.
>
> INTERNAL BUSSES: CPUBUS[0:31], INA[0:31], INB[0:31].
>
> INTERSYSTEM BUSSES: DATA[0:31], ADIN[0:31], **read, write**.
>
> NAME: SP = REG^{63}.
>
> 1. AD = PC; **read** = 1; IR ← DATA.
> 2. PC ← INC[PC];
>   next: 60 (IR$_0$), 3 (else).

Addressing

> (3.) next: 12 (IR$_{12}$), 4 (else).
> 4. next/IR$_{13:15}$: 5, 1, 6, 1, 1, 1, 10, 11.

Register

> (5.) WORK ← REG/IR$_{26:31}$;
>   next: 20.

Register Indirect

> (6.) EA ← REG/IR$_{26:31}$;
>   next: 18.

Page Zero

> (10.) EA ← 0000, IR$_{16:31}$;
>   next: 18.

Relative

> (11.) IR$_{16}$: EA ← ADD$_{1:32}$[FFFF, IR$_{16:31}$; PC; 0];
>   IR$_{16}$': EA ← ADD$_{1:32}$[0000, IR$_{16:31}$; PC; 0];
>   next: 18.

Read second word, direct

> 13. AD = PC; **read** = 1; EA ← DATA.

14.   PC ← INC [PC];
      next/$IR_{13:15}$: 18, 15, 1, 1, 16, 1, 1, 1.

Indirect

15.   AD = EA; **read** = 1; EA ← DATA;
      next: 18.

Immediate

16.   WORK ← EA;
      next: 20.

Data read

18.   AD = EA; **read** = 1; WORK ← DATA;
      next: 20.

20.   "Instruction decode"*

LOD

(25.) REG/$IR_{6:11}$ ← WORK; **z** ← (OR[CPUBUS])';
      n ← $CPUBUS_0$;
      next: 1.

STO

(26.) WORK ← REG/$IR_{6:11}$.

(27.) next: 28(IR_{12}' · IR_{13}' · IR_{14}' · IR_{15}'),
      1 (IR_{13} · IR_{14}' · IR_{15}'), 29 (else).

28.   REG/$IR_{26:31}$ ← WORK;
      next: 1.

29.   ADIN = EA; DATA = WORK; **write** = 1;
      next: 1.

ADD

(30.) **c**, REG/$IR_{6:11}$ ← ADD[REG/$IR_{6:11}$; WORK; 0];
      z ← (OR[CPUBUS])'; **n** ← $CPUBUS_0$;
      v ← INA_0 · INB_0 · $CPUBUS_0$' +
      INA_0' · INB_0' · $CPUBUS_0$;
      next: 1.

ADC

(31.) **c**, REG/$IR_{6:11}$ ← ADD[REG/$IR_{6:11}$ WORK; **c**];
      z ← (OR[CPUBUS])'; **n** ← $CPUSUB_0$;

---

*The details of this step (or steps) are not shown, since we are implementing the controller for only a few of the instructions.

$\mathbf{v} \leftarrow INA_0 \cdot INB_0 \cdot CPUBUS_0{}' +$
$INA_0{}' \cdot INB_0{}' \cdot CPUBUS_0;$
next: 1.

SUB

(32.) $\mathbf{c}, REG/IR_{6:11} \leftarrow ADD[REG/IR_{6:11}; WORK'; 1];$
$\mathbf{z} \leftarrow (OR[CPUBUS])'; \mathbf{n} \leftarrow CPUBUS_0;$
$\mathbf{v} \leftarrow INA_0 \cdot INB_0 \cdot CPUBUS_0{}' +$
$INA_0{}' \cdot INB_0{}' \cdot CPUBUS_0;$
next: 1.

CMP

(34.) $\mathbf{c} \leftarrow ADD_0[REG/IR_{6:11}; WORK9; 1];$
$CPUBUS = ADD_{1:32}[REG/IR_{6:11}; WORK'; 1];$
$\mathbf{z} \leftarrow (OR[CPUBUS])'; \mathbf{n} \leftarrow CPUBUS_0;$
$\mathbf{v} \leftarrow INA_0 \cdot INB_0 \cdot CPUBUS_0{}' +$
$INA_0{}' \cdot INB_0{}' \cdot CPUBUS_0;$
next: 1.

INC

(36.) $WORK \leftarrow ADD_{1:32}[00000001; WORK; 0];$
$\mathbf{z} \leftarrow (OR[CPUBUS])'; \mathbf{n} \leftarrow CPUBUS_0;$
next: 27.

NOT

(40.) $WORK \leftarrow WORK'; \mathbf{z} \leftarrow (OR[CPUBUS])';$
next: 27.

AND

(42.) $REG/IR_{6:11} \leftarrow REG/IR_{6:11} \cdot WORK;$
$\mathbf{z} \leftarrow (OR[CPUBUS])'; \mathbf{n} \leftarrow CPUBUS_0;$
next: 1.

Shifts and rotates

43. $IR_{7:11} \leftarrow DEC[IR_{7:11}];$
next: 44 $(OR[IR_{7:11}])$, 27 (else).
44. next: 45 (IR_4), 47 (else).

ASR

(45.) $WORK \leftarrow WORK_0, WORK_{0:30};$
$\mathbf{z} \leftarrow (OR[CPUBUS])';$
next: 43.

ROR

(47.) WORK $\leftarrow$ WORK$_{31}$, WORK$_{0:30}$;
z $\leftarrow$ (OR[CPUBUS])';
next: 43.

JMP

(50.) **br** = OR[DCD(IR$_{8:11}$) · (**z, z', n, n', c,
c', v, v'**, 0, 0, 0, 0, 0, 0, 0, 1)]
br: PC $\leftarrow$ EA;
next: 1.

CLL

(51.) **br** = OR[DCD(IR$_{8:11}$) · (**z, z', n, n', c,
c', v, v'**, 0, 0, 0, 0, 0, 0, 0, 1)]
next: 1 (**br**); 52 (else)
(52.) ADIN = SP; DATA = PC; **write** = 1.
53.   SP $\leftarrow$ DEC[SP].
54.   PC $\leftarrow$ EA;
next: 1.

PSH

(65.) ADIN = SP; DATA = REG/IR$_{6:11}$; **write** = 1.
66.   SP $\leftarrow$ DEC[SP];
next: 1.

POP

(67.) SP $\leftarrow$ INC[SP].
68.   ADIN = SP; **read** = 1; REG/IR$_{6:11}$ $\leftarrow$ DATA;
z $\leftarrow$ OR[CPUBUS]; n $\leftarrow$ CPUBUS$_0$;
next: 1.

RTS

(70.) SP $\leftarrow$ INC[SP].
71.   ADIN = SP; **read** = 1; PC $\leftarrow$ DATA;
next: 1.

END DESCRIPTION

Appendix

Answers to Selected Exercises

B

B.1 Chapter 1 Answers

1. a. 31   d. 47   h. 0
2. a. 000001001001
   e. 001111101000
   g. $4200 > 2^{12} = 4096$ Thus, can't represent in 12 bits
3. a. 96B
   c. 317
4. c. 1023
5. a. 001111 $3 + 12 = 15$
   d. 000001 $51 + 14 = 65$ overflow
   e. 110010 $11 + 39 = 50$
6. a. 011001   c. cannot be stored
   e. 110001
7. c. $+21$ d. -28 h. -32
8. c. 10001111
   d. cannot store numbers larger than $+127$
9. a. 000100 $-11 + (+15) = +4$
   d. 010000 $-22 + (-26) = $ overflow
   f. 101101 $-3 + (-16) = -19$
10. b. 111001   i. $17 - 24 = $ overflow
                    ii. $+17 - (+24) = -7$
    c. 110011   i. $58 - 7 = 51$
                    ii. $-6 - (+7) = -13$
    d. 001100   i. $36 - 24 = 12$
                    ii. $-28 - (+24) = $ overflow
11. a. 0 11001000 0010100
    d. 0 00000000 0000001
12. a. 0 10000110 10010000010100000000000
    d. 0 01111000 01000111101011100001010
13. b. $.21364 \times 10^7$ e. $-.8 \times 10^{-1}$
14. a. i.   0001 0000 0011
        ii.   0001 0000 0011
       iii.   0001 0000 0011
       iv.   0100 0011 0110
         v.   10100 11000 10001

15.

		i.	ii.	iii.	iv.	v.	vi.
	b.	no	18	15	no	27	+27
	d.	95	no	no	62	149	−107

16. a. ii. 0100010 1001111 1001011 0100010

b. iii. $9/3 = 3$

17. a. ii. 0110011

b. i. 1010 (no error)

iii. 1110 (bit 3 error)

B.2 Chapter 2 Answers

2. a.

w	x	y	z	1	2	3
0	0	0	0	1	1	1
0	0	0	1	1	1	1
0	0	1	0	1	1	1
0	0	1	1	1	1	1
0	1	0	0	1	1	1
0	1	0	1	1	1	1
0	1	1	0	1	1	1
0	1	1	1	0	1	1
1	0	0	0	0	1	1
1	0	0	1	0	1	1
1	0	1	0	0	1	1
1	0	1	1	0	0	1
1	1	0	0	0	0	0
1	1	0	1	0	1	0
1	1	1	0	0	0	0
1	1	1	1	0	1	0

d.

A	B	C	D	F
0	0	0	0	1
0	0	0	1	1
0	0	1	0	0
0	0	1	1	0
0	1	0	0	1
0	1	0	1	1
0	1	1	0	1
0	1	1	1	0
1	0	0	0	0
1	0	0	1	1
1	0	1	0	1
1	0	1	1	1
1	1	0	0	0
1	1	0	1	0
1	1	1	0	1
1	1	1	1	1

h.

a	b	c	d	g
0	0	0	0	1
0	0	0	1	0
0	0	1	0	1
0	0	1	1	0
0	1	0	0	1
0	1	0	1	0
0	1	1	0	1
0	1	1	1	1
1	0	0	0	0
1	0	0	1	1
1	0	1	0	0
1	0	1	1	1
1	1	0	0	X
1	1	0	1	X
1	1	1	0	X
1	1	1	1	X

3. a.

4. a.

X	Y	Z	F
0	0	0	1
0	0	1	0
0	1	0	1
0	1	1	1
1	0	0	1
1	0	1	0
1	1	0	0
1	1	1	1

5. b. $f = h$, but $\neq g$ because of row 011

6. b.   ii.   sum of three product terms
    d.   iv.   product of two sum terms
    f.   i.   product of 1 literal   iii.   sum of 1 literal
         ii.   sum of 1 product term   iv.   product of 1 sum term
    g.   none

7. b. 4   d. 3   f. 1   g. 6

8. a. $= z$
    d. $= a'b' + ac$
    f. $= x'y' + x'z + xy$
         also $= x'y' + yz + xy$

9. c. $(a + c')\,(a' + c)\,(a' + b') = (a + c')\,(a' + c)\,(b' + c')$

10. c.

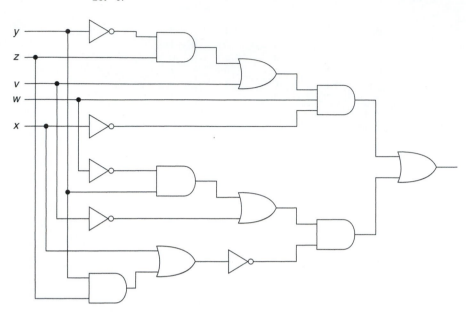

11. c. i. $h = a'c(b + d) + a(c' + bd)$
    ii. $= a'bc + a'cd + ac' + abd$

12. a. $f' = (a' + b' + d)(b + c)(a + c' + d')(a + b' + c + d')$

14. a. $f(a, b, c) = \Sigma m(1, 5, 6, 7)$
    $g(a, b, c) = \Sigma m(0, 1, 4, 5, 6)$

  b. $f = a'b'c + ab'c + abc' + abc$
    $g = a'b'c' + a'b'c + ab'c' + ab'c + abc'$

  c. $f = b'c + ab$
    $g = b' + ac'$

  d. $f'(a, b, c) = \Sigma m(0, 2, 3, 4)$
    $g'(a, b, c) = \Sigma m(2, 3, 7)$

  e. $f = (a + b + c)(a + b' + c)(a + b' + c')(a' + b + c)$
    $g = (a + b' + c)(a + b' + c')(a' + b' + c')$

  f. $f = (b + c)(a + b')$
    $g = (a + b')(b' + c)$

16. a. yes   b. no   c. yes   d. no   e. no   f. yes

17. a. $f = a(bc)' + (c + d')' = ab' + ac' + c'd$
    f. $f = 1 \oplus (ab + cd) = a'c' + a'd' + b'c' + b'd'$

18. d.

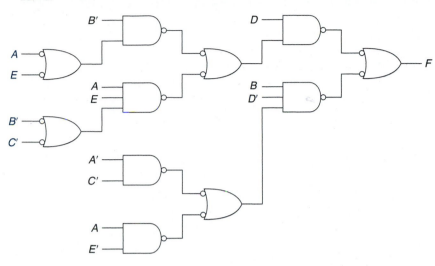

19. c. $f = b + a'c$

20. c. $F = W'Z' + Y'Z + WXY$

    e. $G = B'D + BC + A'D$

    g. $g = bc'd + abc + a'bd'$

         $= a'bc' + abd + bcd'$

21. a. $f = a'b'c' + a'bd + a'cd' + abc + a'c'd$

         $+ a'b'd' + a'bc + bcd + bcd'$

         $= bc + a'c'd + a'b'd'$

22. b. $g = x'y'z' + x'y'z + x'yz' + x'yz + xyz + xy'z'$

        $g(w, x, y, z) = \Sigma m(0, 1, 2, 3, 4, 7)$

23. c. $xy + w'z$

24. c. $(b' + d)(c + d)(a' + b + d')(b' + c' + d')$

25. a. $f = w(y' + xz') + z(y' + w'x')$

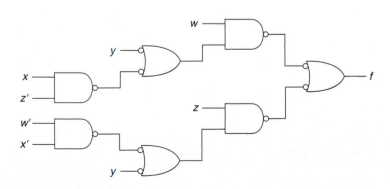

d. $F = B'[D'(A' + CE) + A'C] + B(AC' + C'D)$

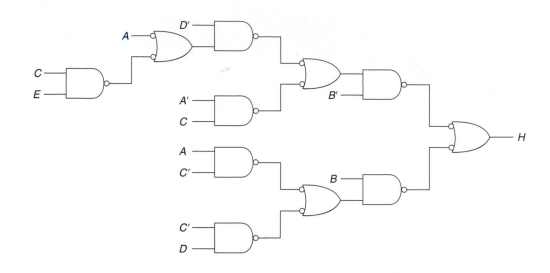

26. a. $F = BE(ACD + C'D' + A'C') + B'(E' + A'C) + CD'E'$
$3 3 3 2 232223$ 3 packs
$= BE(C'(A' + D') + ACD) + B'E' + CD'E' + A'B'C$
322234233 3 packs

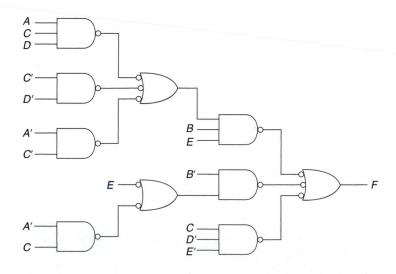

B.3 Chapter 3 Answers

1. b.

yz \ wx	00	01	11	10
00			X	X
01	1	1	1	
11	1	1		
10		1	1	X

c.

cd \ ab	00	01	11	10
00		1		
01		1	1	1
11	1	1		1
10	1	1		1

2. b. $g = w'x' + wx + wy$ $g = w'x' + wx + x'y$

e. $G = X'Z' + W'XZ + WXY'$

i. $h = pq + qr' + r's' + p'q'r + prs$
$h = pq + qr' + r's' + p'q'r + q'rs$
$h = pq + qr' + r's' + q'rs + p'q's'$

l. Prime Implicants: $xy, yz, xz, wz, w'x, w'y'z', x'y'z', wx'y'$
Minimum: $g = yz + xy + w'x + wz + x'y'z'$

m. $H = X'Z' + W'X'Y + W'XZ + WXY'$
$H = X'Z' + W'YZ + W'XZ + WXY'$
$H = X'Z' + W'YZ + XY'Z + WXY'$
$H = X'Z' + W'YZ + XY'Z + WY'Z'$

n. $f = a'c' + ab' + cd' + bd$
$f = b'c' + a'b + cd' + ad$
$f = c'd + ac + a'b + b'd'$
$f = a'c' + ad + bc + b'd'$
$f = b'c' + bd + ac + a'd'$
$f = c'd + bc + ab' + a'd'$

3.   b. $g = wx + yz + xy + xz + wy + wz$

4.   b. $f_1 = ab' + b'd' + cd + a'bc'$
$f_2 = ab' + b'd' + cd + a'bd$
$f_3 = ab' + b'd' + b'c + a'bd$

    e. $f_1 = cd' + a'b + b'd' + ac'd$
$f_2 = cd' + a'b + b'd' + ab'c'$
$f_3 = cd' + a'b + a'd' + ab'c'$

5.   a. $f = A'B + C'D + AD$
$f = (B + D)(A + B + C')\,(A' + D)$

    c. $f_1 = a'd' + ad + bc + ab$
$f_2 = a'd' + ad + bc + bd'$
$f_3 = (a' + b + d)(a + c + d')(a + b + d')$

    g. $f_1 = w'z + wy + xz$
$f_2 = w'z + wy + wx$
$f_3 = w'z + wx + x'z$
$f_4 = w'z + wx + yz$
$f_5 = w'x' + wx + yz$
$f_6 = w'x' + wy + xz$
$f_7 = (w + z)(w' + x + y)$

6.   b. $H = AB'E + BD'E' + BCDE + A'CD'E$

    e. $H = V'W'Z + V'WY + VWY' + W'X'Z' + VWXZ$
$H = V'W'Z + V'WY + VWY' + W'X'Z' + WXYZ$

    g. $G = X'Y' + V'XZ + \{VWZ \text{ or } WXZ\}$

7.   a. $f = a'b'd + ab'c' + bc'd + acd'$
$g = a'b + bc'd + acd'$

    f. $f = c'd' + a'cd + bd$
$g = bd + a'c'd + ab' + \{abc \text{ or } acd'\}$
$h = b'cd' + bd + a'c'd + a'bc' + \{abc \text{ or } acd'\}$

    h. $f = b'c'd + a'b' + a'c'd'$ or
$f = b'c'd + a'b' + bc'd'$ or
$f = b'c'd + b'c + a'c'd'$
$g = b'c'd + cd'$

B.4   Chapter 4 Answers

2. The truth table for this module is

a	b	c	y	s	t
0	0	0	0	1	0
0	0	1	0	1	1
0	1	0	0	1	1
0	1	1	1	0	0
1	0	0	1	0	0
1	0	1	1	0	1
1	1	0	1	0	1
1	1	1	1	1	0

$$y = a + bc \quad s = a'b' + a'c' + abc \quad t = b'c + bc'$$

The delay from c to y is 2 for each module. The total delay is $32 + 1$.

7.

a	b	c	X	Y
0	0	0	0	0
0	0	1	0	1
0	1	0	0	0
0	1	1	1	1
1	0	0	0	0
1	0	1	1	1
1	1	0	1	0
1	1	1	1	1

9.

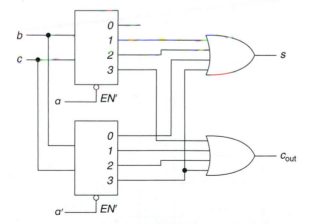

12.

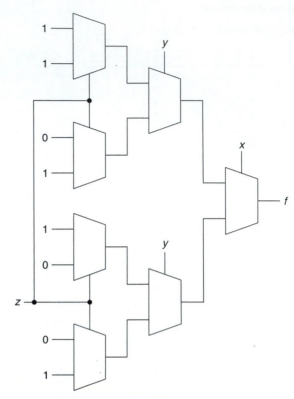

16. a.

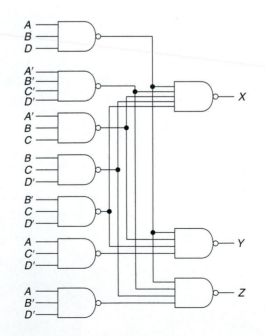

b. The solution is straightforward; the diagram is not shown.

c. We need two decoders. A is connected to the enable of the first. The outputs correspond to the first eight minterms. A' is used to enable the second, producing the other eight minterms. Only three OR gates are needed.

d. The solution of part a is implemented on a PLA with seven terms

$$X = ABD_1 + A'B'C'D'_2 + A'BC_3 + BCD'_4 + B'CD'_5$$
$$Y = AC'D' + ABD_1 + A'BC_3 + B'CD'_5$$
$$Z = ABD_1 + A'B'C'D'_2 + AB'D' + BCD'_4$$

e. The PAL would be implemented with a solution using only prime implicants of individual functions:

$$X = A'B'D' + CD' + ABD + BC$$
$$Y = AC'D' + ABD + A'BC + B'CD' \quad \text{or}$$
$$\quad = A'CD' + BCD + ABC' + AB'D'$$
$$Z = B'C'D' + ABD + BCD' + \{AB'D' \text{ or } ACD'\}$$

19. a. $X1 = B'D'_2 + BD + AC'_1 + A'C$

   $X2 = B' + C'D' + AD' + AC'_1 + A'CD$

   $X3 = D + B'C' + A'B + AC_4$

   or

   $\quad = D + A'C' + BC + AB'$

   $X4 = B'D'_2 + A'B'C_5 + A'CD'_6 + BC'D + ABD + AC'_1$

   $X5 = B'D'_2 + A'CD'_6 + AC'D'$

   $X6 = A'BC' + ABC + AB'C' + \{B'C'D' \quad \text{or} \quad A'C'D'\}$
   $\qquad + \{ACD' \quad \text{or} \quad AB'D'\} + \{BCD' \quad \text{or} \quad A'BD'\}$

   $X7 = BC' + AC'_1 + AB_3 + A'B'C_5 + \{A'CD'_6* \text{ or } BD'\}$

   $X8 = AB_3 + AC_4$

Package Count

X1:	2	2	2	2			4
X2:	0	2	2	(2)	3		5
X3:	0	2	2	2			4
X4:	(2)	3	3	3	3	(2)	6
X5:	(2)	(3)	3				3
X6:	3	3	3	3	3	3	6
X7:	2	(2)	2	(3)	2		5
X8:	(2)	(2)					2

2's:	13	7430s:	4	32 gates/95 inputs	
3's:	13	7420s:	1		
4's:	2	7410s:	5	(2 left over)	
5's	2	7400s:	3	(use one 3-input)	
6's:	2			Total: 13 packages	

---

*Solving $X7$ alone, you would use BD' in place of $A'CD'$. But, the latter is also a prime implicant and can be shared, saving one gate and two inputs. Gate count is based on BD'.

b. $X1 = B'D'_1 + AC'_3 + A'CD_2 + BD$

$X2 = B' + A'CD_2 + AC'_3 + C'D' + ACD'_8$

$X3 = D + ACD'_8 + B'C'D'_{10} + A'BD'_5$

$X4 = A'B'C_4 + B'D'_1 + AC'_3 + A'CD'_7 + A'BC'D_6 + ABCD_9$

$X5 = B'D'_1 + A'CD'_7 + AC'D'$

$X6 = ACD'_8 + B'C'D'_{10} + ABCD_9 + A'BC'D_6 + AB'C' + A'BD'_5$

$X7 = A'B'C_4 + AC'_3 + A'BC'D_6 + AB_{11} + A'BD'_5$

$X8 = AC + AB_{11}$

Package Count

$X1$:	2	2	3	2			4
$X2$:	0	(3)	(2)	2	3		5
$X3$:	0	(3)	3	3			4
$X4$:	3	(2)	(2)	3	4	4	6
$X5$:	(2)	(3)	3				3
$X6$:	(3)	(3)	(4)	(4)	3	(3)	6
$X7$:	(3)	(2)	(4)	2	(3)		5
$X8$:	2	(2)					2

2's:	7	7430s:	4	24 gates/79 inputs
3's:	9	7420s:	2	
4's:	4	7410s:	3	
5's	2	7400s:	2	
6's:	2			Total: 11 packages

c. The PLA implementation of part b would require 18 product terms, one for each of the product terms shown, including the single literal terms (B' in $X2$ and D in $X3$). We could do this with only 16 product terms if we treated the PLA as a ROM (that is, created the 16 minterms). This would not have worked for part b, since it requires gates of more than eight inputs for those functions with more than eight minterms (all but $X5$ and $X8$).

B.5 Chapter 5 Answers

1. b.

x	1	1	0	1	0	1	0	1	0	0	1	0	1	1
q	A	B	B	C	D	C	D	C	D	C	A	B	C	D	B
z	0	0	0	0	1	0	1	0	1	0	0	0	0	1	0	0

4. c.

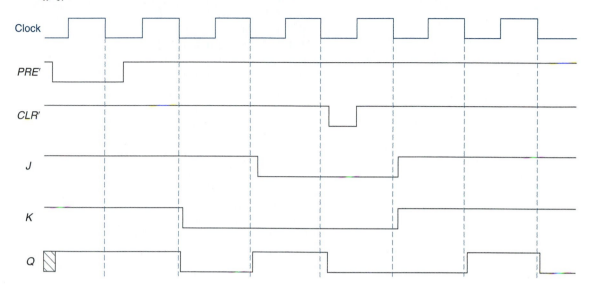

7. b.

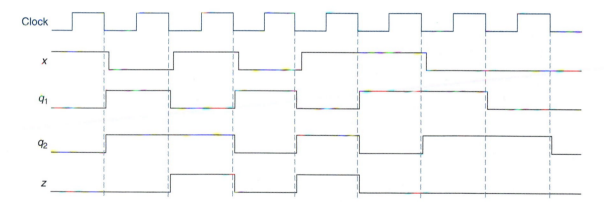

8. a.

q_1q_2	$q_1^\star q_2^\star$		z
	$x = 0$	$x = 1$	
0 0	1 0	1 0	1
0 1	0 0	1 0	0
1 0	1 1	1 1	1
1 1	0 1	1 1	1

$$x \quad 0\ 0\ 1\ 1\ 0\ 0\ 1\ 1\ 0$$
$$q_1 \quad 0\ 1\ 1\ 1\ 1\ 0\ 0\ 1\ 1\ 0\ ?\ 1\ ?$$
$$q_2 \quad 0\ 0\ 1\ 1\ 1\ 1\ 0\ 0\ 1\ 1\ 0\ ?\ 1$$
$$z \quad 1\ 1\ 1\ 1\ 1\ 0\ 1\ 1\ 1\ 0\ 1\ 1\ ?$$

9. c.
$$x \quad 0\ 1\ 1\ 0\ 0\ 1\ 1\ 1\ 0$$
$$A \quad 0\ 0\ 0\ 1\ 1\ 1\ 1\ 0\ 1\ 1\ 1$$
$$B \quad 0\ 1\ 1\ 1\ 0\ 0\ 0\ 0\ 1\ 0\ 0\ 0$$
$$C \quad 0\ 1\ 0\ 0\ 1\ 1\ 0\ 0\ 0\ 1$$
$$z \quad 0\ 1\ 0\ 0\ 0\ 0\ 0\ 0\ 0\ 0\ 0\ 0$$

B.6   Chapter 6 Answers

2. a.   The output equation is the same for all types of flip flop:

$$z = x'B + xB'$$
$$D_A = x'B' + xA \quad D_B = x' + A$$
$$S_A = x'B' \quad R_A = x'B \ (\text{or } x'A) \quad S_B = x' \quad R_B = xA'$$
$$T_A = x'A + x'B' \quad T_B = x'B' + xA'B$$
$$J_A = x'B' \quad K_A = x' \ J_B = x' \quad K_B = xA'$$

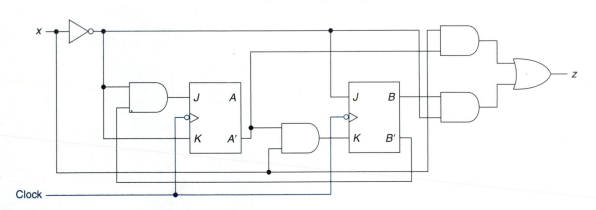

f. $z = A'$
$$D_A = x'A' + x\,AB' \quad D_B = x'B + xB'$$
$$J_A = x' \qquad K_A = x' + B \qquad J_B = x \qquad K_B = x$$
$$S_A = x'A' \qquad R_A = x'A + AB \qquad S_B = xB' \qquad R_B = xB$$
$$T_A = x' + AB \qquad T_B = x$$

3. c. $z = q'_1 q'_2$
$$D_1 = x'q'_1 + xq_1 \qquad D_2 = xq'_1 q'_2$$
$$J_1 = x' \quad K_1 = x' \qquad J_2 = xq'_1 \ K_2 = 1$$

4. b.   (i) $D_1 = xq'_1 q'_2$
$$D_2 = q_1 + x'q'_2 + xq_2 = q_1 + x'q'_1 q'_2 + xq_2$$
$$z = x'q'_1 q'_2 + xq_2$$

(ii) $D_1 = xq'_2$
$$D_2 = q_1 + q'_2 + x$$
$$z = x'q'_2 + xq'_1 q_2$$

(iii) $D_1 = x + q_2'$

$\qquad D_2 = xq_1 + xq_2'$

$\qquad z = xq_2 + x'q_1'$

7. a. $D_D = CBA + DB' + DA'$ $\qquad J_D = CBA$ $\qquad K_D = BA$

$\qquad D_C = D'C'BA + CB' + CA'$ $\qquad J_C = D'BA$ $\qquad K_C = BA$

$\qquad D_B = B'A + BA'$ $\qquad J_B = K_B = A$

$\qquad D_A = A'$ $\qquad J_A = K_A = 1$

8. b. $D_C = BA + \{CB'$ or $B'A'\}$ $\qquad J_C = B$ $\qquad K_C = BA'$

$\qquad D_B = B' + CA$ $\qquad J_B = 1$ $\qquad K_B = C' + A'$

$\qquad D_A = B' + A'$ $\qquad J_A = 1$ $\qquad K_A = B$

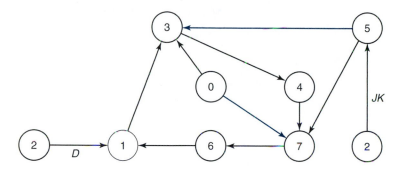

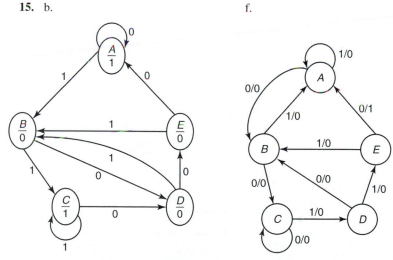

Green path from 0 and 5 when $D_C = BA + B'A'$

10. a. $J_A = B$ $\quad \cdot K_A = x + B$ $\qquad J_B = x' + A'$ $\qquad K_B = 1$

b. $11 \rightarrow 00$

15. b. $\qquad\qquad\qquad\qquad\qquad$ f.

k.

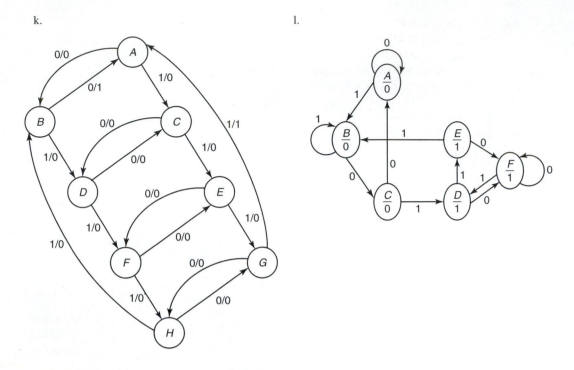

l.

B.7   Chapter 7 Answers

4. a.   Assume CLR' is clocked, but does not require counter to be enabled.

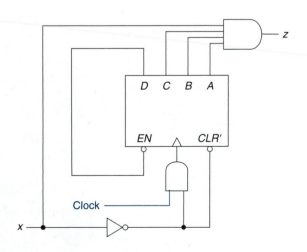

b. $z = x\,q_1'q_2'q_3'q_4'q_5'q_6'q_7'q_8$

$= x(q_1 + q_2 + q_3 + q_4 + q_5 + q_6 + q_7)'q_8$

8.

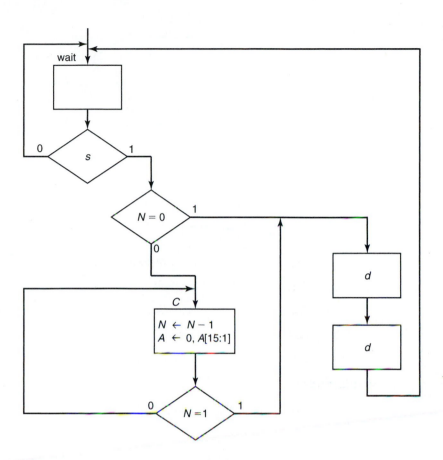

9. a. $J_A = B + C$ $K_A = \{(BD + BC)$ or $(BD + CD')$
                              or $(BC + C'D)\}$

  $J_B = D$ $K_B = C + D$
  $J_C = AD' + B'D'$ $K_C = A'D + \{AD'$ or $BD'\}$
  $J_D = 1$ $K_D = 1$

In some cases, the next state depends on the choice for K_A or K_C. Those transitions are shown with dashed lines. In any case, the sequence is reached within three clocks.

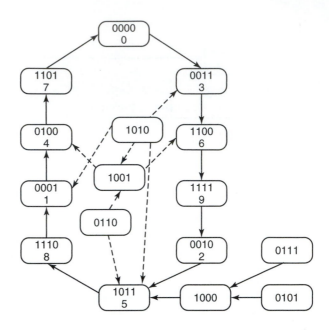

b.   A table for the minimal sum of product expressions is shown.

	X1	X2	X3	X4	X5	X6	X7
A′B′D′	X			X	X		
B′CD	X		X	X			X
ABC	X	X					X
ABD	X	X	X				
A′C′D′		X	X			X	
A′B′C′		X	X				
A′B′C		X					X
ABD′			X	X	X	X	
ACD						X	
BC′D′							X
OR inputs	4	5	5	3	2	3	4

12. The state table for this counter follows

| | $A^\star B^\star C^\star$ | |
ABC	x = 0	x = 1
0 0 0	0 0 1	0 1 1
0 0 1	0 1 0	0 1 1
0 1 0	0 1 1	0 1 1
0 1 1	1 0 0	1 0 0
1 0 0	0 0 0	1 0 1
1 0 1	0 1 1	1 1 0
1 1 0	0 1 1	1 1 1
1 1 1	0 1 1	0 1 0

a.   i.   For the D flip flop, we have

$D_A = A'BC + xAB' + xAC'$

$D_B = B'C + BC' + xA'B' + \{AB \text{ or } AC\}$

$D_C = x'AC + xA'B' + xAC' + BC' + A'C'$

The NAND gate requirements are

Size	Number	Packages
1	1 (x')	0 (from 4)
2	4	1
3	6	2
4	1	1
5+	1	1

The cost is thus $1.25 for gates plus the flip flops.

ii.   Using JK flip flops, we get

$J_A = BC$ $K_A = x' + BC$

$J_B = C + xA'$ $K_B = A'C$

$J_C = x + A' + B$ $K_C = x'A' + xA + \{xB \text{ or } A'B\}$

For this, the NAND gate requirements are

Size	Number	Packages
1	3	1
2	8	2
3	2	1

The two extra NOT gates (1-input) are needed to create the AND for J_A and K_B. The cost is thus $1.00 for gates plus $2.00 for the flip flops, a total of $3.00.

b.   Thus, if the D flip flop packages cost less than $0.875, the first solution is less expensive.

   If we can use one D package and one JK package, the best option is to use the JK package for B and C, and one of the Ds for A (using xB and a shared xAB' in place of xA in K_C). That would require

Size	Number	Packages
1	2	0 (from 2's)
2	5	2
3	6	2

This solution would cost $2.00 plus the cost of the D package. If the D package cost between $0.75 and $0.875, this solution would be better.

c.   This flip flop will be set when the system is in state 5, 6, or 7 and x is 0, or when in state 0 or 1 and the input is 1. It can be cleared whenever the system is in state 3. Thus, for the new flip flop,

$J = xA'B' + x'AB + x'AC$

$K = A'BC$

and the output is just the state of that flip flop.

d.   All of the outputs come from flip flops. We can compute the inputs for a D flip flop for Q using

$D = Q^{\star} = JQ' + K'Q$

and then simplifying the algebra. The result is

$D = AQ + B'Q + C'Q + xA'B' + x'AB + x'AC$

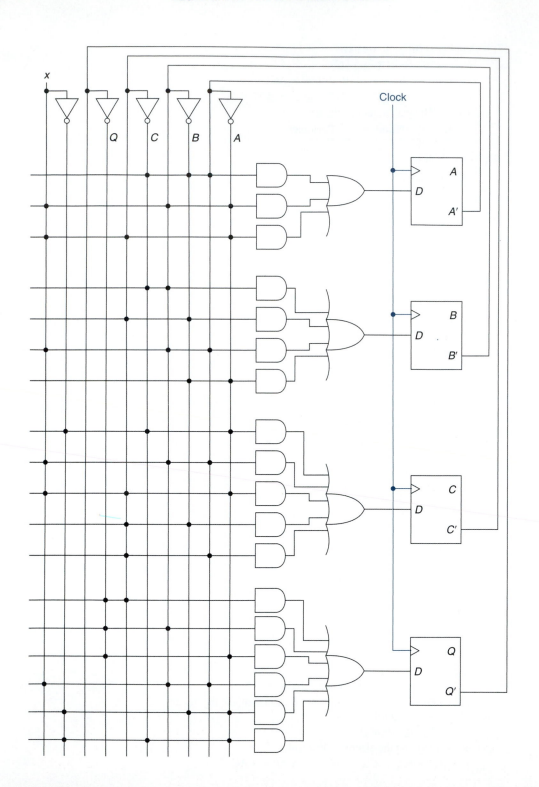

B.8 Chapter 8 Answers

3. a. $REG^5 \leftarrow 12345678$ $PC \leftarrow 1234F$

    b. $REG^5 \leftarrow FFEEDCBA$ $PC \leftarrow 1234F$

    c. $REG^5 \leftarrow FFEEDCBA$ $PC \leftarrow 1234F$

      $REG^2 \leftarrow 12345679$

    d. $REG^5 \leftarrow FFFFEDC2$ $PC \leftarrow 1234F$

    e. $REG^5 \leftarrow 12345666$ $PC \leftarrow 1234F$

    f. $REG^5 \leftarrow 11223344$ $PC \leftarrow 1234F$

    g. $REG^5 \leftarrow FFFFFFFF$ $PC \leftarrow 1234F$

    h. $REG^5 \leftarrow 11223344$ $PC \leftarrow 1234F$

      $M[FEDC2] \leftarrow 12345667$

5b. a. 1

    b. $1 + 1 = 2$

    c. $1 + 1 = 2$

    d. 1

    e. $1 + 1 = 2$

    f. $1 + 1 + 1 = 3$

    g. $1 + 1 = 2$

    h. $1 + 1 + 2 = 4$

7. a. $REG^2 \leftarrow ABCDEF01$ $PC \leftarrow 11112223$

      Memory: $1 + 1 = 2$

    b. $REG^2 \leftarrow 10102323$ $PC \leftarrow 11112223$

      Memory: 1

    c. $M[10102323] \leftarrow 10203040$ $PC \leftarrow 11112223$

      Memory: $1 + 1 = 2$

    d. $REG^{36} \leftarrow 33333333$ $PC \leftarrow 11112223$

      Memory: 1

    e. $REG^{15} \leftarrow 225486B8$ $PC \leftarrow 11112224$

      Memory: $2 + 1 = 3$

    f. $REG^{15} \leftarrow 20305363$ $PC \leftarrow 11112223$

      Memory: 1

    g. $REG^{15} \leftarrow BBEE14F2$ $PC \leftarrow 11112223$

      Memory: $1 + 1 = 2$

    h. $REG^{15} \leftarrow 00100D1D$ $PC \leftarrow 11112223$

      Memory: 1

    i. $M[12345678] \leftarrow 00000000$ $PC \leftarrow 11112224$

      Memory: $2 + 1 + 2 = 5$

    j. $M[10102323] \leftarrow 22334456$ $PC \leftarrow 11112223$

      $REG^{36} \leftarrow 10102324$

      Memory: $1 + 2 = 3$

    k. Stack: | 679ACE00 | $PC \leftarrow 11112223$

      Memory: $1 + 3 = 4$

    l. $REG^{15} \leftarrow 00002000$ $PC \leftarrow 11112223$

      Memory: $1 + 1 = 2$

m. $REG^{15} \leftarrow 10002000$ $PC \leftarrow 11112223$
    Memory: 1

n. $REG^0 \leftarrow 3337777F$ $PC \leftarrow 11112224$
    Memory: $2 + 1 = 3$

p. $M[10102323] \leftarrow EDCBA987$ $PC \leftarrow 11112224$
    Memory: $2 + 2 = 4$

q. $REG^{36} \leftarrow 80811918$ $PC \leftarrow 11112223$
    Memory: 1

r. $M[00009876] \leftarrow 0ABCDEF0$ $PC \leftarrow 11112223$
    Memory: $1 + 2 = 3$

s. $M[00009876] \leftarrow FABCDEF0$ $PC \leftarrow 11112223$
    Memory: $1 + 2 = 3$

t. $M[12345678] \leftarrow FFFFFFFF$ $PC \leftarrow 11112224$
    Memory: $2 + 1 + 2 = 5$

u. $PC \leftarrow 12304560$
    Memory: 2

v. $PC \leftarrow 10102323$
    Memory: 1

11112224
11223344
56789ABC

w. $PC \leftarrow 12345678$ Stack:
    Memory: $2 + 1 + 1$

x. $PC \leftarrow 11223344$ Stack:
    Memory: $1 + 1 = 2$

56789ABC

B.9 Chapter 9 Answers

4. a. $N < 8: 2N + 2$
      $N \geq 8: N + 9$

b.

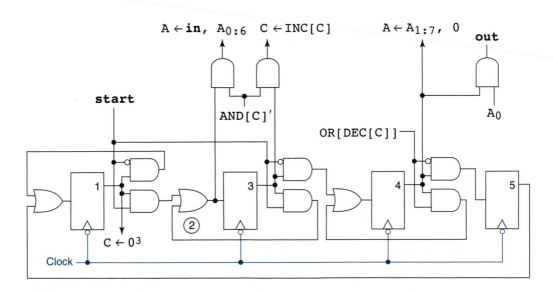

c.

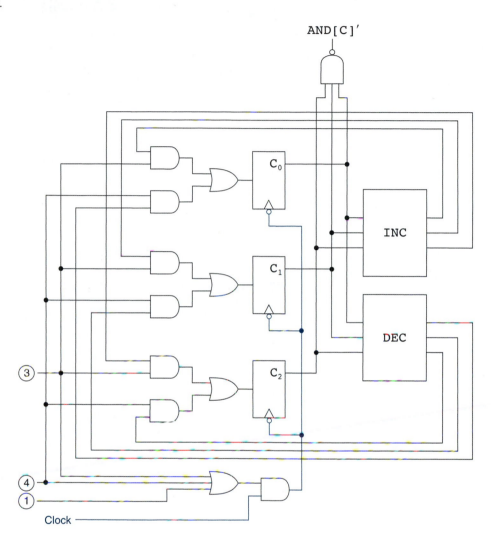

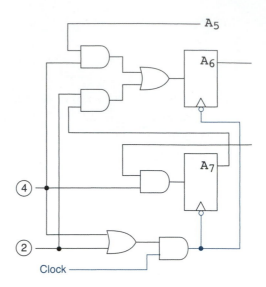

d.   When **start** goes to **1,** the system begins inputting a string of bits on line **in.** (There is an input whenever **start** = **1.**) It continues inputting bits until it has 8 or until **start** goes to **0.** After **start** goes to 0 it outputs *all but the first input* of the string (*up to 7*) on line **out** in reverse order, and a 1 on line **out.** (Note that up to 7 bits are output, but only after **start** goes to 0.)

11.   SYSTEM NAME: COUNT

    INPUT LINE: **go.**

    OUTPUT LINES: **done,** OUT[0:3].

    FLIP FLOPS: C[0:3].

    1.   **go:** CT ← 1^4;

        next: 2 (**go**), 1 (else).

    2.   **go** · AND[C]′: C ← INC[C];

        next: 2 (**go**), 3 (else).

    3.   ·

    4.   OUT = C; **done** = 1;

        next: 1.

  END DESCRIPTION

—or—

    1.   CT ← 0^4;

        next: 2 (**go**), 1 (else).

    2.   AND[C]′: C ← INC[C];

  (3.) next: 2 (**go**), 4 (else).

    4.   ·

    5.   OUT = C; **done** = 1;

        next: 1.

13.   SYSTEM NAME: HPONE

    INPUT LINES: **start**, X[0:19], **ok**.

    OUTPUT LINES: Z[0:7], ready.

    FLIP FLOPS: R[0:19].

    1.   next: 2 (**start**), 1 (else).

    2.   next: 2 (**start**), 3 (else).

    (3.) R ← X.

    4.   **ready** = 1;

      next: 5 (**ok**), 4 (else).

    (5.) $R'_0 \cdot R'_1$: Z = $R_{4:11}$;

      $R'_0 \cdot R_1$: Z = $R'_{4:11}$;

      $R_0 \cdot R'_1$: Z = $R_{12:19}$;

      $R_0 \cdot R_1$: Z = $R'_{12:19}$.

    6.   ·

    7.   ·

    8.   **ready** = 1;

      next: 9 (**ok**), 8 (else).

    (9.) $R'_2 \cdot R'_3$: Z = $R_{4:11}$;

      $R'_2 \cdot R_3$: Z = $R'_{4:11}$;

      $R_2 \cdot R'_3$: Z = $R_{12:19}$;

      $R_2 \cdot R_3$: Z = $R'_{12:19}$.

      next: 1.

  END DESCRIPTION

If ok can be 1 for more than one clock,

    6.   next: 5 (**ok**), 7 (else).

Branch at 9 becomes

    next: 10 (**ok**), 1 (else).

    10.   next: 9.

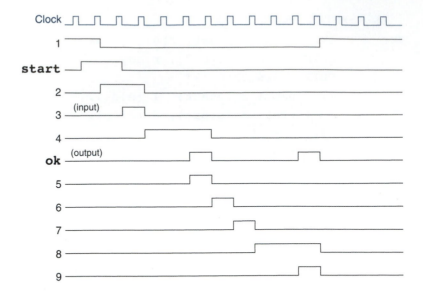

B.10   Chapter 10 Answers

1. ii.   Only REG^2 and the PC are changed

	REG^2	PC
a.	12341134	76543211
b.	22442244	76543211
c.	35764657	76543211
d.	23564534	76543211
e.	12341235	76543212
f.	34563456	76543212
g.	34564567	76543212

3. b. $PC \leftarrow 11111118$
$REG^{3F} \leftarrow FFFFFFF1$
$M[FFFFFFEF] \leftarrow 12345678$
$M[FFFFFFF0] \leftarrow 12345678$
$REG^3 \leftarrow FFFFFFFF$
$REG^4 \leftarrow 12345678$
$REG^5 \leftarrow 12345678$
$REG^6 \leftarrow 22334455$
$z \leftarrow 0 \qquad n \leftarrow 0$

8. a.   1.   AD = PC; **read** = 1; IR ← DATA.
2.   PC ← INC[PC];
next: 60 (IR_0), 3 (else).

Addressing

(3.) next: 12 (IR_{12}), 4 (else)
4.   next/$IR_{13:15}$: 5, 1, 6, 1, 1, 1,
10, 11.

Register

(5.) IR_2': WORK ← REG/$IR_{26:31}$;
      IR_2: WORK ← REG/($IR_{26:30}$, 1);
      next: 5a (IR_2), 20 (else).
5a.   WORK2 ← REG/($IR_{26:30}$, 0);
      next: 20.

Register indirect

(6.) EA ← REG/$IR_{26:31}$;
      next: 18.

Page zero

(10.) EA ← 0000, $IR_{16:31}$;
      next: 18.

Relative

(11.) IR_{16}: EA ← $ADD_{1:32}$[FFFF, $IR_{16:31}$; PC; 0]
      IR_{16}': EA ← $ADD_{1:32}$[0000, $IR_{16:31}$; PC; 0]
      next: 18.

Read second word, direct

13.   AD = PC; **read** = 1; EA ← DATA.
14.   PC ← INC[PC];
      next/$IR_{13:15}$: 18, 15, 1, 1, 16, 1, 1, 1.

Indirect

15.   AD = EA; **read** = 1: EA ← DATA;
      next: 18.

Immediate

16.   WORK ← EA;
      next: 17 (IR_2); 20 (else).
17.   AD = PC; **read** = 1; WORK2 ← DATA.
17a. PC ← INC[PC];
      next: 20.

Data read

18.   AD = EA; **read** = 1; WORK ← DATA;
      next: 19 (IR_2), 20 (else).
19.   EA ← DEC[EA].
19b. AD = EA; **read** = 1; WORK2 ← DATA;
      next: 20.

12. a.

```
SYSTEM NAME: DESIGN PROJECT
  FLIP FLOPS: PC[0:24], IR[0:19],W2[0:19],
  WW2[0:19], W1[0:19],WW1[0:19], REG[0:31; 0:19],
  EA2[0:24], EA1[0:24], z, s.
  OUTPUT LINES: ADIN[0:24], read, write.
  COMMUNICATION BUS: DATA[0:19].
```

1. $ADIN = PC$; **read** $= 1$; $PC \leftarrow ADD25[1^{25}; PC]$.
2. $IR \leftarrow DATA$.
3.   next: 30 (IR_0); 4 (else).

Address two

(4.)   next: 15 (IR_{12}), 5 (else).
(5.)   next/$IR_{13:14}$; 6, 8, 9, 1.

Register

(6.) $W2 \leftarrow REG/IR_{15:19}$;
       next: 7 ($IR_0' \cdot IR_1' \cdot IR_3$), 30 (else).
7. $WW2 \leftarrow REG/(IR_{15:16}, 1)$;
       next: 30.

Register indirect

(8.) $EA2 \leftarrow 0^5$; $REG/IR_{15:19}$;
       next: 26.

Register indirect/pre dec

(9.) $EA2 \leftarrow ADD25[(1)^{25}; 0^5, REG/IR_{15:19}]$;
       $REG/IR_{15:19} \leftarrow ADD25[1FFFFFF; 0^5,$
       $REG/IR_{15:19}]$;
       next: 26.

Second word fetch

(15.) $ADIN = PC$; **read** $= 1$;
       $PC \leftarrow ADD25[1^{25}; PC]$.
16. $EA2 \leftarrow IR_{15:19}, DATA$;
       next/$IR_{13:14}$: 26, 17, 19, 1.

Indirect

17. $ADIN = EA2$; **read** $= 1$.
18. $EA2_{5:24} \leftarrow DATA$;
       next: 26.

Immediate

19. $W2 \leftarrow EA2_{5:24}$;
       next: 25 ($IR_0' \cdot IR_1' \cdot IR_3$), 30 (else).
20. $ADIN = PC$; **read** $= 1$; $PC \leftarrow ADD25[1^{25}; PC]$.
21. $WW2 \leftarrow DATA$;
       next: 30.

Data fetch

26.   ADIN = EA2; **read** = 1.
27.   W2 ← DATA;
      next: 28 (IR_0' · IR_1' · IR_3), 30 (else).
28.   ADIN = $EA2_{0:23}$, 1; **read** = 1.
29.   WW2 ← DATA.

Address one

(30.) next: 50 (IR_4), 31 (else).
31.   next/$IR_{5:6}$: 32, 34, 35, 1.

Register

(32.) W1 ← REG/$IR_{7:11}$;
      next: 33 (IR_0' · IR_1' · IR_3), 60 (else).
33.   WW1 ← REG/($IR_{7:10}$, 1);
      next: 60.

Register indirect

(34.) EA1 ← 0^5, REG/$IR_{7:11}$;
      next: 55.

Register indirect /pre dec

(35.) EA1 ← ADD25[1FFFFFF; 0^5, REG/$IR_{7:11}$];
      REG/$IR_{7:11}$ ← $ADD25_{5:24}$[1FFFFFF; 0^5,
      REG/$IR_{7:11}$];
      next: 55.

Second/third word fetch

50.   ADIN = PC; **read** = 1; PC ← ADD25[1^{25}; PC].
51.   EA1 ← $IR_{7:11}$, DATA;
      next/$IR_{13:14}$: 55, 52, 54, 1.

Indirect

52.   ADIN = EA1; **read** = 1.
53. $EA1_{5:24}$ ← DATA;
      next: 55.

Relative

54. $EA1_5'$: EA1 ← ADD25[00, $IR_{7:11}$; PC];
      $EA1_5$: EA1 ← ADD25[1F, EA1; PC];
      next: 55.

Data fetch

(55.) next: 60 (IR_0 + (IR_1 · IR_2)), 58 (else).
56.   ADIN = EA1; **read** = 1.
57.   W1 ← DATA;
      next: 58 (IR_0' · IR_1' · IR_3), 60 (else).

58. $\text{ADIN} = \text{EA1}_{0:23}$, 1; **read** = 1.
59. $\text{WW1} \leftarrow \text{DATA}$.

Instruction decode

60. $\text{next}/\text{IR}_{0:3}$: 61, 65, 75, 65, 80, 85, 90, 95, 105, 110, 115, 120, 1, 1, 1, 1.

Add

(61.) $\text{W1} \leftarrow \text{ADD20}_{1:20}[\text{W1}; \text{W2}; 0]$;
$\mathbf{z} \leftarrow (\text{OR}[\text{CPUBUS}])'$; $\mathbf{s} \leftarrow \text{CPUBUS}_0$;
next: 91.

Add/sub double (assume low order word first
in even address or register)

(65.) IR_2': $\mathbf{s}$, $\text{W1} \leftarrow \text{ADD20}[\text{W1}; \text{W2}; \mathbf{s}]$;
IR_2: $\mathbf{s}$, $\text{W1} \leftarrow \text{ADD20}[\text{W1}; \text{W2}'; \mathbf{s}]$;
$\mathbf{z} \leftarrow (\text{OR}[\text{CPUBUS}])'$.
(66.) IR_2': $\text{WW1} \leftarrow \text{ADD20}_{1:20}[\text{WW1}; \text{WW2}; \mathbf{s}]$;
IR_2: $\text{WW1} \leftarrow \text{ADD20}_{1:20}[\text{WW1}; \text{WW2}'; \mathbf{s}]$;
$\mathbf{z} \leftarrow \mathbf{z} \cdot (\text{OR}[\text{CPUBUS}])'$; $\mathbf{s} = \text{CPUBUS}_0$.
(67.) next: 70 $(\text{IR}_4' \cdot \text{IR}_5' \cdot \text{IR}_6')$, 68 (else).
·68. $\text{ADIN} = \text{EA1}_{0:23}$, 1; $\text{DATA} = \text{WW1}$; **write** = 1.
69. next: 92.
70. $\text{REG}/(\text{IR}_{7:10}, 1) \leftarrow \text{WW1}$;
next: 94.

Subtract

(75.) $\text{W1} \leftarrow \text{ADD20}_{1:20}[\text{W1}; \text{W2}'; 1]$;
$\mathbf{z} \leftarrow (\text{OR}[\text{CPUBUS}])'$; $\mathbf{s} \leftarrow \text{CPUBUS}_0$;
next: 91.

Compare

(80.) $\text{CPUBUS} = \text{ADD20}_{1:20}[\text{W1}; \text{W2}'; 1]$;
$\mathbf{z} \leftarrow (\text{OR}[\text{CPUBUS}])'$; $\mathbf{s} \leftarrow \text{CPUBUS}_0$;
next: 1.

AND

(85.) $\text{W1} \leftarrow \text{W1} \cdot \text{W2}$;
$\mathbf{z} \leftarrow (\text{OR}[\text{CPUBUS}])'$; $\mathbf{s} \leftarrow \text{CPUBUS}_0$;
next: 91.

Move and store results

(90.) $\text{W1} \leftarrow \text{W2}$; $\mathbf{z} \leftarrow (\text{OR}[\text{CPUBUS}])'$; $\mathbf{s} \leftarrow \text{CPUBUS}_0$.
(91.) next: 94 $(\text{IR}_4' \cdot \text{IR}_5' \cdot \text{IR}_6')$, 92 (else).
92. $\text{ADIN} = \text{EA1}$; $\text{DATA} = \text{W1}$; **write** = 1.

93. next: 1.
94. REG/IR$_{7:11}$ ← W1;
     next: 1.

Move block

(95.) W2 ← 0^{20}.
96. EA2 ← ADD25[0000001; EA2];
     next: 99.
97. ADIN = EA2; **read** = 1.
     EA2 ← ADD25[0000001; EA2].
98. W1 ← DATA.
99. ADIN = EA1; DATA = W1; **write** = 1.
100. EA1 ← ADD25[0000001; EA1].
101. W2 ← ADD20$_{1:20}$[00001; W2; 0];
     next: 1 (AND[W2$_{16:19}$]), 97 (else).

Increment

(105.) W1 ← ADD$_{1:20}$[W1; 00001; 0];
     z ← (OR[CPUBUS])'; **s** ← CPUBUS$_0$;
     next: 91.

Decrement

(110.) W1 ← ADD$_{1:20}$[W1; FFFFF; 0];
     z ← (OR[CPUBUS])'; **s** ← CPUBUS$_0$;
     next: 91.

JSR

(115.) REG/IR$_{15:19}$ ← PC.
116. PC ← EA1;
     next: 1.

JMP

(120.) next: 126 (IR$_{17}$'), 121 (next).
(121.) next/IR$_{18:19}$; 122, 123, 124, 125.
(122.) next: 126 (**z**), 1 (else).
(123.) next: 126 (**z**'), 1 (else).
(124.) next: 126 (**s**), 1 (else).
(125.) next: 126 (**s**'), 1 (else).
(126.) PC ← EA1;
     next: 1.

END DESCRIPTION

b.   All instructions: 3 plus

AD2

Register:	0^*
Register ind	$2^\dagger$
Reg ind dec	$2^\dagger$
Direct	$3^\dagger$
Indirect	$5^\dagger$
Immediate	$2^\dagger$

AD1

Register:	1^*
Register ind	$1 + 2^\dagger$ if data needed
Register ind dec	$1 + 2^\dagger$ if data needed
Direct	$3 + 2^\dagger$ if data needed
Indirect	$5 + 2^\dagger$ if data needed
Relative	$2 + 2^\dagger$ if data needed

Execution

Add, Sub, And, Inc, Dec, Mov	2/3	(register/memory)
Add/Subtract double	4/6	
Compare	1	
Jump	1	
JSR	2	
Move block	80	

Examples:

Add both Direct: $3 + 3 + 5 + 3 = 14$

Add double AD2 Register indirect, AD1 register:
$3 + 4 + 2 + 4 = 13$

Jump Relative: $3 + 0 + 2 + 1 = 6$

---

*one extra for double precision

†two extra for double precision

Chapter Test Answers

C.1 Chapter 1

1. a. 101011011   b. 533

2.

```
   1 1 1 0                    1 1 0 1 1
   0 1 0 1 1    1 1          1 0 1 0 1 1   4 3
   0 1 1 1 0    1 4          0 1 1 0 0 1   2 5
0  1 1 0 0 1    2 5     1    0 0 0 1 0 0   looks like 4—overflow
```

3. a. 149   115   b. -107 $+115$ c. 95   73

4.

```
     1 0 0                 1 1 0                1 1 1
     1 1 0 0   −4          1 0 1 0   −6         0 1 0 1   +5
     1 1 0 1   −3          0 1 1 1   +7         0 0 1 1   +3
(0)  1 0 0 1   −7   (1)    0 0 0 1   +1   (0)   1 0 0 0   overflow
```

5. a. $13 - 12 = 1$ $10 - 6 = 4$

    b. $-3 - (-4) = +1$ $-6 - (+6) =$ overflow

6. a. 1 10001000 00000001101000000000000

    b. 0 10000010 01001111110101110000101

7. $.24368 \times 10^2 + .98142 \times 10^3 = .10058 \times 10^4$

C.2 Chapter 2

1.

A	B	C	D	X	Y	Z
0	0	0	0	0	0	0
0	0	0	1	0	0	1
0	0	1	0	0	1	0
0	0	1	1	0	1	1
0	1	0	0	1	0	1
0	1	0	1	0	0	0
0	1	1	0	0	0	1
0	1	1	1	0	1	0
1	0	0	0	1	1	0
1	0	0	1	1	0	1
1	0	1	0	0	0	0
1	0	1	1	0	0	1
1	1	0	0	1	1	1
1	1	0	1	1	1	0
1	1	1	0	1	0	1
1	1	1	1	0	0	0

2.

a	b	c	f	g
0	0	0	1	1
0	0	1	1	1
0	1	0	1	1
0	1	1	0	0
1	0	0	0	0
1	0	1	0	0
1	1	0	1	1
1	1	1	1	0

NOT equal

3. $a'c + ab'$

4. a.

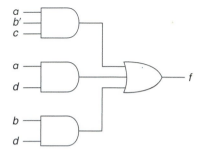

b.

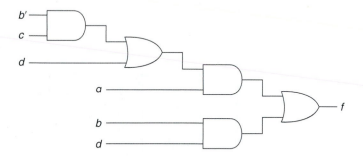

5. a. $f(x, y, z) = \Sigma m(0, 2, 3, 5, 7)$
b. $f = x'y'z' + x'yz' + x'yz + xy'z + xyz$
c. $f = x'z' + x'y + xz = x'z' + xz + yz$
d. $f = (x + y + z')(x' + y + z)(x' + y' + z)$
e. $f = (x + y + z')(x' + z)$

6. a.

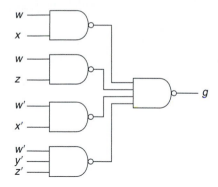

b.

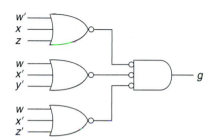

c.

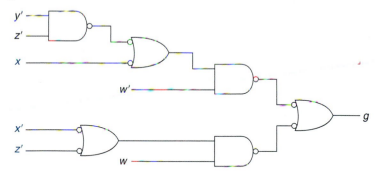

7. a. $f = (b'd' + b'cd') + (bc'd + bcd) + ab'd$
$= b'd' + bd + ab'd$
$= b'd' + d\,(b + b'a) = b'd' + bd + ad$
$= b'(d' + ad) + bd = b'd' + ab' + bd$

b. $g = (xy'z' + xy'z) + yz + wxy + xz$
$= xy' + yz + wxy + xz = x\,(y' + yw) + yz + xz$
$= xy' + wx + yz + xz$
$= xy' + wx + yz$ (consensus)

8. a. $a'b'c' + a'b'c + a'bc' + a'bc + ab'c + abc$

b. $w'x'y' + x'y'z' + wyz$

9.

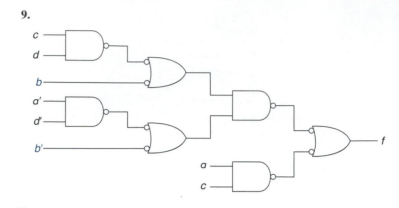

10.

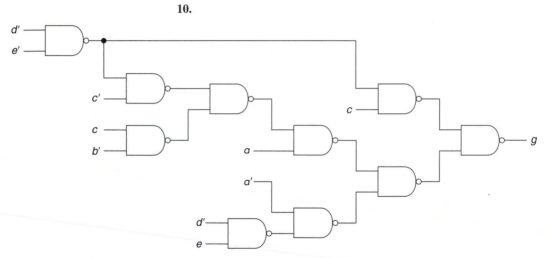

C.3   Chapter 3

1. a. $f(x, y, z) = \Sigma m\,(1, 2, 7) + \Sigma d(4, 5)$

   b. $g = a'c + ab'c'd + a'bd + abc'$

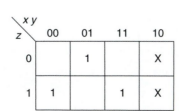

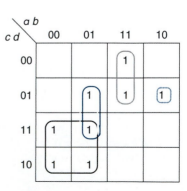

2. a. $wx'y'z' + wyz + w'x$ b. $acd + a'c' + a'd' + ab$

3. $b'd + bd' + ac + \{ab \text{ or } ad\} + \{a'b'c' \text{ or } a'c'd'\}$

4. $wz' + \{x'z \text{ or } wx'\} + \{xy'z' \text{ or } w'xy'\}$

5. $f = a'd + \{c'd \text{ or } b'd\}$
  $f = d(a' + b') = d(a' + c')$

6. $f = wx + \{xy'z \text{ or } w'y'z\} + \{wyz \text{ or } x'yz\}$
  $f = (w + z)(x + y)\{(x + z) \text{ or } (y' + z)\}\{(x' + y') \text{ or } (w + y')\}$

7. $A'B'C' + ACE + ABC'D + BCD'E' + \{A'B'D'E \text{ or } B'CD'E\}$

8. $ACE' + CDE + A'C'E' + BC'E + AB'C'$
  $ACE' + CDE + B'C'E' + A'BC' + AC'E$

9. a. $f = xy'z' + wx' + wz'$
    $g = w'z + w'xy + x'z$

  b. $f = xy'z' + wz' + wx'z$
    $g = w'z + w'xy + wx'z$

10. a. $f = w'z + w'y + yz + wx'z'$
    $g = w'yz' + xz' + wxy + wy'z'$
    $h = w'z + w'x + xyz + wx'y'z'$

  b. $f = w'z + w'yz' + wx'y'z' + wxyz + x'y$
    $g = w'yz' + xz' + wx'y'z' + wxyz$
    $h = w'z + wx'y'z' + wxyz + w'x$

C.4   Chapter 4

1.

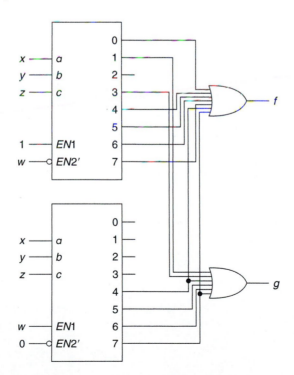

2.

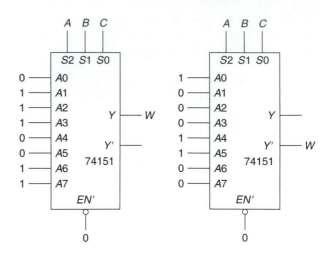

3.

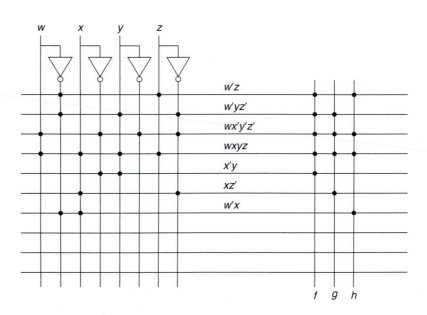

4.

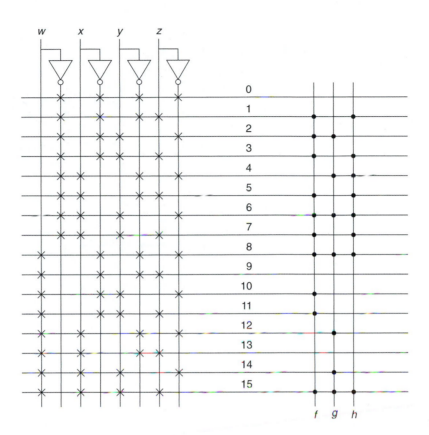

5.

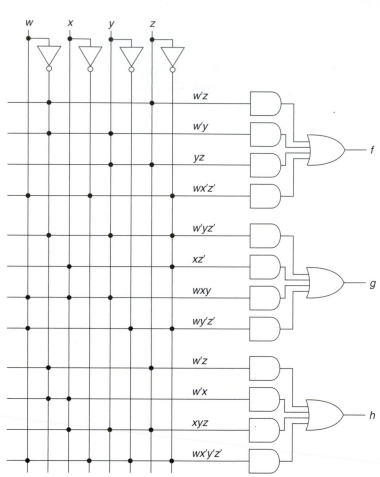

6.

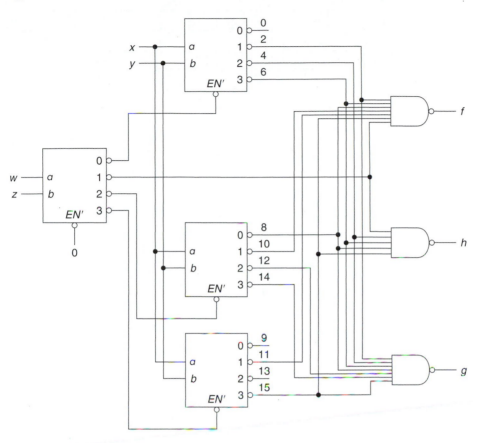

C.5 Chapter 5

1. x 0 0 1 1 0 0 0 1 0 1
 q A C B D B A C B D B D B
 z 0 0 1 0 1 0 0 1 0 1 0 1 0

2.

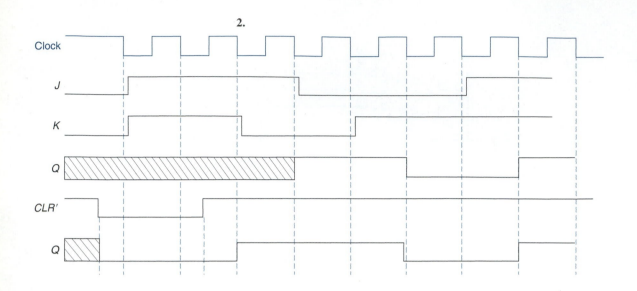

3. $D = xB + x'B'$ $T = A' + x$ $z = A' + B$

AB	$A^\star B^\star$		z
	$x = 0$	$x = 1$	$x = 1$
0 0	1 1	0 1	1
0 1	0 0	1 0	1
1 0	1 0	0 1	0
1 1	0 1	1 0	1

4. $D_A = xB' + x'B$ $D_B = x + A'$ $z = AB$

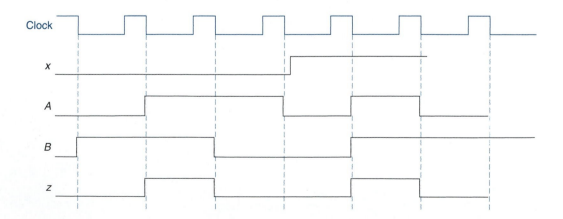

C.6 Chapter 6

1. $D_A = x'B' + xB$ $J_B = K_B = A' + x$ $z = x'A + xB'$
2. $S_1 = x$ $R_1 = x'q_2$ $J_2 = xq_1$ $K_2 = x'$ $z = q_2'$
3. a. $D_1 = x'q_1' + x'q_2 + q_1'q_2 + xq_1q_2'$
        $D_2 = x + q_1'q_2$ $z = q_1'q_2'$
    b. $D_1 = x + q_1q_2$ $D_2 = q_2'$ $z = q_1'q_2'$
    c.

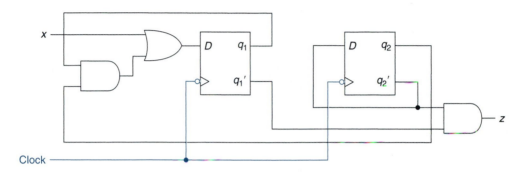

4. $D = A'$ $J = C'$ $K = A'C'$ $T = A' + B'C'$

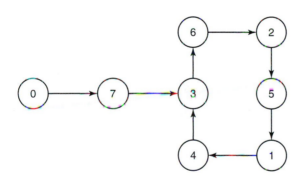

5.   a.

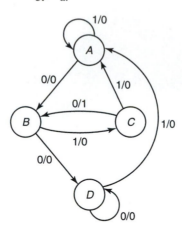

b.

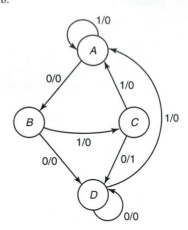

6.

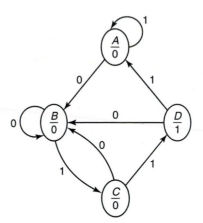

C.7 Chapter 7

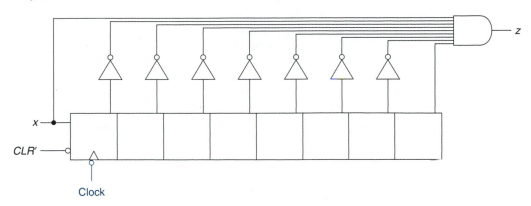

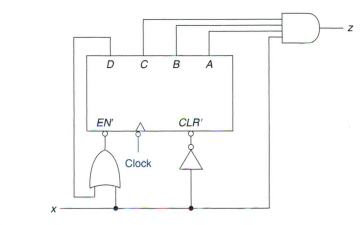

C.8 Chapter 8

1.   a.   b.

A	B	B
C	C	D
E	E	F
G	G	H
H		

A	no-op	no-op
B	B	C
C	D	E
E	F	no-op
G	G	H
H		

2.

before   a.   b.   c.   d.   e.

	a.	b.	c.	d.	e.
			4567		
	1234	1234	1234	1234	
		1234	1234	1234	1234

  d. $REG^3 \leftarrow 4567$

  e. $REG^7 \leftarrow 1234$

3. a. i. 010203

  ii. 6789AB

  iii. ABCDEF

  iv. FFFFFF

  v. 000046

  vi. 123456

  b. i. $M[12345646] \leftarrow 444444$, PC $\leftarrow 00112224$

  Memory: $2 + 1 = 3$

  ii. 010203

  <u>444444</u>

  $454647 \rightarrow REG^7$, PC $\leftarrow 00112223$

  Memory: $1 + 1 = 2$

  iii. $M[123456FF] \leftarrow 776656$, PC $\leftarrow 00112224$

  Memory: $2 + 2 + 2 = 6$

  iv. 0000 0001 0000 0010 0000 0011 OR

  0100 0100 0100 0100 0100 0100 $\rightarrow 454647 \rightarrow REG^7$,

  PC $\leftarrow 00112223$

  Memory: $1 + 1 = 2$

  v. Data: 0110 0111 1000 1001 1010 1011

  $M[00000046] \leftarrow$ 1100 1111 0001 0011 0101 0110

  $= CF1356$, PC $\leftarrow 00112223$

  Memory: $1 + 2 = 3$

  vi. PC $\leftarrow 12345646$

  Memory: 2

C.9 Chapter 9

  1. a.

```
FLIP FLOPS: A[0:3]
INPUT LINES: B[0:3], go, x.
OUTPUT LINES: y.
```

b, c.

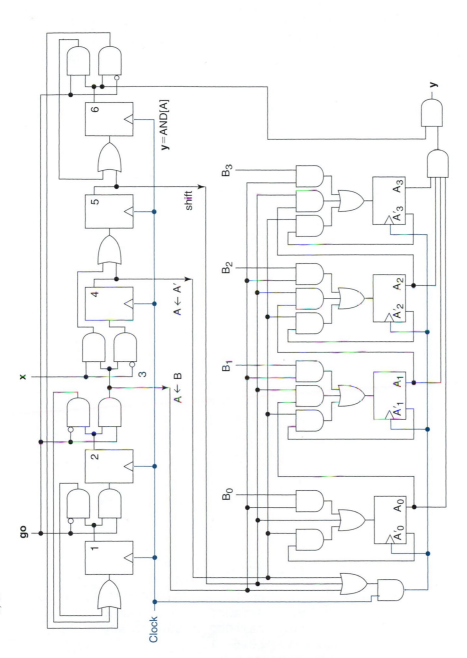

d.

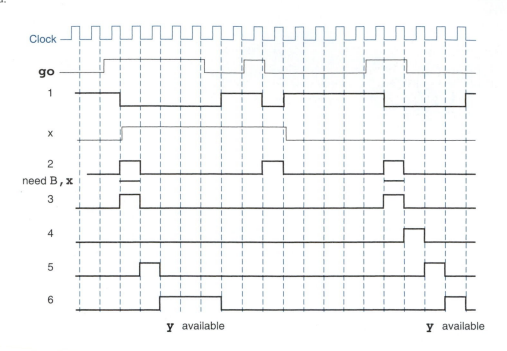

2.

```
SYSTEM NAME: TWO.
    FLIP FLOPS: CT[0:4], SUM[0:15].
    INPUT LINES: go, IN[0:4], DATAIN[0:10].
    OUTPUT LINES: ready, DATAOUT[0:15].
    1.   next: 2 (go), 1 (else).
    2.   next: 3 (go), 1 (else).
    3.   next: 4 (go), 1 (else).
    4.   next: 4 (go), 5 (else).
   (5.)  CT ← IN.
    6.   SUM ← 0¹⁶.
    7.   SUM ← ADD[0⁵, DATAIN; SUM].
    8.   CT ← DEC[CT];
         next: 7 (OR[DEC[CT]]), 9 (else).
    9.   DATAOUT = SUM; ready = 1.
    10.  DATAOUT = SUM; ready = 1;
         next: 1.
END DESCRIPTION
```

C.10 Chapter 10

1. a. $REG^2 \leftarrow 00000000$ $z \leftarrow 1$ $n \leftarrow 0$ $PC \leftarrow 12000124$
      3 memory references
   b. $M[00004567] \leftarrow 98765432$ $PC \leftarrow 12000123$
      2 memory references
   c. $REG^3 \leftarrow 18877665$ $z \leftarrow 0$ $n \leftarrow 0$ $c \leftarrow 1$ $v \leftarrow 1$
      $PC \leftarrow 12000124$ 3 memory references
   d. $REG^3 \leftarrow 98000010$ $z \leftarrow 0$ $n \leftarrow 1$ $PC \leftarrow 12000124$
      4 memory references
   e. $PC \leftarrow ABFF0123$ 1 memory reference

2. 60. EA $\leftarrow$ ADD$_{1:16}$ [00000001; EA; 0].
   61. ADIN = EA; **read** = 1; TEMP $\leftarrow$ DATA.
   62. next: 1 (ADD$_0$ [TEMP; WORK'; 1]), 63 (else).
   63. ADIN = EA; DATA = WORKING; **write** = 1.
   64. EA $\leftarrow$ ADD$_{1:16}$[FFFFFFFF; EA; 0].
   65. ADIN = EA; DATA = TEMP; **write** = 1;
       next: 1.

3. In what follows, we treat all unused combinations as no-ops.

   ```
   SYSTEM NAME: SMALL
       OUTPUT LINES: read, write, ADIN[0:15].
       COMMUNICATION BUS: DATA[0:15].
       INTERNAL BUSSES: CPUBUS[0:15],
       INA[0:15], INB[0:15].
       FLIP FLOPS: PC[0:9], EA[0:15],
       IR[0:15], W[0:15].
   ```

   1.   ADIN = 00, PC; **read** = 1;
          IR $\leftarrow$ DATA.
   2.   PC $\leftarrow$ INC[PC];
          next: 10 (IR$_0$ · IR$_1$), 3 (else).
   3.   next/IR$_{4:5}$: 4, 1, 5, 6.
   (4.)   EA $\leftarrow$ 00, IR$_{6:15}$;
            next: 8.
   (5.)   ADIN $\leftarrow$ 00, IR$_{6:15}$; **read** = 1;
            EA $\leftarrow$ DATA;
            next: 8.
   (6.)   W $\leftarrow$ 00; IR$_{6:15}$;
            next: 10.
   (8.)   next: 10 (IR$_0$), 9 (else).

9.   ADIN ← 00, $IR_{6:15}$; **read** = 1;
        EA ← DATA.

10.   next/$IR_{0:2}$: 11, 12, 13, 1, 14, 1,
        15, 20.

(11.)   REG/IR_3 ← W;
        next: 1.

(12.)   REG/IR_3 ← REG/IR_3 · W;
        next: 1.

(13.)   REG/IR_3 ← ADD[REG/IR_3; W];
        next: 1.

(14.)   ADIN = EA; DATA = REG/IR_3;
        write = 1;
        next: 1.

(15.)   next/$IR_{4:5}$: 16, 17, 18, 19.

(16.)   PC ← $IR_{6:15}$;
        next: 1.

(17.)   next: 1 (OR[REG/IR_3]), 16 (else).

(18.)   next: 1 (REG_0/IR_3)+
        (OR[REG/IR_3])'), 16 (else).

(19.)   next: 16 (REG_0/IR_3), 1 (else).

(20.)   REG/IR_3 ← ADD[REG/IR_3; FFFF];
        next: 1 (OR[REG/IR_3]), 16 (else).

END DESCRIPTION

INDEX

transistor-transistor logic (TTL), 57
translation lookaside buffer (TLB), 601–602
truth tables, 2
  algebraic expressions from, 60–65
  combinational design, 36–37
  consensus operator, 74
  development of, 39–42
  don't care conditions, 38
  switching algebra, 44, 60–65
  for system design, 328
2 of 5 code, 18–19
2421 code, 18–19
two-level circuit, 54
two's complement format, 10–12

U

uncomplemented inputs, 55
Unconditional Branch instruction, 464
unsigned numbers, 3–9, 10

V

valid bits, 593
vectors, 498
Verilog, 220–223, 424–425
very-large-scale integration (VLSI), 57
VHDL, 220
virtual memory, 601–602

W

weighted codes, 18
word, memory, 448
word problems, 39–42
write through, 598

Z

zero-extending, 455